东莞统计年鉴

DONGGUAN STATISTICAL YEARBOOK

2011

(总第21期 NO.21)

东 莞 市 统 计 局
国家统计局东莞调查队 编

Compiled by

Dongguan Municipal Bureau of Statistics

Survey Office of the National Bureau of Statistics in Dongguan

中国统计出版社
China Statistics Press

（京）新登字 041 号

图书在版编目（CIP）数据
东莞统计年鉴. 2011 / 东莞市统计局，国家统计局东莞调查队编.
—北京：中国统计出版社，2011.9
ISBN 978 - 7 - 5037 - 6336 - 6

Ⅰ. ①东…
Ⅱ. ①东… ②国…
Ⅲ. ①统计资料 - 东莞市 - 2011 - 年鉴
Ⅳ. ①C832.653 - 54

中国版本图书馆 CIP 数据核字（2011）第 175139 号

东莞统计年鉴 - 2011

作　　者/ 东莞市统计局　国家统计局东莞调查队
责任编辑/ 陈越月
责任校对/ 李妙荷　蔡盟芳
封面设计/ 张永艳　钟锦漩
出版发行/ 中国统计出版社
通信地址/ 北京市西城区月坛南街 57 号
邮　　编/ 100826
办公地址/ 北京市丰台区西三环南路甲 6 号
电　　话/（010）63376907
E - mail / yearbook@ gj. stats. cn
印　　刷/ 东莞市本色印刷有限公司
经　　销/ 新华书店
开　　本/ 880 × 1230 毫米　1/16
字　　数/ 130 万字
印　　张/ 35.5 印张
印　　数/ 1500 册
版　　别/ 2011 年 9 月第 1 版
版　　次/ 2011 年 9 月第 1 次印刷
书　　号/ ISBN 978 - 7 - 5037 - 6336 - 6/C · 2554
定　　价/ 350.00 元

《东莞统计年鉴－2011》
编委会和编辑出版人员

编 者 说 明

一、《东莞统计年鉴－2011》（以下简称年鉴）是一部反映东莞国民经济和社会发展情况的资料性年刊，本书收录了东莞2010年大量的统计数据和历史主要年份的一些主要统计数据，旨在全面系统地反映东莞在经济和社会方面的发展变化，为社会各界和海内外人士了解和研究东莞提供翔实的资料。

二、全书分三部分。第一部分，概述；第二部分，统计资料，具体分为综合、人口与劳动力、农业、工业、固定资产投资与建筑业、运输邮电、国内贸易、物价、外经旅游、财政与金融、人民生活、社会事业、能源、镇街主要指标、村（居）委会主要指标、历年国民经济和社会发展主要指标、东莞与全国、全省、三角洲主要指标比较等17部分；第三部分，基本单位情况。

三、本年鉴资料大部分来自政府统计部门和调查队的各种定期统计报表和抽样调查资料，部分来自中央省属单位和市属各主管部门的统计资料。

四、使用本年鉴时，请注意指标的统计口径，计量单位及计算价格。本年鉴指标计算所采用的价格除注明外均为当年价格。

五、年鉴统计表中的符号说明："#"表示其中主要项；"空格"表示该项统计指标数据不详或无该项数据。

六、本年鉴在编辑出版过程中，得到有关部门和镇街的大力支持，在此表示衷心感谢。限于编辑水平，本书难免有疏漏之处，敬请批评指正。

目　　录
CONTENTS

第一部分　概　述
Part One　Outline

第二部分　统计资料
Part Two　Statistics

一、综　合
General Survey

二、人口与劳动力
Population and Labor Force

三、农业
Agriculture

四、工业
Industry

五、固定资产投资与建筑业
Investment in Fixed Assets and Construction

六、运输邮电
Transport, Postal and Telecommunication Services

七、国内贸易
Domestic Trade

八、价格指数
Price Indices

九、对外经济贸易与旅游
Foreign Trade and Tourism

十、财政、金融与保险
Finance, Banking and Insurance

十一、人民生活
People's Living Conditions

十二、社会事业
Social Undertakings

十三、能源
Energy

十四、镇街主要指标
Main Indicators of Towns

十五、村（居）委会主要指标
Main Indicatory of Villagers'（Neighborhood）Committees

十六、历年国民经济和社会发展主要指标
Main Indicators of National Economy and Social Development over Years

十七、东莞与全国、全省、三角洲主要指标比较
Comparison of Main Indicators between Dongguan and China, Guangdong Province, the Cities of the Pearl River Delta

第三部分　基本单位情况
Part Three　Basic Units

东莞市生产总值(亿元)

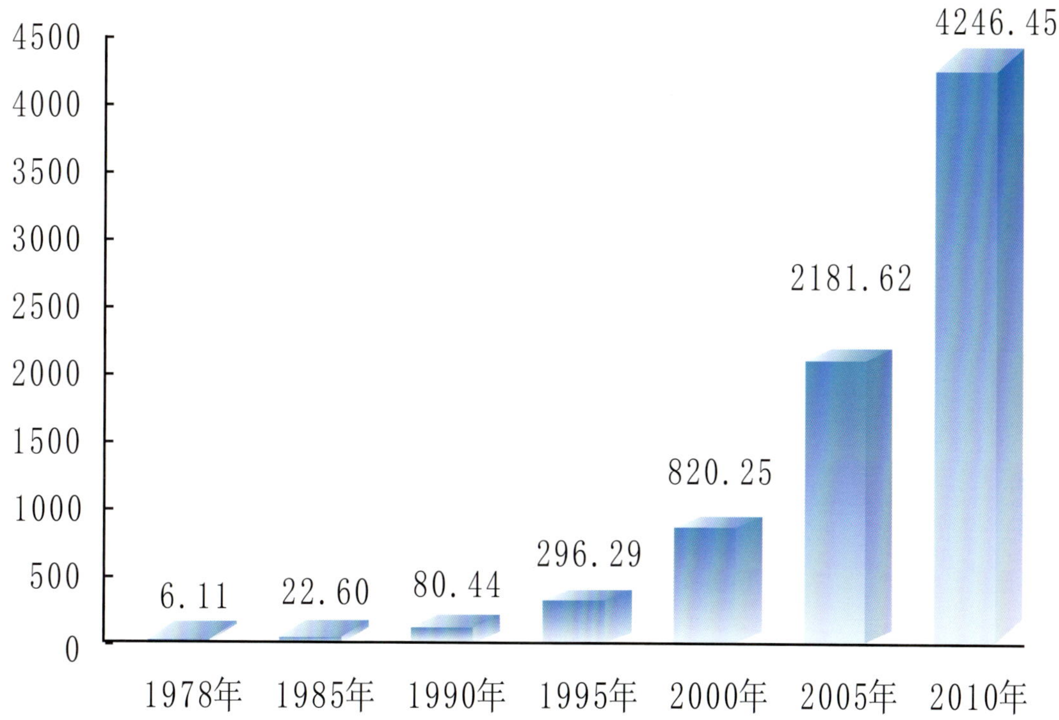

东莞市生产总值构成(%)

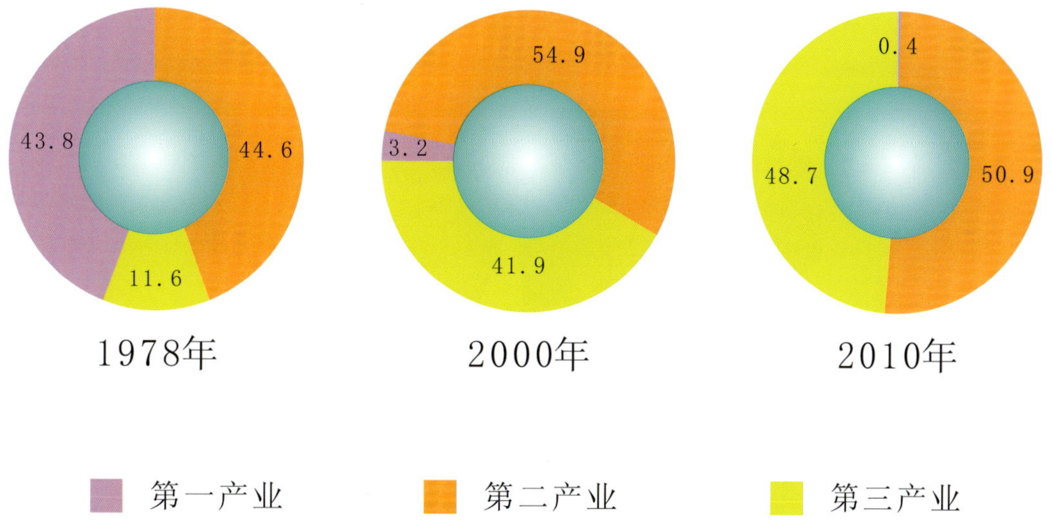

工业增加值（亿元）

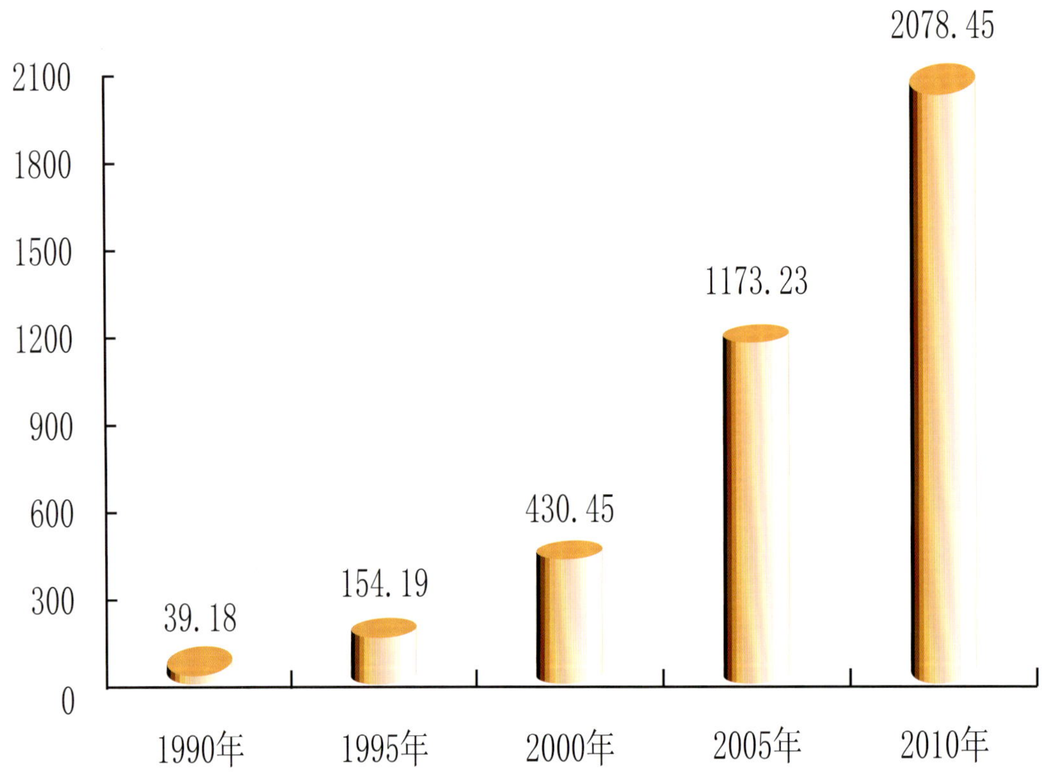

规模以上制造业增加值行业结构(%)

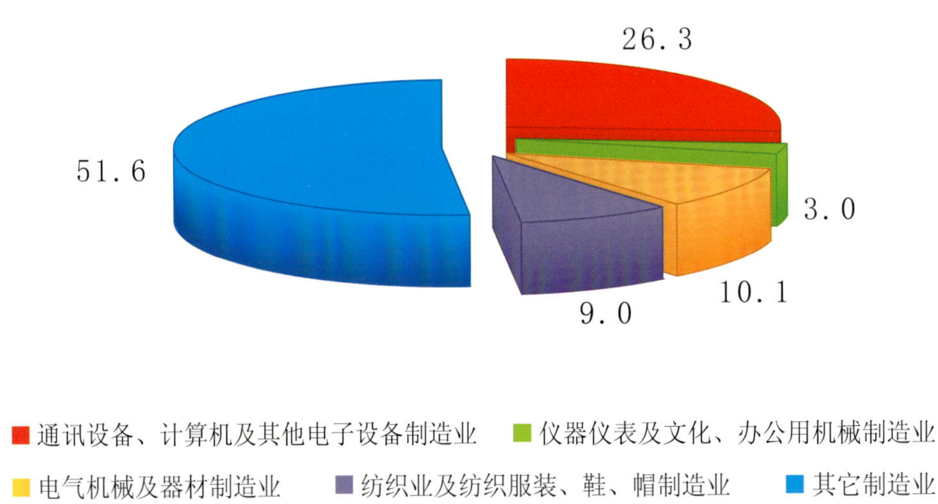

进口总额、出口总额（亿美元）

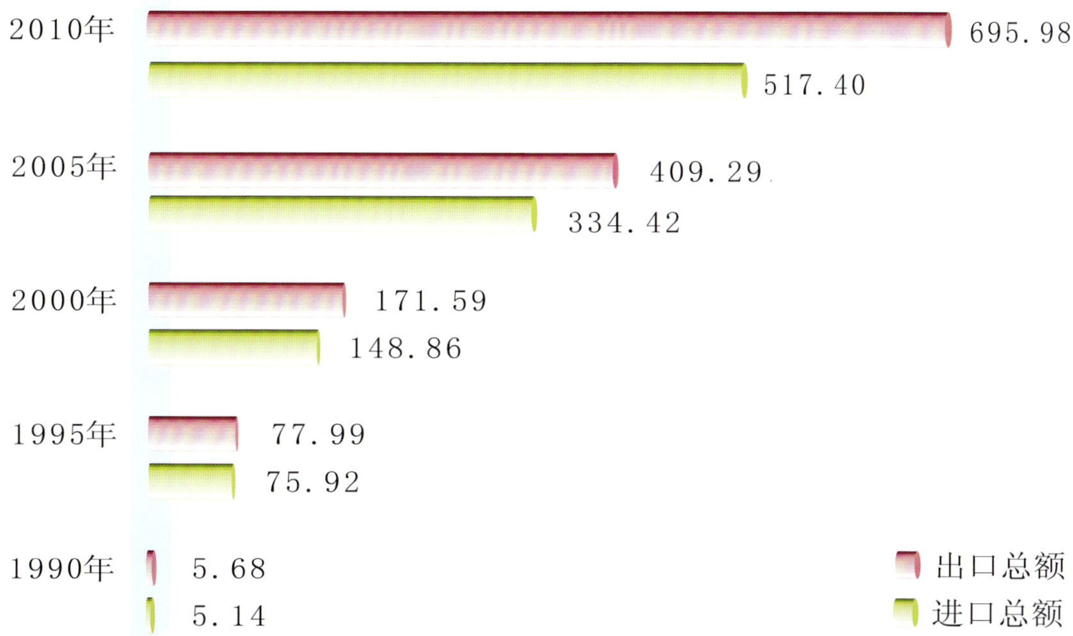

当年实际利用外资（新口径）（亿美元）

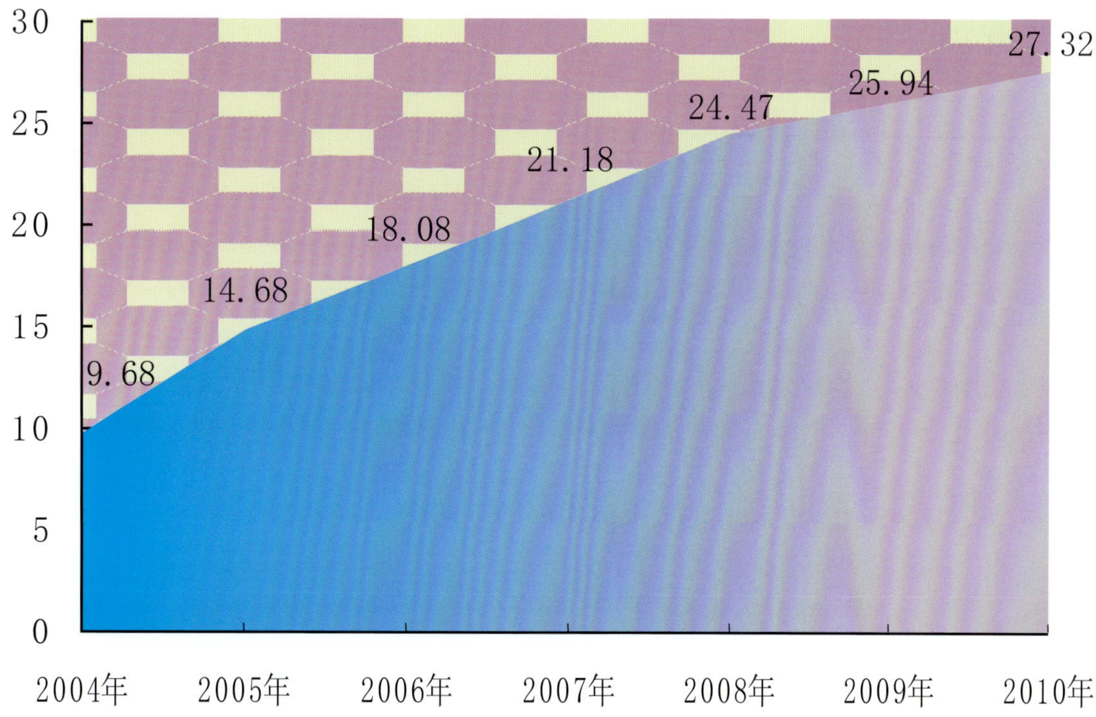

来源于东莞的财政收入(不含关税)(亿元)

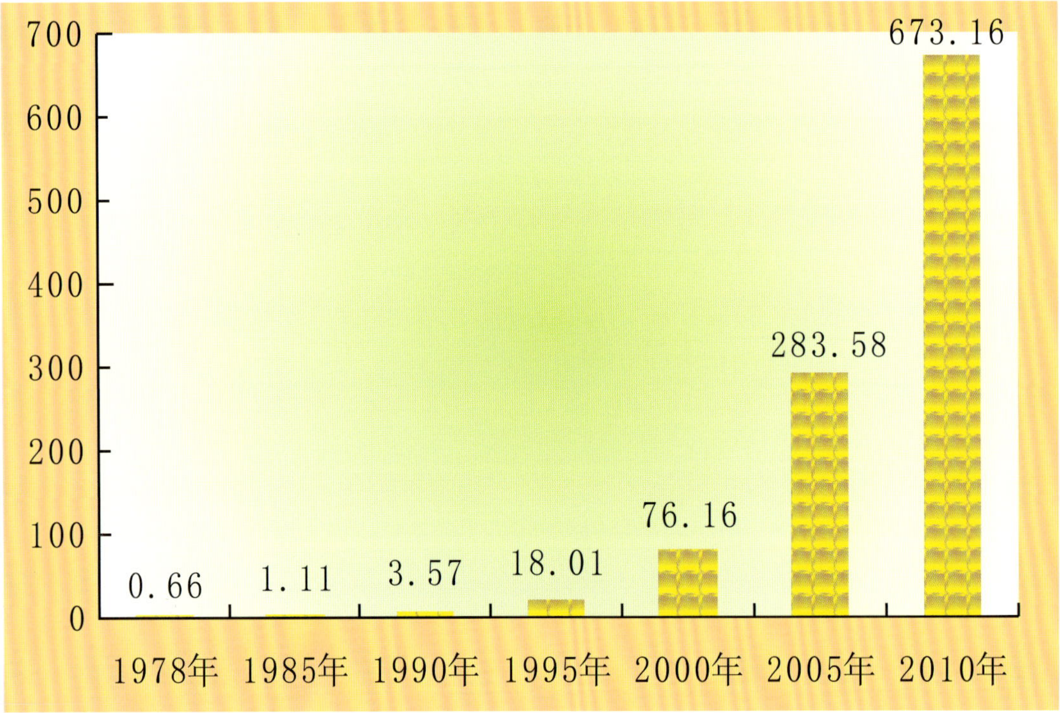

各项人民币存贷款余额(亿元)

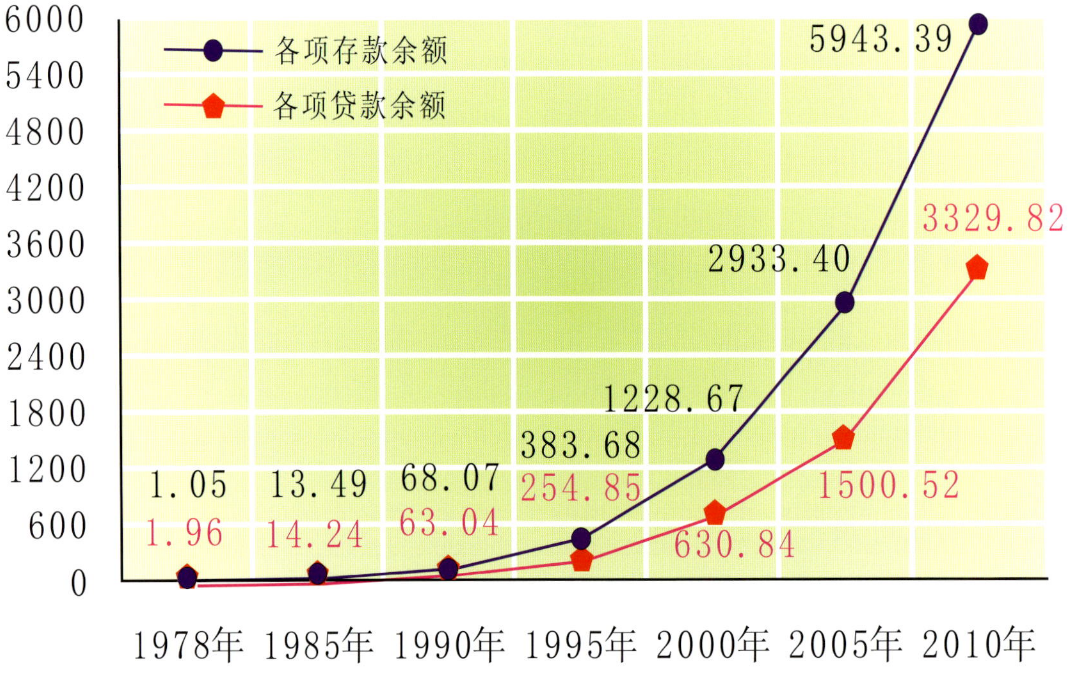

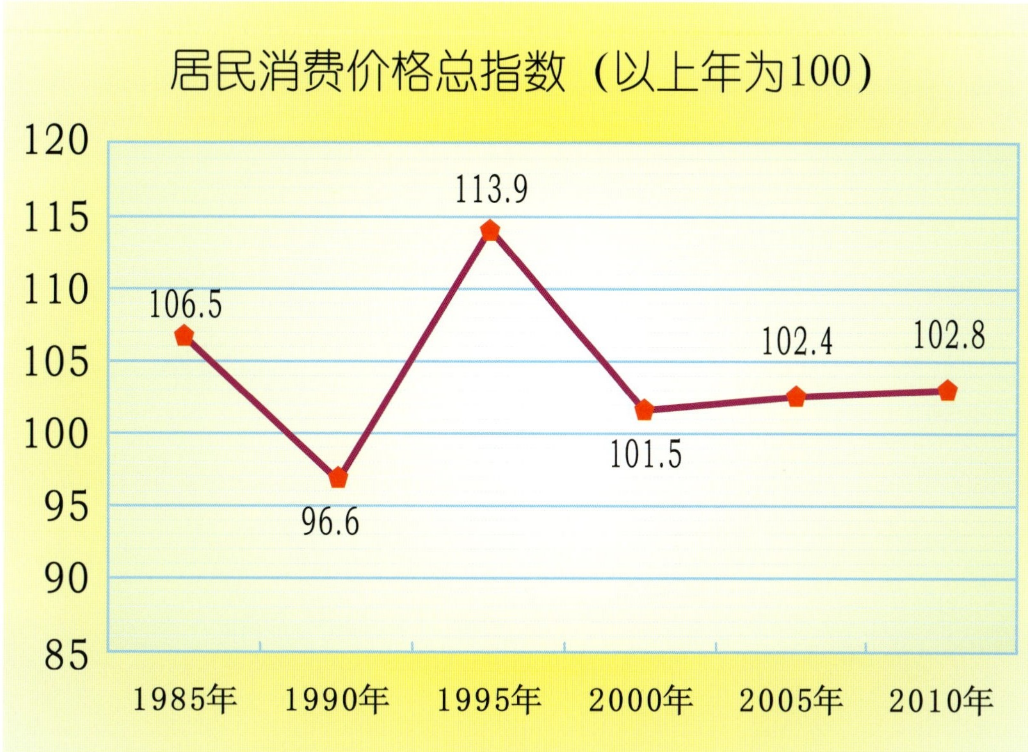
居民消费价格总指数（以上年为100）
120
115
110
105
100
95
90
85
106.5
96.6
113.9
101.5
102.4
102.8
1985年
1990年
1995年
2000年
2005年
2010年

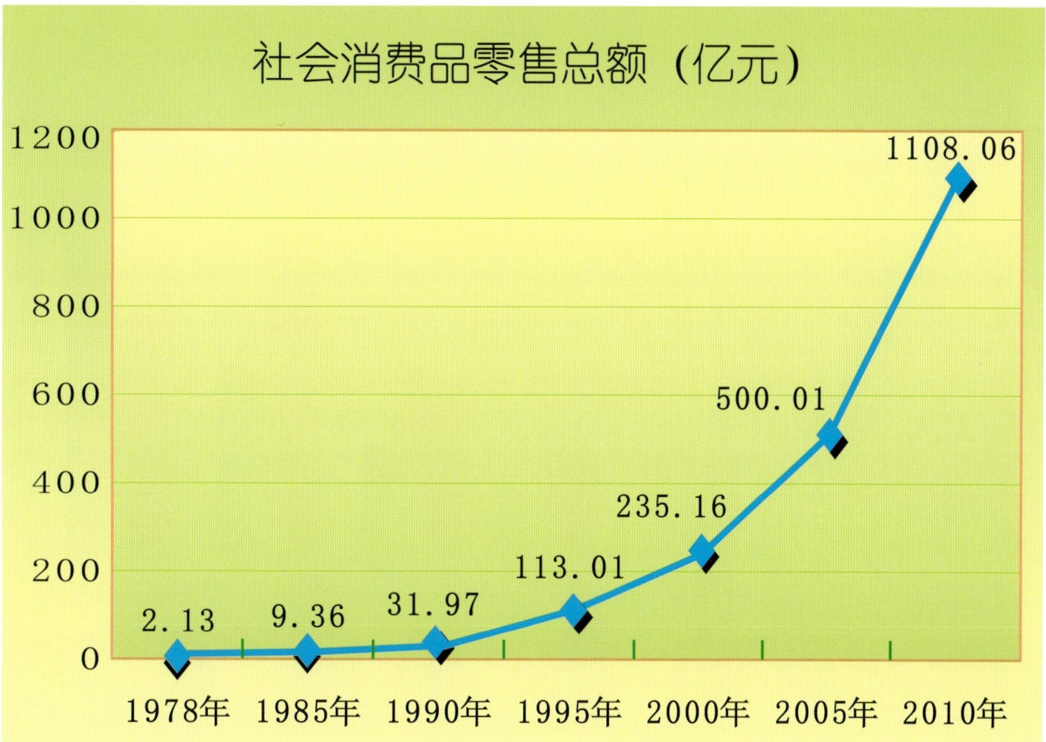
社会消费品零售总额（亿元）
1200
1000
800
600
400
200
0
2.13
9.36
31.97
113.01
235.16
500.01
1108.06
1978年
1985年
1990年
1995年
2000年
2005年
2010年

城乡居民人民币储蓄存款余额(亿元)

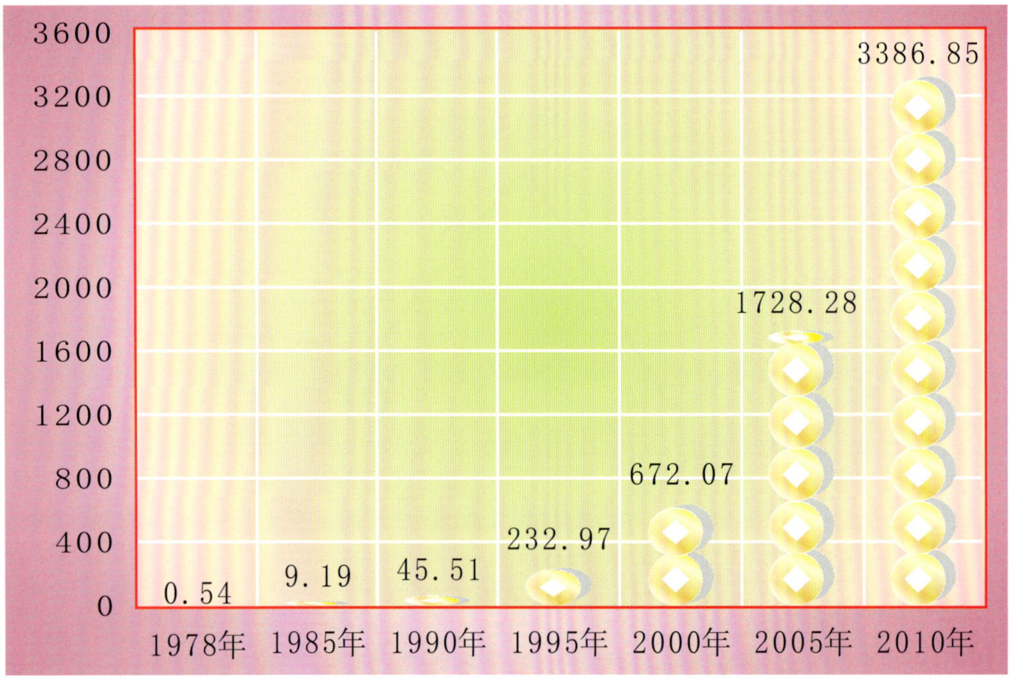

城乡居民收入(元)

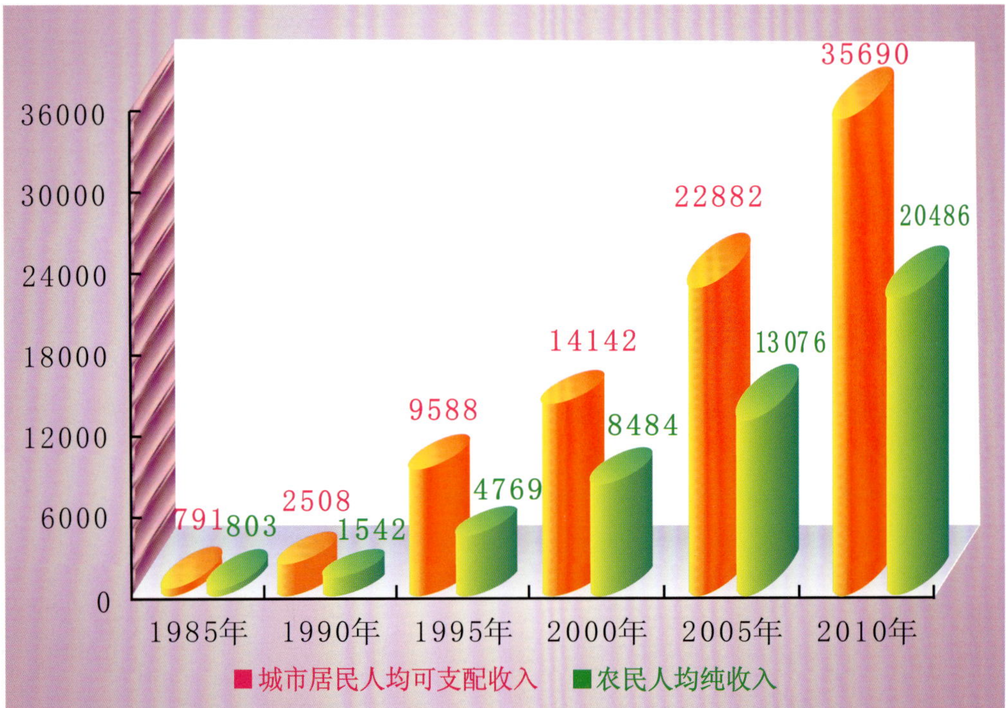

注：农民人均纯收入采用农村住户抽样调查口径，相应调整了往年数。

全社会固定资产投资总额(亿元)

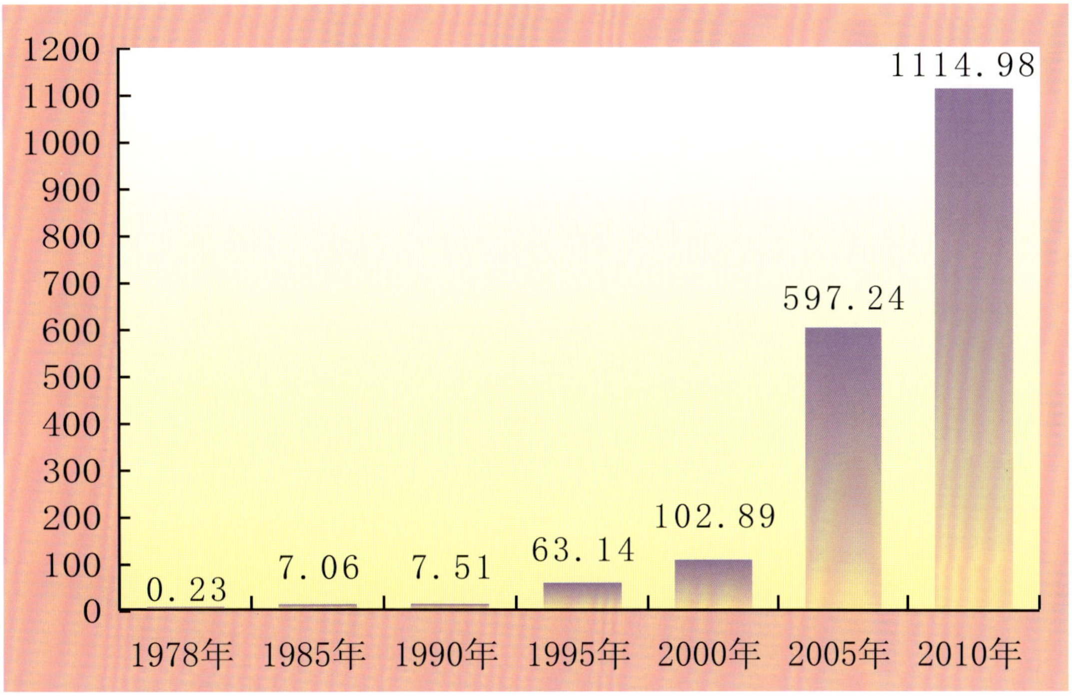

总供电量和总售电量(亿千瓦时)

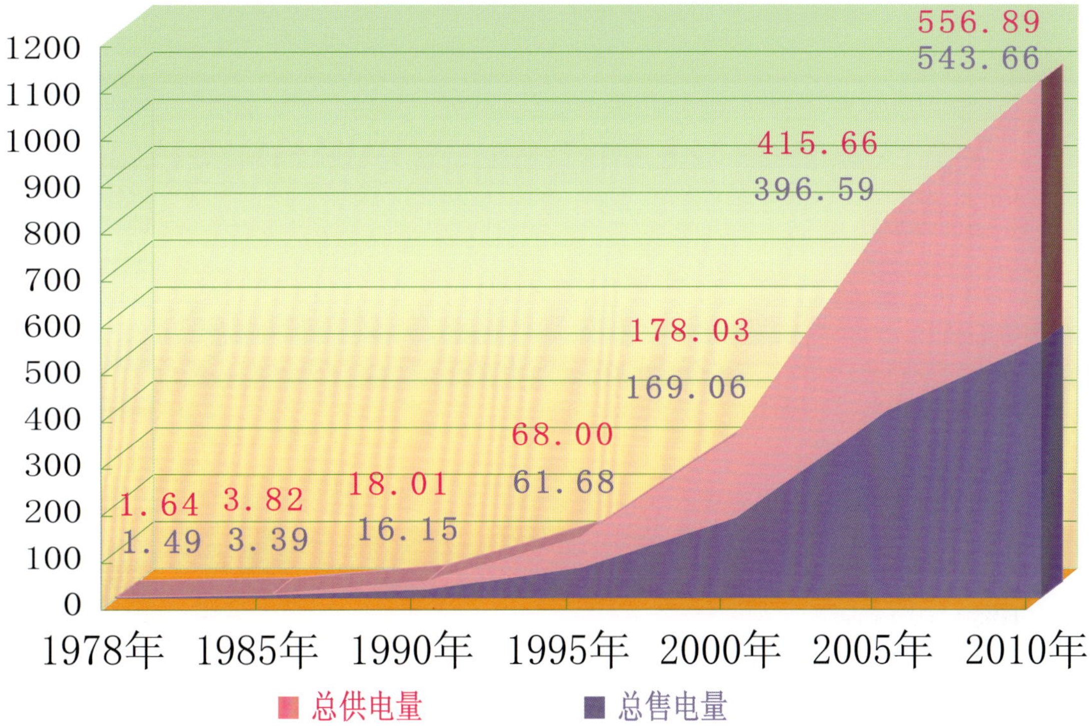

公路密度(公里/百平方公里)

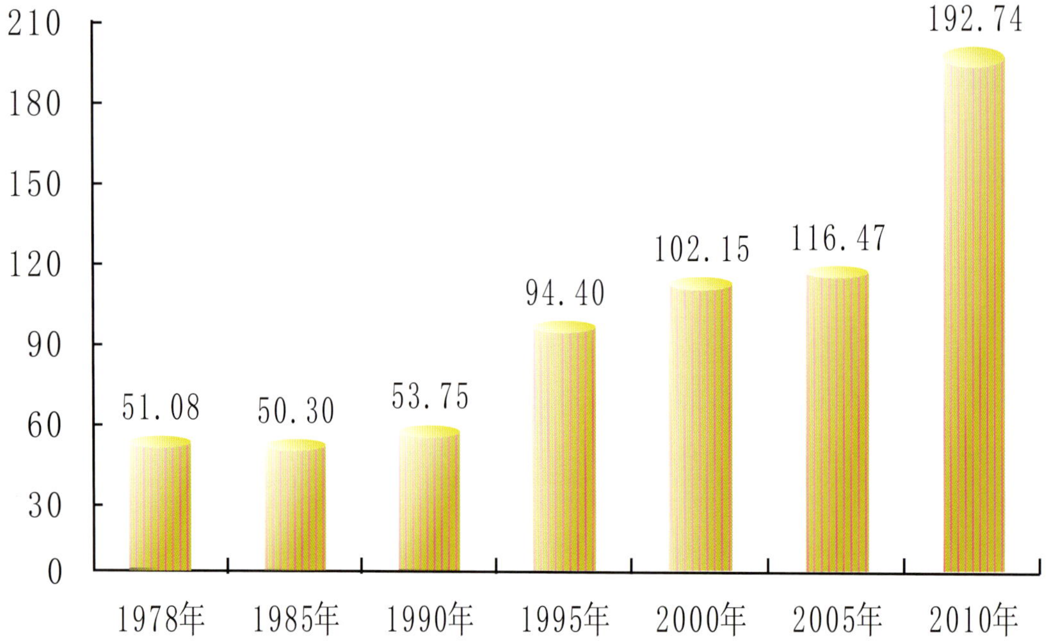

注：公路密度2000年起含高速公路，2006年起含专用公路和村道。

本地电话用户、移动电话用户(万户)

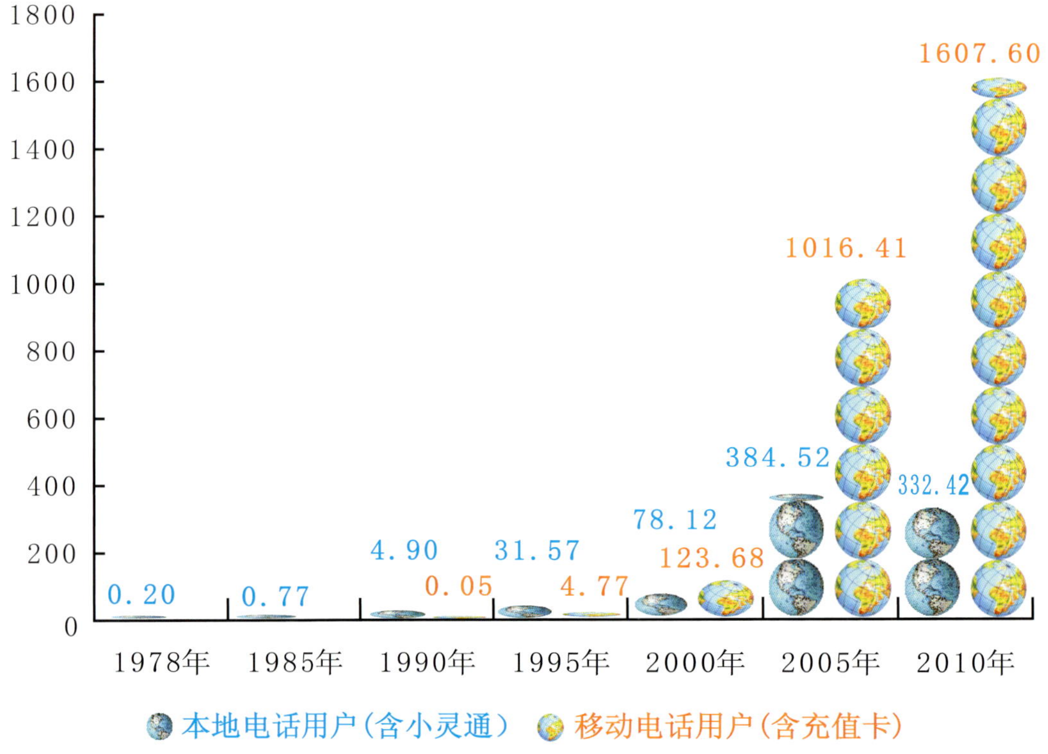

第一部分　概　述

Part One　Outline

2010 年东莞市国民经济和社会发展统计公报

2010 年，东莞人民在市委、市政府的坚强领导下，以科学发展观统领全局，全面实施《珠三角地区改革发展规划纲要（2008－2020 年）》，突出以转变发展方式为主线，继续稳增长，加力调结构，积极优环境，全面强管理，继续巩固应对国际金融危机取得的成果，国民经济发展逐步摆脱了金融危机带来的影响，呈现出经济平稳较快增长，社会事业不断进步的格局。

一、经济发展

经济总量

初步核算，2010 年东莞市生产总值（GDP）4246.25 亿元，按可比价格计算，比上年增长 10.3%。其中第一产业增加值 16.64 亿元，增长 1.9%；第二产业增加值 2183.18 亿元，增长 16.8%；第三产业增加值 2046.43 亿元，增长 3.9%。三大产业比例为 0.4∶51.4∶48.2。在第三产业中，交通运输、仓储和邮政业增长 6.9%，批发和零售业增长 9.1%，住宿和餐饮业增长 0.9%，金融业增长 4.5%，房地产业下降 1.1%，其他服务业增长 3.4%。

图一 2005-2010 年地区生产总值及增长速度

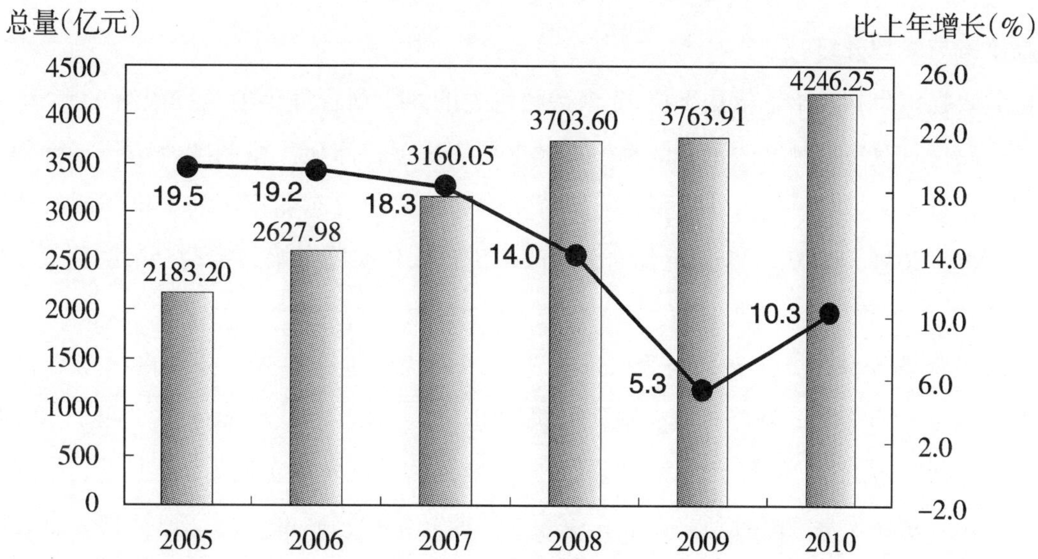

全年来源于东莞的财政收入 785.10 亿元，比上年增长 25.1%。其中市财政一般预算收入 277.84 亿元，增长 20.2%。在市财政一般预算收入中，增值税 62.63 亿元，增长 17.2%；营业税 45.87 亿元，增长 2.6%；企业所得税 24.80 亿元，增长 40.3%；个人所得税 11.04 亿元，增长 26.5%；城市维护建设税 11.38 亿元，增长 23.6%；房产税 9.27 亿元，增长 22.3%；契税 18.70 亿元，增长 18.7%。全年全市工商税收总额 688.72 亿元，比上年增长 25.8%。其中国税 439.44 亿元，增长 29.8%；地税 249.29 亿元，增长 19.3%。全年地方一般财政支出 308.61 亿元，比上年增长 32.7%。其中，一般公共服务支出 16.77 亿元，公共安全支出 28.86 亿元，教育支出 41.30 亿元，科学技术支出 8.60 亿元，

文化体育与传媒支出3.66亿元，社会保障和就业支出19.05亿元，医疗卫生支出3.21亿元，环境保护支出12.26亿元，城乡社区事务支出3.19亿元，农林水事务支出9.86亿元，交通运输支出26.17亿元。

所有制构成

初步核算，在全市生产总值中，公有制经济增加值1095.53亿元，比上年增长6.3%，占25.8%；民营经济增加值1536.47亿元，增长13.1%，占36.2%；外资经济增加值1614.25亿元，增长9.4%，占38.0%。

在全市规模以上工业增加值中，国有控股工业增加值122.14亿元，比上年增长9.0%；集体工业增加值68.93亿元，增长9.1%；外商投资工业增加值584.09亿元，增长22.3%；港澳台投资工业增加值799.90亿元，增长16.6%。私营工业增加值192.19亿元，增长18.9%。

在固定资产投资总额中，国有经济投资162.84亿元，占固定资产投资总额的比重为14.6%；集体经济投资148.23亿元，占13.3%；民营经济投资450.85亿元，占40.4%；外商及港澳台投资223.89亿元，占20.1%。

在限额以上批发零售贸易业零售额中，内资企业实现零售额425.92亿元，比上年增长26.3%，占贸易业零售额的比重为90.0%。其中，国有企业占2.5%，集体企业占4.1%，有限责任公司占33.0%，股份有限公司占13.9%，私营企业占34.2%；外商及港澳台投资企业实现零售额40.34亿元，增长24.3%，占9.8%；个体户实现零售额0.94亿元，占0.2%。

在出口总额中，国有企业出口额110.27亿美元，比上年下降0.9%；三资企业出口额442.62亿美元，增长32.3%；集体企业出口额14.16亿美元，增长50.8%。

体制改革与转型升级

深化简政强镇事权改革，依法下放33个行政机关的542项管理事项及权限给11个中心镇和3个市属园区；深化行政审批制度改革，调整了审批事项232项；深化户籍制度改革，实行积分制入户和居住证制度，近1.2万名新莞人获得积分入户资格；编制实施《东莞市医药卫生体制改革近期重点实施方案（2009－2011年）》，初步拟定公立医院改革试点工作实施方案，推动全市医药卫生体制改革取得积极进展。

加快加工贸易转型升级，支持企业引进先进技术、优化生产模式、拓展内销市场。全年共受理1250家来料加工企业转型，新增外资企业研发机构150个。认定现代产业体系“四个30项目”、商贸流通业“四个十大项目”、民营工业50强、服务业50强和首批总部企业等，实施重点扶持。推动3家企业成功上市。加快发展战略性新兴产业，薄膜太阳能光伏和物联网2个基地被列为全省战略性新兴产业基地。

固定资产投资

全年全社会固定资产投资1114.98亿元，比上年增长1.9%。

在固定资产投资总额中，新建713.12亿元，比上年下降1.0%；扩建73.58亿元，下降9.4%；改建和技术改造投资112.03亿元，增长33.4%；房地产开发投资298.99亿元，增长7.7%。从产业投向看，投资集中在二、三产业。第二产业投资407.9亿元，占36.6%，其中制造业投资338.75亿元；第三产业投资706.89亿元，占63.4%。

图二　2005-2010 年全社会固定资产投资总额及其增长速度

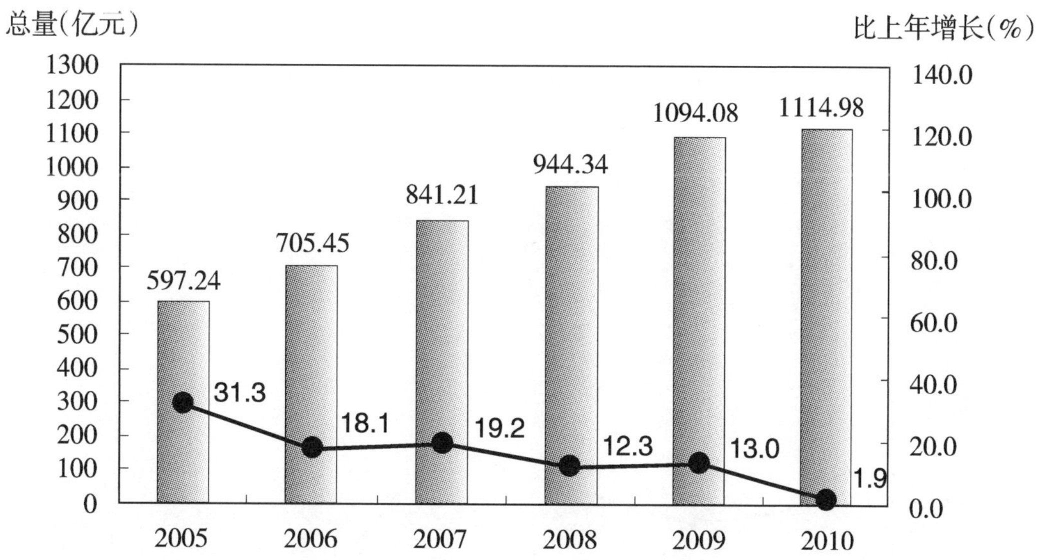

注：从 2009 年起全社会固定资产投资总额数包含跨区项目金额，2009 年增速按同口径计算，比上年增长 13.0%。

表一：2010 年分行业固定资产投资额情况

单位：万元

行　业	投资额	增长%
总计	11149822	1.9
农、林、牧、渔业	1922	-68.7
制造业	3387524	0.6
电力、燃气及水的生产和供应业	687134	15.4
建筑业	4051	157.4
交通运输、仓储和邮政业	1240268	-1.8
信息传输、计算机服务和软件业	200850	-3.1
批发和零售业	201106	23.3
住宿和饮食业	109330	-51.5
金融业	26286	133.8
房地产业	3646832	3.3
租赁和商务服务业	66834	-55.6
科研、技术服务和地质勘查业	93236	87.8
水利、环境和公共设施管理业	793687	2.3
居民服务和其他服务业	29535	48.2
教育	221760	57.9
卫生、社会保障和社会福利业	145102	-31.7
文化、体育和娱乐业	122797	64.4
公共管理和社会组织	171241	18.7

价格

全年居民消费价格总水平比上年上涨 2.8%。其中居住类价格上涨 5.1%，娱乐教育文化用品及服务类价格上涨 3.7%，食品类价格上涨 4.6%，医疗保健和个人用品类价格上涨 1.9%，烟酒及用品类价格上涨1.7%，交通和通信类价格上涨0.4%，家庭设备用品及维修服务类价格上涨0.3%，衣着类价格下降2.1%。商品零售价格上涨3.2%。工业品出厂价格上涨2.6%。

图三　2005－2010年居民消费价格涨跌幅度

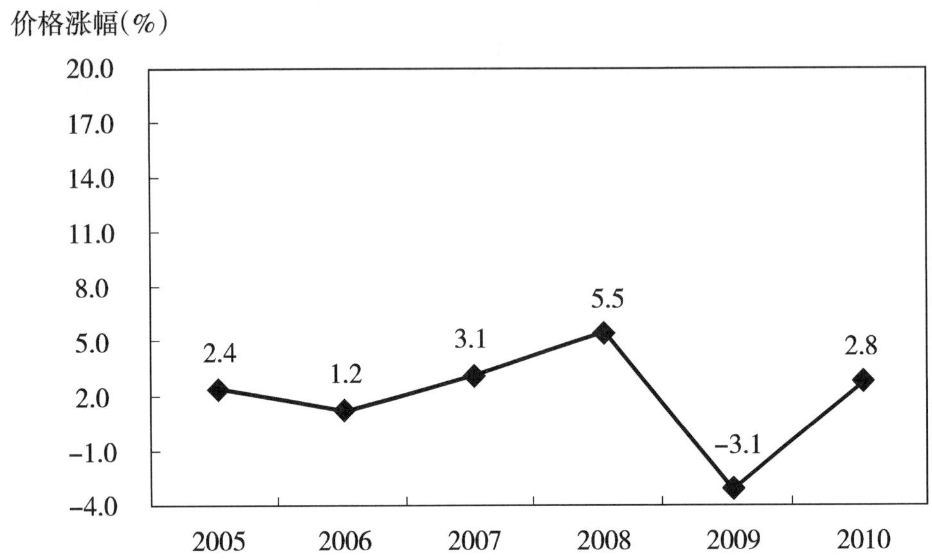

表二：2010年价格变动情况

类　　别	价格指数（%）	比上年升降幅度（%）
居民消费价格指数	102.8	2.8
食　品	104.6	4.6
其中：粮食	104.0	4.0
肉禽及其制品	103.6	3.6
油脂	104.9	4.9
蛋	100.8	0.8
鲜菜	114.5	14.5
水产品	104.5	4.5
烟酒及用品	101.7	1.7
衣　着	97.9	-2.1
家庭设备用品及服务	100.3	0.3
医疗保健及个人用品	101.9	1.9
交通和通信	100.4	0.4
娱乐教育文化用品及服务	103.7	3.7
居　住	105.1	5.1
商品零售价格指数	103.2	3.2
工业品出厂价格指数	102.6	2.6

农业

全年全市完成农业总产值28.31亿元，按可比价计算，比上年增长3.3%。其中种植业产值14.82亿元，下降1.6%，占总产值的52.3%；林业产值0.29亿元，增长14.7%，占1.0%；牧业产值5.55亿元，增长13.1%，占19.6%；渔业产值6.80亿元，增长5.7%，占24.0%。全年粮食种植面积4.19万亩，粮食产量1.25万吨；水产品产量7.63万吨，增长4.1%；蔬菜产量39.29万吨，下降1.8%；生猪出栏数33.64万头，增长19.8%；家禽出栏数746.21万只，下降0.8%。

全年新增省级农业龙头企业1家、市级农业龙头企业1家、新增农民专业合作组织4家。年末全市共有20家农业龙头企业和29家农民专业合作组织，其中省级以上龙头企业7家、国家级2家。年末全市共有广东省名牌产品（农业类）28个、无公害农产品49个、绿色食品44个、有机食品9个。

工业

全年全市规模以上工业增加值1812.86亿元，增长19.0%。其中，重工业增加值960.81亿元，增长20.1%，所占比重为53.0%；轻工业增加值852.05亿元，增长17.8%，占47.0%。大中型工业企业增加值1265.95亿元，占规模以上工业增加值的69.8%。规模以上工业实现利润总额274.87亿元，比上年增长66.3%；资产负债率为60.94%；工业经济综合效益指数为132.63，比上年上升15.43个点。

全年规模以上八大支柱产业增加值1100.12亿元，比上年增长20.0%。其中通信设备、计算机及其他电子设备制造业增加值426.68亿元，增长22.5%。规模以上电子信息制造业增加值668.92亿元，增长22.6%；实现利润总额87.71亿元，增长89.94%。

表三：2010年规模以上工业主要产品产量

产品名称	计量单位	产 量	比上年增长%
电子元件	万只	91845707.91	34.5
机制纸及纸板	吨	9331823.42	10.5
瓷质砖	平方米	20873228.66	8.0
发电量	万千瓦时	3563821.51	4.4
家具	件	73902146.42	18.0
服装	万件	140556.06	7.5
玩具	千元	8279161.78	16.5
钢化玻璃	平方米	7081445.50	4.7
模具	套	303389.13	57.6
不锈钢日用制品	吨	45888.71	24.2
皮革鞋靴	万双	43061.65	16.5
电话单机	部	48092167.00	25.3
组合音响	台	36368747.59	41.5
印制电路板	平方米	18011668.38	34.4
彩色电视机	台	5358975.00	9.3
金属切削工具	万件	1949.04	47.0
电力电缆	千米	383829.09	70.6
布	万米	15794.13	20.7
表	只	21675597.00	58.7
化学纤维	吨	11178.40	37.9
光电子器件	万只	1030151.59	41.8
印刷专用设备	吨	9456.80	34.5
移动通信手持机（手机）	台	19952986.00	71.2
电工仪器仪表	台	5320941.00	44.5
塑料加工专用设备	台	38860.91	87.0
家用电风扇	台	20813012.00	3.2
显示器	台	1573415.00	-3.6

建筑业

全年全市建筑业增加值82.37亿元，比上年下降2.9%。

建筑企业完成产值115.58亿元，比上年增长16.7%；施工面积709.91万平方米，下降2.8%；竣工面积306.9万平方米，下降10.8%。建筑企业按产值计算的全员劳动生产率为22.6万元/人，比上年增长23.5%。

交通运输、仓储和邮政业

全年全市交通运输、仓储和邮政业增加值86.51亿元，比上年增长6.9%。

年末全市境内公路通车里程（含乡村道路）4750.99公里，公路密度192.74公里/百平方公里。其中等级公路4673.04公里，密度189.58公里/百平方公里；高速公路216.74公里，密度8.79公里/百平方公里。年末全市机动车保有量134.75万辆，比上年增长6.2%。其中汽车保有量92.08万辆，增长15.7%。公路货物运输7640万吨，公路货物周转量51.08亿吨公里；水路货物运输1672万吨，水路货物周转量57.95亿吨公里。全年公路运输完成旅客客运量7.74亿人，旅客周转量128.87亿人公里；水路运输31万人，旅客周转量2017万人公里。全年港口旅客吞吐量30.62万人，港口货物吞吐量5657.29万吨。

全年完成邮电业务收入157.93亿元，比上年增长1.0%。其中电信业务收入149.81亿元，增长0.4%；移动业务收入106.58亿元，增长5.2%；邮政业务收入8.12亿元，增长13.6%。全年发送信函4507万件，增长5.4%；邮政特快专递627万件，增长12.6%；全年邮政汇款汇出金额280.51亿元，增长26.2%。

国内贸易

全年全市批发和零售业增加值406.84亿元，比上年增长9.1%；住宿和餐饮业增加值147.82亿元，增长0.9%。

全年全市社会消费品零售总额1108.06亿元，比上年增长15.9%，扣除物价因素影响，实际增长12.3%。分行业看，批发零售贸易业零售额1005.53亿元，增长16.6%；住宿餐饮业零售额102.53亿元，增长9.1%。

在限额以上贸易业中，五金、电料类零售额增长36.3%；家用电器和音像器材类增长32.6%；汽车类增长30.1%；食品、饮料、烟酒类增长18.7%；日用品类增长16.9%；服装鞋帽、针、纺织品类增长6.9%。

全年批发零售贸易业实现商品销售总额1957.18亿元，比上年增长23.7%。

图四　2005-2010年社会消费品零售总额及其增长速度

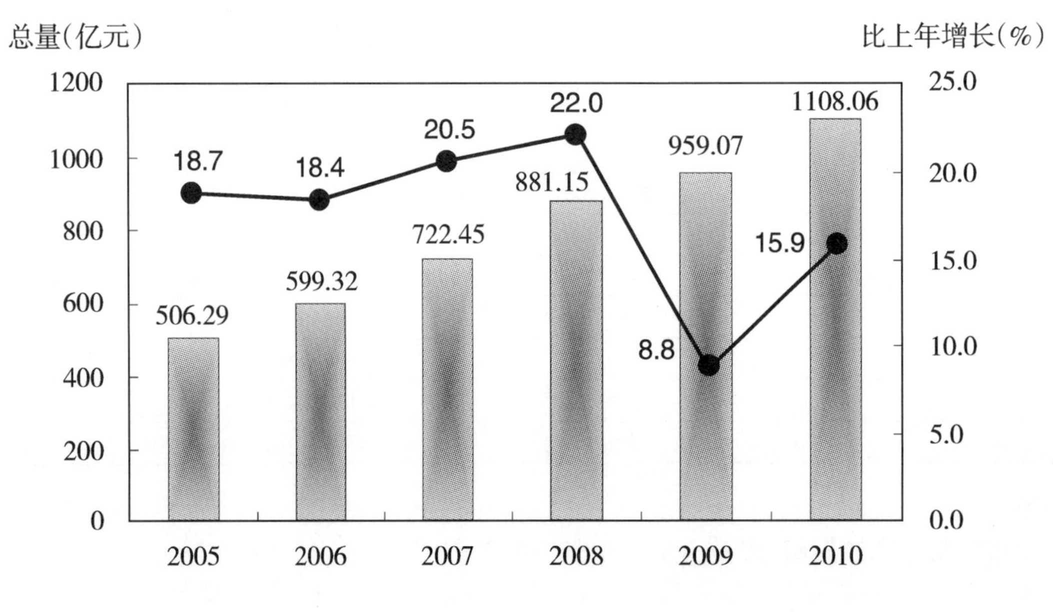

金融业

全年全市金融业增加值165.44亿元，比上年增长4.5%。

全年新增各类金融机构7家。年末全市有各类金融机构83家，其中银行类机构26家，证券期货类机构20家，保险类机构37家。

年末全市金融机构各项人民币存款余额5943.39亿元，比年初增长19.2%。其中企业存款余额1521.56亿元，增长15.2%；财政性存款余额46.58亿元，下降11.2%。各项人民币贷款余额3329.82亿元，比年初增长14.7%。在个人消费贷款余额中，个人住房按揭贷款余额704.63亿元，增长16.1%；个人汽车消费贷款余额20.71亿元，下降13.9%。全年金融机构现金收入9867.57亿元，现金支出10084.22亿元，收支相抵现金净投放216.65亿元。年末全市金融机构不良贷款率比年初下降0.52个百分点。

年末全市各类证券公司共有开户数82.07万户，比上年增加4.47万户。全年股票总成交额10989.84亿元，比上年下降5.9%。年末保证金余额136.33亿元，比上年下降16.2%。

年末全市有各类保险公司38家；保险中介机构44家，比上年增加13家。保险从业人员2.7万人。全年保费收入159.72亿元，比上年增长38.8%。其中财产险保费收入46.72亿元，增长32.1%；人寿险保费收入113亿元，增长41.7%。全年保险赔款与给付金额35亿元，其中财产险赔款21.8亿元，综合赔付率为46.7%。人寿险赔款与给付13.2亿元。

房地产业

全年全市房地产业增加值288.36亿元，比上年下降1.1%。

全年完成房地产开发投资298.99亿元，比上年增长7.7%。商品房施工面积2060.54万平方米，下降11.7%；竣工面积296.59万平方米，下降4.4%；销售面积511.25万平方米，下降14.8%，其中商品住宅销售面积469.9万平方米，下降18.8%。全年商品房销售额373.77亿元，增长5.9%，其中商品住宅销售额334.15亿元，下降0.03%。

民营经济

年末全市民营单位登记注册户数49.28万户，比上年末增长3.1%。其中私营企业增长较快，达到8.87万户，增长19.4%；个体工商户40.24万户，下降0.2%。全年规模以上民营工业完成总产值1195.19亿元，增长21.4%；民营经济完成固定资产投资450.85亿元，增长4.5%；民营经济消费品零售额929.83亿元，增长15.9%；民营经济缴税总额261.05亿元，增长31.9%。

区域经济

年末全市32个镇街本级总资产1070.18亿元，净资产703.70亿元，分别比上年增长10.5%和10.3%；年末全市村组两级集体总资产1230.91亿元，增长4.7%；净资产942.29亿元，增长5.3%；全年镇街本级可支配收入217.42亿元（包含土地和物业转让收入），增长14.2%。当年可支配财政收入超10亿元的镇街有6个。可支配收入（扣除土地物业转让纯收入）超1亿元的村有20个；超5千万的村有69个；超1千万的村有419个。

突出加快园区开发建设。松山湖成功晋升国家级高新区，台湾高科技园开园，粤港澳文化创意产业实验园在莞落户。虎门港泊位码头建设加快，保税物流中心投入运行，对台直航航线正式通航。东莞生态园基础设施建设加快，生态修复初见成效，首次对外公开招商。长安新区用海申报、规划编制等工作扎实推进。

二、对外开放

对外贸易

全年全市进出口总额 1213.38 亿美元，比上年增长 28.8%。其中进口总额 517.40 亿美元，增长 32.7%；出口总额 695.98 亿美元，增长 26.1%。

按贸易方式分，一般贸易出口 95.41 亿美元，比上年增长 66.9%；加工贸易出口 590.16 亿美元，增长 21.0%；其他出口 10.40 亿美元，增长 55.4%。

按出口的国家和地区分，对亚洲出口 354.36 亿美元，比上年增长 29.6%；对欧洲出口 121.37 亿美元，增长 26.0%；对北美洲出口 189.88 亿美元，增长 20.4%；对拉丁美洲出口 17.50 亿美元，增长 32.1%；对大洋洲出口 8.60 亿美元，增长 5.9%。

全年机电产品出口 494.83 亿美元，比上年增长 24.1%，占出口总额的比重为 71.1%。高新技术产品出口 241.95 亿美元，增长 23.0%，占 34.8%。

表四：2010 年主要商品出口情况

单位：万美元

商 品 名 称	金额	比上年增长%
自动数据处理设备及其部件	528199	25.0
服装及衣着附件	389784	38.7
自动数据处理设备的零件	333050	24.8
鞋类	309561	26.0
家具及其零件	320917	32.3
静止式变流器	359806	55.5
游戏机	84546	-53.7
有线电话机（包括无绳电话机）	164438	10.8
纺织纱线、织物及制品	152070	11.2
数字式相机	160842	26.5
电视、收音机及无线电讯设备的零附件	161166	27.9
玩具	163174	32.9
旅行用品及箱包	156455	36.8
电线和电缆	152169	40.8
电视机（包括整套散件）	96536	-5.3
通断保护电路装置及零件	133965	29.2
塑料制品	113700	25.1
录、放像机	132369	57.3
手持或车载无线电话机	96899	21.2

吸收外资

按新口径统计，全年全市新签外商直接投资项目 869 宗，合同外资金额 25.97 亿美元，比上年增长60.7%。实际利用外资27.32亿美元，增长5.3%。全市新签投资总额超1000万美元的项目46宗，增加19宗；新签第三产业项目合同外资金额3.60亿美元，占全市的13.8%。外商投资进入商贸领域加快。全市新签批发和零售业项目有109宗，合同吸收外资2.07亿美元，增长66.5%，占第三产业吸收外资的57.5%。

表五：2010年分行业利用外资及其增长速度

单位：万美元

行业名称	合同外资金额	比上年增长%	实际利用外资	比上年增长%
总计	259740	60.7	273171	5.3
农、林、牧、渔业	1010	7699.2	62	77.1
制造业	222761	62.7	241618	3.2
其中：纺织业	12908	136.5	7225	-10.4
纺织服装、鞋、帽制造业	13120	277.7	9137	-21.0
家具制造业	1825	-44.5	6155	-9.8
普通机械制造业	6530	118.1	7541	6.1
专用设备制造业	19263	209.2	15589	17.4
电气机械及器材制造业	20868	66.2	25260	47.9
电子及通信设备制造业	66565	80.0	60796	-3.6
金属制品业	10391	16.0	10371	24.5
塑料制品业	17764	55.5	14007	21.4
文教体育用品制造业	4873	27.8	8439	-22.5
造纸及纸制品业	8057	269.1	21188	-12.4
其他制造业	40597	4.5	55910	7.0
信息、计算机服务和软件业	782	232.8	109	-80.9
批发和零售业	20655	66.5	13271	74.7

旅游

年末全市有星级酒店97家。其中五星级酒店22家，四星级酒店25家，三星级酒店35家，二星级酒店14家，一星级酒店1家。全市有旅行社54家，其中国际旅行社9家，国内旅行社41家，其他4家。全年接待国际及港澳台旅游入境人数327.4万人次，比上年增长14.5%。其中入境外国人108.69万人次，增长4.3%；港澳台同胞218.71万人次，增长20.3%。国际旅游外汇收入6.76亿美元，增长30.6%。全年接待国内旅游人数1923.83万人次，增长9.9%。旅游总收入191.32亿元，增长26.3%。

全年东莞组团外出旅游人数153.8万人次，比上年增长21.0%。其中，国内旅游人数139.09万人次，增长21.5%；出境旅游人数14.71万人次，增长16.3%。

三、城市建设

城市绿化

年末全市建成区土地面积798.48平方公里，公共设施用地面积61.31平方公里。全市林业用地面积91.0万亩，森林覆盖率为36.7%，林地绿化率为98.7%；城市建成区绿地率为41.16%，绿化覆盖率为44.31%；全市已建成公园广场1004个，面积11130公顷。

公用事业

年末全市有公交线路96条，公交运营车辆1443辆。全年市内公共汽车旅客客运量2.31亿人次。

全市自来水日供水能力达到700万立方米，全年自来水供水总量16.56亿立方米。年末供水管道总长度16268.01公里。全年全社会用电量562亿千瓦时，增长13.4%。其中工业用电435.57亿千瓦时，增长15.8%；照明用电107.07亿千瓦时，增长5.9%。年末全市液化石油气家庭用户87.09万户，天然气家庭用户14.60万户。全年液化石油气供应量34.46万吨，天然气供气量2.96亿立方米。

信息化

2010年信息化综合指数为74.6%。年末全市普通固定电话225.64万户，比上年增加19.08万户；移动电话用户1632.90万户，增加223.61万户，其中充值卡用户1452.01万户，增加180.86万户。全年长途电话通话时长188.43亿分钟，其中对国际及港澳台电话通话时长3.08亿分钟。年末互联网用户153.92万户，比上年增加35.90万户；宽带接入用户150.08万户，增加35.87万户。

四、社会事业

科技

全年新增省级产业集群升级示范区2个、国家高新技术企业91家、省民营科技企业126家、省级以上技术工程中心14个、企业博士后科研工作站5个、省级以上名牌名标56个，参与制订各类技术标准37项，获批省创新科研团队3个。预计全市高新技术产业产值2579.1亿元，比上年增长19.1%。

全年专利申请量21654件、授权量20397件，分别比上年增长13.3%和57.9%。其中发明专利申请量3143件，授权量442件；实用新型申请量7677件，授权量7529件；外观设计申请量10834件，授权量12426件。

教育

全市共有幼儿园727所，比上年增加47所，其中公立集体办园169所，民办园558所。共有省、市一级幼儿园101所。3－6周岁在园（班）幼儿共20.84万人，入园（班）率达95.15%，比上年提高0.05个百分点。

全市共有小学330所，比上年减少7所；在校学生55.24万人；适龄儿童入学率达100%，本市户籍毕业生升学率达100%。全市有初中150所，初中在校学生18.79万人，户籍适龄少年入学率为100%，辍学率为0.22%，毕业生升学率为97.9%。

全市高中阶段学校有66所（含民办学校18所），在校学生11.79万人（含技校），其中普通高中（含完中）40所，在校学生7.04万人，中职学校26所（含技工学校1所），在校学生4.75万人（含技校）。本市户籍初中毕业生35744人，升入各类高中阶段学校就读的学生34985人，其中普通高中21155人，中职学校13830人。本市户籍学生高中阶段毛入学率为94.9%，比上年提高1.3个百分点。

全市有成人高等教育机构1所、镇街成人文化技术学校32所、民办成人非学历教育机构231个，各类成人教育年培训量达52万多人次。

全市有普通高等院校5所。其中本科院校2所，专科院校3所。在校学生3.83万人。全年普通高等院校共招收本科、专科学生1.27万人。毕业生8105人。

2010年全市参加高考总人数24712人，其中普通类21076人，高职类3636人。在普通类考生中，上重点线2353人，比上年增加124人；上本科线9878人，增加1494人。

文化

年末全市有群众艺术馆1个，文化站33个，公共图书馆505个，博物馆30个，文化广场511个，艺术表演场所63个，电影放映单位46个，网吧1053间，公共文化设施建筑面积1160.5万平方米。全市有公共广播节目57套，公共电视节目49套。广播、电视综合覆盖率均达到100%。有线电视“村村通”工程继续推进，全市覆盖率达100%。全年共出版报纸8229.5万份，各类杂志刊物132.38万册（含内部刊物），图书7.56万册，《东莞日报》发行量4562.5万份，电影放映11.52万场次，观众387.74万人次。

卫生

年末全市有医疗机构2229个，其中门诊、诊所、卫生站、医务室、社区卫生服务等基层医疗机构2151个，卫生技术人员37487人，医院病床19980张。全市建成并投入使用的社区卫生服务中心388个，覆盖了全市300多个村（社区）。全年诊疗总人数上升11.9%。

体育

全年东莞运动员共获得50枚金牌（省级以上）、56枚银牌、46枚铜牌。其中夺得国际赛金牌4枚，银牌2枚；夺得全国赛金牌6枚，银牌12枚，铜牌10枚；夺得广东省赛金牌40枚、银牌42枚、铜牌36枚。

全年举办市级综合和单项比赛16次，参加人数1.43万人次；举办镇街级单项比赛578次，参加人数65.62万人次。全市有体育彩票发行网点880个，销售总额7.62亿元，体彩公益金0.13亿元。

社会福利与救助

年末全市有敬老院35个，敬老院供养老人894人。全年社会救济人数3.65万人。城市居民最低生活保障支出2018.3万元，社会救济福利费用4448.6万元，自然灾害救济费用139.4万元。全市纳入“五保户”对象有1263人，“五保户”费用支出1535.73万元。32个镇街全部建立了社会保障网络，纳入街道级最低生活保障范围的有1595户共3629人，纳入镇级最低生活保障范围的有12218户共30799人。

社会稳定

严厉打击恶性和多发性犯罪，大力开展扫黄禁赌等专项行动，深入整治治安重点区域和行业，加强巡逻防控与校园安保。新建省“六好”平安和谐社区41个，市平安社区218个，全年刑事案件破案宗数增长29.9%。深入推进危险化学品、“三小”场所、出租屋、建筑安全、食品药品质量等专项整治，开展创新消防管理试点，落实挂牌督办任务，排查和整改了一批安全隐患。新建镇街应急避灾中心17个，建成食品安全样板市场67个。全市各类安全事故宗数、死亡人数分别下降3.2%和1.4%。完成镇街综治信访维稳中心和村（社区）综治工作站的建设，落实领导接访包案和带案下访等制度，群众信访总量下降23.4%，纠纷调处成功率达93%。加强劳动执法监察和劳资关系调解，劳资突发事件、欠薪逃匿案件分别下降3.4%和37%。

安全生产

全年全市共发生各类生产事故4910宗，比上年下降3.2%；死亡574人，受伤5365人，分别下降

1.4% 和 3.6%；直接经济损失 896.7 万元，上升 12.6%。其中，道路交通事故 4872 宗，下降 3.3%；造成死亡 526 人，受伤 5355 人，分别下降 3.5% 和 3.7%。亿元地区生产总值生产安全事故死亡率为 0.135，工矿商贸 10 万人生产安全事故死亡率为 0.62，道路交通万车死亡率为 3.93。

资源和环境保护

全年雨日天数 202 天，全年日照时数 1699.7 小时，平均气温 22.4 摄氏度，相对湿度 73%。全年降水量 2165.9 毫米。

年末全市有森林公园 17 个，生态公益林 37.63 万亩，林木积蓄量 255.82 万立方米，林木总生长量 15.52 万立方米。全年完成造林 1829.05 公顷，种植乡土阔叶树 135.9 万株；全市参与义务植树人数 85.32 万人，种植树木 329 万株；共投入 1695.9 万元创建林业生态文明村，完成 110.9 公里的道路补绿和 84.2 公顷的闲置地增绿。

全年空气污染指数平均值为 56，空气质量优良天数占 97.8%。全年投入 1.2 亿元，建成樟村水质净化厂污泥初级处置项目，日处理污泥 500 吨。投入 3.9 亿元基本建成污泥处理厂黄江项目。全市新规划的 34 项污水处理工程建成 33 座，截污主干管道完成 86% 工程量。

五、人民生活

人口

年末全市户籍人口 181.77 万人。全年出生人口 1.95 万人，出生率为 10.90‰；死亡人口 8367 人，死亡率为 4.67‰；人口自然增长率为 6.23‰。

居民收入

2010 年全市职工年平均工资 16108 元，比上年增长 11.7%。城镇在岗职工年平均工资 46576 元，增长 9.4%。城市居民人均可支配收入 36350 元，农村居民人均纯收入 20486 元，分别比上年增长 10.0% 和 13.2%。

图五　2005-2010 年城市居民人均可支配收入及其增长速度

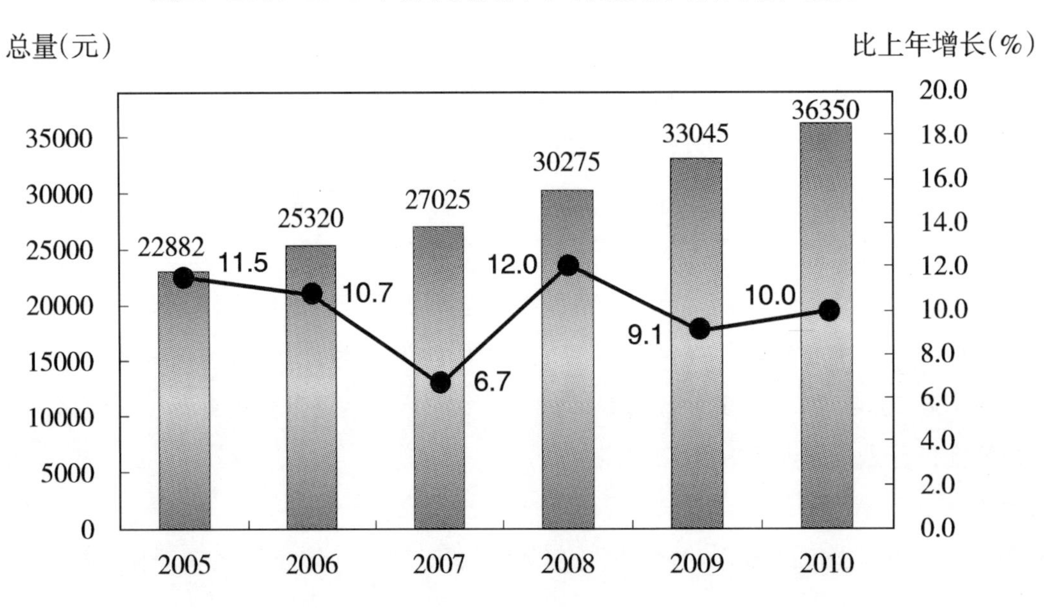

图六　2005-2010 年农民人均纯收入及其增长速度

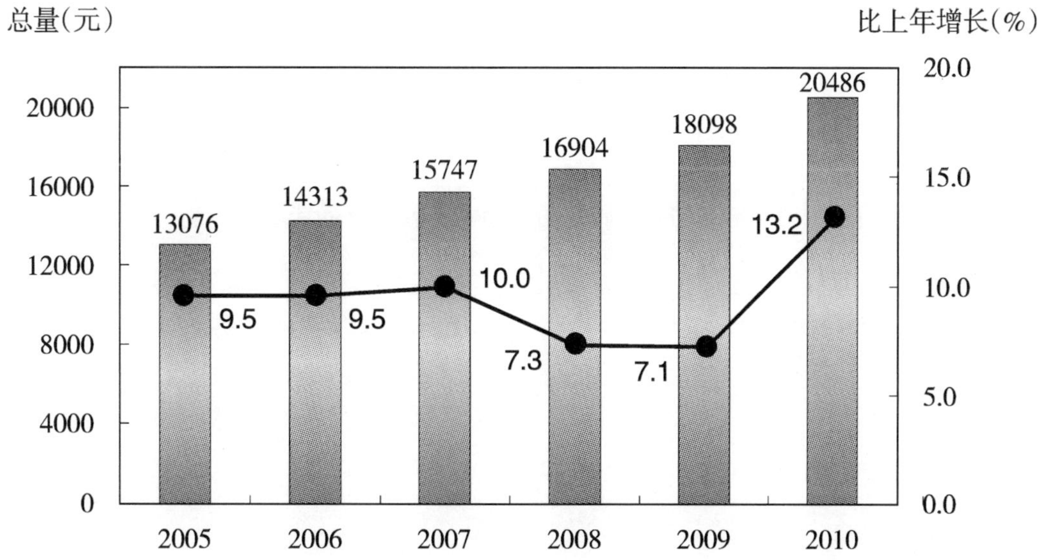

居民消费

全年城市居民人均消费性支出 25733 元，比上年增长 6.0%。其中食品消费支出 8733 元，增长 9.5%；衣着消费支出 1706 元，增长 14.3%；居住消费支出 2089 元，下降 6.4%；家庭设备用品及服务支出 1771 元，增长 9.6%；医疗保健支出 1294 元，下降 7.6%；交通和通信支出 5925 元，增长 8.6%；教育文化娱乐服务支出 3443 元，增长 3.5%；其他商品和服务支出 773 元，下降 0.5%。城市居民家庭恩格尔系数为 33.9%。在农民生活消费现金支出中，食品消费支出占 37.5%，衣着消费支出占 5.2%，居住消费支出占 15.6%，家庭设备用品及服务支出占 4.2%，医疗保健支出占 4.7%，交通通讯支出占 17.9%，文教娱乐用品及服务支出占 9.4%，其他商品和服务消费支出占 5.5%。

表六：2010 年城市居民收支情况

指　　标	金额（元）	比上年增长（%）
城市居民人均可支配收入	36350	10.0
#工资性收入	26860	13.2
财产性收入	4889	16.1
转移性收入	3541	14.4
城市居民人均消费性支出	25733	6.0
食品	8733	9.5
衣着	1706	14.3
居住	2089	-6.4
家庭设备用品及服务	1771	9.6
医疗保健	1294	-7.6
交通和通信	5925	8.6
教育文化娱乐服务	3443	3.5
其他商品和服务	773	-0.5

年末平均每百户城市居民家庭耐用消费品拥有量：家用空调 259 台，组合音响 68 套，移动电话 267 部，家用电脑 129 台，淋浴热水器 134 台，家用汽车 68 辆。年末城市居民人均住房建筑面积 58.58 平方

米。平均每百户农村居民家庭耐用消费品拥有量：彩电 164 台，摩托车 87 辆，洗衣机 106 台，淋浴热水器 132 台，移动电话 268 部，影碟机 71 台，家用空调 218 台，家用电脑 104 台，家用汽车 57 辆。

居民储蓄

年末全市城乡居民人民币储蓄存款余额 3386.85 亿元，比年初增加 500.41 亿元。其中，定期储蓄存款余额 1354.23 亿元，增加 88.66 亿元；活期储蓄存款余额 2032.62 亿元，增加 411.75 亿元。

图七　2005-2010 年城乡居民储蓄存款余额及其增长速度

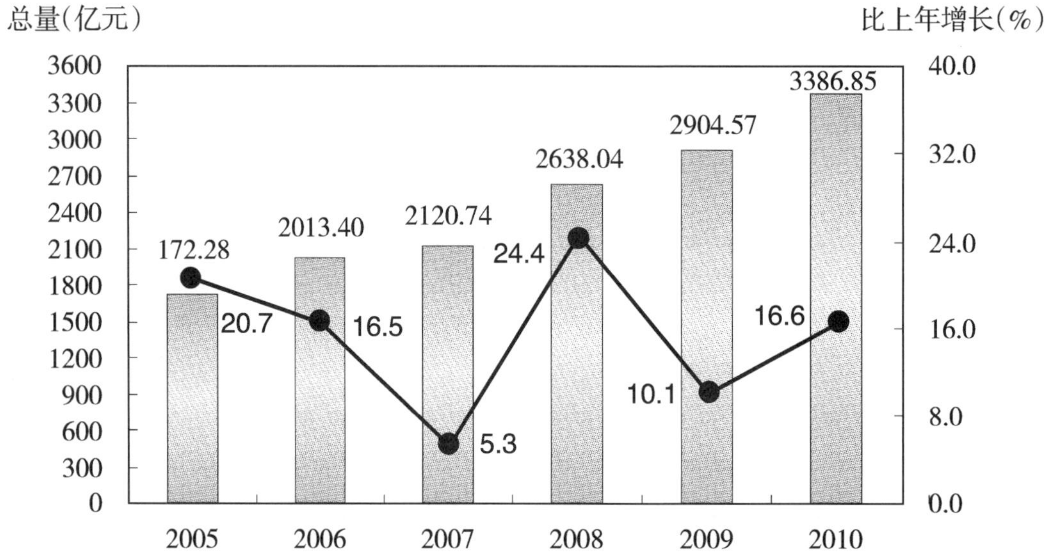

社会保障

年末全市参加职工基本养老保险 421.84 万人，基本医疗保险 592.27 万人，失业保险 279.90 万人，工伤保险 469.08 万人，地方养老保险 371.01 万人。全年社会保险基金总收入 154.41 亿元，保险基金总支出 65.05 亿元，年末保险基金累计余额 413.71 亿元。

国民经济和社会发展中存在的主要困难和问题是：经济回升基础仍不牢固，结构调整力度仍需加大，企业总体技术水平和自主创新能力有待进一步提升。土地、能源等资源制约突出，污染治理与环境保护力度仍需加大。改善民生任务繁重。

注：1. 本公报数为初步统计数，最后统计数据以《东莞统计年鉴 -2011》为准。

2. 地区生产总值、各行业增加值、农业总产值绝对数按当年价格计算，增长速度按可比价格计算。

3. 2010 年人口普查结果需等国家和省批复，统计公报暂不公布常住人口数据。

4. 全市职工年平均工资的调查范围为东莞市辖区内除农户以外各类经济实体，具体包括：①辖区内中央、省、市属各类企业、事业、机关单位；②各镇街办企业；③村及村以下办企业；④私营企业和个体工商户。

城镇在岗职工年平均工资的调查范围包括：①东莞市辖区内中央、省、市属全部独立核算的企业、事业、机关单位；②莞城、石龙、虎门 3 个镇街范围内镇街属单位（不包括莞城、石龙、虎门 3 个镇街以下及其它镇街的单位、全市的私营单位和个体工商户）。

以上两个指标的调查范围不同，调查结果不同，请勿误用。

5. 农村居民人均纯收入采用农村住户抽样调查口径。

6. 阅读本公报时，请注意统计指标的时间、口径和计算方法等。

Dongguan Statistical Communiqué on National Economic and Social Development 2010

In 2010, under the strong leadership of the municipal government, with the guidance of scientific concept of development, in full operation of the 《regional reform and development planning programs of the pearl river delta (2008 - 2020)》, giving prominence to changing the way of development, ensuring the growth of economy, modulating the industry structure effortfully, optimizing the environment, strengthening the management roundly, the people of Dongguan city, have consolidated the achievement of coping with the international financial crisis, bring the economy get rid of the impact of it step by step, the economic growth was fast yet steady, social undertakings got continued progress.

Economical development

Ⅰ Economic aggregate

According to preliminary accounting, Dongguan realized a GDP of RMB 424.63 billion in 2010, up by 10.3% over the previous year calculating at comparable price. In specific terms, primary industry contributed RMB 1.664 billion to the overall growth, up by 1.9%; secondary industry contributed RMB 218.32 billion, up by 16.8%; and tertiary industry contributed RMB 204.64 billion, showing an increase of 3.9%. The added value of primary, secondary and tertiary industries respectively accounted for 0.4%, 51.4% and 48.2% of the GDP of Dongguan for the year 2010. In the tertiary industry, the growth of the transportation, storage and postal services 6.9%, of the wholesales and retail trade 9.1%, of the housing and catering services 0.9%, of the finance 4.5%, of the real estate down by 1.1%, of the others 3.4%.

Figure 1: Gross Domestic Product and Its Growth, 2005–2010

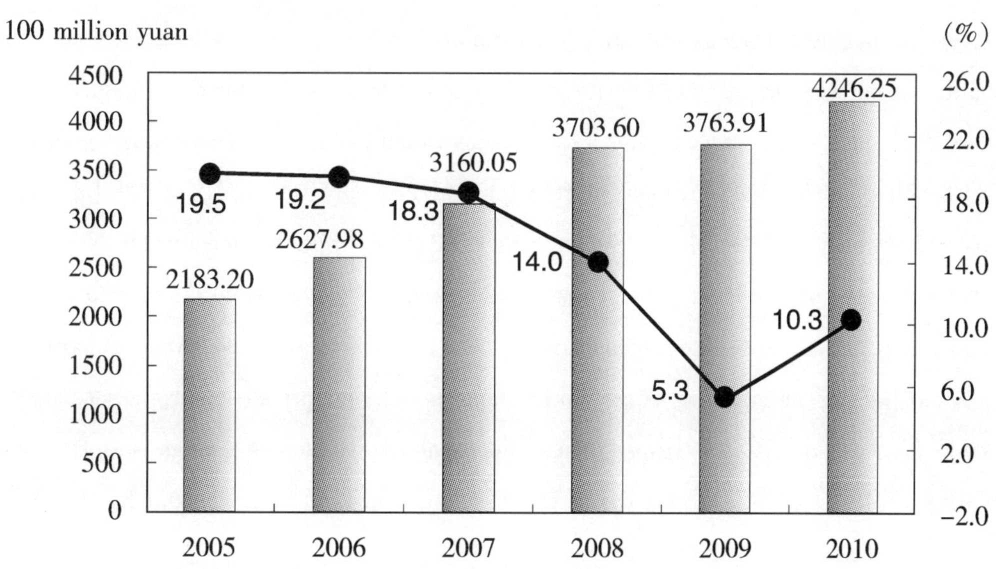

Fiscal revenue rooted in Dongguan was RMB 78. 51 billion for the year, up by 25. 1% , in which, the General budgeted revenue was RMB 27. 78 billion, up by 20. 2%. Among the General budgeted revenue, for the value-added tax revenue was RMB 6. 26 billion, up by 17. 2% ; for the business tax revenue was RMB 4. 59 billion, up by 2. 6% ; for the enterprise income tax revenue was RMB 2. 48 billion, up by 40. 3% ; for the individual income tax revenue was RMB 1. 10 billion, up by 26. 5% ; for the city maintenance and construction tax revenue was RMB 1. 138 billion, up by 23. 6% ; for the house property tax revenue was RMB 0. 93 billion, up by 22. 3% ; for the deed tax revenue was RMB 1. 87 billion, up by 18. 7%. Industrial and commercial tax revenue for the year was RMB 68. 87 billion, up by 25. 8% , in which, the national tax revenue was RMB 43. 94 billion, up by 29. 8% , and the local tax revenue was RMB 24. 93 billion, up by 19. 3%. General budget expenditures amounted to RMB 30. 86 billion, increasing by 32. 7% , in which, the general public services expenditures totaled RMB 1. 68 billion; the expenditure for public security amounted to RMB 2. 89 billion; for education was RMB 4. 13 billion; for science and technology was RMB 0. 86 billion; for culture, sports and media expenditures totaled RMB 0. 37 billion; for safety net and employment effort was RMB 1. 91 billion; for medical and health care services was RMB 0. 32 billion; for environmental protection was RMB 1. 23 billion; for urban and rural community affairs was RMB 0. 32 billion; for agriculture, forestry and water conservancy was RMB 0. 99 billion; for transportation was RMB 2. 62 billion.

II Structure of ownership

According to preliminary accounting, the added value of the public ownership economy was RMB 109. 55 billion, up by 6. 3% ; the private ownership economy was RMB 153. 65 billion, up by 13. 1% ; the foreign investment economy was RMB 161. 43 billion, up by 9. 4%. The added value of public ownership economy, private ownership economy and foreign investment economy respectively accounted for 25. 8% , 36. 2% and 38. 0% in the GDP of Dongguan for the year 2010.

The added value of state-owned enterprises, in which of industrial enterprises above designated size in Dongguan was RMB 12. 21 billion, up by 9. 0% ; collective-owned industrial enterprises was RMB 6. 89 billion, increasing 9. 1% than previous year; industrial enterprises with foreign funds was RMB 58. 41 billion, up by 22. 3% ; HK/Macao/Taiwan-invested industrial enterprises realized RMB 79. 99 billion, up by 16. 6% ; private industrial enterprises increased 18. 9% to RMB 19. 22 billion.

With regard to the sources of the Investment in fixed assets, investment from state-owned economy amounted to RMB 16. 28 billion, account for 14. 6% ; investment from collective-owned economy was RMB 14. 82 billion, account for 13. 3% ; investment from private economy was RMB 45. 09 billion, account for 40. 4% ; funds from foreign and HK/Macao/Taiwan was RMB 22. 39 billion, account for 20. 1%.

The total retail sales of domestic enterprises of wholesale and retail enterprises above designated size increased 26. 3% to RMB 42. 59 billion, account for 90. 0%. Of the total, state-owned enterprises, collective enterprises, limited liability enterprises, share-holding enterprises and private enterprises account for 2. 5% , 4. 1% , 33. 0% , 13. 9% and 34. 2% respectively. The total retail sales of foreign and HK/Macao/Taiwan enterprises realized RMB 4. 03 billion, increased 24. 3% than previous year, account for 9. 8% of the total, self-employed entrepreneurs was RMB 94 million, account for 0. 2%.

In specific terms, the value of export by state-owned enterprises was $11.03 billion, down by 0.9%; the foreign enterprise was $44.26 billion, up by 32.3%; the collective enterprise was $1.42 billion, up by 50.8%.

Ⅲ Structural reform & economy structure transformation and upgrading

Deepen the reform of simplifying the organization and strength authority of towns, delegate 33 administrate 542 authorities to local governments that of 11 central towns and 3 municipality spaces. Deepen the reform of administrative examination and approval by adjusting 232 approvals, deepen the reform of the household registration system by carrying out the integration system for approval addition and residence permit system, 12 thousand new comings got the qualification for approval addition; compiling to carry out the 《Program on medicine and hygiene system reform (2009 - 2011)》, protocol the pilot program of the public hospital reform preliminary, promote it in progress.

Accelerated the improvement trade transformation and upgrading, importation advanced technology, optimized production pattern, expanded the national market for enterprises. 1250 enterprises of improvement trade transformation and upgrading accepted, 150 new R&D foreign organizations added. Identified 30 projects in 4 of modern industry system, 10 projects in 4 of business trade, 50 private industries, 50 service industries and first branch headquarter enterprises by emphasis supports. Promoting 3 enterprises be listed. Developed the strategy emerging industries accelerate, 2 basements of the thin film solar photovoltaic and the internet of things industries identified the provincial strategy emerging industries.

Ⅳ Investment in fixed assets

The total investment in fixed assets reached RMB 111.50 billion in 2010, an increase of 1.9% over previous year. Specifically, the investment in new projects realized RMB 71.31 billion, down by 1.0%; the investment in expansion projects realized RMB 7.36 billion, down by 9.4% and reconstruction & renovation was RMB 11.20, up by 33.4%; the investment in real estate development increased 7.7% to RMB 29.90 billion. With regard to industry, the investment was concentrated toward the secondary and tertiary industries. Investment in secondary industry was RMB 40.79 billion, including manufacturing industry investment of RMB 33.88 billion; investment in tertiary industry was RMB 70.69 billion, account for 63.4% of the investment.

Figure 2: Investment in Fixed Assets and Its Growth, 2005-2010

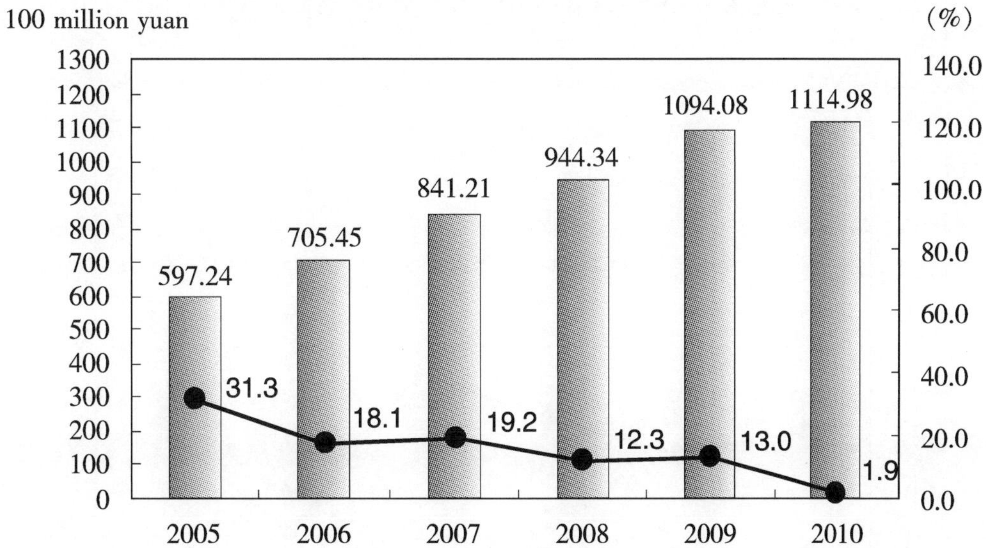

Notes: Investment in Fixed Assets include inter-regional projects from 2009, calculating at same caliber, an increase of 13.0% in 2009.

Table 1: Investment in Fixed Assets by Sector in 2010

Sector	Investment	% over the previous year
Total	11149822	1.9
Farming, Forestry, Animal Husbandry and Fishery	1922	-68.7
Manufacture	3387524	0.6
Production and Supply of Electric power, Gas and Water	687134	15.4
Construction	4051	157.4
Transport, Storage and Postal Services	1240268	-1.8
Information Transmission, Computer Services and Software	200850	-3.1
Wholesale and Retail Trade	201106	23.3
Hotel and Catering Services	109330	-51.5
Finance	26286	133.8
Real Estate	3646832	3.3
Leasing and Business Services	66834	-55.6
Scientific Research, Technical Services and Geological Prospecting	93236	87.8
Water Conservancy, Environment and Public Facilities Management	793687	2.3
Resident Services and Other Services	29535	48.2
Education	221760	57.9
Health Care, Social Security and Social Welfare	145102	-31.7
Culture, Sports and Recreation	122797	64.4
Public Administration and Social Organization	171241	18.7

V Prices

2010 CPI (consumer price index) waw up by 2.8% in Dongguan, among which residence up by 5.1%, recreational, education and culture articles up by 3.7%, clothing down by 2.1%, food prices went up by 4.6%, healthy care and personal articles down by 1.9%, tobacco, liquor and articles up by 1.7%, transportation and communication up by 0.4%, household facilities, articles and services up by 0.3%. 2010 retail price up by 3.2% and PPI (producer price index) up by 2.6% over the pervious year.

Figure 3: Change in Consumer Prices, 2005-2010

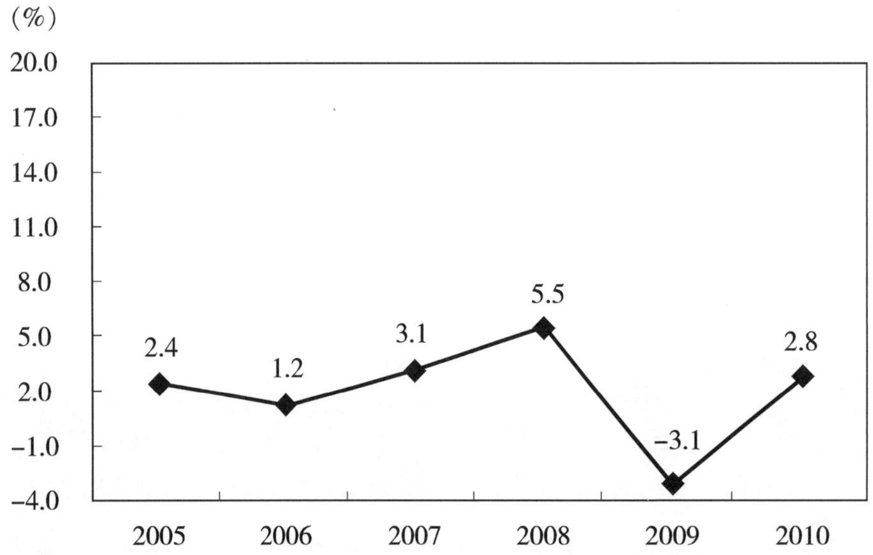

Table 2: Change of Prices in 2010

Item	Price Index (%)	Increase over 2009 (%)
Consumer Price Index	102. 8	2. 8
Food	104. 6	4. 6
Of Which: Grain	104. 0	4. 0
Meal, Poultry and Processed Products	103. 6	3. 6
Oil or Fat	104. 9	4. 9
Eggs	100. 8	0. 8
Fresh	114. 5	14. 5
Aquatic Products	104. 5	4. 5
Tobacco, Liquor and Articles	101. 7	1. 7
Clothing	97. 9	-2. 1
Household Facilities, Articles Services	100. 3	0. 3
Health Care and Personal Articles	101. 9	1. 9
Transportation and Communication	100. 4	0. 4
Recreation, Education and Culture Articles	103. 7	3. 7
Residence	105. 1	5. 1
Retail Price Index	103. 2	3. 2
Producer Price Index	102. 6	2. 6

Ⅵ Agriculture

In 2010, the gross output value of agriculture forestry animal husbandry and fishery was RMB 2. 83 billion, up by 3. 3% calculating at comparable price. Specifically, the output value of agriculture was RMB 1. 48 billion, down by 1. 6%, account for 52. 3%; the output value of forestry was RMB 29 million, up by 14. 7%, account for 1. 0%; the output value of animal husbandry was RMB 555 million, up by 13. 1%, account for 19. 6%; the output of fishery increased 5. 7% to RMB 680 million, account for 24. 0%. In 2010, the sown area of grain was 27. 93 million m^2. The total output of grain was 12. 5 thousand tons; the total output of aquatic products was 76. 3 thousand tons, up by 4. 1%; the total output of vegetables was 392. 9 thousand tons, down by 1. 8%. The number of slaughtered fattened hogs was 336. 4 thousand heads, up by 19. 8%; and that of poultry was 7. 46 million (heads), down by 0. 8%.

In 2010, there was a newly approved leading agricultural enterprises at the provincial level, 1 at the municipality level, 4 new farmer's specialized cooperation units. At the end of 2010, there were 20 leading agricultural enterprises; 29 farmers's specialized cooperation units, 7 provincial level and 2 state level leading enterprises on agricultural industrialization respectively. By the years-end, Dongguan boasted 28 province-level famous brand names in agriculture, 49 pesticide-free farming producers, 44 eco-friendly foods and 9 organic foods.

Ⅶ Industry

In 2010, the total added value of the sector industry above the designated size was RMB 181. 29 billion, up by 19. 0%. Specifically, heavy industry realized an output value of RMB 96. 08 billion, up 20. 1%, accounting for 53. 0% of the output value of industry above the designated size; that of light industry was RMB 85. 21

billion, up by 17.8%, accounting for 47.0%. The output value of large and medium sized enterprises was RMB 126.60 billion, accounting for 69.8% of the added value of the industrial enterprises above the designed size. Which realized total profit RMB 27.49 billion, up by 66.3% over the previous year, the assets liability ratio was 60.94%; and the comprehensive index of economic efficiency levels was 132.63, increased 15.34 index points.

In 2010, the added total value of 8 pillar industry was RMB 110.01 billion, up by 20.0%, among them, the added value of communication equipment, computer and other electronic equipment manufacturing was RMB 42.67 billion, up by 22.5%. The added value of electronic information and manufacturing enterprises above designated size was RMB 66.89 billion, up by 22.6%, showing a total profit of RMB 8.77 billion, up by 89.94% over the previous year.

Table3: Output of Major Industrial Products of Industrial Enterprises above the Designated Size and the Growth Rates in 2010

Industry	Unit	Qty	Increase over 2009 (%)
Electronic Components	10000 Pcs	91845707.91	34.5
Machine-made Paper &Paperboard	Tons	9331823.42	10.5
Porcelain	Sqm	20873228.66	8.0
Electricity	10000 kilowatt-hours	3563821.51	4.4
Furniture	Pcs	73902146.42	18.0
Garment	10000 Pcs	140556.06	7.5
Toy	1000 Yuan	8279161.78	16.5
Tempered glass	Sqm	7081445.50	4.7
Mould	Sets	303389.13	57.6
Daily stainless steel products	tons	45888.71	24.2
Leather Shoes	10000 pairs	43061.65	16.5
Telephone sets	Sets	48092167.00	25.3
Hi-Fi stereo Components Players	Sets	36368747.59	41.5
Print circuit board	Sqm	18011668.38	34.4
Color TV	Sets	5358975.00	9.3
Metal-cutting Tools	10000 units	1949.04	47.0
Power Cable	1000 meters	383829.09	70.6
Fabric	10000 meters	15794.13	20.7
Watch	Pcs	21675597.00	58.7
Chemical Fibers	Tons	11178.40	37.9
Opto-electronic instruments	10000 Pcs	1030151.59	41.8
Printing equipment	Tons	9456.80	34.5
Mobile Telephone	Sets	19952986.00	71.2
Electricians Instruments and Meters	Sets	5320941.00	44.5
Equipments for plastics processing	Sets	38860.91	87.0
Household electric fan	Sets	20813012.00	3.2
Monitor	Sets	1573415.00	-3.6

Ⅷ Construction

The added value of construction was RMB 8. 24 billion, down by 2. 9% over the previous year.

The output value of buildings completed of construction enterprises in Dongguan was RMB 11. 56 billion, up by 16. 7% over the previous year; the floor space of buildings under construction was 7. 09 million m^2, down by 2. 8% ; the floor space of buildings completed was 3. 07 million m^2, down 10. 8%. Calculated at the output value of buildings completed, the overall labor productivity was RMB 226000 per person, up by 23. 5% over the previous year.

Ⅸ Transportation, storage, post and telecommunications

The added value of the transportation, storage, post and telecommunications sector reached RMB 8. 65 billion in 2010, up by 6. 9% over the previous year.

At the end of 2010, the total length of highways in Dongguan (including the highway in the rural area) was 4750. 99 kilometers; the highway density was 192. 74 kilometers per 100 km^2. Among them, the length of expressway and class I to IV highways was 4673. 04 km, the density was 189. 58km per 100 km^2; Among which, the length of expressways in the whole city reached 246. 74 kilometers, and the density reached 8. 79 km per 100 km^2. The possession of motor vehicles reached 1. 35 million units, up by 6. 2%. The possession of civil motor vehicles was 920. 8 thousand units, up by 15. 7%. The freight traffic of highways was 76. 4 million tons, the freight ton-kilometers of highways was 5. 11 billion ton-kilometers; the freight traffic of waterways was 16. 72 million tons, the freight ton-kilometers of waterways was 5. 80 billion ton-kilometers. The passenger traffic of highways was 0. 77 billion by the end of 2010, the passenger-kilometers of highways was 12. 89 billion passenger-km, the passenger traffic of waterways was 310 thousand persons by the end of 2010, the passenger-kilometers of waterways was 20. 17 million passenger-km. The volume of freight handled in Dongguan's coastal ports was 56. 57 million tons and passenger traffic was 0. 31 million persons.

The total business volume of postal and telecommunication services was RMB 15. 79 billion in the year, up by 1. 0% over the previous year. Specifically, the business volume of telecommunications was RMB 14. 98 billion, up by 0. 4% ; the business volume of mobile telephone services was RMB 10. 66 billion, up by 5. 2% ; the business volume of post was RMB 0. 81 billion, up by 13. 6%. In 2010, 45. 07 million letters were posted, up by 5. 4% ; 6. 27 million EMS were posted, up by 12. 6% ; the amount of postal remittance was RMB 28. 05 billion, up by 26. 2%.

Ⅹ Domestic trade

The total value-added of wholesale & retail sales was RMB 40. 68 billion in 2010, up by 9. 1% over the previous year; that of the lodging and catering industry was RMB 14. 78 billion, up by 0. 9%.

The total retail sales of consumer goods reached RMB 110. 81 billion, up by 15. 9% over the previous year (up by 12. 3% in real terms) . Specifically, the retail value of wholesale and retail trades reach RMB 100. 55 billion, up by 16. 6% , the lodging and catering industry reached RMB 10. 25 billion, up by 9. 1%.

With regard to enterprises above designated size of wholesale and retail trades, the sales value of hardware, electrical materials and appliances, audio-visual equipment, household appliances, automobiles, food, beverages, tobacco and liquor, daily necessities, clothing, shoes, hats and textiles increased 36. 3% , 32. 6% , 30. 1% , 18. 7% , 16. 9% and 6. 9% over the previous year.

The total sales value of wholesales and retail trades increased 23. 7% over the previous year, reaching RMB 195. 72 billion.

Figure 4: The Retail Sales of Consumer Goods and Its Growth, 2005 – 2010

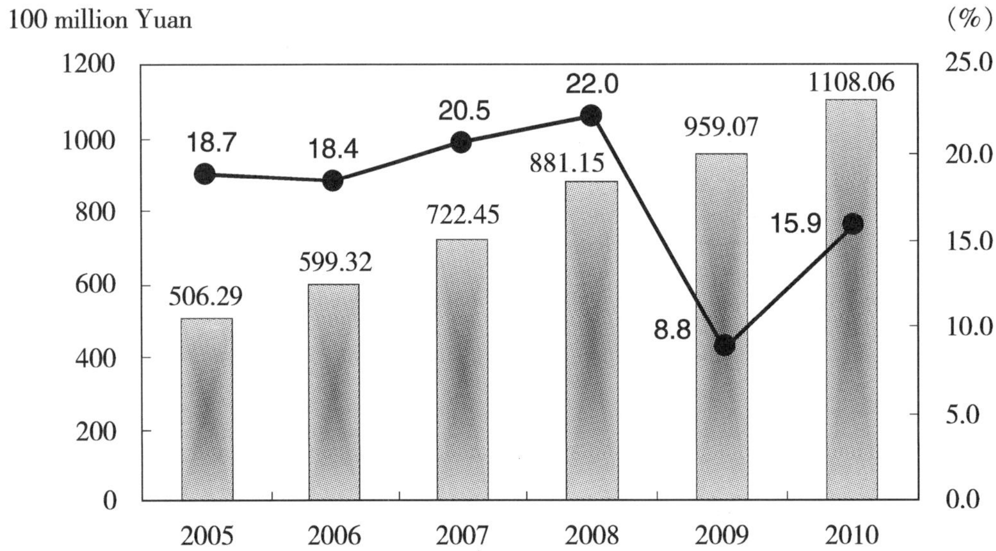

XI Finance

By the end of 2010, the added value of finance was RMB 16. 54 billion, up by 4. 5%.

In 2010, Dongguan had 83 financial institutions, including 7 newly added. Specifically, there were 26 banking institutions, 20 insurance companies, 37 security companies.

The year-end balance of RMB savings in domestic financial institutions totaled 594. 34 billion, up by 19. 2% since the beginning of the year, in which, deposits by enterprises totaled RMB 152. 16 billion, an increase of 15. 2% over the previous year; fiscal deposits amounted to RMB 4. 66 billion, down by 11. 2%. The year-end balance of RMB loans in domestic financial institutions totaled RMB 332. 98 billion, up by 14. 7% since the beginning of the year. With respect to the personal individual consumption loans, the balance of personal housing loans reached RMB 70. 46 billion, up by 16. 1% over the previous year; personal auto loans totaled RMB 2. 07 billion, down by 13. 9%. The cash income of financial institutions totaled RMB 986. 76 billion, cash expenditure totaled RMB 1008. 42 billion, withdrawal of currency from circulation in balance totaled RMB 21. 67 billion. The NPLs of Dongguan financial institutions reduced 0. 52 index over the beginning of the year.

The total investors of all kinds of security companies was 820. 7 thousand by the end of 2010, increased about 44. 7thousand accounts over the previous year. The total turnover of stock trading waw down by 5. 9% to RMB 1098. 98 billion. The guarantee fund balance totaled RMB 13. 63 billion, down by 16. 2% over the previous year.

The total number of insurance institutions reached 38 units, The insurance intermediary institutions increased by 13 amounts to 44. the employee of them amount to 27 thousand. insurance institutions earned premiums of RMB 15. 97 billion, up by 38. 8% over the previous year, in which, property insurance premiums was RMB 4. 67 billion, up by 32. 1% , and life insurance premiums was RMB 11. 3 billion, up by 41. 7%. The claim and payment reached RMB 3. 5 billion, including property insurance indemnity of RMB 2. 18 billion, the loss ratio reached 46. 7% , and life insurance indemnity of RMB 1. 32 billion.

Ⅻ Real estate

The value-added of real estate was RMB 28. 84 billion, down by 1. 1% over the previous year.

The total investment in real estate reached RMB 29. 90 billion in 2010, an increase of 7. 7% over the previous year. The total floor space under construction of commercialized buildings was 20. 6 million m^2, down by 11. 7% over the previous year; the total floor space completed reached 2. 97 million m^2, down by 4. 4% ; the floor space of commercialized buildings sold amounted to 5. 11 million m^2, down by 14. 8% , in which, the floor space of residential buildings sold this year was 4. 70 million m^2, down by 18. 8% over the previous year. The total sales value of commercialized buildings was RMB 37. 38 billion, up by 5. 9% over the previous year, specifically the sales value of residential buildings was RMB 33. 42 billion, down by 0. 03%.

ⅩⅢ Private economy

The number of private units registered was 492. 8 thousand, up by 3. 1% over the previous year, in which, private enterprises was 88. 7 thousand units, and up by 19. 4% over the pervious year and self-employed individuals was 402. 4 thousand, down by 0. 2% over the previous year. The gross output value of the private enterprises above designated size was RMB 119. 52 billion, up by 21. 4% over the previous year; the total investment in fixed asset of the private economy reached RMB 45. 09 billion, up by 4. 5% ; the total retail sales of consumer goods of private economy was RMB 92. 98 billion, up by 15. 9% over the previous year; the total tax payable was RMB 26. 11 billion, up by 31. 9%.

ⅩⅣ Regional economy

The total assets of the 32 towns in Dongguan was recorded at RMB 107. 02 billion, the net assets was RMB 70. 37 billion, up by 10. 5% and 10. 3% respectively over the previous year. The total collective assets of suburban & village groups was RMB 123. 09 billion, up by 4. 7% over the previous year, the net assets was RMB 94. 23 billion, up by 5. 3% over the previous year, the net disposable income was RMB 21. 74 billion, up by 14. 2%. The number of disposable fiscal revenue over RMB 1 billion was 6 towns, and the number of disposable income (excluding the income of land & tenement transferred) over RMB 100 million was 20 villages and, over RMB 50 million was 69 villages and, over RMB 10 million was 419 villages.

Accelerate the development and construction of Industrial Park. The Song Shan lake successful promotion of National High-tech Zone, Taiwan high-tech park opened, Guangdong and Hong Kong and Macao cultural creativity industry garden of experiment settled in Dongguan. Construction of harbor berth wharf in Humen could be accelerated. Bonded logistics center put into operation, flights to Taiwan on officially directed exchanges of shipping. Dongguan ecological park infrastructure construction could be accelerated, Ecological rehabilitation initial results and foreign public investments for the first time. Declarations of the using sea areas in Changan new zone and planning work have been solid advanced.

Reformand opening up

Ⅰ Foreign trade

The total value of imports and exports in 2010 reached US $121.34 billion, up by 28.8% over the previous year, of which the total value of imports reached US $51.74 billion, up by 32.7%; the total value of exports reached US $69.60 billion, up by 26.1%.

Divided by mode of trade, the export value of general trade reached US $9.54 billion, an increase of 66.9%; The export value of processing trade reached US $59.02 billion, up by 21.0%; other trades for export reached US $1.04 billion, representing an increase of 55.4%.

Divided by countries and regions of export, the exports to Asia reached US $35.44 billion, up by 29.6%; the exports to EU reached US $12.14 billion, up by 26.0%; the exports to North America reached US $18.99 billion, up by 20.4%; the exports to Latin America reached US $1.75 billion, up by 32.1%; the exports to Oceania reached US $0.86 billion, up by 5.9%.

The total export volume of electromechanical products reached US $49.48 billion, up by 24.1%, accounting for 71.1% of the total exports. The export of hi-tech products reached US $24.20 billion, up by 23.0%, accounting for 34.8% of total export value of the entire city.

Table 4: Main Export Commodities in Value and the Growth Rates in 2010

Unit: 10000 US dollars

Commodities	Value	Increase over 2009 (%)
Automatic Data processing machines and components	528199	25.0
Clothes and clothing accessories	389784	38.7
Parts of automatic Data processing machines	333050	24.8
Shoes	309561	26.0
Furniture and components	320917	32.3
Static converters	359806	55.5
Game machines	84546	-53.7
Cable telephone (including cordless telephone)	164438	10.8
Spinning Yarn, Fabric and Products	152070	11.2
Digital cameras	160842	26.5
Parts of Television, Radio and Wireless Telecommunication Equipment	161166	27.9
Toys	163174	32.9
Traveling articles and cases (value)	156455	36.8
Insulated Wire or Cable	152169	40.8
TV sets (including a complete set of spare parts)	96536	-5.3
Electric Apparatus for Switching or Protecting Electrical Circuits	133965	29.2
Plastic Articles	113700	25.1
Video Recorder and Video Player	132369	57.3
Handle Mobiles and Car Telephones	96899	21.2

Ⅱ Foreign investment absorbance

According to new statistical information, the number of recently signed projects of foreign direct investment was 869, the amount of contracted foreign capital reached US $2.60 billion, up by 60.7% over the previous year. The amount of foreign capital actually utilized reached US $2.73 billion, up by 5.3%. The number of recently signed projects which investments were over US $10 million was 46, representing an increase of 19 over the previous year; the recently signed projects of tertiary industry reached US $0.36 billion, accounting for 13.8% of the entire city. The step of foreign inverstment entering business domain was getting faster. The number of recently signed projects of wholesale and retail trade was 109 units, the amount of contracted foreign capital reached US $0.21 billion, up by 66.5%, accounting for 57.5% of total contracted foreign capital of tertiary industry.

Table 5: Total Value of Foreign Capital Actually Utilized and the Growth Rates by Sector in 2010

Unit: 10000 US dollar

Sector	contracted foreign capital	Increase over 2009 (%)	Foreign Capital Actually Utilized Value	Increase over 2009 (%)
Total	259740	60.7	273171	5.3
Agriculture, Forestry, Animal Husbandry and Fishing	1010	7699.2	62	77.1
Manufacturing	222761	62.7	241618	3.2
Of Which: Textile Industry	12908	136.5	7225	-10.4
Manufacture of Textiles, garments, shoes and hats	13120	277.7	9137	-21.0
Manufacture of furniture	1825	-44.5	6155	-9.8
Manufacture of General Machinery	6530	118.1	7541	6.1
Manufacture of Special Purpose Machinery	19263	209.2	15589	17.4
Manufacture of Electric Machinery and Equipment	20868	66.2	25260	47.9
Manufacture of Electronic Equipment and Communication Equipment	66565	80.0	60796	-3.6
Manufacture of Metal Products	10391	16.0	10371	24.5
Manufacture of Plastics Products	17764	55.5	14007	21.4
Manufacture of stationery and sporting Products	4873	27.8	8439	-22.5
Manufacture of papermaking and Paper Products	8057	269.1	21188	-12.4
Manufacture of others	40597	4.5	55910	7.0
Information Transmission, Computer Services and Software	782	232.8	109	-80.9
Wholesale and Retail Trade	20655	66.5	13271	74.7

Ⅲ Tourism

At the end of 2010, there were 97 star-rated hotels in the city, including 22 five-star hotels, 25 four-star hotels, 35 three-star hotels, 14 two-star hotels and 1 one-star hotels. There were 54 travel agencies, including 9 international travel agencies, 41 domestic travel agencies and 4 other travel agencies. The number of tourists from foreign economic zones, including Hong Kong, Macao and Taiwan was 3.27 million, up by 14.5% over the previous year, among them, the number of foreign tourists was 1.09 million, up by 4.3% over the previous year; the number of tourists from Hong Kong, Macao and Taiwan was 2.19 million, up by 20.3%. The foreign exchange income from international tourism increased 30.6% to US $0.68 billion. The number of domestic tourists was 19. 24 million, up by 9. 9% over the previous year, and the total income from domestic tourism increased 26. 3% to RMB 19. 13 billion.

The number of tourists of Dongguan out on tours was 1. 54 million in 2010, up by 21. 0%, of which, the tourists who were traveling domestic areas totaled 13. 91 million, up by 21. 5%; traveling aboard totaled 147. 1 thousand, up by 16. 3%.

Urban construction

Ⅰ Urban greening

At the end of 2010, the total developed areas reached 798. 48 sq km. in Dongguan. The land used for public facilities reached 61. 31 sq km. The area of afforested land in Dongguan was 91. 0 thousand hectares; forest cover rate reached 36. 7%, the green cover rate in afforested land reached 98. 7%. The green covered area of completed area reached 41. 16% in the city, the green covered area was 44. 31% of completed areas. The number of park plaza was 1004 and the total area numbered 11130 hectares.

Ⅱ Public utilities

There were 96 bus lines and 1443 vehicles for public transition at year-end of 2010. Passenger's traffic numbered 231 million by public transportation for the year.

The daily water supply capacity was 7 million cubic meters and the annual volume of water supply totaled 1. 66 billion cubic meters in Dongguan. At the end of 2010, the total length of water supply pipelines reached 16. 27 thousand kilometers. Electricity consumption overall the society was 56. 2 billion Kwh, an increase of 13. 4%. In specific terms, industrial electricity was 43. 56 billion Kwh, up by 15. 8% and lighting electricity was 10. 71 billion Kwh, up by 5. 9%. At the end of 2010, the total of households using liquefied petroleum gas numbered 870. 9 thousand, and the households using natural gas numbered 146 thousand. The total LPG supply was 344. 6 thousand tons, and the supply of natural gas was 296 million cubic meters.

Ⅲ Infomationization

In 2010 the general informationization index was 74. 6% in Dongguan. The number of fixed telephone subscribers at year-end was 2. 26 million, an increase of 190. 8 thousand subscribers over 2009. The number of mobile phone subscribers reached 16. 33 million, an increase of 2. 24 million subscribers, of which by recharge card was 14. 52 million, increasing by 1. 81 million. The length of long-distance calls totaled 18. 84 billion minutes in 2010, of which those connected to overseas nations and to Hong Kong, Macao and Taiwan were 308 million minutes. At the end of 2010, there were 1. 54 million internet subscribers, and 1. 5 million broad band subscribers, both increasing by 359 thousand.

Social Undertaking

Ⅰ Science and technology

2 new provincial demonstration districts of industry upgrade clusters, 91 new national hi-tech enterprises, 126 new provincial private hi-tech enterprises, 14 new provincial-level and above technical centers, 5 new post-

doctoral research stations and 3 new provincial innovation research team were approved in 2010. There were 56 new provincial famous brands or famous trademarks and 37 projects participated in technical standards development. The gross output value of high-tech industry is expected to RMB 257. 91 billion in 2010, up by 19. 1% over the previous year.

In 2010, the number of patents application accepted and granted reached 21654 units and 20397 units, up by 13. 3% and 57. 9% respectively over the previous year. Of the total, 3143 patent applications of inventions were accepted, and 442 of them were granted; 7677patent applications of utility model were accepted, and 7529 of them were granted; 10834 patent applications of designing were accepted, and 12426 patent applications were granted.

Ⅱ Education

There were 727 kindergartens in Dongguan, 47 more than the previous year, of which 169 were founded by education departments and collectives and 558 were founded by private institutions. 101 kindergartens were certified as Provincial or Municipal 1st Class kindergarten. There were 208. 4 thousand three to six year old children enrolled, and the enrollment rate of kindergarten reached 95. 15% , 0. 05 points of percentage over the previous year.

There were 330 primary schools in Dongguan, decreased 7 units over the previous year; there were 552. 4 thousand students enrolled in primary school; school-age children enrollment ratio had reached 100% , and the promotion rate from primary schools to junior secondary schools of Dongguan residents was 100%. There were 150 junior secondary schools, with 187. 9 thousand enrolled students. For Dongguan's registered residents, the net enrollment ratio of junior secondary schools, drop-out rate and graduation rate were 100% , 0. 22% and 97. 9% respectively.

There were 66 senior secondary schools (including 18 private schools) with 117. 9 thousand students enrolled (including technical school) in Dongguan. Of the total, there were 40 senior secondary schools (including six-grade secondary schools) with 70. 4 thousand students and 26 secondary vocational schools (including technical school) with 47. 5 thousand students. The junior secondary school graduates of Dongguan residents were 35. 7 thousand, and 35 thousand of them entered various types of senior secondary schools. of the total, the graduates who entered into senior secondary schools and enrolled into vocational secondary schools were 21. 2 thousand and 13. 8 thousand respectively. The promotion rate from junior secondary schools to senior secondary school of Dongguan residents was 94. 9% , 1. 3 points of percentage over the previous year.

There were 1 adult institution of higher education, 32 township cultural and technical schools for adults, and 231 private non-degree adult education institutions. More than 520 thousand people participated in various types of training by adult education.

There were 5 institutions of regular higher education. 2 of them were universities with full undergraduate courses and the other 3 were collages with specialized courses. There were 38. 3 thousand total enrollments. In 2010, in institutions of higher education, there were totally 12. 7 thousand students new-enrolled and 8105 students graduated.

In 2010, there were 24. 71 thousand students participated the entrance examinations for colleges and universities, in special terms, 21. 08 thousand students participated the general colleges, that of the students participated the general colleges, 3.63 thousand for the vocational colleges. 2.35 thousand on the key line, 124 students over the previous year; 9.88 thousand entered the general colleges, 1494 students over the previous year.

Ⅲ Culture

At the end of 2010, there were 1 mass art center, 33 cultural stations, 505 public libraries, 30 museums, 511 cultural squares, 63 arts performance places, 46 movie screening units and 1053 internet cafes. Public cultural facilities construction area reached 11.61 million square meters. Dongguan had 57 public radio programs and 49 public television programs. Radio and television coverage of population had reached 100%. CATV for " Every Village" project be continued to promote. Coverage of households has reached 100%. In 2010, 82.3 million copies of newspapers, 1.32 million copies of magazines and 76 thousand copies of books were published. Dongguan Daily had 45.63 million copies circulation. There were 115.2 thousand film screenings and 3.88, million viewers in 2010.

Ⅳ Health and medicine

At the end of 2010, Dongguan had 2229 heath care institutions, including 2151 grass-roots health care institutions such as outpatient departments, clinics, health stations, infirmaries and community health service centers, with 37487 medical technical personals and 19980 hospital beds. In Dongguan, 388 community health service institutions had been built and put into service, covering more than 300 villages (communities) throughout the city. The patients who received treatment throughout the year were increased by 11.9%.

Ⅴ Sports

Dongguan athletes won 50 gold (above provincial level), 56 silver and 46 bronze medals in 2010, including 4 gold and 2 silver medals in international tournaments, 6 gold, 12 silver and 10 bronze medals in national tournaments. In provincial tournaments, athletes won 40 gold, 42 silver and 36 bronze medals.

Dongguan held 16 municipal integrated and individual competitions, in which over 14.3 thousand people participated. There were 656.2 thousand participants who took part in 578 township individual competitions. Dongguan had 880 sports lottery networks, which total sale was RMB 762 million and public welfare fund of sports lottery was RMB 13 million.

Ⅵ Social welfare and relief

At the end of 2010, there were 35 gerocomiums where 894 old people were maintained. 36.5 thousand persons received social assistance in 2010. The expenditure of urban minimum living allowance was RMB 20.18 million. Expenditure of social relief totaled RMB 44.5 million. Expenditure of social relief for natural disaster was RMB1.39 million. 1263 persons were brought into the "Five-Guaranteed households" project, and which cost RMB 15.36 million. All the 32 towns in Dongguan had established social security network. 1595 households counting up to 3629 persons were brought into the minimum living allowance project and 12218 households counting up to 30799 persons were brought into township receiving minimum living allowance project.

Ⅶ Social stability

Crack down on major and multiple crimes, vigorously carry out anti-vice and gambling special operations, further improve security in the key areas and industries, and strengthen patrols and campus security. 41 New provincial " six-good" safe & harmonious communities and 218 municipal safe communities have been built. The detected criminal cases increased by 29. 9%. Further promote the hazardous chemicals, " Three small" sites, rental, construction safety, food and drug quality special rectification. Carry out the innovative fire management pilot, Implement the task of listing and supervision, and investigated and rectificated a number of security risks. 17 new town emergency disaster prevention centers and 67 food safety markets have been built. Cases of accidents occurred and people died in accidents dropped by 3. 2% and 1. 4% over the previous year. The construction of town comprehensive govern, petition and stability maintenance centers and village (community) comprehensive govern workstation had been completed. The institution of leaders' cases reception and return visit has been implemented. A decline of 23. 4% was shown in total acceptance of mass petitions and the success rate of dispute mediation was 93%. Strengthen labor law enforcement and supervision, and mediate employment relationship, the Labor emergencies and cases of escaping from owing wages were dropped by 3. 4% and 37% respectively.

Ⅷ Safe production

In 2010, 4910 cases of industrial accident occurred in Dongguan, decreased by 3. 2% over the previous year; 574 people died and 5365 people were injured, decreased by 1. 4% and 3. 6% respectively; direct economic losses was RMB 8. 97 million, increasing by 12. 6%. Of the total, the number of road traffic accidents was 4872, decreased by 3. 3%, which resulted in 526 deaths and 5355 injured, a decrease of 3. 5% and 3. 7% respectively. Production-related accident mortality rate per 100 million GDP was 0. 135, mining and commercial production-related accident mortality rate per 100 thousand people was 0. 62, and road traffic mortality rate per 10 thousand vehicles was 3. 93.

Ⅸ Resource and environmental protection

Throughout the year, rainy days numbered 202 days; sunshine hours were 1699. 7 hours; average temperature was 22. 4 degrees Celsius; relative humidity was 73%. Precipitation of the year was 2165. 9 millimeters.

At the end of 2010, there were 17 forest parks and 250. 86 square kilometers of ecological public forest, which contained 2. 56 million cubic meters of tree storage and 155. 2 thousand cubic meters of total tree growth in Dongguan. All year around, 1829. 05 hectares of afforestation has been completed and 1. 36 million native broad-leaved trees had been planted. 853. 2 thousand persons participated in voluntary tree planting activity with 3. 29 million trees had been planted. The investment to forestry and ecologically civilized villages totaled RMB 16. 96 million. 110. 9 kilometers of road Green-fill project and 84. 2 hectares of idle land Green-increase project were completed.

Annual average air pollution index was 56, good air quality days accounted for 97. 8%. That of RMB 120 million had been invested to the primary sludge disposal project of Zhangcun water purification plant, which daily sludge treatment was 500 tons. That of RMB 390 million has been invested to the Huangjiang sludge treatment plant project which has been basically completed. There were 33 new sewage treatment projects had been completed, 86% of the interception trunk pipeline project has been completed.

People's living conditions

Ⅰ Population

At the end of 2010, Dongguan's registered population reached 1.82 million. The year 2010 saw 19.5 thousand births, a crude birth rate of 10.90 per thousand, and 8367 deaths, or a crude death rate of 4.67 per thousand. The natural growth rate was 6.23 per thousand.

Ⅱ Income

In 2010, the average annual salary was RMB 16108, up by 11.7% over the previous year. Of this total, the average annual wage of the urban full-employed staff and workers was RMB 46576, up by 9.4%. The per capital annual disposable income of urban households increased by 10.0% over the previous year to RMB 36350, and the per capita annual disposable income of rural households increased by 13.2% over the previous year to RMB 20486.

Figure 5: Per Capital Disposable Income of Urban Households and Its Growth, 2005–2010

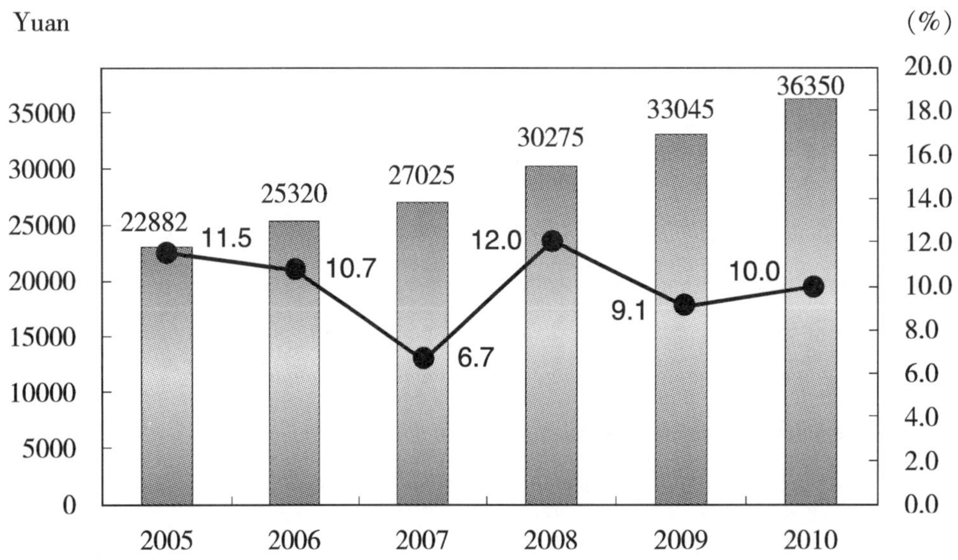

Figure 6: Per Capital Disposable Income Of Rural Households and Its Growth, 2005–2010

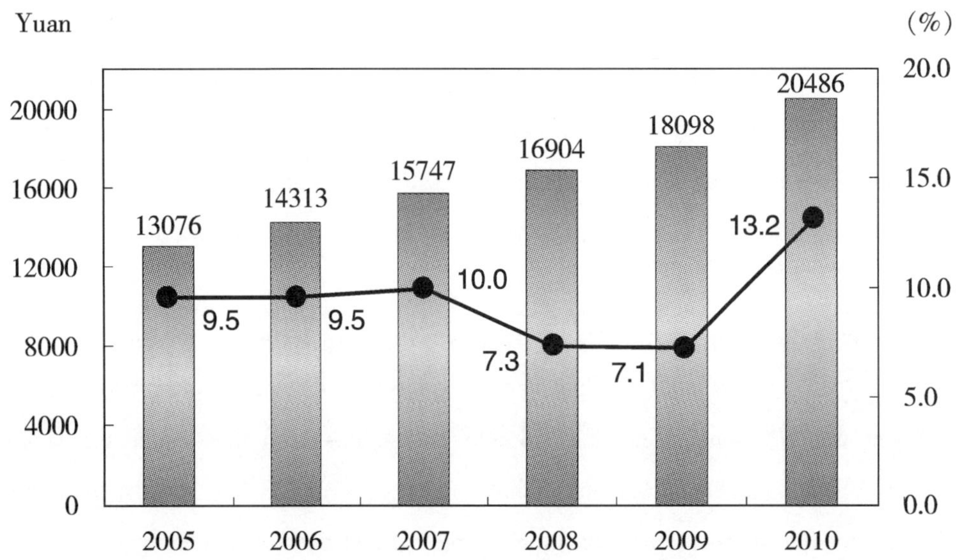

Ⅲ Consumer expenditure

The annual per capital consumption expenditure of urban residents was RMB 25733, increased by 6.0%. Of this total, the expenditure on food was RMB 8733, up by 9.5%; the expenditure on clothing was RMB 1706, up by 14.3%; the expenditure on residence was RMB 2089, down by 6.4%; the expenditure on household facilities, articles and services was RMB 1771, up by 9.6%; the expenditure on health care and medical services was RMB 1294, down by 7.6%; the expenditure on transport and communications was RMB 5925, up by 8.6%; the expenditure on education, cultural and recreation services was RMB 3443, up by 3.5%; and the expenditure on miscellaneous goods and services was RMB 773, down by 0.5%. The Engel's Coefficient of Urban households was 33.9%. In consumption expenditure of rural households, 37.5% was spent on food; 5.2% on clothing; 15.6% on living; 4.2% on household facilities, articles and services; 4.7% on health care and medical services; 17.9% on transport and communications; 9.4% on education, cultural and recreation services; 5.5% on miscellaneous goods and services.

Table 6: Income and Expenditure Of Urban Households 2010

Item	Income or expenditure (yuan)	Increase over 2009 (%)
Per Capita Disposable Income of Urban Residents	36350	10.0
Income from Wages and Salaries	26860	13.2
Income from Properties	4889	16.1
Income from Transfer	3541	14.4
Per Capita Consumption Expenditure of Urban Residents	25733	6.0
Food	8733	9.5
Clothing	1706	14.3
Residence	2089	-6.4
Household Facilities, Articles and Services	1771	9.6
Health Care and Medical Services	1294	-7.6
Transport and Telecommunication	5925	8.6
Educational, Cultural Recreation Services	3443	3.5
Miscellaneous Goods and Services	773	-0.5

The ownership of major durable consumer goods per 100 urban households at the year-end were: 259 air conditioners, 68 Hi-Fi stereo component system, 267 mobile phones, 129 computers, 134 water heaters, 68 cars. The per capita housing floor space of urban households was 58.58 square meters. The ownership of major durable consumer goods per 100 rural households at the year-end were: 164 color TV, 87 motorcycles, 106 washing machines, 132 water heaters, 268 mobile phones, 71 disc players, 218 air conditioner, 104 computers, 57cars.

Ⅳ Household savings

At the end of 2010, the balance of savings deposit of urban and rural households was RMB 338.69 billion, an increase of RMB 50.04 billion over the beginning of the year. Of the total, the fixed deposits was RMB

135. 42 billion, an increase of RMB 8. 87 billion; the current deposits were RMB 203. 26 billion, an increase of RMB 41. 18 billion.

Figure 7: Savings Deposits Of Urban And Rural Households And Its Growth,2005–2010

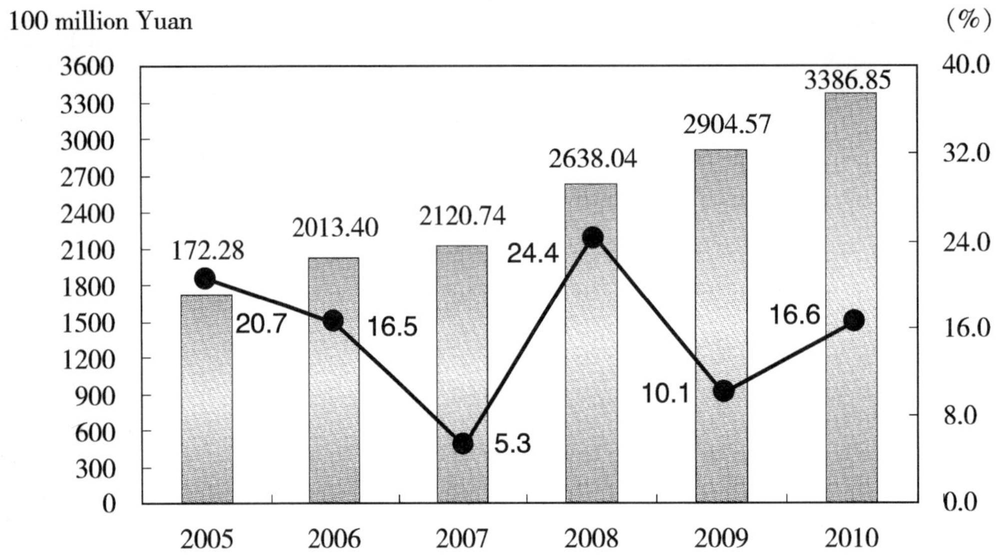

V **Social security**

At year-end, the number of employee joining basic pension insurance was 4. 22 million , in special terms, the basic medical care system was 5. 92 million, the unemployment insurance was 2. 80 million persons; the injury insurance was 4. 69 million persons, and the local basic pension insurance was 3. 71 million persons. The annual total revenue of social insurance fund was RMB 15. 44 billion, the total expense at year-end of the insurance fund was RMB 6. 51 billion, and the accumulated balance of the insurance fund was RMB 41. 37 billion.

The main difficulties and problems in national economic and social development were: the basis of economic recovery was not solid, strength restructuring should be increased, and the overall technical level of enterprises independent innovation ability should be furtherly improved. Land, energy and other resource restraints outstanding efforts in pollution treatment and environment protection still increased. There is heavy task of improving people' s livelihood.

政府工作报告

REPORT ON THE WORK OF THE GOVERNMENT

——2011年1月17日在东莞市第十四届人民代表大会第六次会议上

东莞市人民政府市长　李毓全

各位代表：

现在，我代表市人民政府向大会作政府工作报告，请予审议，并请政协各位委员和其他列席人员提出意见。

2010年及“十一五”时期工作回顾

刚刚过去的2010年，是我市继续巩固应对国际金融危机成果、加快转变经济发展方式的重要一年。面对有所好转但仍然复杂的外部形势，面对繁重艰巨的转型发展任务，面对深层矛盾日益凸显、利益深刻变动的社会格局，我们在上级和市委的坚强领导下，以科学发展观统领全局，全面实施珠三角规划纲要，突出以转变发展方式为主线，继续稳增长，加力调结构，积极优环境，全面强管理，锐意抓改革，着力保民生，推动经济社会在平稳发展的基础上加快转型，取得了扎实成效。东莞成为全国加工贸易转型升级试点城市，获评中国全面小康特别贡献城市、中国十佳绿色城市、中国十大最关爱民生的城市，创建国家环保模范城市通过了国家验收。具体体现在以下六个方面：

一、力保平稳增长，切实巩固了经济回升势头。紧紧抓住外部环境有所好转的时机，深入实施刺激经济增长的一系列政策措施，巩固应对金融危机的成果，保持了经济平稳较快增长。预计全市实现生产总值4246亿元，比上年增长10.3%，人均生产总值66344元，增长14.6%。来源于东莞的财政总收入785亿元，增长25.1%，其中市财政一般预算收入278亿元，增长20.2%。金融机构本外币各项存款余额6078亿元，比年初增长19.3%。坚持不懈帮扶企业。认真落实“六个10亿元”政策，加强用工、用电保障和融资、通关等服务，加快发展保税物流，开展人民币贸易结算试点业务。企业经营明显好转，外资企业关停外迁数比上年减少11%，增资扩产617宗，增加133宗。工业生产和出口均超过危机前的水平，全市规模以上工业增加值1813亿元，增长19%；进出口总额1213亿美元，增长28.8%，其中出口696亿美元，增长26.1%。坚持不懈扩大内需。落实领导挂钩督导和审批绿色通道等制度，加快重点基础设施和优质产业项目建设，完成固定资产投资1115亿元。实施八大商贸促进工程，培育和引导消费，社会零售总额1108亿元，增长15.9%。优化外企内销通道，成功举办外博会、台博会、动漫展等，开展莞货展销活动，筹建工厂直销中心，全市工业产品内销总额3537亿元，增长23.6%。坚持不懈扶持镇村。落实财政超收分成、公共管理支出补助、生态补偿等政策，对镇街统筹土地给予借款支持，实施市内“双到”扶贫。全年市财政共安排65亿元支持镇村建设，预计32个镇街可支配收入280.7亿元，村组两级可支配收入183亿元，分别增长14.8%和6.1%。城市居民人均可支配收入36350元，农村居民人均纯收入14254元，分别增长10%和9.1%。

二、加力调整结构，产业转型迈出了坚实步伐。把调整产业结构作为核心任务，推进经济发展方式有效转变。*突出抓好外经贸“五个1000”专项工作。*加快加工贸易转型升级，支持企业引进先进技术、优化生产模式、拓展内销市场，全年共受理1250家来料加工企业转型，新增外资企业研发机构150个，是历年总数的1.5倍。着力提高利用外资质量，积极组织赴美加、日韩台等地招商，主动拜访外企总部，邀请重点企业来莞考察，全年合同利用外资26亿美元，实际利用外资27.3亿美元，分别增长60.7%和5.3%。*突出培育重点企业和新兴产业。*认定现代产业体系“四个30项目”、商贸流通业“四个十大”项目、民营工业50强、服务业50强和首批总部企业等，实施重点扶持。推动3家企业成功上市。加快发展战略性新兴产业，薄膜太阳能光伏和物联网2个基地被列为全省战略性新兴产业基地。制定珠三角新兴物流城市发展规划。*突出增强自主发展能力。*完善科技东莞政策，深化产学研合作，开展质量强市活动，推动“两自”企业发展。全市工业企业技改投资198亿元，增长28.2%，专利授权量增长70%。新增省级产业集群升级示范区2个、国家高新技术企业91家、省民营科技企业126家、省级以上技术工程中心14个、企业博士后科研工作站5个、省级以上名牌名标56个，参与制修订各类技术标准37项，获批省创新科研团队3个。完善和落实民营经济扶持措施，加强内资引进，民营企业登记户数增长3.1%，实际引进内资176.2亿元，增长45.4%。*突出加快园区开发建设。*松山湖成功晋升国家级高新区，台湾高科技园开园，粤港澳文化创意产业实验园落户，工业产值和税收总额分别增长23.7%和53.9%。虎门港泊位码头建设加快，保税物流中心投入运行，对台直航航线正式通航。东莞生态园基础建设加快，生态修复初见成效，首次对外公开招商。长安新区用海申报、规划编制等工作扎实推进。基本建成7个农业产业园。*突出推进节能降耗减排。*落实企业主体责任，强化重点企业监管，加快高耗能、高污染企业的治理改造，淘汰落后产能，推广清洁生产，加强土地执法监察和闲置地处置。全市单位生产总值耗地、耗能分别下降8.3%和2%。预计二氧化硫和化学需氧量排放分别下降4.2%和3.7%。

三、统筹规划建设，持续改善了城乡环境。坚持规划先行、城乡统筹，推进环境整治，创建宜居城乡。*着力抓好基础设施建设。*环莞快速一期等39项市属重点工程竣工，市轨道交通R2线试验段等26项工程动工。完成3个市区内涝点整治和75个欠发达村老化水管改造。建成镇村联网路31条、110千伏及以上输变电工程21项、水利防灾减灾工程71宗、天然气管网131公里。*着力抓好城乡环境整治。*扎实推进绿道网建设，建成区域绿道225公里。加快森林公园设施配套，植树造林1800多公顷。全面完成在建污水处理厂主体工程，完成运河整治应急工程，全市污水处理能力大大提高，内河涌和水库污染治理有效加强。*着力抓好“三旧”改造。*出台土地出让金调整、容积率计算、拆迁补偿指引等配套文件，完成30万亩土地的专项规划和标图建库，各镇街编制了5年专项规划和年度实施计划，全市启动改造地块174宗、约3.4万亩。

四、强化社会管理，有效维护了安全稳定。落实综治维稳责任，促进了社会安定有序。*加强治安综合治理。*严厉打击恶性和多发性犯罪，大力开展扫黄禁赌等专项行动，深入整治治安重点区域和行业，加强巡逻防控与校园安保。新建省“六好”平安和谐社区41个，市平安社区218个，全年刑事案件破案宗数增长26.9%。*加强安全防范工作。*深入推进危险化学品、“三小”场所、出租屋、建筑安全、食品药品质量等专项整治，开展创新消防管理试点，落实挂牌督办任务，排查和整改了一批安全隐患。新建镇街应急避灾中心17个，建成食品安全样板市场67个，全市各类安全事故宗数、死亡人数分别下降3.2%和2.2%。*加强市政交通管理。*强化城管综合执法，深入整治城市“六乱”，加强市政设施、环卫绿化等管理养护。完善道路护栏设施和步行系统，完成一批交通隐患点的整治，严查酒后驾驶。发展公共交通，新增公交运力120辆、线路12条，更新出租车600辆，新建了一批首末站和候车亭，建成运河路自行车专用道示范工程。*加强矛盾纠纷调解*。完成镇街综治信访维稳中心和村（社区）综治工作站的建设，落实领导接访包案和带案下访等制度，群众信访总量下降23.4%，纠纷调处成功率达93%。加强劳动执法监察和劳资关系调解，劳资突发事件、欠薪逃匿案件分别下降3.4%和37%。

五、办好民生实事，全面发展了社会事业。市财政用于民生事业支出116.4亿元，基本完成向市民承诺的十件实事。*切实做好就业培训工作*。加强就业服务，提高最低工资标准，推广“村民车间”模式，继续实施免费技能培训、工资差额补贴、岗位津贴等政策，全年共培训劳动力13.1万人次，发放就业补贴2.7亿元，户籍大学应届毕业生就业率96%，城镇登记失业率控制在2%以内。*切实提高社会保障水平*。两次调整医保待遇，最高支付额提至15万元，职工和农（居）民退休金分别增长10.2%和44.8%。建立低保标准自然增长机制，向困难人群发放临时物价补贴，发放高龄津贴，设立自然灾害人身保障金。加强住房保障工作，帮助2978户低收入家庭解决住房困难。开展“广东扶贫济困日”和首届“东莞慈善日”活动。积极做好残疾人康复、教育、就业服务。*切实繁荣文化教育事业*。出台文化名城建设规划纲要和若干政策，举办各级各类文化系列活动，新入选3项国家级非物质文化遗产，东莞文艺作品首获文华大奖，东莞作家首获鲁迅文学奖。加快学校布局调整，完成扩建新建6所中学。出台助学贷款和学历进修补助政策。新招收近1.5万名新莞人子女入读公办学校，设立民办学校扶持专项资金。高考每万户籍人口升大学人数居全省首位。*切实推动医疗、体育等事业发展*。完善社区卫生服务体系，加快市中医院新院等大型医疗机构建设，有效防控基孔肯雅热等疫情。广泛开展群众体育运动，成功承办第16届亚运会举重赛事，参加第13届省运会取得佳绩，宏远男篮第六次夺取全国联赛冠军。优化计生服务，开展第六次全国人口普查，人口自然增长率6.23‰。国防人防、拥军优属、科普法普、外事侨务、海洋渔业、工青妇幼、民族宗教、统计审计、气象测报、档案方志、志愿服务、打私等各项工作扎实推进。

六、深化各项改革，激发了体制机制活力。坚持先行先试，锐意改革创新，加强法治政府建设，提升行政服务效能。*深化政府机构改革*。完成部门“三定”方案，市政府工作部门从37个调整为32个，市直临时议事协调机构精简53%。*深化事业单位改革*。实施事业单位岗位设置和人员聘用制度，新进人员实行公开招考。*深化镇村管理体制改革*。推进石龙、塘厦简政强镇试点工作，扩大下放事项，优化机构设置，并在中心镇和市属园区铺开。村级体制改革试点工作稳步推进。基本完成集体林权改革。*深化行政审批制度改革*。开展第四轮清理工作，调整审批事项232项，精简32%。积极推进并联审批、网上审批和电子监察。*深化户籍制度改革*。实行积分制入户和居住证制度，近1.2万名新莞人获得积分入户资格。*深化公共事业改革*。推动医疗卫生事业改革，建立基本药物制度，确立4家公立医院改革试点。认真履行部省协议，推进民政工作改革，推行居家养老服务，开展社会工作试点。完成水务一体化管理以及农村公路养护改革。*深化机关作风建设*。加强廉政和执行力建设，将加工贸易转型等13项重要工作和十件实事纳入行政问责范围。落实重大行政决策程序和政务公开制度，市长办公会向媒体开放。深入开展财政绩效评价。实施大规模干部培训。继续开展市民评机关活动。*深化区域合作发展*。推进深莞惠一体化发展，制定“四年大发展”工作方案，三市在界河污染共治、交通对接、社会管理联动和社保卡互通等方面取得了积极进展。落实“双转移”战略，市财政投入1亿元推进莞韶、莞惠产业转移园区建设。投入援建资金9亿元，提前完成援建四川映秀任务。制定支援新疆农三师图木舒克市总体方案和规划，3个试点项目竣工。落实推进与云浮、韶关两市“双到”扶贫开发，筹集帮扶资金2.2亿元，帮助50.8%的贫困户实现了脱贫。捐赠甘肃玉树灾区6311万元，援助广西河池、西藏林芝、新疆伊吾等对口帮扶地区财物1986万元。

刚刚过去的2010年，也是实施“十一五”规划的最后一年。五年来，我们积极稳妥地推进经济社会双转型，较好地完成了“十一五”各项目标任务，经济社会发展取得了新的成就。

这五年，是综合实力稳步增强的五年。我们在极其困难的情况下，努力实现了高基数上的平稳较快发展。全市生产总值五年增加2000亿元，财政总收入增长1.3倍，年度固定资产投资、社会零售总额均突破1000亿元，各项存款余额突破6000亿元，出口总额稳居全国第四。镇街平均可支配收入达到8.7亿元，村组平均可支配收入超3000万元。东莞被列为全国改革开放18个典型地区之一。

这五年，是结构调整逐步加速的五年。我们解放思想，科学谋划，以深入发动强化共识，以激励政策明确导向，以罕见力度稳企扶企，以危机倒逼助推转型，结构调整明显加快。呈现出三大产业结构、内外经济结构、企业经营形态、产品市场结构优化，以及人均经济指标、自主创新能力、节能减排水平、产业集聚程度提升的良好态势。工业技改投资五年增长4倍，专利授权量跃居全省第二。

这五年，是城乡环境持续优化的五年。我们加强统筹，以城带乡，全社会投入2300多亿元推进城市建设，投入200多亿元治理水污染，建成数百宗工程防灾减灾，扎实推进“四清理”、“五整治”以及森林公园建设。城乡一体化程度更高，市中心区地位更加凸显，镇村形象更加靓丽，水环境明显好转，空气质量持续改善。先后获得了全国绿化模范城市、国际花园城市、国家园林城市等荣誉。

这五年，是社会管理全面提升的五年。我们强力打好“治摩”、“治吧”、整治出租屋、扫除黑诊所等战役，全面推进消防安全大排查、大整改、大培训、大建设，坚持开展民间纠纷调处、劳动争议调解、市镇领导接访等行动，建立健全维稳综治、安全生产、应急管理长效机制。各类事故指标、刑事案件和信访数量稳步下降，群众安全感明显增强，社会管理水平不断提升。东莞获评全国社会治安综合治理优秀市。

这五年，是群众得到更多实惠的五年。我们始终坚持民生为本，市财政累计投入453.4亿元用于发展社会事业，公办义务教育实现了全免费，教育强镇和社区医疗卫生服务实现了全覆盖，基本医疗和养老保险实现了城乡统筹，公园和博物馆等实现了免费开放。城市居民和农民收入稳步增长，最低工资和最低生活保障标准逐步提高。城乡公共服务更加完善，市民素质不断提升。东莞进入全国文明城市行列。

各位代表！

五年的发展令人鼓舞，奋斗的历程让人铭记。五年风雨兼程，五年春华秋实，我们在困难中保持了平稳发展，在危机中加快了转型步伐，在磨砺中经受了严峻考验，在奋进中坚定了信心决心，在实干中铸就了新的辉煌。这离不开上级和市委的坚强领导，离不开市人大、市政协与各民主党派的监督支持，离不开广大市民、新莞人和外来投资者以及驻莞部队的共同努力，离不开港澳台同胞、海外侨胞以及国际友人的关心帮助。在此，我们表示衷心的感谢！

五年的发展启示良多，积累的经验弥足珍贵。我们深切地体会到：*必须强化转型才有出路的共识。*只有深入践行科学发展观，切实转变发展方式，推动经济社会双转型，才能增强核心竞争力和抗风险能力。*必须坚定制造业立市的方向。*实体经济是持续发展的重要支撑，制造业是东莞经济的品牌和特色。只有坚定不移地建设现代制造业名城，才能强化产业依托，发挥比较优势。必须坚守强镇才能强市的理念。镇村是东莞的发展之基、实力所在、惠民所依，只有坚持不懈地做强镇域经济，才能筑牢全市发展根基。必须坚持实施环境取胜的战略。城乡一体、组团发展、绿色宽畅是东莞城市环境的独特优势，只有坚定生态宜居的发展定位，深入实施环境取胜战略，才能赢得主动。必须发扬实干创新发展的精神。实干铸就了东莞“海纳百川、厚德务实”的城市精神，培育了东莞人开拓创新的胆识和勇气，成就了东莞经济社会发展的领先地位。只有发扬实干精神，永不止步，永不懈怠，才能永葆活力，开创未来。

五年的发展攻坚克难，当前的问题仍有不少。我们清醒地看到：经济回升基础仍不牢固。尽管已基本走出金融危机的低谷，但部分经济指标与危机前比，与珠三角其他城市比，还存在一定差距。结构调整力度仍需加大。外向依赖、资源依赖程度还比较高，优质品牌企业还不够多、不够强，企业总体技术水平和自主创新能力有待进一步提升。环境资源压力仍然较大。土地、能源等资源制约突出，污染治理与环境保护力度仍需加大。均衡发展水平仍待提升。镇村之间发展不平衡，村组集体收不抵支现象有所增多。社会管理工作仍需加强。社会不稳定因素依然较多，治安管理、安全生产、信访矛盾、教育公平、医疗改革等仍然面临较大压力，近来物价的持续上涨也给群众生活造成了一定影响。政府服务效率仍待提高。机关作风有待深入改进，办事难等依然是群众反映强烈的问题之一。对此，我们将高度重视，积极应对，努力破解。

“十二五”时期奋斗目标和主要任务

“十二五”时期将是世界经济格局的复杂变革期，是全球新兴产业、新兴市场孕育发展的重大机遇期，是我国加快转变经济发展方式的攻坚期。对东莞来讲，这将是深入推进双转型、加快现代化建设的重要五年。虽然我们面临着外向依存度过高、先发优势弱化、企业成本上升、节能减排和人民币升值压力增大等挑战，中央货币政策收紧、积极财政政策力度减弱以及国内较大的通胀压力等，也将对东莞经济带来一定的影响。但与此同时，我们也拥有许多有利条件：外部经济环境有望逐步好转，我国城镇化建设加快，内需拉动效果逐步显现；全市发展基础扎实，政府和民间的创造力较强，推动转型发展的思想更加统一、目标更加明确、方法更加对头，东莞和谐的人文环境、舒适的城市环境、公平的市场环境以及完备的产业体系仍然受到客商信赖。因此，我们必须准确把握国内外的形势变化，增强机遇意识、忧患意识和创新意识，既要对困难有充分的估计和应对的准备，又要坚定信心决心，扬长避短，主动作为，努力推动东莞经济社会沿着科学发展的道路稳步前进。

“十二五”时期东莞发展的**总体要求**是，以科学发展为主题，以加快转变经济发展方式为主线，以“加快转型升级，建设幸福东莞”为核心，以产业结构调整升级和城市升级为重点，深入推进经济社会双转型，努力当好推动科学发展、促进社会和谐的排头兵。**主要发展目标：**生产总值年均增长8%，结构调整取得明显突破，城市软实力明显提升，体制机制明显完善，人民幸福感明显增强。

要实现上述目标，必须处理好发展速度与发展方式、硬实力与软实力、经济增长与民生福祉、政府与市场、改革发展与稳定的关系。必须坚持先行先试、转型发展，坚持调整结构、创新发展，坚持节能减排、绿色发展，坚持统筹协调、和谐发展，坚持以人为本、惠民发展，坚持扩大开放、合作发展。要重点在以下四大方面下功夫：

一、深入提升“东莞制造”品牌。毫不动摇加快产业结构调整，推动经济发展方式从资源主导、粗放增长向创新主导、绿色低碳转变，从多轮驱动、零散发展向园区带动、集群发展转变，从外向依赖向内外并重转变。大力调整产业存量，深入开展全国加工贸易转型升级试点，改造提升传统产业，加大扶优扶强力度，促进现有企业做大做强。大力提升产业增量，提高利用内外资水平，实施战略性新兴产业五年倍增计划，努力实现以大补小、以优代劣。大力提高产业质量，加强科技创新和品牌建设，壮大民营经济，扩大内需市场，落实节能减排，实现高端化、本土化、集约化发展。大力强化产业服务，加快现代服务业发展，建设金融强市、珠三角新兴物流城市、会展休闲之都。大力优化产业布局，加快形成“一个核心区、三大经济带、五大产业集聚区”的产业空间布局，打造更多更高层次的产业集群。全面构建起先进制造业实力较强、现代服务业支撑有力、都市农业高效集约的现代产业体系，切实提高核心竞争力和抗风险能力。

二、深入打造生态宜居城市。对城市总体规划进行修编，按照“强核、宜居、内畅、外联”的思路，进一步完善城市格局、提升城市品位、塑造城市性格。坚持基础设施先行，以构建内聚外联的轨道交通为突破，完善一环六横六纵三连的高快速路网、四通八达的主干支次路网和便捷顺畅的公交体系，推动市民出行方式转变，建成市内半小时生活圈；以打造“智慧东莞”为方向，推进电信网、广播电视网、互联网三网融合，加快物联网发展，完善城乡全覆盖的水电气设施和通讯网络。坚持组团发展，大力提升以中央商务区、商贸区、生态休闲区为重点的市中心区建设，推进各镇标志性片区和成熟社区的建设，力争把主城区建设成为城市形象展示区、高级人才集聚区和成熟社区示范区，各个镇建设成为具有“小市富县”配套水平的城市支点。坚持环境取胜战略，突出以绿为魂、水气同治，深入推进环境整治，努力做到天更蓝、水更清、城更绿。坚持建管并重，大力推进城市管理精细化、数字化、社会化。努力争创国家生态城市。

三、深入推进文化名城建设。紧紧把握住提高人的素质这个核心要求，深化精神文明建设，发展文化教育事业，全面提升城市软实力。培育现代城市文明，弘扬“海纳百川、厚德务实”的城市精神，加强思想道德建设，建设学习型城市，形成良好社会风尚，践行社会主义核心价值观，巩固全国文明城市地位。加快教育事业改革发展，实施学前教育三年行动计划，推动义务教育优质均衡发展，提高普通高中教育水平，打造职业教育品牌特色，促进高等教育跨越发展、成人教育多元发展，努力建设全省推进教育现代化先进市、珠三角重要人力资源培训配置基地和人才高地。推进文化名城建设，打响东莞特色文化品牌，促进文化事业产业繁荣发展，初步建成全国公共文化服务名城、国家历史文化名城、全国现代文化产业名城、岭南文化精品名城。

四、深入建设和谐幸福家园。坚持发展民生社会事业，维护安定局面，增进社会和谐，不断提高市民幸福指数。推动公安护民，努力实现社会治安根本性好转，信访数量和安全生产事故逐年降低，预防和处置突发公共事件的能力切实提高，市民安全感显著增强，建成全国和谐劳动关系示范区。推动强镇富民，推动镇村集体经济增资减债，扶持欠发达地区加快发展，打造更多的名镇名村，进一步健全覆盖城乡的就业服务体系，以此为依托促进充分就业和自主创业，实现居民收入增长与经济发展同步。推动卫生健民，建立起比较完善的公共医疗卫生服务体系，看病难、看病贵问题得到明显缓解，人民健康水平不断提高。推动社保惠民，全市居民的参保面不断扩大，人人享有保障的目标基本实现。推动服务便民，建立现代社会工作制度，建成覆盖城乡的养老服务网络，建成10分钟公共服务圈，初步实现基本公共服务均等化。

2011年工作安排

2011年是“十二五”开局之年，做好今年政府工作，意义十分重大。综合考虑各方面因素，2011年全市发展的**主要目标**是：生产总值增长8.5%，市财政一般预算收入增长10%，固定资产投资总额增长9%、社会消费品零售总额增长14%、外贸出口总额增长8%，城市居民人均可支配收入和农民人均纯收入增长8%，单位生产总值能耗下降2.52%，城镇登记失业率、居民消费价格涨幅分别控制在3%以内和4%左右。

今年政府工作的**总体要求**是：全面贯彻中央十七届五中全会、中央经济工作会议、省委十届八次全会和市委十二届七次全会精神，坚持以科学发展为主题，以“加快转型升级，建设幸福东莞”为核心，认真落实国家宏观调控政策，着力调整产业结构、转变发展方式，着力增强内需拉动、力促平稳增长，着力加强建设管理、提升发展环境，着力办好社会事业、保障民生改善，巩固和扩大应对金融危机成果，促进经济社会又好又快发展，为“十二五”发展奠定坚实的基础。

围绕以上目标要求，今年要重点抓好以下九方面工作：

一、着力调整产业结构，加快构建现代产业体系

扎实推进产业结构调整，加快转变经济发展方式，不断提升经济发展质量。

加快加工贸易转型。抓好全国加工贸易转型升级试点工作，制定方案，争取政策支持，用好专项资金，加强转型服务，推动来料加工企业转“三资”或民营，支持企业向研发和销售环节拓展。加快发展保税物流，继续举行“莞货全国行”活动，加强与大型零售、电子商务机构的合作。改革加工贸易管理模式，推进外经贸、海关、企业三方联网管理。

加快传统产业改造升级。制定传统产业集群发展和转型升级的指导意见。坚持专业兴镇，扶持各镇集中精力发展1—2个优势传统产业。推广专业镇、专业市场与会展业联动发展模式，加强专业市场整合培育，办好各类知名展会。探索建立工业设计中心。加强“东莞老字号”宣传推介，扶持传统特色企业发展。

加快战略性新兴产业培育。制定战略性新兴产业发展规划及配套政策，重点推动半导体照明、高端新型电子信息、电动汽车、太阳能光伏四大产业发展。加快省市共建产业基地建设，争取电动汽车等产业纳入省级基地。加大新兴产业骨干企业的引进培育，实行用地用电优先保障，政府采购优先考虑，带动形成新兴产业集群。

加快现代服务产业发展。落实新兴物流城市实施意见，推动“一港三带六园区”的规划建设，加快海港航运、城市配送等发展。推进市金融商务区建设，深化区域金融合作，发展新型金融机构，促进地方金融改革创新。加快商业网点规划修编，整合完善西正、东纵、世博、鸿福、华南摩尔等商贸集聚区，提升主城区商业档次。发展旅游、设计、会计、法律等产业。

二、着力加强科技创新，不断提高自主发展能力

整合完善现有政策，五年投入100亿元，深入实施科技东莞工程，提升产业竞争力和自主发展能力。

积极培育“两自”企业。支持企业组建研发中心、重点实验室，资助重大科技专项、粤港招标项目和科技合作交流项目，提升企业技术创新水平。落实税收减免政策，引导企业加强技术改造。深入

开展质量强市活动，扶持品牌经营，试行品牌质押，加强区域品牌培育与保护，支持企业参与行业标准制订。

*加强创新平台建设。*加快建设中科院信息技术研发中心等公共平台，支持半导体照明等行业以及茶山食品、沙田港口物流等专业镇创新平台建设，抓紧建设国家半导体光源产品质检中心、国家城市能源计量中心等检测平台。加强对已建平台的运营管理。落实人才引进政策，积极引进培育科技创新团队和领军人才，建立高层次人才列席重大会议制度。

*深化产学研合作。*设立产学研合作专项资金，推动科技金融结合，支持技术研发。建设一批产学研示范基地，组建太阳能、云计算、物联网等产学研联盟，加快散裂中子源与民用核技术产业基地建设。实施科技特派员计划，办好科技合作周，推动企业与高校院所交流对接。推进专利培育、知识产权优势企业认定工作，发展知识产权交易市场。

*引导扶持民营经济发展。*完善和落实扶持民营经济政策措施，选定一批成长型民营企业进行重点帮扶，引导民间资本投向先进制造业领域，加强技术引进消化吸收再创新。发挥行业协会和商会作用，支持兴建市民营大厦。

三、着力实施引优扶强，提升产业集约发展水平

充分发挥园区的产业集聚和辐射带动作用，加力引进和培育优质企业，不断壮大产业实力。

*加大园区开发建设力度。*加强松山湖招商推介，用好国家级园区优惠政策，完善各项配套，推动落户项目尽快投产。抓好虎门港二期市政工程及麻涌港区建设，建成东莞保税物流中心和虎门港数据中心，提升港口吞吐量。加快生态园基础设施建设，全面开展招商活动。完成长安新区总体规划编制，争取尽快进入开发阶段。制定镇街工业集聚区整合改造指导意见。

*加大优质项目引进力度。*完善招商引资目录，建立重大项目洽谈、决策快速反应机制，积极引进跨国企业、央企和大型民企。开展日韩台驻点招商，逐步建立政企高层沟通机制。完善用地指标分配机制，优先解决一批优质项目用地问题。加强对镇街招商的协调指导，鼓励合作引进大项目。

*加大龙头企业培育力度。*落实能源保障、办事优先等政策，大力扶持521家重点工业企业、现代产业体系“四个30项目”、商贸流通业“四个十大”项目、民营工业50强和服务业50强等。选定一批具备潜力的企业进行重点扶持，力争两年内培育主营业务收入超50亿元企业15家以上，超100亿元3家以上，并对实现目标的企业给予奖励。认定第四批上市后备企业，力争新增上市3—5家。

四、着力加快改旧建新，推动城乡环境持续优化

启动城市总体规划修编，以重点项目、“三旧”改造、环保工程等为抓手，深入推进城乡规划建设，进一步扩大投资拉动，完善城市功能，增创环境新优势。

*推动交通项目建设全面提速。*积极配合穗莞深、穗莞惠城际轨道交通工程，加快市轨道交通R2线建设，加强沿线土地规划统筹。推进东莞新火车站及其配套建设，加快东莞东站升级改造。建成广深沿江高速东莞段一期、虎门港支线一期、东莞大道延长线，加快从莞高速、深圳外环、博深高速、莞番高速东莞段和虎岗高速延长线、环莞快速二期、松山湖大道常平连接线，以及东江梨川、东平大桥等建设。完成中麻公路、S120石排至桥头段、S256南城至虎门段、S358长安至虎门段改造，抓紧石大公路、东部快速企石至桥头段改造，推进沿海公路、疏港大道等建设。

*推动城市功能配套加快完善。*加快中央商务区、商贸区、生态休闲区的规划建设，抓紧推进南城总部经济片区、东城中心片区、东莞火车站石龙茶山新片区等建设，建成广电中心、市中医院新院、

篮球中心等项目，加快工人文化宫、市民艺术中心等项目，进一步增强主城区功能。继续完善城市水电气网络，推进水利防灾减灾工程，建成110千伏及以上输变电工程16项、天然气管网140公里、改造供水管网600公里。加快信息基础设施建设，提升城市信息化水平。

*推动“三旧”改造取得突破。*用好政策优惠期，加快解决历史用地手续问题。加强改造方向引导，注重开发产业性项目和公益性项目。实行领导挂钩督导，简化工作流程，推行并联审批和逾期同意制，加强政策宣传辅导，加快解决征地、拆迁、审批等难题。抓好试点建设，强化示范带动，推动已批项目加快开工建设。

*推动环境整治工程深入实施。*严格落实生态控制和耕地保护红线，研究分期实施生态保护区退果还林工程。编制全市绿道网总体规划，启动市级和社区绿道建设。加快黄旗山城市公园的建设和已建森林公园的配套，启动凤岗南门山、清溪山水天地等森林公园建设。加强社区绿化，新建一批乡村公园，创建一批宜居社区。加强污水处理厂运营管理，加快支次截污管网建设，推进运河及挂影洲中心涌综合整治。加快4座垃圾处理厂和7个环保专业基地建设。严格落实节能减排责任，加强排污监控和环境监测，实施清洁空气行动计划，推广节能技术和清洁生产，强化土地执法监察，盘活存量土地。

五、着力扶持镇村发展，切实增强基层活力

镇村是全市发展的重要基础，集体经济是东莞的特色和优势，必须促进镇村持续稳定发展，打造更多的名镇名村。

*加力推进市内帮扶。*改革市镇财政管理体制，通过提高分成、超收奖励、增加补助等措施，每年增加镇街财力约15亿元。出台激励村一级转型的财政政策。开展市内“双到”扶贫，继续实施原有扶贫贷款贴息、公共管理支出补助等措施，设立定点帮扶资金，延长借款期限，扩大使用范围，对所有基本农田实行生态补偿，实施用地收费返还。年内帮助60%的欠发达村和贫困户脱贫。

*理顺镇村管理体制。*深入推进简政强镇，推动中心镇和三大市属园区加快改革，用好下放事权。推进黄江、厚街村级体制改革试点。设立农村经济风险储备金，加强镇村集体资产和债权债务管理，出台农村干部薪酬管理办法，制定政经分账核算和集体经济多元化经营的指导意见，严控非生产性支出和超前分配。做好镇村（居）班子和农村股份经济组织换届工作。

*发展现代都市农业。*加快农业产业园建设，加强项目引进，打造精细农业示范区。推进标准化基本农田建设，促进农业用地集约和规模经营，培育农业龙头企业和专业合作社。开展科技下乡，落实农机购置补贴，推广先进装备，提高生产效益。加快渔区建设改造，稳定海洋渔业发展。

六、着力强化社会管理，维护和谐稳定局面

坚持防范与打击并重、服务与管理并举，不断提高社会管理水平，努力维护社会稳定。

*继续狠抓社会治安和安全生产。*保持高压态势，加强治安复杂场所整治，严厉打击恶性犯罪和多发性犯罪，突出打击汽车抢劫、入室盗窃、黄赌毒等。推进“平安公交”建设，加强出租屋管理。探索推动巡警体制改革，强化公安信息化和执法规范化建设。加大安全宣教和隐患排查整治力度，实施消防“防火墙”工程，加快“三镇一港”化工园区建设。完善各级应急机构建设，建成市安全生产应急救援指挥中心，提高突发事件联合处置能力。

*继续狠抓劳动监察执法和信访调解。*加强人文关怀，改善用工环境。开展劳动监察网格化和网络化建设，提高劳动仲裁处理效率，严厉打击欠薪逃匿等行为。建成市人民来访接待厅，完善基层综治信访维稳机构，强化矛盾排查化解，落实领导接访包案和干部下访制度，妥善解决群众合理诉求。

继续狠抓市政交通和综合执法管理。增加公交运力和线路，加快完善公交站点和公共停车场建设，提升公交服务质量。加强交通疏导和执法值勤，加快交通拥堵点的改造，完善步行系统、自行车道以及视频监控、护栏设施。加强城乡内涝整治，修缮农村巷道和排污排水设施。探索生活垃圾分类收集处理，继续改进环卫保洁工作。加强城市管理综合执法，深入整治城市“六乱”，抓好流动商贩管理和违法建筑整治。

继续狠抓平安和谐社区建设。启动“幸福家园”社区服务体系建设，实施社区工作人员培训工程，打造社区优质服务示范点，继续抓好省“六好”平安和谐社区、市平安社区创建工作。加大社会工作力度，完善相关配套政策，建立政府购买公共服务制度。加快成熟社区建设，出台考核验收标准，推动社区功能配套加快完善。

七、着力发展各项事业，有效保障民生改善

坚持以人为本，大力改善民生，继续办好十件实事，推动社会事业发展，促进社会全面进步。

铺开文化名城建设。设立5年共50亿元的专项资金，出台配套政策。推进全国公共文化服务示范区建设，完善城乡文化设施，实施文化惠民工程。启动国家历史文化名城创建，加强非物质文化遗产保护，建设中国近代史主题公园。加快印刷、创意设计、现代传媒等行业发展。打造具有岭南文化特色的艺术精品。实施城市形象塑造和提升工程。力保蝉联全国文明城市。

提升教育发展水平。增加财政对教育的投入，提高公办中小学的生均经费标准。加大市镇财政对学前教育的支持力度，壮大公办幼儿园规模，提升民办发展水平，落实村（社区）和新建小区办园，提高幼师待遇，规范学前教育管理。完成10所高中学校新建扩建和职教城一期工程，落实省职业教育综合改革试验区各项工作，支持高等教育发展。

推进健康城市建设。深化医药卫生体制改革，完善基本医疗保障制度，实施基本药物制度，稳妥开展公立医院改革试点。健全基层医疗卫生服务体系，完善社区卫生服务功能，提高服务质量。加强重大传染病和职业病防控。强化食品药品安全监管，加大检测抽查力度。完善各项体育设施，推动群众体育和竞技体育蓬勃发展。继续做好人口计生工作。

做好就业社保等工作。鼓励开办“村民车间”，实施青年见习培训计划，开展农民工专场招聘，帮助市民充分就业创业。完善城乡一体社保体系，提高离退休人员基本养老金，将低保标准从400元提高到440元，实施低保动态管理，增加特困低保家庭生活补助。制定临时救助办法，探索为困难人群购买重大疾病保险，完善专项慈善基金运行机制。落实积分制入户和居住证制度，探索基本公共服务积分制管理。抓好“菜篮子”工程，加强物价管理，向困难群众发放临时物价补贴。加强住房保障，建设雅园新村二期。扎实开展双拥共建，争创全国双拥模范城“七连冠”。继续做好国防人防、科普法普、外事侨务、工青妇幼、民族宗教、统计审计、档案方志、气象、打私等工作。

八、着力落实规划纲要，积极扩大开放合作

深入实施珠三角规划纲要，积极落实内地与港澳台相关经贸合作协议，落实对口帮扶任务，推动区域合作与协调发展。

强化深莞惠一体化合作。共同编制深莞惠区域协调发展总体规划，论证建立产业合作示范区。加快跨界路网对接，优化跨界公交线路，推进车辆通行年票互通。加强界河联合整治，开展大气污染联合防治。加强水资源开发利用、流动人口服务管理、打击跨区域犯罪和处置突发事件的协作。推进职称鉴定和证书互认互通、医疗保险异地结算、养老保险无障碍转移，以及劳动监察、劳动仲裁合作。

强化与港澳台等交流合作。加强与香港、澳门在城市管理、金融、会展、旅游、教育、卫生等方面的合作，落实产业服务制度，促进在莞港资企业转型升级。加强与台湾高科技产业、现代农业等合作，推动松山湖台湾高科技园尽快形成规模效益，推进虎门港与高雄港、基隆港的合作。加强与东盟合作，开拓新兴市场。

强化对口援建与扶贫协作。落实援疆、援藏计划，抓紧启动一批民生项目。扎实推进与云浮、韶关两市“双到”扶贫开发，力争提前实现80%贫困户脱贫的目标。用好省市扶持资金，加强莞韶、莞惠产业转移园基础设施建设和招商引资。完成援建汶川映秀收尾工作。继续做好对广西河池等地的对口帮扶。

九、着力加强自身建设，打造廉洁高效政府

坚持依法行政，优化政府服务，狠抓工作落实，提高政府公信力和执行力。

进一步加强依法行政。认真执行人大决议，主动接受社会监督。落实重大行政决策程序规定，健全行政决策合法性审查机制，促进科学民主决策。制定行政处罚裁量标准，完善处罚程序，开展执法评议考核，进一步规范执法行为。推进电子政务建设，完善网络问政平台及政务信息共享平台。推动中心镇成立法制机构，提高依法行政水平。

进一步提升服务效能。深化行政审批制度改革，完善和落实重点项目并联审批、超时默认制度，推动一批群众常办事务上网审批。完善政府采购实施办法，加强财政资金绩效评价，全面推行市级财务核算信息集中监管改革，提高资金使用效率。推广“一站式服务”，严格执行首问责任、限时办结、责任追究等六项制度。加快事业单位分类改革。落实各项扶企制度，帮助解决好用工、用电、用地、融资等问题。

进一步改进机关作风。加强重大决策和重点工作的跟踪督查，落实现场办公和季度片会制度，促进难点问题解决。严格厉行节约，严控会议和庆典活动，建设全市视频会议系统。落实《廉政准则》，推进廉政建设和反腐败斗争，建设综合型纪检监察平台。健全明查暗访机制，坚决纠正不正之风。

各位代表！“十二五”的蓝图已经绘就，各项目标任务已经明确。站在新的起点上，我们必须恪守主抓执行的职责，拿出只争朝夕的干劲、不甘人后的拼劲，在抓落实上见分晓、比高低；必须牢记执政为民的宗旨，坚持一切为了群众，一切依靠群众，在惠民生上办实事、办好事；必须提振奋发有为的精神，坚定改革创新的决心，强化攻坚克难的锐气，在促转型上求突破、勇争先，为建设幸福东莞而努力奋斗！

名词注解：

“双到”扶贫：指扶贫开发“规划到户责任到人”。省委省政府提出，从2009年开始，用3年时间，对省内欠发达地区的贫困村、贫困户，通过“规划到户责任到人”进行帮扶，确保基本实现脱贫。其中我市承担韶关、云浮两地的帮扶任务。参照省的做法，我市对市内的欠发达村、低保困难户也开展“双到”扶贫。

外经贸“五个1000”专项工作：即推动1000家来料加工企业转变形态、推动1000家加工贸易企业拓展内销市场、推动1000家加工贸易企业提升生产力水平、拜访1000家目标引进企业（机构）、邀请1000家海外企业（机构）深入考察我市投资环境。

现代产业体系“四个30项目”：即30个战略性新兴产业项目、30个先进制造业项目、30个优势传统产业项目、30个现代服务业项目。

商贸流通业"四个十大"项目：即十大连锁经营企业、十大专业市场、十大物流企业和十大会展项目。

一个核心区、三大经济带、五大产业集聚区：一个核心区即中心城区建设现代产业核心区；三大经济带即以松山湖为龙头的园区经济带、以虎门港为依托的物流经济带、以主城区为核心的商贸经济带；五大产业集聚区即先进制造业集聚区、高新技术产业集聚区、现代服务业集聚区、临港产业集聚区、现代农业集聚区。

"强核、宜居、内畅、外联"："强核"是指强化主城区和各镇中心区的城市功能；"宜居"是指营造生态宜居环境；"内畅"是指打造连接顺畅的市内交通网络；"外联"是指打通对外连接通道。

物流"一港三带六园区"：一港即虎门港物流基地；三带即西部沿海物流产业带、东部铁路物流产业带、中部城市物流产业带；六园区即东莞市保税物流园、立沙岛石化物流园、常平大京九物流园、石龙红海物流园、茶山铁路物流园、生态园城市配送物流园。

消防"防火墙"工程：全面加强消防建设，力争通过三年努力，形成政府部门、社会单位、群众共同参与的群防群控格局，推动消防安全环境明显改善，重特大尤其是群死群伤火灾事故有效遏制。

"三镇一港"化工园区：在谢岗、大岭山、清溪、虎门港建立危险化学品生产、储存、经营重点规划区域。

"幸福家园"社区服务体系：今年启动体系建设，到2015年基本建成，主要包括打造社区生活服务中心示范点、培育社区社会组织、培训社会建设人才、建立社区政务服务中心、建设物业管理型社区等。

2011年市政府十件实事

一、加强社会治安治理。严厉打击入室盗窃及路面"双抢"违法犯罪活动，全市社区警情同比下降12%、路面"双抢"警情下降10%；打造"平安公交"，全市50%以上公交企业成立内保机构，二级以上车站全部成立警务室，创建700台平安车厢、15个平安车站，全市公交治安警情下降15%。

二、建设一批学校。投入23亿元，建成市第六高级中学、市第七高级中学、市第八高级中学、市信息职业技术学校、石龙中学、万江中学、厚街专业技术学校、市卫生学校，完成市第五高级中学、长安职业高级中学扩建工程，基本完成职教城一期工程建设。

三、完善公共卫生服务。投入8亿元，全面实施建立居民健康档案、健康教育、免疫规划、传染病报告处理、儿童保健、孕产妇保健、老年人健康管理、高血压和糖尿病管理、重性精神疾病管理等9项基本公共卫生服务项目，实现基本公共卫生服务覆盖城乡居民；建成市中医院新院和广东医学院附属松山湖医院（市第二人民医院）并投入使用。

四、加大就业保障和扶贫力度。投入8亿元，实现城镇登记失业率控制在3%以内、东莞生源应届高校毕业生初次就业率达90%以上；将退休人员养老保险待遇提高10%以上；将低保标准从400元提高到440元；年内实现60%的欠发达村村组两级集体经营性年纯收入达到150万元，实现60%以上已结对帮扶的有劳动能力的低保户脱贫。

五、建设宜居社区和社区生活服务中心。投入2亿元，年内建成80个宜居社区（村），创建20个社区生活服务中心示范点。

六、整治市区内涝。投入8亿元，基本完成鸿福河和四环路宏远路段内涝整治工程，动工建设东纵路内涝整治工程。

七、保障食品安全。加强食品抽检，确保蔬菜农药残留检测合格率达97%以上、生猪"瘦肉精"残留检测合格率达99%以上、水产品药物残留检测合格率达95%以上、食品生产环节抽检合格率85%以上；新建30个食品安全样板市场；创建5条餐饮服务食品安全示范街。

八、建设城市绿道和森林公园。投入7亿元，建成260公里城市绿道，基本建成凤岗镇南门山和清溪镇山水天地两个森林公园，规划建设黄江镇黄牛埔、清泉，凤岗镇碧湖，寮步镇佛灵湖等4个森林公园。

九、治理垃圾填埋场、汽车尾气和工业锅炉。投入8000万元，整改塘厦、虎门、樟木头三座垃圾填埋场，实现无害化处理；治理营运客货车尾气，抽检达标率达78%以上，淘汰或改造工业锅炉400个，改善全市空气质量。

十、实施"文化惠民"工程。投入5亿元，实现全市镇街文化站全部达到省"特级文化站"标准；实现全市村（社区）公共文化服务设施达到"五个有"的标准；实现全市镇街24小时自助图书借阅全覆盖；组织"万场电影、千场演出、百场培训"到村（社区）、到企业。

第二部分　统计资料

Part Two　Statistics

一、综　合
General Survey

1-1 东莞行政区划（2010年）

Divisions of Administrative Areas in Dongguan (2010)

镇 街	村（居）委会		
	个 数		名 称
合 计	村委会	383	
	社区居委会	216	
莞 城	社区居委会	8	东正 市桥 罗沙 北隅 西隅 博厦 兴塘 创业
石 龙	村委会	7	西湖 忠维 林屋 蒲溪 新维 王屋洲 黄家山
	社区居委会	3	中山东 中山西 兴龙
虎 门	社区居委会	30	虎门寨 东方 则徐 大宁 树田 白沙 沙角 怀德 博涌 镇口 村头 新联 九门寨 居岐 金洲 南面 北栅 小捷滘 北面 陈村 东风 武山沙 黄村 南栅 龙眼 宴岗 赤岗 路东 新湾 民泰
东 城	社区居委会	23	岗贝 花园新村 东泰 温塘 桑园 周屋 余屋 鳌峙塘 峡口 柏洲边 上桥 下桥 樟村 梨川 堑头 主山 石井 同沙 光明 牛山 立新 火炼树 星城
万 江	社区居委会	28	万江墟 万江 石美 莫屋 拔蛟窝 黄粘洲 蚬涌 谷涌 小享 滘联 上甲 新村 新谷涌 共联 水蛇涌 大莲塘 牌楼基 严屋 大汾 流涌尾 金泰 曲海 坝头 胜利 官桥滘 简沙洲 新和 新城
南 城	社区居委会	17	宏远 胜和 元美 亨美 三元里 篁村 新基 周溪 袁屋边 白马 石鼓 蛤地 西平 雅园 水濂 新城 鸿福
中 堂	村委会	15	潢涌 三涌 湛翠 凤冲 袁家涌 吴家涌 鹤田 中堂 一村 东向 蕉利 槎滘 下芦 马沥 四乡
	社区居委会	5	中心 斗朗 红锋 东泊 江南
望牛墩	村委会	21	李屋 望东 扶涌 赤滘 五涌 下漕 上合 聚龙江 望联 洲湾 洲涡 杜屋 寮厦 芙蓉沙 官桥涌 横沥 福安 石排 官洲 朱平沙 锦涡
	社区居委会	1	望牛墩
麻 涌	村委会	13	麻一 麻三 麻四 大步 东太 新基 川槎 鸥涌 华阳 南洲 大盛 漳澎 黎滘
	社区居委会	2	麻涌 麻二
石 碣	村委会	14	石碣 唐洪 黄泗围 西南 单屋 梁家村 沙腰 刘屋 水南 四甲 鹤田厦 涌口 横滘 桔洲
	社区居委会	1	城中
高 埗	村委会	18	冼沙 卢溪 宝莲 塘厦 草墩 护安围 保安围 三联 横滘头 低涌 朱磡 新联 欧邓 芦村 高埗 凌屋 上江城 下江城
	社区居委会	1	新创
道 滘	村委会	13	南城 南丫 闸口 大鱼沙 小河 永庆 北永 昌平 厚德 九曲 大罗沙 大岭丫 蔡白
	社区居委会	1	兴隆
洪 梅	村委会	9	洪屋涡 新庄 梅沙 氹涌 黎洲角 夏汇 尧均 乌沙 金鳌沙
	社区居委会	1	洪梅
沙 田	村委会	16	中围 和安 大流 泥洲 杨公洲 福禄沙 阇西 民田 先锋 西大坦 穗丰年 大泥 齐沙 稔洲 义沙 西太隆
	社区居委会	2	横流 滨港
厚 街	村委会	22	厚街 珊美 宝屯 三屯 陈屋 赤岭 河田 寮厦 汀山 环冈 大迳 新围 桥头 南五 新塘 涌口 双岗 溪头 沙塘 宝塘 下汴 白濠
	社区居委会	1	竹溪
长 安	社区居委会	13	涌头 沙头 霄边 上沙 咸西 厦岗 锦厦 厦边 上角 乌沙 新民 长盛 新安

1-1　续表

(2010年)

镇　街	村　(居)　委　会		
	个　数		名　　称
寮　步	村委会	20	西溪　凫山　石龙坑　石步　良边　富竹山　塘唇　向西　霞边　上屯　下岭贝　竹园　上底　药勒　刘屋巷　浮竹山　陈家埔　井巷　小坑　长坑
	社区居委会	10	寮步　塘边　横坑　岭厦　新旧围　缪边　牛杨　泉塘　坑口　良平
大岭山	村委会	21	太公岭　大塘朗　下高田　连平　鸡翅岭　马蹄岗　金桔　大沙　百花洞　大塘　水朗　杨屋　矮岭冚　颜屋　大片美　梅林　元岭　大岭　新塘　旧飞鹅　大环
	社区居委会	3	大岭山　农场　领居
大　朗	村委会	16	高英　洋乌　洋坑塘　松柏朗　黎贝岭　松木山　犀牛陂　水平　宝陂　石厦　杨涌　沙步　新马莲　佛子凹　蔡边　水口
	社区居委会	12	大朗　佛新　巷头　巷尾　大井头　屏山　竹山　求富路　长塘　黄草朗　圣堂　长富
黄　江	村委会	11	社贝　鸡啼岗　袁屋围　合路　北岸　田心　龙见田　大冚　长龙　星光　旧村
	社区居委会	3	新市　田美　三新
樟木头	社区居委会	9	圩镇　樟罗　百果洞　樟洋　石新　柏地　官仓　裕丰　金河
清　溪	村委会	20	浮岗　上元　清厦　铁松　铁场　谢坑　青皇　大埔　长山头　三中　九乡　三星　渔樑围　厦坭　大利　土桥　重河　松岗　罗马　荔横
	社区居委会	1	清溪
塘　厦	社区居委会	22	塘厦　三局　林村　石潭埔　四村　振兴围　大坪　莆心湖　平山　诸佛岭　桥陇　龙背岭　石鼓　田心　横塘　蛟乙塘　凤凰岗　莲湖　沙湖　石马　清湖头　塘新
凤　岗	村委会	11	雁田　官井头　油甘埔　凤德岭　塘沥　黄洞　竹塘　竹尾田　三联　五联　天堂围
	社区居委会	1	凤岗
谢　岗	村委会	11	黎村　窑山　南面　大龙　大厚　赵林　稔子园　五星　曹乐　谢岗　谢山
	社区居委会	1	泰园
常　平	村委会	31	岗梓　塘角　苏坑　袁山贝　金美　还珠沥　朗贝　桥沥　卢屋　九江水　朗洲　陈屋贝　司马　霞坑　漱旧　漱新　黄泥塘　元江元　横江厦　沙湖口　白石岗　松柏塘　上坑　木棆　下墟　板石　田尾　白花沥　桥梓　麦元　土塘
	社区居委会	2	常平　新民
桥　头	村委会	11	田头角　李屋　朗厦　岗头　屋厦　禾坑　邓屋　邵岗头　东江　山和　石水口
	社区居委会	6	桥头　田新　莲城　大洲　迳联　岭头
横　沥	村委会	16	石涌　隔坑　半仙山　田头　田坑　横沥　村头　长巷　田饶步　六甲　村尾　水边　新四　山厦　月塘　张坑
	社区居委会	1	恒泉
东　坑	村委会	14	东坑　坑美　角社　塔岗　黄麻岭　初坑　凤大　黄屋　寮边头　长安塘　新门楼　井美　彭屋　丁屋
	社区居委会	2	草塘　骏达
企　石	村委会	19	铁岗　深巷　湖美　博夏　上洞　江边　旧围　清湖　东平　上截　下截　东山　莫屋　杨屋　新南　南坑　铁炉坑　企石　霞朗
	社区居委会	1	宝石
石　排	村委会	18	石排　下沙　福隆　庙边王　沙角　黄家壆　赤坎　向西　水贝　田寮　横山　埔心　谷吓　塘尾　李家坊　田边　中坑　燕窝
	社区居委会	1	太和
茶　山	村委会	16	上元　茶山　下朗　横江　增埗　卢边　寒溪水　南社　塘角　博头　冲美　粟边　孙屋　超朗　京山　刘黄
	社区居委会	2	茶山圩　茶溪
松山湖	社区居委会	1	松山湖
虎门港	社区居委会	1	虎门港

1-2 历年东莞行政区划

Divisions of Administrative Areas in Dongguan over Years

单位：个

年 份	镇 街	村(居)委会	村委会	社区居委会
1978	33	526	496	30
1979	33	531	501	30
1980	33	545	515	30
1981	34	554	524	30
1982	34	561	531	30
1983	34	561	531	30
1984	34	542	512	30
1985	33	546	516	30
1986	33	560	530	30
1987	34	580	537	43
1988	33	582	542	40
1989	33	583	544	39
1990	33	583	543	40
1991	33	586	546	40
1992	33	590	549	41
1993	33	590	549	41
1994	33	592	551	41
1995	33	592	551	41
1996	33	593	552	41
1997	33	594	551	43
1998	32	594	551	43
1999	32	593	546	47
2000	32	675	546	129
2001	32	678	546	132
2002	32	678	546	132
2003	32	616	487	129
2004	32	596	440	156
2005	32	596	404	192
2006	32	596	394	202
2007	32	591	386	205
2008	32	591	383	208
2009	32	598	383	215
2010	32	599	383	216

注：2010年起社区居委会数含松山湖及虎门港。

1-3 主要年份户数、人口与自然资源

Number of Households, Population and Natural Resources in Main Years

项　　目	单 位	1978年	1985年	1990年	1995年	2000年	2005年	2009年	2010年
一、户　数									
年末户籍总户数	万户	24.82	28.95	32.73	36.43	41.40	46.50	52.12	53.05
#非农业户	万户	4.37	6.97	8.91	10.06	11.44	18.90	24.05	27.08
二、人口与劳动力									
年末常住人口	万人			175.62	336.45	644.84	656.07	786.08	822.48
年末户籍人口	万人	111.23	120.85	131.85	143.65	152.61	165.65	178.73	181.77
#非农业人口	万人	18.49	25.49	30.87	35.38	39.61	65.84	81.46	92.09
年末户籍从业人员数	万人	54.97	67.35	75.10	82.40	88.62	101.30	112.18	114.44
#企事业机关	万人	8.20	12.30	13.16	18.40	16.80	19.14	15.07	14.92
人口密度(常住人口)	人/平方公里			712	1365	2616	2662	3189	3343
人口密度(户籍人口)	人/平方公里	451	490	535	583	619	672	725	739
三、土　地									
土地面积	平方公里	2465	2465	2465	2465	2465	2465	2465	2460
年末耕地面积	万亩	118.39	96.67	88.26	70.86	66.33	50.29	51.66	57.69
人均耕地面积	亩	1.06	0.80	0.67	0.49	0.43	0.30	0.29	0.32
建成区面积	平方公里				82.48	147.68	620.31	780.15	798.48
#城区建成区面积	平方公里					28.13	108.10	87.29	91.65
四、气　候									
年降水量	毫米	1748.3	1678.0	1602.9	1664.8	2019.3	1837.6	1881.6	2165.9
年平均气温	摄氏度	21.9	21.8	22.8	22.4	23.2	22.7	22.8	22.4
极端最高气温	摄氏度	35.7	35.8	37.8	36.2	37.0	37.4	36.3	36.1
极端最低气温	摄氏度	2.7	4.2	4.3	6.7	5.6	1.8	5.3	1.9
年日照时数	小时	1958.8	1671.7	1910.2	1935.7	2059.5	1736.3	1967.8	1699.7
五、森　林									
有林地面积	万亩		78.34	83.48	91.48	92.16	89.23	90.05	87.30
林木蓄积量	万立方米		155.97	167.18	123.02	136.11	175.38	241.41	255.82
森林覆盖率	%		28.6	31.4	29.7	30.6	33.1	36.5	36.7
六、水资源									
大陆海岸线总长度	公里	61.4	61.4	61.4	61.4	115.9	92.1	97.2	97.2
海水养殖可养面积	万亩	5.0	5.0	5.0	5.5	2.6	16.9	2.0	2.0
淡水养殖可养面积	万亩	30.0	30.0	30.0	28.0	14.3	30.7	10.0	10.0

注：1. 人均耕地面积按户籍人口计算。
2. 大陆海岸线从2000年起以咸水为界定。
3. 常住人口2006-2010年数据，根据东莞市第六次全国人口普查数据结果重新修订，下同。

1-4 历年土地与自然资源

Land and Natural Resources over Years

年 份	土地面积(平方公里)	气候				
		年降水量(毫米)	年平均气温(摄氏度)	极端最高气温(摄氏度)	极端最低气温(摄氏度)	年日照时数(小时)
1978	2465	1748.3	21.9	35.7	2.7	1958.8
1979	2465	2007.1	21.9	36.5	2.9	1991.4
1980	2465	1434.7	22.3	37.7	3.3	2157.1
1981	2465	2394.9	22.1	35.6	3.2	1792.2
1982	2465	1454.1	22.1	37.5	3.8	1754.1
1983	2465	1947.1	21.8	35.8	3.3	1909.7
1984	2465	1444.5	21.5	35.9	3.1	1749.2
1985	2465	1678.0	21.8	35.8	4.2	1671.7
1986	2465	1665.2	22.2	35.9	3.0	2098.1
1987	2465	1908.8	22.9	37.0	4.3	1816.6
1988	2465	1735.0	22.0	37.0	7.0	1836.5
1989	2465	1567.2	22.5	37.6	5.2	1926.0
1990	2465	1602.9	22.8	37.8	4.3	1910.2
1991	2465	1219.6	23.0	36.6	1.2	1968.8
1992	2465	1827.1	22.3	37.0	4.5	1854.5
1993	2465	2393.6	22.5	35.6	3.0	1965.7
1994	2465	1809.1	23.0	38.2	5.4	1828.6
1995	2465	1664.8	22.4	36.2	6.7	1935.7
1996	2465	1547.4	22.7	37.1	3.4	2036.0
1997	2465	2074.0	22.8	36.3	6.1	1558.1
1998	2465	1844.5	23.6	36.5	5.6	1699.0
1999	2465	1614.5	23.3	37.8	3.1	2015.8
2000	2465	2019.3	23.2	37.0	5.6	2059.5
2001	2465	2042.6	23.3	36.6	6.6	1978.2
2002	2465	1557.4	23.6	36.7	4.5	2046.9
2003	2465	1416.7	23.0	36.1	3.8	2268.7
2004	2465	1705.8	22.8	38.0	3.5	2192.9
2005	2465	1837.6	22.7	37.4	1.8	1736.3
2006	2465	2412.0	22.7	36.8	4.7	1616.4
2007	2465	1806.9	22.9	35.9	6.7	1876.7
2008	2465	2710.9	22.2	36.8	4.8	1879.3
2009	2465	1881.6	22.8	36.3	5.3	1967.8
2010	2460	2165.9	22.4	36.1	1.9	1699.7

注：土地面积数据由市国土资源局提供，下同。

1-4 续表

年份	森林			水资源		
	森林面积(万亩)	林木蓄积量(万立方米)	森林覆盖率(%)	大陆海岸线总长度(公里)	海水养殖可养面积(万亩)	淡水养殖可养面积(万亩)
1978				61.4	5.0	30.0
1979	44.4	110.3	14.7	61.4	5.0	30.0
1980				61.4	5.0	30.0
1981				61.4	5.0	30.0
1982				61.4	5.0	30.0
1983				61.4	5.0	30.0
1984	76.6	160.5	21.9	61.4	5.0	30.0
1985	78.3	156.0	28.6	61.4	5.0	30.0
1986	82.4	157.8	30.0	61.4	5.0	30.0
1987	83.9	183.9	34.5	61.4	5.0	30.0
1988	84.3	169.1	34.7	61.4	5.0	30.0
1989	80.9	164.8	31.1	61.4	5.0	30.0
1990	83.5	167.2	31.4	61.4	5.0	30.0
1991	85.0	169.2	31.6	61.4	5.0	29.0
1992	86.3	169.8	31.3	61.4	5.5	29.0
1993	87.3	168.9	31.9	61.4	5.5	28.0
1994	86.1	116.8	28.3	61.4	5.5	28.0
1995	91.5	123.0	29.7	61.4	5.5	28.0
1996	91.9	115.7	29.9	61.4	5.5	28.5
1997	93.5	121.1	29.9	61.4	5.7	28.7
1998	93.4	126.0	30.1	61.4	5.7	28.7
1999	92.2	120.4	30.1	115.9	4.8	28.7
2000	92.2	136.1	30.6	115.9	2.6	14.3
2001	93.3	146.0	31.2	116.0	2.8	12.9
2002	93.8	155.0	31.7	115.9	4.1	11.7
2003	93.3	165.1	32.2	92.1	4.2	10.4
2004	93.3	165.1	32.2	92.1	4.0	10.0
2005	89.2	175.4	33.1	92.1	16.9	30.7
2006	88.9	194.4	35.1	92.1	16.6	30.5
2007	89.1	215.1	35.5	92.1	16.9	30.7
2008	88.6	227.9	36.2	97.2	2.5	15.0
2009	90.1	241.4	36.5	97.2	2.0	10.0
2010	87.3	255.8	36.7	97.2	2.0	10.0

1-5 主要年份国民经济主要指标

Main Indicators on National Economy in Main Years

项　　目	单位	1978年	1985年	1990年	1995年	2000年	2005年	2009年	2010年
一、经济总量指标									
地区生产总值	亿元	6.11	22.60	80.44	296.29	820.25	2183.20	3763.91	4246.45
第一产业	亿元	2.72	6.15	13.28	21.43	25.91	20.55	14.79	16.57
第二产业	亿元	2.68	11.66	40.53	166.97	450.71	1227.86	1823.08	2160.82
#工业	亿元			39.18	154.19	430.45	1173.23	1741.53	2078.45
第三产业	亿元	0.71	4.80	26.63	107.89	343.64	934.78	1926.04	2069.07
二、农村经济									
农业总产值(当年价)	亿元	4.24	9.12	23.64	42.69	54.64	42.05	25.31	28.31
农村集体经营总收入	亿元			7.18	41.23	77.50	120.57	136.10	143.38
年末耕地面积	万亩			88.26	70.86	66.33	50.29	51.66	57.69
三、工　业									
工业增加值(当年价)	亿元			39.18	154.19	430.45	1173.23	1741.53	2078.45
规模以上工业企业财务指标									
主营业务收入	亿元	2.69	9.23	47.27	275.84	988.91	3912.15	6007.76	7708.17
年末固定资产原值	亿元	0.78	1.68	14.29	60.14	728.85	1856.09	3079.92	3216.25
年末固定资产净值	亿元	0.51	1.20	11.95	46.26	470.19	1105.26	1724.00	1783.69
年末流动资产余额	亿元	0.26	0.58	1.74	21.28	529.82	1873.28	3165.25	3788.83
资产总额	亿元		1.73	13.51	52.98	1122.60	3345.33	5286.18	6001.71
负债总额	亿元					563.04	1858.09	3043.46	3525.30
资产负债率	%					50.2	55.5	57.6	58.7
利税总额	亿元					84.10	183.10	403.47	469.59
综合效益指数	%					114.0	119.9	127.2	130.3
四、能源及水的消费									
地区能源消费总量(等价值)	万吨标准煤						1885.78	2603.52	2812.65
地区能源消费总量(当量值)	万吨标准煤						1800.14	2311.86	2438.84
电力消耗	亿千瓦时						419.83	495.58	562.00
单位GDP能耗（等价值，2005年可比价）	吨标准煤/万元						0.864	0.705	0.619
单位GDP能耗（当量值，2005年可比价）	吨标准煤/万元						0.825	0.626	0.599
单位GDP电耗(2005可比价)	千瓦小时/万元						1923.00	1341.26	1380.10
规模以上工业综合能源消费量(当量值)	万吨标准煤						1203.77	1367.94	1496.06
规模以上工业增加值能耗(当量值,2005年可比价)	吨标准煤/万元						1.1	0.82	0.728

注：1. 2005年以前地区生产总值采用全国第一次经济普查资料修订的数据；2005-2008年采用第二次经济普查资料修订的数据；2004年以前使用旧行业分类，2004年起使用新行业分类，下同。
2. 规模以上工业企业1997年及以前年份为独立核算工业企业口径，1998-2005年为全部国有工业及年销售收入500万元以上非国有工业企业口径，2006年起为年主营业务收入500万元及以上工业企业口径，下同。
3. 2005年以前工业相关数据采用第一次经济普查资料修订的数据，2008年采用第二次经济普查资料修订的数据，下同。

1-5 续表 1

项　　目	单 位	1978年	1985年	1990年	1995年	2000年	2005年	2009年	2010年
五、运输邮电									
公路通车里程	公里	1259	1240	1325	2327	2518	2871	4713	4751
#高速公路	公里					89	154	207	217
旅客周转量	亿人公里	0.94	9.52	32.22	44.62	100.19	118.53	105.35	129.07
水　运	亿人公里	0.43	0.43	0.15	0.19	0.14	0.33	0.21	0.20
公　路	亿人公里	0.51	9.10	32.07	44.43	100.05	118.20	105.13	128.87
货物周转量	亿吨公里	1.51	17.16	18.47	26.46	40.47	42.48	101.65	109.03
水　运	亿吨公里	1.42	5.86	11.25	13.66	15.86	15.23	56.36	57.95
公　路	亿吨公里	0.09	11.30	7.22	12.80	24.60	27.25	45.29	51.08
港口货物吞吐量	万吨	293	276	233	201	746	2280	3530	5657
邮政业务收入	亿元							7.15	6.32
电信业务收入	亿元							149.16	149.02
局用交换机容量	万门		1.14	6.98	52.29	103.13	286.25	347.15	365.02
年末移动电话交换机总容量	万户				4.80	154.20	1059.10	1621.60	1657.00
本地电话用户	万户	0.20	0.77	4.90	31.58	78.12	384.52	378.40	332.42
移动电话用户(含充值卡)	万户			0.05	4.77	123.68	1016.41	1409.29	1607.60
#充值卡	万户					42.71	839.58	1271.15	1433.56
互联网用户	万户				0.05	13.78	52.90	118.02	153.92
六、供用电									
总供电量	亿千瓦时	1.64	3.82	18.01	68.00	178.03	415.66	488.85	556.89
#网供	亿千瓦时	1.64	3.39	11.18	38.48	134.91	342.26	431.89	547.33
总售电量	亿千瓦时	1.49	3.39	16.15	61.68	169.06	396.59	478.19	543.66
#工业用电	亿千瓦时	1.08	2.21	11.93	48.79	134.58	330.31	376.10	435.57
七、固定资产投资									
全社会固定资产投资总额	亿元	0.23	7.06	7.51	63.14	102.89	597.24	1094.08	1114.98
#房地产开发	亿元				8.52	11.25	144.43	277.66	298.99
房地产开发当年房屋施工面积	万平方米						1160.20	2333.90	2060.54
房地产开发当年房屋竣工面积	万平方米						132.90	310.22	296.59
商品房销售面积	万平方米						321.90	600.27	511.25
商品房销售额	亿元						119.40	353.00	373.77
新增固定资产	亿元						173.30	542.16	577.86
固定资产交付使用率	%						29.0	49.6	51.8
八、国内商业									
社会商业商品销售总额	亿元	7.49	23.16	43.41	155.69	279.19	824.82	1581.91	1957.18
社会消费品零售总额	亿元	2.13	9.36	31.97	113.01	235.16	506.29	959.07	1108.06

注：1. 2006年起公路通车里程含专用公路和村道，与往年数据不可比，下同。
2. 1995年全社会固定资产投资总额含沙角C厂投资126374万元。
3. 2009年起，客货运输量中，公路和水路运输量统计改用新调查方法，与往年不可比，下同。
4. 2005年以前国内商业相关数据采用第一次经济普查资料修订的数据，2005-2008年采用第二次经济普查资料修订的数据，下同。

1-5 续表 2

项目	单位	1978年	1985年	1990年	1995年	2000年	2005年	2009年	2010年
九、物价指数(以上年价格为100)									
商品零售物价总指数	%	100.4	106.9	94.9	109.7	100.1	103.0	95.3	103.2
居民消费价格总指数	%		106.5	96.6	113.9	101.5	102.4	96.9	102.8
消费品价格指数	%		106.9	94.9	109.7	100.1	103.0	97.1	102.8
服务项目价格指数	%		103.3	111.0	128.9	112.8	100.4	96.3	102.6
十、外经、外贸、旅游									
进出口总额(海关口径)	亿美元			10.82	153.91	320.45	743.72	941.55	1213.38
进口总额	亿美元			5.14	75.92	148.86	334.42	389.86	517.40
出口总额	亿美元			5.68	77.99	171.59	409.29	551.69	695.98
#一般贸易	亿美元				2.32	2.09	17.55	57.17	95.41
来料加工装配	亿美元				43.46	83.43	161.17	182.32	195.54
进料加工	亿美元				32.02	85.84	230.43	305.50	394.62
其他	亿美元				0.19	0.22	0.14	6.70	10.40
新签利用外资协议(合同)数	宗						773	579	869
合同外资金额(新口径)	亿美元						29.80	16.16	25.97
实际利用外资(新口径)	亿美元						14.68	25.94	27.32
全年接待旅游人数	万人次			125	89	291	1156	2037	2251
#国际及港澳台旅游者	万人次			27	27	106	169	286	327
旅游外汇收入	万美元					7617	28189	51756	67592
十一、财政、金融									
来源于东莞的财政收入(不含关税)	亿元	0.66	1.11	3.57	18.01	76.16	283.58	553.36	673.16
市财政一般预算收入	亿元				11.56	30.47	103.97	231.16	277.84
市财政一般预算支出	亿元	0.18	0.50	2.28	12.42	33.61	117.04	232.62	289.83
金融机构各项人民币存款余额	亿元	1.05	13.49	68.07	383.68	1228.67	2933.40	4986.61	5943.39
金融机构各项人民币贷款余额	亿元	1.96	14.24	63.04	254.85	630.84	1500.52	2903.80	3329.82
现金总支出	亿元	2.21	17.32	125.88	897.43	3718.78	7178.50	8486.22	10084.22
现金总收入	亿元	2.08	14.03	120.97	858.45	3594.58	7375.25	8449.47	9867.57
十二、人民生活									
全市职工平均工资	元							14416	16108
城镇在岗职工平均工资	元	474	1456	3552	9682	14051	28253	42585	46576
城市居民人均可支配收入	元		791	2508	9588	14142	22882	33045	35690
城市居民人均消费性支出	元		689	2038	9220	12529	21768	24270	25733
农民人均纯收入	元	149	803	1542	4769	8484	13076	18098	20486
城乡居民人民币储蓄存款余额	亿元	0.54	9.19	45.51	232.97	672.07	1728.28	2904.57	3386.85

注：1. 现金总支出与现金总收入1997年及以前年份是银行口径，1998年起为金融机构口径。
2. 城镇在岗职工工资总额和人均工资2000年前是城镇职工工资，2000年起是城镇在岗职工工资，不含乡镇及以下办企业职工，下同。
3. 接待过夜旅客数、国际旅客数和旅游外汇收入2002年起是旅游局口径，与往年数不可比。
4. 农民人均纯收入采用农村住户抽样调查口径，相应调整了往年数，下同。

1-6 主要年份国民经济和社会发展主要比例与效益指标

Main Indicators on National Economy and Social Development in Main Years

项目	单位	1990年	1995年	2000年	2005年	2009年	2010年
一、户籍人口							
出生率	‰	17.07	17.59	12.11	10.62	10.67	10.90
死亡率	‰	4.76	4.84	4.59	4.60	4.36	4.68
自然增长率	‰	12.31	12.75	7.52	6.02	6.31	6.23
人口性别比(男/女)	%	97.1	100.4	102.4	103.1	103.2	103.1
二、就业(按户籍人口计算)							
就业者负担人口	人	1.8	1.7	1.7	1.6	1.6	1.6
各产业劳动力比例							
第一产业	%	36.2	23.7	19.6	8.6	5.1	4.7
第二产业	%	40.6	46.1	46.8	45.6	41.2	39.5
第三产业	%	23.2	30.2	33.6	45.9	53.7	55.9
三、地区生产总值中三次产业比重							
第一产业	%	16.5	7.2	3.2	0.9	0.4	0.4
第二产业	%	50.4	56.4	54.9	56.2	48.4	50.9
工业	%	48.7	52.0	52.5	53.7	46.3	48.9
建筑业	%	1.7	4.3	2.5	2.5	2.2	1.9
第三产业	%	33.1	36.4	41.9	42.8	51.2	48.7
四、全社会劳动生产率	元/人	**10794**	**36261**	**92978**	**218685**	**339314**	**374750**
(按户籍从业人员、增加值计算)							
第一产业	元/人	4853	10934	13841	21794	25243	30029
第二产业	元/人	13581	44828	113318	267365	417944	472766
第三产业	元/人	15380	43395	115595	210172	313439	333238
五、农业							
农业总产值中“五业”比例							
种植业	%	54.9	45.7	39.6	27.0	55.4	55.4
林业	%	1.8	2.1	0.7	0.4	0.9	1.0
牧业	%	19.2	30.0	41.4	57.7	19.7	19.6
副业	%	11.1	6.2	3.5			
渔业	%	13.3	16.1	14.9	14.9	24.0	24.0

注：2002年起农业中副业并入种植业。

1-6 续表 1

项　　目	单 位	1990年	1995年	2000年	2005年	2009年	2010年
六、工　业							
规模以上工业企业效益							
固定资产利税率	%	8.5	10.7	11.5	9.9	23.4	26.3
资金利税率	%	6.3	7.7	7.5	5.5	7.6	7.8
产值利税率	%	5.4	10.0	9.2	4.6	6.6	6.1
七、建筑业							
技术装备率	万元/人		0.37	0.43	0.68	1.37	1.02
产值利税率	%		3.9	5.4	7.5	10.0	8.1
劳动生产率(按总产值计算)	元/人	18636	42766	60849	108136	184034	218076
八、固定资产投资							
全社会固定资产投资相当于地区生产总值比例(投资率)	%	9.3	17.0	12.5	27.4	29.1	26.3
全社会房屋建筑面积竣工率	%	45.2	34.1	60.7	22.5	19.9	20.7
九、财　政							
来源于东莞的财政收入(不含关税)相当于地区生产总值比例	%	4.4	6.1	9.3	13.0	14.7	15.9
市财政一般预算支出相当于地区生产总值比例	%	2.8	4.2	4.1	5.4	6.2	6.5
十、外经外贸							
利用外资结构							
外商直接投资	%	41.2	63.6	66.0	75.2	88.2	86.4
外商其他投资	%	58.8	36.4	34.0	24.8	11.8	13.6
实际利用外资额相当于协议规定外商投资额比例(旧口径)	%	80.6	31.9	89.7	78.9	144.9	103.0
进出口总额比例							
进口总额	%	47.5	49.3	46.5	45.0	41.4	42.6
出口总额	%	52.5	50.7	53.6	55.0	58.6	57.4
#一般贸易	%		3.0	1.2	4.3	10.4	13.7
来料加工装配	%		55.7	48.6	39.4	33.0	28.1
进料加工	%		41.1	50.0	56.3	55.4	56.7
其他	%		0.2	0.2		1.2	1.5

1-6 续表 2

项　　目	单 位	1990年	1995年	2000年	2005年	2009年	2010年
十一、交通、邮电通信业							
货运量中各种运输方式比例							
公　路	%	58.2	55.7	63.3	71.7	79.5	82.0
水　运	%	41.8	44.3	36.7	28.3	20.5	18.0
十二、金　融							
各项人民币存款相当于生产总值比例	%	84.6	129.5	149.8	134.5	132.5	140.0
各项人民币贷款相当于生产总值比例	%	78.4	86.0	76.9	68.8	77.1	78.4
金融机构现金支出相当于收入的比例	%	104.1	104.5	103.5	97.3	100.4	102.2
各项人民币存款余额中主要存款比例							
#企业存款	%	17.1	23.3	35.7	29.2	28.5	25.6
财政性存款	%	1.2	2.2	0.3	0.9	1.1	0.8
储蓄存款	%	66.9	60.7	54.7	58.9	58.2	57.0
农业存款	%	7.4	6.2	5.9	4.1	4.2	5.8
各项人民币贷款余额中主要贷款比例							
#短期贷款	%	90.5	64.6	84.2	48.9	43.4	37.1
#农业贷款	%	10.8	3.2	3.4	0.3	0.05	
中长期贷款	%	2.1	10.8	7.4	46.7	50.0	59.1
十三、科技、教育、文化、卫生							
科教文卫事业费占财政支出比例	%	28.7	24.5	25.8	17.8	31.5	27.9
学龄儿童入学率	%	99.9	100.0	100.0	100.0	100.0	100.0
小学毕业生升学率	%	95.4	99.2	99.8	99.9	100.0	100.0
初中毕业生升学率	%	44.1	85.4	90.3	94.1	97.0	97.9
普通高中毕业生升学率	%	31.2	64.9	70.5	96.5	87.5	95.1
学校教师负担学生数							
普通高等学校	人		13.7	20.1	15.4	18.0	17.6
中等职业技术学校	人	20.6	21.8	19.0	18.2	20.0	20.3
普通中学	人	20.7	21.1	22.4	19.8	18.3	17.7
小学	人	24.0	24.2	34.3	27.5	24.2	23.3
每万人有电影放映单位	个	0.87	1.53	1.27	0.43	0.22	0.25
每万人《东莞日报》发行量	万份	1.36	6.93	10.40	16.79	26.55	25.11
十四、人民生活							
城市居民消费结构							
食品类	%	63.5	39.5	32.3	27.7	32.8	33.9
衣着类	%	4.7	6.6	3.9	5.9	6.1	6.6
其　他	%	31.8	53.9	63.8	66.4	61.1	59.5

注：本表中人均指标按户籍人口计算。

1-7 国民经济主要指标分月变化情况（2010年，累计绝对数）

Main Indicators on National Economy by Month
(2010, Accumulative Figures in Value Terms)

项　　目	单位	1 月	1-2 月	1-3 月	1-4 月	1-5 月	1-6 月
规模以上工业增加值	亿元		213.97	322.46	499.80	641.82	800.84
#国有经济	亿元		14.16	18.82	19.15	24.43	30.87
外资型经济	亿元		160.93	238.54	380.61	490.77	613.26
#民营企业	亿元		28.10	48.51	74.04	93.27	115.12
#八大支柱产业	亿元		126.17	188.54	302.13	388.65	485.42
规模以上工业销售产值	亿元		964.88	1447.10	2117.74	2719.94	3384.03
规模以上工业出口产品产值	亿元		495.94	733.96	1093.19	1419.33	1785.20
规模以上工业产品产销率	%		99.8	99.1	99.2	99.1	98.8
规模以上工业企业主营业务收入	亿元		973.41	1480.24	2161.24	2789.64	3422.62
规模以上工业企业利税总额	亿元		45.35	61.66	107.47	139.47	167.12
全社会固定资产投资总额	亿元		67.07	148.72	233.78	325.27	420.77
#房地产开发	亿元		15.07	40.78	65.33	81.30	106.42
来源于东莞的财政收入	亿元	80.30	129.11	211.66	277.57	328.87	391.83
市财政一般预算收入	亿元	25.32	44.82	72.61	94.62	112.05	132.19
市财政一般预算支出	亿元	19.38	44.45	72.27	93.79	114.20	146.28
金融机构各项人民币存款余额	亿元	5029.96	5002.61	5225.30	5193.57	5241.55	5428.31
#城乡居民储蓄存款余额	亿元	2851.15	2923.30	3003.74	2984.15	3016.02	3134.09
金融机构各项人民币贷款余额	亿元	2951.29	3022.35	3036.59	3117.48	3164.20	3194.99
货币总投放(现金支出)	亿元	825.44	1564.53	2350.71	3144.08	3906.05	4697.31
货币总回笼(现金收入)	亿元	778.29	1457.14	2265.23	3026.42	3801.84	4584.21
进出口总额(海关口径)	亿美元	86.53	150.33	244.29	340.39	441.22	547.12
#出口总额	亿美元	49.53	86.15	137.36	189.78	247.26	307.89
新签项目宗数	宗	68	104	158	208	288	353
合同规定外商投资额	亿美元	1.49	3.58	5.07	6.71	8.83	11.13
实际利用外资(不含对外借款)	亿美元	2.36	4.14	6.88	8.87	11.50	13.95
社会消费品零售总额	亿元		185.69	268.66	356.08	443.72	535.85
居民消费价格总指数	%	99.4	101.1	101.1	101.4	101.9	102.1
#服务项目价格指数	%	96.0	99.2	99.8	100.3	101.0	101.6
总供电量	亿千瓦时	41.55	67.45	110.75	153.83	202.81	252.86
总售电量	亿千瓦时	44.02	86.87	115.43	156.90	197.39	246.09
邮电业务收入	亿元	12.86	25.40	39.02	51.94	64.23	77.00
城市居民人均可支配收入	元			12053			19634
城市居民人均消费性支出	元			7194			13331

注：1. 物价指数与上年同期相比；各项指标1-12月累计不等于年报数。
　　2. 城市居民收支为季报数据。

1-7　续表

(2010年，累计绝对数)

项　　目	单位	1-7 月	1-8 月	1-9 月	1-10 月	1-11 月	1-12 月
规模以上工业增加值	亿元	952.96	1114.50	1282.66	1452.62	1629.23	1812.86
#国有经济	亿元	37.24	44.16	51.17	57.57	63.76	68.93
外资型经济	亿元	728.83	853.32	983.37	1114.80	1248.62	1383.99
#民营企业	亿元	137.61	160.20	183.37	206.97	234.15	265.52
#八大支柱产业	亿元	579.38	675.09	776.83	882.53	989.25	1100.12
规模以上工业销售产值	亿元	4029.66	4712.75	5418.77	6137.37	6865.12	7544.09
规模以上工业出口产品产值	亿元	2136.20	2499.33	2874.43	3260.98	3649.25	4006.84
规模以上工业产品产销率	%	98.8	99.0	99.1	99.1	99.0	97.8
规模以上工业企业主营业务收入	亿元	4071.46	4728.71	5452.98	6171.08	6810.62	7512.83
规模以上工业企业利税总额	亿元	196.89	228.13	264.08	307.42	344.57	385.63
全社会固定资产投资总额	亿元	500.89	600.55	743.79	820.00	904.00	1114.98
#房地产开发	亿元	131.92	162.13	208.72	225.36	246.28	298.99
来源于东莞的财政收入	亿元	457.79	519.27	572.90	654.28	705.57	785.10
市财政一般预算收入	亿元	151.71	173.66	193.52	216.09	234.61	277.84
市财政一般预算支出	亿元	169.06	188.67	218.28	241.21	264.50	308.61
金融机构各项人民币存款余额	亿元	5377.81	5457.47	5677.02	5659.10	5756.12	5943.39
#城乡居民储蓄存款余额	亿元	3130.70	3157.47	3307.15	3246.12	3273.33	3386.85
金融机构各项人民币贷款余额	亿元	3220.09	3262.24	3291.16	3308.18	3316.43	3329.82
货币总投放(现金支出)	亿元	5558.52	6426.83	7359.58	8171.45	9075.24	10084.22
货币总回笼(现金收入)	亿元	5422.49	6274.17	7165.68	7987.24	8894.48	9867.57
进出口总额(海关口径)	亿美元	657.96	770.98	885.14	990.80	1102.33	1213.38
#出口总额	亿美元	372.05	438.47	505.33	567.14	632.00	695.98
新签项目宗数	宗	420	526	621	691	777	869
合同规定外商投资额	亿美元	14.01	17.49	20.38	22.22	24.36	25.97
实际利用外资(不含对外借款)	亿美元	16.73	20.12	23.28	24.92	25.98	27.32
社会消费品零售总额	亿元	627.56	721.75	818.46	914.81	1012.68	1108.06
居民消费价格总指数	%	102.2	102.3	102.4	102.6	102.7	102.8
#服务项目价格指数	%	102.0	102.3	102.6	102.8	102.6	102.6
总供电量	亿千瓦时	311.30	369.12	422.28	469.43	513.67	556.89
总售电量	亿千瓦时	295.31	350.15	406.95	457.82	504.35	543.66
邮电业务收入	亿元	90.36	103.98	117.50	131.55	144.40	157.93
城市居民人均可支配收入	元			27606			36350
城市居民人均消费性支出	元			19161			25733

1-8 国民经济主要指标分月变化情况（2010年，比上年同期增长）

Main Indicators on National Economy by Month (2010, Compare with Same Period of Preceding Year %)

项目	单位	1 月	1-2 月	1-3 月	1-4 月	1-5 月	1-6 月
规模以上工业增加值	%		9.8	14.8	22.0	23.2	24.0
#国有经济	%		6.6	7.9	12.7	13.6	15.1
外资型经济	%		9.8	14.3	21.1	22.6	23.5
#民营企业	%		9.7	18.8	29.8	28.6	28.6
#八大支柱产业	%		13.9	17.8	25.4	26.4	27.3
规模以上工业销售产值	%		15.7	20.5	29.1	30.6	32.6
规模以上工业出口产品产值	%		9.4	15.5	26.0	29.0	32.3
规模以上工业产品产销率	%		0.1	-0.7	-0.5	-0.6	-0.1
规模以上工业企业主营业务收入	%		19.5	22.4	31.0	33.6	34.4
规模以上工业企业利税总额	%		70.3	59.1	108.9	118.0	104.1
全社会固定资产投资总额	%		13.4	13.3	3.4	3.5	4.1
#房地产开发	%		5.4	6.9	12.0	-2.5	2.4
来源于东莞的财政收入	%	42.3	15.7	34.5	28.2	22.9	22.9
市财政一般预算收入	%	14.9	10.4	26.4	22.0	17.8	16.1
市财政一般预算支出	%	-25.6	21.1	33.9	28.0	32.4	38.5
金融机构各项人民币存款余额	%	0.9	0.3	4.8	4.2	5.1	8.9
#城乡居民储蓄存款余额	%	-0.3	1.3	4.1	3.4	4.5	8.6
金融机构各项人民币贷款余额	%	1.6	4.1	4.6	7.4	9.0	10.0
货币总投放(现金支出)	%	2.0	16.7	18.5	18.5	19.6	18.7
货币总回笼(现金收入)	%	8.2	12.7	15.7	15.9	17.4	16.3
进出口总额(海关口径)	%	55.4	37.3	36.5	35.0	35.4	35.4
#出口总额	%	34.5	28.0	26.4	26.2	27.6	29.4
新签项目宗数	%	88.9	48.6	37.4	33.3	60.0	63.4
合同规定外商投资额	%	22.5	31.2	39.0	45.2	78.0	99.1
实际利用外资(不含对外借款)	%	4.8	4.9	5.1	4.9	5.6	5.0
社会消费品零售总额	%		16.7	14.4	14.6	14.8	14.8
居民消费价格总指数	%	-0.6	1.1	1.1	1.4	1.9	2.1
#服务项目价格指数	%	-0.4	-0.8	-0.2	0.3	1.0	1.6
总供电量	%	69.9	26.8	23.7	21.9	21.8	19.7
总售电量	%	13.0	29.0	15.2	13.3	13.8	15.6
邮电业务收入	%	-0.7	-0.4	-0.2	0.1	-1.1	-1.1
城市居民人均可支配收入	%			6.9			7.7
城市居民人均消费性支出	%			14.6			10.4

1-8 续表

(2010年，比上年同期增长)

项　　目	单位	1-7 月	1-8 月	1-9 月	1-10 月	1-11 月	1-12 月
规模以上工业增加值	%	22.8	24.4	22.4	21.1	20.6	19.0
#国有经济	%	15.6	15.1	12.8	12.1	11.6	9.1
外资型经济	%	24.4	24.3	22.4	21.4	21.0	19.0
#民营企业	%	26.6	27.3	24.8	21.8	21.2	20.8
#八大支柱产业	%	28.0	27.4	24.8	23.1	22.1	20.0
规模以上工业销售产值	%	32.5	32.0	30.0	28.1	27.1	23.6
规模以上工业出口产品产值	%	33.4	32.1	29.6	27.9	27.2	23.5
规模以上工业产品产销率	%	-0.7	-0.6	-0.1	-0.1	-0.2	-1.4
规模以上工业企业主营业务收入	%	33.6	33.3	32.7	30.4	29.0	24.8
规模以上工业企业利税总额	%	87.5	75.3	65.0	56.6	49.5	48.8
全社会固定资产投资总额	%	4.5	5.1	6.5	6.7	6.0	1.9
#房地产开发	%	14.9	17.5	19.7	21.8	20.3	7.7
来源于东莞的财政收入	%	22.80	24.6	21.4	23.3	21.9	25.1
市财政一般预算收入	%	14.5	16.6	15.1	14.9	13.0	20.2
市财政一般预算支出	%	32.7	28.9	33.9	35.4	34.9	32.7
金融机构各项人民币存款余额	%	7.8	9.8	13.8	13.5	15.4	19.2
#城乡居民储蓄存款余额	%	8.5	9.4	14.6	12.5	13.4	17.3
金融机构各项人民币贷款余额	%	10.9	12.3	13.3	13.9	14.2	14.7
货币总投放(现金支出)	%	18.1	18.2	17.7	18.2	18.7	18.8
货币总回笼(现金收入)	%	15.7	15.7	15.5	16.0	16.6	16.8
进出口总额(海关口径)	%	33.9	33.6	31.5	30.3	29.9	28.8
#出口总额	%	29.3	29.9	28.4	27.3	26.9	26.1
新签项目宗数	%	51.6	59.4	59.2	53.6	46.1	50.1
合同规定外商投资额	%	92.6	89.7	84.9	79.9	70.2	60.7
实际利用外资(不含对外借款)	%	7.0	7.3	6.5	7.1	5.8	5.3
社会消费品零售总额	%	14.5	14.7	15.2	15.4	15.7	15.9
居民消费价格总指数	%	2.2	2.3	2.4	2.6	2.7	2.8
#服务项目价格指数	%	2.0	2.3	2.6	2.8	2.6	2.6
总供电量	%	18.8	17.7	15.9	15.1	14.5	13.9
总售电量	%	15.0	14.6	14.3	14.1	14.8	13.7
邮电业务收入	%	-0.8	-0.6	-0.1	0.4	0.7	1.0
城市居民人均可支配收入	%			7.1			10.0
城市居民人均消费性支出	%			5.5			6.0

1-9 历年地区生产总值

Gross Domestic Product over Years

年 份	地区生产总值（万元）	第一产业	第二产业	第三产业	人均生产总值（元）
1978	61122	27235	26781	7106	553
1979	66233	26460	29244	10528	593
1980	72199	26323	33290	12586	643
1981	91131	32772	42980	15379	802
1982	114322	37257	58137	18927	991
1983	130340	39847	68962	21531	1115
1984	159632	45671	78091	35869	1350
1985	226033	61475	116584	47973	1885
1986	300167	81416	135735	83016	2462
1987	392859	98236	177249	117373	3170
1988	554583	118888	282771	152924	4408
1989	609202	126568	279724	202910	4768
1990	804401	132787	405290	266325	6173
1991	959073	134523	503220	321330	5095
1992	1108922	144115	592701	372106	5038
1993	1570491	143953	873114	553424	5850
1994	2170341	174796	1194928	800616	6357
1995	2962892	214306	1669723	1078863	7421
1996	3617502	248645	1994826	1374031	8444
1997	4485981	256388	2432816	1796777	9747
1998	5579964	259437	3056779	2263749	11265
1999	6672386	257863	3670519	2744004	12494
2000	8202530	259087	4507072	3436372	13679
2001	9918905	260968	5405092	4252845	15268
2002	11869374	248791	6488109	5132474	18131
2003	14525186	228165	7981954	6315068	22174
2004	18060258	227087	10160382	7672789	27554
2005	21831961	205546	12278624	9347791	33287
2006	26279791	120089	15065985	11093717	39173
2007	31600489	118991	17546573	13934924	45057
2008	37036004	148251	19016068	17871685	50471
2009	37639142	147877	18230836	19260428	48988
2010	42464527	165719	21608153	20690656	52798

注：1. 地区生产总值绝对值按当年价计算，指数按可比价计算,下同。
2. 人均生产总值1990年以前按户籍人口计算，1991年起按常住人口计算，与以前年份不可比。
3. 人均生产总值2006-2010年数据，根据东莞市第六次全国人口普查数据结果重新修订，下同。

1-10 历年地区生产总值指数

Indices of Gross Domestic Product over Years

上年=100

年份	地区生产总值指数	第一产业	第二产业	第三产业	人均生产总值指数	人均GDP指数与GDP指数之比(%)
1979	99.5	86.5	107.0	146.4	98.6	0.991
1980	102.7	90.3	117.3	113.9	102.0	0.993
1981	116.6	115.0	122.1	110.8	115.4	0.989
1982	116.9	105.3	131.0	117.6	115.1	0.985
1983	110.4	104.8	115.7	111.3	108.9	0.987
1984	114.2	109.0	107.0	140.9	112.9	0.988
1985	132.3	118.9	144.5	132.7	130.5	0.986
1986	126.1	111.9	110.3	174.7	124.0	0.983
1987	122.5	111.6	127.7	126.0	120.5	0.984
1988	115.7	90.6	143.7	103.0	114.0	0.985
1989	107.1	99.8	106.2	113.7	105.5	0.985
1990	123.2	104.4	127.6	128.0	120.8	0.980
1991	117.5	103.1	121.5	118.6	108.8	0.926
1992	108.3	100.0	112.6	105.1	92.6	0.855
1993	127.9	79.4	139.2	129.0	104.8	0.820
1994	122.5	107.2	124.7	122.3	96.3	0.786
1995	127.4	110.5	135.1	116.8	108.9	0.855
1996	117.5	109.4	115.5	123.5	109.5	0.932
1997	119.6	104.5	119.8	121.8	111.3	0.931
1998	121.8	100.9	122.1	124.5	113.1	0.929
1999	119.7	102.3	120.6	120.3	111.0	0.928
2000	119.7	99.8	120.7	120.0	106.6	0.891
2001	119.9	103.0	121.6	118.9	110.7	0.923
2002	120.5	97.6	122.6	119.1	119.6	0.992
2003	120.5	90.2	122.3	119.7	120.4	0.999
2004	121.0	90.0	125.6	115.8	120.9	0.999
2005	119.5	102.3	120.0	119.3	119.4	0.999
2006	119.2	58.9	121.9	117.1	116.6	0.978
2007	118.3	89.9	114.8	123.3	113.1	0.957
2008	114.0	110.6	106.1	124.0	109.0	0.956
2009	105.3	102.3	99.7	111.4	100.5	0.955
2010	110.3	101.6	116.7	104.1	105.3	0.955

1-11　历年地区生产总值产业构成

Composition of Gross Domestic Product over Years

单位：%

年　份	地区生产总　值	第一产业	第二产业	第三产业
1978	100.0	44.6	43.8	11.6
1979	100.0	40.0	44.2	15.9
1980	100.0	36.5	46.1	17.4
1981	100.0	36.0	47.2	16.9
1982	100.0	32.6	50.9	16.6
1983	100.0	30.6	52.9	16.5
1984	100.0	28.6	48.9	22.5
1985	100.0	27.2	51.6	21.2
1986	100.0	27.1	45.2	27.7
1987	100.0	25.0	45.1	29.9
1988	100.0	21.4	51.0	27.6
1989	100.0	20.8	45.9	33.3
1990	100.0	16.5	50.4	33.1
1991	100.0	14.0	52.5	33.5
1992	100.0	13.0	53.5	33.6
1993	100.0	9.2	55.6	35.2
1994	100.0	8.1	55.1	36.9
1995	100.0	7.2	56.4	36.4
1996	100.0	6.9	55.1	38.0
1997	100.0	5.7	54.2	40.1
1998	100.0	4.7	54.8	40.6
1999	100.0	3.9	55.0	41.1
2000	100.0	3.2	55.0	41.9
2001	100.0	2.6	54.5	42.9
2002	100.0	2.1	54.7	43.2
2003	100.0	1.6	55.0	43.5
2004	100.0	1.3	56.3	42.5
2005	100.0	0.9	56.2	42.8
2006	100.0	0.5	57.3	42.2
2007	100.0	0.4	55.5	44.1
2008	100.0	0.4	51.3	48.3
2009	100.0	0.4	48.4	51.2
2010	100.0	0.4	50.9	48.7

1-12 各行业增加值项目（2010年）

Composition of Value-added by Industry (2010)

单位:万元

项　　目	增加值	劳动者报酬	生产税净额	固定资产折旧	营业盈余
地区生产总值	**42464527**	**18528289**	**4402306**	**7143414**	**12390519**
第一产业	165719	151471		14248	
第二产业	21608153	11435509	1789639	2427874	5955131
工业	20784479	11060885	1653834	2367617	5702142
建筑业	823674	374623	135805	60257	252989
第三产业	20690656	6941308	2612667	4701292	6435388
交通运输、仓储和邮政业	810778	320992	61292	244422	184072
交通运输和仓储业	769969	303166	59567	239398	167838
邮政业	40809	17826	1725	5024	16235
信息传输、计算机服务和软件业	1750307	282898	92295	300362	1074753
批发和零售业	4058051	1778715	1560878	160442	558017
住宿和餐饮业	1476753	1206313	79315	196961	-5836
金融业	1752289	499852	245052	36317	971068
#银行业	1406175	419254	121167	31852	833902
房地产业	3164428	141546	359901	2180227	482755
房地产开发经营	811451	61970	311671	27169	410640
物业管理	169638	58747	11324	84068	15498
房地产中介服务	19303	8884	2582	2635	5203
其他房地产活动	141341	11945	34324	43659	51414
居民自有住房服务	2022695			2022695	
租赁和商务服务业	4167292	355528	136231	713991	2961542
科学研究、技术服务和地质勘查业	261103	71597	12338	111575	65593
水利、环境和公共设施管理业	91962	43354	3452	26752	18403
居民服务和其他服务业	787164	641490	24904	72849	47921
教育	680379	554289	3467	114760	7863
卫生、社会保障和社会福利业	399797	279279	6839	56652	57029
文化、体育和娱乐业	205681	101282	25915	66278	12207
#娱乐业	129515	61078	20858	53243	-5663
公共管理和社会组织	1084671	664176	789	419705	

1-13 主要年份支出法地区生产总值

Gross Domestic Product by Expenditure Approach in Main Years

项　　目	1995年	2000年	2005年	2009年	2010年
支出法地区生产总值(万元)	2962892	8202530	21831961	37639142	42464527
最终消费	1502524	4342481	11201390	19971108	22984391
资本形成总额	1210079	2369818	7148513	11972192	12757774
货物和服务净出口	250290	1490232	3482058	5695842	6722362
资本形成率(投资率)(%)	40.8	28.9	32.7	31.8	30.0
最终消费率(消费率)(%)	50.7	52.9	51.3	53.1	54.1

1-14 主要年份资本形成总额及构成

Gross Capital Formation and Its Composition in Main Years

项　　目		1995年	2000年	2005年	2009年	2010年
资本形成总额(万元)		1210079	2369818	7148513	11972192	12757774
固定资产形成总额		884671	1775228	6115306	10122708	10513989
存货增加		325407	594590	1033207	1849484	2243785
比重(资本形成总额=100)	固定资产形成总额	73.1	74.9	85.5	84.6	82.4
	存货增加	26.9	25.1	14.5	15.4	17.6

1-15 主要年份最终消费支出及构成

Final Consumption Expenditure and Its Composition in Main Years

项　　目		1995年	2000年	2005年	2009年	2010年
最终消费(万元)		1502524	4342481	11201390	19971108	22984391
居民消费		1262972	3752814	9798031	17408587	19852461
政府消费		239552	589666	1403359	2562521	3131930
比重(最终消费=100)	居民消费	84.1	86.4	87.5	87.2	86.4
	政府消费	15.9	13.6	12.5	12.8	13.6

1-16 主要年份全市企业和个体工商户登记注册年末实有数量

Enterprises and Self-employed Individuals Registered at Year-end

单位：户

项　　目	2001年	2005年	2006年	2007年	2008年	2009年	2010年
工商登记户数合计	**163743**	**353266**	**403403**	**476125**	**504978**	**505502**	**518513**
内资企业	18055	13898	12953	13401	13074	12493	12439
#国有	3119	1977	1554	1404	1313	1141	1058
集体	12142	6478	4989	4487	3385	2899	2180
有限责任公司	2573	1606	1468	1493	7017	7886	9165
外商投资企业	4815	7675	7695	7973	9437	9748	10113
#合资	1412	1013	822	718	860	1206	1120
合作	751	482	379	307	218	197	179
独资	2649	6177	6492	6946	6956	7678	8280
“三来一补”企业	11310	9552	8206	7417	6552	5748	4906
私营企业	9260	29017	38282	48955	63241	74229	88650
个体工商户	120303	293124	336267	398379	412674	403284	402405

注：本表数据来源于市工商局。

1-17 个体工商户情况（2010年）

Statistics on Self-employed Individuals (2010)

项　　目	户　数 （户）	从　业 人　员 （人）	资　金 数　额 （万元）	其中城镇		
				户　数 （户）	从业人员 （人）	资金数额 （万元）
合　　计	**402405**	**930265**	**891793**	**216294**	**465266**	**454328**
农、林、牧、渔业	215	826	5024	96	372	1873
工　业	60119	275122	320162	23968	105937	122746
建筑业	1031	2751	4505	585	1443	1950
交通运输、仓储和邮政业	1646	4434	6348	1128	2678	4359
信息传输、计算机服务和软件业	3050	4532	2522	1585	2276	1237
批发和零售业	264138	460883	373658	148578	248772	215262
住宿和餐饮业	34628	93806	93551	19260	53747	57131
房地产业	124	244	377	83	160	217
租赁和商务服务业	2356	5613	6789	1599	3750	4378
居民服务和其他服务业	34177	79152	69640	18821	44275	39104
卫生、社会保障和社会福利业	27	55	98	23	46	86
文化、体育和娱乐业	484	1817	7730	296	1154	5169
其他行业	410	1030	1387	272	656	817

注：本表数据来源于市工商局。

1-18 私营工商企业基本情况（2010年）

Basic Statistics on Private Industrial & Commercial Enterprises (2010)

项目	户数（户）	投资者人数（人）	雇工人数（人）	注册资本（万元）	其中：1. 独资企业 户数（户）	投资者人数（人）	雇工人数（人）	注册资本（万元）
合计	**88650**	**163472**	**556881**	**10931555**	**7792**	**7615**	**80142**	**276790**
农、林、牧、渔业	646	1004	10461	71173	371	351	8079	29761
工业	30001	57374	224537	3066833	4064	4044	49414	120939
建筑业	4060	7558	24691	761216	40	40	233	338
交通运输、仓储和邮政业	1678	3069	9078	253280	23	22	101	230
信息传输、计算机服务和软件业	1945	3559	12825	222123	520	515	4988	51911
批发和零售业	31028	54692	162942	2437525	1510	1481	5449	13503
住宿和餐饮业	1100	1740	13494	200390	351	329	4709	36362
房地产业	2850	5731	14860	880118	5	5	16	38
租赁和商务服务业	7713	15297	40759	1548765	223	202	771	2552
居民服务和其他服务业	3791	5833	21373	214031	551	491	4857	14402
卫生、社会保障和社会福利业	23	39	308	24213				
文化、体育和娱乐业	622	1132	4373	76069	99	99	1353	6143
其他行业	3193	6444	17180	1175819	35	36	172	611

1-18 续表

项目	2. 合伙企业 户数（户）	投资者人数（人）	雇工人数（人）	注册资本（万元）	3. 有限责任公司 户数（户）	投资者人数（人）	雇工人数（人）	注册资本（万元）
合计	**942**	**2342**	**7883**	**100546**	**79672**	**152995**	**467564**	**10311525**
农、林、牧、渔业	98	248	1378	6368	174	381	897	30044
工业	384	924	3444	22079	25527	52237	171333	2834099
建筑业	1	3	5	25	4010	7515	24401	760854
交通运输、仓储和邮政业	3	8	12	95	1648	3037	8942	252455
信息传输、计算机服务和软件业	143	356	855	14280	1273	2688	6923	155932
批发和零售业	86	191	327	3225	29345	52793	156920	2391270
住宿和餐饮业	51	134	895	11165	695	1277	7866	152863
房地产业	4	11	12	30	2835	5708	14814	863122
租赁和商务服务业	84	253	357	38457	7393	14806	39571	1485235
居民服务和其他服务业	66	158	473	2672	3163	5184	16017	196957
卫生、社会保障和社会福利业					22	39	303	24213
文化、体育和娱乐业	14	33	91	808	508	1000	2921	69118
其他行业	8	23	34	1343	3079	6330	16656	1095364

注：本表数据来源于市工商局。

1-19 历年总供用电

Gross Electricity Supply over Years

单位：万千瓦时

年 份	总供电量	#网供	总用电量	#工业用电	#农村工业用电	照明用电
1978	16375	16376	14909	10828		1741
1979	19271	19271	17325	12474		2338
1980	21659	21569	19663	13407		3372
1981	22247	22247	19902	14194		4650
1982	26871	26351	23502	14618		6272
1983	31527	31527	27461	17496		8052
1984	32617	28566	28403	18019		9484
1985	38183	33907	33907	22139		9934
1986	39305	35100	35099	25567		10204
1987	64258	45129	57083	38076		16657
1988	94842	66295	84738	60226		22347
1989	120861	76762	108387	80050	60116	26139
1990	180142	111800	161479	119322	70459	39677
1991	240471	139841	216657	157062	99767	56504
1992	320003	180902	288688	210373	144391	25578
1993	436231	242205	393962	287400	205687	103583
1994	585763	393312	530232	416128	297479	110357
1995	680030	384764	616788	487873	386413	125135
1996	800300	506062	727093	569317	423898	153093
1997	949296	612907	866456	702811	519325	180583
1998	1094816	724758	1009086	781811	597601	221750
1999	1327788	973427	1234183	965945	756713	261629
2000	1780290	1349134	1690557	1345766	1104301	337044
2001	2077248	1649458	1965858	1567083	1400915	584700
2002	2585474	2219054	2471342	2070709	1877278	392879
2003	3216468	2846679	2835389	2401970	2071712	424869
2004	3728441	3196454	3502821	2966131	2539962	527332
2005	4156629	3422603	3965892	3303140	2873734	652514
2006	4644506	3676492	4455157	3686266	3234929	759384
2007	5078933	4167125	4825614	3956118	3483474	859851
2008	5073489	4423085	4873204	3928108	3424868	935510
2009	4888467	4318868	4781895	3761046	3292716	1011494
2010	5568902	5473261	5436637	4355690	3841990	1070692

1-20 企业景气指数（2010年）

Business Climate Index (2010)

项　目	一季度	二季度	三季度	四季度
企业景气指数	**136.08**	**135.80**	**143.78**	**143.47**
按行业门类分				
工业	138.13	141.84	144.75	146.64
建筑业	113.33	133.33	140.00	140.00
交通运输、仓储和邮政业	120.00	120.00	120.00	120.00
批发和零售业	150.38	140.69	149.20	147.05
房地产业	142.31	109.17	113.89	133.38
社会服务业	120.00	125.00	160.00	145.00
信息传输、计算机服务和软件	145.76	153.67	160.34	147.91
住宿和餐饮业	115.59	124.45	130.59	121.53
按企业登记注册类型分				
国有企业	161.96	161.96	174.46	174.46
集体企业	121.05	115.79	121.05	131.58
股份合作企业				
有限责任公司	126.86	128.07	137.00	131.93
股份有限公司	147.24	138.27	153.65	145.96
私营企业	125.00	139.09	162.50	150.00
港、澳、台投资企业	126.57	137.21	154.95	144.13
外商投资企业	140.17	139.36	132.57	134.46
按企业规模分				
大型	162.59	161.87	167.97	159.44
中型	120.00	123.33	131.11	133.33
小型	123.19	128.99	133.33	130.43
按观察指标分				
生产总量	91.18	130.13	134.98	99.87
盈利(亏损)变化	89.29	115.89	115.82	114.05
流动资金	130.77	129.09	130.81	130.88
货款拖欠	114.72	108.85	105.01	108.91
劳动力需求	135.40	122.17	134.74	135.02
固定资产投资	93.63	113.65	119.45	114.22
产品订货	110.36	122.06	125.22	119.48
企业融资	115.14	119.43	118.86	107.28

1-21　企业家信心指数（2010年）

Entrepreneurs' Confidence Index (2010)

项　　目	一季度	二季度	三季度	四季度
企业家信心指数	**137.75**	**135.42**	**138.73**	**142.00**
按行业门类分				
工业	142.23	144.22	143.57	141.32
建筑业	113.33	133.33	126.67	133.33
交通运输、仓储和邮政业	113.33	120.00	113.33	113.33
批发和零售业	145.07	138.40	146.03	148.82
房地产业	123.97	72.94	91.16	139.18
社会服务业	130.00	140.00	150.00	145.00
信息传输、计算机服务和软件	153.33	153.67	153.67	173.67
住宿和餐饮业	109.67	121.53	130.59	117.69
按企业登记注册类型分				
国有企业	161.96	161.96	161.96	149.46
集体企业	126.32	100.00	115.79	142.11
股份合作企业				
有限责任公司	134.00	132.05	135.90	138.26
股份有限公司	138.78	123.40	147.53	139.84
私营企业	135.91	137.42	131.17	160.91
港、澳、台投资企业	135.11	145.37	147.37	141.21
外商投资企业	119.43	136.00	130.09	129.20
按企业规模分				
大型	152.97	163.20	158.56	166.26
中型	128.89	125.56	132.22	125.56
小型	124.64	123.19	127.54	136.23

1-22 各行业企业景气指数（2010年）

Business Climate Index by Sector (2010)

指　　标	一季度	二季度	三季度	四季度
总指数	**136.08**	**135.80**	**143.78**	**143.47**
工业				
企业综合生产经营	138.13	141.84	144.75	146.64
生产成本	68.53	53.98	67.13	68.57
生产总量	79.63	149.61	141.90	90.15
产品订货	114.25	136.24	127.95	113.75
#国外订货	103.16	125.64	115.63	112.17
产品销售量	77.05	148.90	130.98	95.81
产品销售价格	94.48	114.75	98.36	110.68
产成品库存	126.84	124.06	124.42	121.25
盈利(亏损)变化	88.03	122.93	121.12	111.33
流动资金	137.15	140.17	137.64	136.61
企业融资	120.30	127.50	127.07	111.46
货款拖欠	115.51	104.53	100.31	97.89
劳动力需求	142.64	133.12	142.32	144.56
固定资产投资	89.68	120.38	130.18	121.72
科技创新	104.85	109.75	106.28	105.08
原材料及能源购进价格	60.54	46.29	61.81	50.92
原材料及能源供应	135.95	127.15	138.39	135.56
建筑业				
企业综合生产经营	113.33	133.33	140.00	140.00
工程合同	106.67	126.67	126.67	113.33
#国(境)外合同	93.33	106.67	100.00	113.33
建筑工程量	86.67	140.00	126.67	126.67
新开工工程量	113.33	126.67	100.00	100.00
技术设备能力	166.67	160.00	166.67	173.33
工程进度	126.67	120.00	153.33	153.33
工程结算收入	86.67	126.67	120.00	113.33
建筑材料购进价格	80.00	86.67	46.67	53.33
工程结算成本	86.67	86.67	46.67	46.67
盈利(亏损)变化	60.00	133.33	126.67	126.67
流动资金	146.67	146.67	166.67	160.00
企业融资	120.00	120.00	133.33	126.67
工程款拖欠	133.33	126.67	133.33	120.00
劳动力需求	86.67	126.67	146.67	126.67
固定资产投资	106.67	106.67	106.67	106.67
交通运输、仓储及邮政业				
企业综合生产经营	120.00	120.00	120.00	120.00
业务预订	86.67	93.33	133.33	100.00
业务量	93.33	93.33	126.67	86.67
业务收费价格	113.33	73.33	100.00	106.67

1-22 续表 1

指　　标	一季度	二季度	三季度	四季度
业务成本	66.67	60.00	46.67	40.00
盈利(亏损)变化	86.67	100.00	120.00	66.67
流动资金	113.33	120.00	126.67	113.33
企业融资	120.00	126.67	106.67	100.00
货款拖欠	106.67	106.67	100.00	106.67
劳动力需求	106.67	80.00	113.33	93.33
固定资产投资	106.67	113.33	106.67	113.33
批发和零售贸易业				
企业综合生产经营	150.38	140.69	149.20	147.05
购货合同	113.26	122.75	130.38	137.12
商品购进价格	77.00	83.37	67.50	60.23
商品销售	104.23	104.79	105.75	110.09
#出口	103.33	90.00	106.67	93.33
商品销售价格	126.22	107.30	105.30	101.04
商品库存	126.76	131.63	111.72	123.86
经营费用	64.39	84.61	59.85	60.65
竞争能力	129.50	132.83	128.29	124.96
盈利(亏损)变化	102.17	125.50	122.29	123.27
流动资金	122.59	122.59	112.59	117.32
企业融资	107.91	112.21	104.58	113.60
货款拖欠	102.06	89.28	103.33	105.39
劳动力需求	146.06	119.61	121.96	124.87
固定资产投资	112.06	105.39	112.72	107.55
房地产业				
企业综合生产经营	142.31	109.17	113.89	133.38
土地开发	121.11	84.34	106.08	96.46
完成投资	110.27	63.82	108.71	76.06
新开工面积	83.90	96.34	73.16	59.40
房屋竣工面积	103.88	72.09	87.59	103.34
商品房预售面积	66.46	74.85	64.37	137.19
商品房销售面积	86.46	53.86	49.06	114.40
商品房销售价格	98.66	71.07	79.57	121.44
空置商品房面积	160.06	133.30	150.01	150.01
盈利(亏损)变化	106.70	90.89	47.95	130.54
流动资金	132.94	113.89	113.80	109.99
企业融资	122.16	91.58	87.68	81.02
货款拖欠	129.26	151.65	151.65	130.69
劳动力需求	136.07	84.34	92.69	102.39
固定资产投资	102.92	85.66	82.20	103.32
社会服务业				
企业综合生产经营	120.00	125.00	160.00	145.00
服务预订	135.00	105.00	150.00	120.00

1-22 续表 2

指　　标	一季度	二季度	三季度	四季度
竞争能力	150.00	160.00	165.00	170.00
旅游客源	116.67	100.00	200.00	100.00
收费服务价格	100.00	90.00	115.00	85.00
业务量	125.00	120.00	150.00	115.00
营业成本	60.00	60.00	40.00	60.00
盈利(亏损)变化	90.00	100.00	125.00	115.00
流动资金	105.00	100.00	120.00	130.00
企业融资	90.00	105.00	115.00	100.00
货款拖欠	110.00	110.00	95.00	130.00
劳动力需求	110.00	110.00	140.00	130.00
固定资产投资	85.00	105.00	110.00	90.00
信息传输、计算机服务和软件业				
企业综合生产经营	145.76	153.67	160.34	147.91
产品销售	87.34	147.91	134.58	147.58
产品订货	94.01	140.34	127.01	114.58
竞争能力	159.09	172.42	172.42	172.09
销售(收费)价格	67.91	93.33	93.67	94.58
营业收入	54.92	127.91	121.25	126.67
营业成本	98.75	52.09	65.42	46.33
盈利(亏损)变化	65.76	121.25	141.25	119.66
流动资金	138.75	133.67	146.67	153.67
企业融资	119.09	132.09	125.76	106.67
货款拖欠	113.67	107.01	107.01	120.34
劳动力需求	134.24	120.91	134.24	133.67
固定资产投资	107.58	134.24	121.25	127.01
住宿和餐饮业				
企业综合生产经营	115.59	124.45	130.59	121.53
业务预订	78.24	80.00	124.39	134.72
业务量	88.83	102.08	134.39	144.72
竞争能力	129.08	129.08	150.00	147.10
客房出租	40.00	60.00	60.00	80.00
收费服务价格	100.00	110.00	104.06	104.06
营业收入	67.28	88.47	114.39	124.72
营业成本	81.75	70.81	60.81	57.08
盈利(亏损)变化	71.73	95.02	109.39	104.72
流动资金	108.86	108.86	115.94	102.10
企业融资	105.02	113.86	113.86	108.86
货款拖欠	92.36	110.25	85.59	133.25
劳动力需求	119.98	125.92	145.55	149.98
固定资产投资	99.06	110.88	115.55	117.69

1-23 企业宏观经济景气状况

Macro Economic Climate Situations of Enterprises

指　　标	2003年	2004年	2005年	2006年	2007年	2008年	2009年	2010年
一季度								
企业家信心指数	140.35	140.73	133.95	137.41	144.75	136.51	85.12	137.75
企业家对本行业景气状况判断(%)								
乐观	49.22	49.12	39.84	45.56	53.43	44.86	21.32	42.95
一般	41.90	42.49	54.26	46.28	37.89	46.78	42.48	51.84
不乐观	8.88	8.39	5.90	8.16	8.68	8.36	36.20	5.21
二季度								
企业家信心指数	130.04	139.03	132.04	134.53	142.57	131.96	96.52	135.42
企业家对本行业景气状况判断(%)								
乐观	44.42	49.19	40.67	45.15	53.04	41.18	24.00	43.01
一般	41.20	40.65	50.71	44.22	36.51	49.61	48.52	49.40
不乐观	14.38	10.16	8.63	10.63	10.45	9.21	27.48	7.59
三季度								
企业家信心指数	140.85	139.05	131.86	140.03	143.21	120.04	122.30	138.73
企业家对本行业景气状况判断(%)								
乐观	46.18	49.10	41.32	46.79	52.47	32.49	32.43	45.56
一般	48.49	40.85	49.22	46.46	38.28	55.07	57.44	47.61
不乐观	5.33	10.05	9.46	6.75	9.25	12.45	10.13	6.83
四季度								
企业家信心指数	140.20	133.60	133.05	141.76	148.18	88.10	128.02	142.00
企业家对本行业景气状况判断(%)								
乐观	47.03	45.05	43.59	49.91	54.11	19.81	36.40	49.37
一般	46.13	43.51	45.86	41.94	39.96	48.46	55.22	43.25
不乐观	6.83	11.45	10.54	8.15	5.93	31.72	8.38	7.38

1-24 企业综合生产经营状况

Comprehensive Production and Management Situations of Enterprises

指　　标	2003年	2004年	2005年	2006年	2007年	2008年	2009年	2010年
一季度								
企业景气指数	138.81	135.69	132.79	133.80	138.02	131.94	98.83	136.08
企业家对生产经营景气状况判断(%)								
良好	46.13	41.55	42.26	42.90	49.06	43.76	23.01	44.87
一般	46.55	52.59	48.27	48.00	39.90	44.41	52.81	46.33
不佳	7.32	5.86	9.47	9.10	11.04	11.83	24.18	8.79
二季度								
企业景气指数	119.33	138.85	134.75	135.51	141.44	127.50	114.33	135.80
企业家对生产经营景气状况判断(%)								
良好	38.17	45.61	43.39	43.95	48.04	37.58	27.65	42.61
一般	43.00	47.64	47.96	47.61	45.36	52.34	59.03	50.57
不佳	18.84	6.75	8.65	8.44	6.60	10.08	13.31	6.82
三季度								
企业景气指数	139.73	138.48	131.49	141.85	147.21	122.32	131.17	143.78
企业家对生产经营景气状况判断(%)								
良好	43.67	46.38	38.46	47.09	52.18	34.90	39.20	50.79
一般	52.40	45.74	54.57	47.67	42.84	52.53	52.78	42.20
不佳	3.93	7.89	6.97	5.24	4.98	12.58	8.02	7.01
四季度								
企业景气指数	142.20	135.06	131.09	141.19	142.76	100.50	133.40	143.47
企业家对生产经营景气状况判断(%)								
良好	46.34	44.44	39.85	45.90	51.67	24.31	41.72	49.68
一般	49.52	46.18	51.39	49.38	39.42	51.89	49.96	44.11
不佳	4.14	9.38	8.76	4.72	8.91	23.81	8.32	6.21

1-25 历年国民经济主要指标人均水平

The Per Capita Level of Main National Economic Indicators over Years

年　份	人均生产总　值（元）	人均地方财政收入（元）	人均出口总　额（美元）	人均消费品零售额（元）	人均固定资产投资额（元）	人　均用电量（千瓦时）	年末人均储蓄存款余额（元）
1978	553	60	36	192	21	135	49
1979	593	59	48	224	15	155	64
1980	643	60	69	281	21	175	104
1981	802	60	81	354	33	175	178
1982	991	70	94	417	157	204	238
1983	1115	73	102	447	157	235	328
1984	1350	72	110	625	254	240	520
1985	1885	93	146	781	589	283	761
1986	2462	132	191	1004	945	288	1068
1987	3170	163	216	1214	1145	461	1519
1988	4408	215	253	1959	1315	674	1965
1989	4768	250	273	2116	392	848	2529
1990	6173	274	436	2454	576	1239	2592
1991	5095	236	879	1943	732	1154	3074
1992	5038	263	1217	2073	883	1350	3580
1993	5850	385	1318	2615	1345	1617	4131
1994	6357	277	1548	3070	5074	1911	5130
1995	7421	366	2468	3577	1998	1952	6924
1996	8444	268	2553	3489	1879	2021	8300
1997	9747	278	2774	3564	1608	2114	9758
1998	11265	324	2799	3753	1650	2162	10740
1999	12494	344	2851	3806	1662	2322	10890
2000	13679	503	2834	3884	1700	2792	10422
2001	15268	693	2923	4244	1932	3026	12212
2002	18131	845	3626	4907	2926	3775	15297
2003	22174	1030	4275	5645	4876	4329	18788
2004	27554	1261	5369	6506	6940	5344	21836
2005	33287	1585	6240	7719	9106	6047	26343
2006	39173	1922	7062	8934	10516	6641	29364
2007	45057	2658	8588	10301	11994	6881	29577
2008	50471	2851	8931	12008	12869	6641	35146
2009	48988	3009	7180	12482	14239	6224	36950
2010	52798	3455	8653	13777	13863	6760	41179

注：1. 人均指标1991年以前按户籍人口计算，1991年起按常住人口计算；时点数按年末人口计算，时期数按年平均人口计算。
2. 人均指标2006-2010年数据，根据东莞市第六次全国人口普查数据结果重新修订，下同。

主要统计指标解释

Explanatory Notes on Main Statistical Indicators

国内（地区）生产总值 指按市场价格计算的一个国家（或地区）所有常住单位在一定时期内生产活动的最终成果。国内（地区）生产总值有三种计算方法，即生产法、收入法和支出法。三种方法分别从不同的方面反映国内（地区）生产总值及其构成。

增加值 指常住单位生产过程创造的新增价值和固定资产的转移价值。它可以按生产法计算，也可以按收入法计算，按生产法计算，它等于总产出减去中间投入；按收入法计算，它等于劳动者报酬、生产税净额、固定资产折旧和营业盈余之和。

劳动者报酬 指劳动者因从事生产活动所获得的全部报酬，包括劳动者获得的各种形式的工资、奖金和津贴，既包括货币形式的，也包括实物形式的，还包括劳动者所享受的公费医疗和医药卫生费、上下班交通补贴和单位支付的社会保险费、住房公积金等。对于个体经济来说，其所有者所获得的劳动报酬和经营利润不易区分，这两部分统一作为劳动者报酬处理。

生产税净额 指生产税减生产补贴后的差额。生产税指政府对生产单位从事生产、销售和经营活动以及因从事生产活动使用某些生产要素（如固定资产、土地、劳动力）所征收的各种税、附加费和规费。生产补贴与生产税相反，指政府对生产单位的单方面转移支付，因此视为负生产税，包括政策性亏损补贴、价格补贴等。

固定资产折旧 指一定时期内为弥补固定资产损耗按照规定的固定资产折旧率提取的固定资产折旧，或按国民经济核算统一规定的折旧率虚拟计算的固定资产折旧。它反映了固定资产在当期生产中的转移价值。各类企业和企业化管理的事业单位的固定资产折旧是指实际计提的折旧费；不计提折旧的政府机关、非企业化管理的事业单位和居民住房的固定资产折旧是按照统一规定的折旧率和固定资产原值计算的虚拟折旧。

营业盈余 指常住单位创造的增加值扣除劳动者报酬、固定资产折旧和生产税净额后的余额。它相当于企业的营业利润加上生产补贴，但要扣除从利润中开支的工资和福利等。

三次产业 根据社会生产活动历史发展的顺序对产业结构的划分，产品直接取自自然界的部门称为第一产业，初级产品进行再加工的部门称为第二产业，为生产和消费提供各种服务的部门称为第三产业。它是世界上通用的产业结构分类，但各国的划分不尽一致。我国的三次产业划分是：

第一产业：农林牧渔业

第二产业：工业（包括采矿业，制造业，电力、燃气及水的生产和供应业）和建筑业。

第三产业：除第一、二产业以外的其他行业。第三产业包括：交通运输、仓储和邮政业，信息传输、计算机服务和软件业，批发和零售业，住宿和餐饮业，金融业，房地产业，租赁和商务服务业，科学研究、技术服务和地质勘查业，水利、环境和公共设施管理业，居民服务和其他服务业，教育，卫生、社会保障和社会福利业，文化、体育和娱乐业，公共管理和社会组织，国际组织。

景气指数 亦称景气度，是对企业景气调查中的定性指标通过定量方法加工汇总，综合反映某一特定调查群体或某一社会经济现象所处的状态或发展趋势的一种指标，景气指数介于0－200之间，100为景气指数的临界值；当景气指数大于100时，表明经济状况趋于上升或改善，处于景气状态；当景气指数小于100时，表明经济状况趋于下降或恶化，处于不景气状态。

企业景气指数 亦称企业综合生产经营景气指数，是根据企业家对本企业综合生产经营情况的判断与预期（通常为对“良好”、“一般”、“不佳”的选择）而编制的指数，用以综合反映企业的生产经营状况。

企业家信心指数 亦称宏观经济景气指数，.是根据企业家对企业对外部市场经济环境与宏观政策的认识、看法、判断与预期（通常为对“乐观”、“一般”、“不乐观”的选择）而编制的指数，用以综合反映企业家对宏观经济环境的感受与信心。

发展速度 用以反映社会经济发展程度的相对指标，根据两个时期发展水平的对比而得。由于比较的标准时期不同，发展速度可分为定基发展速度和环比发展速度两种。

增长速度 发展速度 - 1（或 100%）就是增长速度。即增长速度=发展速度 - 1（或 100%）。

平均每年增长速度 我国计算平均增长速度有两种方法，一种是习惯上经常使用的“水平法”，又称几何平均法，是以间隔最后一年的水平同基期水平对比来计算平均每年增长（或下降）的速度；另一种是“累计法”又称代数平均法或方程法，是以间隔年内各年水平的总和同基期水平对比来计算平均每年增长（或下降）的速度。具体计算方法，可参照中国财经出版社出版的《平均增长速度查对表》。

在一般正常情况下，两种方法计算的平均每年增长速度比较接近，但在经济发展不平衡出现大起大落时，两种方法计算的结果差别较大。

本《年鉴》内所列的平均每年增长速度都是用水平法计算的。从某年到某年平均增长速度的年份，均不包基期年在内。如 1981-2010 年平均每年增长速度，是以 1980 年为基期，2010 年为报告期，年份从 1981 年算起，共 30 年。

二、人口与劳动力

Population and Labor Force

2-1 历年总人口数与人口密度

Total Population and Density over Years

单位：万人

年 份	户籍人口	按性别分		按农业、非农业分		外来暂住人口	常住人口	人口密度(人/平方公里)
		男	女	农业人口	非农业人口			
1949	68.24	32.87	35.37	56.29	11.95			
1952	71.68	34.53	37.15	58.69	12.99			
1957	77.48	37.50	39.98	62.52	14.96			
1962	79.64	38.07	41.57	64.42	15.22			
1965	86.46	41.83	44.63	70.28	16.18			
1970	98.56	47.91	50.65	81.26	17.30			
1975	107.94	52.70	55.24	90.37	17.57			
1978	111.23	54.34	56.89	92.74	18.29			451
1979	112.04	54.45	57.59	92.86	19.18			455
1980	112.70	54.43	58.27	92.87	19.83			457
1981	114.46	55.36	59.10	94.08	20.38			464
1982	116.19	56.28	59.91	95.32	20.87			471
1983	117.59	57.05	60.54	96.36	21.23			477
1984	118.95	57.80	61.15	96.47	22.48			483
1985	120.85	58.84	62.01	95.36	25.49			490
1986	123.01	59.95	63.06	96.53	26.48	15.62		499
1987	124.86	61.02	63.84	97.20	27.66	25.29		507
1988	126.76	62.09	64.67	97.96	28.80	36.89		514
1989	128.76	63.27	65.49	98.82	29.94	47.19		522
1990	131.85	64.96	66.89	100.99	30.86	65.59	175.62	712
1991	133.65	66.10	67.55	101.79	31.86	80.58	200.01	811
1992	136.06	67.55	68.51	103.35	32.71	114.48	227.78	924
1993	138.92	69.20	69.72	105.18	33.74	121.70	259.41	1052
1994	141.40	70.64	70.76	106.85	34.55	139.09	295.43	1198
1995	143.65	71.97	71.68	108.27	35.38	142.18	336.45	1365
1996	145.25	72.92	72.33	109.11	36.14	143.32	383.17	1554
1997	147.12	74.04	73.08	110.15	36.97	144.68	436.38	1770
1998	148.77	74.99	73.78	110.93	37.84	199.11	496.97	2016
1999	150.82	76.18	74.64	112.09	38.73	244.81	565.98	2296
2000	152.61	77.22	75.39	113.00	39.61	254.72	644.84	2616
2001	153.89	77.94	75.95	113.52	40.37	457.82	654.43	2655
2002	156.19	79.14	77.05	115.17	41.02	433.65	654.84	2657
2003	158.96	80.65	78.31	102.09	56.87	440.45	655.25	2658
2004	161.97	82.25	79.72	100.49	61.48	486.95	655.66	2660
2005	165.65	84.07	81.58	99.81	65.84	584.98	656.07	2662
2006	168.31	85.43	82.88	97.89	70.42	586.76	685.66	2782
2007	171.26	87.00	84.26	97.59	73.67	557.80	717.02	2909
2008	174.86	88.88	85.98	98.06	76.80	552.50	750.60	3045
2009	178.73	90.78	87.95	97.27	81.46	429.96	786.08	3189
2010	181.77	92.27	89.50	89.68	92.09	411.47	822.48	3343

注：1. 人口密度1990年以前户籍人口计算，1990年起按常住人口计算。
2. 常住人口2006-2010年数据，根据东莞市第六次全国人口普查数据结果重新修订，下同。

2-2 主要年份户籍人口与劳动力指标

Main Indicators of Household Population and Labor in Main Years

指 标	单 位	1985年	1990年	1995年	2000年	2005年	2009年	2010年
年末户籍人口	人	1208515	1318526	1436525	1526090	1656541	1787288	1817709
#农业人口	人	953582	1009857	1082703	1130002	998159	972706	896789
人口性别比(女性人口=100)	%	94.9	97.1	100.4	102.4	103.1	103.2	103.1
人口密度	人/平方公里	490	535	583	619	672	725	739
人口出生率	‰	15.4	17.1	17.6	12.1	10.6	10.7	10.9
人口死亡率	‰	4.5	4.8	4.8	4.6	4.6	4.4	4.7
人口自然增长率	‰	10.8	12.3	12.8	7.5	6.0	6.3	6.2
人口净迁移率	‰	3.0	1.9	1.9	2.2	16.4	16.2	12.0
户籍从业人员总数	人	673494	750980	824014	886169	983628	1121839	1144444
按类型分								
企事业机关从业人员	人	122951	131631	184047	168013	178495	150747	149212
国有单位	人	56534	63469	75308	79738	86665	99804	98084
企业	人			32080	32964	22225	15033	17388
事业和机关	人			43228	46774	64440	84771	80696
城镇集体单位	人	63383	58749	65145	51088	45654	20893	21121
其他所有制单位	人	3034	9413	43594	37187	46176	30050	30007
#外商经济单位	人				11208	9725	6711	8688
港澳台经济单位	人				17482	25479	12608	9554
城镇私营个体劳动者人数	人	5809	20438	45122	83457	178793	351366	369247
农村乡镇劳动者人数	人	544734	598911	594845	634699	626340	619726	625985
按产业分								
第一产业劳动者人数	人	285857	271513	194895	173829	101936	57012	53361
第二产业劳动者人数	人	233231	305190	380101	414273	457039	462281	451836
第三产业劳动者人数	人	154406	174277	249018	298067	424653	602545	639248
城镇新登记的失业人员人数	人			6536	6524	7080	15150	3207
城镇失业人员安置就业人数	人				5683	6088	11923	3796

2-3 历年户籍人口自然变动情况

Changes of Household Population over Years

年份	出生		死亡		自然增长	
	人数(人)	出生率(‰)	人数(人)	死亡率(‰)	人数(人)	自然增长率(‰)
1978	20728	18.73	5451	4.92	15277	13.81
1979	26931	24.13	5755	5.13	21176	19.00
1980	27428	24.41	5747	5.10	21681	19.31
1981	24828	21.86	6016	5.29	18812	16.57
1982	21991	19.07	5681	4.93	16310	14.14
1983	19573	16.74	6100	5.21	13473	11.53
1984	18380	15.54	5841	4.94	12539	10.60
1985	18432	15.37	5439	4.54	12993	10.83
1986	20049	16.44	5955	4.88	14094	11.56
1987	19962	16.11	5502	4.44	14459	11.67
1988	21077	16.75	5863	4.66	15214	12.09
1989	23457	17.06	5966	4.67	17491	12.39
1990	22238	17.07	6208	4.76	16030	12.31
1991	23771	17.91	6070	4.57	17701	13.34
1992	26040	19.31	6485	4.81	19555	14.50
1993	25270	18.38	6833	4.97	18437	13.41
1994	24152	17.88	6319	4.51	17833	13.37
1995	25312	17.59	6898	4.84	18414	12.75
1996	24635	17.05	7333	5.08	17302	11.97
1997	24106	16.50	6448	4.41	17658	12.09
1998	22563	15.31	6553	4.45	16010	10.86
1999	21673	14.55	6460	4.34	15213	10.22
2000	18260	12.11	6923	4.59	11337	7.52
2001	17083	11.16	6344	4.14	10739	7.01
2002	16029	10.35	6873	4.44	9156	5.91
2003	16204	10.34	7346	4.69	8858	5.65
2004	17312	10.86	7814	4.90	9498	5.96
2005	17301	10.62	7497	4.60	9804	6.02
2006	16819	10.14	7103	4.28	9716	5.86
2007	17482	10.39	7418	4.41	10064	5.98
2008	18382	10.77	7752	4.54	10630	6.23
2009	18584	10.67	7587	4.36	10997	6.31
2010	19509	10.90	8367	4.68	11142	6.23

2-4 历年户籍人口迁移变动情况

Changes of Household Migration over Years

年 份	迁 入		迁 出		总迁移		净迁移	
	人 数 (人)	迁入率 (‰)	人 数 (人)	迁出率 (‰)	人 数 (人)	总迁移率 (‰)	人 数 (人)	净迁移率 (‰)
1978	10148	9.2	13179	11.9	23327	21.1	-3031	-2.7
1980	13345	11.9	28624	25.5	41969	37.4	-15279	-13.6
1985	19205	16.0	15636	13.0	34841	29.1	3569	3.0
1990	13485	10.4	11061	8.5	24546	18.8	2424	1.9
1991	12628	9.5	12531	9.4	25159	19.0	97	0.1
1992	14622	10.8	11168	8.3	25790	19.1	3454	2.5
1993	10801	7.9	4886	3.6	15687	11.4	5915	4.3
1994	10127	7.2	6406	4.6	16533	11.8	3721	2.7
1995	10312	7.2	7675	5.4	17987	12.6	2637	1.9
1996	9273	6.4	11508	8.0	20781	14.4	-2235	-1.6
1997	10284	7.0	9469	6.5	19753	13.5	815	0.6
1998	12400	8.4	11253	7.6	23653	16.0	1147	0.8
1999	15049	10.0	11497	7.6	26546	17.6	3552	2.4
2000	15618	10.2	12314	8.1	27932	18.3	3304	2.2
2001	15968	10.4	11099	7.2	27067	17.6	4869	3.2
2002	20214	12.9	8033	5.1	28247	18.1	12181	7.8
2003	27143	17.1	7173	4.5	34316	21.6	19970	12.6
2004	29621	18.3	7618	4.7	37239	23.0	22003	13.6
2005	43026	26.0	15798	9.5	58824	35.5	27228	16.4
2006	30710	18.2	11442	6.8	42152	25.0	19268	11.4
2007	26940	15.7	4847	2.8	31787	18.6	22093	12.9
2008	33595	19.2	5974	3.4	39569	22.6	27621	15.8
2009	36387	20.4	7381	4.1	43768	24.5	29006	16.2
2010	28534	15.7	6651	3.7	35185	19.4	21883	12.0

2-5 主要年份新莞人和劳动力

Migrant Population and Labor in Main Years

单位：人

项　　目	1995年	1996年	1997年	1998年	1999年	2000年	2001年	2002年
一、新莞人总计	**1421754**	**1433157**	**1446830**	**1991122**	**2448134**	**2547221**	**4578163**	**4336453**
（一）按性别分								
男	581304	606524	554193	850266	1084492	1155277	2138218	1973316
女	840450	826633	892637	1140856	1363642	1391944	2439945	2363137
（二）按来自地区分								
省内	371816	305821	298510	402267	504722	485889	731931	722894
省外	1023510	1106749	1130981	1569963	1921206	2041959	3826830	3593034
#湖南省	253574	232329	243384	330241	391491	377257	718295	685311
四川省	223727	223315	227077	294149	387730	319039	622166	555569
广西自治区	149478	137933	140483	183734	236936	240923	442904	394088
湖北省	84727	90528	89140	143662	173787	196697	359872	389735
江西省	67562	79730	83272	118685	149000	157323	294740	294086
港澳台	23729	18094	16048	17557	20664	17547	17975	18856
国外	2699	2493	1291	1335	1542	1826	1427	1669
二、新莞人劳动力总计	**1265368**	**1276626**	**1307279**	**1831939**	**2161487**	**2448415**	**4496771**	**4260142**
按行业分								
工业	1084860	1084330	1114235	1577922	1609539	2043270	3681099	3573355
农业	54714	64732	57214	68143	113324	88195	174936	127584
商业	52965	61092	67242	100041	282938	187015	283277	300642
服务业	72829	66472	68588	85833	155686	129935	357459	258561

注：本表根据市公安局统计数据整理。

2-5 续表

单位：人

项　　目	2003年	2004年	2005年	2006年	2007年	2008年	2009年	2010年
一、新莞人总计	**4404467**	**4869462**	**5849785**	**5867555**	**5577988**	**5525022**	**4299615**	**4114745**
（一）按性别分								
男	2198324	2347115	2746833	2775718	2666292	2657712	2093055	2010869
女	2206143	2522347	3102952	3091837	2911696	2867310	2206560	2103876
（二）按来自地区分								
本省	665549	747804	1036417	1012637	986062	1012341	889160	791665
外省	3720408	4096599	4747692	4807064	4551507	4468505	3367565	3275768
#湖南省	663487	812976	844053	875904	816688	828779	604891	587153
四川省	591145	581272	642170	617644	553907	533496	441758	411005
广西自治区	432738	483329	574634	556961	497438	488226	396425	405051
湖北省	443603	490063	514760	531987	521529	517519	391650	353414
江西省	339518	329715	376526	367094	355798	353738	269133	252936
港澳台	16986	21700	59798	44653	36321	37329	35630	37665
国外	1524	3359	5878	3201	4098	6847	7260	9647
二、新莞人劳动力总计	**4327312**	**4733903**	**5534248**	**5669798**	**5389490**	**5303008**	**4134581**	**3912274**
按行业分								
工业	3753904	4078400	4676454	4820388	4480800	4227211	3361306	3191436
农业	85109	98272	107933	124942	102519	97597	74982	92451
商业	278632	315021	420810	412180	460114	560345	430183	402786
服务业	209667	242210	329051	312288	346057	417855	268110	225601

2-6 历年新莞人与劳动力

Migrant Population and Labor over Years

单位：人

年份	新莞人总计	按性别分		按省内省外分		新莞人劳动力	工业	农业	商业	服务业
		男性	女性	本省	外省					
1986	156222					104091	87154	9849	2509	4579
1987	252895					180285	154842	13110	4181	8152
1988	368913					292499	260237	16911	5797	9554
1989	481850					405287	365840	19893	7763	11791
1990	655902			333180	322722	572044	518971	25576	10793	16704
1991	805790			360379	445411	701982	633400	25838	17945	24799
1992	1144753	440500	704253	494278	650475	1071048	874149	62324	88087	46488
1993	1217010	529096	687914	370770	846240	1126813	933147	40177	88524	64965
1994	1390884	547435	843449	380790	1010094	1241814	1069478	52146	39869	80321
1995	1421754	581304	840450	371816	1023510	1265368	1084860	54714	52965	72829
1996	1433157	606524	826633	305821	1106749	1276626	1084330	64732	61092	66472
1997	1446830	554193	892637	298510	1130981	1307279	1114235	57214	67242	68588
1998	1991122	850266	1140856	402267	1569963	1831939	1577922	68143	100041	85833
1999	2448134	1084492	1363642	504722	1921206	2161487	1609539	113324	282938	155686
2000	2547221	1155277	1391944	485889	2041959	2448415	2043270	88195	187015	129935
2001	4578163	2138218	2439945	731931	3826830	4496771	3681099	174936	283277	357459
2002	4336453	1973316	2363137	722894	3593034	4260142	3573355	127584	300642	258561
2003	4404467	2198324	2206143	665549	3720408	4327312	3753904	85109	278632	209667
2004	4869462	2347115	2522347	747804	4096599	4733903	4078400	98272	315021	242210
2005	5849785	2746833	3102952	1036417	4747692	5534248	4676454	107933	420810	329051
2006	5867555	2775718	3091837	1012637	4807064	5669798	4820388	124942	412180	312288
2007	5577988	2666292	2911696	986062	4551507	5389490	4480800	102519	460114	346057
2008	5525022	2657712	2867310	1012341	4468505	5303008	4227211	97597	560345	417855
2009	4299615	2093055	2206560	889160	3367565	4134581	3361306	74982	430183	268110
2010	4114745	2010869	2103876	791665	3275768	3912274	3191436	92451	402786	225601

2-7 历年户籍社会劳动者人数

Social Laborers of Household Registration over Years

单位：万人

年份	合计	企事业机关从业人员	国有单位	城镇集体	其他	城镇私营个体从业人员人数	农村劳动者人数
1957	37.57	4.65	3.90	0.75			32.92
1962	36.78	3.94	2.93	1.01			32.84
1965	40.56	4.61	3.17	1.44			35.95
1970	49.97	5.39	3.29	2.10			44.58
1975	51.44	6.32	3.80	2.52			45.12
1978	54.97	8.20	4.84	3.36			46.78
1979	56.51	9.68	5.17	4.51		0.02	46.81
1980	57.86	9.86	4.94	4.92		0.14	47.86
1981	59.42	10.66	5.19	5.47		0.32	48.43
1982	61.76	11.41	6.14	5.27		0.11	50.24
1983	63.25	11.59	6.12	5.48		0.43	51.22
1984	65.51	11.76	5.40	6.37		1.07	52.68
1985	67.35	12.30	5.65	6.34	0.30	0.58	54.47
1986	69.68	13.27	6.17	6.77	0.34	0.70	55.70
1987	71.63	13.67	6.20	6.85	0.61	0.85	57.11
1988	71.99	12.71	6.15	5.70	0.86	1.04	58.24
1989	73.95	13.10	6.17	6.37	0.56	1.85	58.99
1990	75.10	13.16	6.35	5.87	0.94	2.04	59.89
1991	76.99	14.59	6.54	6.42	1.63	2.26	60.15
1992	77.55	15.47	6.81	6.68	1.98	2.85	59.23
1993	79.36	17.66	6.92	7.37	3.37	3.41	58.30
1994	81.02	17.78	7.36	6.83	3.59	3.00	60.24
1995	82.40	18.40	7.53	6.51	4.36	4.51	59.48
1996	83.52	18.05	7.66	6.37	4.03	5.77	59.70
1997	84.78	16.73	7.38	5.90	3.45	6.51	61.54
1998	85.98	16.45	7.57	5.36	3.51	5.14	64.39
1999	87.82	16.66	7.74	5.32	3.61	8.67	62.49
2000	88.62	16.80	7.97	5.11	3.72	8.35	63.47
2001	90.80	16.98	8.02	4.82	4.14	8.78	65.03
2002	92.93	17.23	7.93	5.36	3.94	11.44	64.27
2003	95.64	16.88	8.50	4.36	4.02	14.52	64.24
2004	98.36	17.85	8.67	4.57	4.62	17.88	62.63
2005	101.30	19.14	9.91	4.48	4.75	21.18	60.99
2006	103.76	20.23	10.61	4.38	5.24	23.18	60.35
2007	106.65	21.44	11.65	4.02	5.77	25.58	59.63
2008	109.67	13.68	10.45	1.55	1.68	35.96	60.03
2009	112.18	15.08	9.98	2.09	3.01	35.14	61.97
2010	114.44	14.92	9.81	2.11	3.00	36.92	62.60

注：2008年起采用新口径，与往年数不可比。

2-8 主要年份分行业年末户籍从业人员数

Number of Employed Resident Persons at Year-end by Sector in Main Years

单位：人

项　　目	1985年	1990年	1995年	2000年	2005年	2009年	2010年
合　计	**673494**	**750980**	**824014**	**886169**	**1013029**	**1121839**	**1144444**
第一产业	**285857**	**271513**	**194895**	**173829**	**86694**	**57012**	**53361**
第二产业	**233231**	**305190**	**380101**	**414273**	**461451**	**462281**	**451836**
工　业	195846	266867	348107	382674	435208	432464	420497
采矿业			121	75	707	61	17
制造业			341954	377632	426649	425852	413942
电力、燃气及水的生产和供应业			6032	4967	7852	6551	6538
建筑业	37385	38323	31994	31599	26243	29817	31339
第三产业	**154406**	**174277**	**249018**	**298067**	**464884**	**602546**	**639248**
#金融业	2942	5635	12900	20380	18446	15636	18018
房地产业			2377	3774	777	3122	4254
公共管理和社会组织	5854	7887	9407	14829	27987	36872	36721

2-9 主要年份城镇职工年末人数

Number of Employed Persons in Urban Areas at Year-end in Main Years

单位：人

项　　目	1985年	1990年	1995年	2000年	2005年	2009年	2010年
合　计	**122951**	**131631**	**178724**	**164080**	**188579**	**225990**	**226268**
第一产业	**2432**	**2053**	**620**	**476**	**483**	**477**	**625**
第二产业	**64525**	**72993**	**110885**	**76153**	**80596**	**94365**	**87136**
工　业	60571	68508	105782	68354	79359	92943	84992
采矿业			130	62	59	50	52
制造业			99194	62790	71569	85496	77544
电力、燃气及水的生产和供应业			6458	5502	7731	7397	7396
建筑业			5103	7799	1237	1422	2144
第三产业	**55994**	**56585**	**67219**	**87451**	**107500**	**131148**	**138507**
#金融业	2270	4291	9487	13945	16584	18290	20706
房地产业	1551	2529	73	387	427	472	488
公共管理和社会组织	5854	7887	9711	15733	28542	39017	41676

注：2000年起为城镇在岗职工人数。

2-10 历年分行业户籍从业人员与城镇职工人数

Number of Employed Persons in Resident and Urban Areas by Sector over Years

单位：人

年 份	年末户籍从业人员	第一产业	第二产业	#工业	第三产业	年末城镇职工人数合计	第一产业	第二产业	#工业	第三产业
1978	549728	393460	92601	85380	63667	81971	2875	41179	38729	37917
1979	565106	376489	130211	127797	58406	96807	3051	44905	42251	48851
1980	578587	370959	142273	139636	65355	98587	2637	47374	44737	48576
1981	594207	370122	139996	137728	84089	106626	2897	52638	50370	51091
1982	617578	362320	162932	145325	92326	114119	2133	56391	52418	55595
1983	632486	307693	204435	178546	120358	115926	1978	58139	53246	55809
1984	655121	250339	240330	204914	164452	117627	1933	59129	54916	56565
1985	673494	285857	233231	195846	154406	122951	2432	64525	60571	55994
1986	696758	279337	264289	218257	153132	132744	2252	73922	65674	56570
1987	716287	272343	281926	238059	162018	136666	2359	76393	69985	57914
1988	719942	273059	286785	246743	160098	127098	2702	69385	64631	55011
1989	739474	275774	291640	254727	172060	131039	2397	73042	68738	55600
1990	750980	271513	305190	266867	174277	131631	2053	72993	68508	56585
1991	769895	263385	323235	285691	183275	145873	2083	84992	79389	58798
1992	775498	238442	337736	300848	199320	154712	2043	89713	82611	62956
1993	793618	212881	357969	313281	222769	176578	1933	107296	92212	67349
1994	810180	197120	364846	324883	248213	160872	621	95378	83322	64873
1995	824014	194895	380101	348107	249018	178724	620	110885	105782	67219
1996	835174	199715	377401	343021	258058	174964	497	98061	91228	76406
1997	847812	203616	378073	338911	266123	164987	616	82513	76619	81858
1998	859797	202926	381278	344588	275594	164047	779	80510	70499	82758
1999	878242	200559	381198	346341	296485	163917	583	76905	68860	86429
2000	886169	173829	414273	382674	298067	164080	476	76153	68354	87451
2001	907962	159116	436684	407142	312162	164226	444	76181	69260	87601
2002	929321	132403	439266	402030	357652	164209	431	75384	68348	88394
2003	956442	114911	449963	424507	391568	165978	522	73357	72118	92099
2004	983628	101936	457039	427880	424653	175415	565	78003	76786	96847
2005	1013029	86694	461451	435208	464884	188579	483	80596	79359	107500
2006	1037587	67300	468080	440192	502207	199878	483	84618	83328	114777
2007	1066498	61555	450004	421588	554940	205640	487	81448	79949	123705
2008	1096704	60150	410124	379780	626430	207234	459	77982	76563	128793
2009	1121839	57012	462281	432464	602546	225990	477	94365	92943	131148
2010	1144444	53361	451836	420497	639248	226268	625	87136	84992	138507

注：2000年起城镇职工为城镇在岗职工口径。

2-11 主要年份国有单位分行业年末职工人数

Number of Employed Persons in State-owned Units at Year-end by Sector in Main Years

单位：人

指　　标	1985年	1990年	1995年	2000年	2005年	2009年	2010年
合　计	**56534**	**63469**	**71165**	**78216**	**94902**	**116088**	**121690**
按企业、事业、机关单位分							
企业	40201	43538	38022	31988	20401	19873	20348
事业	11362	13072	23147	31506	46382	57846	60310
机关	4971	6859	9996	14722	28119	38369	41032
按国民经济行业分							
第一产业	2264	1956	712	476	483	477	625
第二产业	22373	22877	17363	11658	4442	4687	4888
工　业	20919	19390	14610	10119	3471	3465	3638
采矿业	423	72	130	62	59	50	52
制造业	19625	16912	12908	6611	1217	940	981
电力、燃气及水的生产和供应业	871	2406	1572	3446	2195	2475	2605
建筑业	1454	3487	2753	1539	971	1222	1250
第三产业	31897	38571	53090	66082	89977	110924	116177
交通运输、仓储及邮政业					3381	2263	2182
信息传输、计算机服务和软件业					2243	2281	2275
批发和零售业					1582	1377	1790
住宿和餐饮业							
金融业	943	2215	5634	7343	9401	9293	9319
房地产业	138	149	44	98	244	310	329
租赁和商务服务业					676	1438	1437
科学研究、技术服务和地质勘查业					1496	1854	1928
水利、环境和公共设施管理业					484	516	542
居民服务和其他服务业					95	108	105
教育					23301	25778	26138
卫生、社会保障和社会福利业					17134	24904	26795
文化、体育和娱乐业					1398	1785	1661
公共管理和社会组织	4971	6859	9563	15372	28542	39017	41676
国际组织							

注：2000年起为城镇在岗职工人数，下同。

2-12 主要年份城镇集体单位分行业年末职工人数

Number of Employed Persons in Urban Collective-owned Units at Year-end by Sector in Main Years

单位：人

指　　标	1985年	1990年	1995年	2000年	2005年	2009年	2010年
合　计	**63383**	**58749**	**64923**	**50592**	**44251**	**35159**	**35106**
按企业、事业、机关单位分							
企业	58258	54671	63194	49257	43200	34269	34245
事业	4062	3050	1581	974	1051	890	861
机关	1063	1028	148	361			
按国民经济行业分							
第一产业	168	97	33				
第二产业	39858	41795	52334	34958	32778	23586	23765
工　业	37358	40979	49984	28698	32527	23397	22879
采矿业		433					
制造业		40458	48600	27268	30772	21931	21497
电力、燃气及水的生产和供应业		88	1384	1430	1755	1466	1382
建筑业	2500	998	2350	6260	251	189	886
第三产业	23357	16857	12556	15634	11473	11573	11341
交通运输、仓储及邮政业					3446	3845	3543
信息传输、计算机服务和软件业					45	40	40
批发和零售业					2078	1897	1818
住宿和餐饮业					307	272	289
金融业	1327	2076	3844	3437	4184	4349	4533
房地产业			29	289	183	162	159
租赁和商务服务业					843	703	677
科学研究、技术服务和地质勘查业					16	56	56
水利、环境和公共设施管理业					237	117	112
居民服务和其他服务业							
教育							
卫生、社会保障和社会福利业					92	66	64
文化、体育和娱乐业					42	66	50
公共管理和社会组织	1063	1028	148	361			
国际组织							

2-13 主要年份其他所有制单位分行业年末职工人数

Number of Employed Persons in Other Ownership Units at Year-end by Sector in Main Years

单位：人

指　　标	1985年	1990年	1995年	2000年	2005年	2009年	2010年
合　计	**3034**	**9413**	**42636**	**35272**	**49426**	**74743**	**69472**
按企业、事业、机关单位分							
企业	2312	9413	42597	35272	49426	74743	69472
事业	722		39				
机关							
按国民经济行业分							
第一产业							
第二产业	2294	8321	41188	29537	43376	66092	58483
工　业	2294	8321	41188	29537	43361	66081	58475
采矿业		48					
制造业		8273	37686	28911	39580	62625	55066
电力、燃气及水的生产和供应业			3502	626	3781	3456	3409
建筑业					15	11	8
第三产业					6050	8651	10989
#交通运输、仓储及邮政业					412	682	702
信息传输、计算机服务和软件业					240	220	220
批发和零售业					1530	2523	2607
住宿和餐饮业					678	450	450
金融业			9	3165	2999	4648	6854
房地产业	722						
租赁和商务服务业					191	128	156
卫生、社会保障和社会福利业							

2-14 主要年份工业、建筑业企业年末城镇职工人数

Number of Urban Employed Persons in Industrial and Construction Enterprises at Year-end in Main Years

单位：人

指标	1985年	1990年	1995年	2000年	2005年	2009年	2010年
一、工业总计	**105782**	**91228**	**82474**	**68354**	**79359**	**92943**	**84992**
（一）按经济类型分							
国有经济单位	14610	15121	14477	10119	3471	3465	3638
城镇集体经济单位	49984	38822	32620	28698	32527	23397	22879
其他各种经济单位	41188	37285	35377	29537	43361	66081	58475
（二）按工业行业分(大类)							
非金属矿采选业	130	43	66	62	59	50	52
农副食品加工业	4664	4419	3978	2884	249	397	398
食品制造业	1842	542	583	368	159	138	137
饮料制造业	3944	2976	2814	584	570	1400	1400
烟草制品业							
纺织业	2722	1561	1547	1990	1928	1499	1252
纺织服装、鞋、帽制造业	11769	13199	6749	4162	5068	6687	6628
皮革、毛皮、羽毛(绒)及其制品业	3692	2756	1688	106	209	5692	167
木材加工及木、竹、藤、棕、草制品业	1190	1056	910	362	45		
家具制造业	433	192	154	29	5246	4888	6036
造纸及纸制品业	1697	1540	938	1079	1241	928	976
印刷业和记录媒介的复制	2065	1493	1734	773	1074	1015	986
文教、体育用品制造业	7192	1463	1173	9	254	1003	249
石油加工、炼焦及核燃料加工业							
化学原料及化学制品制造业	1921	1325	1284	869	662	1053	1204
医药制造业	1115	915	689	2719	1890	1846	1927
化学纤维制造业	25	25					
橡胶制品业		9	520	148			
塑料制品业	3783	3855	3235	1418	1739	3265	2259
非金属矿物制品业	4909	3882	3159	1939	3556	671	1126
黑色金属冶炼及压延加工业							
有色金属冶炼及压延加工业	59	205	205	86	74	83	83
金属制品业	2862	1767	1664	2226	768	476	482
通用设备制造业	2097	2825	2666	1308	890	1048	1093
专用设备制造业	1819	942	1968	560	240	509	1533
交通运输设备制造业	1729	972	827	375	329	2681	1976
电气机械及器材制造业	14755	10017	11197	16028	13638	10857	12792
通信设备、计算机及其他电子设备制造业	14129	12589	14310	14121	17812	20958	21330
仪器仪表及文化、办公用机械制造业	4884	6617	8107	7262	13759	17635	12812
工艺品及其他制造业				1385	130	745	673
电力、热力的生产和供应业	6068	4993	5199	4579	6487	5731	5687
水的生产和供应业	390	415	590	923	1244	1666	1709
二、建筑业总计	**5103**	**6833**		**7799**	**1237**	**1422**	**2144**
国有经济单位	2753	1462	1362	1539	971	1222	1250
城镇集体经济单位	2350	4771	4532	6260	251	189	886
其他各种经济单位		600			15	11	8

2-15 主要年份城镇职工变动情况

Changes of Employed Persons in Urban Areas in Main Years

单位：人

项　　目	1995年	1996年	1997年	1998年	2000年	2005年	2009年	2010年
当年增加人数	**25995**	**12155**	**10658**	**14326**	**17604**	**35604**	**37712**	**53694**
从农村招收	13318	4883	4007	6551	7208	17746	16737	25032
从城镇招收	3025	2059	2269	2241	2391	4109	3930	5238
录用退伍军人	299	183	144	240	306	412	229	227
录用大、中专、技工学校毕业生	3082	1894	2527	3230	4852	7409	8778	10400
调入	1806	1021	912	1135	947	1156	1425	1256
其他	4465	2115	799	929	1900	4772	6613	11541
当年减少人数	**19109**	**14039**	**11565**	**16349**	**12881**	**29785**	**39481**	**53505**
离、退休、退职	2784	2230	3040	2682	2764	8532	15121	18899
开除、除名、辞退	6561	2887	2170	2483	2565	3491	1618	1684
终止解除合同	4695	4989	4136	7544	3989	12587	17396	20501
离开本单位仍保留劳动关系	1131			1127	634	74	36	31
调出	30	932	726	555	524	610	1190	1035
其他	3908	3001	1493	1958	2405	4491	4120	11355

2-16 单位从业人员变动情况（2009-2010年）

Changes of Employed Persons in Units (2009-2010)

单位：人

项　　目	2009年				2010年			
	总　计	国有单位	城镇集体单位	其他单位	总　计	国有单位	城镇集体单位	其他单位
当年增加人数	**37712**	**7431**	**8725**	**21556**	**53694**	**8017**	**8976**	**36701**
从农村招收	16737	556	5398	10783	25032	585	4633	19814
从城镇招收	3930	781	639	2510	5238	846	904	3488
录用退伍军人	229	128	31	70	227	125	21	81
录用大、中专、技工学校毕业生	8778	3246	884	4648	10400	3425	694	6281
调入	1425	1139	19	267	1256	1194	26	36
#由外省、自治区、直辖市调入	340	320	1	19	263	250	1	12
其他	6613	1581	1754	3278	11541	1842	2698	7001
当年减少人数	**39481**	**3805**	**10156**	**25520**	**53505**	**4162**	**9979**	**39364**
离、退休、退职	15121	710	2802	11609	18899	748	2690	15461
开除、除名、辞退	1618	441	675	502	1684	298	408	978
终止解除合同	17396	1335	4559	11502	20501	1744	4254	14503
离开本单位仍保留劳动关系	36	14	20	2	31	18	8	5
调出	1190	864	33	293	1035	644	33	358
#调往外省、自治区、直辖市	29	27		2	58	29		29
其他	4120	441	2067	1612	11355	710	2586	8059

2-17 按经济类型分行业城镇职工人数及构成（2010年）

Employed Persons in Urban Areas by Registration Status and Sector (2010)

项　　目	合　计	国有经济单位	城镇集体经济单位	其他经济单位
合　计(人)	**226268**	**121690**	**35106**	**69472**
第一产业	625	625		
第二产业	87136	4888	23765	58483
工　业	84992	3638	22879	58475
采掘业	52	52		
制造业	77544	981	21497	55066
电力、燃气及水的生产和供应业	7396	2605	1382	3409
建筑业	2144	1250	886	8
第三产业	138507	116177	11341	10989
交通运输、仓储及邮政业	6427	2182	3543	702
信息传输、计算机服务和软件业	2535	2275	40	220
批发和零售业	6215	1790	1818	2607
住宿和餐饮业	739		289	450
金融业	20706	9319	4533	6854
房地产业	488	329	159	
租赁和商务服务业	2270	1437	677	156
科学研究、技术服务和地质勘查业	1984	1928	56	
水利、环境和公共设施管理业	654	542	112	
居民服务和其他服务业	105	105		
教育	26138	26138		
卫生、社会保障和社会福利业	26859	26795	64	
文化、体育和娱乐业	1711	1661	50	
公共管理和社会组织	41676	41676		
国际组织				
占全部职工人数的比重(%)	**100.00**	**53.78**	**15.52**	**30.70**
第一产业	0.28	0.28		
第二产业	38.51	2.16	10.50	25.85
工　业	37.56	1.61	10.11	25.84
采矿业	0.02	0.02		
制造业	34.27	0.43	9.50	24.34
电力、燃气及水的生产和供应业	3.27	1.15	0.61	1.51
建筑业	0.95	0.55	0.39	
第三产业	61.21	51.34	5.01	4.86
交通运输、仓储及邮政业	2.84	0.96	1.57	0.31
信息传输、计算机服务和软件业	1.12	1.01	0.02	0.10
批发和零售业	2.75	0.79	0.80	1.15
住宿和餐饮业	0.33		0.13	0.20
金融业	9.15	4.12	2.00	3.03
房地产业	0.22	0.15	0.07	
租赁和商务服务业	1.00	0.64	0.30	0.07
科学研究、技术服务和地质勘查业	0.88	0.85	0.02	
水利、环境和公共设施管理业	0.29	0.24	0.05	
居民服务和其他服务业	0.05	0.05		
教育	11.55	11.55		
卫生、社会保障和社会福利业	11.87	11.84	0.03	
文化、体育和娱乐业	0.76	0.73	0.02	
公共管理和社会组织	18.42	18.42		
国际组织				

2-18 主要年份私营企业和个体劳动者分行业年末从业人数

Number of Employed Persons in Private Enterprises and Self-employed Individuals at Year-end by Sector in Main Years

单位：人

项　目	1985年	1990年	1995年	2000年	2005年	2009年	2010年
合　计	**18813**	**64875**	**171136**	**356748**	**1120116**	**1506355**	**1487146**
第一产业(农、林、牧、渔业)			**83**	**395**	**43784**	**12515**	**11287**
第二产业	**575**	**19924**	**54174**	**122907**	**362041**	**486890**	**527101**
工　业	575	19548	51968	119342	344854	461867	499659
采矿业			1230	81	5884	77	45
制造业			50738	119261	338737	461393	499234
电力、煤气及水的生产和供应业					233	397	380
建筑业		376	2206	3565	17187	25023	27442
第三产业	**18238**	**44951**	**116879**	**233446**	**714291**	**1006950**	**948758**
交通运输、仓储及邮政业					12031	12045	13512
信息传输、计算机服务和软件业					17493	18138	17357
批发和零售业					484087	684682	623825
住宿和餐饮业					83895	118441	107300
房地产业					9190	14385	15104
租赁和商务服务业					21529	41072	46372
居民服务和其他服务业					75334	98271	100525
卫生、社会保障和社会福利业					122	399	363
文化、体育和娱乐业					2818	5356	6190
其他行业					7792	14161	18210

注：本表根据工商登记注册资料整理。

主要统计指标解释

Explanatory Notes on Main Statistical Indicators

人口数　指一定时点、一定地区范围内的有生命的个人的总和。年度统计的年末人口数是指每年 12 月 31 日 24 时的人口数。

常住人口包括　居住在本乡镇街道、户口在本乡镇街道或户口待定的人；居住在本乡镇街道、离开户口所在的乡镇街道半年以上的人；户口在本乡镇街道、外出不满半年或在境外工作学习的人。

外来暂住人口　指户口登记地在外县、市而目前在本市暂住的人口。

性别比　反映两性人口之间比例的指标。指在总人口中或在各年龄人口中，男性人数与女性人数之比。通常用每 100 个女性人口相应有多少男性人口表示。

出生率（又称粗出生率）　指在一定时期内（通常为一年）平均每千人所出生的人数的比率，一般用千分率表示。

死亡率（又称粗死亡率）　指在一定时期内（通常为一年）一定地区的死亡人数与同期平均人数（或期中人数）之比，一般用千分率表示。

人口自然增长率　指在一定时期内（通常为一年）人口自然增加数（出生人数减死亡人数）与该时期内平均人口数（或期中人数）之比，一般用千分率表示。

总迁移率　是反映人口迁移变动总规模的相对指标，是某地区一定时期内（通常为一年）迁入人数及迁出人数之和与同时期平均人口数之比，一般用千分率表示。

净迁移率　是反映人口迁移变动的相对指标之一，是某地区一定时期内（通常为一年）迁入与迁出相抵销后的余额与同时期平均人口数之比，一般用千分率表示。

计划生育率　是指一定时期内（通常为一年）计划内出生人数与总出生人数之间的比率，一般用百分率表示。

节育率　指一定时期内（通常为一年）已落实节育措施的已婚育龄妇女人数与同期已婚育龄妇女人数之间的比率，一般用百分率表示。

从业人员　指在劳动年龄内，有劳动能力，参加社会劳动取得劳动报酬或经营收入的人口。

职工　在单位工作，以工资为生活费主要来源的从业人员。

城镇集体经济单位职工　指在城镇集体经济单位及其管理部门工作，并由其支付工资的各类人员。

其他经济单位职工　指在联营经济、股份制经济、外商投资经济、港、澳、台投资经济单位工作，并由其支付工资的各类人员。

三、农　业

Agriculture

3-1 主要年份农业指标

Main Indicators of Agriculture in Main Years

指　　标	单　位	1978年	1980年	1985年	1990年	1995年	2000年	2001年	2002年
镇(街)户籍总户数	户	248167	256572	289512	327344	364273	414007	421177	431459
镇(街)户籍总人口数	人	1112299	1126973	1208515	1318526	1436525	1526090	1538919	1561884
镇(街)农村劳动力	人	467757	478599	544734	598911	639985	727328	743662	754294
第一产业	人	390585	368322	283425	269460	202138	189349	174786	151487
第二产业	人	51422	94576	167116	228114	283050	362666	383363	394770
第三产业	人	25750	15701	94193	101337	154797	175313	185513	208037
年末耕地面积	亩	1183926	1177400	966725	882602	708595	663304	643648	500694
农业机械总动力	千瓦	248760	354250	667750	1003980	795120	586063	515689	361552
水利建设总投资	万元	413	927	886	5428	16900	35550	33416	38921
化肥施用量(实物量)	吨	113296	100776	150083	235836	124263	103570	99146	76634
农药施用量	吨	4276	3382	2951	3453	1924	1836	1819	1485
农村用电量	万千瓦时	5667	7355	14365	82545	406327	1312931	1475778	1927589
农业总产值(当年价)	万元	42394	41943	91244	236412	426901	546383	559280	536729
主要农产品产量									
粮　食	吨	532308	529381	488705	494259	227441	204136	128366	53732
糖　蔗	吨	508976	447318	526033	538712	233803	49359	24768	15025
花　生	吨	14157	29015	20963	13411	3724	1960	1556	865
水　果	吨	26457	23688	189350	282410	243231	129367	150115	189343
水产品	吨	30900	25471	32641	68508	74778	95076	89599	82361
肉　类	吨	26920	27652	33298	62191	97572	179032	198423	188774
#猪 肉	吨	22790	23461	25759	40130	68649	149648	168353	165344
禽　蛋	吨	425	398	2424	6906	5431	4367	4441	4052
森林覆盖率	%			28.6	31.4	29.2	30.6	31.2	31.7

注：本表部分镇街农村劳动力含部分外来劳动力，下同。

3-1 续表

指　　标	单　位	2003年	2004年	2005年	2006年	2007年	2008年	2009年	2010年
镇(街)总户数	户	445001	454605	465008	477046	492510	506357	521190	530497
镇(街)总户籍人口数	人	1589611	1619690	1656541	1683078	1712593	1748658	1787288	1817709
镇(街)总劳动力	人	851484	798954	830705	847361	837283	842933	870156	878912
第一产业	人	130930	119347	110612	92819	85246	82059	77502	72856
第二产业	人	486298	434172	447207	460758	441523	436029	447662	448637
第三产业	人	234256	245435	272886	293784	310514	324845	344992	357419
年末耕地面积	亩	492433	489448	502937	491535	483740	479260	516623	576883
农业机械总动力	千瓦	308159	299152	229297	212312	192990	154344	159010	367988
水利建设总投资	万元	40320	66726	59437	53583	73032	96075	64935	78308
化肥施用量(实物量)	吨	69896	59126	52749	49716	47661	43699	43364	41445
农药施用量	吨	1355	1201	1090	1017	1000	1006	1060	819
农村用电量	万千瓦时	2239886	2880220	2970738	2979221	3489058	3373402	3567469	3950486
农业总产值(当年价)	万元	490206	441912	420496	212632	199782	255307	253077	283092
主要农产品产量									
粮　食	吨	30500	30374	20004	10040	9864	11902	11912	12482
糖　蔗	吨	2564	1437	450	379	1953	2580	1249	800
花　生	吨	395	216	114	99	73	130	113	115
水　果	吨	146414	175389	151255	139582	131571	101541	91544	75540
水产品	吨	75756	71526	67381	47059	47292	72282	73323	76268
肉　类	吨	154615	146184	171737	34891	20257	24052	25457	28830
#猪　肉	吨	135344	128286	159169	30199	14862	17946	19095	22339
禽　蛋	吨	3597	3435	1355	371	361	146	515	386
森林覆盖率	%	32.2	33.0	33.1	35.1	35.5	36.2	36.5	36.7

注：2010年起，农业机械总动力数据采用农业局统计口径，下同。

3-2 主要年份农村经济比例和效益指标

Main Indicators of Proportions and Efficiency in Rural Economy in Main Years

指　　标	单　位	1985年	1990年	1995年	2000年	2005年	2009年	2010年
一、农村各产业劳动力比例								
第一产业	%	52.0	45.0	31.6	26.0	13.3	8.9	8.3
第二产业	%	30.7	38.1	44.2	49.9	53.8	51.4	51.0
第三产业	%	17.3	16.9	24.2	24.1	32.9	39.7	40.7
二、劳动生产条件								
平均每一农业人口用电量	千瓦时	150	826	3778	11666	29762	36676	44051
每亩耕地农业机械总动力	瓦特	691	1138	1122	884	455	308	638
平均每亩耕地化肥施用量	公斤	155	267	175	156	105	84	72
平均每亩耕地农药施用量	公斤	3.05	3.91	2.72	2.77	2.17	2.10	1.42
三、增加值率								
农业增加值率	%			57.8	56.9	51.9	58.4	58.5
四、劳动生产率（平均每个劳动力创造或生产的）								
农业总产值	元	1703	3977	6737	7828	5062	2908	3221
农业增加值	元			3892	4453	2627	1699	1886
粮食产量	吨	0.91	0.83	0.36	0.29	0.02	0.01	0.01
蔬菜产量	吨	0.59	0.75	0.88	0.94	0.55	0.46	0.45
糖蔗产量	吨	0.98	0.91	0.37	0.07			
水果产量	吨	0.35	0.48	0.38	0.19	0.18	0.11	0.09
畜牧总肉产量	吨	0.06	0.10	0.15	0.26	0.21	0.03	0.03
#猪　肉	吨	0.05	0.07	0.11	0.21	0.19	0.02	0.03
水产品产量	吨	0.06	0.12	0.12	0.14	0.08	0.08	0.09

注：劳动生产率中产值部分按当年价计算。

3-3 农村集体(经联社、经济社两级)资产负债及收益分配

Assets，Liabilities and Income Distribution of Rural Collective Economy

单位：亿元

指　　标	2005年	2007年	2008年	2009年	2010年
一、资产负债情况					
资产总额	929.60	1088.58	1135.14	1173.48	1228.20
负债总额	221.56	267.42	275.38	283.25	292.15
资产负债率(%)	23.83	24.57	24.25	24.14	23.79
净资产	708.04	821.16	859.70	890.23	936.05
二、收益分配情况					
经营总收入	120.57	140.19	141.02	136.10	143.38
#直接经营收入	12.83	14.31	12.73	12.92	14.39
物业出租收入	77.02	86.44	89.79	86.39	91.65
管理费收入	13.07	10.30	8.66	7.94	7.51
结汇收入		6.41	5.12	3.77	3.52
农业发包及上交收入	3.17	2.57	2.25	2.14	2.09
投资收益	5.07	6.87	7.43	6.60	7.07
其他收入	9.40	13.29	15.05	16.35	17.15
经营总费用	48.05	58.39	63.34	63.78	66.45
#直接经营费用	6.46	8.11	8.50	8.49	8.59
租赁费用	24.05	26.41	28.61	30.47	32.62
经营税金		1.37	1.51	1.67	1.90
管理费用	9.34	11.50	12.61	12.01	12.46
其他支出	7.92	10.99	12.11	11.14	10.89
经营纯收入	72.52	81.80	77.68	72.32	76.93
收益分配总额	64.57	77.32	82.90	82.39	92.79
可弥补分配的收益总额	3.29	7.92	8.71	12.31	15.79

3-4 历年农产品人均拥有量

Per Capita Possession of Agricultural Products over Years

单位：公斤

年份	粮食		#稻谷		蔬菜	
	按总人口	按农业人口	按总人口	按农业人口	按总人口	按农业人口
1949	312	378	304	368		
1952	379	463	364	444		
1957	373	463	337	419		
1962	414	514	392	486		
1965	513	632	502	618		
1970	463	562	451	546		
1975	473	565	452	539		
1980	471	570	462	558	111	134
1985	408	510	397	497	260	330
1990	379	495	368	480	337	440
1995	160	211	148	196	388	515
1996	168	224	155	207	411	548
1997	169	225	155	207	436	582
1998	167	224	151	203	450	603
1999	165	222	149	200	443	597
2000	135	181	121	163	431	582
2001	83	113	71	97	459	623
2002	34	54	27	43	418	653
2003	19	30	13	20	352	549
2004	19	30	8	12	329	530
2005	12	20	7	12	278	461
2006	6	10	4	8	212	364
2007	6	10	4	7	200	351
2008	7	12	3	6	224	399
2009	7	12	4	7	224	412
2010	7	14	5	10	216	438

注：本表按户籍人口计算。

3-4 续表

单位：公斤

年份	水果		猪肉		水产品	
	按总人口	按农业人口	按总人口	按农业人口	按总人口	按农业人口
1949					5	6
1952					5	6
1957					5	7
1962					8	10
1965	53	66			12	14
1970	71	87			17	20
1975	34	41			20	24
1980	21	26	21	25	23	27
1985	158	197	21	27	27	34
1990	218	283	31	40	53	69
1995	171	226	48	64	52	70
1996	143	190	58	77	56	76
1997	113	151	68	91	63	84
1998	77	103	84	112	65	88
1999	91	122	87	117	63	84
2000	85	115	97	131	61	82
2001	98	132	109	148	58	79
2002	121	190	106	165	53	82
2003	92	143	85	133	48	74
2004	108	175	79	128	44	71
2005	91	152	96	159	41	68
2006	83	143	18	31	28	48
2007	77	135	9	15	28	48
2008	58	104	10	18	41	74
2009	51	94	11	20	41	75
2010	42	84	12	25	42	85

3-5 主要年份基层组织情况

Basic Statistics on Rural Grassroots Units in Main Years

指　　标	单位	1985年	1990年	1995年	2000年	2005年	2009年	2010年
一、农村基层组织								
镇街政府	个	33	33	33	32	32	32	32
社区居委会、村委会	个	528	583	594	593	596	598	599
二、镇街户籍总户数	**户**	**289512**	**327344**	**364273**	**414007**	**465008**	**521190**	**530497**
#农业户	户	219846	238221	263669	299576	275988	280737	259691
三、镇街户籍总人口	**人**	**1208515**	**1318526**	**1436525**	**1526090**	**1656541**	**1787288**	**1817709**
#农业人口	人	953582	1009857	1082703	1130002	998159	972706	896789
四、镇街劳动力	**人**	**544734**	**598911**	**639985**	**727328**	**830705**	**870156**	**878912**
按性别分								
男性	人	260439	289258	315892	364866	427840	468137	475996
女性	人	284295	309653	324093	362462	402865	402019	402916
按行业分								
农、林、牧、渔业	人	283425	269460	190061	174201	110612	77502	72856
工业	人	133685	194485	254999	335545	414017	413929	416197
建筑业	人	33431	33629	28051	27121	33190	33733	32440
交运仓储和邮政业	人	20142	29005	40032	31291	40619	40299	40124
信息传输、计算机服务和软件业	人					16889	28283	31432
批发与零售业	人					65051	79491	82662
住宿和餐饮业	人					32953	44140	48728
其他行业	人					117374	152779	154473

3-6 历年耕地面积

Area of Cultivated Land over Years

单位：亩

年 份	年末实有耕地面积	当 年新增面积	当 年减少面积	粮食占用耕地面积
1949	1398338			1260357
1952	1445016			1283151
1957	1435861			1199575
1962	1214417	15405	75905	1053985
1965	1199611	4142	11473	956906
1970	1203350	11359	8818	944903
1975	1193180	1246	6402	922916
1978	1183926	288	6515	874967
1979	1182292	120	1754	896347
1980	1177400	177	5069	856824
1981	1159963	279	17716	824166
1982	1146458	1086	14591	834028
1983	1121311	216	25363	837642
1984	1077659	664	44316	784763
1985	966725	1655	112589	691895
1986	889780	2350	79295	624471
1987	887369	1986	22271	618066
1988	877308	12374	22435	609332
1989	885694	13885	5499	626334
1990	882602	6991	10083	621564
1991	878980	962	4584	614994
1992	845159	100	33921	532296
1993	753746	6319	97732	391736
1994	718144	11169	46771	382238
1995	708595	12227	21776	394913
1996	674588	6270	40277	391610
1997	663013	6350	17925	382890
1998	663045	156	124	376133
1999	663122	1684	1607	381933
2000	663304	1632	1450	354980
2001	643648	4410	24066	255771
2002	500694		150	116989
2003	492433	1922	10183	81939
2004	489448	625	3610	85988
2005	502937	291	4302	76037
2006	491535		11403	34366
2007	483740		7795	32314
2008	479260	375	4855	40795
2009	516623	9	1212	41561
2010	576883	65649	5362	41922

3-7 历年耕地面积变动情况

Changes of Cultivated Land over Years

单位：亩

年 份	当年增加耕地面积	#新开荒	围海造田	当年减少耕地面积	#国家基建占用	种果占用	鱼塘占用
“六五”时期累计	**3900**	**1152**		**214575**	**6687**	**148244**	**33462**
1981	279	91		17716	1275	7577	4507
1982	1086	215		14591	505	3345	8073
1983	216	135		25363	788	19590	2152
1984	664	148		44316	1122	31072	7694
1985	1655	563		112589	2997	86660	11036
“七五”时期累计	**33250**	**2507**	**600**	**38017**	**9587**	**9138**	**2698**
1986							
1987							
1988	12374	1199		22435	6971	5379	1871
1989	13885	651	100	5499	1433	330	151
1990	6991	657	500	10083	1183	3429	676
“八五”时期累计	**30777**	**569**	**150**	**204784**	**5339**	**101880**	**44542**
1991	962	95	150	4584	1463	430	57
1992	100	5		33921	1090	17435	3154
1993	6319	270		97732	808	64790	19032
1994	11169	139		46771	645	16031	16162
1995	12227	60		21776	1333	3194	6137
“九五”时期累计	**16092**	**443**	**175**	**61383**	**2824**	**26550**	**9637**
1996	6270	194	19	40277	532	16382	5597
1997	6350			17925	797	10168	4027
1998	156		156	124	85		
1999	1684	148		1607	128		
2000	1632	101		1450	1282		13
“十五”时期累计	**7248**			**42311**	**3114**	**14531**	**5704**
2001	4410			24066	1406	14434	5704
2002				150			
2003	1922			10183	1587		
2004	625			3610	121		
2005	291			4302		97	
“十一五”时期累计	**66033**	**23627**		**30627**			
2006				11403			
2007				7795			
2008	375			4855			
2009	9			1212			
2010	65649	23627		5362			

3-8 历年农村劳动力(按性别、产业分)

Rural Labor Force over Years (by Sex and Industry)

单位：人

年 份	合 计	按性别分		按产业分		
		男	女	第一产业	第二产业	第三产业
1949	329182			281700		
1952	280506			228550		
1957	329204			269365		
1962	328354			267466		
1965	359464			294760		
1970	445768			376585		
1975	451207			427304		
1978	467757			390585	51422	25750
1979	468059			373438		
1980	478599	227496	251103	368322	94576	15701
1981	484346	231033	253313	367225		
1982	502066	239398	262668	360387	106294	35385
1983	512240	262608	249632	305715	145787	60738
1984	526766	253922	272844	248406	178527	99833
1985	544734	260439	284295	283425	167116	94193
1986	557048	265132	291916	277085	187920	92043
1987	571077	272044	299033	269984	204802	96291
1988	582425	281299	301126	270357	216508	95560
1989	589920	281420	308500	273377	215634	100909
1990	598911	289258	309653	269460	228114	101337
1991	601467	286328	315139	261271	232797	107399
1992	612142	298997	313145	239845	253218	119079
1993	625571	311208	314363	219230	267438	138903
1994	627366	313942	313424	200833	245562	180971
1995	639985	315892	324093	202138	283050	154797
1996	639492	316928	322564	206543	286166	146783
1997	643671	320844	322827	208030	284919	150722
1998	661604	329713	331891	205300	297418	158886
1999	668473	333136	335337	207432	300506	160535
2000	727328	364866	362462	189349	362666	175313
2001	743662	377491	366171	174786	383363	185513
2002	754294	384417	369877	151487	394770	208037
2003	851484	439406	412078	130930	486298	234256
2004	798954	412687	386267	119347	434172	245435
2005	830705	427840	402865	110612	447207	272886
2006	847361	445915	401446	92819	460758	293784
2007	837283	446755	390528	85246	441523	310514
2008	842933	451325	390608	82059	436029	324845
2009	870156	468137	402019	77502	447662	344992
2010	878912	475996	402916	72856	448637	357419

注：本表农村劳动力包含部分外来劳动力。

3-9 历年农村劳动力(按主要行业分)

Rural Labor Force over Years (by Main Sectors)

单位：人

年 份	合 计	农 业	工 业	建筑业	交通仓储邮电通讯业	商饮业
1949	329182	281700				
1952	280506	228550				
1957	329204	269365				
1962	328354	267466				
1965	359464	294760	2626			
1970	445768	376585	9178			
1975	451207	427304	10293			
1978	467757	390585	46651	4771	2515	2441
1979	468059	373438	85306			
1980	478599	368322	94576			
1981	484346	367225	87204			
1982	502066	360387	92860	13434	15580	3158
1983	512240	305715	124791	20996	8129	5916
1984	526766	248406	147324	31203	15804	12808
1985	544734	283425	133685	33431	20142	16970
1986	557048	277085	150136	37784	25049	18417
1987	571077	269984	167354	37448	25832	20919
1988	582425	270357	181234	35274	27280	21698
1989	589920	273377	183107	32527	28491	21582
1990	598911	269460	194485	33629	29005	22652
1991	601467	261271	201152	31645	29787	25813
1992	612142	239845	222722	30496	32777	29991
1993	625571	219230	236994	30444	39612	33629
1994	627366	200833	245562	28425	39479	35798
1995	639985	202138	254999	28051	40032	36974
1996	639492	206543	258227	27939	41092	40166
1997	643671	208030	258432	26487	37375	37702
1998	661604	205300	271099	26319	36939	38880
1999	668473	207432	273914	26592	37323	39284
2000	727328	189349	335545	27121	31291	48088
2001	743662	174786	357527	25836	32153	50512
2002	754294	151487	361418	33352	34919	57997
2003	851484	130930	451920	34378	35517	62978
2004	798954	119347	398596	35576	38406	83901
2005	830705	110612	414017	33190	40619	98004
2006	847361	92819	427500	33258	43295	102259
2007	837283	85246	406910	34613	41687	113141
2008	842933	82059	402895	33134	40827	117545
2009	870156	77502	413929	33733	40299	123631
2010	878912	72856	416197	32440	40124	131390

注：本表农村劳动力包含部分外来劳动力。

3-10 历年农业总产值及指数

Gross Output Value and Indices of Agriculture over Years

年　份	农　业总产值	种植业	#粮食	水果	林业	牧业	副业	渔业
一、农业总产值(万元)								
1978	42394	29425	21006	1404	312	5665	3843	3149
1980	41943	28054	17178	1570	238	6313	4460	2878
1985	91244	57684	19986	1913	759	12652	13930	6219
1986	122988	79251	18869	34831	2425	18078	14294	8940
1987	148414	90502	21593	39295	2330	23324	20328	11930
1988	203685	109531	29776	33939	4732	36915	26007	26500
1989	221079	117464	35488	30276	4316	45313	25491	28495
1990	236412	129032	34543	44268	4324	45405	26202	31449
1991	242587	130986	30256	44250	4038	47839	27084	32640
1992	271293	148412	28551	56967	5307	57163	22384	38026
1993	284539	130666	18519	39505	5489	78919	22728	46737
1994	347451	158315	22426	44798	6735	101117	21020	60263
1995	426901	194921	29030	59567	8850	128089	26494	68547
1996	497161	213018	33620	55763	9149	155112	32890	86992
1997	514373	232721	35329	53483	4383	176254	19442	81573
1998	536047	220614	34338	29852	5472	193404	23467	93090
1999	537442	236429	35549	47159	5640	197474	22404	75495
2000	546383	216318	19893	46423	3649	226293	19006	81118
2001	559280	228740	12895	48496	5309	245444	7655	72132
2002	536729	224452	5680	49790	2346	242928		67003
2003	490206	218039	3377	54346	1414	203477		67276
2004	441912	172481	3489	46992	2247	199912		67272
2005	420496	113577	4194	35130	1746	242534		62639
2006	212632	126923	2232	29801	3101	50638		31968
2007	199782	124627	2446	27434	3238	38354		33562
2008	255307	138205	3326	22551	3585	53221		60296
2009	253077	140221	3170	22986	2232	49982		60642
2010	283092	156698	3389	22804	2937	55499		67958

注：绝对数按当年价格计算，指数按可比价格计算。从2002年起种植业包含副业产值。下同。

3-10 续表

年份	农业总产值	种植业	#粮食	水果	林业	牧业	副业	渔业
二、指数(1978=100)								
1978	100.0	100.0	100.0	100.0	100.0	100.0	100.0	100.0
1980	98.0	100.3	98.1	89.0	65.6	81.4	146.7	88.3
1985	138.9	131.3	84.6	719.8	154.2	130.7	411.3	127.5
1986	174.6	158.0	78.8	1159.9	677.2	183.5	470.3	166.7
1987	186.4	160.1	80.0	1354.9	416.9	194.9	637.0	241.0
1988	182.1	143.5	79.8	959.0	476.4	215.1	766.8	262.2
1989	181.9	138.0	84.5	784.5	372.4	225.4	812.9	288.4
1990	195.3	150.6	85.7	1005.4	320.6	238.5	827.4	316.2
1991	199.5	149.4	77.3	961.8	286.4	262.1	859.5	335.9
1992	211.3	163.7	60.0	1255.3	325.7	289.3	697.3	356.7
1993	175.5	115.7	32.9	720.2	281.8	320.1	670.2	332.3
1994	188.4	123.9	32.8	905.8	235.5	364.3	582.0	382.1
1995	207.8	132.8	36.8	1022.0	337.0	410.4	731.1	407.0
1996	216.3	122.6	39.3	791.4	312.7	465.1	900.2	467.4
1997	225.0	129.1	40.0	835.4	167.7	532.0	563.1	540.4
1998	227.3	103.6	39.9	407.7	225.3	612.8	612.0	659.7
1999	242.8	140.2	39.9	981.4	297.4	616.2	52.7	686.0
2000	243.3	111.5	32.9	593.1	214.9	697.5	269.1	769.6
2001	246.3	111.8	20.5	634.6	233.4	750.0	146.4	766.0
2002	263.2	150.9	8.5	1336.5	124.5	730.2		652.5
2003	209.7	105.7	4.6	654.3	62.1	600.5		666.2
2004	213.5	118.0	3.3	899.9	123.9	563.1		647.9
2005	222.2	107.7	2.2	861.4	171.4	662.2		653.8
2006	121.0	108.3	2.4	683.1	246.6	155.2		590.7
2007	105.6	102.7	2.3	667.9	261.7	93.6		584.9
2008	118.3	106.0	3.9	520.6	286.3	109.5		899.5
2009	122.2	109.4	4.3	507.1	178.9	116.9		929.2
2010	126.2	107.6	4.6	415.3	205.2	132.2		982.2

3-11 历年农业增加值

Added Value of Agriculture over Years

单位：万元

年份	农业增加值	种植业	林业	牧业	副业	渔业
1978	27235	18903	200	3639	2469	2023
1980	26323	17606	149	3962	2799	1806
1985	61475	38864	511	8524	9385	4190
1986	81416	52463	1605	11967	9462	5918
1987	98236	59904	1542	15438	13455	7897
1988	118888	63932	2762	21547	15180	15468
1989	126568	67248	2471	25942	14594	16313
1990	132787	72474	2429	25503	14717	17664
1991	134523	72636	2239	26528	15019	18100
1992	144115	78839	2819	30366	11891	20200
1993	143953	66106	2777	39926	11498	23645
1994	174796	79645	3388	50870	10575	30317
1995	214306	97851	4443	64301	13300	34411
1996	248645	106537	4576	77576	16449	43507
1997	256388	115999	2185	87853	9691	40660
1998	259437	106773	2648	93604	11358	45054
1999	257863	113438	2706	94747	10749	36222
2000	259087	102575	1730	107305	9012	38465
2001	260968	106733	2477	114528	3572	33658
2002	248791	104041	1087	112605		31058
2003	228165	101486	658	94708		31313
2004	227087	88633	1155	102730		34569
2005	218212	84774	1162	97864		34412
2006	123936	88073	1913	17938		16011
2007	118991	86597	1997	13586		16810
2008	148250	96984	2212	18851		30202
2009	147877	98420	1378	17703		30375
2010	165719	110209	1812	19658		34040

注：绝对数按当年价格计算，从2002年起种植业包含副业产值。

3-12 历年农作物播种面积

Total Sown Area of Farm Crops over Years

单位：亩

年 份	农作物总播种面积	粮食	#稻谷	薯类	大豆	甘蔗	#糖蔗	花生	蔬菜（瓜）
1949	2118931	1908828	1783035	100391	40369	32165		39038	30000
1952	2514170	2245205	2035558	170547	37000	60682		47305	32000
1957	2834694	2482883	2015230	303587	53598	87062		53009	41934
1962	2339543	2072742	1795654	222978	31356	70793		67854	36415
1965	2384567	1824562	1681802	105758	24329	102528		113797	48988
1970	2618966	1908766	1752465	102205	31519	116639		118469	56668
1975	3029981	2055514	1739862	82594	43076	129778		141213	68061
1978	2859494	2072184	1715230	66400	36764	131200	130676	155021	68743
1979	2585334	1937441	1676936	62537	37993	110580	110123	185434	63959
1980	2436118	1756854	1624873	49665	39261	92397	91908	232541	58550
1981	2267521	1606926	1525072	48999	32143	131453	131103	264903	63768
1982	2204381	1600137	1511345	57188	35450	125787	124431	217612	82982
1983	2193087	1635344	1530918	71430	32029	110684	109283	152335	119370
1984	2165276	1576777	1468801	77105	31718	98449	96224	173198	153636
1985	1950081	1395692	1293847	70997	28982	96627	91884	159918	139795
1986	1791221	1257126	1174464	54993	31469	67920	63729	152214	159100
1987	1795990	1250934	1165554	57850	28471	63655	59637	130292	184744
1988	1792952	1236359	1151493	55368	27929	69694	66505	113882	208930
1989	1834039	1284184	1199979	55964	26200	85238	82666	101077	211217
1990	1848814	1286028	1194153	61281	26444	85977	83246	97808	229532
1991	1791266	1226573	1138043	60107	22785	90137	87356	85537	238418
1992	1561497	963947	889074	51273	20688	76184	72845	67897	318193
1993	1068053	551155	499223	34449	12843	43720	40594	39062	361826
1994	1009468	536191	482051	32615	7542	36346	34621	25344	367122
1995	1078363	598547	527594	43346	7058	28521	26488	24779	379362
1996	1083418	628347	559499	37989	8276	32620	30880	20805	363331
1997	1082610	624091	560506	32629	8190	41427	40166	18490	369113
1998	1101826	624383	558668	34799	7028	48602	47772	16824	385151
1999	1088854	626481	558508	36329	5597	31641	30889	14305	388173
2000	986022	527689	465616	31754	5290	7566	6775	11969	407304
2001	854229	338467	283351	31214	3947	4610	3290	9405	465659
2002	634205	148184	112388	18265	1983	3193	2299	4746	445447
2003	509504	84782	54970	11154	1550	1879	626	2823	380252
2004	462244	81207	31108	24683	816	868	373	1544	350412
2005	410648	62084	34356	9390	1006	950	55	574	315537
2006	333854	34366	25159	4100	183	575	55	556	241070
2007	320500	32314	19534	5330	253	1676	281	340	236490
2008	352222	40352	18781	4381	443	2330	340	586	287618
2009	370740	41421	18629	5047	140	4144	209	838	306270
2010	369257	41922	26124	3192		2944	100	713	300622

3-13 历年农作物产量

Total Output of Farm Crops over Years

单位：吨

年　份	粮食	#稻谷	薯类	大豆	甘蔗	#糖蔗	花生	蔬菜（瓜）
1949	210694	205180	4889		52229	49229	1464	
1952	269458	258860	9641		181901	177696	3545	
1957	288047	260432	22623		170880	160314	3280	
1962	331207	313352	15213		134012	133755	3813	
1965	437106	427809	8165		348519	293622	7232	
1970	450808	438293	9703		397251	395964	9629	
1975	507151	484425	7685		361756	359666	11108	
1978	532308	501074	6458	1948	511492	508976	14157	135603
1979	535342	516263	6568	1982	366424	364084	19100	127918
1980	529381	518591	5432	2245	449907	447318	29015	124859
1981	447540	439534	6318	1722	678160	676074	35506	132846
1982	543349	532998	8430	2162	707764	699174	29930	123117
1983	561246	548073	11345	1875	553174	553105	19662	168878
1984	558216	545548	10946	1980	569225	554919	23076	230454
1985	488705	476399	10304	1771	556983	526033	20963	314539
1986	455243	443760	9422	2050	382608	354759	20056	427138
1987	462830	451032	10058	1920	378094	349749	17019	414261
1988	460929	448923	9950	1965	420391	400045	15119	412436
1989	487648	474476	11052	2023	528463	511031	13746	410879
1990	494259	479350	12452	2184	557102	538712	13411	444377
1991	473663	458425	12998	1838	619884	601734	11510	446204
1992	368083	354298	11070	1763	543657	523271	9323	523806
1993	202097	192018	7366	1035	343133	326389	5594	572376
1994	202356	189688	7929	668	313851	302669	3678	537442
1995	227441	210876	10758	647	246707	233803	3724	557807
1996	243204	224469	11271	806	285732	274531	3120	597732
1997	246901	227163	11487	811	354420	346469	2879	641403
1998	247194	223938	13916	758	411555	406644	2588	668753
1999	247287	223403	14580	566	242773	238774	2204	668822
2000	204136	183485	9730	610	54095	49359	1960	658196
2001	128366	109881	9920	426	33387	24768	1556	706775
2002	53732	42508	5420	244	20224	15025	865	653272
2003	30500	20423	3415	215	8019	2564	395	560523
2004	30374	12230	9803	138	4763	1437	216	532116
2005	20004	11941	2733	147	4433	450	114	460204
2006	10040	7548	1314	31	3167	379	99	356347
2007	9864	6467	1732	48	10834	1953	73	342703
2008	11902	6007	1381	95	15286	2580	130	391192
2009	11912	6560	1437	19	23044	1249	113	400335
2010	12482	8768	668		15952	800	115	392904

3-14 主要年份农作物播种面积、亩产及总产量

Sown Area, Yield Per Acreage and Total Output of Farm Crops in Main Years

单位：亩、公斤、吨

指　　标	1978年			1985年			1990年		
	播种面积	亩产	总产量	播种面积	亩产	总产量	播种面积	亩产	总产量
一、粮食作物	**2072184**	**257**	**532308**	**1395692**	**350**	**488705**	**1286028**	**384**	**494259**
按品种分									
稻谷	1715230	292	501074	1293847	368	476399	1194153	401	479350
小麦									
旱粮	290554	85	24776	30848	65	2002	30594	80	2457
薯类	66400	97	6458	70997	145	10304	61281	203	12452
按季节分									
春收				30978	131	4042	33352	174	5790
夏收	1127790	248	279552	649856	377	244755	614059	399	244890
#早稻	814852	309	251907	620409	389	241413	587821	410	241018
秋收	944394	268	252757	714858	336	239907	638617	381	243579
#晚稻	900378	277	249167	673438	349	234985	606332	393	238332
二、大豆	**36764**	**53**	**1948**	**28982**	**61**	**1771**	**26444**	**83**	**2184**
三、经济作物				**306406**			**209120**		
#甘蔗	131200	3899	511492	96627	5765	556983	85977	6480	557102
糖蔗	130676	3895	508976	91884	5725	526033	83246	6471	538712
果蔗	524	4802	2516	4743	6525	30950	2731	6734	18390
油料作物				160186	131	20974	97808	137	13411
#花生	155021	91	14157	159918	131	20963	97808	137	13411
四、其他作物				**219001**			**327222**		
#蔬菜	68743	1973	135603	139795	2250	314539	229532	1936	444377

3-14 续表 1

单位：亩、公斤、吨

指 标	1995年			2000年			2005年		
	播种面积	亩产	总产量	播种面积	亩产	总产量	播种面积	亩产	总产量
一、粮食作物	**598547**	**380**	**227441**	**527689**	**387**	**204136**	**62084**	**322**	**20004**
按品种分									
稻谷	527594	400	210876	465616	394	183485	34356	348	11941
小麦									
旱粮	27607	210	5807	30319	360	10921	18338	291	5330
薯类	43346	248	10758	31754	306	9730	9390	291	2733
按季节分									
春收	17880	224	4008	20787	287	5966	9665	312	3019
夏收	282978	388	109914	245110	392	96015	23286	306	7136
#早稻	255886	405	103592	225985	397	89729	14713	351	5164
秋收	297689	381	113519	261792	390	102155	29133	338	9850
#晚稻	271708	395	107284	239631	391	93756	19643	345	6777
二、大豆	**7058**	**92**	**647**	**5290**	**115**	**610**	**1006**	**146**	**147**
三、经济作物	**62092**			**35221**			**18011**		
#甘蔗	28521	8650	246707	7566	7150	54095	950	4666	4433
糖蔗	26488	8827	233803	6775	7285	49359	55	8182	450
果蔗	2033	6347	12904	791	5987	4736	895	4450	3983
油料作物	24779	150	3724	11969	164	1960	574	199	114
#花生	24779	150	3724	11969	164	1960	574	199	114
四、其他作物	**410666**			**417822**			**329547**		
#蔬菜	379362	1470	557807	407304	1616	658196	315537	1458	460204

3-14 续表 2

单位：亩、公斤、吨

指　　标	2008年			2009年			2010年		
	播种面积	亩产	总产量	播种面积	亩产	总产量	播种面积	亩产	总产量
一、粮食作物	**40352**	**295**	**11902**	**41421**	**288**	**11912**	**41922**	**298**	**12482**
按品种分									
稻谷	18781	320	6007	18629	352	6560	26124	336	8768
小麦									
旱粮	17190	262	4514	17745	221	3915	12606	242	3046
薯类	4381	315	1381	5047	285	1437	3192	209	668
按季节分									
春收	6629	267	1767	6257	254	1588	5202	221	1150
夏收	16466	306	5039	17314	302	5221	17948	306	5501
#早稻				9117	332	3031	12017	330	3965
秋收	17257	295	5096	17850	286	5103	18772	311	5831
#晚稻				9512	371	3529	14107	340	4803
二、大豆	**443**	**214**	**95**	**140**	**136**	**19**			
三、经济作物	**14423**			**16440**			**14084**		
#甘蔗	2330	6560	15286	4144	5561	23044	2944	5418	15952
糖蔗	340	7588	2580	209	5976	1249	100	8000	800
果蔗	1990	6384	12706	3935	5539	21795	2844	5328	15152
油料作物	586	221	130	838	135	113	713	161	115
#花生	586	221	130	838	135	113	713	161	115
四、其他作物	**297004**			**312739**			**313251**		
#蔬菜	287618	1360	391192	306270	1307	400335	300622	1307	392904

3-15 主要年份农机总动力、水利、化肥、农药及农村用电量

Basic Statistics on Total Power of Agricultural Machinery, Water Conservancy, Consumption of Chemical Fertilizers and Pesticides, and Electricity Consumed in Rural Areas in Main Years

指　标	单　位	1978年	1985年	1990年	1995年	2000年	2005年	2009年	2010年
一、农业机械总动力	**千瓦**	**248760**	**667750**	**1003980**	**795120**	**586063**	**229297**	**159010**	**367988**
#耕作机械	千瓦	42550	116200	157910	83482	51848	16386	13959	24079
排灌机械	千瓦	104050	149900	178280	112392	91745	36251	26186	99716
收获机械	千瓦	6180	39130	84130	54722	51084	969	599	2280
运输机械	千瓦	16930	273270	322950	397735	184949	41678	18423	12463
二、水利建设完成土石方	**万立方米**	**957**	**295**	**737**	**891**	**927**	**682**	**520**	**442**
土方	万立方米	932	266	693	835	864	611	445	386
石方	万立方米	25	29	44	56	63	71	75	56
水利建设总投资	万元	413	886	5428	16900	35550	59437	64935	78308
#各级自筹资金	万元	247	720	4956	14500	33026			
水利建设使用劳动工日	万工日	696	136	994	1019	1200	732	984	
三、化肥施用实物量	**吨**	**113296**	**150083**	**235836**	**124263**	**103570**	**52749**	**43364**	**41445**
#氮肥	吨	86371	66846	84642	43441	30214	14439	11024	10214
磷肥	吨	23164	37147	52483	28939	23939	10967	8555	8055
钾肥	吨	3761	13544	26131	16915	14606	6403	5376	5030
复合肥	吨		13117	39098	34968	34811	20940	18409	18146
四、农药施用量	**吨**	**4276**	**2951**	**3453**	**1924**	**1836**	**1090**	**1060**	**819**
五、农村用电量	**万千瓦时**	**5667**	**14365**	**82545**	**406327**	**1312931**	**2970738**	**3567469**	**3950486**
#农村工业用电量	万千瓦时			70459	386413	1104301	2873735		
平均每一农业人口用电量	千瓦时		150	826	3778	11666	29762	36676	44051

注：农业机械总动力数据从2010年起采用农业局统计口径，数据与往年不可比，下同。

3-16 历年水果面积及产量

Planted Area and Output of Fruits over Years

年 份	年末实有水果面积(亩)	#香(大)蕉	荔 枝	水 果总产量(吨)	#香(大)蕉	荔 枝
1949		15659	19300		15911	1391
1952		21827	20050		21633	1976
1957		21827	18242		19469	1976
1962		15547	22844		7766	255
1965		19343	27966	45421	28259	14259
1970		24831	37482	69480	47257	18775
1975		24232	41045	36821	32238	2727
1978	93245	18828	46678	26457	18867	4959
1979	91021	17977	46697	23346	12165	8667
1980	88444	15582	46743	23688	10894	7884
1981	97468	18042	48230	46909	25513	15599
1982	114730	28439	50669	58196	40872	7042
1983	159260	39749	63349	77225	42079	20724
1984	235311	66506	84183	105851	69186	14714
1985	407416	125998	115428	189350	133503	19304
1986	609347	171168	168820	307743	210439	18577
1987	609569	158874	175366	363085	222826	17439
1988	548482	99256	176979	263710	126655	7699
1989	476598	54867	164782	221418	69410	6165
1990	452729	54185	160355	282410	73555	16994
1991	440442	56481	154456	343155	85702	6201
1992	420661	81331	139584	344751	97986	22972
1993	360130	86299	117557	271346	80982	717
1994	325336	67595	121236	264875	92072	12703
1995	322876	62351	142370	243231	86466	23324
1996	326291	59822	159403	206276	77768	14804
1997	319556	57583	188220	165016	80355	22572
1998	310873	46377	208899	114106	78978	2885
1999	285514	48975	198144	136317	82169	35218
2000	297618	71454	189862	129367	108913	9107
2001	275428	86578	156019	150115	132292	7059
2002	209924	76764	109948	189343	135209	45339
2003	199634	82024	95812	146414	130688	9012
2004	183375	84812	80115	175389	150669	18312
2005	176845	75452	83357	151255	123986	21026
2006	173470	73493	81395	139582	124601	8615
2007	163448	66904	80313	131571	116833	10107
2008	178337	64141	94953	101541	86817	8498
2009	177281	52761	103364	91544	75341	10240
2010	170536	47420	100136	75540	60236	8266

3-17 历年林业生产

Basic Statistics on Forestry Production over Years

年 份	林业用地面积（亩）	#杉	松	桉	当年育苗面积（亩）	当年幼林抚育面积（亩）	当年迹地更新面积（亩）	当年四旁植树（万株）
1952					15			3
1957					144			15
1962					333	3740		47
1965					2028			307
1970	711996	20266	596098	8100	531	6783	423	12
1975	711375	59992	572746	35216	693	29200	4343	40
1978	700570	63994	541492	49008	485	32900	5365	44
1979	705764	67104	543210	50439	880	14900	4745	30
1980	740052	70665	568729	56272	316	9500	3924	15
1981	743697	67236	584674	49994	133	12500	931	12
1982	698715	63730	535072	52925	500	11945	2531	19
1983	769893	67423	574171	56724	361	40464	3193	17
1984	739402	66107	552721	58092	501	106982	5120	16
1985	761460				801	120000	4479	150
1986	706823	61438	510042	60581	33231	210540	16908	22
1987	714664	57824	526254	75498	1728	53759	28007	35
1988	729896	59351	512451	90998	3667	70275	34467	37
1989	691944	53293	490370	103887	2101	64950	31241	58
1990	709240	47054	484397	133706	3464	56647	15782	54
1991	709306	44432	459015	148127	609	53827	22294	63
1992	662919	39326	422527	149944	762	60764	28184	49
1993	628612	36213	400816	144346	677	28511	13318	57
1994	1016138	43815	382482	129473	2492	28127	9689	34
1995	1015223	43661	360591	125133	4273	25130	11140	48
1996	1014972	9654	248288	115878	699	21000	23143	133
1997	1014954	8843	235410	113928	823	23745	22462	218
1998	1014876	8367	222147	112005	387	36000	22273	417
1999	1009965	10890	221585	133500	506	29863	29000	522
2000	1009037	29940	526797	280618	625	47145	13515	425
2001	1007298	9678	189930	133464	705	45000	38000	357
2002	900335	8265	187665	138525	516	46500	13700	98
2003	890877	6540	66206	105666	420	38910	10425	147
2004	980942				255	60000	8472	625
2005	934700	3086	2860	100145	195	61005	3383	253
2006	930162	3716	60890	162125	15	25320	3900	480
2007	926760	3870	62363	149440	255	43320	4701	600
2008	923097	3873	59864	145340	255	49571	4548	610
2009	921000	3719	58375	143690	610	56545	6184	60
2010	909900	3719	56987	142971	285	37278	5889	18

3-18 历年畜牧业生产及产品产量

Production of Animal Husbandry and Output of Livestock Products over Years

年 份	耕牛年末存栏量(头)	羊年末存栏量(头)	生猪饲养量(头)	生猪存栏量(头)	生猪出栏量(头)	三鸟饲养量(万只)	三鸟出栏量(万只)	畜牧总肉量(吨)	#猪肉	禽蛋总产量(吨)
1949	52475		147266	82266	65000	256	159			
1952	58530		243000	117082	125918	329	205			
1957	62444		300529	154756	145773	400	249			339
1962	47004		185961	103034	82927	339	248			394
1965	53105		640968	369391	271577	421	276			2989
1970	56665		900481	593310	307171	310	163			1614
1975	55292		920100	633527	286573	364	187			1141
1978	53004		1018060	672919	345141	428	219	26920	22790	425
1979	50595		995408	626435	368973	379	187	29209	25647	367
1980	53385		799568	501380	298188	420	209	27652	23461	444
1981	58619		703659	449638	254021	476	252	28011	23387	1284
1982	64067		791518	526106	265412	568	309	33037	27374	679
1983	69117		842198	489887	352311	630	370	35695	28872	1256
1984	70992		784473	458804	325669	652	369	33260	26301	1899
1985	62763		790505	471268	319237	832	414	33298	25759	2424
1986	62874		812102	428545	383557	940	655	43302	30920	5159
1987	58577		781957	396082	385875	1235	862	46120	32588	5478
1988	54723		811945	402035	409910	1400	1020	56125	35067	6734
1989	52713		846598	407317	439281	1565	1136	58563	38270	7109
1990	48760	1559	870782	410875	459907	1592	1188	62191	40130	6906
1991	44121	1396	930377	420919	509458	1806	1336	68844	44702	5924
1992	32259	1068	981698	448586	533112	1889	1419	67983	45492	5845
1993	18688	783	982084	404352	577732	2185	1647	76562	49470	4990
1994	14219	863	1089793	434904	654889	2334	1730	85448	57920	5521
1995	12207	1593	1250597	469355	781242	2501	1881	97572	68649	5431
1996	12945	1806	1407080	490161	916919	2418	1851	116058	83404	5862
1997	12675	2391	1772892	619114	1153778	2608	1863	128992	99300	6295
1998	10522	2159	2217247	776851	1440396	2291	1742	153513	123874	4738
1999	6811	1508	2573310	900285	1673025	2228	1667	159889	130494	4742
2000	5550	1675	2894126	967056	1927070	2362	1784	179032	149648	4367
2001	4618	1851	3255780	1079397	2176383	2226	1683	198423	168353	4441
2002	2919	1931	3075523	927477	2148046	1962	1557	188774	165344	4052
2003	1727	1789	2525252	742101	1783151	1652	1282	154615	135344	3597
2004	1024	1936	2444990	785289	1659701	1396	1048	146184	128286	3435
2005	827	998	2487962	214120	2273842	1314	1072	171737	159169	1355
2006	82	242	530959	110396	420563	485	312	34891	30199	371
2007	399	415	292234	88648	203586	525	341	20257	14862	361
2008	55		454117	195016	259101	758	574	24052	17946	106
2009	94		464727	183904	280823	767	576	25457	19095	515
2010	224	60	511356	174933	336423	761	591	28830	22339	386

3-19 历年水产品产量及养殖面积

Output and Cultured Area of Aquatic Products over Years

年份	水产品产量(吨)	海水产量	海水捕捞	海水养殖	淡水产量	淡水捕捞	淡水养殖	养殖面积(亩)	海水养殖	淡水养殖
1949	3175	1475	1475		1700		1700	27390		27390
1952	3365	1565	1565		1800		1800	26167		26167
1957	4185	2410	2410		1775		1775	36016		36016
1962	6321	3521	3521		2800		2800	100822		100822
1965	9946	5693	5693		4253		4253	93502		93502
1970	16214	10878	10878		5336		5336	72176		72176
1975	21879	15026	15026		6853		6853	83398		83398
1978	30900	23307	23307		7593		7593	89040		89040
1979	22309	13878	13878		8431		8431	94916		94916
1980	25471	17069	17069		8402		8402	95549		95549
1981	24905	15669	15669		9236		9236	104069		104069
1982	27695	16120	16120		11575		11575	112586		112586
1983	30292	17330	17330		12962		12962	116943		116943
1984	32465	18025	18025		14440		14440	119456		119456
1985	32641	15422	15214	208	17219		17219	131350	5301	126049
1986	46534	28439	25918	2521	18095		18095	138651	16078	122573
1987	65679	45214	42793	2421	20465		20465	163225	15036	148189
1988	68087	44111	42926	1185	23976	182	23794	137966	9670	128296
1989	62306	37189	35372	1817	25117	1194	23923	123090	10350	112740
1990	68508	41002	38423	2579	27506	2177	25329	136174	19286	116888
1991	69025	39906	37209	2697	29119	2147	26972	131849	18446	113403
1992	73164	42429	38033	4396	30735	2590	28145	134558	20400	114158
1993	64973	33745	28192	5553	31228	3120	28108	143696	25855	117841
1994	67420	31284	24059	7225	36136	2565	33571	144869	26583	118286
1995	74778	32132	24637	7495	42646	2084	40562	162609	27795	134814
1996	81067	33363	25471	7892	47704	1940	45764	172656	27791	144865
1997	91901	35407	26704	8703	56494	5157	51337	184889	30326	154563
1998	96872	33618	24319	9299	63254	3146	60108	192381	29223	163158
1999	94023	31332	24257	7075	62691	2747	59944	167880	19440	148440
2000	95076	33234	24180	9054	61842	3135	58707	167841	25695	142146
2001	89599	30877	23726	7151	58722	2285	56437	155720	27928	127792
2002	82361	30800	23474	7326	51561	2762	48799	142167	26696	115471
2003	75756	30151	22826	7325	45605	2121	43484	126660	27097	99563
2004	71526	29289	22382	6907	42237	3078	39159	125116	25652	99464
2005	67381	28319	21622	6697	39062	1783	37279	102023	23530	78493
2006	47059	21152	15256	5897	25907	1062	24845	71745	6345	65400
2007	47292	21637	15992	5645	25655	857	24797	71100	5925	65175
2008	72282	21297	14322	6975	50985	512	50473	137718	17559	120159
2009	73323	19034	13205	5829	54289		54289	129136	4197	124939
2010	76268	19300	13257	6043	56968	1563	55405	132960	4147	128813

3-20 主要农产品产量与最高年份比较（2010年）

Output of Main Agricultural Products in Comparison with Peak Year (2010)

指标	单位	2010年	建国以来最高年份		
			年份	产量	2010年为最高年份的%
一、粮食总产量	**吨**	**12482**	**1977**	**563463**	**2.2**
#稻　谷	吨	8768	1973	548073	1.6
#早　稻	吨	3965	1983	279723	1.4
晚　稻	吨	4803	1984	279898	1.7
二、大　豆	**吨**		**1954**	**2790**	
三、经济作物					
#甘　蔗	吨	15952	1982	707764	2.3
#糖　蔗	吨	800	1982	699174	0.1
花　生	吨	115	1981	35506	0.3
四、其他作物					
#蔬　菜	吨	392904	2001	706775	55.6
五、水果总产量	**吨**	**75540**	**1987**	**363085**	**20.8**
#香(大)蕉	吨	60236	1987	222826	27.0
荔　枝	吨	8266	2002	45339	18.2
六、水产品	**吨**	**76268**	**1998**	**96872**	**78.7**
七、生猪年末存栏量	**头**	**174933**	**2001**	**1079397**	**16.2**
生猪年出栏头数	头	336423	2005	2273842	14.8
猪肉产量	吨	22339	2001	168353	13.3
八、三鸟饲养量	**万只**	**761**	**2000**	**2362**	**32.2**
三鸟出栏量	万只	591	2000	1784	33.1
禽蛋产量	吨	386	1989	7109	5.4

主要统计指标解释

Explanatory Notes on Main Statistical Indicators

耕地面积　指可以用来种植农作物、经常进行耕锄的田地，包括熟地、当年新开荒地、连续撂荒未满三年的耕地和当年的休闲地(轮歇地)，还包括以种植农作物为主并附带种植桑树、茶树、果树和其他林木的土地，以及沿海、沿湖地区已围垦利用的“海涂”、“湖田”等面积。不包括属于专业性的桑园、茶园、果园、果木苗圃、林地、芦苇地、天然或人工草地面积。

农作物播种面积　指实际播种或移植有农作物的面积。凡是实际种植有农作物的面积，不论种植在耕地上还是种植在非耕地上，均包括在农作物播种面积中。在播种季节基本结束后，因遭灾而重新改种和补种的农作物面积，也包括在内。

粮食产量　指全社会的产量。包括国有经济经营的、集体统一经营的和农民家庭经营的粮食产量，还包括工矿企业办的农场和其他生产单位的产量。粮食除包括稻谷、小麦、玉米、高粱、谷子及其他杂粮外，还包括薯类和豆类。其产量计算方法，豆类按去豆荚后的干豆计算；薯类(包括甘薯和马铃薯，不包括芋头和木薯)1963年以前按每4公斤鲜薯折1公斤粮食计算，从1964年开始改为按5公斤鲜薯折1公斤粮食计算。城市郊区作为蔬菜的薯类(如马铃薯等)按鲜品计算，并且不作粮食统计。其他粮食一律按脱粒后的原粮计算。

水产品产量　指人工养殖的水产品和天然生长的水产品的捕捞量。包括海水的鱼类、虾蟹类、贝类和藻类以及内陆水域的鱼类、虾蟹类和贝类，不包括淡水生植物。

猪、牛、羊肉产量　指当年出栏并已屠宰、除去头蹄下水后带骨肉(即胴体重)的重量。

期初(末)畜禽存栏头(只)数　指报告期初(末)农村各种合作经济组织和国营农场、农民个人、机关、团体、学校、工矿企业、部队等单位以及城镇居民饲养的大牲畜、猪、羊、家禽等畜禽的存栏数。

农林牧渔业总产值　指以货币表现的农、林、牧、渔业全部产品的总量，它反映一定时期内农业生产总规模和总成果。农业总产值的计算方法通常是按农林牧渔业产品及其副产品的产量分别乘以各自单位产品价格求得；少数生产周期较长，当年没有产品或产品产量不易统计的，则采用间接方法匡算其产值；然后将四业产品产值相加即为农业总产值。

农业机械总动力　指主要用于农、林、牧、渔业的各种动力机械的动力总和。包括耕作机械、排灌机械、收获机械、农用运输机械、植物保护机械、牧业机械、林业机械、渔业机械和其他农业机械〔内燃机按引擎马力折成瓦(特)计算、电动机按功率折成瓦(特)计算〕。不包括专门用于乡、镇、村、组办工业、基本建设、非农业运输、科学试验和教学等非农业生产方面用的动力机械与作业机械。

农民人均纯收入　**纯收入**指农村住户当年从各个来源得到的总收入相应地扣除所发生的费用后的收入总和。**“农民人均纯收入”**按人口平均的纯收入水平，反映的是一个地区农村居民的平均收入水平。计算方法：纯收入=总收入（包括现金形态和实物形态折算款）-家庭经营费用支出-税费支出-生产性固定资产折旧-赠送农村外部亲友支出

四、工 业

Industry

4-1 主要年份工业主要指标

Main Indicators of Industry in Main Years

指　　　标	单位	1998年	2000年	2001年	2005年	2009年	2010年
全市企业单位数	个	16406	16975	18094	21868	31160	38273
全市工业增加值	万元	2906904	4304525	5170314	11732288	17415347	20784479
规模以上工业:							
企业单位数	个	1500	1663	1680	4505	5801	5899
年末固定资产原值合计	万元	6257040	7288486	8259152	18560858	30799221	32162507
年末固定资产净值合计	万元	4392164	4701886	5354719	11052566	17239987	17836928
年末流动资产	万元	3798813	5298239	5629510	18732801	31652484	37888251
年末资产总额	万元	9267121	11225950	11730032	33453291	52861843	60017098
年末负债总额	万元	4752964	5630399	5796530	18580908	30434568	35252952
所有者权益	万元	4514157	5595551	5933502	14872383	22410155	24750103
工业增加值	万元	1687134	2594352	2906664	10624190	14533667	17083110
主营业务收入	万元	6399088	9889058	11312944	39121487	60077589	77081695
利税总额	万元	447544	841047	789734	1830988	4034721	4695854
#利润总额	万元	255715	503589	433640	1243516	2972487	3523632
全员劳动生产率(按增加值计算)	元/人	26688	36101	39438	53340	56766	60854
综合效益指数	%	94.1	114.0	109.5	119.9	127.2	130.3

注：1. 2005年以前数据根据东莞市第一次经济普查取得，2008年数据根据第二次经济普查取得，下同。
　　2. 规模以上工业企业1997年及以前年份为独立核算工业企业口径，1998-2005年为全部国有工业及年销售收入500万元以上非国有工业企业口径，2006年起为年主营业务收入500万元及以上工业企业口径，下同。

4-2 历年工业企业单位数（按经济成份分）

Number of Industrial Enterprises over Years (by Ownership)

单位：个

年份	全市工业企业单位数	国有	集体企业	港澳台投资企业	外商投资企业	其他类型企业
1949	1	1				
1952	3522	20	3			3499
1957	262	76	186			
1962	280	57	223			
1965	260	61	199			
1970	220	57	163			
1975	324	61	263			
1978	1290	64	1226			
1979	1250	63	1187			
1980	1293	64	1229			
1981	1479	64	1415			
1982	1862	66	1796			
1983	1964	68	1896			
1984	2329	69	2109			151
1985	4187	73	2990	79		1045
1986	5949	81	4263	89		1516
1987	8106	74	5123	175		2734
1988	8408	72	5424	241		2671
1989	8757	76	5835	323		2523
1990	9892	78	6165	521	4	3124
1991	10094	77	6404	754	4	2855
1992	11639	72	6400	932	4	4231
1993	12449	75	7129	1388	24	3833
1994	14086	45	7185	2002	191	4663
1995	15215	70	9345	2631	210	2959
1996	15326	40	8958	2128	253	3947
1997	16857	41	9949	2064	315	4488
1998	16406	29	8814	2050	461	5052
1999	16877	29	10325	2627	731	3165
2000	16975	23	10184	2717	893	3158
2001	18094	20	9978	3605	1186	3305
2002	21313	19	198	10830	907	9359
2003	21935	19	200	10969	958	9789
2004	22156	13	211	9450	1422	11060
2005	21868	10	220	10141	2093	9404
2006	22447	10	211	10271	2190	9765
2007	22587	16	151	10041	2528	9851
2008	26372	35	484	5122	2489	18242
2009	31160	26	313	5141	2439	23241
2010	38273	21	262	5417	2447	30126

注：本表2002年起集体企业不包括“三来一补”企业。

4-3 主要年份工业企业单位数（按不同类型分）

Number of Industrial Enterprises in Main Years (by Ownership)

单位：个

指标	1998年	2000年	2004年	2005年	2009年	2010年
全市企业单位数	**16406**	**16975**	**22156**	**21868**	**31160**	**38273**
轻工业	14389	14440	15270	12651	18618	20651
重工业	2017	2535	6886	9217	12542	17622
在总计中:						
(一)规模以上工业企业	1500	1663	4224	4505	5801	5899
按轻重工业分						
轻工业	1082	1124	2405	2569	3096	3183
重工业	418	539	1819	1936	2705	2716
按登记注册类型分						
国有	29	16	4	5	10	10
集体	204	248	162	162	156	151
私营	24	44	557	621	1101	1159
联营	5	6	4	2	4	5
股份合作	9	6		1	2	2
股份有限公司	6	3	19	18	20	20
外商投资	134	201	787	820	1309	1321
港澳台投资	1082	1119	2367	2481	2571	2564
其他	7	20	324	395	628	667
按企业规模分						
大型企业	16	28	40	39	78	84
中型企业	27	19	592	579	1156	1327
小型企业	1457	1616	3592	3887	4567	4488
(二)规模以下工业企业	14906	15312	20107	17363	25359	32374

4-4 历年工业增加值

Value-added of Industry over Years

年 份	工业增加值	
	绝对值 （万元）	增速 (%)
1986	105398	
1987	142357	25.8
1988	250456	51.4
1989	272185	6.4
1990	391840	30.6
1991	483441	21.8
1992	566316	13.7
1993	828934	38.5
1994	1107729	24.3
1995	1541922	35.3
1996	1878517	16.2
1997	2307863	20.1
1998	2906904	22.2
1999	3495304	20.7
2000	4304525	20.9
2001	5170314	22.0
2002	6218553	23.0
2003	7571849	21.4
2004	9680128	26.5
2005	11732288	20.2
2006	14416864	22.0
2007	16818293	15.0
2008	18192243	6.4
2009	17415347	-0.6
2010	20784479	17.5

注：本表工业增加值绝对值为当年价，增速按可比价计算。

4-5 规模以上工业企业单位数（2010年）

Number of Industrial Enterprises above Designated Size (2010)

单位：个

项目	工业单位数	按登记注册类型分		
		国有及国有控股工业	集体工业	港澳台及外商投资工业
总　计	**5899**	**27**	**151**	**3885**
按轻重工业分				
轻工业	3183	13	106	2052
重工业	2716	14	45	1833
按企业规模分				
大型企业	84	1		74
中型企业	1327	14	17	1088
小型企业	4488	12	134	2723
按工业行业分(大类)				
非金属矿采选业	1			
农副食品加工业	42	3	1	12
食品制造业	48			19
饮料制造业	12	2		8
纺织业	421		3	236
纺织服装、鞋、帽制造业	206	2	5	121
皮革、毛皮、羽绒及其制品业	321		12	255
木材加工及木、竹、藤、棕、草制品业	41			20
家具制造业	269		3	160
造纸及纸制品业	309		19	128
印刷业、记录媒介的复制	114		4	66
文教体育用品制造业	216	1	4	187
石油加工、炼焦及核燃料加工业	7			4
化学原料及化学制品制造业	220	2	2	124
医药制造业	11			5
化学纤维制造业	11			9
橡胶制品业	94			73
塑料制品业	677		17	486
非金属矿物制品业	132	1	2	68
黑色金属冶炼及压延加工业	32			22
有色金属冶炼及压延加工业	72			37
金属制品业	355		4	224
通用设备制造业	241	2	2	152
专用设备制造业	215	2	1	146
交通运输设备制造业	54	1		39
电气机械及器材制造业	583		15	400
通信设备、计算机及其他电子设备制造业	929	2	25	702
仪器仪表及文化、办公用机械制造业	104		2	88
工艺品及其他制造业	107		1	83
电力、热力的生产和供应业	14	6	1	9
燃气生产和供应业	5			2
水的生产和供应业	36	3	28	

4-6 规模以上工业增加值（2010年）

Value-added of Industrial Enterprises above Designated Size(2010)

单位：万元

项目	工业增加值	按登记注册类型分		
		国有及国有控股工业	集体工业	港澳台及外商投资工业
总计	**17083110**	**1168713**	**334288**	**13113781**
按轻重工业分				
轻工业	8243567	101671	239912	6201464
重工业	8839543	1067042	94376	6912317
按企业规模分				
大型企业	4193196	687247		3119222
中型企业	8326994	454842	140979	7044954
小型企业	4562920	26624	193309	2949605
按工业行业分(大类)				
非金属矿采选业	999			
农副食品加工业	305956	45906	625	191827
食品制造业	245923			212943
饮料制造业	210298	9937		199429
纺织业	843671		2127	583955
纺织服装、鞋、帽制造业	593384	7404	3091	230214
皮革、毛皮、羽绒及其制品业	1021419		58394	875784
木材加工及木、竹、藤、棕、草制品业	40291			23008
家具制造业	508839		943	342399
造纸及纸制品业	1016110		37337	740619
印刷业、记录媒介的复制	325386		2823	282112
文教体育用品制造业	537806	1109	5337	508497
石油加工、炼焦及核燃料加工业	10504			6708
化学原料及化学制品制造业	447806	1057	679	360071
医药制造业	38292			5005
化学纤维制造业	6582			4868
橡胶制品业	123513			112212
塑料制品业	1014967		25662	840343
非金属矿物制品业	380964	726	762	307727
黑色金属冶炼及压延加工业	47818			34866
有色金属冶炼及压延加工业	109400			63947
金属制品业	519465		1549	386535
通用设备制造业	414402	5844	2547	334852
专用设备制造业	395342	12670	953	326030
交通运输设备制造业	294508	57562		271386
电气机械及器材制造业	1604721		66675	1278761
通信设备、计算机及其他电子设备制造业	4172746	3920	68296	3648340
仪器仪表及文化、办公用机械制造业	469762		5422	419181
工艺品及其他制造业	182485		162	165592
电力、热力的生产和供应业	1067203	987898	455	321032
燃气生产和供应业	39096			35538
水的生产和供应业	93452	34680	50449	

4-7 规模以上工业企业主要财务指标（2010年）

Main Financial Indicators of Industrial Enterprises above Designated Size (2010)

单位：万元

指　　标	全市总计	按登记注册类型分			按轻重工业分	
		内资企业	港澳台商投资企业	外商投资企业	轻工业	重工业
一、企业单位数(个)	**5899**	**2014**	**2564**	**1321**	**3183**	**2716**
二、年末资产						
流动资产合计	37888251	8639244	17433247	11815760	18394181	19494070
#产成品存货	2926318	674538	1337256	914524	1433584	1492734
固定资产净值	17836928	5126809	8007994	4702125	7429971	10406957
年末资产总额	60017098	15241534	27156478	17619086	27853589	32163509
三、年末负债及所有者权益						
年末负债总额	35252952	10287332	15052899	9912721	16654046	18598906
所有者权益合计	24750103	4943965	12100846	7705292	11196238	13553865
四、损益及分配						
主营业务收入	77081695	19377279	32781458	24922958	33426207	43655488
#主营业务成本	68340953	17254395	28914992	22171566	29215519	39125434
主营业务税金及附加	90326	55267	19434	15625	41676	48650
主营业务利润	8650416	2067617	3847032	2735766	4169012	4481404
营业费用	1568429	446872	564399	557158	954955	613474
管理费用	3748145	775655	1725318	1247172	1794499	1953646
财务费用	260453	151666	82690	26097	121113	139340
#利息支出	264474	143172	78015	43287	113525	150949
利润总额	3523632	777697	1694286	1051649	1448498	2075134
#亏损企业亏损总额	291634	38434	140941	112259	174206	117428
利税总额	4695854	1304791	2064478	1326585	2004048	2691806

4-8 规模以上工业企业主要指标（2010年）

Main Indicators of Industrial Enterprises above Designated Size (2010)

单位：万元

项　　目	企业单位数(个)	#亏损企业	工业销售产值	工业增加值	全部职工平均人数(人)
总　计	**5899**	**954**	**77273008**	**17083110**	**2807246**
按轻重工业分					
轻工业	3183	527	33514672	8243567	1557722
重工业	2716	427	43758336	8839543	1249524
按企业规模分					
大型企业	84	2	21972776	4193196	428606
中型企业	1327	170	33455221	8326994	1465503
小型企业	4488	782	21845011	4562920	913137
按工业行业分(大类)					
非金属矿采选业	1		1463	999	39
农副食品加工业	42	6	2592848	305956	6370
食品制造业	48	6	787265	245923	17188
饮料制造业	12	1	1379614	210298	7057
纺织业	421	47	3439591	843671	181918
纺织服装、鞋、帽制造业	206	32	1848012	593384	124633
皮革、毛皮、羽绒及其制品业	321	58	2785051	1021419	329862
木材加工及木、竹、藤、棕、草制品业	41	7	157750	40291	7732
家具制造业	269	46	2111941	508839	108509
造纸及纸制品业	309	41	4563472	1016110	72427
印刷业、记录媒介的复制	114	17	917667	325386	41238
文教体育用品制造业	216	51	1779699	537806	171992
石油加工、炼焦及核燃料加工业	7		179347	10504	681
化学原料及化学制品制造业	220	28	2256916	447806	34006
医药制造业	11	2	93274	38292	2311
化学纤维制造业	11		38677	6582	1302
橡胶制品业	94	19	455539	123513	28820
塑料制品业	677	112	3927261	1014967	220647
非金属矿物制品业	132	25	1301951	380964	31731
黑色金属冶炼及压延加工业	32	5	420893	47818	2978
有色金属冶炼及压延加工业	72	9	983574	109400	13302
金属制品业	355	58	2352838	519465	99624
通用设备制造业	241	29	2159412	414402	60596
专用设备制造业	215	24	1295094	395342	64869
交通运输设备制造业	54	7	1113662	294508	21652
电气机械及器材制造业	583	94	7237323	1604721	270600
通信设备、计算机及其他电子设备制造业	929	172	22360244	4172746	745639
仪器仪表及文化、办公用机械制造业	104	23	2675851	469762	83267
工艺品及其他制造业	107	23	887857	182485	30487
电力、热力的生产和供应业	14		4721445	1067203	20479
燃气生产和供应业	5		212848	39096	605
水的生产和供应业	36	12	234629	93452	4685

4-8　续表 1

(2010年)

单位：万元

项　　　目	年末资产合计	#流动资产年合计	#产成品	固定资产净值	年末负债合计
总　　计	**60017098**	**37888251**	**2926318**	**17836928**	**35252952**
按轻重工业分					
轻工业	27853589	18394181	1433584	7429971	16654046
重工业	32163509	19494070	1492734	10406957	18598906
按企业规模分					
大型企业	15398710	8001302	618998	6082289	8834441
中型企业	26670501	16968327	1343461	7707741	14787863
小型企业	17947887	12918622	963859	4046898	11630648
按工业行业分(大类)					
非金属矿采选业	2862	1311		1325	207
农副食品加工业	1823136	1489938	85841	225415	1473006
食品制造业	800876	516062	33907	229420	328237
饮料制造业	901178	498817	35417	335591	559646
纺织业	2885857	2047177	160068	698571	1768456
纺织服装、鞋、帽制造业	1403520	1145107	97782	200518	737444
皮革、毛皮、羽绒及其制品业	1739764	1339280	116871	303557	1182030
木材加工及木、竹、藤、棕、草制品业	168078	125297	12063	36789	116621
家具制造业	1648569	1188108	126673	370936	957451
造纸及纸制品业	4838329	2256655	225768	1931691	2752300
印刷业、记录媒介的复制	957819	650408	40858	255621	424281
文教体育用品制造业	1402863	1005451	84952	339599	828408
石油加工、炼焦及核燃料加工业	98925	85226	1813	10273	74380
化学原料及化学制品制造业	1906332	1420917	103386	341006	1125284
医药制造业	211022	162230	3772	22015	36270
化学纤维制造业	30607	23539	2103	5391	15555
橡胶制品业	364114	263279	34375	87445	225507
塑料制品业	3394534	2336691	235121	874092	1951614
非金属矿物制品业	1579901	819790	75936	645934	782636
黑色金属冶炼及压延加工业	315675	274696	22357	31380	227964
有色金属冶炼及压延加工业	600251	501992	55857	84047	386130
金属制品业	1945534	1383714	97282	468337	1121100
通用设备制造业	1660446	1212932	99166	356315	1000300
专用设备制造业	1376419	905620	54744	395811	724215
交通运输设备制造业	1001106	642477	33654	271588	526550
电气机械及器材制造业	5032351	3549306	339668	1021642	2831982
通信设备、计算机及其他电子设备制造业	13653323	9241215	634692	3697740	8259976
仪器仪表及文化、办公用机械制造业	1577056	1113198	61383	373439	1002025
工艺品及其他制造业	652112	471243	35616	141480	402096
电力、热力的生产和供应业	4925716	865128	13934	3511317	2661732
燃气生产和供应业	163048	48846	39	68749	87604
水的生产和供应业	955775	302601	1220	499894	681945

4-8 续表 2

(2010年)

单位：万元

项　　目	主营业务收入	#主营业务税金及附加	成本费用总额	本年应交增值税	亏损企业亏损总额
总　计	**77081695**	**90326**	**73917980**	**1081896**	**291634**
按轻重工业分					
轻工业	33426207	41676	32086085	513874	174206
重工业	43655488	48650	41831895	568022	117428
按企业规模分					
大型企业	21965868	24113	21051577	307847	8461
中型企业	33343209	30681	31768811	459969	111914
小型企业	21772618	35532	21097592	314080	171259
按工业行业分(大类)					
非金属矿采选业	1273	19	741	72	
农副食品加工业	2578388	1622	2490626	19225	21863
食品制造业	786170	1074	698270	39211	2695
饮料制造业	1376443	7447	1301547	49292	620
纺织业	3434533	3381	3369704	60317	15046
纺织服装、鞋、帽制造业	1844028	4193	1731943	50389	6843
皮革、毛皮、羽绒及其制品业	2766985	2293	2697814	25076	13373
木材加工及木、竹、藤、棕、草制品业	158045	580	154023	3167	1601
家具制造业	2111985	2655	2069555	21899	7458
造纸及纸制品业	4548795	5540	4254265	82788	6845
印刷业、记录媒介的复制	916385	758	826945	21300	5897
文教体育用品制造业	1773103	1049	1747825	8938	18857
石油加工、炼焦及核燃料加工业	175583	222	170542	1996	
化学原料及化学制品制造业	2262441	2029	2150968	46705	10991
医药制造业	93052	607	77480	8039	463
化学纤维制造业	39031	31	37596	819	
橡胶制品业	454422	675	448126	5757	4858
塑料制品业	3920708	4295	3796073	49310	27325
非金属矿物制品业	1302568	1557	1163367	43836	5327
黑色金属冶炼及压延加工业	419197	178	401647	2646	678
有色金属冶炼及压延加工业	983795	827	944858	7392	1035
金属制品业	2340872	2022	2273741	35646	8152
通用设备制造业	2151277	2067	2076104	30481	3200
专用设备制造业	1281098	1201	1210422	27767	5371
交通运输设备制造业	1111907	796	1007330	21059	554
电气机械及器材制造业	7202808	4966	6866007	62300	19335
通信设备、计算机及其他电子设备制造业	22324769	18692	21664717	138080	79749
仪器仪表及文化、办公用机械制造业	2671493	1375	2574071	10747	2836
工艺品及其他制造业	885285	532	832125	6715	8953
电力、热力的生产和供应业	4719022	14977	4467238	189206	
燃气生产和供应业	212468	299	178274	1106	
水的生产和供应业	233766	2367	234036	10615	11709

4-8　续表 3

(2010年)

项　　目	利　税 总　额 (万元)	人　均 税　收 (元)	利　润 总　额 (万元)	人　均 利　润 (元)
总　　计	**4695854**	**4176**	**3523632**	**12552**
按轻重工业分				
轻工业	2004048	3566	1448498	9299
重工业	2691806	4935	2075134	16607
按企业规模分				
大型企业	1294462	7745	962501	22457
中型企业	2243528	3348	1752879	11961
小型企业	1157864	3829	808252	8851
按工业行业分(大类)				
非金属矿采选业	675	23359	584	149769
农副食品加工业	100770	32727	79923	125468
食品制造业	132490	23438	92206	53645
饮料制造业	132848	80401	76109	107849
纺织业	140715	3501	77017	4234
纺织服装、鞋、帽制造业	159493	4379	104911	8418
皮革、毛皮、羽绒及其制品业	89874	830	62505	1895
木材加工及木、竹、藤、棕、草制品业	9577	4845	5831	7541
家具制造业	78844	2263	54290	5003
造纸及纸制品业	406012	12195	317685	43863
印刷业、记录媒介的复制	120235	5349	98177	23807
文教体育用品制造业	41694	581	31707	1844
石油加工、炼焦及核燃料加工业	8984	32570	6766	99349
化学原料及化学制品制造业	168799	14331	120066	35307
医药制造业	24686	37413	16039	69405
化学纤维制造业	2468	6525	1619	12434
橡胶制品业	12168	2232	5736	1990
塑料制品业	200398	2429	146794	6653
非金属矿物制品业	195044	14306	149651	47162
黑色金属冶炼及压延加工业	24137	9485	21312	71565
有色金属冶炼及压延加工业	52465	6179	44247	33263
金属制品业	122884	3781	85217	8554
通用设备制造业	130058	5371	97509	16092
专用设备制造业	104591	4466	75623	11658
交通运输设备制造业	139911	10094	118056	54524
电气机械及器材制造业	451713	2486	384447	14207
通信设备、计算机及其他电子设备制造业	885478	2103	728706	9773
仪器仪表及文化、办公用机械制造业	124542	1456	112420	13501
工艺品及其他制造业	63014	2377	55767	18292
电力、热力的生产和供应业	523651	99704	319468	155998
燃气生产和供应业	34694	23220	33290	550240
水的生产和供应业	12942	27723	-46	-98

4-9 规模以上工业企业主要经济效益指标（2010年）

Main Indicators on Economic Benefit of Industrial Enterprises above Designated Size (2010)

项目	工业增加值率 (%)	总资产贡献率 (%)	资产负债率 (%)	流动资产周转率 (次/年)	成本费用利润率 (%)	全员劳动生产率 (元/人)	产品销售率 (%)
总计	**22.1**	**8.3**	**58.7**	**2.0**	**4.8**	**60854**	**99.9**
按轻重工业分							
轻工业	24.6	7.6	59.8	1.8	4.5	52921	100.0
重工业	20.2	8.8	57.8	2.2	5.0	70743	99.7
按企业规模分							
大型企业	19.2	8.9	57.4	2.7	4.6	97833	100.8
中型企业	25.0	8.8	55.5	2.0	5.5	56820	100.5
小型企业	20.5	7.0	64.8	1.7	3.8	49970	98.0
按工业行业分(大类)							
非金属矿采选业	68.3	23.6	7.2	1.0	78.8	256103	100.0
农副食品加工业	12.3	5.9	80.8	1.7	3.2	480307	104.0
食品制造业	31.7	16.8	41.0	1.5	13.2	143078	101.5
饮料制造业	14.8	15.6	62.1	2.8	5.9	297999	97.3
纺织业	24.1	5.2	61.3	1.7	2.3	46376	98.2
纺织服装、鞋、帽制造业	31.4	11.7	52.5	1.6	6.1	47611	97.8
皮革、毛皮、羽绒及其制品业	37.1	5.2	67.9	2.1	2.3	30965	101.1
木材加工及木、竹、藤、棕、草制品业	25.2	6.7	69.4	1.3	3.8	52110	98.8
家具制造业	24.2	5.1	58.1	1.8	2.6	46894	100.6
造纸及纸制品业	22.3	9.2	56.9	2.0	7.5	140294	100.3
印刷业、记录媒介的复制	35.6	12.7	44.3	1.4	11.9	78904	100.3
文教体育用品制造业	30.1	3.2	59.1	1.8	1.8	31269	99.8
石油加工、炼焦及核燃料加工业	5.7	10.1	75.2	2.1	4.0	154250	97.7
化学原料及化学制品制造业	19.6	9.2	59.0	1.6	5.6	131684	98.8
医药制造业	40.3	10.9	17.2	0.6	20.7	165693	98.1
化学纤维制造业	16.4	8.4	50.8	1.7	4.3	50556	96.3
橡胶制品业	27.0	3.4	61.9	1.7	1.3	42857	99.6
塑料制品业	25.6	6.1	57.5	1.7	3.9	46000	99.0
非金属矿物制品业	28.7	13.0	49.5	1.6	12.9	120060	98.0
黑色金属冶炼及压延加工业	11.3	8.6	72.2	1.5	5.3	160569	99.7
有色金属冶炼及压延加工业	11.0	9.7	64.3	2.0	4.7	82243	99.0
金属制品业	22.0	6.6	57.6	1.7	3.8	52143	99.5
通用设备制造业	19.1	8.2	60.2	1.8	4.7	68388	99.6
专用设备制造业	30.4	7.8	52.6	1.4	6.3	60945	99.5
交通运输设备制造业	26.7	14.3	52.6	1.7	11.7	136019	100.8
电气机械及器材制造业	22.0	9.3	56.3	2.0	5.6	59302	99.1
通信设备、计算机及其他电子设备制造业	18.7	6.7	60.5	2.4	3.4	55962	100.4
仪器仪表及文化、办公用机械制造业	17.9	8.0	63.5	2.4	4.4	56416	101.8
工艺品及其他制造业	19.8	10.0	61.7	1.9	6.7	59857	96.4
电力、热力的生产和供应业	22.5	12.1	54.0	5.5	7.2	521121	99.4
燃气生产和供应业	18.3	22.1	53.7	4.3	18.7	646218	99.8
水的生产和供应业	38.0	3.5	71.4	0.8		199474	95.4

4-10 国有及国有控股工业企业主要经济指标（2010年）

Main Indicators of State-owned and State-holding Industrial Enterprises (2010)

项目	企业单位数（个）	#亏损企业	工业增加值（万元）	主营业务收入（万元）	亏损企业亏损总额（万元）
总计	**27**	**4**	**1168713**	**5626897**	**9456**
按轻重工业分					
轻工业	13	2	101671	820480	8782
重工业	14	2	1067042	4806417	674
按企业规模分					
按大中小型企业分					
大型企业	1		687247	3397620	
中型企业	14	1	454842	1799492	429
小型企业	12	3	26624	429785	9027
按销售收入分					
10亿元以上	8		1113916	5290858	
5-10亿元	2		40104	128921	
1-5亿元	5	1	-4851	142630	8254
1亿元以下	12	3	19544	64488	1202
按工业行业分(大类)					
#非金属矿采选业					
农副食品加工业	3		45906	666460	
纺织服装、鞋、帽制造业	2		7404	14307	
木材加工及木、竹、藤、棕、草制品业					
造纸及纸制品业					
通用设备制造业	2		5844	83505	
通信设备、计算机及其他电子设备制造业	2	1	3920	15189	429
电力、热力的生产和供应业	6		987898	4416504	

4-10 续表 1

(2010年)

项　　目	利税总额(万元)	人均税收(元)	利润总额(万元)	人均利润(元)
总　　计	**551733**	**84390**	**328565**	**124244**
按轻重工业分				
轻工业	42957	49533	22549	54731
重工业	508776	90822	306016	137073
按企业规模分				
按大中小型企业分				
大型企业	242087	90672	100340	64184
中型企业	296652	83534	223167	253685
小型企业	12994	39386	5058	25101
按销售收入分				
10亿元以上	533869	105467	323020	161575
5-10亿元	6765	54931	1893	21342
1-5亿元	4726	17861	403	1666
1亿元以下	6373	9932	3249	10326
按工业行业分(大类)				
#非金属矿采选业				
农副食品加工业	33124	132610	21865	257541
纺织服装、鞋、帽制造业	1363	6889	597	5359
木材加工及木、竹、藤、棕、草制品业				
造纸及纸制品业				
通用设备制造业	1609	18574	642	12317
通信设备、计算机及其他电子设备制造业	156	1538	36	460
电力、热力的生产和供应业	478695	106703	279075	149174

4-11 国有及国有控股工业企业主要经济效益指标（2010年）

Main Indicators on Economic Benefit of State-owned and State-holding Industrial Enterprises (2010)

项目	工业增加值率(%)	总资产贡献率(%)	资产负债率(%)	流动资产周转率(次/年)	成本费用利润率(%)	全员劳动生产率(元/人)	产品销售率(%)
总计	**20.7**	**11.5**	**55.9**	**4.8**	**6.2**	**441941**	**99.7**
按轻重工业分							
轻工业	12.4	7.1	74.1	2.5	2.8	246773	100.1
重工业	22.1	12.2	52.9	5.7	6.8	477958	99.7
按企业规模分							
大型企业	20.2	8.7	59.9	17.2	3.1	439613	100.0
中型企业	24.9	17.8	45.1	2.2	13.9	517043	98.7
小型企业	6.3	5.0	76.2	2.8	1.2	132129	102.2
按工业行业分(大类)							
非金属矿采选业							
农副食品加工业	6.9	10.9	71.9	3.0	3.4	540709	101.0
食品制造业							
饮料制造业	30.2	23.8	72.1	1.9	24.1	223308	113.1
纺织业							
纺织服装、鞋、帽制造业	49.9	8.1	29.8	1.3	4.4	66522	96.5
皮革、毛皮、羽绒及其制品业							
木材加工及木、竹、藤、棕、草制品业							
家具制造业							
造纸及纸制品业							
印刷业、记录媒介的复制							
文教体育用品制造业	24.3	6.7	9.8	2.2	0.3	54881	102.6
石油加工、炼焦及核燃料加工业							
化学原料及化学制品制造业	24.0	12.9	68.3	2.5	2.5	150929	89.5
医药制造业							
化学纤维制造业							
橡胶制品业							
塑料制品业							
非金属矿物制品业	14.2	15.0	76.4	1.5	-3.9	33925	100.1
黑色金属冶炼及压延加工业							
有色金属冶炼及压延加工业							
金属制品业							
通用设备制造业	7.1	5.5	57.3	3.9	0.8	112167	101.8
专用设备制造业	30.2	7.2	54.5	1.1	8.4	90307	100.0
交通运输设备制造业	22.9	8.1	66.5	1.5	10.2	595884	99.8
电气机械及器材制造业							
通信设备、计算机及其他电子设备制造业	25.1	1.8	64.3	0.5	0.2	50192	97.2
仪器仪表及文化、办公用机械制造业							
工艺品及其他制造业							
电力、热力的生产和供应业	22.3	12.6	51.8	7.3	6.7	528062	99.6
燃气生产和供应业							
水的生产和供应业	35.4	2.6	80.6	1.5	-7.8	295650	90.1

4-12 规模以上集体工业主要经济指标（2010年）

Main Indicators of Collective-owned Industrial Enterprises above Designated Size (2010)

项目	企业单位数（个）	#亏损企业	工业增加值（万元）	主营业务收入（万元）	亏损企业亏损总额（万元）
总计	**151**	**34**	**334288**	**835782**	**7557**
按轻重工业分					
轻工业	106	24	239912	637158	5787
重工业	45	10	94376	198624	1770
按企业规模分					
按大中小型企业分					
大型企业					
中型企业	17	2	140979	323816	1034
小型企业	134	32	193309	511966	6523
按销售收入分					
10亿元以上	1		12734	108804	
5-10亿元	1		3846	50841	
1-5亿元	16		169034	312645	
1亿元以下	133	34	148674	363492	7557
按工业行业分(大类)					
非金属矿采选业					
农副食品加工业	1		625	2541	
食品制造业					
饮料制造业					
纺织业	3		2127	6525	
纺织服装、鞋、帽制造业	5		3091	8993	
皮革、毛皮、羽绒及其制品业	12	3	58394	74979	48
木材加工及木、竹、藤、棕、草制品业					
家具制造业	3	1	943	3462	34
造纸及纸制品业	19	2	37337	215143	55
印刷业、记录媒介的复制	4		2823	7218	
文教体育用品制造业	4	1	5337	7402	600
石油加工、炼焦及核燃料加工业					
化学原料及化学制品制造业	2		679	3259	
医药制造业					
化学纤维制造业					
橡胶制品业					
塑料制品业	17	3	25662	103045	585
非金属矿物制品业	2		762	4677	
黑色金属冶炼及压延加工业					
有色金属冶炼及压延加工业					
金属制品业	4	2	1549	6907	322
通用设备制造业	2	1	2547	13285	3
专用设备制造业	1		953	3228	
交通运输设备制造业					
电气机械及器材制造业	15	2	66675	123499	753
通信设备、计算机及其他电子设备制造业	25	9	68296	118299	2139
仪器仪表及文化、办公用机械制造业	2		5422	8694	
工艺品及其他制造业	1		162	720	
电力、热力的生产和供应业	1		455	3103	
燃气生产和供应业					
水的生产和供应业	28	10	50449	120803	3018

4-12　续表 1

(2010年)

项　　　目	利税总额(万元)	人均税收(元)	利润总额(万元)	人均利润(元)
总　　计	**89691**	**1349**	**75333**	**7079**
按轻重工业分				
轻工业	79723	2099	66305	10371
重工业	9968	221	9028	2125
按企业规模分				
按大中小型企业分				
大型企业				
中型企业	17457	858	13057	2547
小型企业	72234	1805	62276	11290
按销售收入分				
10亿元以上	5858	23341	2543	17909
5-10亿元	532		532	5092
1-5亿元	46637	532	44262	9911
1亿元以下	36664	1462	27996	4721
按工业行业分(大类)				
非金属矿采选业				
农副食品加工业	143	6978	78	8409
食品制造业				
饮料制造业				
纺织业	2758	304	2701	14490
纺织服装、鞋、帽制造业	599	1307	389	2419
皮革、毛皮、羽绒及其制品业	4228	57	4059	1363
木材加工及木、竹、藤、棕、草制品业				
家具制造业	268	649	228	3715
造纸及纸制品业	16267	12237	10630	23079
印刷业、记录媒介的复制	894	1678	797	13892
文教体育用品制造业	119	119	71	178
石油加工、炼焦及核燃料加工业				
化学原料及化学制品制造业	555	2738	455	12395
医药制造业				
化学纤维制造业				
橡胶制品业				
塑料制品业	10199	468	9809	11769
非金属矿物制品业	178	1969	152	11898
黑色金属冶炼及压延加工业				
有色金属冶炼及压延加工业				
金属制品业	67	872	-43	-341
通用设备制造业	634	3769	361	4970
专用设备制造业	282	140	276	6352
交通运输设备制造业				
电气机械及器材制造业	34578	382	34072	25715
通信设备、计算机及其他电子设备制造业	4390	148	3895	1165
仪器仪表及文化、办公用机械制造业	911	989	705	3389
工艺品及其他制造业	8	395		
电力、热力的生产和供应业	418	55500	396	989750
燃气生产和供应业				
水的生产和供应业	12195	19067	6302	20380

4-13 规模以上集体工业企业主要经济效益指标（2010年）

Main Indicators on Economic Benefit of Collective-owned Industrial Enterprises above Designated Size (2010)

项目	工业增加值率 (%)	总资产贡献率 (%)	资产负债率 (%)	流动资产周转率 (次/年)	成本费用利润率 (%)	全员劳动生产率 (元/人)	产品销售率 (%)
总计	**38.8**	**10.6**	**66.3**	**2.1**	**9.7**	**31412**	**97.4**
按轻重工业分							
轻工业	36.8	11.2	63.2	1.8	11.4	37526	97.9
重工业	45.1	7.3	82.8	4.0	4.7	22212	95.8
按企业规模分							
大型企业							
中型企业	42.9	8.9	72.7	3.4	4.1	27503	99.0
小型企业	36.3	11.0	64.5	1.7	13.6	35044	96.4
按工业行业分(大类)							
非金属矿采选业							
农副食品加工业	21.3	9.9	33.2	2.6	3.1	67204	86.5
食品制造业							
饮料制造业							
纺织业	26.9	14.2	11.2	3.5	69.2	11410	82.6
纺织服装、鞋、帽制造业	31.1	8.5	76.7	1.4	4.5	19225	90.6
皮革、毛皮、羽绒及其制品业	73.9	17.7	47.9	4.6	5.4	19612	94.9
木材加工及木、竹、藤、棕、草制品业							
家具制造业	23.6	5.6	69.1	1.2	6.8	15385	86.5
造纸及纸制品业	17.2	11.8	58.1	2.6	5.2	81062	99.7
印刷业、记录媒介的复制	32.8	7.8	66.6	1.2	11.5	49181	84.2
文教体育用品制造业	62.7	3.9	105.0	4.1	0.8	13392	86.9
石油加工、炼焦及核燃料加工业							
化学原料及化学制品制造业	17.5	8.7	78.4	1.0	16.5	18493	84.1
医药制造业							
化学纤维制造业							
橡胶制品业							
塑料制品业	24.5	30.3	52.8	8.9	10.3	30792	98.2
非金属矿物制品业	16.2	3.4	45.6	1.5	3.4	59539	99.1
黑色金属冶炼及压延加工业							
有色金属冶炼及压延加工业							
金属制品业	19.6	1.0	73.5	1.4	-0.6	12380	87.3
通用设备制造业	15.8	12.9	76.4	2.6	2.8	35083	90.9
专用设备制造业	29.5	13.9	91.8	6.3	8.6	21908	100.0
交通运输设备制造业							
电气机械及器材制造业	53.3	103.3	46.1	12.0	36.5	50320	99.0
通信设备、计算机及其他电子设备制造业	55.4	5.7	92.1	5.5	3.4	20425	96.0
仪器仪表及文化、办公用机械制造业	60.0	14.2	102.1	2.3	8.8	26067	96.2
工艺品及其他制造业	22.5	4.9	23.2	11.4		8105	100.0
电力、热力的生产和供应业	14.7	3.5	101.3	0.7	14.6	1136250	100.0
燃气生产和供应业							
水的生产和供应业	41.3	3.8	67.5	0.6	5.5	163163	99.5

4-14 规模以上外商投资工业企业主要经济指标（2010年）

Main Indicators of Industrial Enterprises above Designated Size with Foreign Funds (2010)

项目	企业单位数（个）	#亏损企业	工业增加值（万元）	主营业务收入（万元）	亏损企业亏损总额（万元）
总计	**1321**	**248**	**5199602**	**24922958**	**112259**
按轻重工业分					
轻工业	610	128	2071098	8556705	61988
重工业	711	120	3128504	16366253	50271
按企业规模分					
按大中小型企业分					
大型企业	46	2	1730536	9434142	8461
中型企业	390	57	2230465	9550725	46555
小型企业	885	189	1238601	5938091	57243
按销售收入分					
10亿元以上	42	3	1918170	11467848	21635
5-10亿元	45	3	741670	3137867	5330
1-5亿元	319	34	1573595	6724552	42922
1亿元以下	915	208	966167	3592691	42372
按工业行业分(大类)					
非金属矿采选业					
农副食品加工业	8	3	156203	835529	21558
食品制造业	5	1	171234	488695	354
饮料制造业	2		100061	329527	
纺织业	47	6	142592	519038	451
纺织服装、鞋、帽制造业	14	3	20938	65033	1204
皮革、毛皮、羽绒及其制品业	87	14	262750	883667	2880
木材加工及木、竹、藤、棕、草制品业	8	4	5649	18278	881
家具制造业	62	11	134997	666366	1620
造纸及纸制品业	26	4	184256	788360	507
印刷业、记录媒介的复制	18	4	84726	213919	597
文教体育用品制造业	55	17	146135	449146	4539
石油加工、炼焦及核燃料加工业					
化学原料及化学制品制造业	47	7	193513	932068	7519
医药制造业					
化学纤维制造业	3		1826	11362	
橡胶制品业	29	9	61156	208136	2687
塑料制品业	157	33	334255	1263356	12558
非金属矿物制品业	22	6	54203	180338	1988
黑色金属冶炼及压延加工业	12	2	12526	152732	560
有色金属冶炼及压延加工业	16	3	24831	296273	534
金属制品业	67	11	116604	633485	1910
通用设备制造业	48	3	123626	584540	99
专用设备制造业	51	5	171247	556158	3853
交通运输设备制造业	22	4	151529	551669	88
电气机械及器材制造业	147	29	419724	2417492	8746
通信设备、计算机及其他电子设备制造业	300	57	1826963	10351331	35311
仪器仪表及文化、办公用机械制造业	36	6	190848	1055675	604
工艺品及其他制造业	27	6	43716	183547	1211
电力、热力的生产和供应业	3		27956	94349	
燃气生产和供应业	2		35538	192889	
水的生产和供应业					

4-14 续表 1

(2010年)

项　　目	利税总额(万元)	人均税收(元)	利润总额(万元)	人均利润(元)
总　计	**1326585**	**3501**	**1051649**	**13392**
按轻重工业分				
轻工业	514381	4468	363704	10785
重工业	812204	2773	687945	15354
按企业规模分				
按大中小型企业分				
大型企业	510212	3656	435806	21415
中型企业	523046	3265	396544	10233
小型企业	293327	3810	219299	11287
按销售收入分				
10亿元以上	653986	7376	541133	35369
5-10亿元	225606	4904	177777	18227
1-5亿元	301529	2297	235643	8214
1亿元以下	145464	1951	97096	3917
按工业行业分(大类)				
非金属矿采选业				
农副食品加工业	-1420	19469	-4128	-29676
食品制造业	101987	37660	73328	96357
饮料制造业	80922	159412	49135	246415
纺织业	24543	2769	17681	7136
纺织服装、鞋、帽制造业	1968	1240	1246	2139
皮革、毛皮、羽绒及其制品业	33870	875	27308	3642
木材加工及木、竹、藤、棕、草制品业	84	4553	-394	-3752
家具制造业	21307	1119	17815	5706
造纸及纸制品业	58199	20384	39809	44124
印刷业、记录媒介的复制	46866	4622	43083	52629
文教体育用品制造业	12506	608	9813	2217
石油加工、炼焦及核燃料加工业				
化学原料及化学制品制造业	58005	21074	34324	30546
医药制造业				
化学纤维制造业	656	6586	347	7403
橡胶制品业	3644	864	2348	1565
塑料制品业	57765	1405	47565	6550
非金属矿物制品业	15853	5397	12782	22460
黑色金属冶炼及压延加工业	3055	13314	1794	18945
有色金属冶炼及压延加工业	10808	7777	8292	25633
金属制品业	28454	3372	22371	12398
通用设备制造业	51263	4243	43467	23658
专用设备制造业	39656	3092	30965	11017
交通运输设备制造业	88533	17651	71766	75551
电气机械及器材制造业	81797	3228	56477	7199
通信设备、计算机及其他电子设备制造业	383028	1940	329474	11936
仪器仪表及文化、办公用机械制造业	53827	1935	48303	16916
工艺品及其他制造业	13118	1095	12271	15858
电力、热力的生产和供应业	24252	33953	22598	464031
燃气生产和供应业	32039	4481	31809	629954
水的生产和供应业				

4-15 规模以上外商投资工业企业主要经济效益指标（2010年）

Main Indicators on Economic Benefit of Industrial Enterprises above Designated Size with Foreign Funds (2010)

项目	工业增加值率(%)	总资产贡献率(%)	资产负债率(%)	流动资产周转率(次/年)	成本费用利润率(%)	全员劳动生产率(元/人)	产品销售率(%)
总计	**20.8**	**7.8**	**56.3**	**2.1**	**4.4**	**66212**	**100.1**
按轻重工业分							
轻工业	24.1	7.4	57.9	1.8	4.4	61414	99.7
重工业	19.2	8.1	55.1	2.4	4.4	69823	100.4
按企业规模分							
大型企业	18.5	9.4	54.2	2.7	4.8	85035	100.9
中型企业	23.5	7.7	55.1	2.1	4.3	57560	100.7
小型企业	20.4	6.1	60.1	1.6	3.8	63751	98.1
按工业行业分(大类)							
非金属矿采选业							
农副食品加工业	18.0	0.3	79.8	1.7	-0.5	1122958	96.2
食品制造业	36.4	21.2	29.5	1.7	17.5	225012	104.1
饮料制造业	29.5	30.7	51.0	1.9	17.7	501809	98.2
纺织业	27.8	6.2	63.6	1.8	3.5	57553	101.8
纺织服装、鞋、帽制造业	31.0	4.7	76.7	2.1	2.0	35951	97.0
皮革、毛皮、羽绒及其制品业	29.6	6.1	64.8	1.9	3.2	35046	100.0
木材加工及木、竹、藤、棕、草制品业	28.1	1.5	74.3	0.5	-2.1	53753	90.4
家具制造业	20.8	4.0	59.4	1.6	2.7	43240	102.7
造纸及纸制品业	22.2	6.2	49.0	1.7	5.3	204229	96.6
印刷业、记录媒介的复制	40.5	20.3	27.6	1.3	24.8	103501	101.6
文教体育用品制造业	33.0	3.3	53.8	1.7	2.2	33008	101.5
石油加工、炼焦及核燃料加工业							
化学原料及化学制品制造业	20.7	6.8	65.1	1.4	3.8	172210	99.5
医药制造业							
化学纤维制造业	15.2	8.1	42.8	1.6	3.1	38930	94.1
橡胶制品业	29.8	2.1	66.0	1.8	1.1	40771	101.5
塑料制品业	26.2	5.4	60.7	1.8	3.9	46028	99.1
非金属矿物制品业	29.8	6.6	51.2	1.8	7.6	95243	99.3
黑色金属冶炼及压延加工业	8.2	3.6	70.7	1.6	1.2	132268	99.7
有色金属冶炼及压延加工业	8.4	7.2	57.6	2.4	2.9	76758	99.9
金属制品业	18.9	5.9	59.3	1.8	3.6	64625	103.0
通用设备制造业	21.2	9.5	54.8	1.5	7.8	67287	100.7
专用设备制造业	31.4	7.0	53.7	1.5	5.9	60927	102.6
交通运输设备制造业	27.8	21.5	39.7	2.0	14.9	159521	101.1
电气机械及器材制造业	17.0	6.0	53.1	2.4	2.4	53504	98.6
通信设备、计算机及其他电子设备制造业	17.8	7.0	55.9	2.7	3.3	66189	100.7
仪器仪表及文化、办公用机械制造业	17.9	9.0	57.3	2.8	4.8	66835	99.0
工艺品及其他制造业	23.4	7.1	63.2	1.3	7.1	56495	99.2
电力、热力的生产和供应业	29.1	13.6	60.8	1.1	21.6	574045	98.1
燃气生产和供应业	18.3	21.9	53.0	4.4	19.8	703745	99.5
水的生产和供应业							

4-16 规模以上港澳台商投资工业企业主要经济指标（2010年）

Main Indicators of Industrial Enterprises above Designated Size with Hong Kong, Macao and Taiwan Funds(2010)

项目	企业单位数(个)	#亏损企业	工业增加值(万元)	主营业务收入(万元)	亏损企业亏损总额(万元)
总计	**2564**	**517**	**7914179**	**32781458**	**140941**
按轻重工业分					
轻工业	1442	296	4130365	16047468	83223
重工业	1122	221	3783814	16733990	57718
按企业规模分					
按大中小型企业分					
大型企业	28		1388686	6839261	
中型企业	698	100	4814489	18265024	61639
小型企业	1838	417	1711004	7677173	79302
按销售收入分					
10亿元以上	44	2	2630228	12273565	10326
5-10亿元	55	3	862967	3771397	492
1-5亿元	498	50	2622544	10288267	42342
1亿元以下	1967	462	1798440	6448229	87781
按工业行业分(大类)					
非金属矿采选业					
农副食品加工业	4	1	35623	386085	72
食品制造业	14	4	41709	128506	1751
饮料制造业	6	1	99368	979191	620
纺织业	189	29	441362	1784787	13943
纺织服装、鞋、帽制造业	107	23	209277	600473	5445
皮革、毛皮、羽绒及其制品业	168	36	613034	1512072	10034
木材加工及木、竹、藤、棕、草制品业	12	2	17359	63803	681
家具制造业	98	24	207402	743818	5143
造纸及纸制品业	102	21	556363	2335533	4843
印刷业、记录媒介的复制	48	11	197386	563939	5125
文教体育用品制造业	132	30	362362	1220063	13628
石油加工、炼焦及核燃料加工业	4		6708	48652	
化学原料及化学制品制造业	77	16	166558	830651	3299
医药制造业	5	2	5005	20115	463
化学纤维制造业	6		3042	15392	
橡胶制品业	44	7	51056	194013	2113
塑料制品业	329	70	506089	1890293	13728
非金属矿物制品业	46	11	253524	805441	2666
黑色金属冶炼及压延加工业	10	1	22340	196883	74
有色金属冶炼及压延加工业	21	4	39116	206334	273
金属制品业	157	36	269931	1097373	4953
通用设备制造业	104	17	211226	1131216	1842
专用设备制造业	95	15	154783	468528	1472
交通运输设备制造业	17	2	119857	466470	329
电气机械及器材制造业	253	45	859038	3341784	8151
通信设备、计算机及其他电子设备制造业	402	81	1821376	8707285	36691
仪器仪表及文化、办公用机械制造业	52	15	228333	1500247	1947
工艺品及其他制造业	56	13	121876	603984	1655
电力、热力的生产和供应业	6		293076	938527	
燃气生产和供应业					
水的生产和供应业					

4-16 续表 1

(2010年)

项目	利税总额(万元)	人均税收(元)	利润总额(万元)	人均利润(元)
总计	**2064478**	**2563**	**1694286**	**11730**
按轻重工业分				
轻工业	843441	2098	660838	7594
重工业	1221037	3267	1033448	17997
按企业规模分				
按大中小型企业分				
大型企业	389754	3388	336664	21485
中型企业	1312200	2561	1092650	12746
小型企业	362524	2266	264972	6156
按销售收入分				
10亿元以上	1034694	5157	903990	35667
5-10亿元	298023	4731	242693	20753
1-5亿元	509533	1844	411439	7736
1亿元以下	222228	1588	136164	2512
按工业行业分(大类)				
非金属矿采选业				
农副食品加工业	24512	115415	16525	238802
食品制造业	17774	14520	11368	25766
饮料制造业	42472	51382	19766	44730
纺织业	63438	2535	36679	3475
纺织服装、鞋、帽制造业	32434	1935	21604	3859
皮革、毛皮、羽绒及其制品业	32929	529	22037	1069
木材加工及木、竹、藤、棕、草制品业	3232	2272	2363	6179
家具制造业	23412	1850	15039	3322
造纸及纸制品业	240109	10378	205741	62127
印刷业、记录媒介的复制	64034	5239	49890	18482
文教体育用品制造业	25146	427	20100	1702
石油加工、炼焦及核燃料加工业	7571	60107	5942	219251
化学原料及化学制品制造业	72803	8477	61006	43836
医药制造业	844	10633	271	5022
化学纤维制造业	1148	4057	942	18537
橡胶制品业	5742	3327	1799	1517
塑料制品业	96905	2297	70439	6113
非金属矿物制品业	152220	19941	122762	83105
黑色金属冶炼及压延加工业	12169	6166	11523	109954
有色金属冶炼及压延加工业	15720	2641	14544	32646
金属制品业	45942	1735	36225	6469
通用设备制造业	51987	4281	39488	13525
专用设备制造业	43651	4696	31133	11679
交通运输设备制造业	43269	2421	40836	40637
电气机械及器材制造业	250656	858	238729	17166
通信设备、计算机及其他电子设备制造业	365592	1129	325918	9277
仪器仪表及文化、办公用机械制造业	54706	810	51152	11653
工艺品及其他制造业	52659	2366	48324	26369
电力、热力的生产和供应业	221402	172119	172141	601475
燃气生产和供应业				
水的生产和供应业				

4-17 规模以上港澳台商投资工业企业主要经济效益指标（2010年）

Main Indicators on Economic Benefit of Industrial Enterprises above Designated Size with Hong Kong, Macao and Taiwan Funds(2010)

项目	工业增加值率(%)	总资产贡献率(%)	资产负债率(%)	流动资产周转率(次/年)	成本费用利润率(%)	全员劳动生产率(元/人)	产品销售率(%)
总计	**24.0**	**7.9**	**55.4**	**1.9**	**5.4**	**54793**	**99.7**
按轻重工业分							
轻工业	25.7	6.5	55.3	1.8	4.3	47467	99.9
重工业	22.4	9.3	55.6	1.9	6.5	65895	99.5
按企业规模分							
大型企业	20.6	7.3	55.8	2.1	5.2	88624	101.5
中型企业	26.4	9.1	53.9	2.0	6.3	56161	100.5
小型企业	21.4	5.6	58.6	1.6	3.6	39752	96.4
按工业行业分(大类)							
非金属矿采选业							
农副食品加工业	9.2	14.7	69.7	3.0	4.5	514785	99.4
食品制造业	31.4	10.9	46.7	1.2	9.7	94536	96.7
饮料制造业	9.8	8.4	66.3	3.3	2.1	224866	96.4
纺织业	24.0	3.9	49.3	1.6	2.1	41810	97.1
纺织服装、鞋、帽制造业	33.7	5.9	54.4	1.4	3.7	37381	97.4
皮革、毛皮、羽绒及其制品业	41.1	3.3	69.1	1.9	1.5	29748	101.8
木材加工及木、竹、藤、棕、草制品业	27.5	4.7	64.6	1.0	3.8	45382	101.5
家具制造业	27.9	3.7	48.1	1.6	2.0	45817	100.1
造纸及纸制品业	24.2	9.2	53.5	2.0	9.6	168004	101.5
印刷业、记录媒介的复制	35.3	10.6	45.4	1.4	9.6	73122	101.1
文教体育用品制造业	29.4	2.9	60.4	1.7	1.7	30689	99.4
石油加工、炼焦及核燃料加工业	11.8	14.5	63.0	1.0	13.3	247528	92.3
化学原料及化学制品制造业	19.7	11.6	43.7	1.7	7.9	119679	97.7
医药制造业	24.3	2.0	46.3	0.7	1.4	92861	97.2
化学纤维制造业	19.2	7.6	38.8	1.3	6.5	59882	96.0
橡胶制品业	25.8	3.5	56.0	1.6	0.9	43070	98.8
塑料制品业	26.6	5.3	51.9	1.4	3.9	43922	99.7
非金属矿物制品业	30.8	16.1	40.3	1.7	17.8	171625	97.7
黑色金属冶炼及压延加工业	11.1	9.1	68.3	1.5	6.1	213169	98.1
有色金属冶炼及压延加工业	19.0	13.3	61.9	2.2	7.5	87803	99.7
金属制品业	24.2	4.7	49.8	1.6	3.4	48203	99.3
通用设备制造业	18.5	7.1	59.7	2.0	3.6	72350	99.5
专用设备制造业	31.6	7.7	44.6	1.2	7.1	58063	97.4
交通运输设备制造业	25.7	8.7	59.9	1.5	9.3	119272	100.1
电气机械及器材制造业	25.6	10.2	56.0	2.0	7.6	61771	99.9
通信设备、计算机及其他电子设备制造业	20.9	5.9	60.7	2.1	3.9	51845	100.3
仪器仪表及文化、办公用机械制造业	15.7	6.2	67.2	2.2	3.5	52016	103.6
工艺品及其他制造业	19.2	14.3	52.1	2.2	8.7	66505	95.3
电力、热力的生产和供应业	30.9	26.3	43.9	2.9	21.2	1024026	99.0
燃气生产和供应业							
水的生产和供应业							

4-18 规模以上私营工业企业主要经济指标（2010年）

Main Indicators of Private Industrial Enterprises above Designated Size (2010)

项　　目	企业单位数（个）	#亏损企业	工业增加值（万元）	主营业务收入（万元）	亏损企业亏损总额（万元）
总　　计	**1159**	**87**	**1668510**	**7912882**	**7268**
按轻重工业分					
轻工业	655	48	1112171	4939718	4183
重工业	504	39	556339	2973164	3085
按企业规模分					
按大中小型企业分					
大型企业	6		242611	738284	
中型企业	131	4	621091	2877577	658
小型企业	1022	83	804808	4297021	6610
按销售收入分					
10亿元以上	5		195042	793829	
5-10亿元	18	1	259945	1267916	10
1-5亿元	140	4	478097	2710342	598
1亿元以下	996	82	735426	3140795	6660
按工业行业分(大类)					
非金属矿采选业					
农副食品加工业	13	1	27204	352968	225
食品制造业	19	1	19091	109810	591
饮料制造业	1		194	771	
纺织业	142	7	202170	937755	353
纺织服装、鞋、帽制造业	53	3	328100	1076419	84
皮革、毛皮、羽绒及其制品业	29	2	39276	132465	280
木材加工及木、竹、藤、棕、草制品业	16	1	13155	52728	40
家具制造业	67	10	102135	457747	661
造纸及纸制品业	98	9	128155	759766	635
印刷业、记录媒介的复制	26	2	22074	72457	175
文教体育用品制造业	17	2	18438	79487	82
石油加工、炼焦及核燃料加工业	2		3048	113858	
化学原料及化学制品制造业	59	2	41072	205666	7
医药制造业	1		696	1050	
化学纤维制造业	1		1288	9329	
橡胶制品业	12	2	6347	23068	17
塑料制品业	118	4	102656	458717	242
非金属矿物制品业	34	4	53339	221950	111
黑色金属冶炼及压延加工业	6	2	2854	17496	44
有色金属冶炼及压延加工业	21		12219	93288	
金属制品业	71	6	84246	408277	601
通用设备制造业	52	4	50409	252450	1063
专用设备制造业	48	3	38063	152210	41
交通运输设备制造业	5	1	4940	15344	138
电气机械及器材制造业	108	10	175835	925541	707
通信设备、计算机及其他电子设备制造业	118	8	165928	893698	971
仪器仪表及文化、办公用机械制造业	7		16171	46168	
工艺品及其他制造业	15	3	9407	42399	200
电力、热力的生产和供应业					
燃气生产和供应业					
水的生产和供应业					

4-18 续表 1

(2010年)

项　　目	利税总额(万元)	人均税收(元)	利润总额(万元)	人均利润(元)
总　计	**507654**	**7337**	**300471**	**10640**
按轻重工业分				
轻工业	325262	6944	192638	10086
重工业	182392	8157	107833	11797
按企业规模分				
按大中小型企业分				
大型企业	108796	8579	74887	18946
中型企业	196518	7106	123672	12064
小型企业	202340	7155	101912	7261
按销售收入分				
10亿元以上	79429	9353	50140	16012
5-10亿元	97721	7910	73455	23945
1-5亿元	159944	8250	95636	12268
1亿元以下	170560	6270	81240	5703
按工业行业分(大类)				
非金属矿采选业				
农副食品加工业	10336	14333	7443	36884
食品制造业	7919	9256	4773	14047
饮料制造业	37	6085	1	237
纺织业	41073	6287	15627	3861
纺织服装、鞋、帽制造业	119470	7522	78946	14654
皮革、毛皮、羽绒及其制品业	7519	5870	2044	2192
木材加工及木、竹、藤、棕、草制品业	5159	9477	3536	20642
家具制造业	15298	3857	7471	3682
造纸及纸制品业	42177	11882	24418	16337
印刷业、记录媒介的复制	3395	6796	1442	5019
文教体育用品制造业	3297	4025	1556	3599
石油加工、炼焦及核燃料加工业	1089	32979	627	44800
化学原料及化学制品制造业	16571	17249	9710	24408
医药制造业	556	25151	423	79717
化学纤维制造业	564	12695	297	14157
橡胶制品业	1172	6014	498	4438
塑料制品业	20620	7048	8868	5318
非金属矿物制品业	16576	11175	7736	9778
黑色金属冶炼及压延加工业	1076	7346	751	16989
有色金属冶炼及压延加工业	4165	9564	2081	9550
金属制品业	31124	7364	19995	13230
通用设备制造业	18320	12556	9631	13917
专用设备制造业	10084	7330	5845	10105
交通运输设备制造业	1702	14080	1122	27221
电气机械及器材制造业	59734	7545	39281	14492
通信设备、计算机及其他电子设备制造业	57563	5043	38822	10447
仪器仪表及文化、办公用机械制造业	8940	11431	6803	36400
工艺品及其他制造业	2118	6884	724	3575
电力、热力的生产和供应业				
燃气生产和供应业				
水的生产和供应业				

4-19 规模以上私营工业企业主要经济效益指标（2010年）

Main Indicators on Economic Benefit of Private Industrial Enterprises above Designated Size (2010)

项　　目	工业增加值率 (%)	总资产贡献率 (%)	资产负债率 (%)	流动资产周转率 (次/年)	成本费用利润率 (%)	全员劳动生产率 (元/人)	产品销售率 (%)
总　计	**20.8**	**10.5**	**70.0**	**2.0**	**4.0**	**59084**	**98.8**
按轻重工业分							
轻工业	22.3	10.8	69.5	2.0	4.1	58232	99.0
重工业	18.4	9.9	70.9	2.0	3.8	60865	98.6
按企业规模分							
大型企业	32.7	18.5	54.6	1.6	11.3	61380	98.8
中型企业	21.6	9.9	66.2	1.8	4.5	60587	100.6
小型企业	18.3	9.1	77.2	2.3	2.4	57341	97.7
按工业行业分(大类)							
非金属矿采选业							
农副食品加工业	7.8	7.7	75.6	2.7	2.1	134805	101.5
食品制造业	16.7	9.6	81.1	1.8	4.5	56183	96.5
饮料制造业	13.4	3.2	77.9	1.3	0.2	32864	53.5
纺织业	21.3	7.0	87.8	1.9	1.7	49954	98.9
纺织服装、鞋、帽制造业	29.9	17.0	48.2	1.7	8.0	60904	98.0
皮革、毛皮、羽绒及其制品业	30.5	15.2	70.3	3.8	1.6	42110	106.8
木材加工及木、竹、藤、棕、草制品业	23.7	18.9	79.1	2.6	7.1	76794	95.8
家具制造业	22.3	6.8	75.9	2.3	1.7	50337	99.8
造纸及纸制品业	16.8	10.3	75.4	2.5	3.3	85745	99.9
印刷业、记录媒介的复制	28.9	6.9	75.7	1.6	2.0	76832	95.3
文教体育用品制造业	22.9	9.3	76.4	2.6	2.0	42641	98.7
石油加工、炼焦及核燃料加工业	2.7	3.5	94.9	3.9	0.6	217721	100.2
化学原料及化学制品制造业	19.3	12.2	68.0	1.9	4.9	103247	96.3
医药制造业	45.2	28.5	8.7	1.1	67.3	131340	70.2
化学纤维制造业	13.6	17.1	81.5	4.6	3.3	61352	98.6
橡胶制品业	26.2	10.4	67.9	2.7	2.2	56621	95.1
塑料制品业	21.9	8.2	77.2	2.2	2.0	61559	97.8
非金属矿物制品业	23.9	9.6	74.3	1.7	3.6	67423	99.2
黑色金属冶炼及压延加工业	15.5	6.0	89.5	1.2	4.5	64559	101.6
有色金属冶炼及压延加工业	12.7	10.1	62.2	2.6	2.3	56076	97.4
金属制品业	19.9	13.0	68.9	2.2	5.1	55744	96.3
通用设备制造业	19.8	9.0	67.7	1.6	4.0	72846	99.4
专用设备制造业	23.7	10.5	79.7	2.0	4.0	65808	94.9
交通运输设备制造业	32.1	17.4	59.0	2.2	8.0	119896	104.7
电气机械及器材制造业	18.8	8.7	62.9	1.6	4.4	64869	99.6
通信设备、计算机及其他电子设备制造业	18.3	11.0	70.6	2.2	4.5	44653	98.9
仪器仪表及文化、办公用机械制造业	34.9	21.2	55.9	1.6	17.0	86522	99.6
工艺品及其他制造业	22.2	8.5	61.0	2.2	1.7	46350	100.0
电力、热力的生产和供应业							
燃气生产和供应业							
水的生产和供应业							

4-20 大中型工业企业主要经济指标（2010年）

Main Indicators of Large and Medium-sized Industrial Enterprises (2010)

项　　目	企业单位数（个）	#亏损企业	工业增加值（万元）	主营业务收入（万元）	亏损企业亏损总额（万元）
总　计	**1411**	**172**	**12520190**	**55309077**	**120374**
按轻重工业分					
轻工业	744	101	5620455	22018681	63048
重工业	667	71	6899735	33290396	57326
按企业规模分					
大型企业	84	2	4193196	21965868	8461
中型企业	1327	170	8326994	33343209	111913
按工业行业分(大类)					
非金属矿采选业					
农副食品加工业	2		35055	396147	
食品制造业	10	1	213122	641144	690
饮料制造业	5		193225	1281696	
纺织业	96	9	571091	2333088	8498
纺织服装、鞋、帽制造业	43	6	451398	1356479	2881
皮革、毛皮、羽绒及其制品业	96	16	786592	2063657	7463
木材加工及木、竹、藤、棕、草制品业	3		12696	56159	
家具制造业	71	10	357740	1442746	4857
造纸及纸制品业	53	5	746871	3221522	1396
印刷业、记录媒介的复制	27	4	200116	588834	416
文教体育用品制造业	73	15	392268	1325769	11459
石油加工、炼焦及核燃料加工业					
化学原料及化学制品制造业	25	7	163896	820479	8228
医药制造业	2		28639	63600	
化学纤维制造业					
橡胶制品业	14	4	50010	175751	1612
塑料制品业	119	15	553308	1969029	12058
非金属矿物制品业	21		297052	914052	
黑色金属冶炼及压延加工业					
有色金属冶炼及压延加工业	10	1	49831	409194	16
金属制品业	60	9	306859	1146942	1470
通用设备制造业	30	1	246294	1208881	37
专用设备制造业	43	2	245792	787523	3717
交通运输设备制造业	17	1	247375	921268	9
电气机械及器材制造业	159	13	1184926	4753809	6587
通信设备、计算机及其他电子设备制造业	375	49	3669950	20008509	48338
仪器仪表及文化、办公用机械制造业	36	4	367294	2370454	642
工艺品及其他制造业	13		59475	260958	
电力、热力的生产和供应业	6		1017468	4534675	
燃气生产和供应业	1		33691	183774	
水的生产和供应业	1		38156	72938	

4-20 续表 1

(2010年)

项目	利税总额(万元)	人均税收(元)	利润总额(万元)	人均利润(元)
总计	**3537990**	**4343**	**2715380**	**14336**
按轻重工业分				
轻工业	1406501	3704	1035774	10350
重工业	2131489	5058	1679606	18801
按企业规模分				
大型企业	1294462	7745	962501	22457
中型企业	2243528	3348	1752879	11961
按工业行业分(大类)				
非金属矿采选业				
农副食品加工业	25128	82851	16445	156922
食品制造业	122240	28630	86397	69013
饮料制造业	120365	94292	69315	128030
纺织业	99891	3975	58502	5619
纺织服装、鞋、帽制造业	137949	5749	93260	11996
皮革、毛皮、羽绒及其制品业	68432	816	47857	1898
木材加工及木、竹、藤、棕、草制品业	2816	2651	2017	6692
家具制造业	57659	2072	42893	6019
造纸及纸制品业	310896	15065	253322	66283
印刷业、记录媒介的复制	69792	3363	60452	21768
文教体育用品制造业	28970	437	23890	2055
石油加工、炼焦及核燃料加工业				
化学原料及化学制品制造业	72397	10837	55644	35995
医药制造业	22480	56522	15200	118012
化学纤维制造业				
橡胶制品业	3511	1527	1416	1031
塑料制品业	108364	2051	84140	7123
非金属矿物制品业	175774	21931	139807	85248
黑色金属冶炼及压延加工业				
有色金属冶炼及压延加工业	26155	3849	23650	36340
金属制品业	68499	3137	50499	8802
通用设备制造业	59446	4127	46494	14814
专用设备制造业	56491	3226	43525	10830
交通运输设备制造业	121542	9937	105015	63136
电气机械及器材制造业	341997	2351	299828	16717
通信设备、计算机及其他电子设备制造业	794127	2107	668339	11195
仪器仪表及文化、办公用机械制造业	100579	1415	92095	15364
工艺品及其他制造业	8815	42	8771	8224
电力、热力的生产和供应业	496213	104709	294146	152423
燃气生产和供应业	31285	4064	31103	691167
水的生产和供应业	6177	59335	1358	16720

4-21 大中型工业企业主要经济效益指标（2010年）

Main Indicators on Economic Benefit of Large and Medium-sized Industrial Enterprises (2010)

项目	工业增加值率 (%)	总资产贡献率 (%)	资产负债率 (%)	流动资产周转率 (次/年)	成本费用利润率 (%)	全员劳动生产率 (元/人)	产品销售率 (%)
总计	**22.7**	**8.8**	**56.2**	**2.2**	**5.1**	**66101**	**100.6**
按轻重工业分							
轻工业	25.6	8.0	56.2	1.9	4.9	56162	100.7
重工业	20.8	9.5	56.1	2.5	5.3	77235	100.6
按企业规模分							
大型企业	19.2	8.9	57.4	2.7	4.6	97833	100.8
中型企业	25.0	8.8	55.5	2.0	5.5	56820	100.5
按工业行业分(大类)							
非金属矿采选业							
农副食品加工业	8.8	15.6	71.9	3.0	4.3	334496	99.4
食品制造业	34.1	18.4	39.4	1.5	15.5	170239	102.7
饮料制造业	14.6	15.9	62.1	2.8	5.7	356899	96.8
纺织业	24.1	5.1	60.3	1.6	2.6	54855	98.8
纺织服装、鞋、帽制造业	32.5	12.9	48.3	1.5	7.4	58065	97.7
皮革、毛皮、羽绒及其制品业	38.7	5.4	68.1	2.1	2.4	31193	102.4
木材加工及木、竹、藤、棕、草制品业	24.2	6.1	59.5	1.5	3.7	42124	105.8
家具制造业	25.4	5.1	55.9	1.7	3.0	50201	102.2
造纸及纸制品业	23.3	8.9	54.2	2.1	8.5	195424	100.9
印刷业、记录媒介的复制	34.5	10.6	41.2	1.3	11.3	72059	101.7
文教体育用品制造业	29.6	3.1	59.4	1.9	1.8	33748	100.6
石油加工、炼焦及核燃料加工业							
化学原料及化学制品制造业	20.7	9.6	54.5	1.5	7.2	106020	102.8
医药制造业	44.8	13.4	5.9	0.5	31.2	222355	100.0
化学纤维制造业							
橡胶制品业	29.2	2.4	63.4	1.9	0.8	36442	103.3
塑料制品业	28.5	6.0	52.7	1.6	4.4	46840	101.6
非金属矿物制品业	32.1	17.1	44.0	1.9	18.0	181129	98.5
黑色金属冶炼及压延加工业							
有色金属冶炼及压延加工业	12.2	11.3	61.9	1.8	6.1	76568	99.9
金属制品业	27.4	7.2	56.2	1.7	4.6	53486	102.9
通用设备制造业	20.6	7.8	61.3	2.1	4.0	78475	101.2
专用设备制造业	31.6	6.8	53.9	1.4	5.8	61159	102.9
交通运输设备制造业	27.1	14.7	52.2	1.7	12.7	148725	101.1
电气机械及器材制造业	24.8	10.4	51.4	2.1	6.7	66066	100.0
通信设备、计算机及其他电子设备制造业	18.5	6.9	60.3	2.5	3.4	61473	100.7
仪器仪表及文化、办公用机械制造业	15.8	7.8	66.4	2.5	4.0	61274	102.3
工艺品及其他制造业	22.8	4.2	35.1	1.9	3.5	55766	99.9
电力、热力的生产和供应业	22.3	12.6	51.9	6.4	6.9	527240	99.5
燃气生产和供应业	18.3	22.9	52.0	4.4	20.5	748684	100.0
水的生产和供应业	48.3	5.4	76.4	1.7	1.9	469910	92.4

4-22 主要年份规模以上工业企业经济效益指标

Main Indicators on Economic Benefit of Industrial Enterprises above Designated Size in Main Years

项　　目	单位	1985年	1990年	1995年	2000年	2004年	2005年	2009年	2010年
产品销售率	%	85.6	94.7	98.7	99.8	99.6	99.5	99.2	99.9
成本费用利润率	%	6.5	1.5	5.0	5.4	3.4	3.3	5.2	4.8
产值利税率	%	6.9	6.4	9.8	9.2	5.6	4.6	6.6	6.1
资金利税率	%	9.0	6.3	6.9	7.5	3.6	5.5	7.6	7.8
销售利税率	%	8.2	6.7	9.1	9.2	5.7	4.7	6.7	6.1
每百元固定资产原值实现的产值	元	174.9	133.6	108.7	125.5	220.3	212.4	197.1	240.6
每百元固定资产原值实现的利税	元	14.2	8.5	10.7	11.5	9.8	9.9	13.1	14.6
每百元固定资产原值实现的利润	元	4.4	1.8	5.5	6.9	6.8	6.7	9.7	11.0
每百元流动资产实现的产值	元	210.2	247.8	169.4	178.6	227.3	216.3	191.8	204.3
每百元流动资产实现的利税	元	17.1	15.7	16.6	16.4	10.2	10.0	12.7	12.4
每百元流动资产实现的利润	元	4.9	3.3	8.6	9.8	7.0	6.8	9.4	9.3
亏损企业亏损面	%	7.2	11.1	25.9	31.3	33.7	30.1	24.1	16.2
全部流动资产周转天数	天	173.7	155.6	201.1	189.0	170.6	169.8	192.3	179.4
增加值全员劳动生产率	元/人	2906	6439	13778	36101	52464	53340	56766	60854
平均每个职工提供利税	元	626	1519	5351	11703	12192	9193	15759	16728

注：由于1993年财务会计制度改革，本表中有关财务指标1993年起数字与往年不可比；全员劳动生产率1993年起按增加值计算，以前年份按净产值计算；1993年以前的流动资产按定额资金计算。下同。

4-23 主要年份国有经济工业企业经济效益指标

Main Indicators on Economic Benefit of State-owned and State-holding Industrial Enterprises in Main Years

项　　目	单位	1985年	1990年	1995年	2000年	2004年	2005年	2009年	2010年
产品销售率	%	89.6	102.0	100.8	98.3	99.9	100.0	99.1	99.8
成本费用利润率	%	8.0	-0.8	15.5	7.0	6.8	5.8	7.1	3.2
产值利税率	%	13.2	9.2	40.6	69.4	98.7	11.3	10.4	7.3
资金利税率	%	20.4	8.3	14.9	21.6	40.8	10.6	9.8	6.7
销售利税率	%	14.8	9.0	20.6	19.2	98.7	11.3	10.5	7.3
每百元固定资产原值实现的产值	元	142.9	85.5	61.1	63.4	44.2	105.0	73.4	79.0
每百元固定资产原值实现的利税	元	21.1	7.8	24.8	44.0	12.2	11.8	7.6	5.7
每百元固定资产原值实现的利润	元	9.6	-0.6	10.8	14.5	8.7	5.6	4.8	2.4
每百元流动资产实现的产值	元	445.1	397.8	96.3	73.4	215.4	443.4	387.9	794.5
每百元流动资产实现的利税	元	65.7	36.4	39.1	50.9	59.3	50.0	40.3	57.7
每百元流动资产实现的利润	元	27.5	-2.4	17.0	16.7	42.3	23.8	25.4	24.6
亏损企业亏损面	%	9.9	16.7	20.9		25.0	20.0	18.5	
全部流动资产周转天数	天	80.9	88.7	299.8	137.7	56.2	83.0	95.3	46.1
增加值全员劳动生产率	元/人	3641	11253	73910	456736	1694891	2320312	416456	405232
平均每个职工提供利税	元	1757	5325	55113	303960	1603751	1197862	171857	144620

4-24 主要年份规模以上集体经济工业企业经济效益指标

Main Indicators on Economic Benefit of Collective-owned Industrial Enterprises above Designated Size in Main Years

项　　目	单位	1985年	1990年	1995年	2000年	2004年	2005年	2009年	2010年
产品销售率	%	85.1	92.2	98.0	97.0	101.2	100.5	100.2	97.4
成本费用利润率	%	5.9	3.3	5.2	2.7	4.5	3.3	8.9	9.7
产值利税率	%	9.3	6.9	9.0	5.1	7.6	5.8	9.8	10.4
资金利税率	%	15.1	9.7	6.0	2.9	5.8	3.2	9.2	9.7
销售利税率	%	11.0	7.5	8.7	5.2	7.6	5.8	9.9	10.7
每百元固定资产原值实现的产值	元	236.7	159.4	128.0	99.3	106.1	98.1	141.4	131.1
每百元固定资产原值实现的利税	元	22.1	11.0	11.5	5.0	7.8	5.7	13.9	13.6
每百元固定资产原值实现的利润	元	10.8	4.5	6.4	2.4	3.8	3.0	11.4	11.5
每百元流动资产实现的产值	元	509.0	225.7	179.5	113.8	194.2	157.7	249.2	214.9
每百元流动资产实现的利税	元	47.5	15.6	16.1	5.7	14.3	9.1	24.4	22.4
每百元流动资产实现的利润	元	23.2	6.4	9.0	2.8	6.9	4.8	20.0	18.8
亏损企业亏损面	%	6.6	8.8	12.8	18.6	19.5	25.9	19.9	22.5
全部流动资产周转天数	天	84.3	175.3	197.4	340.1	207.4	241.7	147.8	175.1
增加值全员劳动生产率	元/人	2664	5437	5820	16344	21711	28414	29447	31412
平均每个职工提供利税	元	715	1058	1533	3135	5702	5241	8800	8428

4-25 主要年份大中型工业企业经济效益指标

Main Indicators on Economic Benefit of Large and Medium-sized Industrial Enterprises in Main Years

项　　目	单位	1985年	1990年	1995年	2000年	2004年	2005年	2009年	2010年
产品销售率	%	104.3	103.5	99.7	98.6	99.5	99.5	99.3	100.6
成本费用利润率	%	14.3	2.2	12.9	12.0	3.9	3.8	5.9	5.1
产值利税率	%	16.1	8.7	19.9	21.4	5.2	4.7	7.2	6.4
资金利税率	%	14.8	6.5	14.0	15.3	6.4	6.1	8.5	8.4
销售利税率	%	15.5	8.4	19.8	21.7	5.3	4.7	7.3	6.4
每百元固定资产原值实现的产值	元	106.0	87.1	112.8	98.4	227.2	229.8	186.3	221.6
每百元固定资产原值实现的利税	元	17.1	7.6	22.4	21.1	11.7	10.7	13.4	14.2
每百元固定资产原值实现的利润	元	11.5	1.7	13.1	13.0	8.8	8.4	10.2	10.9
每百元流动资产实现的产值	元	758.8	329.3	174.3	183.4	242.9	227.4	209.0	220.6
每百元流动资产实现的利税	元	122.4	28.6	34.6	39.2	12.5	10.6	15.0	14.2
每百元流动资产实现的利润	元	82.3	6.4	20.2	24.2	9.4	8.3	11.4	10.9
亏损企业亏损面	%		17.2	22.2	12.8	24.6	20.1	19.8	12.2
全部流动资产周转天数	天	46.1	107.1	209.5	210.2	156.7	160.8	176.3	164.8
增加值全员劳动生产率	元/人	6202	16492	81787	280810	65573	72657	64534	66101
平均每个职工提供利税	元	2601	7883	52997	165448	14187	11918	19234	18679

4-26 主要年份规模以上港澳台商投资工业企业经济效益指标

Main Indicators on Economic Benefit of Industrial Enterprises above Designated Size with Hong Kong, Macao and Taiwan Funds in Main Years

项　目	单位	1990年	1995年	2000年	2004年	2005年	2009年	2010年
产品销售率	%	94.2	99.6	100.8	99.9	99.4	99.4	99.7
成本费用利润率	%	-11.5	2.1	4.6	2.5	3.2	5.9	5.4
产值利税率	%	-9.3	4.9	6.6	3.3	4.0	6.9	6.3
资金利税率	%	-14.3	3.8	5.4	3.5	4.6	7.5	7.6
销售利税率	%	-9.9	4.9	6.5	3.3	4.1	7.0	6.3
每百元固定资产原值实现的产值	元	104.9	114.8	114.5	178.6	198.1	176.8	216.6
每百元固定资产原值实现的利税	元	-9.7	5.6	7.5	8.2	8.0	12.2	13.6
每百元固定资产原值实现的利润	元	-12.6	2.6	5.1	5.5	6.0	9.8	11.1
每百元流动资产实现的产值	元	154.3	165.2	182.2	209.0	192.3	179.7	189.1
每百元流动资产实现的利税	元	-14.3	8.1	12.0	9.5	7.8	12.4	11.8
每百元流动资产实现的利润	元	-18.5	3.7	8.1	6.5	5.8	9.9	9.7
亏损企业亏损面	%	25.0	46.4	36.1	39.9	35.1	30.3	20.2
全部流动资产周转天数	天	251.1	199.1	199.9	207.4	191.1	205.0	194.1
增加值全员劳动生产率	元/人	16962	17478	28933	42634	41933	50040	54793
平均每个职工提供利税	元	-8238	4232	7026	5612	6244	13679	14293

4-27 主要年份规模以上外商投资工业企业经济效益指标

Main Indicators on Economic Benefit of Foreign-funded Industrial Enterprises above Designated Size in Main Years

项　目	单位	1990年	1995年	2000年	2004年	2005年	2009年	2010年
产品销售率	%	94.2	91.0	99.2	98.8	99.4	98.4	100.1
成本费用利润率	%	-11.5	-2.6	4.7	3.2	2.8	5.3	4.4
产值利税率	%	-9.3	-0.6	5.7	3.3	3.2	6.4	5.3
资金利税率	%	-14.3	-0.5	7.4	5.0	4.1	7.6	7.5
销售利税率	%	-9.9	-0.6	5.7	3.3	3.2	6.5	5.3
每百元固定资产原值实现的产值	元	104.9	155.5	231.2	307.9	285.2	228.6	286.9
每百元固定资产原值实现的利税	元	-9.7	-0.9	13.1	9.8	9.2	14.7	15.3
每百元固定资产原值实现的利润	元	-12.6	-1.9	10.3	8.0	7.6	11.2	12.1
每百元流动资产实现的产值	元	154.3	94.3	251.0	252.2	223.6	182.8	211.1
每百元流动资产实现的利税	元	-14.3	-1.5	14.2	8.0	7.2	11.7	11.2
每百元流动资产实现的利润	元	-18.5	5.5	11.1	6.5	5.9	8.9	8.9
亏损企业亏损面	%	25.0	38.2	31.3	29.5	34.5	29.3	18.8
全部流动资产周转天数	天	251.1	174.1	148.4	156.0	164.4	203.3	173.0
增加值全员劳动生产率	元/人	16962	3646	50318	70718	70722	60130	66212
平均每个职工提供利税	元	-8238	-700	13714	12328	8288	16693	16893

4-28 主要年份规模以上工业产品产量

Output of Main Industrial Products of Industrial Enterprises above Designated Size in Main Years

产品名称	单位	1985年	1990年	1995年	2000年	2005年	2009年	2010年
食用植物油	吨	5571	4431	6824	5180	181869	610729	1135677
糖	吨	51858	61016	7841	17869			
饼干	吨		45158	26252	21262	38859	131296	142126
罐头	吨	924	1352	5982			10251	12890
饮料酒	千升	4034	2441	1720			281181	493644
软饮料	吨		44061	71566	158599	861853	2906855	3142076
棉纱	吨		321	9902	3048	49383	10368	11252
布	万米		82	31045	28139	65669	13795	15794
服装	万件	108	1835	112177	85635	70054	117601	140556
#衬衫	万件			2518	3624	2210	5656	6372
西服	万件			205	1761	555	228	204
轻革	万平方米		5	1076	378	1391	374	744
皮鞋	万双	17	457	27184	23474	31942	36297	43062
人造板	立方米		7100	40666		167088	169446	266113
家具	万件	815	8657	77501	151374	7974	5745	7390
机制纸及纸板	吨	30241	106535	339742	618000	4081761	8666746	9331823
玩具	万元			657936	469792	1354386	677938	827916
火柴	万件	19	22	9				
中成药	吨		216	6268	2354	1759	1836	2478
塑料制品	吨	3089	17335	624476	571900	1265865	2228984	3998208
#塑料薄膜	吨		1928	59128	71394	83954	121923	134737
水泥	万吨	41	140	283	435	305	138	249
砖	万块	159305	296962	252783		2903	33	
日用陶瓷	万件	561	480	2414	1860	5745	2005	2426
耐火材料制品	吨	7600	9928	9144			57124	62512
钢材	吨	4678	1730	19690	14550	1087242	30185	191656
铝材	吨		881	3536	4080	61510	64973	69933
输送机械	吨		8622	3736		33200	16368	

注：2000年以前家具的计量单位为“万元”，输送机械的计量单位为“吨”。

4-28 续表

产品名称	单位	1985年	1990年	1995年	2000年	2005年	2009年	2010年
电动工具	万台		1.89	471	357	6		1520
滚动轴承	万套	36	373	691	594	1333	3331	4232
民用钢质船	载重吨	1916	841	3620	2894			18186
交流电动机	万千瓦	23	19	43	87		155	193
变压器	千伏安				6730	816409	4127869	2980343
电力电缆	公里		15091	20694	61996	78266	260739	383829
原电池(折干电池)	万只	12354	7607	63237	69401	214507	316334	417215
吸尘器	万台	0.13	7.35	483	67	464	672	428
电风扇	万台		106	474	436	964	2011	2081
房间空调器	台	31		26480	39582	4941		
排油烟机	台			57551				
缝纫机	台			190		504	123	440
自行车	辆			95439	185608	885211	1271123	1014533
家用电冰箱	台			35336		19360		
白炽灯泡	万只			5778	8560	45164	23536	13198
灯　具	万件		87	42407	25135	14017	20758	22819
电话单机	万部		17	877	1074	3651	2948	4809
移动电话机	万部				619	639	1736	1995
电子计算机	万台				27	180	16	44
彩色显像管	万只			210	394			
电子元件	万只	1422	20487	719259	1039500	46416689	68920968	91845708
显示器	万台						175	157
打印机	万台						54	57
硬盘存储器	万台						50	30
半导体分立器件	万只			2484814	32256	2203170	2628605	4044448
彩色电视机	万台		1.04	81	134	135	514	536
组合音响	万台			1136	1572	2446	2667	3637
照相机	万台		3	374	122	1355	284	210
手　表	万只		15	8514	954	1370	1367	2168
钟	万只			1986	984	1193	2396	3776
发电量	亿千瓦时	0.29	93	139	269	344	337	356
自来水生产量	万吨			21070	102083	94962	169063	179639

4-29 规模以上八大支柱产业主要经济指标（2010年）

Main Indicators of Eight Pillar Industries above Designated Size (2010)

项目	企业单位数（个）	#亏损企业	工业增加值（万元）	主营业务收入（万元）	亏损企业亏损总额（万元）
总计	**3223**	**524**	**10404269**	**49373571**	**167414**
按轻重工业分					
轻工业	1891	299	5187069	21822952	85984
重工业	1332	225	5217200	27550619	81430
按企业规模分					
大型企业	63		2949785	16424993	
中型企业	848	112	5173149	22373349	91627
小型企业	2312	412	2281335	10575229	75787
按工业行业分(大类)					
通信设备、计算机及其他电子制造业	929	172	4172746	22324769	79749
电气机械及仪器仪表制造业	687	117	2074483	9874301	22171
纺织服装鞋帽制造业	627	79	1437055	5278561	21890
造纸及纸制品业	309	41	1016110	4548795	6845
家具制造业	269	46	508839	2111985	7458
玩具制造业	122	34	291010	810107	14995
食品饮料制造业	60	7	456221	2162613	3316
化工制品制造业	220	28	447805	2262440	10990

4-29 续表 1

(2010年)

项目	利税总额（万元）	人均税收（元）	利润总额（万元）	人均利润（元）
总计	**2689724**	**3519**	**2072943**	**11827**
按轻重工业分				
轻工业	1403325	4593	996747	11259
重工业	1286399	2423	1076196	12406
按企业规模分				
大型企业	929003	5178	760800	23419
中型企业	1233206	3014	960395	10609
小型企业	527515	3363	351748	6730
按工业行业分(大类)				
通信设备、计算机及其他电子制造业	885478	2103	728706	9773
电气机械及仪器仪表制造业	576256	2243	496868	14041
纺织服装鞋帽制造业	300207	3858	181928	5935
造纸及纸制品业	406012	12195	317685	43863
家具制造业	78844	2263	54290	5003
玩具制造业	8790	344	5088	473
食品饮料制造业	265338	40018	168315	69422
化工制品制造业	168799	14331	120063	35307

4-30 规模以上电子信息制造业主要指标(2010年)

Main Indicators of Electronic Information Industrial Enterprises above Designated Size(2010)

指　　标	单位	2010年
企业单位数	个	1616
#亏损企业单位数	个	289
工业增加值	亿元	624.72
主营业务收入	亿元	3219.91
成本费用总额	亿元	3110.48
#销售成本及费用	亿元	2955.35
管理费用	亿元	153.14
财务费用	亿元	1.99
利税总额	亿元	146.17
#利润总额	亿元	122.56
应交增值税	亿元	21.11
亏损企业亏损总额	亿元	10.19
企业资产总额	亿元	2026.27
#流动资产	亿元	1390.37
#应收帐款余额	亿元	580.85
产成品存货	亿元	103.57
企业负债总额	亿元	1209.40
企业资产负债率	%	59.69
成本费用利润率	%	3.94

注：本表统计范围为规模以上电子通信类、电气机械及器材类、仪表仪器类制造业。

4-31 规模以上先进制造业企业主要经济指标（2010年）

Main Indicators of Advanced Manufacturing Enterprises above Designated Size (2010)

项 目	企业单位数（个）	#亏损企业	工业增加值（万元）	主营业务收入（万元）	亏损企业亏损总额（万元）
总 计	**2335**	**366**	**6922470**	**35422383**	**110415**
按企业规模分					
大型企业	46	1	1928409	12219874	2893
中型企业	547	66	3356263	14378892	55661
小型企业	1742	299	1637798	8823617	51861
按工业行业分					
1. 装备制造业	1982	314	6292829	32110742	93889
金属制品业	280	44	357337	1827114	5275
通用设备制造业	241	29	414402	2151277	3200
专用设备制造业	206	24	381481	1238954	5371
交通运输设备制造业	45	7	262748	976466	554
电气机械及器材制造业	351	54	882614	4632191	8449
通信设备、计算机及其他电子设备制造业	825	149	3899745	20993299	69952
仪器仪表及文化、办公用机械制造业	34	7	94502	291441	1088
2. 黑色金属冶炼及压延加工业	32	5	47818	419197	678
炼铁					
炼钢					
钢压延加工	30	5	46049	413389	678
铁合金冶炼	2		1769	5808	
3. 石油及化工	321	47	581823	2892444	15848
石油加工、炼焦及核燃料加工业	7		10504	175583	
化学原料及化学制品制造业	220	28	447806	2262441	10991
橡胶制品业	94	19	123513	454420	4857

4-31 续表 1

项　　目	利税总额(万元)	人均税收(元)	利润总额(万元)	人均利润(元)	工业增加值率(%)
总　　计	**1811809**	**3113**	**1464098**	**13109**	**19.5**
按企业规模分					
大型企业	542869	3232	467309	19989	16.0
中型企业	798971	2231	671577	11763	23.4
小型企业	469969	4637	325212	10418	18.0
按工业行业分					
1. 装备制造业	1597722	2737	1310219	12474	19.5
金属制品业	84656	3440	61854	9331	19.5
通用设备制造业	130058	5371	97509	16092	19.1
专用设备制造业	101061	4592	72717	11780	30.3
交通运输设备制造业	128223	12441	107156	63278	27.1
电气机械及器材制造业	286041	2061	254194	16451	18.6
通信设备、计算机及其他电子设备制造业	831425	2152	685547	10111	18.6
仪器仪表及文化、办公用机械制造业	36258	4072	31242	25359	32.6
2. 黑色金属冶炼及压延加工业	24137	9485	21312	71565	11.3
炼铁					
炼钢					
钢压延加工	23284	10164	20527	75661	11.1
铁合金冶炼	853	2532	785	29634	29.9
3. 石油及化工	189950	9036	132567	20874	19.9
石油加工、炼焦及核燃料加工业	8984	32570	6766	99349	5.7
化学原料及化学制品制造业	168799	14331	120066	35307	19.6
橡胶制品业	12167	2232	5735	1990	27.0

4-31 续表 2

项目	总资产贡献率(%)	资产负债率(%)	流动资产周转率(次/年)	成本费用利润率(%)	全员劳动生产率(元/人)	产品销售率(%)
总计	**7.8**	**59.4**	**2.1**	**4.3**	**61980**	**99.9**
按企业规模分						
大型企业	8.3	61.6	2.8	4.0	82487	101.1
中型企业	7.9	56.3	2.0	4.9	58787	100.6
小型企业	7.1	62.0	1.7	3.8	52464	97.1
按工业行业分						
1. 装备制造业	7.7	59.2	2.2	4.2	59909	100.0
金属制品业	6.0	62.2	1.7	3.5	53908	100.5
通用设备制造业	8.2	60.2	1.8	4.7	68388	99.6
专用设备制造业	8.0	52.2	1.4	6.2	61801	99.5
交通运输设备制造业	14.6	51.6	1.7	12.2	155159	100.9
电气机械及器材制造业	10.0	57.3	2.2	5.8	57120	98.0
通信设备、计算机及其他电子设备制造业	6.7	60.5	2.4	3.4	57517	100.4
仪器仪表及文化、办公用机械制造业	14.5	51.3	1.8	11.8	76706	100.2
2. 黑色金属冶炼及压延加工业	8.6	72.2	1.5	5.3	160569	99.7
炼铁						
炼钢						
钢压延加工	8.4	72.1	1.5	5.2	169735	99.7
铁合金冶炼	14.5	78.4	1.7	15.7	66736	98.1
3. 石油及化工	8.3	60.1	1.6	4.8	91616	98.9
石油加工、炼焦及核燃料加工业	10.1	75.2	2.1	4.0	154250	97.7
化学原料及化学制品制造业	9.2	59.0	1.6	5.6	131684	98.8
橡胶制品业	3.4	61.9	1.7	1.3	42857	99.6

4-32 规模以上IT制造业企业主要经济指标（2010年）

Main Indicators of IT Manufacturing Enterprises above Designated Size (2010)

项目	企业单位数(个)	#亏损企业	工业增加值(万元)	主营业务收入(万元)	亏损企业亏损总额(万元)
总计	**1293**	**240**	**5154445**	**27847349**	**98559**
按企业规模分					
大型企业	39		1693761	11361527	
中型企业	440	60	2652617	12069070	57456
小型企业	814	180	808067	4416752	41103
按工业行业分(小类)					
训练健身器材制造	4		4942	25792	
玩具制造	122	34	291010	810107	14995
信息化学品制造	5	4	4918	15986	601
医疗诊断、监护及治疗设备制造	1		396	1281	
微电机及其他电机制造	17	2	71750	262111	172
电线电缆制造	160	25	287999	2182703	2754
光纤、光缆制造					
电池制造	34	3	191906	855812	359
通信交换设备制造	1		270	2196	
通信终端设备制造	11	2	47780	158368	180
移动通信及终端设备制造	13	3	254389	2089899	4998
电子计算机整机制造	18	4	150214	1400107	9241
计算机网络设备制造	6	2	34962	238449	155
电子计算机外部设备制造	115	30	544567	2875401	9321
电子真空器件制造	4	1	51934	515054	52
集成电路制造	14	4	176365	1515050	4248
光电子器件及其他电子器件制造	69	11	301359	1271133	7718
电子元件及组件制造	422	54	1753165	7925786	22404
印制电路板制造	50	14	225681	912146	5051
家用影视设备制造	35	9	94518	620256	4393
家用音响设备制造	69	14	178482	711214	5404
其他电子设备制造	70	15	201278	952944	4500
电子测量仪器制造	4	1	4422	18744	707
照相机及器材制造	10	1	53438	231705	3
复印和胶印设备制造	10	2	121280	1118244	419
计算器及货币专用设备制造	4		54067	711213	
其他未列明的制造业	25	5	53353	425648	884

4-32 续表 1

项目	利税总额(万元)	人均税收(元)	利润总额(万元)	人均利润(元)	工业增加值率(%)
总　计	**1111413**	**2076**	**910207**	**9392**	**18.5**
按企业规模分					
大型企业	502579	3346	433150	20877	15.1
中型企业	436103	1554	352130	6517	21.9
小型企业	172731	2160	124927	5644	17.8
按工业行业分(小类)					
训练健身器材制造	855	1374	651	4370	18.5
玩具制造	8790	344	5088	473	35.3
信息化学品制造	-409	1210	-583	-4056	31.5
医疗诊断、监护及治疗设备制造	3		3	297	32.6
微电机及其他电机制造	10560	394	9890	5822	26.5
电线电缆制造	71502	3217	54082	9988	12.9
光纤、光缆制造					
电池制造	64783	7690	47167	20592	22.8
通信交换设备制造	187	24	184	1842	12.3
通信终端设备制造	5488	864	4228	2897	30.1
移动通信及终端设备制造	94676	10220	66218	23781	12.1
电子计算机整机制造	27092	2378	20362	7194	10.8
计算机网络设备制造	4945	199	4845	9577	13.7
电子计算机外部设备制造	107550	1171	95718	9477	19.0
电子真空器件制造	25295	2504	24653	96149	10.9
集成电路制造	26366	8061	9885	4835	11.5
光电子器件及其他电子器件制造	46945	1351	38590	6238	24.1
电子元件及组件制造	383096	1512	335015	10537	22.0
印制电路板制造	51649	2579	44509	16075	24.6
家用影视设备制造	12476	1845	8586	4071	15.2
家用音响设备制造	41577	1505	34573	7430	25.3
其他电子设备制造	30916	2552	18703	3908	21.2
电子测量仪器制造	460	3083	259	3954	22.5
照相机及器材制造	15248	2380	12527	10954	23.9
复印和胶印设备制造	42794	1920	40284	30824	10.7
计算器及货币专用设备制造	8118	16	8103	8126	8.2
其他未列明的制造业	30451	6699	26667	47278	11.9

4-32 续表 2

项 目	总资产贡献率(%)	资产负债率(%)	流动资产周转率(次/年)	成本费用利润率(%)	全员劳动生产率(元/人)	产品销售率(%)
总 计	**6.6**	**61.2**	**2.3**	**3.4**	**53186**	**100.2**
按企业规模分						
大型企业	8.0	63.5	2.7	4.0	81636	101.3
中型企业	5.7	58.0	2.2	3.0	49094	100.2
小型企业	5.7	64.5	1.9	2.9	36506	97.3
按工业行业分(小类)						
训练健身器材制造	6.1	50.2	2.2	2.6	33191	96.5
玩具制造	1.5	58.0	1.5	0.6	27064	98.6
信息化学品制造	-2.2	15.6	1.1	-3.5	34202	101.7
医疗诊断、监护及治疗设备制造	0.2	61.6	1.0	0.2	39188	100.0
微电机及其他电机制造	7.4	43.3	2.9	3.9	42236	96.6
电线电缆制造	5.7	68.5	2.0	2.5	53188	98.6
光纤、光缆制造						
电池制造	9.5	57.7	1.9	5.8	83780	102.7
通信交换设备制造	2.4	44.4	6.4	9.2	2699	100.0
通信终端设备制造	7.2	66.8	2.6	2.7	32744	99.8
移动通信及终端设备制造	8.9	81.1	2.2	3.3	91359	99.7
电子计算机整机制造	6.0	50.0	5.7	1.5	53070	100.6
计算机网络设备制造	4.7	65.1	2.7	2.1	69109	93.2
电子计算机外部设备制造	7.0	61.8	2.6	3.4	53916	100.8
电子真空器件制造	15.9	43.4	4.4	5.0	202549	108.4
集成电路制造	3.9	89.7	2.9	0.7	86259	99.6
光电子器件及其他电子器件制造	4.7	63.9	2.1	3.1	48715	102.2
电子元件及组件制造	7.2	55.2	2.3	4.4	55143	99.7
印制电路板制造	6.2	47.7	1.7	5.1	81509	99.4
家用影视设备制造	3.9	70.6	2.5	1.4	44817	99.1
家用音响设备制造	7.8	53.5	2.0	5.1	38354	100.9
其他电子设备制造	4.7	56.3	2.1	2.0	42061	100.2
电子测量仪器制造	3.1	43.9	1.8	1.4	67619	95.3
照相机及器材制造	13.2	50.8	2.7	5.6	46728	105.0
复印和胶印设备制造	10.3	56.4	3.8	3.7	92799	99.1
计算器及货币专用设备制造	1.6	81.8	1.7	1.2	54224	107.6
其他未列明的制造业	12.2	69.4	2.1	6.7	94584	95.6

主要统计指标解释

Explanatory Notes on Main Statistical Indicators

工业 指从事自然资源的开采，对采掘品和农产品进行加工和再加工的物质生产部门。具体包括：对自然资源的开采，如采矿、晒盐、森林采伐等（但不包括禽兽捕猎和水产捕捞）；对农副产品的加工、再加工，如粮油加工、食品加工、轧花、缫丝、纺织、制革等；对采掘品的加工、再加工，如炼铁、炼钢、化工生产、石油加工、机器制造、木材加工等，以及电力、自来水、煤气的生产和供应等；对工业品的修理、翻新，如机器制造设备的修理、交通运输工具（包括小卧车）的修理等。

轻工业 是指主要提供生活消费品和制作手工工具的工业。按其所使用的原料不同，可分为两大类：以农产品为原料的轻工业，是指直接或以农产品为基本原料的轻工业，主要包括食品制造、饮料制造、烟草加工、纺织、缝纫、皮革和毛皮制作、造纸以及印刷等工业；以非农产品为原料的轻工业，是以工业品为原料的轻工业，主要包括文教体育用品、化学药品制造、合成纤维制造、日用化学制品、日用玻璃制品、日用金属制品、手工工具制造、医疗器械制造、文化和办公用机械制造等工业。

重工业 是指为国民经济各部门提供物质技术基础的主要生产资料的工业。按其生产性质和产品用途，可以分为下列三类：采掘（伐）工业，是对自然资源的开采，包括石油开采、煤炭开采、金属矿开采等工业；原材料工业，指向国民经济各部门提供基本材料、动力和燃料的工业，包括金属冶炼及加工、炼焦及焦炭化学、化学原料、水泥、人造板以及电力、石油和煤炭加工等工业；加工工业，是指对工业原材料进行再加工制造的工业，包括装备国民经济各部门的机械设备制造工业、金属结构、水泥制造等工业，以及为农业提供的生产资料如化肥、农药等工业。

资产总额 是指企业拥有或控制的能以货币计量的经济资源，包括各种财产、债权和其他权利。资产按其流动性（即资产的变现能力和支付能力）划分为：流动资产、长期投资、固定资产、无形资产、递延资产和其他资产，即为企业资产负债表中的资产总计项。

流动资产 是企业资产的重要组成部分，通常是指一年内或超过一年的一个营业周期内可以变现或耗用的资产。其特点是在企业的生产经营或者业务活动中不断地在生产循环中周转，不断改变其形态。其价值一次性消耗、转移或者实现。包括：货币资金、短期投资、应收票据、应收账款、预付账款、其他应收款、存货、待摊费用、待处理流动资产损失、一年内到期的本期债券投资及其他流动资产。

固定资产原价 是指企业在建造、购置、安装、改建、扩建、技术改造某项固定资产时实际支出的全部货币总额。它一般包括买价、包装费、运杂费和安装费等。

固定资产合计 包括固定资产净值、固定资产清理、在建工程、待处理固定资产净损失所占用的资金合计。

固定资产净值 是指固定资产原价减去历年已提折旧额后的净额。

负债 是指企业所承担的能以货币计量，将以资产或劳务偿付的债务。其偿还形式可以用货币，也可以用资产或提供劳务的方式进行。包括流动负债、长期负债和递延税款贷项等，即为企业资产负债表的负债合计项。

实收资本 是指企业实际收到的投资人投入的资本。包括有国家资本、集体资本、法人资本、个人资本、外商资本、港澳台资本等。

主营业务收入 是企业在销售商品、提供劳务及让渡资产使用权等日常活动中所产生的收入。

主营业务税金及附加 是指企业日常活动应负担的税金及附加，包括营业税、消费税、城市维护建设税、资源税、土地增值税和教育费附加等。

主营业务成本 是指企业因销售商品、提供劳务或让渡资产使用权等日常活动而发生的实际成本。

营业利润 是企业生产经营活动所取得的利润，包括主营业务利润和其他业务利润。

利润总额 是指企业在一定时期内生产经营活动的最终的财务成果，是企业的收入减去有关成本与费用后的差额，收入大于相关的成本费用，企业就盈利，反之则亏损。包括营业利润、补贴收入、投资净收益、营业外收支净额、以前年度损失调整。

应交增值税 是指企业按税法规定，从事货物销售或提供加工、修理修配劳务等增加货物价值的活动本期应交纳的税金，即企业在报告期应交的增值税额。计算公式为：

应交增值税 = 销项税额-(进项税额-进项税额转出)-出口抵减内销产品应纳税额-减免税款+出口退税

从业人员平均人数 从业人员指企业工作并取得劳动报酬的全部人员数。包括在岗职工、再就业的离退休人员、民办教师及在企业工作的外方人员和港澳台方人员、兼职人员、借用的外单位人员和第二职业者。不包括离开本单位但仍保留劳动关系的职工。而从业人员平均人数指报告期内每天平均拥有的从业人员人数。其计算公式为：

月平均人数=报告月内每天实有人数之和÷报告月日历日数

季平均人数=季内各月平均人数之和÷3

年平均人数=全年各月平均人数之和÷12

资产利税率 是在一定时期内已实现的利润、税金总额与同期的资产总额之比。计算公式：

$$资产利税率（\%）=\frac{报告期累计实现利税总额}{资产总额}\times100\%$$

资产利税率反映每单位（通常是每万元）资产所提供的利税金额。它是考察和评价部门或企业资金运用的经济效益，分析资金投入效果的主要分析指标。

产值利税率 是报告期已实现的利润、税金总额（包括利润总额、产品销售税金及附加和应交增值税）占同期全部工业总产值的百分比，计算公式为：

$$产值利税率(\%)=\frac{利税总额}{工业总产值(现价)}\times100\%$$

工业经济效益综合指数 是现行综合评价工业经济效益总体水平及工业经济运行质量的指数，它是以若干项代表性经济效益指标，分别除以各项指标的标准值，再乘以各自的权数，加总后除以总权数求得。其计算公式为：

$$工业经济效益综合指数=\Sigma\left(\frac{某项经济效益指标报告期数值}{该项指标标准值}\times权数\right)\div总权数$$

上式总权数为 100。

工业产品销售率 是反映工业产品已实现销售的程度，是分析工业产销衔接情况、研究工业产品满足社会需求的指标。计算公式是：

$$产品销售率(\%)=\frac{现价工业销售产值}{现价工业总产值}\times100\%$$

总资产贡献率 是指企业一定时期内全部资产获利能力，是企业经营业绩和管理水平的集中体现，是评价和考核企业盈利能力的核心指标。计算公式为：

$$总资产贡献率（\%）= \frac{利润总额+税金总额+利息支出}{平均资产总额} \times 100\% \times \frac{12}{累计月数}$$

注：税金总额为主营业务税金及附加与应交增值税之和，平均资产总额为期初、期末资产总计的算术平均值。

资本保值增值率　是反映企业净资产变动状况的一个重要指标，是企业发展能力的集中体现。是指期末所有者权益总额与期初所有者权益总额的比率。计算公式为：

$$资本保值增值率（\%）= \frac{期末所有者权益}{期初所有者权益} \times 100\%$$

所有者权益等于资产总计减负债总计。

资产负债率　是指反映企业经营风险的大小，反映企业利用债权人提供的资金从事经营活动的能力。计算公式为：

$$资产负债率（\%）= \frac{负债总额}{资产总额} \times 100\%$$

资产及负债均为报告期期末数。

流动资产周转率　是指一定时期内流动资产完成的周转次数，反映投入工业企业流动资金的周转速度，一般以一年内周转多少次表示。计算公式为：

$$流动资产周转率（次）= \frac{产品销售收入}{流动资产平均余额} \times \frac{12}{累计月数}$$

成本费用利润率　是指工业企业投入的生产成本及费用的经济效益，同时也反映企业降低成本所取得的经济效益。计算公式为：

$$成本费用利润率（\%）= \frac{利润总额}{成本费用总额} \times 100\%$$

注：成本费用总额为产品销售成本、销售费用、管理费用、财务费用之和。

全员劳动生产率　是指反映企业的生产效率和劳动投入的经济效益。一般用平均每人一年创造的工业增加值表示。计算公式为：

$$全员劳动生产率（元/人）= \frac{工业增加值}{全部职工平均人数} \times \frac{12}{累计月数}$$

五、固定资产投资与建筑业

Investment in Fixed Assets and Construction

5-1 主要年份固定资产投资与建筑业主要指标

Main Indicators of Investment in Fixed Assets and Construction in Main Years

项　　目	单　位	1985年	1990年	1995年	2000年	2005年	2009年	2010年
全社会固定资产投资总额	万元	70600	75052	631355	1028914	5972443	10940753	11149822
#国有单位	万元	16914	50658	106935	197658	686333	1661417	1479886
私营个体经济	万元					1027969	2378277	2077250
港澳台投资经济	万元			10281	130501	1246450	1114631	1326063
外商投资经济	万元			230409	92699	507322	923601	938943
新增固定资产	万元					1732967	5421597	5778616
固定资产交付使用率	%					29.02	49.55	51.83
房屋竣工面积	万平方米					696.99	951.47	686.22
房屋面积竣工率	%					21.62	25.38	20.65
计划总投资	万元					13905355	31274675	45000174
固定资产投资建设周期	年					2.32	2.86	4.04
固定资产投资资金来源	万元	17000	50100	480875	1047861	6717711	14489422	18550102
#国家预算内资金	万元	1100	3600	10858	10490	536	117904	130717
国内贷款	万元	2800	2900	27439	122561	651723	1014574	1882278
利用外资	万元		17000	194486	207444	940432	1189793	1400920
自筹资金	万元	13100	25400	163090	587176	3901138	8697747	8390847
房地产开发投资	万元			85163	112498	1444277	2776623	2989853
房地产开发当年房屋施工面积	万平方米			160.74	315.45	1160.17	2333.90	2060.54
房地产开发当年房屋竣工面积	万平方米			76.78	103.20	132.88	310.22	296.59
#住宅	万平方米			68.36	77.97	115.23	268.08	256.09
商品房销售面积	万平方米			25.42	63.21	321.85	600.27	511.25
#住宅	万平方米			20.49	51.02	297.19	578.82	469.90
建筑企业(单位)个数	个		8	8	99	361	404	431
建筑企业平均人数	人		6803	22200	64300	79965	55684	57473
建筑企业总产值	万元		12678	94941	404493	843540	994007	1220569
劳动生产率(按总产值计算)	元/人		18636	42766	60849	108136	184034	218076
建筑业房屋施工面积	万平方米		66.30	278.72	1218.00	1234.98	730.61	733.44
建筑业房屋竣工面积	万平方米		29.95	94.99	53.76	707.77	354.08	311.94

注：本表固定资产投资资金来源1990年前是国有单位数，1995年以后是城镇集体以上单位数；1995年固定资产投资含沙角C厂完成的126374万元，2005年起是全社会固定资产投资单位数。

5-2 历年全社会固定资产投资

Total Investment in Fixed Assets over Years

单位：万元

年份	全社会投资总额	#民营	#外资	#港澳台	#房地产开发
1978	2319				
1979	1641				
1980	2395				
1981	3756				
1982	18102				
1983	18370				
1984	30050				
1985	70600				
1986	115173				
1987	141856				
1988	165459				
1989	50135				
1990	75052				
1991	137464				
1992	188824				
1993	327630		62600		52110
1994	1407621		1038599		78392
1995	631355		240690		85163
1996	676185		259705		86258
1997	658941		69055		86662
1998	769953		91719	35868	95451
1999	883201		188036	116708	104411
2000	1028914		146887	96112	112498
2001	1254945		224812	181822	148544
2002	1915741		466569	213458	268350
2003	3193889		888664	619193	551184
2004	4548691		1094045	716611	1144195
2005	5972443		1753772	1246450	1444277
2006	7054511	2410417	2297486	1584104	1642398
2007	8412074	2841860	2356983	1136955	2094187
2008	9443426	3240949	2710398	1469186	2714197
2009	10940753	4279669	2038232	1114631	2776623
2010	11149822	4847208	2265006	1326063	2989853

注：1994、1995、1996年全社会投资总额分别含沙角C厂投资额956758万元、126374万元、102760万元。

5-3 按登记类型和行业分的固定资产投资(2010年)

Total Investment in Fixed Assets by Registration Status and Sector (2010)

单位：万元

项 目	全市合计	#城镇	#房地产	农村
合 计	**11149822**	**7655167**	**2989853**	**3494655**
按登记注册类型分				
内资	8884816	6408350	2704492	2476466
国有	1479886	1452018	17245	27868
集体	1505879	682954	145892	822925
股份合作	20652	19057		1595
国有联营				
集体联营	1856	88		1768
国有与集体联营				
其他联营	2300			2300
国有独资公司	185806	185806	89530	
其他有限责任公司	3102356	2482014	1457683	620342
股份有限公司	191677	71087		120590
私营	1663591	1324244	961717	339347
其他	317154	139878	32425	177276
个体经营：个体户	399853	50575		349278
个人合伙	13806	629		13177
港澳台商投资	1326063	704860	158056	621203
合资经营	156086	117781	50393	38305
合作经营	90813	74609	27640	16204
独资	1068711	502807	80023	565904
股份有限	10453	9663		790
外商投资	938943	541957	127305	396986
合资经营	122892	100442	34385	22450
合作经营	58174	52257	47844	5917
独资	737123	383453	45076	353670
股份有限	20754	5805		14949
按国民经济行业分				
第一产业	1922	1242		680
第二产业	4080358	2083533		1996825
制造业	3388101	1487044		1901057
电力、燃气及水的生产和供应业	687134	594329		92805
建筑业	4796	2160		2636
第三产业	7067542	5570392	2989853	1497150
交通运输、仓储和邮政业	1191693	1052482		139211
信息传输、计算机服务和软件业	200850	197447		3403
批发和零售业	201106	71590		129516
住宿与饮食业	109330	38902		70428
金融业	26286	20195		6091
房地产业	3645313	3239309	2989853	406004
租赁和商务服务业	66834	17031		49803
科学 研究、技术服务和地质勘查业	93236	45177		48059
水利、环境和公共设施管理业	841767	517270		324497
居民服务和其他服务业	29535	5950		23585
教育	221760	140043		81717
卫生、社会保障和社会福利业	145102	111889		33213
文化、体育和娱乐业	122567	64295		58272
公共管理和社会组织	172163	48812		123351

5-4 固定资产投资主要指标（2010年）

Main Indicators of Total Investment in Fixed Assets (2010)

单位：万元

项目	计划总投资	本年完成投资				
			建筑工程	安装工程	设备工器具购置	其他费用
合计	**24846310**	**8159969**	**3773358**	**399624**	**3020012**	**966975**
按登记注册类型分						
内资	21924084	6180324	3491535	377288	1411423	900078
国有	5888137	1462641	1106512	70344	141635	144150
集体	3882644	1359987	933563	74047	96107	256270
股份合作	118296	20652	19652			1000
国有联营						
集体联营	1993	1856	948		908	
国有与集体联营						
其他联营	2500	2300	2300			
国有独资公司	1917083	96276	42008	21365	98	32805
其他有限责任公司	7101933	1644673	639824	117287	598235	289327
股份有限公司	714465	191677	57844	10179	94348	29306
私营个体	1725484	1115533	535126	58972	390224	131211
其他	571549	284729	153758	25094	89868	16009
港澳台商投资	1814516	1168007	172571	16178	932136	47122
外商投资	1107710	811638	109252	6158	676453	19775
按国民经济行业分						
第一产业	2812	1922	1622		250	50
第二产业	6996549	4080358	1061414	126028	2614899	278017
制造业	5106787	3388101	680705	76709	2428455	202232
电力、燃气及水的生产和供应业	1881956	687134	379468	49319	182590	75757
建筑业	7151	4796	914		3854	28
第三产业	17846949	4077689	2710322	273596	404863	688908
交通运输、仓储和邮政业	10319477	1191693	860019	12975	62625	256074
信息传输、计算机服务和软件业	137460	200850	11985	93859	94986	20
批发和零售业	360310	201106	80288	16937	73336	30545
住宿与饮食业	296757	109330	54573	32599	20630	1528
金融业	77465	26286	19080	549	2017	4640
房地产业	1812056	655460	485776	37989	15240	116455
租赁和商务服务业	201852	66834	33198	2735	21186	9715
科学 研究、技术服务和地质勘查业	528342	93236	52674		4082	36480
水利、环境和公共设施管理业	2315565	841767	688500	45484	51550	56233
居民服务和其他服务业	49685	29535	8971	4260	11929	4375
教育	535564	221760	132114	4517	12818	72311
卫生、社会保障和社会福利业	504352	145102	108181	11949	14195	10777
文化、体育和娱乐业	353360	122567	100091	5011	10065	7400
公共管理和社会组织	354704	172163	74872	4732	10204	82355
按建设性质分						
新建	17983987	4141374	2689820	166457	483287	801810
扩建	2388889	735826	420274	120304	169052	26196
改建	1913676	1120253	605485	105571	276718	132479
单纯建造生活设施	18622	18271	8268	7092	1575	1336
迁建	189443	23902	17861	200	687	5154
恢复	103168	31650	31650			
单纯购置	2248525	2088693			2088693	

注：本表不含房地产开发投资。

5-4 续表 1

(2010年)

单位：万元

项　　目	本年新增固定资产	本年施工房屋面积(万平方米)	本年竣工房屋面积(万平方米)	本年资金来源合计	#上年末结余资金
合　　计	**4436871**	**1262.12**	**389.62**	**10060431**	**1187934**
按登记注册类型分					
内资	3087432	1102.13	373.50	7359495	919355
国有	254503	32.64	4.94	1443832	35111
集体	753617	296.70	93.89	1882308	222443
股份合作	20016	17.99	17.00	20652	9304
国有联营					
集体联营	1170	0.60		6185	290
国有与集体联营					
其他联营		1.30		2500	689
国有独资公司	44224			96296	
其他有限责任公司	913666	199.20	39.18	2017324	400126
股份有限公司	137477	39.53	8.42	300873	128094
私营个体	778223	449.05	189.55	1287906	29553
其他	184536	65.12	20.51	301619	93745
港澳台商投资	742385	101.73	10.66	1756607	235052
外商投资	607054	58.26	5.47	944329	33527
按国民经济行业分					
第一产业	1872			1922	
第二产业	2550759	593.37	139.20	5001081	446640
制造业	2404065	582.49	136.87	4181944	385069
电力、燃气及水的生产和供应业	144476	10.47	2.33	813779	60491
建筑业	2043	0.42		5031	1080
第三产业	1884240	668.75	250.42	5057428	741294
交通运输、仓储和邮政业	322993	25.46	9.54	1276384	316040
信息传输、计算机服务和软件业	190411	0.15		200850	
批发和零售业	105009	40.80	8.47	244853	25009
住宿与饮食业	65273	35.01	3.04	140183	2144
金融业	8195	15.50	0.38	65390	5418
房地产业	414119	317.51	155.62	1022584	186054
租赁和商务服务业	46247	19.01	12.48	99542	6143
科学 研究、技术服务和地质勘查业	59095	14.09	0.18	148653	767
水利、环境和公共设施管理业	380806	17.81	1.62	995611	54170
居民服务和其他服务业	11548	2.01	1.67	43772	15246
教育	84778	66.52	16.98	251193	10560
卫生、社会保障和社会福利业	84434	65.64	27.72	164622	19917
文化、体育和娱乐业	59782	17.82	0.62	140349	4832
公共管理和社会组织	51550	31.42	12.11	263442	94994
按建设性质分					
新建	1750867	1024.07	300.75	5417555	831313
扩建	462924	70.86	25.91	790100	199387
改建	550321	159.80	60.57	1294428	54773
单纯建造生活设施	16045	0.21	0.01	18848	442
迁建	18841	7.16	2.37	27982	
恢复	30691	0.02	0.02	31650	
单纯购置	1607182			2479868	102019

5-4 续表 2

(2010年)

单位：万元

项目	本年资金来源					
	#本年资金来源小计	国家预算内资金	国内贷款	利用外资	自筹资金	其他资金来源
合　计	**8872497**	**130717**	**610748**	**1325738**	**6365177**	**416431**
按登记注册类型分						
内资	6440140	130717	535216	13810	5455545	281166
国有	1408721	6231	121244		1221062	50498
集体	1659865	75722	62547	1830	1381654	138112
股份合作	11348		6257		5091	
国有联营						
集体联营	5895				5711	184
国有与集体联营						
其他联营	1811				1811	
国有独资公司	96296	47964			48332	
其他有限责任公司	1617198		227177	5503	1361489	23029
股份有限公司	172779	800	1857	5428	164644	50
私营个体	1258353		114380	1035	1079905	49033
其他	207874		1754	14	185846	20260
港澳台商投资	1521555		58959	759072	641509	62015
外商投资	910802		16573	552856	268123	73250
按国民经济行业分						
第一产业	1922				1362	560
第二产业	4554441	1053	185336	1250811	2910590	182965
制造业	3796875	966	105220	1247568	2285415	143706
电力、燃气及水的生产和供应业	753288		80116	3243	621405	38838
建筑业	3951	87			3443	421
第三产业	4316134	129664	425412	74927	3453225	232906
交通运输、仓储和邮政业	960344	9021	231699	2600	633803	83221
信息传输、计算机服务和软件业	200850			148	200602	100
批发和零售业	219844	3293	11507	22402	181250	1392
住宿与饮食业	138039	100	4600	1980	124732	6627
金融业	59972			680	59292	
房地产业	836530	11000	97565	3500	691423	33042
租赁和商务服务业	93399		5967	1100	82384	3948
科学 研究、技术服务和地质勘查业	147886	4268		433	141041	2144
水利、环境和公共设施管理业	941441	78704	30141	1157	737443	93996
居民服务和其他服务业	28526	924		5968	21634	
教育	240633	16559	34994	8000	178312	2768
卫生、社会保障和社会福利业	144705		6257	26552	111681	215
文化、体育和娱乐业	135517	4854			129963	700
公共管理和社会组织	168448	941	2682	407	159665	4753
按建设性质分						
新建	4586242	52968	360854	173171	3788818	200745
扩建	590713	68704	30353	17136	455860	18660
改建	1239655	9045	184505	86374	852996	92735
单纯建造生活设施	18406			3064	11528	3814
迁建	27982			1550	26432	
恢复	31650				31650	
单纯购置	2377849		35036	1044443	1197893	100477

5-5 固定资产投资分类情况(2010年)

Basic Statistics on Total Investment in Fixed Assets by Type (2010)

单位：万元

项　　目	计　划 总投资	自开始建设 累计完成投资	本年完 成投资	#住宅	本年新增 固定资产
固定资产投资总额	**24846310**	**13671228**	**8159969**	**246625**	**4436871**
#基础设施	14144588	5901960	2762103	6385	1030455
#基础产业	14366100	6119440	2880390	6385	1148784
#城市建设	8086967	2214813	1164364	6385	595595
#原材料	386428	344649	234493		185745
#能源	1011324	713620	462388		47940
#工业合计	6989398	5669850	4075562	12680	2548716
#工业九大产业	3556373	3045611	2256742	1982	1544853
#电子信息业	1140141	976525	792041	1337	586801
电气机械及专用设备	687002	552202	502343	320	313809
石油及化学	151954	117500	108578	125	63755
纺织及服装	280265	242126	234307	200	184128
食品饮料	233052	164473	149889		58022
建筑材料	245217	240442	144963		128335
森工造纸	762592	712556	288194		179545
医药	9606	7645	7645		3404
汽车	46544	32142	28782		27054

注:本表不含房地产开发投资。

5-6 房地产开发主要指标

Main Indicators of Real Estate Development

项　　目	单位	2002年	2003年	2005年	2006年	2007年	2009年	2010年
一、土地开发及购置								
本年土地开发面积	万平方米	111.8	115.6	20.1	63.5	44.3	66.9	
本年土地购置面积	万平方米	93.4	176.5	44.9	73.0	57.7	92.0	135.7
二、本年完成投资额	**万元**	**268350**	**551184**	**1444277**	**1642398**	**2094187**	**2776623**	**2989853**
#住宅	万元	197633	422347	1197154	1475181	1860580	2513852	2504525
三、资金来源	**万元**	**495093**	**676767**	**1632570**	**2120240**	**2900238**	**4281021**	**6533564**
#国内贷款	万元	72221	139527	114755	292488	446710	544169	1271530
利用外资	万元	30213	55616	2075	10140		105397	75182
自筹资金	万元	166636	185201	867824	677095	905912	1840753	2025670
四、房屋建筑面积								
施工面积	万平方米	401.9	689.5	1160.2	1437.6	1521.6	2333.9	2060.5
#住宅	万平方米	340.3	530.0	889.9	1229.4	1371.0	2050.1	1686.6
竣工面积	万平方米	127.7	257.3	132.9	166.3	137.3	310.2	296.6
#住宅	万平方米	117.4	222.0	115.2	114.1	111.9	268.1	256.1
五、商品房屋销售额	**万元**	**282948**	**480189**	**1193991**	**1612449**	**2949939**	**3530040**	**3737742**
#住宅	万元	232269	409037	1091095	1460425	2736729	3342466	3341485
六、商品房屋销售面积	**万平方米**	**95.0**	**165.0**	**321.9**	**382.0**	**573.0**	**600.3**	**511.3**
#住宅	万平方米	82.9	141.9	297.2	353.0	541.1	578.8	469.9

注：从2010年起，取消“本年土地开发面积”指标。

5-7 房地产开发企业主要经济指标（2010年）

Main Indicators of Real Estate Enterprises (2010)

单位:万元

项　目	资产总计	负债总计	主营业务收入	主营业务税金及附加	利润总额	全部从业人员年平均人数（人）
合　计	**15749778**	**12632102**	**3131319**	**301413**	**424122**	**10581**
按登记注册类型分						
#内源型经济	13838576	11251087	2819442	269661	402008	9082
#民营经济	11993677	10002636	2282336	203177	266128	7786
#国有经济	509144	368971	266339	45386	91239	126
集体经济	1153884	737032	266571	20791	43853	1057
私营个体经济	5626893	4628146	1149473	95305	104278	3925
外源型经济	1911202	1381015	311877	31752	22114	1499
#港澳台商投资	1205803	942606	244778	27177	10511	695
外商投资	705399	438409	67099	4575	11603	804
按控股情况分						
国有控股	509144	368971	266339	45386	91239	126
集体控股	1211048	783398	272190	21888	43179	1081
私人控股	10971752	9185552	1849756	164767	144732	7236
港澳台控股	1206803	942606	244778	27177	10512	697
外商控股	847494	573793	147907	8473	21864	829
其他控股	1003537	777782	350349	33722	112596	612
按资质等级分						
一级	1141965	861244	388675	40551	73806	715
二级	2850349	2470040	462892	37641	13955	1559
三级	3401679	2633752	800600	71849	105019	2933
四级	4951464	3934268	1004948	100511	127343	3446
暂定	2460048	2002977	307791	38391	90168	966
其他	944273	729821	166413	12470	13831	962

5-8 房地产开发投资情况（2010年）

Investment in Real Estate Development (2010)

项　　目	房地产开发投资（万元）	土地开发投资	住宅
合　　计	**2989853**	**11988**	**2504525**
内资	2704492	11729	2251889
国有	17245		13409
集体	145892	3256	137529
国有独资公司	89530		74296
其他有限责任公司	1457683	2227	1247415
私营独资	96250		92474
私营有限责任公司	828438	6246	640890
私营股份有限公司	37029		31513
其他内资企业	32425		14363
港澳台商投资	158056	259	126793
外商投资	127305		125843

5-9 房地产开发企业、房屋建筑面积及价值（2010年）

Floor Space and Value of Buildings in Real Estate Development (2010)

项　　目	房屋建筑面积（平方米）		竣工房屋价值（万元）
	施工面积	竣工面积	
合　　计	**20605403**	**2965906**	**1181775**
内资	18931494	2898770	1165633
国有	486747		
集体	1253763	442462	115803
国有独资公司	289615		
其他有限责任公司	8498171	946419	427020
私营独资	624767	101130	25422
私营有限责任公司	7478643	1363247	577096
私营股份有限公司	220044	27504	16502
其他内资企业	79744	18008	3790
港澳台商投资	1291830	67136	16142
外商投资	382079		

5-10 商品房屋销售情况（2010年）

Sale of Commercialized Buildings (2010)

项目	商品房屋销售建筑面积（平方米）	#住宅	商品房屋销售额（万元）	#住宅
合计	**5112506**	**4698970**	**3737742**	**3341485**
内资	4800315	4442831	3484902	3182827
国有	101848	79905	53959	40064
集体	400559	363245	346581	322155
国有独资公司	153161	117098	209356	175567
其他有限责任公司	2128005	2042823	1521572	1437621
私营独资	20695	15675	7037	6001
私营有限责任公司	1895714	1723752	1286363	1141385
私营股份有限公司	88886	88886	52339	52339
其他内资企业	11447	11447	7695	7695
港澳台商投资	224209	177012	187754	103235
外商投资	87982	79127	65086	55423

5-11 建筑施工企业主要指标（2009-2010年）

Main Indicators of Construction Enterprises (2009-2010)

指标	单位	2009年		2010年	
		合计	#国有单位	合计	#国有单位
企业单位数	个	404	1	431	1
年平均人数	人	55684	1842	57473	1841
自有固定资产原价	万元	308231	17893	262771	14485
自有固定资产净值	万元	157630	9810	150269	6921
自有施工机械设备年末总台数	台	16640	423	17596	413
自有施工机械设备年末净值	万元	76006	1529	58404	1503
自有施工机械设备年末总功率	万千瓦	14	1	17	1
建筑业总产值	万元	994007	141397	1220569	197246
建筑工程产值	万元	806862	141139	994608	197246
安装工程产值	万元	150690	258	172772	
其它产值	万元	36455		53189	
建筑业竣工产值	万元	674761	60225	799524	80081
建筑业增加值	万元	815489		823674	
房屋建筑施工面积	万平方米	731	6	733	15
房屋建筑竣工面积	万平方米	351		312	5
利润总额	万元	61495	721	57835	1039
利税总额	万元	99896	6033	99072	8669
劳动生产率(按总产值计算)	元/人	184034	767628	218076	1071407
劳动生产率(按增加值计算)	元/人	150983		147163	
技术装备率	元/人	13650	8301	10162	8164
动力装备率	千瓦/人	2.5	5.0	3.0	5.0
房屋建筑面积竣工率	%	48.0		42.6	33.3
产值利润率	%	6.2	0.5	4.7	0.5
产值利税率	%	10.0	4.2	8.1	4.4

主要统计指标解释

Explanatory Notes on Main Statistical Indicators

固定资产投资额 是以货币形式表现的在一定时期内建造和购置固定资产的工作量以及与此有关的费用的总称。按构成可分为建筑工程、安装工程、设备工器具购置和其他费用。

房屋建筑施工面积 指报告期内施工的全部房屋建筑面积。包括本期新开工的面积和上期开工跨入本期继续施工的房屋面积，以及上期已停建在本期复工的房屋面积。本期竣工和本期施工后又停缓建的房屋，其建筑面积仍计入本期施工房屋面积中。

房屋建筑新开工面积 指报告期内新开工的全部房屋建筑面积，以单位工程为核算对象。房屋新开工面积指整栋房屋的全部建筑面积，不能分割计算。

房屋建筑竣工面积 指在报告期内房屋建筑按照设计要求已全部完工，达到住人和使用条件，经验收鉴定合格(或达到竣工验收标准)，可正式移交使用的各栋房屋建筑面积的总和。

房屋建筑面积竣工率 指一定时期内房屋竣工面积占同期房屋施工面积的比率。它是从房屋建筑施工速度的角度反映投资效果和建筑业经济效益的指标。

固定资产交付使用率 指一定时期新增固定资产与同期完成投资额的比率。它反映各个时期固定资产动用速度、衡量建设过程中投资效果的一个综合性指标。

六、运输邮电

Transport, Postal and Telecommunication Services

6-1 主要年份运输邮电主要指标

Main Indicators of Transport, Postal and Telecommunication Services in Main Years

项　　目	单　位	1985年	1990年	1995年	2000年	2005年	2009年	2010年
公路通车里程	公里	1240	1325	2327	2519	2871	4713	4751
#高速公路	公里				89	154	207	217
一级公路	公里		6	679	782	1315	2389	2394
内河通航里程	公里	532	598	598	798	664	643	643
公路桥梁	座	211	267	338	538	826	1065	1211
民用汽车	辆	7897	19394	88311	153684	406577	795554	920766
#载客	辆	1878	7225	25366	69658	268918	653273	772701
载货	辆	5980	12087	52242	80405	129298	137334	143005
摩托车	辆	11786	47881	255591	482636	775838	470818	423766
机动船	艘	2883	5885	5292	806	467	293	286
机动船净载重	吨位	80324	186056	259329	152661	148737	203820	557846
邮电局(所)	处	52	53	273	594	702	546	555
邮路长度	公里	790	459	685	3550	6835	6198	4667
长途自动交换机容量	路端		2100	15000	42182	510045	864970	419110
局用交换机容量	万门	1.14	6.98	52.29	103.13	286.25	347.15	365.02
移动电话交换机总容量	万户			4.8	154.2	1059.1	1621.6	1657.0
本地电话用户	万户	0.77	4.90	31.58	78.12	384.52	378.40	332.42
移动电话用户(含充值卡)	万户		0.05	4.77	123.68	1016.41	1409.29	1607.60
互联网用户	万户			0.05	13.78	52.90	118.02	153.92
邮政业务收入	万元						71467	63178
电信业务收入	万元						1491610	1490174
客运量	万人	2072	5758	10237	30697	33551	73324	77446
#公路	万人	1940	5728	10210	30680	33510	73291	77415
旅客周转量	万人公里	95237	322236	446230	1001906	1185290	1053469	1290692
#公路	万人公里	90950	320690	444293	1000492	1182000	1051324	1288675
货运量	万吨	2913	2701	4266	5431	6400	8733	9312
#公路	万吨	1922	1571	2377	3440	4586	6944	7640
货物周转量	万吨公里	171591	184700	264605	404678	424829	1016490	1090340
#公路	万吨公里	113038	72162	128026	246046	272500	452880	510801
港口货物吞吐量	万吨	276	233	201	746	2280	3530	5657

注：1. 2006年起公路通车里程含专用公路和村道，下同。
2. 2010年起，长途自动交换机容量统计口径有变，与往年不可比，下同。
3. 2010年起，邮政业务相关指标不包括速递物流及邮政储蓄银行独立运营部分，下同。

6-2 历年运输线路长度与公路密度

Length of Transportation Routes and Road Density over Years

年 份	公路通车里程(公里)	#等级公路	#一级	等外公路	高级、次高级路面通车里程(公里)	内河通航里程(公里)	公路密度(公里/百平方公里)
1978	1259	287		972		530	51.08
1979	1225	355		870		603	49.70
1980	1225	355		870		603	49.70
1981	1225	845		380		415	49.70
1982	1225	845		380		115	49.70
1983	1225	872		353		132	49.70
1984	1240	896		344		132	50.30
1985	1240	490		750	488	132	50.30
1986	1248	977		271		274	50.63
1987	1261	991		270		598	51.16
1988	1302	1068	6	234		598	52.82
1989	1325	1091	6	234		598	53.75
1990	1325	1102	6	223	750	598	53.75
1991	1759	1226	6	533	1137	598	71.36
1992	2055	1431	151	624	1442	599	83.37
1993	2260	1673	315	587	1675	598	91.68
1994	2292	1868	599	424	1773	598	92.98
1995	2327	1930	679	397	1650	598	94.40
1996	2330	2087	689	243	1653	598	94.50
1997	2330	2087	690	243	1563	598	94.50
1998	2429	1897	714	480	1958	598	98.52
1999	2467	1935	717	480	2048	798	100.06
2000	2519	2339	782	91	2253	798	102.15
2001	2570	2393	845	78	2321	798	104.26
2002	2641	2464	908	78	2406	798	107.14
2003	2688	2508	967	75	2472	716	109.05
2004	2759	2609	1148	37	2637	798	111.93
2005	2871	2686	1315	31	2774	664	116.47
2006	3891	3619	1585	117	3823	664	157.85
2007	3924	3650	1591	116	3860	535	159.19
2008	4001	3884	1639	117	3864	643	162.31
2009	4713	4598	2389	115	4643	643	191.21
2010	4751	4637	2394	114	4681	643	192.74

注：公路密度数据来源于交通运输局，下同。

6-3 主要年份运输线路长度

Length of Transport Routes in Main Years

项　　目	单　位	1980年	1985年	1990年	1995年	2000年	2005年	2009年	2010年
一、公路通车里程合计	**公里**	**1225**	**1240**	**1325**	**2327**	**2519**	**2871**	**4713**	**4751**
#按等级分									
等级公路	公里	355	490	1102	1930	2339	2686	4598	4637
高速公路	公里					89	154	207	217
一　级	公里			6	679	782	1315	2389	2394
二　级	公里		58	65	361	684	703	1317	1317
三　级	公里		61	60	135	310	297	153	178
四　级	公里	355	371	971	755	563	371	532	532
等外公路	公里	870	750	223	397	91	31	115	114
#按路面分									
有路面里程	公里		622	800	1808	2508	2858	4650	4689
#高级、次高级	公里		488	750	1650	2253	2774	4643	4681
无路面里程	公里		618	524	519	11	13	63	62
二、桥梁合计	**座**		**211**	**267**	**338**	**538**	**826**	**1065**	**1211**
	延米					39956	112385	138867	162767
三、公路密度	**公里/百平方公里**	**49.70**	**50.30**	**53.75**	**94.40**	**102.15**	**116.47**	**191.21**	**192.74**
#等级公路密度	公里/百平方公里	14.40	19.88	44.71	78.30	94.89	108.97	186.54	188.12
四、内河通航里程	**公里**	**603**	**532**	**598**	**598**	**798**	**664**	**643**	**643**

6-4 主要年份客货运输量

Passenger and Freight Traffic in Main Years

年　份	客运量（万人）	旅客周转量（万人公里）	货运量（万吨）	货物周转量（万吨公里）	港口货物吞吐量（万吨）
1952	86	1350	7	139	
1957	120	2100	10	195	
1962	187	4120	14	293	
1965	193	4725	22	457	
1970	118	2800	36	900	
1975	169	3890	30	694	
1978	403	9425	394	15148	293
1980	572	13584	349	16353	295
1985	2072	95237	2913	171591	276
1990	5758	322236	2701	184700	233
1995	10237	446230	4266	264605	201
1996	10749	477466	4451	267193	289
1997	11300	511592	4644	278649	338
1998	17485	577452	4776	285889	516
1999	25404	804278	5016	300410	654
2000	30697	1001906	5431	404678	746
2001	31220	1031579	5527	406247	883
2002	32100	1091821	5857	420684	1611
2003	32588	1126964	5877	422822	2352
2004	33240	1166262	6054	423669	2600
2005	33551	1185290	6400	424829	2280
2006	35182	1213809	5481	336783	1951
2007	37182	1264982	5676	356677	2017
2008	122468	2248521	9273	1747489	3208
2009	73324	1053469	8733	1016490	3530
2010	77446	1290692	9312	1090340	5657

6-5 客货运输量

Passenger and Freight Traffic

项　　目	单　位	1980年	1985年	1990年	1995年	2000年	2005年	2009年	2010年
一、客运量	**万人**	**572**	**2072**	**5758**	**10237**	**30697**	**33551**	**73324**	**77446**
公　路	万人	362	1940	5728	10210	30680	33510	73291	77415
水　运	万人	210	132	30	27	17	41	33	31
二、旅客周转量	**万人公里**	**13584**	**95237**	**322236**	**446230**	**1001906**	**1185290**	**1053469**	**1290692**
公　路	万人公里	8285	90950	320690	444293	1000492	1182000	1051324	1288675
水　运	万人公里	5299	4287	1546	1937	1414	3290	2145	2017
三、货运量	**万吨**	**349**	**2913**	**2701**	**4266**	**5431**	**6400**	**8733**	**9312**
公　路	万吨	51	1922	1571	2377	3440	4586	6944	7640
#个体及联户	万吨		1906	1557	2368	3440	4586	1973	2080
水　运	万吨	298	991	1130	1889	1991	1814	1789	1672
#个体及联户	万吨		617	837	1599	1660	1484	159	158
四、货物周转量	**万吨公里**	**16353**	**171591**	**184700**	**264605**	**404678**	**424829**	**1016490**	**1090340**
公　路	万吨公里	1479	113038	72162	128026	246046	272500	452880	510801
#个体及联户	万吨公里		113002	72141	127928	246046	272500	126052	131929
水　运	万吨公里	14874	58553	112538	136579	158632	152329	563610	579539
#个体及联户	万吨公里		31784	83094	105099	119855	113249	8787	9399

6-6 主要年份运输工具拥有量

Possession of Main Means of Transport in Main Years

项　　目	单　位	1980年	1985年	1990年	1995年	2000年	2005年	2009年	2010年
一、民用车辆拥有量									
(一)汽车	辆	2009	7897	19394	88311	153684	406577	795554	920766
1. 载客汽车	辆	516	1878	7225	25366	69658	268918	653273	772701
	客位	1909	23462	66361	302844	560155	2420591	4483494	5101240
2. 载货汽车	辆	1457	5980	12087	55000	81623	129298	137334	143005
	吨位	3368	20428	38010	133757	332621	243390	234684	253879
3. 其他汽车	辆	36	39	82	7945	2403	8361	4947	5060
(二)摩托车	辆	170	11786	47881	255591	482636	775838	470818	423766
(三)挂车	辆					8	2222	2697	2983
二、民用运输船舶拥有量									
机动船	艘	1948	2883	5885	5292	806	467	293	286
	净载重吨位	42473	80323	186056	259329	152661	148737	203820	557846
	客位	2107	2056	776	1881	1054	604	902	902
#货船	艘		2866	5875	5259	796	465	290	283
	净载重吨位		80285	186038	259314	152661	148431	203360	557236
客船	艘				26	10	2	3	3
	客位				1295	1054	604	902	902
三、期末机动车驾驶员	**人**		**44186**	**118229**	**351947**	**563564**	**798086**	**1144901**	**1287738**
#汽车驾驶员	人		10661	28768	94778	173865	428912	941097	1110932

注：2002年起民用汽车拥有量按新的口径分类，部分指标数值与往年不可比。

6-7 历年主要运输工具年末拥有量

Possession of Main Means of Transport at Year-end over Years

年　份	民用汽车 (辆)	#客车	#货车	摩托车 (辆)	机动船 (艘)
1978	623	78	506	134	2169
1979	1115	178	1089	156	2034
1980	2009	516	1457	170	1948
1981	3039	751	2031	517	2107
1982	3419	791	2724	1168	2285
1983	4473	854	3580	1636	2313
1984	6059	1243	4822	7060	2563
1985	7897	1878	5980	11786	2883
1986	8632	2245	6334	18006	4368
1987	9983	2954	6973	21308	4884
1988	13581	3456	8690	26995	4911
1989	16340	4214	10434	36820	4901
1990	19394	7225	12087	47881	5885
1991	20734	5206	15423	65770	4405
1992	32625	5753	25048	106013	4351
1993	48145	8710	35421	153014	4379
1994	61572	11550	43925	200543	4562
1995	88311	25366	55000	255591	5292
1996	90793	29430	54870	249492	5313
1997	103425	40101	62507	287076	5064
1998	113435	47769	64434	382010	456
1999	127007	55715	69470	399324	690
2000	153684	69658	82841	482636	806
2001	183638	89677	91304	560310	536
2002	220134	116783	102253	642034	483
2003	255603	155206	97047	692562	392
2004	319725	210531	105050	687651	417
2005	406577	268918	129298	775838	467
2006	489306	351265	131704	697175	440
2007	608933	466999	134825	567002	393
2008	701600	557359	136295	521118	326
2009	795554	653273	137334	470818	293
2010	920766	772701	143005	423766	286

6-8 主要年份邮电通信业务基本情况

Basic Statistics on Postal and Telecommunication Services in Main Years

项　　目	单位	1978年	1985年	1990年	1995年	2000年	2005年	2009年	2010年
一、邮电通信网									
邮电局、所	处	50	52	53	273	594	702	546	555
#设在农村	处	48	50	49	222	539	617	478	415
邮路长度	公里	513	790	459	685	3550	6835	6198	4667
农村投递线路长度	公里	1985	2302	1812	2057	8865	19722	25025	13261
二、邮电通信工具									
邮政汽车	辆		2	7	10	35	192	363	131
长途自动交换机容量	路端			2100	15000	42182	510045	864970	419110
移动电话交换机总容量	万户				4.8	154.2	1059.1	1621.6	1657.0
移动电话用户(含充值卡)	万户					123.68	1016.41	1409.29	1607.60
移动电话用户(不含充值卡)	万户			0.05	4.77	80.97	176.83	138.14	174.04
局用交换机容量	万门		1.14	6.98	52.29	103.13	286.25	347.15	365.02
#市话交换机	万门		0.22	2.10	16.82	21.84	67.68	90.05	94.28
本地电话用户	万户	0.20	0.77	4.90	31.57	78.12	384.52	378.40	332.42
市内电话用户	万户	0.04	0.16	1.50	9.78	19.69	68.30	113.51	85.76
农村电话用户	万户	0.16	0.61	3.40	21.80	58.43	316.22	264.89	246.66
数字数据用户(DDN)	端口					2741	2170	1301	1098
互联网用户	万户				0.05	13.78	52.90	118.02	153.92
三、邮电业务量									
邮电业务收入	亿元							156.31	155.34
#电信业务	亿元							149.16	149.02
#移动通信业务	亿元							101.29	105.78
邮政特快专递	万件						292.17	557.22	183.00
函件	万件		805	3372	10407	8124	9430	4276	4507
长途电话	万次		89	1739	21287	66419	159762	154412	135811

6-9 历年邮电通信业务主要指标

Main Indicators of Postal and Telecommunication Services over Years

年 份	邮 电 局、所 (处)	长途自动 交换机容量 (路端)	局用交 换机容量 (万门)	本地电话 用 户 (万户)	移动电话 用 户 (万户)	邮电业务 收 入 (亿元)
1978	50			0.20		
1979	50			0.21		
1980	50		0.50	0.31		
1981	50			0.34		
1982	51			0.35		
1983	51			0.39		
1984	52			0.48		
1985	52		1.14	0.77		
1986	53			0.88		
1987	45			1.63		
1988	48			2.52		
1989	50			4.30	0.02	
1990	53	2100	6.98	4.90	0.05	
1991	60		9.82	7.50	0.11	
1992	91	3510	11.07	9.70	0.30	
1993	161	3510	21.24	14.98	0.72	
1994	216	11410	36.37	23.19	2.41	
1995	273	15000	52.29	31.57	4.77	
1996	310	15000	52.79	36.91	8.24	
1997	339	15000	57.76	42.65	15.29	
1998	397	25000	73.09	50.13	26.17	
1999	458	40000	84.79	60.87	51.01	
2000	594	42182	103.13	78.12	123.68	
2001	689	59000	155.29	98.96	295.76	
2002	696	59000	176.94	127.93	412.39	90.56
2003	846	129000	220.28	206.11	660.86	105.12
2004	854	200985	265.66	281.35	856.09	120.78
2005	702	510045	286.25	384.52	1016.41	132.82
2006	560	563071	299.19	461.31	1216.34	146.69
2007	567	713290	329.50	469.17	1408.23	161.90
2008	547	766946	340.71	439.41	1454.29	172.38
2009	546	864970	347.15	378.40	1409.29	156.31
2010	555	419110	365.02	332.42	1607.60	155.34

注：本地电话用户含小灵通用户。

6-10 历年邮电通信企业财务指标

Main Financial Indicators of Postal and Telecommunication Enterprises over Years

单位：万元

指　　标	2002年	2003年	2004年	2005年	2006年	2007年	2009年	2010年
职工人数(人)	5035	5269	9485	10730	10881	11309	10901	10050
#固定工	4038	4277	7941	4803	4498	4528	4459	4375
年末资产总额	1211054	1211056	1342540	1465629	1548349	1623628	1585605	1615528
年末流动资产合计	224550	146908	133768	181039	228697	279043	246591	261091
#应收帐款净额	63042	57368	53062	67608	56478	62631	20441	53749
年末固定资产合计	947924	998057	1151720	1238276	1280974	1258143	1160814	1118833
年末固定资产原值合计	1157237	1402762	1534094	1790159	2018571	2252314	2694488	2835390
#生产用	1122155	1386056	1516466	1770843	2006747	2163153	2686818	2827527
累计折旧	348785	472350	531081	664786	860633	1077754	1482506	1647586
#当年折旧	115935	122390	154417	177293	197314	230146	237351	112848
年末固定资产净值合计	808453	930412	1003012	1125360	1157926	1174540	1211982	1187804
无形资产及递延资产	15635	25839	57051	42582	38777	81176	61802	63073
其它资产	12707	11056		2198	2551	5265	116398	172531
负债及所有者权益总计	1211054	1211056	1342540	1465629	1548349	1623628	1585605	1615528
年末流动资产负债合计	244828	194474	202929	365735	451449	465033	474003	570387
#未交税金	19870	17729	29345	39447	42265	33785	10644	17248
短期借款				3000		8000		
年末长期负债合计	95	14175	9932				64537	-2635
期末所有者权益合计	966131	1002408	1129679	1099894	1096900	1158595	1047065	1047776
主营业务收入	890138	1036123	1174265	1326686	1446601	1603151	1636257	1155820
#营业成本	236322	278125	303464	406999	471863	552168	583539	468110
营业税金及附加	26517	34307	36790	41122	41635	48758	46435	32063
其他业务利润	-855	266223	11911	-11316	-15355	1230	2690	-1721
管理费用	24375	214051	84868	99425	56157	54236	47008	34802
财务费用	3910	447	37848	539	897	898	1660	2718
营业外收入	874	1088	1676	879	1809	2135	2204	6093
营业外支出	10122	2424	8424	2838	3325	6132	18017	3281
利润总额	548341	580729	676902	716380	805496	877893	738312	496456
利税总额	576501	627697	713700	756757	835548	926720	777806	520173

主要统计指标解释

Explanatory Notes on Main Statistical Indicators

公路里程 指在一定时点上实际达到交通部规定的公路技术等级标准，并经公路主管部门正式验收交付使用的公路里程数。包括大、中城市的郊区公路以及公路通过城镇（指县城、集镇）街道的里程数。但不包括大、中城市街道，厂矿、林区内部生产用道、农业生产用道，以及新建公路尚未进行验收交付使用的路段里程。公路按工程技术等级分为高速、一、二、三、四级公路；按公路是否铺设路面分为有路面和无路面公路；按公路通车情况分为晴雨通车里程和晴通雨阻里程。计量单位为公里。

货（客）运量 在一定时期内，各运输部门实际运送的货物（旅客）数量。货运按吨计算，客运按人计算。货物不论运输距离长短，货物类型，均按实际重量统计；旅客不论行程远近或票价多少，均按一人一次作为客运量统计。半价票，小孩票也按一人统计。货（客）运量反映运输业为国民经济和人民生活服务的数量，也是制定和检查运输生产计划，研究运输发展规模和速度的重要指标。

货物（旅客）周转量 指在一定时期内，由各种运输工具运输业运送的货物（旅客）数量与其相应运输距离的乘积，通常以吨公里和人公里为计算单位。计算货物周转量通常按发出站与到达站之间的最短距离，也就是计费距离计算。它是反映运输业生产总成果的重要指标，也是编制和检查运输生产计划，计算运输效率，劳动生产率以及核算运输单位成本的主要基础资料。

货物吞吐量 是指经由水运运进、运出港区范围，并经过装卸的货物数量。货物吞吐量分别按国内进口（装卸）、出口（装船），外贸进口、出口统计。货物吞吐量按货物实际重量吨统计，以货物交接清单或货单上记载的重量吨为准。如无实际重量吨，可根据船舶装载情况来推算。在本港区内的水运转口分别按进口和出口各计算一次吞吐量。货物吞吐量是衡量港口生产规模的一个主要数量指标。

邮电业务收入 是指邮电营运企业从事邮政、电信、移动及其他邮电业务所取得的营业收入。

局用电话交换机容量 指安装在本地电信运营商内用于接读本地固定电话的电话交换机容量，有倍增设备按倍增后的数量计数。包括现用和备用的人工或自动交换全部容量。

本地电话用户 是指接入本地电信运营商固定电话网上的电话用户。包括：住宅电话、单位用户、公用电话用户等。

移动电话用户 是指在移动通信部门办理登记手续，通过移动电话交换机进入移动电话网，占用移动电话号码的电话用户。

邮电局所 是指对外营业、直接为用户办理邮电业务的服务机构。一个邮电局所，必须同时具备以下三个条件：①有固定的局所地址；②领有上级发给的日戳或戳记；③至少办理出售邮票和收寄挂号信两种邮政业务或办理一种电信业务。凡是具备上述三个条件的，均按邮电局所统计，计量单位为“处”。邮电局所按经营方式分为自办局所和代办所。

邮电服务网点 指为用户进行邮电服务的地点，包括邮电局所、报刊亭等。

主要统计指标解释

Explanatory Notes on Main Statistical Indicators

七、国内贸易

Domestic Trade

7-1 历年社会消费品零售总额

Total Retail Sales of Consumer Goods over Years

年　份	社会消费品零售总额	
	绝对值（万元）	增速（%）
1978	21269	
1979	24956	17.3
1980	31595	26.6
1981	40201	27.2
1982	48126	19.7
1983	52255	8.6
1984	73930	41.5
1985	93640	26.7
1986	122420	30.7
1987	150511	23.0
1988	246518	63.8
1989	270354	9.7
1990	319738	18.3
1991	364972	14.2
1992	443464	21.5
1993	636882	43.6
1994	851556	33.7
1995	1130081	32.7
1996	1255311	11.1
1997	1460396	16.3
1998	1751551	19.9
1999	2023008	15.5
2000	2351634	16.2
2001	2757143	17.2
2002	3212436	16.5
2003	3697814	15.1
2004	4264704	15.3
2005	5062917	18.7
2006	5993201	18.4
2007	7224491	20.5
2008	8811519	22.0
2009	9590727	8.8
2010	11080592	15.9

注：本表1979-2003年数据根据东莞市第一次全国经济普查结果重新核定，2005-2008年数据根据东莞市第二次全国经济普查结果重新核定。

7-2 历年批发零售贸易企业与个体户数

Wholesale and Retail Trades Enterprises and Self-employed Individuals over years

单位：个

年　份	单位数合计	国有经济	集体经济	其他经济	＃私营个体经济
1979	2459	406	1918	135	135
1980	2613	395	1679	539	537
1981	4603	371	1954	2278	2274
1982	3323	373	1838	1112	1107
1983	8723	401	1539	6783	6783
1984	18917	431	6720	11766	11766
1985	16885	670	4543	11672	11671
1986	18547	823	3063	14661	14660
1987	23468	739	4102	18627	18626
1988	26247	665	4405	21177	21176
1989	28453	695	4196	23562	23561
1990	27931	709	3512	23710	23709
1991	29474	678	3934	24862	24862
1992	34465	803	4193	29469	29469
1993	43511	886	7640	34985	34985
1994	49706	633	11396	37677	37677
1995	56339	745	14492	41102	41101
1996	60078	670	15183	44225	44224
1997	48910	811	8477	39622	39546
1998	52543	1064	4046	47433	46615
1999	55925	1056	3843	51026	50172
2000	57474	1024	3581	5289	51914
2001	68909	866	2960	65083	63760
2002	89246	748	2424	86078	84614
2003	113531	530	2068	110933	109236
2004	149067	539	1941	146587	144304
2005	192525	393	1451	190681	188082
2006	236124	283	1090	234751	231930
2007	284109	268	930	282911	279524
2008	301996	288	833	300875	296613
2009	300088	256	744	299088	294753
2010	300668	239	654	299775	295166

7-3 批发零售业商品销售总额（2010年）

Total Sales of Commodities in Wholesale and Retail Trades(2010)

单位：万元

项　目	商品销售总额	#批发额	零售额
合　计	**19571790**	**9581828**	**9989963**
按行业分			
批发业	9050232	8632055	418177
零售业	10521558	949773	9571785
按规模分			
限额以上企业	12572052	7840126	4731926
粮油、食品、饮料、烟酒类	1403791	1106597	297194
粮油类	211663	132930	78733
肉禽蛋类	50171	22701	27470
水产品类	7241	1260	5981
蔬菜类	19172	666	18506
干鲜果品类	25364	3388	21976
饮料类	119429	66751	52678
烟酒类	654581	626462	28119
服装鞋帽、针纺织品类	928326	702005	226321
服装类	507779	389017	118763
鞋帽类	197124	112829	84295
针、纺织品类	223422	200160	23263
化妆品类	41025	5996	35029
金银珠宝类	22444	12321	10123
日用品类	270578	185640	84938
洗涤用品类	127869	79601	48267
儿童玩具类	30791	25507	5283
五金、电料类	205195	185365	19830
体育、娱乐用品类	21646	9195	12451
书报杂志类	19586	10093	9493
电子出版物及音像制品类	5243	3394	1849
家用电器和音像器材类	688013	319878	368135
中西药品类	318786	177585	141201
西药	178086	71926	106160
中草药及中成药	57616	30918	26698
文化办公用品类	109954	46013	63941
家具类	452627	447959	4668
通讯器材类	394262	336933	57329
煤炭及制品类	399978	398611	1367
木材及制品类	16885	16885	
石油及制品类	2638469	1298790	1339679
化工材料及制品类	1006388	1006388	
化肥类	1856	1856	
金属材料类	349687	349687	
建筑及装潢材料类	98365	77002	21364
机电产品及设备类	213790	199893	13897
农机类	1162	1162	
汽车类	2079021	101258	1977764
种子饲料类	228	228	
棉麻类	543		543
其它	887221	842411	44810
限额以下企业和个体户	6999738	1741702	5258036

7-4 限额以上住宿业和餐饮业经营情况（2010年）

Business of Hotels and Catering Services above Designated Size (2010)

项目	法人企业（个）	从业人数（人）	营业额（万元）	客房收入	餐费收入	商品销售收入	其它收入
总计	**310**	**66267**	**739544**	**169639**	**476274**	**2807**	**90825**
一、住宿业	**170**	**47012**	**483694**	**160746**	**239627**	**971**	**82350**
（一）按登记注册类型分							
内资企业	157	42011	430127	143428	208587	811	77300
港、澳、台商投资企业	8	2957	29414	9991	16779	157	2487
外商投资企业	5	2044	24154	7328	14261	2	2563
（二）按国民经济行业分							
旅游饭店	138	43763	454820	147851	230189	880	75900
一般旅馆	28	3028	26864	11408	9064	91	6301
其它住宿服务业	4	221	2011	1487	374		150
二、餐饮业	**140**	**19255**	**255850**	**8892**	**236647**	**1836**	**8475**
（一）按登记注册类型分							
内资企业	124	12803	149687	4605	136758	1836	6488
港、澳、台商投资企业	7	1746	21999	4021	16753		1225
外商投资企业	9	4706	84164	267	83136		762
（二）按国民经济行业分							
正餐服务业	122	13959	146887	8892	128871	904	8219
快餐服务业	9	4508	103255		102999		256
饮料及冷饮服务业	1	376	998		66	932	
其他餐饮服务业	8	412	4711		4711		

7-5 限额以上批发和零售企业财务状况（2010年）

Main Financial Indicators of Enterprises above Designated Size in Wholesale and Retail Trade (2010)

单位:万元

项目	法人企业数(个)	年末资产负债				
		流动资产合计	存货	固定资产原价	累计折旧	本年折旧
总计	**769**	**4921840**	**862311**	**742620**	**244884**	**53169**
一、批发企业	**321**	**3728708**	**507832**	**277178**	**98075**	**20234**
(一) 按登记注册类型分						
内资企业	311	3619177	493351	265182	93186	18897
港、澳、台商投资企业	7	81812	10683	5083	1294	699
外商投资企业	3	27719	3798	6913	3596	638
(二) 按国民经济行业分						
农畜产品批发业	1	56	50	55	44	3
食品、饮料及烟草制品批发业	35	377836	63488	41134	14781	4254
纺织、服装及日用品批发业	29	323489	13401	39352	14157	1775
文化、体育用品及器材批发业	7	60891	14789	2479	1216	174
医药及医疗器材批发业	11	102000	23860	4485	2049	619
矿产品、建材及化工产品批发业	132	1584564	235890	102935	38433	6788
机械设备、五金交电及电子产品批发业	70	963882	110382	61460	18066	4284
贸易经纪与代理	12	41660	4344	13375	4936	1216
其他批发业	24	274329	41629	11903	4392	1120
二、零售企业	**448**	**1193132**	**354479**	**465442**	**146809**	**32936**
(一) 按登记注册类型分						
内资企业	424	1093241	313523	420194	134904	29501
港、澳、台商投资企业	6	43326	22769	19827	3202	888
外商投资企业	18	56565	18187	25421	8703	2547
(二) 按国民经济行业分						
综合零售业	86	180486	51393	156743	38391	11256
食品、饮料及烟草制品专门零售业	7	7762	2808	2189	1121	104
纺织、服装及日用品专门零售业	6	11896	9853	551	352	68
文化、体育用品及器材专门零售业	5	17021	5505	2051	629	284
医药及医疗器材专门零售业	26	53382	15334	10120	4052	471
汽车、摩托车、燃料及零配件专门零售业	264	778219	212360	266293	91685	18956
家用电器及电子产品专门零售业	23	111537	46595	5379	1953	559
五金、家具及室内装修材料专门零售业	11	6298	2717	6241	4320	310
无店铺及其他零售业	20	26531	7915	15876	4306	927

7-5 续表 1

(2010年)

单位: 万元

项目	年末资产负债				损益及分配	
	资产总计	负债合计	所有者权益合计	实收资本	营业收入合计	主营业务收入
总计	**6946688**	**5234099**	**1712589**	**560035**	**12770201**	**12653094**
一、批发企业	**4520475**	**3832009**	**688466**	**293575**	**8079712**	**8046608**
(一)按登记注册类型分						
内资企业	4397581	3749276	648305	259752	7778535	7748849
港、澳、台商投资企业	85770	65606	20164	13703	166028	164443
外商投资企业	37123	17127	19996	20121	135149	133316
(二)按国民经济行业分						
农畜产品批发业	67	9	58	50	502	502
食品、饮料及烟草制品批发业	774649	486931	287718	74851	1115450	1106302
纺织、服装及日用品批发业	428889	379336	49553	26729	1559468	1554287
文化、体育用品及器材批发业	64693	52814	11879	10516	73277	73172
医药及医疗器材批发业	108981	98884	10098	6637	172044	171704
矿产品、建材及化工产品批发业	1765870	1575472	190398	108120	3404621	3400251
机械设备、五金交电及电子产品批发业	1033659	927382	106277	47354	1017690	1006627
贸易经纪与代理	50686	43132	7553	6068	257313	255695
其他批发业	292981	268050	24932	13251	479348	478069
二、零售企业	**2426213**	**1402090**	**1024124**	**266460**	**4690489**	**4606486**
(一)按登记注册类型分						
内资企业	2286355	1306270	980085	231904	4234441	4157865
港、澳、台商投资企业	61332	35950	25382	12652	203684	201418
外商投资企业	78526	59869	18657	21904	252363	247204
(二)按国民经济行业分						
综合零售业	343396	265390	78006	43381	656126	616539
食品、饮料及烟草制品专门零售业	11596	9581	2015	565	23722	23231
纺织、服装及日用品专门零售业	12515	11857	658	500	60065	59987
文化、体育用品及器材专门零售业	27753	16522	11231	7455	10617	10360
医药及医疗器材专门零售业	62173	47398	14775	3852	128167	127835
汽车、摩托车、燃料及零配件专门零售业	1796006	906861	889145	180591	3376976	3350932
家用电器及电子产品专门零售业	121270	100777	20492	12380	321114	307609
五金、家具及室内装修材料专门零售业	9168	15443	-6275	7653	26787	25527
无店铺及其他零售业	42337	28262	14075	10083	86915	84467

7-5 续表 2

(2010年)

单位: 万元

项目	损益及分配					
	主营业务成本	主营业务税金及附加	主营业务利润	其他业务利润	营业费用	管理费用
总 计	**11519728**	**45678**	**1088049**	**99027**	**501610**	**191869**
一、批发企业	**7527874**	**36291**	**482304**	**28345**	**227732**	**98987**
(一)按登记注册类型分						
内资企业	7279006	35044	434661	25603	196003	94391
港、澳、台商投资企业	130211	111	34121	933	23599	1848
外商投资企业	118657	1136	13522	1810	8130	2748
(二)按国民经济行业分						
农畜产品批发业	472		30		10	17
食品、饮料及烟草制品批发业	932518	30847	142938	8972	37716	22170
纺织、服装及日用品批发业	1512316	327	41645	4268	22254	9231
文化、体育用品及器材批发业	66302	83	6787	105	3645	1619
医药及医疗器材批发业	159599	192	11913	55	5878	3457
矿产品、建材及化工产品批发业	3220345	2261	177644	3519	95636	36878
机械设备、五金交电及电子产品批发业	941491	1435	63562	9254	41593	17147
贸易经纪与代理	250398	755	4542	1033	1737	3090
其他批发业	444433	392	33244	1140	19263	5378
二、零售企业	**3991854**	**9387**	**605745**	**70682**	**273878**	**92882**
(一)按登记注册类型分						
内资企业	3591830	9047	557487	64247	244772	84278
港、澳、台商投资企业	181490	86	19842	2124	8177	4094
外商投资企业	218534	253	28416	4311	20929	4510
(二)按国民经济行业分						
综合零售业	521995	3862	91180	38082	101457	14808
食品、饮料及烟草制品专门零售业	21128	46	2057	49	1162	704
纺织、服装及日用品专门零售业	22256	297	37434	76	19572	10996
文化、体育用品及器材专门零售业	8577	89	1693	257	4334	1702
医药及医疗器材专门零售业	108876	287	18672	297	9692	6924
汽车、摩托车、燃料及零配件专门零售业	2937685	3681	409566	16419	95765	49008
家用电器及电子产品专门零售业	277834	798	28977	12642	31779	3877
五金、家具及室内装修材料专门零售业	20643	128	4757	1247	5077	839
无店铺及其他零售业	72860	198	11408	1612	5041	4023

7-5 续表 3

(2010年)

单位: 万元

项　　目	损益及分配				本年应交增值税	全部从业人员年平均人数（人）
	财务费用	营业利润	利润总额	应交所得税		
总　计	**71456**	**432922**	**518631**	**55445**	**118919**	**63906**
一、批发企业	**49859**	**140676**	**227869**	**36365**	**68467**	**22855**
(一)按登记注册类型分						
内资企业	50295	119876	207756	33309	60837	21332
港、澳、台商投资企业	-169	9776	9738	1901	5319	1010
外商投资企业	-267	11024	10374	1155	2312	513
(二)按国民经济行业分						
农畜产品批发业		3	3	1		16
食品、饮料及烟草制品批发业	10640	81383	158774	22108	28295	3436
纺织、服装及日用品批发业	3974	10480	15524	2936	4321	2248
文化、体育用品及器材批发业	413	1215	1759	126	875	845
医药及医疗器材批发业	1322	1310	1248	333	1934	1176
矿产品、建材及化工产品批发业	28591	26020	29196	5880	20682	5070
机械设备、五金交电及电子产品批发业	3242	10979	11833	2516	7122	7980
贸易经纪与代理	557	656	740	178	576	508
其他批发业	1121	8630	8792	2288	4662	1576
二、零售企业	**21597**	**292246**	**290762**	**19080**	**50451**	**41051**
(一)按登记注册类型分						
内资企业	19777	277085	274189	15266	45940	37666
港、澳、台商投资企业	1021	8674	8674	2090	2032	1082
外商投资企业	800	6488	7899	1723	2479	2303
(二)按国民经济行业分						
综合零售业	2230	11001	13119	4103	9217	13918
食品、饮料及烟草制品专门零售业	17	223	182	94	306	242
纺织、服装及日用品专门零售业	208	6734	2826	1957	1106	999
文化、体育用品及器材专门零售业	83	-393	-441	14	250	766
医药及医疗器材专门零售业	1075	1289	1656	414	2162	3008
汽车、摩托车、燃料及零配件专门零售业	15461	265897	267004	11084	31144	15233
家用电器及电子产品专门零售业	1678	4297	5001	906	4359	4989
五金、家具及室内装修材料专门零售业	389	-301	-320	58	733	552
无店铺及其他零售业	457	3499	1734	450	1173	1344

7-6 限额以上住宿和餐饮企业财务状况（2010年）

Main Financial Indicators of Enterprises above Designated Size in Hotels and Catering Services (2010)

单位:万元

项目	法人企业数(个)	年末资产负债				
		流动资产合计	存货	固定资产原价	累计折旧	本年折旧
总计	**310**	**557774**	**35976**	**1022845**	**443249**	**55093**
一、住宿业	**170**	**458001**	**26530**	**844733**	**358649**	**45716**
（一）按登记注册类型分						
内资企业	157	404457	23377	719918	279652	39635
港、澳、台商投资企业	8	34767	2307	88806	59462	4338
外商投资企业	5	18777	847	36009	19535	1743
（二）按国民经济行业分						
旅游饭店	138	438143	25408	805862	343068	43781
一般旅馆	28	19620	1094	38010	15097	1718
其它住宿服务业	4	238	28	861	484	216
二、餐饮业	**140**	**99773**	**9446**	**178112**	**84600**	**9378**
（一）按登记注册类型分						
内资企业	124	73581	5827	136015	63912	5891
港、澳、台商投资企业	7	9929	903	12260	4784	1399
外商投资企业	9	16263	2716	29837	15904	2088
（二）按国民经济行业分						
正餐服务业	122	42941	6175	148606	70586	7123
快餐服务业	9	54064	3117	29184	13782	2219
饮料及冷饮服务业	1	49	10	27	1	
其他餐饮服务业	8	2719	144	295	231	35

7-6 续表 1

(2010年)

单位: 万元

项目	年末资产负债				损益及分配	
	资产总计	负债合计	所有者权益合计	实收资本	营业收入	主营业务收入
总计	**1453065**	**1251982**	**201083**	**335782**	**861330**	**737111**
一、住宿业	**1157527**	**985480**	**172048**	**221370**	**605884**	**482252**
(一)按登记注册类型分						
内资企业	1045266	898716	146549	172395	432279	428725
港、澳、台商投资企业	74290	48853	25438	39340	149404	29391
外商投资企业	37972	37911	61	9635	24201	24136
(二)按国民经济行业分						
旅游饭店	1101965	959435	142530	205409	576995	453582
一般旅馆	54904	24843	30061	15711	26963	26744
其它住宿服务业	659	1201	-543	250	1926	1926
二、餐饮业	**295538**	**266502**	**29035**	**114412**	**255445**	**254859**
(一)按登记注册类型分						
内资企业	217975	228761	-10786	86284	147638	147152
港、澳、台商投资企业	31131	27935	3197	9500	23537	23527
外商投资企业	46432	9807	36625	18628	84271	84180
(二)按国民经济行业分						
正餐服务业	163180	207635	-44455	82470	146698	146346
快餐服务业	129449	58224	71225	29789	103553	103319
饮料及冷饮服务业	76	9	66	24	458	458
其他餐饮服务业	2833	635	2199	2130	4737	4737

7-6 续表 2

(2010年)

单位: 万元

项　　目	损益及分配					
	主营业务成本	主营业务税金及附加	主营业务利润	其他业务利润	营业费用	管理费用
总　计	**274501**	**44809**	**422700**	**2243**	**274698**	**148147**
一、住宿业	**160689**	**30005**	**296547**	**2156**	**181391**	**116063**
(一)按登记注册类型分						
内资企业	144642	26968	257115	2069	160141	99181
港、澳、台商投资企业	8566	1622	24192	22	11538	11147
外商投资企业	7482	1414	15240	65	9712	5736
(二)按国民经济行业分						
旅游饭店	152746	27895	277931	1937	170100	109572
一般旅馆	7478	1997	17269	219	10146	6364
其它住宿服务业	466	113	1347		1146	128
二、餐饮业	**113811**	**14804**	**126153**	**87**	**93307**	**32084**
(一)按登记注册类型分						
内资企业	76528	9236	61297	148	45750	21349
港、澳、台商投资企业	7716	1277	14534	7	8050	6401
外商投资企业	29567	4291	50322	-68	39507	4334
(二)按国民经济行业分						
正餐服务业	69421	9115	67719	268	49583	24917
快餐服务业	40565	5406	57348	-181	43243	6711
饮料及冷饮服务业	267	25	166		115	1
其他餐饮服务业	3558	259	920		366	456

7-6 续表 3

(2010年)

单位: 万元

项　　目	损益及分配				全部从业人员年平均人数（人）
	财务费用	营业利润	利润总额	应交所得税	
总　　计	**20834**	**-23092**	**-32891**	**4387**	**66267**
一、住宿业	**22085**	**-25796**	**-23496**	**1476**	**47012**
(一)按登记注册类型分					
内资企业	19872	-19979	-17556	1466	42011
港、澳、台商投资企业	1136	-4597	-4720		2957
外商投资企业	1078	-1220	-1220	10	2044
(二)按国民经济行业分					
旅游饭店	21497	-26197	-23953	1243	43763
一般旅馆	569	346	402	215	3028
其它住宿服务业	18	55	56	19	221
二、餐饮业	**-1251**	**2704**	**-9395**	**2911**	**19255**
(一)按登记注册类型分					
内资企业	-1526	-3525	-14866	1068	12803
港、澳、台商投资企业	466	-375	-786	101	1746
外商投资企业	-191	6604	6256	1742	4706
(二)按国民经济行业分					
正餐服务业	-1711	-4197	-15942	1069	13959
快餐服务业	460	6754	6401	1809	4508
饮料及冷饮服务业		50	50	11	376
其他餐饮服务业		98	96	22	412

7-7 历年住宿餐饮企业与个体户数

Enterprises and Self-employed Individuals in Hotels and Catering Services over Years

单位：个

年 份	单位数合 计	国有经济	集体经济	其他经济	#私营个体经济
1979	147	22	115	10	10
1980	182	23	121	38	38
1981	622	24	283	315	315
1982	308	24	102	182	182
1983	2069	31	98	1940	1940
1984	4012	31	445	3536	3536
1985	2982	36	389	2557	2557
1986	3268	38	270	2960	2956
1987	2281	35	308	1938	1934
1988	2265	31	296	1938	1934
1989	2850	32	276	2542	2538
1990	3387	30	439	2918	2914
1991	3438	44	225	3169	3165
1992	4456	25	320	4111	4106
1993	7119	12	1851	5256	5232
1994	7819	12	1748	6059	6051
1995	8918	26	1802	7090	7082
1996	9708	9	1900	7799	7789
1997	9968	28	606	9334	9210
1998	11069	102	368	10599	10532
1999	11904	80	337	11487	11392
2000	8335	78	361	7896	7831
2001	9776	67	343	9366	9318
2002	15128	74	265	14789	14740
2003	17615	64	229	17322	17276
2004	19802	39	424	19339	19224
2005	25972	28	315	25629	25522
2006	27108	16	247	26845	26747
2007	38435	11	219	38205	38094
2008	40154	9	177	39968	39687
2009	38220	5	130	38085	37795
2010	36156	4	113	36039	35728

7-8 历年限额以上企业商品购进、销售、库存总额

Total Purchases, Sales and Stock of Commercial Enterprises above Designated Size over Years

单位：万元

年 份	商品购进总额	商品销售总额	批 发	零 售	年末库存总额
1978	82347	74936	50207	24729	7576
1979	91074	82878	55528	27350	8378
1980	109147	99324	66547	32777	10041
1981	131797	119936	80357	39579	12125
1982	156730	142615	95552	47063	14418
1983	160485	146042	97848	48194	14764
1984	214364	195072	130698	64374	19721
1985	254458	231557	155143	76414	23410
1986	630988	283945	190243	93702	28706
1987	380242	346021	231834	114187	34982
1988	714661	650342	435729	214613	65749
1989	729163	663539	444570	218969	67083
1990	766549	697560	467365	230195	70523
1991	796488	672666	433991	238675	74092
1992	881697	743990	473014	270976	64939
1993	1141163	1063567	725979	337588	92249
1994	1323263	1296363	912457	383906	177377
1995	1584470	1556882	1044334	512548	143404
1996	1694496	1737121	1117111	620010	166267
1997	1857884	1922001	1212399	709602	175715
1998	779319	863214	696921	166293	91640
1999	1064070	1106048	875799	230249	73620
2000	1232026	1354640	1072929	281711	58304
2001	1312924	1405409	1080688	324721	67415
2002	1588853	1682579	1188961	493618	102657
2003	1712564	1805840	1138496	667344	107996
2004		5406921	3479209	1927712	251427
2005	4798504	5683548	3882222	1801326	322445
2006	5324450	6487742	4215562	227179	335108
2007	6706290	8102415	4875668	3226748	485401
2008	8349926	10772768	6604662	4168106	790691
2009	8689984	10167222	6137228	4029994	839175
2010	12846503	14271362	9046899	5224463	1002940

7-9 市场分类基本情况(2010年)

Basic Statistics on Market Classification (2010)

单位：个

项　　目	合　计	城　市	农　村
合　　计	**792**	**194**	**598**
一、消费品市场	**728**	**169**	**559**
(一) 消费品综合市场	198	21	177
(二) 农副产品市场	390	97	293
1. 农副产品综合市场	363	88	275
2. 农副产品专业市场	27	9	18
(三) 工业品消费市场	86	31	55
1. 工业消费品综合市场	56	20	36
2. 工业消费品专业市场	30	11	19
(四) 其他消费品市场	54	20	34
二、生产资料市场	**64**	**25**	**39**
(一) 生产资料综合市场	1		1
(二) 工业生产资料市场	47	13	34
1. 机动车交易市场	4	2	2
2. 钢材交易市场	2	1	1
3. 煤炭交易市场			
4. 木材交易市场	5	1	4
5. 其他工业生产资料市场	36	9	27
(三) 农业生产资料市场			
1. 农业生产资料综合市场			
2. 农业生产资料专业市场			
(四) 其他生产资料市场	16	12	4

注：本表数据来源于市工商局。

7-10 历年城乡集市贸易

Statistics on Urban and Rural Trade Fairs over Years

单位：个

年　份	集贸市场 总　数	城　市	农　村
1978	35		35
1979	35		35
1980	35		35
1981	38		38
1982	40		40
1983	41		41
1984	43		43
1985	48		48
1986	57	7	50
1987	63	10	53
1988	66	12	54
1989	69	11	58
1990	73	10	63
1991	75	10	65
1992	53	7	46
1993	155	13	142
1994	162	12	150
1995	189	17	172
1996	219	20	199
1997	241	23	218
1998	252	25	227
1999	286	36	250
2000	308	29	279
2001	375	31	344
2002	495	28	467
2003	576	34	542
2004	610	35	575
2005	665	36	629
2006	812	39	773
2007	845	36	809
2008	871	228	643
2009	883	225	658
2010	792	194	598

注：1995年前为工商系统口径，从1996年起为全市口径。2008年以前的城市集贸市场数只包括莞城的集贸市场，2008年起包括莞城、东城、南城和万江四大街道办的市场数。

主要统计指标解释

Explanatory Notes on Main Statistical Indicators

社会消费品零售总额　指企业（单位、个体户）通过交易直接售给个人、社会集团非生产、非经营用的实物商品金额，以及提供餐饮服务所取得的收入金额。个人包括城乡居民和入境人员，社会集团包括机关、社会团体、部队、学校、企事业单位、居委会或村委会等。

商品购进总额　指从本企业以外的单位和个人购进（包括从国外直接进口）作为转卖或加工后转卖的商品金额（含增值税）。本指标反映批发和零售业从国内外市场上购进商品的总价。

商品销售总额　指对本单位以外的单位和个人出售的商品金额（包括售给本单位消费用的商品，含增值税），本指标反映批发和零售业在国内市场上销售商品以及出口商品的总量。

期末库存　对于批发和零售业法人企业和个体经营户，是指取得所有权的全部商品金额（含增值税）；对于批发和零售业产业活动单位，是指期末实际在库且归属法人具有所有权的全部商品金额（含增值税）。这个指标反映批发和零售业的商品库存情况，以及对市场商品供应的保证程度。

批发和零售业零售额　指专门从事商品转卖业务的各种经济类型独立核算的批发零售贸易企业、生产活动单位和个体户直接售给居民和社会集团的消费品零售额。

住宿和餐饮业零售额　指住宿和餐饮业单位因为提供就餐服务或销售商品取得的全部收入，包括餐费收入和商品销售收入（含增值税）。

流动资产合计　指企业可以在一年内或者超过一年的一个生产周期内变现或者耗用的资产，包括现金及各种存款、短期投资、应收及预付款项、存货等。

固定资产合计　指企业使用期限超过一年的房屋、建筑物、机器、机械、运输工具以及其他与生产、经营有关的设备、器具、工具等。不属于生产经营主要设备的物品，单位价值在2000元以上，并且使用年限超过2年的，也应当作为固定资产。

所有者权益合计　指企业投资人对企业净资产的所有权。企业净资产为企业全部资产与企业全部负债的差额，包括实收资本、资本公积、盈余公积、未分配利润等。

营业税金及附加　指与企业营业收入有关的，应由各项经营业务分担的税金及附加，包括营业税、消费税、城市维护建设税、资源税、土地增值税、教育费附加等。

利润总额　指企业在生产经营过程中各种收入扣除各种耗费后的盈余，反映企业在报告期内实现的亏盈总额，包括营业利润、补贴收入、投资净收益和营业外收支净额。

应交增值税　指企业按税法规定，从事货物销售或提供加工、修理修配劳务等增加货物价值的活动本期应交纳的税金。指企业在报告期应交增值税额。

计算公式　本年应交增值税＝销项税额－（进项税额-进项税额转出）

－出口抵减内销产品应纳税额－减免税款＋出口退税

批发零售贸易、餐饮业统计限额标准

行业类别	统计指标名称	限额标准
批发业	年主营业务收入	2000万元及以上
零售业	年主营业务收入	500万元及以上
住宿业、餐饮业	年主营业务收入	200万元及以上

说明：

1. 外贸企业包括在批发业中，其年销售额以外币计量的，应折合成人民币，按批发业标准执行。

2. 本限额标准对象为批发和零售业、住宿和餐饮业法人企业和个体经营户、非批发和零售业、住宿和餐饮业法人单位附营的批发和零售业、住宿和餐饮业产业活动单位。

八、价格指数

Price Indices

8-1 历年物价总指数（以上年价格为100）

General Price Indices over Years (Preceding Year=100)

年 份	商品零售价格总指数	#食品	#家用电器及音像器材	居民消费价格总指数	#食品	#服务项目
1978	100.4	101.6				
1979	102.6	107.1				
1980	110.9	114.5				
1981	109.3	110.3				
1982	101.2	100.8				
1983	99.6	99.5				
1984	98.6	97.5		99.3	97.5	102.0
1985	106.9	108.7		106.5	108.7	103.3
1986	104.4	105.0		104.2	105.0	102.3
1987	112.2	113.6		112.0	113.6	109.6
1988	132.8	133.9		136.0	133.9	168.0
1989	122.4	125.7		122.0	127.5	118.8
1990	94.9	92.8		96.6	92.8	111.0
1991	101.4	101.1		102.4	101.1	109.8
1992	107.7	109.0		109.2	109.0	117.9
1993	119.5	123.7		121.8	123.7	134.6
1994	118.4	125.9	99.6	123.5	126.4	141.2
1995	109.7	119.5	95.6	113.9	119.1	128.9
1996	104.7	108.1	94.5	106.8	107.8	115.0
1997	99.7	100.0	92.7	101.5	99.4	113.1
1998	98.7	99.9	93.3	99.9	99.5	108.4
1999	95.9	95.6	94.9	97.9	95.7	109.5
2000	100.1	100.3	97.2	101.5	100.4	112.8
2001	97.8	99.1	97.0	96.6	98.9	101.1
2002	99.1	100.9	98.0	98.1	99.0	98.7
2003	101.7	103.6	99.0	100.7	103.5	97.8
2004	103.2	108.6	98.7	103.0	108.6	99.7
2005	103.0	106.5	101.1	102.4	106.5	100.4
2006	102.8	100.1	100.5	101.2	100.1	101.6
2007	104.2	108.3	98.2	103.1	108.0	100.2
2008	107.9	115.6	100.4	105.5	115.1	100.1
2009	95.3	97.9	95.6	96.9	98.1	96.3
2010	103.2	104.8	95.6	102.8	104.6	102.6

8-2 居民消费价格分类指数(2010年，以上年价格为100)

Consumer Price Indices by Category (2010, Preceding Year=100)

项　　目	指 数
居民消费价格总指数	**102.8**
非食品价格指数	**102.0**
服务项目价格指数	**102.6**
扣除鲜菜鲜果总指数	**102.1**
消费品价格指数	**102.8**
一、食　品	**104.6**
粮食	104.0
大米	104.1
粮食制品	100.2
淀粉	110.3
干豆类及豆制品	90.7
油脂	104.9
肉禽及其制品	103.6
蛋	100.8
水产品	104.5
菜	112.3
鲜菜	114.5
干菜及菜制品	96.2
调味品	100.4
糖	98.6
食糖	91.4
糖果	100.8
茶及饮料	100.5
干鲜瓜果	117.4
鲜瓜果	119.0
糕点饼干	101.3
液体乳及乳制品	99.3
在外用膳食品	100.5
主食	100.0
炒菜	100.9
地方小吃	99.7
其他食品	100.9
二、烟酒及用品	**101.7**
烟草	102.0
酒	99.7
三、衣着	**97.9**
服装	99.1
衣着材料	119.2
棉布	117.3
化纤布	129.7
棉混纺布	126.2
毛线	100.0
鞋袜帽	92.8
鞋	92.7
袜子	92.7
帽子	94.9
衣着加工服务费	100.0
四、家庭设备用品及维修服务	**100.3**
耐用消费品	98.3
家具	98.3
家庭设备	98.3
室内装饰品	103.5
床上用品	101.6
家庭日用杂品	96.1
家庭服务及加工维修服务	108.8
五、医疗保健和个人用品	**101.9**
医疗保健	102.4
中药材及中成药	109.4
西药	100.7
医疗保健服务	100.0
个人用品及服务	100.8
化妆美容用品	96.5
清洁化妆用品	101.3
个人饰品	109.9
个人服务	100.0
六、交通和通信	**100.4**
交通	101.9
交通工具	99.9
市区公共交通费	100.0
城市间交通费	101.3
通信	98.8
通信工具	93.5
通信服务	100.0
七、娱乐教育文化用品及服务	**103.7**
文娱用耐用消费品及服务	96.0
教育	100.1
教材及参考书	101.2
学杂托幼费	100.0
文化娱乐类	99.8
文化娱乐用品	97.8
书报杂志	100.0
文娱费	101.8
旅游	116.2
八、居住	**105.1**
建房及装修材料	103.9
租房	100.0
自有住房	100.7
水、电、燃料	108.4

8-3 居民消费价格分月指数（2010年，以上年同月价格为100）

Consumer Price Indices by Month (2010, Same Month of Preceding Year=100)

项　　目	1 月	2 月	3 月	4 月	5 月	6 月
居民消费价格总指数	**99.4**	**102.8**	**101.0**	**102.4**	**103.6**	**103.4**
非食品价格指数	**99.1**	**101.6**	**101.0**	**101.9**	**103.1**	**103.3**
服务项目价格指数	**96.0**	**102.5**	**100.9**	**101.9**	**103.8**	**104.5**
扣除鲜菜鲜果总指数	**99.1**	**101.5**	**100.5**	**101.4**	**102.5**	**102.9**
消费品价格指数	**100.6**	**103.0**	**101.0**	**102.6**	**103.5**	**103.0**
一、食品	**100.2**	**105.5**	**101.1**	**103.6**	**104.8**	**103.6**
#粮食	105.5	104.0	101.9	101.8	102.8	103.1
肉禽及制品	97.9	106.7	100.2	100.0	101.6	102.5
蛋	95.6	99.7	97.9	97.9	98.2	98.6
水产品	98.3	98.5	96.2	101.0	101.6	105.1
菜	106.3	130.3	103.7	117.8	126.0	107.1
二、烟酒及用品	**99.6**	**99.5**	**100.1**	**102.1**	**102.9**	**101.8**
#烟草	100.1	100.1	100.1	102.3	102.7	102.7
酒	99.6	99.5	99.1	99.1	99.0	98.0
三、衣着	**98.4**	**97.1**	**97.5**	**98.0**	**98.0**	**98.0**
#服装	97.9	97.7	98.1	98.7	99.4	99.4
四、家庭设备用品及维修服务	**95.4**	**100.7**	**98.5**	**96.2**	**98.8**	**101.4**
#耐用消费品	97.5	97.8	99.9	97.4	99.4	99.2
五、医疗保健和个人用品	**100.5**	**101.3**	**100.6**	**100.9**	**101.8**	**102.3**
#医疗保健	100.4	101.6	101.4	102.3	102.8	103.2
个人用品及服务	100.6	100.7	99.2	98.4	100.0	100.8
六、交通和通信	**100.2**	**102.1**	**101.1**	**100.8**	**100.7**	**100.7**
#交通	102.1	105.7	103.9	103.5	103.4	102.0
通信	98.3	98.5	98.2	98.1	98.0	99.4
七、娱乐教育文化用品及服务	**93.5**	**101.1**	**100.8**	**102.7**	**106.9**	**107.4**
#文娱用耐用消费品及服务	95.0	95.1	94.5	94.7	95.0	95.2
教育	100.2	100.2	100.2	100.2	100.2	100.2
文化娱乐类	99.5	100.2	100.1	99.8	100.0	100.2
旅游类	80.0	108.2	107.5	115.1	129.2	131.8
八、居住	**103.6**	**104.1**	**104.1**	**107.3**	**107.5**	**107.3**
#建房及装饰材料	99.3	99.5	100.6	104.8	102.4	107.5
租房	100.0	100.0	100.0	100.0	100.0	100.0
自有住房	100.0	100.0	100.0	100.0	100.0	100.0
水、电、燃料	108.0	108.9	108.2	113.3	115.1	111.6

8-3 续表

项　　目	7 月	8 月	9 月	10 月	11 月	12 月
居民消费价格总指数	**102.8**	**103.2**	**103.3**	**104.2**	**103.5**	**103.8**
非食品价格指数	**102.4**	**102.5**	**102.1**	**102.4**	**101.7**	**102.4**
服务项目价格指数	**104.3**	**105.0**	**104.4**	**104.4**	**101.3**	**102.7**
扣除鲜菜鲜果总指数	**102.2**	**102.7**	**102.6**	**103.1**	**102.8**	**103.5**
消费品价格指数	**102.2**	**102.5**	**102.9**	**104.2**	**104.2**	**104.1**
一、食品	**103.7**	**104.8**	**106.0**	**108.2**	**107.2**	**106.6**
#粮食	102.8	102.8	102.4	103.5	107.0	109.8
肉禽及制品	103.9	105.5	106.1	106.9	105.6	107.2
蛋	97.6	102.1	103.0	103.2	104.0	112.7
水产品	100.4	105.2	109.5	112.0	114.9	113.6
菜	110.2	108.2	113.0	124.8	105.9	99.0
二、烟酒及用品	**102.2**	**102.6**	**102.5**	**102.6**	**102.9**	**101.7**
#烟草	102.7	102.7	102.7	102.7	102.7	102.7
酒	99.4	100.7	100.3	100.7	100.7	100.3
三、衣着	**98.4**	**97.8**	**97.1**	**97.3**	**98.0**	**99.3**
#服装	99.6	99.5	99.3	99.3	99.3	101.6
四、家庭设备用品及维修服务	**100.8**	**100.7**	**100.4**	**102.2**	**101.9**	**107.0**
#耐用消费品	98.7	97.8	97.8	97.6	97.4	99.2
五、医疗保健和个人用品	**101.9**	**102.3**	**102.2**	**102.0**	**102.9**	**103.5**
#医疗保健	102.9	102.8	102.0	102.0	103.7	104.0
个人用品及服务	100.1	101.3	102.6	102.1	101.4	102.8
六、交通和通信	**99.8**	**99.9**	**99.6**	**100.1**	**100.0**	**99.9**
#交通	100.4	100.5	100.0	100.8	100.6	100.6
通信	99.2	99.2	99.2	99.3	99.3	99.1
七、娱乐教育文化用品及服务	**107.2**	**108.4**	**107.5**	**107.3**	**100.3**	**101.1**
#文娱用耐用消费品及服务	96.4	96.1	97.6	97.9	97.3	97.4
教育	100.2	100.2	100.0	100.0	100.0	100.0
文化娱乐类	99.6	99.1	99.7	99.6	99.7	99.6
旅游类	127.1	133.8	128.8	126.8	102.4	106.3
八、居住	**104.5**	**103.6**	**103.3**	**103.8**	**105.9**	**105.8**
#建房及装饰材料	105.4	106.7	105.5	103.4	105.2	106.9
租房	100.0	100.0	100.0	100.0	100.0	100.0
自有住房	100.0	100.0	100.0	101.3	103.4	104.1
水、电、燃料	106.4	103.9	104.0	105.7	108.7	107.6

8-4 居民消费价格分月指数（2010年，以上月价格为100）

Consumer Price Indices by Month (2010, Preceding Month=100)

项　　目	1 月	2 月	3 月	4 月	5 月	6 月
居民消费价格总指数	**100.5**	**102.1**	**98.3**	**100.9**	**100.9**	**99.9**
非食品价格指数	**99.8**	**101.1**	**99.1**	**100.9**	**101.2**	**99.8**
服务项目价格指数	**99.4**	**102.8**	**98.4**	**100.9**	**102.6**	**100.1**
扣除鲜菜鲜果总指数	**100.3**	**101.5**	**98.4**	**100.8**	**100.8**	**99.8**
消费品价格指数	**100.9**	**101.9**	**98.2**	**100.9**	**100.3**	**99.8**
一、食品	**102.1**	**104.2**	**96.7**	**100.8**	**100.3**	**99.9**
#粮食	101.1	100.2	99.8	100.3	100.1	100.7
肉禽及制品	102.8	105.7	92.7	99.6	100.0	99.9
蛋	98.3	103.8	98.2	100.0	100.0	100.0
水产品	103.5	104.9	94.2	102.4	98.1	98.8
菜	103.6	113.1	95.0	99.4	102.5	98.7
二、烟酒及用品	**100.0**	**100.0**	**100.5**	**101.6**	**100.0**	**99.7**
#烟草	101.2	100.0	100.0	101.4	100.0	100.0
酒	98.3	99.9	100.1	100.0	99.9	98.9
三、衣着	**100.1**	**98.6**	**100.2**	**99.9**	**99.6**	**99.9**
#服装	100.0	99.6	100.0	99.9	100.2	100.0
四、家庭设备用品及维修服务	**100.3**	**102.0**	**97.5**	**98.4**	**101.8**	**102.1**
#耐用消费品	99.8	100.0	100.1	98.8	102.1	99.8
五、医疗保健和个人用品	**100.1**	**100.3**	**99.4**	**100.6**	**101.1**	**100.0**
#医疗保健	99.8	100.8	99.8	101.1	100.7	100.1
个人用品及服务	100.6	99.5	98.6	99.6	101.9	99.7
六、交通和通信	**100.3**	**100.9**	**98.9**	**100.1**	**100.0**	**99.8**
#交通	100.6	101.8	98.2	100.3	100.1	99.6
通信	100.0	100.0	99.6	100.0	100.0	99.9
七、娱乐教育文化用品及服务	**98.0**	**103.5**	**99.6**	**101.6**	**105.4**	**99.2**
#文娱用耐用消费品及服务	99.8	99.7	99.3	99.8	99.9	99.8
教育	100.0	100.0	100.0	100.0	100.0	100.0
文化娱乐类	99.9	100.6	99.5	99.7	100.2	100.1
旅游类	92.6	113.6	99.6	106.1	118.8	97.6
八、居住	**100.3**	**100.6**	**98.6**	**102.9**	**99.6**	**99.5**
#建房及装饰材料	99.7	101.4	98.5	105.8	98.0	102.3
租房	100.0	100.0	100.0	100.0	100.0	100.0
自有住房	100.0	100.0	100.0	100.0	100.0	100.0
水、电、燃料	100.8	100.6	97.8	103.4	100.2	97.8

8-4 续表

项　　目	7 月	8 月	9 月	10 月	11 月	12 月
居民消费价格总指数	**100.2**	**99.8**	**100.4**	**100.8**	**99.3**	**100.6**
非食品价格指数	**100.1**	**99.6**	**100.0**	**100.4**	**99.5**	**100.8**
服务项目价格指数	**101.3**	**100.0**	**99.5**	**100.4**	**96.7**	**100.8**
扣除鲜菜鲜果总指数	**100.0**	**100.0**	**100.3**	**100.7**	**99.9**	**101.0**
消费品价格指数	**99.8**	**99.8**	**100.7**	**101.0**	**100.2**	**100.6**
一、食品	**100.4**	**100.4**	**101.3**	**101.6**	**98.8**	**100.2**
#粮食	100.0	100.1	100.2	100.4	103.5	103.1
肉禽及制品	100.2	101.8	101.8	100.9	100.8	101.1
蛋	100.0	104.0	100.7	100.0	100.0	107.4
水产品	97.8	101.2	103.2	105.1	101.0	103.4
菜	104.3	97.8	103.5	108.2	83.1	93.2
二、烟酒及用品	**100.4**	**100.4**	**99.9**	**100.2**	**100.0**	**99.0**
#烟草	100.0	100.0	100.0	100.0	100.0	100.0
酒	101.4	101.3	99.8	100.7	100.0	100.0
三、衣着	**100.1**	**99.5**	**99.3**	**100.1**	**100.9**	**101.2**
#服装	100.0	99.9	99.8	100.0	100.0	102.2
四、家庭设备用品及维修服务	**100.0**	**99.4**	**99.9**	**100.2**	**100.1**	**105.4**
#耐用消费品	98.9	98.3	100.8	99.7	99.3	101.8
五、医疗保健和个人用品	**100.2**	**99.8**	**100.2**	**100.3**	**100.3**	**101.1**
#医疗保健	100.3	100.0	100.1	100.1	100.5	100.5
个人用品及服务	99.9	99.5	100.5	100.6	100.0	102.3
六、交通和通信	**99.7**	**99.6**	**100.0**	**100.3**	**100.3**	**100.0**
#交通	99.7	99.2	100.1	100.5	100.5	100.2
通信	99.8	100.0	100.0	100.0	100.0	99.8
七、娱乐教育文化用品及服务	**102.6**	**99.7**	**99.1**	**100.6**	**92.9**	**99.5**
#文娱用耐用消费品及服务	100.1	99.5	100.1	100.0	99.4	100.1
教育	100.0	100.0	100.0	100.0	100.0	100.0
文化娱乐类	99.8	99.0	100.6	100.0	100.0	100.1
旅游类	108.2	100.0	96.8	101.8	78.9	97.9
八、居住	**98.4**	**99.4**	**101.0**	**100.8**	**103.4**	**101.2**
#建房及装饰材料	99.6	99.9	99.8	97.6	103.5	100.9
租房	100.0	100.0	100.0	100.0	100.0	100.0
自有住房	100.0	100.0	100.0	101.3	102.0	100.7
水、电、燃料	96.8	98.7	102.3	102.6	104.8	101.8

8-5 居民消费价格分月指数(2010年，以上年12月价格为100)

Consumer Price Indices by Month (2010, December of Preceding Year=100)

项　　目	1 月	2 月	3 月	4 月	5 月	6 月
居民消费价格总指数	**100.5**	**102.7**	**100.9**	**101.8**	**102.7**	**102.6**
非食品价格指数	**99.8**	**100.9**	**100.0**	**100.9**	**102.1**	**101.9**
服务项目价格指数	**99.4**	**102.2**	**100.6**	**101.5**	**104.1**	**104.2**
扣除鲜菜鲜果总指数	**100.3**	**101.8**	**100.2**	**101.0**	**101.8**	**101.6**
消费品价格指数	**100.9**	**102.8**	**101.0**	**101.9**	**102.2**	**102.0**
一、食品	**102.1**	**106.4**	**102.9**	**103.6**	**104.0**	**103.9**
#粮食	101.1	101.4	101.2	101.4	101.5	102.2
肉禽及制品	102.8	108.7	100.8	100.4	100.4	100.3
蛋	98.3	102.0	100.2	100.2	100.2	100.2
水产品	103.5	108.6	102.3	104.7	102.6	101.4
菜	103.6	117.1	111.2	110.6	113.3	111.8
二、烟酒及用品	**100.0**	**100.0**	**100.5**	**102.1**	**102.1**	**101.8**
#烟草	101.2	101.2	101.2	102.7	102.7	102.7
酒	98.3	98.1	98.2	98.3	98.2	97.1
三、衣着	**100.1**	**98.6**	**98.9**	**98.7**	**98.3**	**98.2**
#服装	100.0	99.6	99.6	99.5	99.7	99.7
四、家庭设备用品及维修服务	**100.3**	**102.3**	**99.8**	**98.1**	**99.9**	**102.0**
#耐用消费品	99.8	99.8	99.9	98.7	100.7	100.5
五、医疗保健和个人用品	**100.1**	**100.4**	**99.8**	**100.4**	**101.5**	**101.5**
#医疗保健	99.8	100.7	100.5	101.6	102.3	102.4
个人用品及服务	100.6	100.0	98.6	98.3	100.2	99.9
六、交通和通信	**100.3**	**101.2**	**100.1**	**100.2**	**100.3**	**100.0**
#交通	100.6	102.3	100.5	100.8	100.9	100.5
通信	100.0	100.0	99.6	99.6	99.5	99.5
七、娱乐教育文化用品及服务	**98.0**	**101.4**	**101.1**	**102.6**	**108.2**	**107.3**
#文娱用耐用消费品及服务	99.8	99.5	98.8	98.6	98.5	98.3
教育	100.0	100.0	100.0	100.0	100.0	100.0
文化娱乐类	99.9	100.6	100.0	99.7	99.9	100.0
旅游类	92.6	105.3	104.9	111.2	132.1	128.9
八、居住	**100.3**	**100.9**	**99.5**	**102.4**	**102.0**	**101.5**
#建房及装饰材料	99.7	101.1	99.6	105.3	103.2	105.6
租房	100.0	100.0	100.0	100.0	100.0	100.0
自有住房	100.0	100.0	100.0	100.0	100.0	100.0
水、电、燃料	100.8	101.4	99.2	102.6	102.8	100.6

8-5 续表

项目	7月	8月	9月	10月	11月	12月
居民消费价格总指数	**102.8**	**102.6**	**103.0**	**103.9**	**103.1**	**103.8**
非食品价格指数	**102.1**	**101.6**	**101.6**	**102.1**	**101.6**	**102.4**
服务项目价格指数	**105.5**	**105.5**	**105.0**	**105.4**	**101.9**	**102.7**
扣除鲜菜鲜果总指数	**101.6**	**101.6**	**101.9**	**102.6**	**102.4**	**103.5**
消费品价格指数	**101.8**	**101.6**	**102.3**	**103.3**	**103.5**	**104.1**
一、食品	**104.3**	**104.7**	**106.0**	**107.7**	**106.4**	**106.6**
#粮食	102.2	102.3	102.5	102.8	106.5	109.8
肉禽及制品	100.6	102.4	104.2	105.2	106.0	107.2
蛋	100.2	104.2	105.0	105.0	105.0	112.7
水产品	99.1	100.3	103.5	108.8	109.9	113.6
菜	116.7	114.1	118.1	127.8	106.2	99.0
二、烟酒及用品	**102.2**	**102.6**	**102.5**	**102.8**	**102.8**	**101.7**
#烟草	102.7	102.7	102.7	102.7	102.7	102.7
酒	98.5	99.8	99.6	100.3	100.3	100.3
三、衣着	**98.3**	**97.8**	**97.1**	**97.2**	**98.1**	**99.3**
#服装	99.7	99.6	99.4	99.4	99.4	101.6
四、家庭设备用品及维修服务	**102.0**	**101.4**	**101.3**	**101.5**	**101.5**	**107.0**
#耐用消费品	99.5	97.7	98.5	98.2	97.5	99.2
五、医疗保健和个人用品	**101.7**	**101.5**	**101.8**	**102.0**	**102.4**	**103.5**
#医疗保健	102.8	102.7	102.8	102.9	103.5	104.0
个人用品及服务	99.8	99.3	99.8	100.4	100.5	102.8
六、交通和通信	**99.8**	**99.3**	**99.4**	**99.6**	**99.9**	**99.9**
#交通	100.2	99.4	99.4	99.9	100.4	100.6
通信	99.3	99.3	99.3	99.3	99.3	99.1
七、娱乐教育文化用品及服务	**110.1**	**109.8**	**108.7**	**109.4**	**101.6**	**101.1**
#文娱用耐用消费品及服务	98.4	97.9	97.9	97.9	97.4	97.4
教育	100.0	100.0	100.0	100.0	100.0	100.0
文化娱乐类	99.8	98.9	99.4	99.4	99.4	99.6
旅游类	139.5	139.5	135.0	137.5	108.5	106.3
八、居住	**99.9**	**99.3**	**100.3**	**101.2**	**104.6**	**105.8**
#建房及装饰材料	105.2	105.1	104.9	102.4	106.0	106.9
租房	100.0	100.0	100.0	100.0	100.0	100.0
自有住房	100.0	100.0	100.0	101.3	103.4	104.1
水、电、燃料	97.3	96.0	98.3	100.8	105.6	107.6

8-6 商品零售价格分类指数（2010年，以上年价格为100）

Retail Price Indices by Category (2010, Preceding Year=100)

项　　目	指　数	项　　目	指　数
商品零售价格总指数	**103.2**	3. 音像器材类	97.0
一、食品类	**104.8**	**六、文化办公用品**	**97.8**
1. 粮食	104.0	**七、日用品**	**100.2**
2. 淀粉	110.3	1. 日用百货	98.5
3. 干豆类及豆制品	90.7	2. 日用杂品	100.4
4. 油脂	104.9	3. 洗涤用品	102.9
5. 肉禽及其制品	103.6	4. 其他日用品	98.4
6. 蛋	100.8	**八、体育娱乐用品**	**95.9**
7. 水产品	104.5	1. 体育用品	94.1
8. 菜	112.3	2. 娱乐用品	97.7
9. 调味品	100.4	**九、交通、通信用品**	**96.7**
10.糖	98.6	1. 交通运输机械	98.7
11.干鲜瓜果	117.4	2. 通信器材类	94.3
12.糕点饼干面包	101.3	**十、家具**	**98.3**
13.液体乳及乳制品	99.3	**十一、化妆品类**	**96.1**
14.在外用膳食品	100.5	**十二、金银珠宝类**	**111.4**
15.其他食品	100.9	**十三、中西药品及医疗保健用品类**	**103.2**
二、饮料、烟酒	**100.8**	1. 医疗器具及用品	101.4
1. 茶及饮料	100.5	2. 中药材及中成药	109.4
2. 烟草	102.0	3. 西药	100.7
3. 酒	99.7	4. 保健器具及用品	99.4
三、服装、鞋帽类	**97.6**	**十四、书报杂志及电子出版物类**	**100.2**
1. 服装	99.1	1. 教材及参考书	101.2
2. 鞋袜帽	92.8	2. 书报杂志	100.0
3. 其他	100.4	3. 电子音像制品	98.5
四、纺织品类	**106.0**	**十五、燃料类**	**117.3**
1. 衣着材料	119.2	1. 煤炭及制品类	100.0
2. 床上用品	101.6	2. 石油及制品类	117.5
五、家用电器及音像器材	**95.6**	**十六、建筑材料及五金电料类**	**103.5**
1. 家庭设备	98.3	1. 建筑装璜材料	104.6
2. 文娱用耐用消费品	91.0	2. 五金电料类	101.0

8-7 主要年份食品全社会综合平均价格

Comprehensive Average Prices of Food in Main Years

项 目	规 格 等 级	单 位	价 格（元）						
			1985年	1990年	1995年	2000年	2005年	2009年	2010年
大 米	标 二	千克	0.39	0.85	2.93	2.16	2.90	3.43	3.57
面 粉	南 方	千克	0.74	1.70	3.11	3.65	2.53	5.82	6.36
豆 类	一等大豆	千克	1.07	2.94	3.77	3.99	5.57	7.38	7.18
植物油	一级花生油	千克	3.55	7.36	12.53	10.62	11.95	16.95	18.50
猪 肉	鲜上肉	千克	3.55	9.50	15.98	13.78	18.53	21.97	21.89
瘦猪肉	鲜 肉	千克	7.20	13.35	23.73	18.04	25.00	30.08	29.40
牛 肉	去骨统肉	千克	5.60	11.22	22.40	18.61	25.73	45.43	44.00
白条鸡	开 膛	千克		9.21	13.80	14.61	21.82	26.11	27.82
鸡	上等竹丝鸡	千克	7.20	13.04	22.31	15.77	14.99	17.10	17.38
鸭	上等番鸭	千克	3.17	5.81	11.65	14.28	14.33	17.51	17.01
鸡 蛋	新鲜鸡蛋	千克	3.63	6.70	7.91	6.21	7.73	12.42	12.84
再制蛋	皮 蛋	千克	2.40	4.52	6.40	5.85	7.05	8.59	8.82
香 肠	本地产中等	千克	11.60	23.75	52.13	53.67	31.67	90.00	90.00
烧 鹅	本地产	千克	8.53	14.41	32.54	30.67	44.49	55.25	58.20
胖头鱼	中等0.5公斤以上一条	千克	2.91	4.81	9.56	8.80	11.79	14.53	14.32
红三鱼	冰 鲜	千克			9.13	16.20	24.85	28.33	34.30
虾	罗氏虾	千克				40.06	37.18	65.20	74.68
草 鱼	中等1公斤以上一条	千克	2.69	6.67	13.30	10.18	14.25	20.76	20.50
精 盐	再制盐	千克		0.49	1.20	1.60	1.27	1.23	3.25
白砂糖	国家机制一级	千克	1.36	2.71	6.10	4.32	5.23	6.50	6.50
红 糖	一级冰片糖	千克		2.95	6.55	4.95	5.70	9.50	9.50
卷 烟	广州双喜	盒	1.12	1.40	4.87	5.92	6.62	6.50	6.50
白 酒	0.5千克装	瓶	2.30	2.40	5.55	6.58	7.25	6.25	6.25
啤 酒	热 12 度	瓶		1.60	6.40	4.92	4.66	5.00	5.00
红 茶	一 级	千克	3.98	12.76	28.95	64.68	6.91	129.58	127.50
绿 茶	一 级	千克	8.00	10.34	15.40	59.21	27.40	123.00	123.00
苹 果	一 级	千克	2.14	4.89	6.54	5.80	6.44	8.61	11.18
梨	一 级	千克	1.86	4.40	5.46	3.99	3.74	4.40	5.18
柑	一 级	千克	1.75	1.97	3.28	3.27	3.54	3.92	4.84
香 蕉	一 级	千克	1.24	2.22	3.90	3.18	3.04	4.02	4.68
荔 枝	桂味/糯米糍	千克	2.57	7.95	20.50	14.93	11.75	12.70	14.88
面 包	中 等	千克	2.00	5.09	4.39	15.25	7.39	16.70	16.70
饼 干	一 级	千克	2.48	7.88	9.03	22.97	8.80	22.00	22.00
奶 粉	国 产	千克	4.80	5.27	25.12	24.55	22.33	32.00	32.00

注：2000年起茶叶的档次提高。

8-8 工业品出厂价格总指数(2003－2010年，以上年价格为100)

General Producer Price Index (PPI) for Manufactured Goods (2003-2010,Preceding Year=100)

项　　目	2003年	2004年	2005年	2006年	2007年	2008年	2009年	2010年
工业品价格总指数	98.3	101.4	100.4	100.7	101.4	101.7	96.8	102.6
#轻工业	98.2	100.2	99.9	100.2	101.4	102.6	97.7	101.8
重工业	101.7	105.4	100.6	101.1	101.5	101.0	96.1	103.1
#非金属矿采选业	95.6	96.5	97.0	100.1	101.3	101.7	103.9	102.9
农副食品加工业	92.4	107.7	107.5	99.2	106.8	119.1	93.2	107.8
食品制造业	99.1	100.9	100.3	100.2	101.5	101.7	97.2	102.7
饮料制造业	99.4	98.6	99.2	100.8	99.9	103.0	102.2	100.6
纺织业	100.6	103.5	101.5	102.2	101.5	104.2	99.3	100.8
纺织服装、鞋、帽制造业	100.5	109.8	100.9	100.5	100.9	100.5	98.3	101.6
皮革、皮毛、羽毛(绒)及其制品业	103.7	101.4	101.1	101.0	105.6	103.7	100.8	101.7
木材加工及木、竹、藤、棕、草制品业	98.7	100.8	100.5	102.6	101.6	106.3	100.4	102.3
家具制造业	99.6	99.9	100.7	102.2	101.8	103.1	100.9	102.4
造纸及纸制品业	96.8	97.4	100.8	101.8	101.4	104.3	94.3	113.1
印刷业和记录媒介的复制	103.3	102.9	99.6	98.2	100.4	103.7	100.4	101.6
文教体育用品制造业	100.2	100.1	101.8	103.9	103.3	101.6	100.4	99.4
石油加工、炼焦及核燃料加工业	115.8	113.7	122.8	117.0	104.6	120.1	88.5	119.7
化学原料及化学制品制造业	102.5	110.3	103.5	101.2	106.7	104.8	92.7	109.1
医药制造业	101.6	96.9	101.1	100.4	105.7	102.3	97.5	101.7
化学纤维制造业	102.9	105.0	104.4	101.0	101.6	95.1	87.1	120.2
橡胶制品业	96.4	98.5	101.0	104.1	99.8	100.2	97.5	101.5
塑料制品业	99.9	104.3	107.4	101.7	101.0	102.0	96.7	102.9
非金属矿物制品业	99.8	112.4	96.7	100.3	102.2	104.7	99.0	105.1
黑色金属冶炼及压延加工业	108.3	123.8	101.2	94.2	113.4	130.1	79.1	109.1
有色金属冶炼及压延加工业	102.0	118.7	106.8	136.6	110.0	98.7	87.3	122.1
金属制品业	97.6	102.8	100.8	103.0	104.9	105.9	96.2	102.8
通用设备制造业	100.5	101.3	104.0	102.8	100.1	103.8	99.2	103.0
专用设备制造业	96.7	99.1	101.6	100.9	99.7	103.6	99.1	98.3
交通运输设备制造业	97.2	102.1	99.2	96.7	95.7	99.7	100.2	100.4
电气机械及器材制造业	98.4	101.4	103.7	106.6	104.3	99.7	93.0	103.9
通信设备、计算机及其他电子设备制造业	96.7	98.4	96.9	95.9	98.3	97.6	96.1	100.0
仪器仪表及文化、办公用机械制造业	95.3	98.4	100.6	102.2	100.4	100.5	99.1	99.7
工艺品及其他制造业	101.6	100.2	101.6	106.0	102.2	103.9	103.0	103.7
电力、热力的生产和供应业	97.5	101.1	102.3	101.7	101.4	103.4	102.4	98.8
燃气生产和供应业								112.1
水的生产和供应业	103.2	101.7	100.8	103.4	104.1	102.8	101.3	103.1

主要统计指标解释

Explanatory Notes on Main Statistical Indicators

居民消费价格指数　是度量消费商品及服务项目价格水平随着时间而变动的相对数，反映居民家庭购买的消费品及服务价格水平的变动情况。它是宏观经济分析、决策、调控和价格总水平监测以及国民经济核算的重要指标。其按年度计算的变动率通常被用来作为反映通货膨胀(或紧缩)程度的指标。

商品零售价格指数　是度量市场商品零售价格水平变动趋势和变动程度的相对数，反映商品在流通过程中最后一个环节的价格即工业、商业、餐饮业和其他零售企业向城乡居民、机关团体出售生活消费品和办公用品价格水平的变动趋势。它可以为国家宏观调控和国民经济核算提供参考依据，并在此基础上派生其他价格指数。

九、对外经济贸易与旅游

Foreign Trade and Tourism

9-1 主要年份对外经济与旅游业主要指标

Main Indicators of Foreign Trade and Economic Cooperation and Tourism in Main Years

指　　标	单 位	1979年	1985年	1990年	1995年	2000年	2005年	2009年	2010年
进出口总额	万美元			108229	1539112	3204526	7437150	9415458	12133773
出口总额	万美元	5382	17545	56828	779867	1715927	4092905	5516861	6959751
进口总额	万美元			51401	759245	1488599	3344245	3898597	5174022
新签利用外资协议(合同)数	宗	184	625	1267	3077	1276	992	601	875
#增资项目	宗						1138	1123	1059
#“三来一补”项目	宗	184	514	1075	2094	871	219	22	6
“三资”项目	宗		111	192	983	405	773	579	869
合同规定外商投资额	万美元	476	6815	30180	330920	183633	475238	203040	307282
#增资项目	万美元						187422	66735	180723
#“三来一补”项目	万美元	476	1870	12346	97428	69302	166363	41420	47542
“三资”项目	万美元		4945	17834	233492	114331	308875	161620	259740
实际利用外资(不含对外借款)	万美元	173	2894	24319	105665	164712	375139	294157	316287
“三来一补”项目	万美元	173	1511	14309	38418	55975	93023	34758	43116
“三资”项目	万美元		1383	10010	67247	108737	282116	259399	273171
本年止累计“三来一补”企业投产宗数	宗	140	1592	3880	8447	9917	8997	6757	5688
年末“三来一补”企业从业人员	万人	1.15	9.82	21.48	59.44	72.89	126.49	91.24	81.00
本年止累计“三资”企业投产数	宗		51	454	2629	3908	6657	7940	8338
年末“三资”企业从业人员	万人		0.64	3.81	25.01	87.17	145.50	150.00	163.53
当年来料加工企业转为三资或民营企业	家							588	1250
合同规定外商投资额(新口径)	万美元						298029	161620	259740
实际利用外资(新口径)	万美元						146796	259399	273171
全年接待旅游人数	万人次			125	89	291	1156	2037	2251
#国际及港澳台旅游者	万人次			27	27	106	169	286	327
#外国人	万人次			1	6	15	70	104	109
国内旅客	万人次			98	62	185	987	1751	1924
国际旅游收入	万美元			1025	5679	7617	28189	51756	67592
星级以上宾馆酒店客房数	间			3793	7568	18024	18258	16332	16631
宾馆酒店客房开房率	%			60.19	68.80	61.88	58.90	57.96	58.12

注：1. 对外经济部分除有注明新口径的以外均为旧口径，旧口径包括“三资”和“三来一补”，新口径不含“三来一补”且以验资作为统计标准，后同。
2. 2002年起旅游业指标采用旅游局口径，与往年数不可比。

9-2 主要年份进出口贸易

Total Imports and Exports in Main Years

单位：万美元

项目	1995年	2000年	2001年	2002年	2003年	2004年	2005年	2009年	2010年
进出口总额	**1539112**	**3204526**	**3445457**	**4424706**	**5210623**	**6451775**	**7437150**	**9415458**	**12133773**
出口总额	**779867**	**1715927**	**1898924**	**2373646**	**2800227**	**3519237**	**4092905**	**5516861**	**6959751**
按贸易方式分									
#一般贸易	23180	20937	25945	34848	48988	85056	175502	571682	954098
来料加工装配	434646	834347	940908	1171688	1257934	1503757	1611676	1823160	1955379
进料加工	320186	858409	931766	1167047	1492723	1929967	2304325	3055047	3946227
其他	1855	2234	305	63	582	457	1402	66971	104047
按经济类型分									
#国有企业	474304	867501	972541	1189726	991762	1086698	1139776	1112383	1102678
三资企业	305061	835611	908388	1153178	1498993	1948473	2353253	3345624	4426236
集体企业	122	12259	17584	25798	27072	30229	37893	93853	141561
民营企业			143	4905	282079	453457	561650	961892	1285124
进口总额	**759245**	**1488599**	**1546533**	**2051060**	**2410396**	**2932538**	**3344245**	**3898597**	**5174022**
按贸易方式分									
#一般贸易	5394	72475	68392	83522	144235	222262	236133	456075	755349
来料加工装配	353138	645562	684323	922916	962367	1090197	1216566	1297315	1424118
进料加工	259397	616319	656910	886699	1127404	1402413	1625629	1820882	2457194
其他	141316	154243	5513	4112	5551	217666	265917	324325	537362
按经济类型分									
#国有企业	419827	764945	795407	1019994	832593	855107	987421	994470	1076821
三资企业	329164	706145	733492	1002467	1308831	1655308	1882393	2159599	3028036
集体企业	243	10267	12101	17930	19408	24151	32167	56164	78053
民营企业			21	6521	244005	391706	439521	681737	967472
贸易顺差	**20622**	**227328**	**352391**	**322586**	**389831**	**586699**	**748660**	**1618264**	**1785728**

9-3 历年进出口总额

Total Value of Imports and Exports over Years

单位：万美元

年 份	进出口总 额	出口总额	#一般贸易	来料加工装配	进料加工	进口总额	#一般贸易	来料加工装配	进料加工
1978		3938							
1979		5382							
1980		7737							
1981		9173							
1982		10879							
1983		11890							
1984		12966							
1985		17545							
1986		23280							
1987		26755							
1988		31781							
1989		34868							
1990	108229	56828				51401			
1991	317463	165159				152304			
1992	509007	260272				248735			
1993	675647	321137				354510			
1994	882997	429416				453581			
1995	1539112	779867	23180	434646	320186	759245	5394	353138	259397
1996	1784222	918683	16377	496833	405066	865539	8956	383988	309710
1997	2129885	1136768	18020	582863	535708	993117	7598	445237	420014
1998	2327324	1306055	15409	652853	636822	1021269	10406	462194	463450
1999	2846291	1515391	16347	759638	738191	1330900	51726	584224	582721
2000	3204526	1715927	20937	834347	858409	1488599	72475	645562	616319
2001	3445457	1898924	25945	940908	931766	1546533	68392	684323	656910
2002	4424706	2373646	34848	1171688	1167047	2051060	83522	922916	886699
2003	5210623	2800227	48988	1257934	1492723	2410396	144235	962367	1127404
2004	6451775	3519237	85056	1503757	1929967	2932538	222262	1090197	1402413
2005	7437150	4092905	175502	1611676	2304325	3344245	236133	1216566	1625629
2006	8422107	4737640	265784	1661399	2806910	3684467	259709	1265725	1879233
2007	10687290	6023212	357941	2235125	3398212	4664078	371073	1702595	2196521
2008	11329947	6553738	487193	2428365	3585619	4776209	455447	1712939	2206139
2009	9415458	5516861	571682	1823160	3055047	3898597	456075	1297315	1820882
2010	12133773	6959751	954098	1955379	3946227	5174022	755349	1424118	2457194

注：出口总额1990年以前为外经贸口径，1990年起为海关口径。

9-4 分国别(地区)进出口总值 (2009-2010年)

Total Value of Imports and Exports by Countries (Regions)(2009-2010)

单位：亿美元

国别(地区)	实际出口		进口到货	
	2010年	2009年	2010年	2009年
亚洲	354.36	273.35	447.88	340.64
东南亚联盟	27.68	17.78	77.04	54.39
非洲	4.27	2.95	1.60	1.26
欧洲	121.37	96.30	25.78	19.71
欧洲共同体	115.64	92.93	24.50	18.45
拉美洲	17.50	13.24	14.00	9.26
北美洲	189.88	157.70	24.81	16.38
大洋洲	8.60	8.13	3.20	2.44
美国	179.78	149.27	20.31	14.40
香港	219.75	174.49	7.03	4.65
日本	60.88	46.95	88.33	71.70
荷兰	22.90	17.49	2.53	1.63
德国	26.01	23.21	7.71	5.41
英国	18.54	15.96	2.69	1.89
韩国	18.17	14.13	44.83	32.49
台湾	10.04	7.12	96.17	73.39
法国	10.13	7.83	1.35	1.13
加拿大	10.09	8.43	4.50	1.98
澳大利亚	7.96	7.56	2.53	1.80
新加坡	6.31	5.53	11.89	7.57
马来西亚	4.44	3.14	23.00	14.40

9-5 主要商品类别出口总值（2007-2010年）

Total Export Value by Category of Main Commodities (2007-2010)

单位：亿美元

商品名称	2007年	2008年	2009年	2010年
机电产品	436.87	483.66	387.52	494.83
高新技术产品	197.82	201.49	159.39	241.95
自动数据处理设备及其部件	75.93	65.86	42.26	52.82
服装及衣着附件	29.30	31.92	28.11	38.98
录、放像机	11.73	11.64	8.41	13.24
自动数据处理设备的零件	30.63	31.97	26.68	33.31
纺织纱线、织物及制品	16.57	14.69	13.68	15.21
玩具	15.24	14.69	12.28	16.32
鞋类	23.07	27.06	24.57	30.96
家具及其零件	27.44	27.79	24.26	32.09
录音机及收录(放)音组合机(包括整套散件)	11.07	10.62	7.46	8.85
塑料制品	11.76	10.74	9.10	11.37
静止式变流器	21.63	26.71	23.14	35.98
旅行用品及箱包	9.43	10.91	11.43	15.65
灯具、照明装置及类似品	7.64	8.87	7.84	10.37
电线和电缆	11.76	14.03	10.81	15.22
通断及保护电路装置	10.90	12.36	10.37	13.40
有线电话机	15.69	15.37	14.84	16.44
电视、收音机及无线电讯设备的零附件	11.94	16.21	12.59	16.12

9-6 主要商品进口数量与金额(海关口径，2008-2010年)

Main Import Commodities in Volume and Value (Custom Statistics) (2008-2010)

金额单位：万美元

商品名称	数量单位	2008年		2009年		2010年	
		数量	金额	数量	金额	数量	金额
谷物及谷物粉	万吨	1.31	691	3.18	1205	5.24	2039
#小麦粉	吨	60	2	12	2	0.22	0.03
食用植物油	万吨	22.26	23839	3.50	2218	4.43	3524
食糖	万吨	0.23	112	6.63	2187	6.27	2664
天然橡胶(包括胶乳)	万吨	2.22	3737	2.30	3612	2.26	4950
合成橡胶(包括胶乳)	万吨	11.31	21892	9.49	17575	10.09	21424
原木	万立方	4.30	1900	5.50	2664	9.95	4699
锯材	万立方	41.42	11827	32.17	8082	46.71	14312
羊毛(包括羊毛条)	吨	1737	899	1348	818	832	562
纺织用合成纤维	万吨	1.85	3244	1.81	3082	1.68	3299
#聚酯纤维	万吨	2.00	4136	1.15	1829	1.00	1566
纺织用人造纤维	吨	103.40	31	40.92	13	17.47	5
成品油	万吨	0.43	1092	0.36	835	0.92	1769
合成有机染料	吨	2384.71	1577	1471.71	1053	1886.80	1213
初级形状的塑料	万吨	210.78	366351	191.68	308584	216.71	390243
#初级形状的聚乙烯	万吨	17.99	27214	16.66	21793	17.31	24156
初级形状的聚丙烯	万吨	32.14	47116	29.74	39425	34.10	49226
初级形状的苯乙烯聚合物	万吨	73.66	122337	63.05	99175	69.04	119466
初级形状的氯乙烯聚合物	万吨	45.87	81013	24.08	21237	27.52	28931
初级形状的聚酯	万吨	27.79	41324	15.15	39344	20.22	58565
牛皮革及马皮革	万吨	6.91	47354	5.38	42245	7.18	56696
纸及纸板(未切成形的)	万吨	60.74	39163	59.26	34709	44.87	33999
毛纱线	万吨	0.89	5964	0.67	4483	0.76	5678
合成纤维纱线	万吨	5.44	16151	4.86	15035	5.54	18795
棉机织物	万米	15848.24	22938	13525.38	19178	13572.82	20279
涂覆浸渍塑料的织物	万吨	4.58	11596	3.16	9184	3.59	12218
针织或钩编织物	万米		35766	25197.31	27452	24854.37	27468
鞋靴零件	万吨	0.42	3332				
钢材	万吨	155.84	168061	110.17	109430	141.82	152727
#钢铁板材	万吨	143.10	147777	100.54	94963	126.45	128706
未锻造的铜及铜材	万吨	31.25	214850	24.12	130340	25.18	174812
#铜材	万吨	22.23	151154	17.24	96339	18.19	122608
未锻造的铝及铝材	万吨	10.03	34795	8.92	29377	8.40	33203
#铝材	万吨	4.82	22431	4.41	20253	4.58	24723

9-6 续表

金额单位：万美元

商品名称	数量单位	2008年		2009年		2010年	
		数量	金额	数量	金额	数量	金额
钢材或铝制结构体及其部件	吨	867	210	934	285	955	377
蒸汽锅炉及过热水锅炉	台	6	23	7	18	2	8
液泵及液体提升机	台	1958356	1134	1362113	1155	1108302	1417
冷冻机和制冷设备	台		407		90		283
机械提升搬运装卸设备及零件	台		3405		2892		5335
制造纸及纸制品用机械及零件	金额		11477		11023		15077
印刷、装订机械及零件	金额		59061		44739		79242
纺织机械及零件	金额		26378		8668		12500
#针织机及缝编机	台	6418	23494	1764	5834	2248	10785
花边绣品饰带织机、簇绒机	台	359	1068				
纱线织物等后整理机器	台	490	1147	974	690	279	829
工业用缝纫机	台	7225	1563	2262	343	3521	1135
制革、制鞋机器	台	602	519				
金属加工机床	台	4834	20192	1635	7283	3687	20131
橡胶或塑料加工机械及零件	金额		11989		5487		11352
型模及金属铸造用型箱	吨	229	4732		4547		6458
自动数据处理设备及其部件	万台	4080	104516	2744	59580	2646	59022
自动数据处理设备的零件	吨	17536	69482	17967	73356	22515	107192
电动机及发电机	万台	33202	24974	32351	22938	39427	29339
发电机组及旋转式变流机	台	175	2284	80	961	28	471
旋转式电力设备的零件	吨	17831	13926				
焊接机器及零件	金额		3343				
电视、收音机及无线电讯设备	吨	8677	70241	8153	60863	7731	85203
通断及保护电路装置	万吨		109681		89996		130794
电视显像管	万只	30.40	184	2.98	23	0.79	7
#彩色显像管	万只	5.58	119	0.75	19	0.50	6
二极管、晶体管及类似半导体	亿个	471.88	176757	419.24	147379	512.09	196257
电线和电缆	吨	38492	35692	28328	27093	33507	36761
计量检测分析自控仪器及器具	金额		27297		19697		28444
钟表机芯及钟表零件	金额		8660				
塑料制品	吨	30749	13271	22961	10870	24384	13805
玩具	金额		1627				

9-7 主要商品出口数量与金额（海关口径，2008-2010年）

Main Export Commodities in Volume and Value (Custom Statistics) (2008-2010)

金额单位：万美元

商品名称	数量单位	2008年		2009年		2010年	
		数　量	金　额	数　量	金　额	数　量	金　额
活猪(种猪除外)	万头	1.40	268	1.13	217		157
活家禽	万只	18.86	64				
水海产品	万吨	0.60	155	0.04	253	0.02	245
谷物及谷物粉	万吨				1		1
蔬菜	万吨		13	0.02	19	0.16	173
#鲜蔬菜	万吨		2				
鲜、干水果及坚果	万吨	0.21	188		2		7
食用植物油(包括棕榈油)	吨	9.58	3	24.75	9	324.35	127
药材	吨					44.37	8
锯材	立方米	250	12	200	10		1
成品油	万吨		17	0.03	50	0.03	54
合成有机染料	吨	282.92	426	319.02	315	198.91	70
医药品	吨	5570.22	3005	2480.77	1425	1437.78	779
美容化妆品及护肤品	吨	3274.45	1072	2888.88	1226	3476.26	1449
洗衣粉	吨	8165.15	553	11106.46	687	17887.35	1098
烟花、爆竹	吨	1460.68	132	998.44	95	416.28	63
初级形状的聚氯乙烯	吨	6479.68	914	3500	533	6000	900
家用或装饰用木制品	吨	13297.37	1651	8900	1321	9500	1828
纸及纸板(未切成形的)	万吨	15.15	7717	5.09	2773	3.37	2675
纺织纱线、织物及制品	金额		146949		136789		152070
#棉纱线	吨	24549.17	9197	25499.61	9265	25927.56	10422
亚麻及苎麻纱线	万米	208.33	82			43.25	116
棉机织物	万米	3716.00	4728	2093.69	2870	2349.16	4058
玻璃制品	金额		2618		2616		3790
家用陶瓷器皿	吨	24723.98	2481	20900	2335	26100	4312
装饰用陶瓷制品	吨	17375.97	2000				
钢材	万吨	3.27	4184	2.39	2839	4.40	5098
未锻造的铜及铜材	吨	33181.98	26575	24790.85	15726	28597.01	22750
未锻造的铝及铝材	吨	9517.93	3675	4800	1874	7600	3191
手用或机用工具	吨	12456.81	8385	9200	6544	10300	9527

9-7 续表

金额单位：万美元

商品名称	数量单位	2008年		2009年		2010年	
		数量	金额	数量	金额	数量	金额
锁	吨	6861	3512				
电扇	万台	10600.7	28595	9316.9	25552	11169.8	31980
纺织机械及零件	金额		1564		1928		2005
金属加工机床	万台	2.4	1524	0.8	1068	0.2	1488
电子计算器	亿台	0.6	17698	0.4	11829	0.5	12682
电动机及发电机	亿台	8.1	46148	6.1	41501	7.2	60650
静止式变流器	亿个	5.2	267124	4.4	231369	6.9	359806
原电池	亿个	12.9	12902	11.5	11942	13.7	16375
蓄电池	亿个	2.5	49461	2.2	27656	2.4	31218
有线电话机	万个	4965.9	153716	4240.1	148365	5011.5	164438
扬声器	亿个	2.0	45902	1.4	34594	1.8	50717
收音设备（包括收录音组合机）	万台	4494.4	106267	3337.9	74636	4124.6	88472
电视机	万台	451.1	79805	568.7	101880	518.0	96536
#彩色电视机	万台	451.1	79805	568.7	101880	517.5	96529
电视、收音机及无线电讯零附件	万吨	9.7	162116	6.9	125973	7.2	161166
电容器	吨	13049	44385	11598	49340	14790	72468
通断及保护电路装置	亿个		123618		103732		133965
二极管及类似半导体器件	亿个	358.0	42912	350.8	36080	479.4	54844
电线和电缆	万吨	23.0	140256	17.5	108069	20.8	152169
照相机	万架	208	159	2144	127230	2582	160905
医疗仪器及器械	金额		10557		8573		12824
手表	亿只	0.6	9826	0.6	8562	0.5	11268
#电动手表	亿只	0.6	9384	0.6	8306	0.5	11028
家具	金额		277855		242625		320917
灯具、照明装置及类似品	金额		88680		78441		103738
箱包及类似容器	金额		109052		114374		156455
服装及衣着附件	金额		319244		281057		389784
#织物制服装	金额		268855		242454		342793
裘皮服装	吨	190	2444	157	2013	145	1857
帽类	万个	15416.3	7993	9939.9	8992	15532.2	11470
鞋	亿双	5.5	261248	2.4	237001	2.7	297056
塑料制品	万吨	54.5	107390	44.6	90913	51.1	113700
玩具	金额		146857		122821		163174
贵金属或包贵金属的首饰	金额		2435		5934		15089
人造花	吨	22103	5145				

9-8 历年新签利用外资协议(合同)宗数

Number of Signed Agreements or Contracts of Utilization of Foreign Capital over Years

单位：宗

年 份	新签协议(合同)数	“三来一补”企业	“三资”企业
1979	184	184	
1980	415	415	
1981	555	553	2
1982	470	468	2
1983	454	447	7
1984	551	508	43
1985	625	514	111
1986	618	559	59
1987	824	729	95
1988	2048	1839	209
1989	939	779	160
1990	1267	1075	192
1991	1636	1268	368
1992	2232	1374	858
1993	3118	1773	1345
1994	2678	1521	1157
1995	3077	2094	983
1996	1678	1343	335
1997	1685	1492	193
1998	1383	1051	332
1999	1362	1135	227
2000	1276	871	405
2001	1395	705	690
2002	1391	524	867
2003	1524	392	1132
2004	1423	391	1032
2005	992	219	773
2006	786	177	609
2007	790	82	708
2008	588	35	553
2009	601	22	579
2010	875	6	869

9-9　历年新签利用外资协议(合同)规定外商投资额

Amount of Signed Agreements or Contracts of Utilization of Foreign Capital over Years

单位：万美元

年　份	协议(合同)规定外商投资额	"三来一补"企业	"三资"企业
1979	476	476	
1980	1055	1055	
1981	806	784	22
1982	787	771	16
1983	1616	841	775
1984	3217	1013	2204
1985	6815	1870	4945
1986	3398	1593	1805
1987	18513	14082	4431
1988	62173	42507	19666
1989	23365	9268	14097
1990	30180	12346	17834
1991	64483	19348	45135
1992	208825	29720	179105
1993	355515	54823	300692
1994	349703	47700	302003
1995	330920	97428	233492
1996	208861	62811	146050
1997	121351	62114	59237
1998	163677	58709	104968
1999	147247	69756	77491
2000	183633	69302	114331
2001	209779	56833	152946
2002	248914	47285	201629
2003	325633	59538	266095
2004	413216	124089	289127
2005	475238	166363	308875
2006	552758	197836	354922
2007	625088	176903	448185
2008	393701	134952	258749
2009	203040	41420	161620
2010	307282	47542	259740

9-10 历年实际利用外资

Foreign Capital Actually Utilized over Years

单位：万美元

年 份	累计实际利用外资	当年实际利用外资	“三来一补”企业	“三资”企业
1979	173	173	173	
1980	1107	934	934	
1981	1642	535	528	7
1982	2357	715	668	47
1983	3258	901	871	30
1984	5175	1917	1233	684
1985	8069	2894	1511	1383
1986	11111	3042	1553	1489
1987	22370	11259	9185	2074
1988	46496	24126	17717	6409
1989	71445	24949	16559	8390
1990	95764	24319	14309	10010
1991	121918	26154	11478	14676
1992	168510	46592	13716	32876
1993	261938	93428	14181	79247
1994	366750	104812	26938	77874
1995	472415	105665	38418	67247
1996	579979	107564	38061	69503
1997	701406	121427	33467	87960
1998	835219	133813	40780	93033
1999	980951	145732	48620	97112
2000	1145663	164712	55975	108737
2001	1327225	181562	66841	114721
2002	1542073	214848	68980	145868
2003	1798409	256336	80936	175400
2004	2101839	303430	89555	213875
2005	2476978	375139	93023	282116
2006	2910751	433773	98543	335230
2007	3415146	504395	94365	410030
2008	3737716	322570	77902	244668
2009	4031873	294157	34758	259399
2010	4348160	316287	43116	273171

注：本表数据不含对外借款。

9-11 主要年份“三资”企业利用外资

Utilization of Foreign Capital of Enterprises with Foreign Investment in Main Years

项　　目	计量单位	1985年	1990年	1995年	2000年	2005年	2009年	2010年
一、全部“三资”企业利用外资情况								
当年新签协议宗数	宗	111	192	983	405	773	579	869
本年止累计执行宗数	宗	51	591	2807	4012	6657	7940	8338
#已投产	宗	47	454	2629	3908	5870	7282	7469
项目(协议)终止宗数	宗	3	24	48	338	193	286	471
实际投资总额	万美元	2565	18642	75853	115801	290553	264549	277547
境内资金总额	万美元	1182	8632	8606	7064	8437	5150	4376
中方实际投资	万美元	1182	5515	6448	4445	8337	5150	4376
企业境内借款	万美元		3117	2158	2619	100		
境外资金总额	万美元	1383	10010	67247	108737	282959	259399	273171
外商实际投资	万美元	1383	8934	65416	108468	282116	259399	273171
企业境外借款	万美元		1076	1831	269	842		
引进设备价值	万美元	995	6619	50267	80215	118401	37922	63822
出口总值	万美元	799	13439	178351	835600	2353253	3345624	4426236
期末职工人数	万人	0.54	3.81	25.01	87.17	145.50	150.00	163.53
二、中外合作企业利用外资情况								
当年新签协议宗数	宗	86	72	195	19	2	2	
本年止累计执行宗数	宗	43	237	730	705	337	281	184
#已投产	宗	41	177	682	700	299	279	184
项目(协议)终止宗数	宗	3	15	12	130	25	7	23
实际投资总额	万美元	1301	5072	15159	10045	13529	4563	1345
境内资金总额	万美元	423	1427	176	1731	860	328	169
中方实际投资	万美元	423	651	136	1486	860	328	169
企业境内借款	万美元		776	40	245			
境外资金总额	万美元	878	3645	14983	8314	12669	4235	1176
外商实际投资	万美元	878	3642	14981	8314	12669	4235	1176
企业境外借款	万美元		3	2				
引进设备价值	万美元	290	2411	9320	5033	4060	509	651
出口总值	万美元	534	2423	35718	92100	116157	117228	117188
期末职工人数	万人	0.33	1.02	5.82	13.57	10.38	5.70	3.50

注：本表2000年起出口总值是海关口径。

9-11　续表

项　　　目	计量单位	1985年	1990年	1995年	2000年	2005年	2009年	2010年
三、中外合资企业利用外资情况								
当年新签协议宗数	宗	25	93	378	29	31	15	18
本年止累计执行宗数	宗	8	338	1590	1690	712	663	507
#已投产	宗	6	251	1498	1650	668	648	489
项目(协议)终止宗数	宗		9	31	159	53	23	99
实际投资总额	万美元	1264	13070	39659	23966	25672	40650	36342
境内资金总额	万美元	759	7199	8345	5333	7477	4822	4207
中方实际投资	万美元	759	4864	6312	2959	7477	4822	4207
企业境内借款	万美元		2335	2033	2374			
境外资金总额	万美元	506	5871	31314	18633	18195	35828	32135
外商实际投资	万美元	506	4798	29496	18364	18195	35828	32135
企业境外借款	万美元		1073	1818	269			
引进设备价值	万美元	705	3920	25557	14365	4060	15742	28850
出口总值	万美元	265	10934	90357	248800	289344	265929	348622
期末职工人数	万人	0.20	2.69	13.51	24.68	17.95	13.07	11.60
四、外商独资企业利用外资情况								
当年新签协议宗数	宗		27	410	357	740	562	851
本年止累计执行宗数	宗		16	487	1614	5607	6996	7641
#已投产	宗		8	449	1555	4903	6263	6790
项目(协议)终止宗数	宗			5	49	115	256	349
实际投资总额	万美元		500	21035	79113	252194	218703	239860
境内资金总额	万美元		6	85		100		
中方实际投资	万美元							
企业境内借款	万美元		6	85		100		
境外资金总额	万美元		494	20950	79113	252094	218703	239634
外商实际投资	万美元		494	20939	79113	251252	218703	239634
企业境外借款	万美元			11		842		
引进设备价值	万美元		288	15390	58140	91288	21670	34321
出口总值	万美元		82	52276	494700	1947751	2962467	3960425
期末职工人数	万人		0.10	5.67	48.92	117.17	131.23	148.43

9-12 主要年份分方式、分国别(地区)实际利用外资

Foreign Capital Actually Utilized by Type and Countries(Regions) in Main Years

单位：万美元

项目	1990年	1995年	2000年	2001年	2003年	2005年	2009年	2010年
一、按引进方式分								
总计	**10167**	**68438**	**164712**	**181562**	**256336**	**375139**	**294157**	**316287**
外商直接投资	10010	67247	108737	114721	175400	282116	259399	273171
合资经营企业	5871	31314	18865	16413	12938	18195	35828	32135
合作经营企业	3645	14983	8305	6798	8608	12669	4235	1176
外资(独资)经营企业	494	20950	78890	88413	153854	251252	218703	239634
外商投资股份公司			2677	3097			633	226
外商其他投资	157	1191	55975	66841	80936	93023	34758	43116
国际租赁								
补偿贸易								
加工装配	157	1191	55975	66841	80936	93023	34758	43116
二、按国家和地区分								
总计	**10167**	**67247**	**164712**	**181562**	**256336**	**375139**	**294157**	**316287**
香港	10167	58333	88950	89559	122639	185214	169794	182600
澳门		13				44	824	442
台湾		3016	23722	32130	30005	130682	81208	82674
日本		391	7476	6994	11037	25253	13556	12861
泰国		96	33	108		20		
新加坡		822	3511	5595	5003	3994	6121	6094
德国		3	1884	1210	5265	487	494	1488
法国			89			20	542	688
瑞士			546	426			41	127
加拿大		46	15	142	56	99	195	568
美国		3230	2391	2576	5987	8122	6054	3309
澳大利亚		56	14	118	252	48	193	61
韩国			2362	2792	5012	6958	4962	5955
利比亚			153					
英国		79		570	194	12	2576	277
其他		1162	33566	39342	70886	14186	7597	19143

注：1995年分国别地区的外商投资额是外商直接投资额。

9-13 外商直接投资分行业情况（2010年）

Foreign Direct Investment by Sector (2010)

单位：万美元

行业	项目个数(个)	合同外资金额	实际投资金额
总计	**869**	**259740**	**273171**
农、林、牧、渔业		1010	62
采矿业		64	32
制造业	732	222480	241560
#纺织业	45	12908	7225
化学原料及化学制品制造业	7	2353	4209
医药制造业		-768	1185
通用设备制造业	28	6530	7541
专用设备制造业	38	19263	15589
通信设备、计算机及其他电子设备制造业	110	66565	60796
电力、燃气及水的生产和供应业	1	193	2864
建筑业			112
交通运输、仓储和邮政业	1	1594	1104
信息传输、计算机服务和软件业	4	782	109
批发和零售业	109	20655	13271
住宿和餐饮业	1	305	691
金融业			
房地产业	4	11250	11223
#房地产开发经营	1	7791	11174
租赁和商务服务业	12	945	1225
科学研究、技术服务和地质勘查业	4	320	331
居民服务和其他服务业		116	409
卫生、社会保障和社会福利业			178
公共管理和社会组织	1	26	

9-14 主要年份宾馆酒店接待能力和接待人数

Capacity and Tourists Received by Hotels in Main Years

项目	单位	1990年	1995年	2000年	2005年	2009年	2010年
一、三星级以上宾馆(酒店)	家	3	16	30	63	80	82
三星级	家	3	16	23	27	35	35
四星级	家			6	22	26	25
五星级	家			1	14	19	22
二、客房（已评1星以上）	间	3793	7568	18024	18258	16332	16631
床位（已评1星以上）	张	8531	15136	30895	25014	24389	24841
开房率	%	60.2	68.8	61.9	58.9	58.0	58.1
三、全年接待人数	万人次	125	89	291	1156	2037	2251
(一) 国际及港澳台旅游者	万人次	27	27	106	169	286	327
#外国人	万人次	1	6	15	70	104	109
港澳台同胞	万人次	26	21	89	99	182	219
(二) 国内旅客	万人次	98	62	185	987	1751	1924

9-15 历年旅游业情况

Basic Statistics on Tourism over Years

年份	三星级以上宾馆(酒店)(家)	客房(已评1星以上)(间)	床位(已评1星以上)(张)	开房率(%)	全年接待人数(万人次)	国际及港澳台旅游者	外国人	港澳台同胞	国内游客	国际旅游外汇收入(万美元)
1978										
1979										
1980										
1981										
1982										
1983										
1984										
1985										
1986					80	11		10	69	554
1987					107	19	1	18	87	453
1988		6435	7641	65.8	125	20		19	105	710
1989		3324	7376	64.8	115	18		18	97	504
1990		3793	8531	60.2	125	27	1	26	98	1025
1991		4004	8701	64.9	155	37	1	36	118	2443
1992		4042	8770	72.6	172	47	2	46	125	2473
1993		4258	8517	75.1	169	52	2	50	117	2888
1994		3542	7443	77.6	119	44	4	40	75	3464
1995	16	7568	15136	68.8	89	27	6	21	62	5679
1996	16	13409	26818	50.3	175	36	6	29	139	6464
1997	19	10420	19142	50.6	171	59	5	54	112	6778
1998	20	17428	31987	53.3	216	75	11	63	141	6601
1999	20	17931	25482	63.5	253	97	17	77	156	7055
2000	30	18024	30895	61.9	291	106	15	89	185	7617
2001	48	20572	32789	62.0	327	110	22	88	217	8200
2002	53	9427	14652	69.0	930	108	22	86	822	11847
2003	52	8170	12599	65.0	1086	80	24	56	1006	13825
2004	60	10530	14934	61.2	1131	149	66	83	982	23437
2005	63	18258	25014	58.9	1156	169	70	99	987	28189
2006	71	18258	25014	60.1	1363	193	81	112	1170	33180
2007	74	19023	26132	63.4	1725	248	102	146	1477	42702
2008	77	19510	26864	58.9	1872	268	103	165	1604	45614
2009	80	16332	24389	58.0	2037	286	104	182	1751	51756
2010	82	16631	24841	58.1	2251	327	109	219	1924	67592

注：国际旅游外汇收入1995年以前单位为万元(外汇券)，1995年起为万美元。

9-16 外出旅游情况（2008-2010年）

Basic Statistics on Domestic amd Outbound Tourism (2008-2010)

项　　目	单位	2008年	2009年	2010年
外出旅游人数	万人次	108.32	127.1	153.8
(一)国内旅游人数	万人次	97.78	114.45	139.09
(二)出国(境)游人数	万人次	10.54	12.65	14.71
#旅行社组团出境旅游合计	人次	105400	126500	147055
香港游	人次	42350	35507	45100
澳门游	人次	11986	53952	57519
港澳游	人次	7981	5154	5622
泰国	人次	2981	2055	2670
泰港	人次	1954	1790	2061
泰港澳	人次	4800	112	137
新马港	人次	3596	4631	5650
新泰港	人次	5874	2209	2467
新马泰港	人次	3618	1355	1662
韩国	人次	5875	1853	2486
韩港	人次	3873	2583	3094
菲律宾	人次	2516	1218	1240
澳大利亚	人次	1079	207	260
日本	人次	3936	4521	5070
其他	人次	2981	9353	12017

主要统计指标解释

Explanatory Notes on Main Statistical Indicators

海关进出口总额　指实际进出我国国境的货物（包括贸易和非贸易）的价值总和。主要包括对外贸易实际进出口货物，来料加工装配、补偿贸易、进料加工进出口货物，国家间及国际组织无偿援助物资和赠送品，华侨、港澳台同胞和外籍华人捐赠品，租赁期满归承租人所有的租赁货物，边境地方贸易及边境地区小额贸易进出口货物（边民互市贸易除外），中外合资、合作经营企业、外商独资经营企业进出口货物和公用物品，到、离岸价格在规定限额以上的进出口货样和广告品（无商业价值、无使用价值和免费提供出口的除外），从保税仓库提取在中国境内销售的进出口货物，以及其他进出口货物。海关进出口总额反映一个国家在对外经济贸易方面实际进出口货物的总规模。

创汇总额　包括一般贸易出口、"三来一补"出口应收工缴费、三资企业出口和非贸易。

贸易出口　指由外贸进出口公司、工农贸易进出口公司和地方性的进出口公司由国家统一安排的出口、代理出口和自营、联营出口，其中包括进料加工出口，以及各进出口公司在国内以外汇结算方式售给友谊商店、华侨商店、出国人员服务公司和中外合资、合作经营和外资企业等的出口商品。

"三来一补"出口　指来料加工装配出口按工缴费计算，中小型补偿贸易按金额计算。

"三资"企业出口　指三资企业自己出口的本企业产品。不包括委托外贸进出口公司出口的商品。

利用外资　指我国各级政府、部门、企业和其他经济组织通过对外借款、吸收外商直接投资以及向境外发行债券、股票等方式筹措的境外资金。

外资的形式可以是现汇、实物、工业产权或专有技术等有形资本和无形资本。

我国自有外汇如国家外汇、中国银行等金融机构用自有资金发放的外汇贷款等，华侨、港澳同胞的捐赠，联合国或其他国际组织的无偿赠送资金、无偿援建的项目均不属于外资范围。

利用外资的方式有：对外借款，外国（或港澳地区）企业和经济组织或个人在我国境内开办独资企业，与我国境内的企业或组织共同开办合资企业合作经营（企业）项目或合作开发资源，以及补偿贸易、国际租赁等。

对外借款　指我国政府、部门、企业和中国银行等单位向国际金融组织、外国政府、企业等借用的长期、短期资本，到期需还本付息。借款按不同渠道划分为：1.外国政府贷款；2.国际金融组织贷款；3.外国银行贷款；4.出口信贷；5.发行债券、股票。

外商直接投资　指外国企业和经济组织或个人（包括华侨、港澳同胞以及我在境外注册的企业）按我国有关政策、法规，在我国境内开办外商独资企业，与我国境内的企业或经济组织共同举办中外合资企业、合作经营企业或合作开发资源的投资以及外商从企业得到收益的再投资。

新口径合同利用外资　根据2003年修订的《利用外资统计制度》，明确指出合同外资的统计指外商直接投资（三资企业）企业设立时，根据合同（章程）规定，外方投资者应缴付的注册资本。

国际旅游（外汇）收入　指国内各部门为来我国旅游的外国人、华侨、港澳和台湾同胞提供商品和劳务而得到的外汇收入。包括供应商品、饮食和提供住宿、交通、邮电、文化娱乐、导游等各项服务所得的全部外汇收入。

十、财政、金融与保险

Finance, Banking and Insurance

10-1 主要年份财政收支主要指标

Main Indicators of Government Revenue and Expenditure in Main Years

单位：万元

项　　目	1978年	1980年	1985年	1990年	2000年	2005年	2006年
一、财政收入							
来源于东莞的财政收入(含关税)					1035562	3319079	4065412
中央财政收入					617151	1935069	2323977
#关税和海关代征税					273972	483327	526251
省级财政收入					113681	344330	451990
市财政一般预算收入					304730	1039680	1289445
来源于东莞的财政收入(不含关税)	6604	6710	11118	35719	761590	2835752	3539161
中央财政收入					343179	1451742	1797726
省级财政收入					113681	344330	451990
市财政一般预算收入	6604	6710	11118	35719	304730	1039680	1289445
各项税收	6595	6699	10998	33544	265565	879653	1077152
工商税收	5826	5785	9708	31911	248159	797038	990029
农业税类	769	914	1290	1633	17406	82615	87123
专项收入				686	14709	36423	49285
其他收入	9	11	120	1489	24456	123604	163008
二、工商税收							
工商税收总额					867584	2923001	3593704
国税(不含关税)					607216	1849818	2208722
地税					260368	1073183	1384982
三、财政支出							
市财政一般预算支出	1792	2015	4999	22779	336102	1170427	1478955
#基本建设支出					27426	276646	242829
企业挖潜改造支出		88	15	37	1584	9107	9691
科技三项费用支出		7		140	9963	31572	87397
农林水气部门事业费支出		304	1154	3261	40097	62181	64911
工交部门事业费支出		2	7	180	192	20499	18552
城市维护费支出		31	219	1350	41267	162370	205426
科教文卫体事业费支出		1051	2139	7357	86737	210620	291467
#科学事业费				404	936	3956	3874
教育事业费		760	1504	3786	68194	171055	244113
卫生事业费		185	262	743	12083	11469	12826
体育事业费		18	50	827	1517	2860	3266
抚恤和社会福利救济支出		75	132	368	2888	8335	34050
行政管理费支出		293	320	1324	29817	102296	119034
公检法司支出			92	740	46446	166055	225382

注：从2007年起财政收支按新的分类项目，在10-2表中反映。

10-2 财政收支主要指标（2006-2010年）

Main Indicators of Government Revenue and Expenditure (2006-2010)

单位：万元

指　　标	2006年	2007年	2008年	2009年	2010年
来源于东莞的财政收入(含关税)	4065412	5395362	6010642	6278114	7851003
财政总收入	3358095	4574778	5234746	5402140	6542697
#中央	1638195	2151906	2476902	2392927	2940745
省级	430455	558404	665596	697658	823548
市财政一般预算收入	1289445	1864468	2092248	2311555	2778404
#增值税	347153	474288	552515	534382	626301
营业税	291122	380958	422427	446884	458712
企业所得税	145739	173566	184478	176786	247986
个人所得税	60518	75765	87895	87313	110441
房产税	51622	63228	65560	75806	92706
契税	80793	355039	113509	157533	186994
罚没收入	75238	81766	79104	72888	78400
市财政一般预算支出	1478955	1930968	2182626	2326216	2898306
#一般公共服务	161657	220367	234172	259865	269505
公共安全	233413	324714	365387	367266	388243
教育	293000	412347	499978	553429	653090
科学技术	10593	91232	93518	112506	79830
社会保障和就业	27100	104264	232742	194637	264017
农林水事务	77188	116452	143695	131828	229613
交通运输	14439	54144	49759	73635	90609
工商税收总额	3593704	4709341	5361733	5475100	6887249
#国税(不含关税)	2208722	3057525	3390812	3384667	4394366
地税	1384982	1651816	1970921	2090433	2492883

10-3 历年财政收入

Government Revenue over Years

单位：万元

年 份	来源于东莞的财政总收入（含关税）	来源于东莞的财政总收入（不含关税）	中央财政收入	省级财政收入	市财政一般预算收入	各项税收	工商税收	专项收入	其他收入
1978		6604			6604	6595	5826		9
1979		6634			6634	6625	5725		9
1980		6710			6710	6699	5785		11
1981		6823			6823	6805	5942		18
1982		8103			8103	8068	7184		35
1983		8578			8578	8501	7599		77
1984		8469			8469	8385	7442		84
1985		11118			11118	10998	9708		120
1986		16053			16053	15865	14574	45	143
1987		20221			20221	19989	18551	50	182
1988		27076			27076	26837	25309	76	163
1989		31888			31888	30997	29331	116	775
1990		35719			35719	33544	31911	686	1489
1991		44374			44374	41659	39302	913	1802
1992		56204			56204	52620	48272	1351	2233
1993		93828			93828	88920	83462	1947	2961
1994		130531	53591		76940	70451	60889	2697	3792
1995		180051	64433		115618	106388	95463	4070	5160
1996	283506	201579	78403	26635	96541	85648	74323	4470	6423
1997	335044	237391	94320	29002	114069	96980	85245	4794	12295
1998	472422	342792	133803	57977	151012	123816	106700	5693	21503
1999	717847	438761	182160	74024	182577	159873	134852	8759	13945
2000	1035561	761590	343179	113681	304730	265565	248159	14709	24456
2001	1259961	1100212	477826	172223	450163	402668	381660	18356	29139
2002	1678848	1510978	710391	247654	552933	489780	467998	26438	36715
2003	2064052	1811345	864349	272535	674461	575342	536390	30710	68409
2004	2591086	2232480	1099129	306962	826389	707954	655571	35273	83162
2005	3319079	2835752	1451742	344330	1039680	879653	797038	36423	123604
2006	4065412	3539161	1797726	451990	1289445	1077152	990029	49285	163008
2007	5395362	4738885	2316013	558404	1864468	1652620	1291335	55863	155985
2008	6010642	5376839	2476902	665596	2092248	1682270	1555499	60590	10085
2009	6278114	5533562	2392927	697658	2311556	1822650	1618514	60007	40700
2010	7851003	6731600	2940745	823548	2778404	2217675	1950773	72153	12207

10-4 历年财政支出

Government Expenditure over Years

单位：万元

年 份	预算内地方财政支出总额	#基本建设支出	#科技三项费用	#农林水气等部门事业费	#城市维护费	#科教文卫体育事业费	#教育事业费	#行政管理费
1978	1792							
1979	1908		20	451	74	852	618	202
1980	2015		7	304	31	1051	760	293
1981	2139		4	341	36	1182	818	246
1982	2612		1	359	141	1346	912	336
1983	2804		1	413	28	1672	1004	287
1984	3013			264	48	1868	1309	340
1985	4999			1154	219	2139	1504	320
1986	9916			2541	1431	2887	1793	330
1987	12512			3479	1624	4759	1871	510
1988	17475		100	4094	1614	6950	3339	888
1989	21623		103	3509	2286	7958	3733	1159
1990	22779		140	3261	1350	7357	3786	1324
1991	27499		30	4938	866	7956	4720	1484
1992	38162		50	5637	567	17505	7682	2348
1993	72910	5400	1289	8882	5737	25716	14427	4002
1994	88984	14575	1496	12835	5254	20725	13552	6158
1995	124173	13736	441	15798	9947	31021	23110	8433
1996	124059	17285	1332	14962	5199	28927	21237	10384
1997	148510	16923	1479	15349	6258	36614	23262	11691
1998	179064	26144	1164	19255	7264	36710	25578	11082
1999	212641	40681	1429	26648	12994	40863	30631	12979
2000	336102	27426	9963	40097	41267	86737	68194	29817
2001	478646	119692	4113	28957	43706	105990	85544	28961
2002	649606	165283	28013	37348	64483	143225	120195	43678
2003	765190	201077	30062	41164	44240	193138	163390	50022
2004	941554	179039	27110	53855	164770	162573	139337	84798
2005	1170427	276646	31572	62181	162370	210620	171055	102296
2006	1478955	242829	87397	64911	205426	291467	244113	119034

注：从2007年起财政支出按新的分类项目，在10-2表中反映。

10-5 税务登记情况及税种征收情况（2009-2010年）

Taxes (2009-2010)

指　　标	国税		地税	
	2009年	2010年	2009年	2010年
税务登记情况（户）	**205588**	**247277**	**237858**	**304204**
#国有企业	360	358	874	1334
集体企业	5742	5057	7122	7787
私营企业	29684	33986	24244	31641
港澳台投资企业	5445	5823	5783	8455
外商投资企业	3850	4010	3170	3843
个体经营	127726	157155	148353	183214
工商税收总额（万元）	**3384667**	**4394366**	**2090433**	**2492883**
#国有企业	10420	9933	56759	35701
集体企业	37186	41161	237882	245968
私营企业	300923	432581	203804	234451
港澳台投资企业	787927	902769	256827	399846
外商投资企业	641713	713086	282171	341140
个体经营	276327	367881	190681	229409
#增值税	2859992	3586480		
消费税	22848	38528		
营业税			875821	919809
企业所得税	374517	588256	438967	550874
个人所得税	7825	1484	363805	460168
房产税			75806	92704
印花税			37672	89081
城镇土地使用税			79479	94552
土地增值税			100970	142003
车船税			27410	31869
车辆购置税	117778	177508		
#第一产业	968	1113	848	1310
第二产业	2054904	2478868	779784	1022327
#采矿业	745	597	808	1314
制造业	1859444	2264031	499247	711871
农副食品加工业	8965	9554	6482	8266
食品制造业	56991	72742	26221	37054
饮料制造业	34716	33733	10055	7793
纺织业	91797	93705	11067	16803
纺织服装、鞋、帽制造业	126588	149890	21183	28726
皮革、毛皮、羽绒及其制品业	48555	76543	11473	15626
木材加工及竹、藤、棕草制品业	9986	10646	1683	2762
家具制造业	67214	79142	11217	18627
造纸及纸制品业	103606	125648	12176	20058

注：2009和2010年国税的工商税收总额含代地税征收的城市维护建设税分别为1707万元和2110万元。

10-5 续表

单位：万元

指标	国税		地税	
	2009年	2010年	2009年	2010年
印刷业、记录媒介的复制	41117	54974	9772	14419
文教体育用品制造业	36737	47221	14150	18048
石油加工、及炼焦业及核燃业	1868	7960	1934	3205
化学原料及化学制品制造业	61011	68698	12406	15444
医药制造业	11303	12690	2920	4825
化学纤维制造业	2723	3256	105	172
橡胶制品业	17312	22984	5716	7901
塑料制品业	128595	156955	34944	49300
非金属矿物制品业	47204	69141	5860	9436
黑色金属冶炼及压延加工业	170	311	1429	1636
有色金属冶炼及压延加工业	3263	5228	1626	1935
金属制品业	101350	132603	25235	39579
通用设备制造业	52259	86175	17815	24233
专用设备制造业	58774	81485	13963	20194
交通运输设备制造业	35556	46474	21366	12473
电气机械及器材制造业	135985	164802	34476	63890
通信设备、计算机及其他电子设备制造业	419887	476071	149515	220276
仪器仪表及文化、办公用机械制造业	37341	44861	6484	9280
其他制造业	118571	130539	27974	39910
电力、热力的生产和供应业	167255	208102	58666	61702
建筑业	6248	6138	221063	247440
房屋和土木工程建筑业	773	785	44822	66006
建筑安装业	2413	2045	145732	151391
建筑装饰业	1645	1468	14751	15103
其他建筑业	1417	1840	15758	14940
第三产业	1328795	1914386	1309801	1469246
#交通运输、仓储及邮政业	3681	6263	67782	84894
信息传输、计算机服务和软件业	2494	2349	70474	58352
批发和零售业	361715	501711	97468	124125
住宿和餐饮业	1013	1633	74341	78305
金融业	91444	109961	187363	224405
房地产业	79321	121515	480420	515796
租赁和商务服务业	11156	11259	79964	104598
居民服务和其他服务业	12915	18188	157730	174026
教育	112	193	4728	4082
卫生、社会保险和社会福利业	351	414	6662	5992
文化、体育和娱乐业	210	256	21558	21611
公共管理和社会组织	1	10	21696	25531
其他行业	764382	1140634	39615	47529

10-6 历年金融机构各项人民币存款余额

Balance of RMB Deposits of Financial Institutions over Years

单位：万元

年　份	各项存款余额	#企业存款余额	#城乡居民储蓄存款余额	#财政性存款余额
1978	10497	1431	5409	963
1979	14875	2319	7184	1028
1980	26093	5107	11718	1481
1981	38003	6546	20339	1503
1982	45120	8169	27650	1937
1983	60547	10190	38597	3343
1984	110265	22510	61823	5060
1985	134867	23367	91941	3488
1986	195948	35422	131352	5801
1987	284819	49618	189654	5321
1988	380511	73733	249134	6724
1989	468203	75491	325670	9202
1990	680696	116074	455140	7953
1991	949713	164519	614737	10313
1992	1473354	319933	815404	19926
1993	1798346	423791	1071715	33016
1994	2497834	616328	1515445	60551
1995	3836761	895021	2329685	83933
1996	4896463	1114040	3180215	56860
1997	6711687	1595280	4258238	48923
1998	8640053	2515686	5337482	49729
1999	10408377	3268530	6163430	35166
2000	12286706	4385202	6720704	39949
2001	14586491	5032045	7991768	57056
2002	17901799	5775722	10016909	78673
2003	21267775	6378486	12310616	110077
2004	24628693	7546584	14316777	164648
2005	29334026	8558552	17282760	259771
2006	33656508	10111005	20133979	298793
2007	37518345	11624537	21207413	568912
2008	43545340	11839005	26380433	495375
2009	49866108	14199448	29045704	524501
2010	59433885	15215577	33868535	465766

10-7 历年金融机构各项人民币贷款余额及现金收支

Balance of RMB Loans, Cash Income and Expenditure of Financial Institutions over Years

单位：万元

年 份	各项贷款余额	#短期贷款	#中长期贷款	现金收入合计	#商品销售收入	现金支出合计	现金净投放(+)净回笼(−)
1978	19607	19607		20774	14102	22122	1348
1979	21301	21301		24534	16526	26866	2332
1980	30797	29669	403	31479	20608	35825	4346
1981	40243	38365	765	46686	27780	56128	9442
1982	45525	44081	690	61297	33398	69210	7913
1983	57618	56063	837	70482	35539	92040	21558
1984	121891	114522	3365	88743	36275	143081	54338
1985	142437	130716	6230	140341	48661	173190	32849
1986	206813	193501	9486	176408	57195	231184	54776
1987	312431	292104	7162	286438	75083	346268	59830
1988	415818	381957	12351	547812	136849	577049	29237
1989	493737	456504	12338	843887	181085	856946	13059
1990	630355	570324	13427	1209730	195286	1258795	49065
1991	783957	714848	17385	1798653	247206	1923571	124918
1992	1059794	935064	23000	3038847	369975	3445508	406661
1993	1343103	923157	237985	4901078	562202	5403709	502631
1994	1734350	1246772	250806	6808963	636843	7217477	408504
1995	2548512	1645696	274157	8584483	752404	8974313	389830
1996	3128076	2053343	353298	11245241	764331	11935860	690619
1997	3826560	2737916	205486	13909740	852965	14381835	472095
1998	4427394	3666563	155295	24885265	1963439	25150137	264872
1999	5243735	4628058	328875	29970415	2541776	30985960	1015545
2000	6308405	5313933	469249	35945777	3277631	37187782	1242005
2001	7501801	5341925	1436127	38494378	3451596	38583059	88681
2002	9334054	5731973	2312883	45085355	4071749	44611686	-473669
2003	12067237	6918877	3730104	55556021	5374491	54193508	-1362513
2004	14052461	7118671	5222504	68687707	5675223	67287198	-1400509
2005	15005217	7341939	7007138	73752467	5532266	71784959	-1967507
2006	17305554	7792175	8684306	78759519	6057902	77137021	-1622498
2007	21547660	9245906	11427676	90319897	6045894	89760923	-558973
2008	23803585	10132902	12052974	91343779	5997521	90710505	-633274
2009	29037984	12604957	14519686	84494728	5218187	84862223	367496
2010	33298244	12340319	19675448	98675665	6458444	100842157	2166492

注：现金收入与支出1997年及以前年份为国家银行口径，1998年起为金融机构口径。

10-8 历年各项人民币存贷款余额与现金收支增加额

Balance of RMB Deposits and Loans, Increase of Cash Income and Expenditure over Years

单位：万元

年 份	各项存款余额		各项贷款余额		现金收入		现金支出	
	年末数	年增加额	年末数	年增加额	合 计	年增加额	合 计	年增加额
1978	10497		19607		20774		22122	
1979	14875	4378	21301	1694	24534	3760	26866	4744
1980	26093	11218	30797	9496	31479	6945	35825	8959
1981	38003	11910	40243	9446	46686	15207	56128	20303
1982	45120	7117	45525	5282	61297	14611	69210	13082
1983	60547	15427	57618	12093	70482	9185	92040	22830
1984	110265	49718	121891	64273	88743	18261	143081	51041
1985	134867	24602	142437	20546	140341	51598	173190	30109
1986	195948	61081	206813	64376	176408	36067	231184	57994
1987	284819	88871	312431	105618	286438	110030	346268	115084
1988	380511	95692	415818	103387	547812	261374	577049	230781
1989	468203	87692	493737	77919	843887	296075	856946	279897
1990	680696	212493	630355	136618	1209730	365843	1258795	401849
1991	949713	269017	783957	153602	1798653	588923	1923571	664776
1992	1473354	523641	1059794	275837	3038847	1240194	3445508	1521937
1993	1798346	324992	1343103	283309	4901078	1862231	5403709	1958201
1994	2497834	699488	1734350	391247	6808963	1907885	7217477	1813768
1995	3836761	1338927	2548512	814162	8584483	1775520	8974313	1756836
1996	4896463	1059702	3128076	579564	11245241	2660758	11935860	2961547
1997	6711687	1815224	3826560	698484	13909740	2664499	14381835	2445975
1998	8640053	1928366	4427394	600834	24885265	10975525	25150137	10768302
1999	10408377	1768324	5243735	816341	29970415	5085150	30985960	5835823
2000	12286706	1878329	6308405	1064670	35945777	5975362	37187782	6201822
2001	14586491	2299785	7501801	1193396	38494378	2548601	38583059	1395277
2002	17901799	3315308	9334054	1832253	45085355	6590977	44611686	6028627
2003	21267775	3365976	12067237	2733183	55556021	10470666	54193508	9581822
2004	24628693	3360918	14052461	1985224	68687707	13131686	67287198	13093690
2005	29334026	4705333	15005217	952756	73752467	5064760	71784959	4497761
2006	33656508	4322482	17305554	2300337	78759519	5007052	77137021	5352062
2007	37518345	3861837	21547660	4242106	90319897	11560378	89760923	12623902
2008	43545340	6026995	23803585	2255925	91343779	1023882	90710505	949582
2009	49866108	6320728	29037984	5234399	84494728	-6849051	84862223	-5848282
2010	59433885	9567777	33298244	4260260	98675665	14180937	100842157	15979934

注：现金收入与支出1998年以前是国家银行口径，1998年起是金融机构口径。

10-9 保险行业主要指标(2006-2010年)

Main Indicators of Insurance (2006-2010)

指　　标	单位	2006年	2007年	2008年	2009年	2010年
保险公司	家	26	30	35	37	37
保险业从业人员	人	11714	17846	24771	27386	27281
保费收入	万元	473835	676062	902986	1150795	1597166
寿险类	万元	277769	397962	583983	797192	1129950
#传统寿险	万元	51772	57890	61255	63681	72494
分红险	万元	157264	190521	355674	572703	867738
万能险	万元	34050	51114	73233	85142	110035
投连险	万元	1750	60993	38195	18481	18953
意外险	万元	12382	14490	17188	17143	18718
健康险	万元	20477	22954	38438	40043	42012
财险类	万元	196066	278100	319010	353602	467216
#机动车险	万元	155067	231073	270082	301526	400405
企财险	万元	17160	21254	22626	24276	32123
家财险	万元	3228	3393	1373	1113	1832
货运险	万元	1985	2514	2819	3648	4576
责任险	万元	4179	5477	6571	7273	9772
短健险	万元	1448	271	759	8058	4289
短意险	万元	10536	12945	13145	6184	11073
农业险	万元	23	43	17		55

主要统计指标解释

Explanatory Notes on Main Statistical Indicators

财政收入 国家财政参与社会产品分配所取得的收入，是实现国家职能的财力保证，主要包括：

（1）各项税收 包括增值税、营业税、消费税、土地增值税、城市维护建设税、资源税、城市土地使用税、印花税、个人所得税、企业所得税、关税、农牧业税和耕地占用税等。

（2）专项收入 包括征收排污费收入、征收城市水资源费收入，教育费附加收入等。

（3）其他收入 包括基本建设贷款归还收入、基本建设收入、捐赠收入等。

（4）国有企业计划亏损补贴 这项为负收入，冲减财政收入。

财政支出 国家财政将筹集起来的资金进行分配使用，以满足经济建设和各项事业的需要，主要包括：基本建设支出、企业挖潜改造资金、地质勘探费用、科技三项费用、支援农村生产支出、农林水利气象等部门的事业费用、工业交通商业等部门的事业费、文教科学卫生事业费、抚恤和社会福利救济费、国防支出、行政管理费、价格补贴支出等项目。

银行信贷存款 指企业、机关、团体或居民把货币资金存入银行或其他信用机构保管并取得一定利息的一种信用活动形式。根据存款对象的不同可划分为：企业存款、财政存款、机关团体存款、基本建设存款、城镇居民储蓄存款、农村存款等科目。它是银行信贷资金的主要来源。

银行信贷贷款 银行或其他信用机构根据必须归还的原则，按一定利率，为企业、个人等提供资金的一种信用活动形式。我国银行贷款，分流动资金贷款、固定资产贷款、城乡个体工商户贷款以及农业贷款等科目。

十一、人民生活

People's Living Conditions

11-1 主要年份人民生活主要指标

Basic Statistics on People's Living Conditions in Main Years

指　　标	单位	1985年	1990年	1995年	2000年	2005年	2009年	2010年
城镇职工年平均工资	元	1456	3552	9682	14051	28253	42585	46576
国有单位	元	1400	3600	9390	16371	37919	56129	57275
城镇集体单位	元	1501	3507	7507	10475	15958	22077	27391
其他各种单位	元	1571	3525	7891	14218	20882	31195	37803
城市居民家庭每一就业者负担人口	人	1.58	1.70	1.50	1.54	1.58	1.54	1.60
城市居民家庭人均可支配收入	元	791	2508	9588	14142	22882	33045	35690
城市居民家庭人均总支出	元	718	2152	10049	14193	25822	29647	32140
城市居民家庭人均消费性支出	元	689	2038	9220	12529	21768	24270	25733
食品	元	493	1295	3644	4048	6035	7972	8732
衣着	元	28	95	604	487	1285	1492	1706
家庭设备用品及服务	元	48	153	694	623	1165	1616	1771
医疗保健	元	14	42	258	431	811	1400	1294
交通和通讯	元	4	25	1562	3309	7482	5456	5925
教育文化娱乐服务	元	21	113	991	1517	3205	3326	3443
居住	元	58	184	1084	1218	1242	2232	2089
杂项商品和服务	元	23	131	383	896	543	776	773
城市居民家庭人均非消费性支出	元		12	829	1664	4054	5377	6407
农民人均纯收入	元	803	1542	4769	8484	13076	18098	20486
全市职工年平均工资	元				7765	10639	14416	16108

注：1. 职工年平均工资从2000年起是城镇在岗职工工资,不含乡镇及以下办企业职工，下同。
　　2. 全市职工年平均工资统计是根据中央、省、市属各类企事业机关单位，各镇街、村及村以下非农企业,个体私营非农企业以及"三资"、"三来一补"非农企业的在岗从业人员劳动报酬抽样调查计算所得。
　　3. 本表城市居民人均可支配收入1997年以前是生活费收入口径，1997年起是可支配收入口径。
　　4. 农民人均纯收入采用农村住户抽样调查口径，相应调整了往年数，下同。

11-2 历年城镇职工工资总额与平均工资

Total and Average Wage of Employed Persons in Urban Areas over Years

项 目	工资总额(万元)	国有单位	城镇集体单位	其他单位	平均工资(元)	国有单位	城镇集体单位	其他单位
1978	4485	2911	1574		474	630	325	
1979	5869	3611	2258		650	708	574	
1980	7255	4210	3045		750	867	632	
1981	9416	5000	4416		887	979	801	
1982	11839	6440	5399		1095	1089	1102	
1983	12808	6834	5974		1197	1138	1273	
1984	14963	7002	7961		1383	1333	1431	
1985	17260	7619	9238	403	1456	1400	1501	1571
1986	20980	10336	10026	618	2616	1698	1525	1940
1987	27610	12300	14159	1151	2067	2028	2094	2166
1988	35007	17931	14854	2222	2757	2942	2588	2574
1989	42947	20340	20808	1799	3320	3355	3295	3236
1990	46780	22321	21012	3447	3552	3600	3507	3525
1991	54002	24456	23268	6278	3777	3841	3674	3933
1992	68360	30469	28886	9005	4531	4610	4404	4696
1993	107088	47088	40171	19829	6228	7007	5583	6044
1994	131160	61869	49323	19968	8360	9390	7507	7891
1995	171543	75157	51398	44988	9682	10802	8007	10367
1996	178968	83372	52581	43015	10382	11623	8658	10775
1997	175156	87890	47185	40081	10691	12160	8774	10610
1998	187636	98109	50302	39225	11422	13123	9362	10959
1999	204550	109437	52217	42896	12557	14601	9966	12062
2000	229404	125711	53903	49790	14051	16371	10475	14218
2001	261645	152564	52645	56436	16183	19869	11001	15238
2002	291778	165611	58907	67260	17804	22228	11640	17348
2003	362935	230464	55866	76605	22598	29773	12940	19140
2004	432893	282512	62898	87483	25326	35163	13954	19223
2005	518216	349572	70872	97772	28253	37919	15958	20882
2006	608670	413718	74637	120315	31135	41457	17174	23032
2007	707007	487826	74408	144773	35284	46197	18807	26218
2008	809893	570134	82432	157327	39516	51441	20833	28838
2009	944243	639161	76001	229081	42585	56129	22077	31195
2010	1029873	678673	96664	254537	46576	57275	27391	37803

注：2000年起本表统计口径为城镇在岗职工工资总额和平均工资。

11-3 城镇在岗职工工资总额及平均工资(2010年，按经济类型、行业分)

Total and Average Wage of Fully Employed Persons in Urban Areas (2010,by Status of Registration and Sector)

项目	工资总额(万元)	国有单位	城镇集体单位	其他单位	平均工资(元)	国有单位	城镇集体单位	其他单位
总计	**1029874**	**678673**	**96664**	**254537**	**46576**	**57275**	**27391**	**37803**
一、按企业、事业和机关分								
企业	524498	176714	93248	254537	43121	88998	27071	37803
事业	277655	274239	3416		46478	46564	40476	
机关	227720	227720			57300	57300		
二、按国民经济行业分								
农、林、牧、渔业	3709	3709			61606	61606		
工业	255405	25894	49470	180041	30418	73230	21350	31444
建筑业	6648	4783	1847	18	31020	38451	20725	22000
交通运输、仓储及邮政业	26444	11586	12054	2804	40809	53639	33115	41238
信息传输、计算机服务和软件业	26306	24308	60	1938	110207	114339	13378	89708
批发和零售业	23470	5370	5352	12749	38986	30545	30082	51343
住宿和餐饮业	1427		456	971	21955		22810	21576
金融业	185715	108124	23083	54508	94569	118324	52200	89681
房地产业	2665	2214	450		53939	67920	26810	
租赁和商务服务业	10651	6448	2694	1509	47505	46255	39103	94874
科学研究、技术服务和地质勘查业	9811	9616	194		51017	51507	34679	
水利、环境和公共设施管理业	3368	3062	307		51426	56590	26921	
居民服务和其他服务业	608	608			56776	56776		
教育	97647	97647			37734	37734		
卫生、社会保障和社会福利业	136731	136300	431		52867	52834	66308	
文化、体育和娱乐业	9838	9572	266		58317	58473	53180	
公共管理和社会组织	229431	229431			56817	56817		
国际组织								

11-4　主要年份各种分组的城镇职工平均工资

Average Wage of Employed Persons in Urban Areas by Item in Main Years

单位：元

项　　目	1980年	1985年	1990年	1995年	2000年	2005年	2009年	2010年
职工平均工资	**750**	**1456**	**3552**	**9682**	**14051**	**28253**	**42585**	**46576**
一、按企业事业和机关分								
企　业				9316	13501	24152	38522	43121
事　业				10872	15485	32203	44369	46478
机　关				12171	15383	38441	53588	57300
二、按经济类型分								
国有单位	867	1400	3600	10802	16371	37919	56129	57275
城镇集体单位	632	1501	3507	8007	10475	15958	22077	27391
其他单位		1571	3525	10367	14218	20882	31195	37803
三、按国民经济行业分								
农、林、牧、渔业	694	1312	3639	12412	14000	37046	70827	61606
工　业	769	1450	3481	8945	12316	18371	25401	30418
建筑业	1018	2052	3813	9125	9820	18385	25787	31020
交通运输、仓储及邮政业						31989	40725	40809
信息传输、计算机服务和软件业						71801	117960	110207
批发和零售业						28565	37224	38986
住宿和餐饮业						18257	21035	21955
金融业	685	1500	3303	13254	20560	40655	97728	94569
房地产业	577	1779	4414	11184	17993	34805	47933	53939
租赁和商务服务业						29824	41545	47505
科学研究、技术服务和地质勘查业						37423	49231	51017
水利、环境和公共设施管理业						34573	49269	51426
居民服务和其他服务业						44853	52269	56776
教　育						27255	37639	37734
卫生、社会保障和社会福利业						37991	49246	52867
文化、体育和娱乐业						37710	49378	58317
公共管理和社会组织	695	1519	3666	12347	15424	37888	53017	56817
国际组织								

注：2000年起本表统计口径为城镇在岗职工工资总额和平均工资。

11-5 各种经济类型分行业职工工资总额、平均工资(2009-2010年)

Total and Average Wage of Employed Persons by Status of Registration and Sector (2009-2010)

项　　目	国有经济		城镇集体经济		其他经济类型	
	2009年	2010年	2009年	2010年	2009年	2010年
一、职工工资总额(万元)	**639161**	**678673**	**76001**	**96664**	**229081**	**254537**
农、林、牧、渔业	3364	3709				
工业	24738	25894	43724	49470	163874	180041
建筑业	3225	4783	358	1847	27	18
交通运输、仓储及邮政业	12971	11586	11944	12054	2578	2804
信息传输、计算机服务和软件业	27912	24308	60	60	1730	1938
批发和零售业	4623	5370	5264	5352	10992	12749
住宿和餐饮业			441	456	939	971
金融业	116141	108124	10259	23083	48446	54508
房地产业	1742	2214	477	450		
租赁和商务服务业	6259	6448	2390	2694	495	1509
科学研究、技术服务和地质勘查业	8899	9616	194	194		
水利、环境和公共设施管理业	2721	3062	265	307		
居民服务和其他服务业	544	608				
教育	96261	97647				
卫生、社会保障和社会福利业	119180	136300	384	431		
文化、体育和娱乐业	8687	9572	241	266		
公共管理和社会组织	201894	229431				
国际组织						
二、职工平均工资(元)	**56129**	**57275**	**22077**	**27391**	**31195**	**37803**
农、林、牧、渔业	70827	61606				
工业	71188	73230	19112	21350	25168	31444
建筑业	26875	38451	18963	20725	24364	22000
交通运输、仓储及邮政业	58298	53639	30586	33115	41313	41238
信息传输、计算机服务和软件业	124774	114339	13378	13378	73309	89708
批发和零售业	33941	30545	28544	30082	45745	51343
住宿和餐饮业			22273	22810	20500	21576
金融业	126254	118324	24258	52200	108549	89681
房地产业	57125	67920	30190	26810		
租赁和商务服务业	45091	46255	34845	39103	38976	94874
科学研究、技术服务和地质勘查业	49686	51507	34679	34679		
水利、环境和公共设施管理业	54849	56590	24109	26921		
居民服务和其他服务业	52269	56776				
教育	37639	37734				
卫生、社会保障和社会福利业	49220	52834	59092	66308		
文化、体育和娱乐业	49753	58473	38806	53180		
公共管理和社会组织	53017	56817				
国际组织						

注：本表统计口径为城镇在岗职工工资总额和平均工资。

11-6 国有企、事业和机关单位从业人员工资总额及平均工资(2010年)

Total and Average Wage of Employed Persons in State-owned Enterprises, Institutions and Government Agencies (2010)

项目	单位从业人员劳动报酬(万元)	在岗职工工资总额	其他从业人员工资总额	在岗职工平均工资(元)
总计	**690373**	**678673**	**11700**	**57275**
一、按企事业机关分				
企业	181657	176714	4943	88998
#地方	145652	144381	1272	86825
事业	277757	274239	3518	46564
#地方	276065	272547	3518	46412
机关	230960	227720	3240	57300
#地方	230960	227720	3240	57300
二、按行业分				
农、林、牧、渔业	3907	3709	198	61606
工业	25914	25894	20	73230
建筑业	4783	4783		38451
交通运输、仓储及邮政业	11592	11586	6	53639
信息传输、计算机服务和软件业	24308	24308		114339
批发和零售业	5895	5370	525	30545
住宿和餐饮业				
金融业	111785	108124	3661	118324
房地产业	2243	2214	29	67920
租赁和商务服务业	6541	6448	93	46255
科学研究、技术服务和地质勘查业	10376	9616	760	51507
水利、环境和公共设施管理业	3124	3062	62	56590
居民服务和其他服务业	755	608	147	56776
教育	97760	97647	113	37734
卫生、社会保障和社会福利业	138223	136300	1923	52834
文化、体育和娱乐业	9901	9572	328	58473
公共管理和社会组织	233266	229431	3835	56817
国际组织				

注：本表统计口径为城镇在岗职工工资总额和平均工资。

11-7 主要年份工业、建筑业职工工资总额和平均工资

Total and Average Wage of Employed Persons in Industrial and Construction Units in Main Years

项　　目	2000年		2005年		2010年	
	工资总额(万元)	平均工资(元)	工资总额(万元)	平均工资(元)	工资总额(万元)	平均工资(元)
一、工业总计	**85303**	**12316**	**142060**	**18371**	**255405**	**30418**
(一) 按经济类型分						
国有单位	18184	17409	21272	61692	25894	73230
城镇集体单位	26612	9021	44574	13593	49470	21350
其他各种单位	40507	13815	76214	18548	180041	31444
(二) 按工业行业分(大类)						
非金属矿采选业	95	15557	212	36586	311	61000
木材及竹材采运业						
食品加工业	4074	12987	410	17172	1164	29628
食品制造业	357	10037	256	15172	315	19000
饮料制造业	600	9367	576	10105	1851	13661
烟草加工业						
纺织业	2045	10137	2411	12947	1588	13159
服装及其他纤维制品制造业	4566	10761	6759	14469	8313	14007
皮革、毛皮、羽绒及其制品	74	7500	217	10757	244	14263
木材加工及竹、藤、棕、草制品业	488	12728	57	10942		
家具制造业	21	6118	7424	17079	21359	38708
造纸及纸制品业	1099	11458	1406	12281	1894	17359
印刷业、记录媒介的复制	709	9275	1270	12423	1518	16255
文教、体育用品制造业	6	7111	254	9922	459	15831
石油加工及炼焦业						
化学原料及化学制品制造业	961	10934	648	9336	2564	21689
医药制造业	3707	13695	3189	17351	6572	36011
化学纤维制造业						
橡胶制品业	60	4082				
塑料制品业	1244	9228	1959	11793	6541	26929
非金属矿物制品业	1487	9124	4621	13149	2281	19987
黑色金属冶炼及压延加工业						
有色金属冶炼及压延加工业	130	15140	105	13513	112	13802
金属制品业	4812	20636	1055	12964	816	15877
普通机械制造业	1768	12832	1768	20583	4100	39380
专用设备制造业	719	12703	309	13214	4588	29715
交通运输设备制造业	490	12519	965	32163	7525	39113
电气机械及器材制造业	13773	8039	16399	11894	28457	23419
电子及通信设备制造业	22371	16436	35289	20038	78943	35391
仪器、仪表及文化办公用品制造业	6123	8418	16175	11973	28057	22242
其他制造业	1445	9846	173	13872	967	14071
电力蒸汽热水生产和供应业	10342	22136	34588	53575	37150	64834
煤气生产和供应业	755	28614				
自来水生产和供应业	982	14496	3507	28861	7654	46051
二、建筑业总计	**7689**	**9820**	**2261**	**18385**	**6648**	**31020**
国有单位	1911	12418	1693	17603	4783	38451
城镇集体单位	5778	9184	542	21235	1847	20725
其他单位			26	20308	18	22000

注：2000年起本表劳动工资统计口径为城镇在岗职工工资总额和平均工资。

11-8 历年居民收支、农民收入

Income and Expenditure of Urban Households and Net Income of Rural Households over Years

年 份	城市居民人均可支配收入（元）	城市居民人均消费性支出（元）	农民人均纯收入（元）
1978			149
1979			188
1980			272
1981			463
1982			567
1983			618
1984			691
1985	791	689	803
1986	1033	883	951
1987	1247	1174	1142
1988	1778	1583	1325
1989	2282	1980	1424
1990	2508	2038	1542
1991	3068	2481	1673
1992	4026	3901	2290
1993	5970	5533	2903
1994	8270	7270	3769
1995	9588	9220	4769
1996	10824	8585	5554
1997	11032	8309	6132
1998	11506	8644	6830
1999	12954	11348	7704
2000	14142	12529	8484
2001	16938	14669	9383
2002	16949	15157	10178
2003	18471	15446	11033
2004	20526	18426	11941
2005	22882	21768	13076
2006	25320	18995	14313
2007	27025	21545	15747
2008	30275	23208	16904
2009	33045	24270	18098
2010	35690	25733	20486

注：本表城市居民人均可支配收入1997年以前是生活费收入口径，1997年起是可支配收入口径，下同。

11-9 历年城市居民家庭户基本情况

Basic Conditions of Urban Households over Years

年　份	平均每户家庭人口（人）	平均每户家庭就业人口（人）	平均每户住房使用面积（平方米）	平均每户家庭可支配收入（元）	平均每户家庭消费性支出（元）
1985	3.89	2.30	42.79	3077	2680
1986	4.01	2.13	48.12	4142	3541
1987	4.02	2.09	52.26	5013	4719
1988	4.08	2.17	61.20	7254	6459
1989	3.88	2.01	65.96	8854	7682
1990	4.06	2.09	64.96	10182	8274
1991	4.08	2.14	65.28	12517	10122
1992	4.06	2.06	69.02	16346	15838
1993	3.86	2.68	77.20	23044	21357
1994	3.86	2.26	88.78	31922	28062
1995	3.94	2.18	78.80	37777	36327
1996	4.07	2.31	85.47	44054	34941
1997	4.02	2.30	84.42	44349	33402
1998	3.92	2.17	101.92	45104	33884
1999	4.05	2.38	120.29	52464	45959
2000	3.89	2.69	121.10	55012	48738
2001	3.75	2.30	149.59	63518	55009
2002	3.66	2.47	152.99	62033	55475
2003	3.57	2.11	147.73	65941	55142
2004	3.50	2.17	145.53	71841	64491
2005	3.38	2.14	144.26	77341	73576
2006	3.68	2.31	166.23	93178	69902
2007	3.41	2.09	147.11	92155	73468
2008	3.43	1.81	138.06	103843	79603
2009	3.38	2.00	136.59	111692	82033
2010	3.32	2.08	146.23	118491	85434

注：平均每户住房使用面积2002年以前为平均每户居住面积口径。

11-10 历年人均总收入分类

Per Capita Total Income over Years

单位：元

年 份	年人均总收入	#工资性收入	经营净收入	财产性收入	转移性收入	#可支配收入
1985	837	603				791
1986	1111	974				1033
1987	1364	989				1247
1988	1889	1097				1778
1989	2439	1185				2282
1990	2678	1459	46	30	417	2508
1991	3343	2160	226	55	534	3062
1992	4520	2560	411	175	709	4026
1993	6623	3684	749	889	319	5969
1994	9131	5758	840	553	994	8270
1995	10491	6260	1210	659	1329	9588
1996	11640	8428	1127	455	1273	10824
1997	11063	8024	625	349	1544	11032
1998	11551	8334	884	319	1207	11506
1999	13009	7910	1799	357	1541	12954
2000	14231	8702	2740	895	720	14142
2001	17062	11037	2643	895	1879	16938
2002	17711	13050	1662	1076	1923	16949
2003	19478	15282	1598	1210	1388	18471
2004	21875	17153	1634	1553	1535	20526
2005	24663	18524	2709	1894	1536	22882
2006	27157	18318	4389	2504	1946	25320
2007	29335	18930	3359	4849	2101	27025
2008	31967	20872	4521	3527	3047	30275
2009	35750	23723	4724	4209	3094	33045
2010	38961	26799	4171	4771	3220	35690

注：1、本表2007年以前采用50户抽样调查的统计口径,2007年起采用250户抽样调查的统计口径，下同。
2、本表年人均总收入指标2002年以前采用年人均实际收入统计口径，2002年起采用年人均总收入统计口径，下同。

11-11 历年人均消费性支出分类

Per Capita Living Expenditure over Years

单位：元

年份	年人均消费性支出	食品	衣着	家庭设备用品及服务	医疗保健	交通与通讯	教育文化娱乐服务	居住	杂项商品和服务	恩格尔系数(%)
1985	689	493	28	48	14	4	21	58	23	71.6
1986	883	588	43	84	15	6	46	66	35	66.6
1987	1174	709	64	128	55	9	106	79	24	60.4
1988	1583	977	64	171	22	12	124	136	77	61.7
1989	1980	1235	101	196	55	24	115	156	98	62.4
1990	2038	1295	95	153	42	25	113	184	131	63.5
1991	2481	1476	188	122	47	47	211	254	136	59.5
1992	3901	1834	259	263	94	587	331	369	164	47.0
1993	5533	2615	373	583	133	855	389	333	252	47.3
1994	7270	3172	420	925	192	850	714	761	236	43.6
1995	9220	3644	604	694	258	1562	991	1084	383	39.5
1996	8585	3682	706	660	225	990	847	674	802	42.9
1997	8309	3681	594	435	415	916	939	880	449	44.3
1998	8644	3785	457	612	455	1025	1074	659	577	43.8
1999	11348	3712	400	601	371	3398	1043	898	923	32.7
2000	12529	4048	487	623	431	3309	1517	1218	896	32.3
2001	14669	4572	648	746	513	4258	1429	1173	1330	31.2
2002	15157	4818	748	611	529	4303	2660	1060	428	31.8
2003	15446	4804	921	1093	693	2062	2512	2966	395	31.1
2004	18426	5041	1134	925	811	4973	2673	2517	352	27.4
2005	21768	6035	1285	1165	811	7482	3205	1242	543	27.7
2006	18995	6321	1238	1229	809	3531	3001	2341	525	33.3
2007	21545	6966	1213	1342	860	5208	3515	1903	538	32.3
2008	23208	7778	1349	1539	1332	4462	3464	2585	699	33.5
2009	24270	7972	1492	1616	1400	5456	3326	2232	776	32.8
2010	25733	8732	1706	1771	1294	5925	3443	2089	773	33.9

11-12 不同收入等级年人均可支配收入与消费性支出水平

Per Capita Annual Disposable Income and Consumption Expenditure by Level of Income

单位：元

年份	年人均可支配收入	#最低收入户	低收入户	高收入户	最高收入户	年人均消费性支出	#最低收入户	低收入户	高收入户	最高收入户
1985	791					689				
1986	1033					883				
1987	1247					1174				
1988	1778					1583				
1989	2282					1980				
1990	2508	1391	1744	3774	4546	2038	1170	1539	2099	4156
1991	3068	1665	2286	4092	4592	2481	1725	1877	2699	3784
1992	4026	2053	2650	5988	7275	3901	1966	2648	4690	6070
1993	5970	2977	4203	8484	9852	5533	3046	3685	6691	6956
1994	8270	4157	5248	12217	14265	7270	4477	5762	10839	8378
1995	9588	4539	5867	13828	18771	9220	4362	6912	12194	19353
1996	11639	5627	7142	15377	19224	8585	5152	6278	11496	10498
1997	11032	5778	7214	16496	22069	8309	5298	5963	15265	12323
1998	11506	6136	7853	16660	21591	8644	4888	6259	11774	14733
1999	12954	5998	7944	18951	23447	11348	4777	7755	18118	26001
2000	14142	6826	7806	19104	28769	12529	6706	7211	10297	25896
2001	16938	7174	10365	25167	33526	14669	6990	7425	18880	29834
2002	16949	6374	9398	23342	45001	15157	7224	8974	29735	21807
2003	18471	4535	9146	27000	48849	15446	6436	7990	25065	26683
2004	20526	8548	11658	31923	39058	18426	8047	9190	30530	45944
2005	22882	9590	13348	35885	43010	21768	10038	8908	31542	31498
2006	25320	13551	15633	37559	51957	18995	8841	11781	32568	39862
2007	27025	12073	16207	39071	55821	21545	12862	14547	31653	36732
2008	30275	11172	17340	46744	66034	23208	10927	14275	37741	53404
2009	33045	13642	19311	47680	71031	24270	12793	13654	27597	42949
2010	35690	18466	23384	48582	69968	25733	14073	15412	39674	46282

11-13 主要年份城市居民家庭基本情况

Basic Conditions of Urban Households in Main Years

项　　目	单 位	1985年	1990年	1995年	2000年	2005年	2009年	2010年
一、调查户数	**户**	**50**	**50**	**50**	**50**	**50**	**250**	**250**
二、平均每户家庭人口	**人**	**3.90**	**4.06**	**3.94**	**3.89**	**3.38**	**3.38**	**3.32**
三、平均每户家庭就业人口	**人**	**2.30**	**2.09**	**2.18**	**2.69**	**2.14**	**2.00**	**2.08**
四、平均每一就业者负担人口	**人**	**1.58**	**1.70**	**1.50**	**1.54**	**1.58**	**1.54**	**1.60**
五、平均每人每年可支配收入	**元**	**791**	**2508**	**9588**	**14142**	**22882**	**33045**	**35690**
#工薪收入	元	603	1459	6260	8702	18524	23723	26799
六、平均每人每年消费性支出	**元**	**689**	**2038**	**9220**	**12529**	**21768**	**24270**	**25733**
(一)食　品	元	493	1295	3644	4048	6035	7972	8732
(二)衣　着	元	28	95	604	487	1285	1492	1706
(三)家庭设备用品及服务	元	48	153	694	623	1165	1616	1771
#耐用消费品	元	21	93	368	18	425	522	460
(四)医疗保健	元	14	42	258	431	811	1400	1294
(五)交通与通讯	元	4	25	1562	3309	7482	5456	5925
(六)娱乐教育文化服务	元	21	113	991	1517	3205	3326	3443
#文化娱乐用品	元	13	36	521	532	610	734	687
文化娱乐服务	元	5	37	173	286	1112	1603	1691
教　育	元	3	40	297	699	1482	989	1065
(七)居　住	元	58	184	1084	1218	1242	2232	2089
(八)杂项商品和服务	元	23	131	383	896	543	776	773
七、平均每人住房使用面积	**平方米**	**10.98**	**16.61**	**20.00**	**31.13**	**42.68**	**40.41**	**44.05**
八、平均每人每年购买商品								
1.粮　食	元	106	109	74	66	65	393	466
2.油脂类	元	5	5	7	8	8	141	121
3.肉禽及其制品	元	37	48	40	50	72	1694	1692
4.蛋　类	元	6	6	10	9	8	81	77
5.水产品	元	23	29	25	29	22	644	660
6.鲜　菜	元	90	100	117	116	114	529	591
7.烟草类	元	3	18	52	94	53	168	192
8.酒和饮料	元	16	25	48	78	132	286	324
9.干鲜瓜果	元	11	84	258	298	344	564	628
10.糕点、奶及奶制品	元		13	42	105	264	301	484
11.服　装	元	28	95	434	356	944	1108	1297

注：1. 工薪收入2002年以前为基本工资收入口径，2002年起为工薪收入口径。
　　2. 平均每人住房使用面积2002年以前为平均每人居住面积口径。
　　3. 粮食、油脂类、肉禽及其制品、蛋类、水产品、鲜菜2008年以前以公斤为计量单位。

11-14 主要年份城市居民消费性支出及构成

Consumption Expenditure of Urban Households in Main Years

项　　目	单位	1985年	1990年	1995年	2000年	2005年	2009年	2010年
一、年消费性支出	**元**	**689**	**2038**	**9220**	**12529**	**21768**	**24270**	**25733**
(一)食　品	元	493	1295	3644	4048	6035	7972	8732
(二)衣　着	元	28	95	604	487	1285	1492	1706
(三)家庭设备用品及服务	元	48	153	694	623	1165	1616	1771
#耐用消费品	元	21	93	368	18	425	522	460
(四)医疗保健	元	14	42	258	431	811	1400	1294
#药品费	元			109	240	276	442	466
滋补保健品	元			46	178	207	544	434
(五)交通与通讯	元	4	25	1562	3309	7482	5456	5925
交通	元	4	25	1245	2154	6381	4153	4473
通讯	元			317	1155	1101	1303	1452
(六)娱乐教育文化服务	元	21	113	991	1517	3205	3326	3443
文化娱乐用品	元	13	36	521	532	610	734	687
文化娱乐服务	元	5	37	173	286	1112	1603	1691
教　育	元	3	40	297	699	1482	989	1065
(七)居　住	元	58	184	1084	1218	1242	2232	2089
#住房	元	7	92	725	455	34	837	482
水电燃料	元	51	92	358	763	972	1188	1299
(八)杂项商品和服务	元	23	131	383	896	543	776	773
二、消费性支出构成								
(一)食　品	%	71.55	63.54	39.52	32.31	27.72	32.85	33.93
(二)衣　着	%	4.06	4.66	6.55	3.89	5.90	6.15	6.63
(三)家庭设备用品及服务	%	6.97	7.51	7.53	4.97	5.35	6.65	6.88
#耐用消费品	%	43.76	60.78	53.03	2.89	1.95	2.15	1.79
(四)医疗保健	%	2.03	2.06	2.80	3.44	3.73	5.77	5.03
(五)交通与通讯	%	0.58	1.23	16.94	26.41	34.37	22.48	23.02
(六)娱乐教育文化服务	%	3.05	5.54	10.75	12.11	14.72	13.70	13.38
(七)居　住	%	8.42	9.03	11.76	9.72	5.71	9.20	8.12
(八)杂项商品和服务	%	3.34	6.43	4.15	7.15	2.50	3.20	3.00

11-15 历年城市居民家庭平均每百户主要耐用消费品拥有量

Ownership of Durable Consumer Goods Owned per 100 Urban Households over Years

年份	汽车（辆）	电冰箱（台）	洗衣机（台）	空调器（台）	组合音响（套）	彩色电视机（台）	电话机（部）	移动电话（部）	电脑（台）
1985		22	56			22			
1986		26	66			40			
1987		42	72			52			
1988		52	86			66			
1989		72	96		4	84			
1990		84	54	16	14	92			
1991		98	106	16	14	100			
1992		96	112	12	18	98	64		
1993		108	108	28	34	102	60		
1994		110	114	60	52	114	72		
1995		110	108	82	54	138	82		
1996		104	110	128	68	132	98		
1997		106	108	100	68	116	98		22
1998	2	110	112	122	64	146	96	28	28
1999	10	116	118	130	84	178	100	72	34
2000	12	108	114	150	88	178	100	126	68
2001	16	118	110	184	76	176	100	186	98
2002	24	126	112	204	76	192	100	200	102
2003	26	134	108	226	82	194	104	224	96
2004	32	132	118	258	80	192	112	264	108
2005	42	124	110	264	72	200	112	294	114
2006	44	130	112	280	80	218	116	255	90
2007	54	115	110	271	82	206	115	272	111
2008	47	110	103	200	59	180	108	248	100
2009	63	113	105	233	69	184	105	261	112
2010	68	118	107	259	68	186	110	267	129

11-16 按收入等级分的城市居民家庭基本情况(2010年)

Basic Conditions of Urban Households by Level of Income (2010)

项目	单位	总平均	最低收入户	低收入户	中等偏下户	中等收入户	中等偏上户	高收入户	最高收入户
调查户数	户	250	25	25	50	50	50	25	25
平均每户家庭人口	人	3.32	3.72	3.68	3.32	3.35	3.17	3.32	2.84
平均每户家庭就业人口	人	2.08	2.07	1.82	2.06	2.07	2.21	2.20	2.08
平均每一就业者负担人口	人	1.60	1.80	2.02	1.61	1.62	1.43	1.51	1.37
平均每户就业面	%	62.65	55.65	49.46	62.05	61.79	69.72	66.27	73.24
平均每人总收入	元	38961	20511	25077	30356	36718	45245	52567	76597
平均每人可支配收入	元	35690	18466	23384	27786	33483	41443	48582	69968
平均每人总支出	元	32140	16975	20417	22853	32305	37478	47363	58803
平均每人消费性支出	元	25733	14073	15412	18686	24499	30741	39674	46282
平均每一就业者总收入	元	62189	36860	50705	48923	59423	64898	79328	104584
平均每人住房建筑面积	平方米	58.58	46.62	48.64	65.35	52.68	62.74	60.36	73.85
平均每百户家庭年末主要耐用消费品拥有量									
家用汽车	辆	68	24	40	58	76	78	92	104
洗衣机	台	107	100	100	110	104	104	116	120
电冰箱	台	118	112	104	108	124	118	132	132
彩色电视机	台	186	180	144	180	186	198	184	228
家用电脑	台	129	104	100	122	126	146	144	152
组合音响	套	68	60	48	74	60	78	64	80
照相机	架	79	60	52	72	74	84	96	124
钢琴	架	4	4		2	4	4	4	12
空调器	台	259	236	212	230	248	272	292	348
淋浴热水器	台	134	120	128	140	130	124	144	164
消毒碗柜	台	78	76	64	72	74	86	88	92
健身器材	套	12	4	28	12	8	20		12
固定电话	部	110	108	100	124	100	110	108	120
移动电话	部	267	264	284	270	250	260	272	292

11-17 按收入等级分的城市居民家庭平均每人全年现金收入(2010年)

Per Capita Annual Cash Income of Urban Households by Level of Income (2010)

项目	单位	总平均	最低收入户	低收入户	中等偏下户	中等收入户	中等偏上户	高收入户	最高收入户
一、平均每户家庭就业人口	**人**	**2.08**	**2.07**	**1.82**	**2.06**	**2.07**	**2.21**	**2.20**	**2.08**
国有单位职工人数	人	0.39	0.08	0.24	0.54	0.32	0.40	0.44	0.64
集体单位职工人数	人	0.49	0.36	0.45	0.44	0.62	0.42	0.52	0.64
其它各类经济类型单位职工人数	人	0.37	0.49	0.36	0.34	0.24	0.54	0.36	0.24
个体雇主与自营者人数	人	0.22	0.08	0.16	0.04	0.36	0.26	0.24	0.44
个体被雇人员数	人	0.42	0.72	0.56	0.46	0.35	0.40	0.44	0.08
其他就业人员人数	人	0.17	0.34	0.04	0.22	0.18	0.18	0.12	0.04
二、家庭总收入	**元**	**38961**	**20511**	**25077**	**30356**	**36718**	**45245**	**52567**	**76597**
#可支配收入	元	35690	18466	23384	27786	33483	41443	48582	69968
#工资性收入	元	26799	14866	16621	23611	23382	31863	36920	47993
#工资及补贴收入	元	26795	14864	16621	23606	23373	31862	36920	47983
经营净收入	元	4171	633	1707	539	5609	4788	6165	13386
财产性收入	元	4771	2750	3844	3892	3528	6482	5472	8976
#股息与红利收入	元	1787	1619	2348	1582	1516	1758	2780	1308
租金收入	元	2662	1037	1399	1971	1594	4504	1923	7313
转移性收入	元	3220	2262	2905	2314	4198	2112	4011	6243
#离退休金	元	1919	1653	2072	992	2959	1030	2282	3338
赠送收入	元	713	237	433	698	732	655	862	1648

11-18 城市居民家庭平均每人全年消费性支出（2010年）

Per Capita Annual Consumption Expenditure of Urban Households (2010)

项目	单位	总平均	最低收入户	低收入户	中等偏下户	中等收入户	中等偏上户	高收入户	最高收入户
平均每人年消费性支出	**元**	**25733**	**14073**	**15412**	**18686**	**24499**	**30741**	**39674**	**46282**
(一)食　品	**元**	**8732**	**6718**	**6119**	**7533**	**8904**	**9791**	**11997**	**10983**
粮油类	元	655	566	523	632	699	734	612	772
肉禽蛋水产品类	元	2428	2272	1966	2343	2686	2542	2434	2559
水产品	元	660	594	536	610	769	681	661	713
蔬菜类	元	653	592	566	653	704	671	636	701
调味品	元	58	51	41	54	61	62	60	79
糖烟酒饮料类	元	591	429	465	488	537	647	1149	561
干鲜瓜果类	元	628	482	508	609	685	705	667	668
糕点、奶及奶制品	元	484	362	418	486	509	516	569	496
其他食品	元	64	49	44	60	66	63	94	78
在外用餐和饮食服务	元	3171	1915	1587	2207	2957	3850	5776	5070
(二)衣　着	**元**	**1706**	**821**	**936**	**1177**	**1820**	**2210**	**2186**	**3143**
#服　装	元	1297	602	679	854	1385	1702	1628	2548
(三)居　住	**元**	**2089**	**1201**	**1623**	**1460**	**2371**	**2247**	**2124**	**4265**
#住房	元	482	137	286	49	854	390	331	1701
水电、燃料及其它	元	1298	945	1207	1184	1233	1426	1457	1829
(四)家庭设备用品及服务	**元**	**1771**	**944**	**1302**	**1054**	**1596**	**2182**	**1770**	**4638**
#耐用消费品	元	460	181	385	165	486	524	189	1725
(五)医疗保健	**元**	**1294**	**1152**	**618**	**676**	**982**	**1979**	**1968**	**2218**
#药品费	元	466	572	268	261	412	570	706	676
滋补保健品	元	434	335	227	171	320	723	555	934
(六)交通与通讯	**元**	**5925**	**1543**	**2156**	**3685**	**5224**	**7072**	**12161**	**13584**
#交通	元	4473	556	1136	2421	3877	5355	10284	11366
通讯	元	1452	987	1021	1264	1347	1717	1877	2218
(七)教育文化娱乐服务	**元**	**3443**	**1388**	**2285**	**2647**	**2754**	**4523**	**5516**	**6284**
文化娱乐用品	元	687	350	341	562	677	701	1232	1219
文化娱乐服务	元	1691	357	891	1004	1362	2365	3278	3501
教育	元	1065	681	1053	1082	715	1457	1006	1564
(八)杂项商品和服务	**元**	**773**	**305**	**373**	**453**	**849**	**738**	**1953**	**1168**

11-19 按收入等级分的城市居民平均每人(每户)全年主要非食品购买量（2010年）

Per Capita or Household Annual Purchases of Main Non-food Commodities of Urban Households by Level of Income (2010)

项　目	单 位	总平均	最低收入户	低收入户	中等偏下户	中等收入户	中等偏上户	高收入户	最高收入户
其它商品和服务	元/人	773	305	373	453	849	738	1953	1168
(一)其它商品	元/人	513	204	215	266	628	445	1358	779
#金银珠宝饰品	元/人	163	29	37	65	336	81	424	202
化妆品	元/人	220	96	109	117	179	221	662	344
其它杂品	元/人	119	70	65	77	103	131	259	202
(二)服务	元/人	259	101	157	187	221	293	595	389
#理发洗澡费	元/人	145	56	101	107	127	161	300	235
美容费	元/人	57	20	22	37	58	65	123	94
耐用消费品	元/人	460	181	385	165	486	524	189	1725
微波炉	台/百户	3.52	0.40	2.40	2.20	7.40	6.60		
洗衣机	台/百户	3.96	4.80	1.60	2.40	4.20	2.60	1.20	13.60
淋浴热水器	台/百户	3.96		0.80	0.80	5.80	2.40	3.20	17.60
空调器	台/百户	7.64	8.40	16.20	1.00	6.40	5.80	4.00	29.20
彩色电视机	台/百户	2.76		0.40	2.60	3.40	2.60	8.40	1.60
家用电脑	台/百户	7.08	5.20	6.00	6.60	4.00	5.40	20.00	7.60
移动电话	部/百户	50.96	9.60	30.80	31.80	55.20	56.20	107.60	75.20
汽　车	台/百户	1.64			2.00			8.00	4.40

11-20 农村居民人均实际收入与实际支出（2006-2010年）

Per Capita Actual Income and Expenditure of Rural Households (2006-2010)

单位：元

年　份	家庭现金收入	#纯收入	家庭现金支出	#生活消费现金支出	#食品消费支出
2006	17676	14313	12173	9370	3380
2007	19945	15747	13078	10771	3805
2008	20622	16904	13154	10887	3823
2009	22077	18098	14643	10598	3711
2010	22537	20486	16245	11842	4447

11-21 农村居民人均实际收入（2006-2010年）

Per Capita Actual Income of Rural Households (2006-2010)

单位：元

年　份	家庭现金收　入	#工资性收入	家庭经营收入	财产性收入	转移性收入
2006	17676	8522	4195	4171	789
2007	19945	9446	4388	5191	920
2008	20622	9876	4326	5531	889
2009	22077	10442	4517	6210	908
2010	22537	11201	3629	6402	1305

11-22 农村居民人均消费支出（2006-2010年）

Per Capita Consumption Expenditure of Rural Households (2006-2010)

单位：元

年份	生活消费现金支出	#食品	衣着	家庭设备及服务	医疗保健	交通通讯	教育文化娱乐服务	居住	杂项商品和服务
2006	9370	3380	448	474	510	1543	932	1458	625
2007	10771	3805	602	581	494	1953	1029	2001	306
2008	10887	3823	691	622	545	1799	1198	1500	709
2009	10598	3711	633	471	565	1764	1223	1485	746
2010	11842	4447	627	480	569	2120	1082	1877	640

11-23 每百户农村居民家庭主要耐用消费品拥有量（2006-2010年）

Ownership of Durable Consumer Goods Owned per 100 Rural Households (2006-2010)

项目	单位	2006年	2007年	2008年	2009年	2010年
洗衣机	台	101	105	107	103	106
电冰箱	台	108	111	111	109	110
空调机	台	210	223	234	209	218
微波炉	台	37	45	50	46	46
热水器	台	137	143	142	129	132
摩托车	辆	134	95	84	83	87
生活用汽车	辆	49	59	67	53	57
固定电话机	部	139	137	137	122	120
移动电话	部	240	251	261	257	268
彩色电视机	台	175	178	183	160	164
影碟机	台	92	95	95	74	71
摄像机	台	15	17	21	13	17
照相机	架	54	59	64	53	55
家庭计算机	台	84	97	107	98	104
中高档乐器	件	8	9	10	10	11

主要统计指标解释

Explanatory Notes on Main Statistical Indicators

城市居民家庭可支配收入 指调查户可用于最终消费支出和其它非义务性支出以及储蓄的总和，即居民家庭可以用来自由支配的收入。它是家庭总收入扣除交纳的所得税、个人交纳的社会保障费以及调查户的记帐补贴后的收入。计算公式为：

可支配收入=家庭总收入-经营性支出-交纳所得税-个人交纳的社会保障支出-记帐补贴

城市居民家庭消费性支出 指调查户用于本家庭日常生活的全部支出，包括食品、衣着、家庭设备用品及服务、医疗保健、交通和通讯、娱乐教育文化服务、居住、其他商品和服务八大类等，均按商品（服务）的用途分类。

农村居民家庭总收入 是指农村住户年内从各种来源得到的全部实际收入（包括现金收入和实物收入）。由基本收入、转移性收入和财产性收入三部分组成。

农村居民家庭纯收入 是农村常住居民家庭总收入扣除相应的各项费用性支出后，归农民所有的收入。它既可以用于生产、非生产投资、改善物质和文化生活，以及用于再分配的支出和结余的收入。这个指标用来观察农民实际收入水平，以及农民扩大再生产和改善生活的能力。

农村居民家庭生活费支出 是指农民住户年内用于物质生活和精神生活方面的实际支出，直接反映农民的生活水平、研究农民消费结构变化的基本指标。生活消费支出包括食品，衣着、居住，家庭设备，用品及服务，医疗保健，交通和通讯，文化教育娱乐用品及服务，其他商品和服务等消费支出。

单位从业人员劳动报酬 指各单位在一定时期内直接支付给本单位在岗职工的工资总额和其他从业人员的劳动报酬。

在岗职工工资总额 指各单位在一定时期内直接支付给本单位在岗职工的劳动报酬总额。

不在岗职工（离岗职工）生活费 指各单位在一定时期内按政策直接支付给本单位中离开本单位仍保留劳动关系的这部分不在岗职工的最低生活保障费。

职工工资总额 指各单位在一定时期内直接支付给本单位在岗职工的工资总额和不在岗职工（离岗职工）的生活费。

单位从业人员劳动报酬和职工工资总额的计算原则应以直接支付给职工的全部劳动报酬为根据。各单位支付给职工的劳动报酬以及其他根据有关规定支付的工资，不论是计入成本的还是不计入成本的，不论是按国家规定列入计征奖金税项目的，还是未列入计征奖金税项目的，不论是以货币形式支付的还是以实物形式支付的，均包括在内。

职工平均工资 指企业、事业、机关单位的职工在一定时期内平均每人所得的货币工资额。它表明一定时期职工工资收入的高低程度，是反映职工工资水平的主要指标。计算公式为：职工平均工资=报告期实际支付全部职工工资总额/报告期全部职工平均人数

职工平均实际工资 指扣除物价变动因素后职工平均工资。计算公式为：

职工平均实际工资=报告期职工平均工资/报告期城镇居民消费价格指数

十二、社会事业

Social Undertakings

12-1 主要年份社会事业主要指标

Main Indicators of Social Undertakings in Main Years

项　　目	单位	1985年	1990年	1995年	2000年	2005年	2009年	2010年
国有企事业单位科学技术人员数	人	9166	11629	16856		42593	55097	40025
三种专利申请量	件		34	325	1653	6694	19106	21654
三种专利授权量	件		30	262	1399	3114	12918	20397
各类技术合同签订项目数	项		5	46	110	50	60	70
各类技术合同签订项目金额	万元		12	1804	3469	4058	6996	15760
在校学生数								
普通高等学校	人			1628	3241	16645	33992	38293
成人高等学校	人	403	531	1254	3642	12665	21464	21703
中等职业技术学校	人	3363	8919	18737	23144	29487	46538	47531
普通中学	人	46596	61188	92481	112418	191044	249464	258276
小学	人	134421	162664	195063	272793	480923	511160	552377
学龄儿童入学率	%	99.8	99.9	100.0	100.0	100.0	100.0	100.0
小学毕业生升学率	%	79.5	95.4	99.2	99.8	99.9	100.0	100.0
初中毕业生升学率	%	38.5	43.6	85.4	90.3	94.1	97.0	97.9
普通高中毕业生升学率	%	26.5	31.2	64.9	70.5	96.5	87.5	95.1
高考省线入围人数	人	285	224	809	2646	11196	12569	13761
电影放映单位	个	60	114	218	192	70	40	46
艺术表演团体	个	1	7	2	1		4	4
文化馆(群众艺术馆)	个	1	1	1	1	1	1	1
公共图书馆(室)	个	3	5	15	18	473	504	505
博物馆	个	2	2	2	3	16	31	30
档案馆	个	1	1	1	1	1	1	1
《东莞日报》发行量	万份		177	987	1578	2751	4745	4563
广播电台	座		1	1	1	1	1	1
电视台	座	1	1	1	1	1	1	1
病床床位数	张	2323	3866	5798	7081	11972	18080	19980
卫生技术人员数	人	3305	3902	5290	6915	16608	35766	37487
#执业（助理）医师	人	1201	1721	2299	3309	6901	12884	13214
举办镇街级及以上体育运动会	次	72	114	14	5	8	5	58
参加运动会的运动员人数	万人次	3.60	6.38	5.15	1.70	1.36	0.30	10.18
执业律师人数	人	6	12	85	130	625	1223	1366
公证人员数	人	6	10	19	20	48	90	96
人民调解委员会调解人员数	人	3603	3664	3664	3644	4556	16248	17438
优抚收养单位收养人数	人		19	11	7	8	7	8
工业固体废物综合利用率	%	37.5	17.9	18.2	63.8	86.5	95.0	95.0
城市环境空气质量优良天数	天						361	357

注：1. 2010年起，国有企事业单位科学技术人员数只统计在编在岗人员数，因此与往年不可比。
2. 中等职业技术学校包含市技工学校，不含一般成人中专。
3. 2004年起，卫生方面包含诊所、卫生所、医务室及村卫生室的数据，与往年数不可比。

12-2 科技活动基本情况(2010年)

Basic Statistics on Scientific and Technological Activities (2010)

项　目	单位	2010年	项　目	单位	2010年
一、科技企业			专利申请数	件	245
企业数	个	3353	获专利授权数	件	196
#国家高新技术企业	个	336	营业收入	万元	28574
省创新型试点企业	个	15	四、科技园区和基地		
省创新型企业	个	7	国家级高新区	个	1
省创新百强企业	个	8	省级高新区	个	
省民营科技企业	个	688	专业镇	个	15
重点培育上市后备科技企业	个	53	#工业总产值	万元	41164221
市民营科技企业	个	2246	专业镇科技投入	万元	260913
二、科技合作			国家高新技术企业数	家	161
国际合作项目立项数	项	6	火炬计划特色产业基地	个	8
#国家立项数	项	2	#工业总产值	万元	14286530
省级立项数	项	4	国家高新技术企业数	家	91
国际科技合作示范基地	个	7	科技企业孵化器/加速器	个	7
#国家级基地	个	2	#建筑场地面积	万平方米	15.47
省级基地	个	5	在孵企业数	个	268
产学研项目立项数	项	111	毕业企业数	个	42
#省部合作	项	97	五、工程中心		
省院合作	项	14	国家级工程中心	个	1
总投入	万元	38175	省级工程中心	个	40
资助金额	万元	7635	#工程中心职工总数	人	6794
市配套金额	万元	7635	经费收入	万元	126168
省部产学研示范基地	个	28	研究开发课题(项目)	项	416
省部产学研创新联盟	个	6	专利授权数	项	361
三、科技机构			研究与发展(R&D)人员	人	3480
机构数	个	43	研究与发展经费	万元	101962
从业人员	人	1961	市级工程中心	个	82
#科技活动人员	人	1179	#工程中心职工总数	人	11037
#本科及以上	人	863	经费收入	万元	180057
#中级及以上职称	人	393	研究开发课题(项目)	项	852
科技经费筹集额	万元	25831	专利授权数	项	858
#政府拨款	万元	19439	研究与发展(R&D)人员	人	8118
企业自筹	万元	6014	研究与发展经费	万元	147358
科技经费内部支出	万元	21975	六、科技金融		
项目(课题)数	项	223	科技贷款机构	个	
项目(课题)经费支出额	万元	10567	上市后备企业	个	36
论文数	篇	213	创业风险机构	个	5
科技专著数	篇	3			

12-3 主要年份国有企事业单位科学技术人员

Scientific and Technical Personnel in State-owned Enterprises and Institutions in Main Years

单位：人

项　　目	1990年	1995年	2002年	2004年	2005年	2009年	2010年
国有企事业单位科技人员数	**11629**	**16856**	**28154**	**39398**	**42593**	**55097**	**40025**
#工程技术人员	1084	1718	1651	1752	1839	2302	1438
农业技术人员	432	230	183	276	290	284	172
卫生技术人员	1430	1988	6155	14541	16188	21679	11171
科学研究人员	21	52	19	141	77	43	16
教学人员	7524	11553	18599	20905	21717	26741	24010
经济人员	278	329	555	561	636	1129	1184
财会人员	581	484	500	613	1299	1940	1454
统计人员	170	77	70	74	82	122	91

注：2010年国有企事业单位科技人员为在编在岗人员数。

12-4 主要年份三种专利申请量与授权量

Three Kinds of Patents Application Accepted and Granted in Main Years

单位：件

项　　目	1990年	1995年	1999年	2000年	2002年	2004年	2005年	2009年	2010年
一、申请量	**34**	**325**	**1221**	**1653**	**3100**	**4325**	**6694**	**19106**	**21654**
发　　明	1	5	15	35	90	185	245	1593	3143
实用新型	5	70	305	386	937	1523	1971	6557	7677
外观设计	28	250	901	1232	2073	2617	4478	10956	10834
二、授权量	**30**	**262**	**819**	**1399**	**2680**	**3167**	**3114**	**12918**	**20397**
发　　明	1	8	16	4	10	26	24	254	442
实用新型	4	41	157	344	669	919	1116	4370	7529
外观设计	25	213	646	1051	2001	2222	1974	8294	12426

12-5 主要年份各类技术合同签订情况

Basic Statistics on Technical Contracts Signed by Type in Main Years

项　　目	1990年	1995年	1999年	2000年	2002年	2004年	2005年	2009年	2010年
一、技术合同项目数(项)	**5**	**46**	**20**	**110**	**91**	**69**	**50**	**60**	**70**
#技术开发合同	3			1	5	62	41	46	62
技术咨询合同							2		
技术转让合同	2	44	20	78	81	6	1	3	2
技术服务合同		2		31	5	1	6	11	6
二、技术合同金额(万元)	**12**	**1804**	**1124**	**3469**	**766**	**4278**	**4058**	**6996**	**15760**
#技术开发合同				1000	110	4175	1888	6031	4325
技术咨询合同			1124				80		
技术转让合同	12	1656		2007	637	91	2000	270	11046
技术服务合同		148		1362	19	13	90	695	389
三、技术合同实现金额(万元)	**7**	**1623**	**1077**	**2398**	**730**	**2726**	**2522**	**6264**	**15572**
#技术开发合同				700	110	2623	1427	5299	2748
技术咨询合同							35		
技术转让合同	7	1535	1077	1260	601	91	1000	270	11211
技术服务合同		88		438	19	13	60	695	1612

12-6 主要年份高新科技发展情况

Basic Statistics on High-tech Development in Main Years

项　　目	单 位	1995年	1999年	2000年	2002年	2004年	2005年	2009年	2010年
一、高新技术企业									
企业数	个	11	53	66	102	201	247	246	334
总产值	亿元	30.55	215.00	274.41	405.32	690.00	925.07	780.97	1240.59
总收入	亿元	26.76	213.00	266.49	409.93	691.00	927.72	797.10	1249.50
出口总额	亿美元	0.54	14.40	7.34	20.16	45.00	71.59	58.26	99.08
从业人员数	人	6400	29840	36304	50955	107541	171812	171813	246134
#科技活动人员	人	832	6424	8663	14426	26885	34448	56478	72833
二、高新技术产品									
产品	个	27	159	177	619	668	947	1828	1430
总产值	亿元	31.43	144.00	186.00	430.23	711.11	1062.40	1778.97	2353.70
#电子与信息技术	亿元				289.99	355.63	726.92	1351.58	1407.39
生物技术	亿元				3.63	8.45	8.20	17.79	51.93
新材料技术	亿元				22.80	34.48	51.43	213.39	115.46
光机电一体化技术	亿元				54.05	91.36	146.94	101.16	153.74
新能源高效节能技术	亿元				4.80	11.40	32.71	61.94	95.52
环保技术	亿元				0.53	1.07	6.58	33.11	4.95
其他	亿元				54.43	208.71	89.63		524.70

注：1. 高新技术企业情况2009年以前为省级高新技术企业情况，2009年起为国家级高新技术企业情况。
　　2. 高新技术产品情况从2010年起，统计口径为规模以上工业企业。

12-7 主要年份科学技术成果项数

Achievements for Scientific and Technological Research in Main Years

单位：项

项　　目	1985年	1990年	1995年	1999年	2000年	2002年	2004年	2005年	2009年	2010年
获省级科技进步奖		**1**	**4**	**9**	**6**	**3**	**6**	**3**	**19**	**4**
市级科技进步奖	**68**	**31**	**22**	**39**	**47**	**47**	**60**	**75**	**85**	**87**
1. 农业方面	**30**	**8**	**3**	**11**	**13**	**4**	**10**	**9**	**8**	**7**
一等奖	1	4		1	2		1	1	2	2
二等奖	3	3		3	5	3	2	3	2	2
三等奖	18	1	3	6	6	1	7	5	4	3
四等奖	8									
2. 工业方面	**32**	**18**	**14**	**19**	**24**	**23**	**27**	**42**	**62**	**57**
特等奖					1		1	2		
一等奖	1	3		3	5	4	4	7	19	13
二等奖	8	11	5	8	8	6	11	19	16	21
三等奖	10	4	9	8	10	13	11	14	27	23
四等奖	13									
3. 医药卫生方面	**6**	**5**	**5**	**5**	**10**	**20**	**22**	**25**	**15**	**23**
特等奖										
一等奖			1	1		3	1		1	5
二等奖		1			2	6	6	4	6	6
三等奖	2	4	4	4	8	11	15	19	8	12
四等奖	4									
市长奖									**5**	**5**
技术成果类									1	1
荣誉类									4	4
创新企业奖									**8**	**4**

12-8 科技创新平台情况（2009-2010年）

Basic Statistics on Technology Innovation Platform (2009-2010)

单位：个

项　　目	2009年	2010年
科技创新平台合计	156	207
#公共科技创新平台	9	10
行业性科技创新平台	26	34
#行业性科技创新平台(企业研究院)	9	11
专业镇技术创新平台	11	15
科技行业技术联盟	6	8
企业创新平台	104	125
#企业工程技术研究开发中心	104	125
#国家级	1	1
省级	34	40
市级	69	84
实验室	17	38
#国家级	4	10
#资助获中国合格评定国家认可委员会认可实验室	4	10
省级	2	5
市级	11	23

12-9 历年国有企事业单位科学技术人员数

Scientific and Technical Personnel in Enterprises and Institutions over Years

单位：人

年 份	科学技术人员	工程技术人员	农业技术人员	卫生技术人员	科学研究人员	教学人员	经济人员	会计人员	统计人员
1980	6619	370	190	1076	19	4282		564	99
1981	7473	463	217	1166	23	4978		501	109
1982	7547	468	243	1241	28	4954		509	101
1983	8453	525	315	1699		5257		109	109
1984	9033	615	307	1791		5534		261	201
1985	9166	663	318	2319	6	5129		491	214
1986	9490	768	358	2398	5	5222		501	203
1987	10945	797	378	2426	6	6495		583	222
1988	12495	1014	359	3093	24	7064	72	590	197
1989	11306	960	388	1393	19	7394	281	632	181
1990	11629	1084	432	1430	21	7524	278	581	170
1991	15004	2170	405	3347	13	7843	308	558	153
1992	16809	2522	375	3690	18	8659	313	613	153
1993	18491	2871	264	4074	112	9511	290	916	141
1994	20198	3490	272	4513	57	9949	300	657	112
1995	23104	3944	255	4878	66	11613	329	750	171
1996	24693	4037	263	5356	51	12287	360	740	143
1997	26103	4258	294	5504	48	13371	418	882	280
1998	26582	4321	310	4862	48	14316	376	894	171
1999	28789	4620	288	5246	48	15604	416	946	152
2000									
2001	24677	795	121	5493	31	17309	252	273	40
2002	34168	5261	246	6538	28	18756	555	1319	184
2003	33070	996	159	11145	44	19614	314	741	57
2004	39398	1752	276	14541	141	20905	561	613	74
2005	42593	1839	290	16188	77	21717	636	1299	82
2006	46371	1913	462	18401	70	22434	763	1512	93
2007	49032	2037	492	19528	71	23364	892	1832	92
2008	51729	2375	343	20955	50	24063	1048	1827	100
2009	55097	2302	284	21679	43	26741	1129	1940	122
2010	40025	1438	172	11171	16	24010	1184	1454	91

注：2010年为在编在岗人员数。

12-10 历年三种专利与技术合同签订情况

Basic Statistics on Three Kinds of Patents and Technical Contracts Signed by Type over Years

年 份	三种专利申请量(件)	#发明	三种专利授权量(件)	#发明	技术合同签订项目数（项）	技术合同签订金额(万元)	技术合同实现金额(万元)
1990	34	1	30	1	5	12	7
1991	70	3	50	1	4	10	10
1992	102	5	78	2	3	23	10
1993	100	3	90	1	2	24	2
1994	104	4	100	2	14	2537	1756
1995	325	5	262	8	46	1804	1623
1996	333	3	312	4	133	4839	3756
1997	725	1	321		78	2036	800
1998					62	3048	2398
1999					20	1124	1077
2000	1653	35	1399	4	110	3469	2398
2001	2914	71	1753	5	89	1335	953
2002	3100	90	2680	10	91	766	730
2003	3865	93	2858	14	58	700	680
2004	4325	185	3167	26	69	4278	2726
2005	6694	245	3114	24	50	4058	2522
2006	9879	553	4872	28	25	13644	13402
2007	13842	876	6752	44	53	8510	8138
2008	14406	1188	8093	115	54	12838	3694
2009	19106	1593	12918	254	60	6996	6264
2010	21654	3143	20397	442	70	15760	15572

12-11 历年科学技术成果项数

Scientific and Technological Achievements over Years

单位：项

年 份	获国家级科技进步奖	获省级科技进步奖	获市级科技进步奖	特等奖	一等奖	二等奖	三等奖	四等奖
1979			25			5	4	16
1980			27			2	11	14
1981			35		2	4	11	18
1982			62		1	3	21	37
1983			38		2	6	11	19
1984			35			11	11	13
1985			68		2	11	30	25
1986			86		5	14	27	40
1987			59		2	19	25	13
1988		1	37		6	10	16	5
1989		1	32		4	6	22	
1990		1	31		7	15	9	
1991		4	35	1	3	18	13	
1992		3	19		4	7	8	
1993			18	1	3	8	6	
1994		6	23		4	9	10	
1995		4	22		1	5	16	
1996		3	32		7	6	19	
1997		4	32		7	6	19	
1998		6	38	1	2	11	24	
1999		9	39		6	11	22	
2000		6	47	1	7	15	24	
2001		4	51		4	23	24	
2002		3	47		7	15	25	
2003		4	50		7	14	29	
2004		6	60	1	6	19	34	
2005		3	75	2	10	25	38	
2006		3	70	1	8	24	37	
2007		4	83	1	18	26	38	
2008		10	83		19	28	36	
2009		19	85		22	24	39	
2010		4	87		20	29	38	

12-12 主要年份各类学校情况

Basic Statistics on Schools by Type in Main Years

项　　目	单位	1985年	1990年	1995年	2000年	2005年	2009年	2010年
一、普通高等专业学校								
学校数	所			1	1	4	5	5
毕业生数	人			395	985	1439	7292	8105
招生数	人			576	1440	7273	12863	12660
在校学生数	人			1628	3241	16645	33992	38293
教职工数	人			262	293	1761	3068	3192
#专任教师	人			119	161	1081	1890	2174
二、中等职业技术学校								
学校数	所	3	17	20	23	21	26	26
毕业生数	人	234	2210	4641	9554	9062	11927	14028
招生数	人	1508	3866	8697	8759	10971	15767	18477
在校学生数	人	3363	8919	18737	23144	29487	46538	47531
教职员工数	人	217	619	1134	1608	2230	3112	2996
#专任教师	人	150	434	859	1221	1621	2321	2341
三、普通中学								
学校数	所	106	64	69	77	134	186	190
毕业生数	人	12317	18688	24165	30261	48935	71811	73810
#高中生	人	2055	2527	3231	7120	12233	20550	20816
招生数	人	16978	20441	33086	41488	70843	88325	93196
#高中生	个	2915	3389	6099	9048	19540	23631	24668
在校学生数	人	46596	61188	92481	112418	191044	249464	258276
#高中生	人	6304	8572	13653	24677	52283	66750	70398
教职员工数	人	3266	4001	5900	6012	12177	17212	16946
#专任教师	个	2420	2963	4381	5027	9640	13598	14572
四、小　学								
学校数	所	583	570	595	552	414	337	330
毕业生数	人	17901	18262	27257	33684	61173	78027	77429
招生数	人	20264	26158	36702	53786	84784	92281	108900
在校学生数	人	134421	162664	195063	272793	480923	511160	552377
教职员工数	人	7009	7797	9560	9131	21964	26605	28298
#专任教师	人	6017	6785	8060	7946	17478	21130	23733

注：中等职业技术学校包含市技工学校，不含一般成人中专，下同。

12-12 续表

项目	单位	1985年	1990年	1995年	2000年	2005年	2009年	2010年
五、成人高等专业教育								
当年招生人数	人				1697	6387	8092	6086
在校学生数	人	403	531	1254	3642	12665	21464	21703
#广播电视大学	人	403	531	1254	1362	4169		
六、学龄儿童入学								
学龄儿童总数	人	103460	133011	177791	247555	423058	441557	511439
已入学学龄儿童数	人	103282	132934	177787	247539	423058	441557	511439
学龄儿童入学率	%	99.8	99.9	100.0	100.0	100.0	100.0	100.0
七、小学毕业生升学								
小学毕业生人数	人	17901	18262	27257	33684	61173	78027	77429
已升学人数	人	14235	17413	27166	33627	61095	78027	77429
小学毕业生升学率	%	79.5	95.4	99.2	99.8	99.9	100.0	100.0
八、初中毕业生升学								
初中毕业生人数	人	10262	16161	20933	23141	36702	51261	52994
已升学人数	人	3955	7134	17876	20896	34536	49723	51881
初中毕业生升学率	%	38.5	43.6	85.4	90.3	94.1	97.0	97.9
九、普通高中毕业生升学								
高考省线入围人数	人	285	224	809	2646	6455	12569	13761
高考录取人数	人	543	759	2095	5017	12461	18767	20099
#高考升本科人数	人	274	250	697	1678	5161	9571	11033
普通高中毕业生升学率	%	26.5	31.2	64.9	70.5	96.5	87.5	95.1
十、幼儿园								
幼儿园数	所	83	86	258	452	511	680	727
在园幼儿数	人	31382	47040	84263	111763	111330	176249	208373
幼教职工数	人	984	1387	1427	7517	12567	21347	22122
#专任教师	人	841	1160	1160	4618	7002	12419	13947
十一、全国各类大中专院校招生人数								
国家各大(学)专院校在我市招生人数	人				11680	35831	38364	40795
国家各中专学校在我市招生人数	人				3359	2768		
全市教育经费投入总额	亿元				15.5	50.2	78.8	94.4

12-13 历年各类学校在校学生数

Number of Students Enrollment by Type of School over Years

单位：人

年份	普通高等学校	中等职业技术学校	#技工学校	普通中学	#高中	小学	幼儿园
1949		151		1960	318	52781	
1952		543		3394	296	70359	
1957		561		6652	848	88001	
1962		380		9736	1513	119998	
1965		358		10469	1397	160931	
1970				60150	9873	118128	
1975		689		49569	10847	168236	
1978		595		76025	12092	161114	18228
1979		450		62292	7010	158008	12774
1980		386		54829	6909	154871	7630
1981		450		43514	5755	150857	8103
1982		661		41683	4654	144754	14650
1983		967		42777	4798	135440	15436
1984		1070		46488	5766	134567	23702
1985		3363		46596	6304	134421	31382
1986		3891	60	49445	7880	140700	38195
1987		5847	117	54435	8367	144287	42569
1988		7120	229	59268	8201	150097	42845
1989		7878	293	61955	7687	155852	44110
1990		8919	582	61188	8572	162664	47040
1991		10938	915	60146	8725	170064	51051
1992		13161	1277	65171	9711	175203	57537
1993	1079	14176	1516	75305	10297	180114	65310
1994	1451	16084	2025	85827	11409	186244	72552
1995	1628	18737	2404	92481	13653	195063	84263
1996	1771	22614	2567	95150	16887	205957	85709
1997	2025	24821	2598	98005	20609	221838	100059
1998	2171	25588	2291	101202	22490	235787	103585
1999	2241	25073	2001	105518	23084	248759	109773
2000	3241	23144	1746	112418	24677	272793	111763
2001	3802	23638	2039	122115	28232	295384	112963
2002	5144	25363	2152	135256	32398	342804	108898
2003	6884	27664	2564	149656	38143	386890	104832
2004	9104	28487	2559	171336	45050	448296	112538
2005	16645	29487	2618	191044	52283	480923	111330
2006	22005	35403	2905	214638	57662	496828	118683
2007	25178	40429	3063	234578	61151	520684	130932
2008	28656	45419	3238	248442	63962	528644	156362
2009	33992	46538	3268	249464	66750	511160	176249
2010	38293	47531	2955	258276	70398	552377	208373

12-14 历年各类学校当年招收学生数

Number of New Students Enrollment by Type of School over Years

单位：人

年 份	普通高等学校	中等职业技术学校	#技工学校	普通中学	#高中	小 学
1949		102				
1952		285		1666	190	
1957		80		2516	259	
1962		45		3716	566	
1965		134		3656	476	
1970				45069	7919	
1975		188		28329	5930	
1978		250		29788	3436	30152
1979		200		25364	3900	28315
1980		186		24083	3906	26857
1981		266		16808	2594	26461
1982		162		17492	2317	23970
1983		573		18111	2344	19604
1984		1964		16609	2477	17644
1985		1508		16978	2915	20264
1986		1977	60	17944	2781	25867
1987		2883	64	21720	2665	28926
1988		2832	112	23280	2925	29437
1989		2966	124	21877	2686	27539
1990		3866	343	20441	3389	26158
1991		5008	445	21430	3266	27539
1992		5696	487	26161	3751	28804
1993	567	5835	633	29948	3944	31841
1994	569	7064	952	32229	4440	34495
1995	576	8697	996	33086	6099	36702
1996	711	10119	978	33576	7385	39689
1997	750	9718	798	35140	8273	42066
1998	750	9664	852	36423	8118	43802
1999	802	9060	665	38400	8199	47715
2000	1440	8759	527	41488	9048	53786
2001	1597	8850	1116	44729	10727	56521
2002	2190	9417	1153	49881	11852	65066
2003	3104	9809	874	55564	15147	71476
2004	3804	10618	1044	63085	17467	80525
2005	7273	10971	1100	70843	19540	84784
2006	8032	13357	1250	79985	20866	89663
2007	8519	16491	1297	85816	21146	92860
2008	10218	17475	1163	89808	22313	94641
2009	12863	15767	1598	88325	23631	92281
2010	12660	18477	2052	93196	24668	108900

12-15 历年各类学校当年毕业生数

Number of Graduates by Type of School over Years

单位：人

年 份	普通高等学校	中等职业技术学校	#技工学校	普通中学	#高中	小 学
1949				414	83	
1952		48		588	44	14349
1957		87		1365	203	59056
1962		209		2680	468	28418
1965		44		2363	393	32508
1970				15081	1954	26187
1975		374		20842	4937	25009
1978		244		43035	8533	30480
1979		244		33554	8004	28925
1980		250		19578	3096	27294
1981		191		13308	3046	27215
1982				10483	3004	27348
1983		260		10752	1940	26723
1984		230		10969	1404	17870
1985		234		12317	2055	17901
1986		660		13527	1271	17533
1987		819		13895	2296	23183
1988		1323		15322	2966	23054
1989		1960	60	15310	2716	20315
1990		2210	57	18688	2527	18262
1991		2634	112	19820	2559	19186
1992		2126	123	19323	2643	23308
1993	30	2915	390	18363	3020	26893
1994	197	5035	445	20360	2787	28500
1995	395	4641	541	24165	3231	27257
1996	560	5813	753	27675	3483	27156
1997	484	6745	691	28729	3834	27992
1998	556	8316	918	29839	5448	29794
1999	714	9044	796	30109	6585	31426
2000	985	9554	634	31291	7120	33684
2001	1019	7748	684	32409	7553	37077
2002	753	7171	542	34204	8277	40611
2003	1350	7217	509	39031	8784	45599
2004	1506	8630	917	43471	10676	51831
2005	1439	9062	777	48935	12233	61173
2006	2269	9422	677	55856	15486	70474
2007	5096	10061	754	60436	17354	74681
2008	6486	10728	821	66594	19315	78037
2009	7292	11927	962	71811	20550	78027
2010	8105	14028	956	73810	20816	77429

12-16 历年各级各类学校专任教师数

Number of Full-time Teachers by Level and Type of School over Years

单位：人

年 份	普通高等学校	中等职业技术学校	技工学校	普通中学	高中	小 学	幼儿园
1978		34		3641	638	5641	
1979		31		3367	369	6136	
1980		29		2996	370	6022	
1981		32		2343	344	6433	
1982		38		2210	284	6186	
1983		61		2361	296	5830	
1984		63		2352	309	5971	
1985		150		2420	354	6017	841
1986		168	5	2463	407	6515	720
1987		208	7	2709	490	6878	941
1988		306	9	3007	540	7112	967
1989		422	11	2949	462	6743	980
1990		434	12	2963	488	6785	1160
1991		513	15	3019	500	6831	1470
1992		600	17	3198	479	7164	1569
1993	99	737	16	3583	610	7314	1773
1994	113	767	26	4001	710	7610	1920
1995	119	859	34	4381	733	8060	1160
1996	119	924	40	4310	886	7410	2175
1997	123	1151	89	4404	991	7518	2753
1998	125	1338	93	4632	1065	7912	3247
1999	133	1205	92	4699	1149	7198	3715
2000	161	1221	84	5027	1310	7946	4618
2001	231	1286	121	5348	1411	8693	4701
2002	290	1445	125	6373	1769	10880	5351
2003	312	1548	124	7069	1976	12490	5505
2004	560	1531	134	8437	2367	15512	6218
2005	1081	1621	150	9640	2817	17478	7002
2006	1357	1801	122	10953	3215	18717	7919
2007	1569	1965	156	12272	3678	20511	9279
2008	1691	2218	161	12995	3976	21203	11072
2009	1890	2321	160	13598	4178	21130	12419
2010	2174	2341	171	14572	4541	23733	13947

12-17 历年各类学校入(升)学率与高考入围人数

Number of Passing College Entrance Examination and Proportion of Students Entering Schools over Years

年 份	学龄儿童入学率(%)	小学毕业生升学率(%)	初中毕业生升学率(%)	高中毕业生升学率(%)	高考入围人数(人)	省线入围人数
1978	98.36	85.80	14.30	8.14	846	250
1979	98.70	76.00	16.00	6.71	566	166
1980	98.85	73.40	25.40	7.15	222	140
1981	98.72	50.56	27.40	8.64	239	154
1982	99.06	54.40	34.40	8.04	252	115
1983	99.75	57.60	37.40	12.34	245	150
1984	99.65	70.80	29.86	43.32	619	220
1985	99.83	79.52	38.54	26.50	534	285
1986	99.90	84.71	33.89	43.69	595	228
1987	99.94	83.60	40.10	27.09	644	297
1988	99.93	89.88	42.00	30.63	925	315
1989	99.92	96.18	43.30	32.92	977	284
1990	99.94	95.35	43.60	31.20	759	224
1991	99.92	96.18	45.20	26.22	861	268
1992	99.94	97.58	56.00	35.59	994	312
1993	99.95	97.79	68.50	39.23	1102	423
1994	99.96	98.94	79.02	62.75	1823	586
1995	99.99	99.16	85.40	64.90	2095	809
1996	99.98	96.45	86.70	66.80	2160	1093
1997	99.99	99.90	87.35	60.00	2212	1215
1998	99.99	99.86	88.25	47.69	2348	1315
1999	99.99	99.87	89.80	53.15	3501	1790
2000	99.99	99.83	90.30	70.50	5017	2646
2001	100.00	99.77	90.50	74.82	5651	3225
2002	100.00	99.80	91.10	83.00	6873	3759
2003	100.00	99.80	92.10	93.60	9167	4509
2004	100.00	99.90	93.30	96.70	10756	5452
2005	100.00	99.90	94.10	96.50	11196	6455
2006	100.00	100.00	94.80	82.90	11359	7652
2007	100.00	100.00	95.20	89.10	13275	9185
2008	100.00	100.00	96.60	91.00	15047	9987
2009	100.00	100.00	97.00	87.50	17487	12569
2010	100.00	100.00	97.90	95.10	18845	13761

12-18 历年文化艺术、文物事业机构数

Number of Institutions in Culture and Cultural Relics over Years

年 份	电影放映单位(个)	#影剧院(座)	艺术表演团体(个)	群 众艺术馆(个)	文化站(广电文化中心)(个)	公 共图书馆(座)	公共图书馆藏书量(万册)	博物馆(座)	档案馆(座)
1949	5	2							
1952	8	3							
1957	14	5							
1962	28	4	2	1	4	1		2	1
1965	28	4	2	1	4	1		2	1
1970	28	4	3	1	33	1		2	1
1975	33	4	3	1	33	1		2	1
1978	167	5	1	1	33	1	11	2	1
1979	157	5	1	1	33	1	15	2	1
1980	65	5	1	1	33	1	16	2	1
1981	75	6	1	1	33	1	17	2	1
1982	53	6	1	1	33	1	19	2	1
1983	49	6	1	1	33	1	19	2	1
1984	65	6	1	1	33	1	24	2	1
1985	60	7	1	1	33	3	30	2	1
1986	61	9	2	1	33	3	30	2	1
1987	70	13	4	1	33	8	30	2	1
1988	78	15	5	1	33	3	30	2	1
1989	102	26	6	1	33	3	30	2	1
1990	114	26	7	1	33	5	30	2	1
1991	126	36	5	1	33	6	31	2	1
1992	150	50	2	1	33	8	37	2	1
1993	163	53	2	1	33	11	47	2	1
1994	193	63	2	1	33	14	58	2	1
1995	218	97	2	1	33	15	68	2	1
1996	225	111	4	1	33	16	73	2	1
1997	229	130	4	1	33	26	84	2	1
1998	233	147	4	1	32	26	106	3	1
1999	210	87	4	1	32	20	133	3	1
2000	192	87	1	1	32	18	97	3	1
2001	145	84	1	1	32	21	99	3	1
2002	162	81	2	1	32	24	109	3	2
2003	107	55	2	1	32	346	289	3	2
2004	88	78		1	32	397	631	6	2
2005	70	31		1	32	473	660	16	2
2006	51	34		1	33	1222	771	21	2
2007	51	34		1	33	1271	896	23	2
2008	40	34	1	1	33	387	515	23	1
2009	40		4	1	33	504	599	31	1
2010	46		4	1	33	505	701	30	1

12-19 主要年份广播电视事业发展情况

Basic Statistics on Radio and Television Industry in Main Years

项　目	单位	1985年	1990年	1995年	1999年	2000年	2004年	2005年	2009年	2010年
广播电台	座		1	1	1	1	1	1	1	1
电视台	座	1	1	1	1	1	1	1	1	1
镇街文化广电服务中心	个								28	28

12-20 主要年份安全生产事故中火灾事故情况

Basic Statistics on Fire of Production Accidents in Main Years

项　目	单位	1995年	1998年	1999年	2000年	2002年	2004年	2005年	2009年	2010年
一、发生起数	起	24	24	33	60	25	13	13	5	13
二、受伤人数	人	8	15	22	34	15	7	7	1	8
三、死亡人数	人	12	18	40	31	24	18	18	6	15
四、损失折款	万元	1596	1111	1016	1022	592	208	22	6	21
五、平均每起事故损失	万元	66.50	46.29	30.79	17.03	23.68	15.98	1.67	1.20	1.63

注：本表数据来源于市安监局。

12-21 主要年份交通事故发生情况

Basic Statistics on Traffic Accidents in Main Years

项目	单位	1995年	1998年	1999年	2000年	2002年	2004年	2005年	2009年	2010年
一、发生起数	起	2015	4248	6619	7386	9393	8029	7124	5039	4874
二、受伤人数	人	2061	4681	6843	8217	10410	9655	8642	5560	5355
三、死亡人数	人	692	858	902	903	1263	978	921	546	528
四、损失折款	万元	685	1213	1418	1759	1538	1038	934	670	682
五、平均每起事故损失	元	3400	2855	2142	2382	1637	1293	1312	1330	1400

注：本表数据来源于市安监局，含道路和水上交通事故。

12-22 各类卫生事业机构及床位、人员数（2010年）

Number of Health Care Institutions, Beds and Employed Personnel by Type of Institution(2010)

项目	机构数(个)	实有床位数(张)	人员数(人)	卫生技术人员	执业(助理)医师
总计	**2229**	**19980**	**46102**	**37487**	**13214**
医疗机构	2225	19980	45742	37202	13121
县及县以上及其他医院	71	19571	33521	26792	9123
#综合医院	53	17509	30546	24690	8431
中医医院	2	754	1163	947	325
专科医院	16	1308	1812	1155	367
社区卫生服务中心	388		4711	3529	1303
村(社区)卫生站	1244		3655	3655	1445
门诊部	257		2150	1738	647
诊所、卫生所、医务室	262		746	706	361
妇幼保健院	1	326	714	600	193
专科疾病防治院	1	83	215	163	49
急救中心(站)	1		30	19	
采供血机构	1		104	78	7
疾病预防控制中心	1		162	140	86
卫生监督所	1		94	67	
健康教育所	1				
其他卫生机构					

12-23 主要年份卫生事业机构各类人员数

Number of Personnel in Health Institutions in Main Years

单位：人

项　　目	1980年	1985年	1990年	1995年	2000年	2002年	2005年	2009年	2010年
总　　计	**3599**	**3945**	**4503**	**6149**	**9289**	**10692**	**22127**	**43561**	**46102**
一、卫生技术人员	2960	3305	3902	5290	6915	9011	16608	35766	37487
执业（助理）医师	980	1177	1724	2326	2819	3523	5981	12884	13214
注册护士	584	643	1164	1751	2673	3462	6303	13638	14689
药剂人员	236	572	546	602	706	794	1281	2001	2284
检验人员	120	147	152	216	367	476	781	1257	1412
其　他	1040	766	316	395	350	756	2262	5986	5888
二、其他技术人员	8		13	96	174	215	786	1065	1217
三、管理人员	299	282	243	432	597	745	1080	2416	2418
四、工勤人员	332	358	345	331	453	721	1504	4314	4980

注：1. 从2002年起卫生技术人员按新口径分类。
　　2. 2004年起，卫生方面包含诊所、卫生所、医务室及村卫生室的数据，与往年数不可比。

12-24 医疗机构服务情况（2010年）

Services in Medical Institutions (2010)

指 标 名 称	诊疗人数（人次）	门、急诊	入院人数（人）	治愈率（%）	病死率（%）	健康检查人数(人次)
总　　计	**57724621**	**57591760**	**740455**	**68.9**	**0.48**	**3642902**
医院	32534974	32412675	719264	68.7	0.49	3369556
#综合医院	30641171	30526946	677148	68.4	0.51	3255303
中医医院	1210379	1208856	20209	57.9	0.52	38470
专科医院	683424	676873	21907	87.7	0.02	75783
#民营医院	4343108	4321436	152832	73.9	0.50	971166
社区卫生服务中心(站)	12152109	12145019				225776
村卫生站	8351407	8351407				
门诊部(所)	3594137	3590665				13609
妇幼保健院(所、站)	909804	909804	20206	78.2	0.03	5151
专科疾病防治院(所、站)	182190	182190	985	9.9	0.21	28810

12-25 历年卫生事业机构、床位、人员数

Number of Health Care Institutions, Beds and Personnel over Years

年 份	机 构 (个)	床 位 (张)	卫生工作人员 (人)	#卫生技术人员	#执业(助理)医师
1949	5	219	170	156	
1952	6	179	124	109	
1957	26	403	287	252	
1962	37	1376	1572	1262	
1965	38	1308	1932	1618	
1970	39	1476	2135	1678	
1975	40	1970	2840	2282	
1978	82	2257	3242	2636	768
1979	81	2271	3466	2863	971
1980	83	2207	3599	2960	1167
1981	83	2210	3724	3091	1102
1982	83	2292	3886	3253	1097
1983	83	2098	3985	3335	1088
1984	83	2231	4005	3351	1132
1985	87	2323	3945	3305	1201
1986	88	3054	4084	3454	1179
1987	88	3393	4475	3490	1304
1988	87	3640	4582	3829	1537
1989	87	3677	4522	3874	1620
1990	85	3866	4503	3902	1721
1991	85	4085	4578	3946	1755
1992	83	4517	4705	4127	1832
1993	99	4940	5247	4524	2023
1994	98	5365	5689	4930	2221
1995	99	5798	6149	5290	2299
1996	99	5288	6712	5766	2449
1997	151	5505	7286	6283	2605
1998	171	5892	8306	7139	2955
1999	176	6241	8697	7575	3080
2000	174	7081	9289	8065	3309
2001	173	7474	9323	8064	3429
2002	178	8641	10692	9011	3523
2003	172	9820	11584	9807	3758
2004	944	10797	15058	13053	4870
2005	874	11972	22127	18757	6901
2006	1210	13293	27128	22904	8629
2007	1649	15227	34151	28758	10446
2008	2106	16778	40449	33113	11869
2009	2106	18080	43561	35766	12884
2010	2229	19980	46102	37487	13214

注：2004年起本表包含诊所、卫生所、医务室及村卫生室的数据，与往年数不可比。

12-26 历年体育运动情况

Basic Statistics on Sports over Years

年 份	破（超）世 界 纪 录（次）	破（超）亚 洲 纪 录（次）	破（超）全 国 纪 录（次）	在国际比赛中获得金牌总数（枚）	在全国比赛中获得金牌总数（枚）	在省级比赛中获得金牌总数（枚）	市级运动会参赛运动员人数（人）	为国家省输送运动员（人）
1978			9	1	7	26	2500	11
1979	2		2	1	7		2250	18
1980			12		2		2400	14
1981			11	4	19		2500	13
1982			14	4	30	15	2650	9
1983	1		7	5	6		2420	7
1984			1	16	5		2500	33
1985		2	1	5	2		1960	7
1986		7	4	7	4	52	2420	16
1987	1	1	8	35	9		2130	19
1988	3	1	4	14	25		2540	15
1989			27	5	43	92	6430	18
1990	13	5		4	6		2370	25
1991	2	1	8	12	14		4800	16
1992	2	3	21	10	6		15000	30
1993	2	8	5	12	9		10350	16
1994	34	2	24	6	23	157	2720	14
1995	10	1		5	37		1500	14
1996				3	16		7800	13
1997	10	9		1	6	36	6000	74
1998	2	4	28	4	28	87	1560	74
1999				4	33		6000	6
2000			3	4	91		4000	6
2001				13	22	48	8000	5
2002				2	35	58		11
2003		7		2	31	82		6
2004	3	4	4	49	34			18
2005				2	13	46	8564	44
2006				20	21	32	16000	
2007				3	25	46	2740	9
2008				3	16	49	630	17
2009		1	3	8	20	94	1550	17
2010				4	6	40	9895	64

12-27 主要年份体育比赛成绩

Basic Statistics on Sports Achievements in Main Years

项　　目	单位	1980年	1985年	1990年	1995年	2000年	2005年	2009年	2010年
破世界纪录	次			13	10				
获得国际赛冠军	个		5	4	5	4		8	4
破亚洲纪录	次		2	5	1			1	
破全国纪录	次	12	1			3		3	
获国际比赛奖牌									
金牌	枚		5	4	5	4	2	8	4
银牌	枚			4	3	2	1	3	2
铜牌	枚						2	4	
获全国比赛金牌	枚	2	2	6	37	91	13	20	6

注：“获得国际赛冠军”及“获国际比赛奖牌”含地区赛。

12-28 主要年份群众体育活动情况

Basic Statistics on Activities of Mass Sports in Main Years

项　　目	单位	1980年	1985年	1990年	1995年	2000年	2005年	2009年	2010年
举办市级运动会	次	5	4	9	4	2	4	1	16
市级运动会参赛运动员人数	人	2400	1960	2370	1500	4000	8564	1550	9895
举办镇街级运动会	次	57	68	105	10	3	4	4	58
镇街级运动会参赛运动员人数	人	17100	34300	61500	50000	13000	5000	1437	101760
为国家和省输送运动员	人	14	7	25	14	6	47	17	64

12-29 历年治安案件情况

Basic Statistics on Public Security Cases over Years

项　　目	单位	2005年	2006年	2007年	2008年	2009年	2010年
治安案件受理数	起	13760	17537	32293	42270	64506	44979
扰乱公共秩序	起	2816	1525	741	645	514	198
妨害公共安全	起	243	445	496	598	592	630
侵犯人身、财产权利	起	6044	9328	20171	25446	25157	24551
#盗窃	起	2599	2984	6229	11633	10192	10513
妨害社会管理秩序	起	4296	6239	10885	15581	38243	19600
#吸毒	起	2697	3214	4180	3850	4164	4455
卖淫、嫖娼	起	153	376	351	386	481	663
赌博或为赌博提供条件	起	942	1431	3123	6312	30416	10464
治安案件查处数	起	12490	16711	29533	36081	58868	37818
扰乱公共秩序	起	2797	1523	729	623	503	186
妨害公共安全	起	237	418	476	592	569	583
侵犯人身、财产权利	起	4865	8538	17504	19438	19706	17687
#盗窃	起	2007	2479	4559	7416	6241	5476
妨害社会管理秩序	起	4246	6232	10824	15428	38090	19362
#吸毒	起	2665	3211	4179	3805	4059	4317
卖淫、嫖娼	起	147	376	349	382	481	659
赌博或为赌博提供条件	起	938	1430	3113	6260	30402	10408
查处违法人员数	人	20692	24539	36382	36081	65351	42815
扰乱公共秩序	人	4486	1696	909	1118	457	363
妨害公共安全	人	218	477	565	641	573	618
侵犯人身、财产权利	人	6769	12010	19598	19353	15748	14145
#盗窃	人	2676	2969	4222	5967	4448	3802
妨害社会管理秩序	人	8201	10356	15310	19736	48573	27689
#吸毒	人	3922	3842	4675	4145	4442	4885
卖淫、嫖娼	人	415	850	737	814	1143	1506
赌博或为赌博提供条件	人	3179	4089	6395	9672	39732	17191

注：本表数据来源于市公安局。

12-30 历年刑事案件情况

Basic Statistics on Criminal Cases over Years

项　　目	单位	2005年	2006年	2007年	2008年	2009年	2010年
刑事案件立案数	起	44641	35528	33837	33880	33309	36965
危害公共安全	起	264	293	263	205	348	586
破坏市场经济秩序	起	451	373	531	418	492	577
侵犯公民人身权利	起	3748	3328	3658	3634	3365	3587
#杀人	起	87	70	72	52	67	69
伤害	起	3071	2703	2873	2840	2509	2882
强奸	起	266	229	293	263	270	336
侵犯财产	起	39657	31045	28909	29120	28298	31251
#抢劫	起	9144	7862	7380	7331	6704	5045
抢夺	起	3736	2563	2343	2181	2364	3250
入室盗窃	起	4150	3038	3327	5804	6834	8779
盗窃机动车	起	16050	10588	7876	7264	4962	3526
诈骗	起	897	953	1136	1587	2513	3203
妨害社会管理秩序	起	571	488	458	503	805	963
#毒品犯罪	起	215	258	261	257	424	587
刑事案件破案数	起	13682	13477	12729	8342	12525	16271
危害公共安全	起	161	191	131	103	301	550
破坏市场经济秩序	起	439	283	243	273	239	388
侵犯公民人身权利	起	2037	1896	2077	1732	1748	1933
#杀人	起	73	52	65	40	60	61
伤害	起	1586	1472	1527	1282	1231	1449
强奸	起	171	147	192	152	165	224
侵犯财产	起	10598	10672	9870	5856	9543	12534
#抢劫	起	3582	3707	3527	2474	3136	2531
抢夺	起	1525	1328	1113	610	929	1700
入室盗窃	起	1081	864	891	796	2422	4182
盗窃机动车	起	1880	1717	703	526	761	631
诈骗	起	202	278	285	154	572	536
妨害社会管理秩序	起	490	429	387	378	693	866
#毒品犯罪	起	210	247	239	243	412	569

注：本表数据来源于市公安局。

12-31　历年道路交通违法情况

Basic Statistics on Traffic Offense over Years

项　　目	单位	2005年	2006年	2007年	2008年	2009年	2010年
处理违法起数	万起	61.04	92.71	94.95	266.96	294.27	282.48
#机动车	万起		90.29	92.05	263.86	291.69	280.44
非机动车	万起		1.04	1.88	1.9	1.11	1.01
行人和乘车人	万起		1.15	1.03	1.19	1.48	1.03
教育人次	万人次		10.76	13.05	15	24.37	26.14
#机动车	万人次		8.76	11.17	13.27	22.51	25.38
非机动车	万人次		0.93	0.98	0.79	0.62	0.35
行人和乘车人	万人次		1.07	0.90	0.93	1.24	0.41
罚款总额	万元	9991.7	19072.80	19705.00	43761.11	24534.65	44359.52
#机动车	万元		19069.10	19689.00	43744.65	24531.19	44355.07
非机动车	万元		2.00	16.00	17.14	2.98	2.8
行人和乘车人	万元				0.32	0.48	1.65

注：本表数据来源于市公安局。

12-32　主要年份律师、公证、基层司法及普法教育

Basic Statistics on Lawyers, Notarization, Grassroots Judicial Work and Law Education in Main Years

项　　目	单位	1990年	1995年	2000年	2005年	2009年	2010年
一、律师工作							
律师事务所	个	2	8	22	46	90	115
律师	人	12	85	221	625	1223	1366
担任常年法律顾问	家	102	364	416	1426	2316	2752
民事诉讼代理	件	145	343	1203	6543	13172	12041
非诉讼法律事务	件	110	1162	2079	13391	22427	19967
刑事辩护及代理	件	295	235	438	2496	2447	2776
国内经济案件诉讼代理	件	107	348	1100	1801	790	1133
涉外及港澳台经济案件诉讼代理	件	165	11	27	160	615	299
二、公证工作							
公证处	个	1	1	1	1	3	3
公证人员	人	10	19	20	48	90	96
办结公证总数	件	5347	11377	28910	60685	41055	48296
#国内民事公证	件	113	2795	19607	19627	27808	35104
国内经济公证	件	236	898	1776	34015	2474	3536
涉外公证	件	4998	7684	4809	4607	10773	9656
三、基层司法工作							
法律服务所	个	24	29	32	32	32	32
基层法律工作人员	人	70	115	117	191	285	360
担任法律顾问	家	62	482	695	1208	830	724
民事诉讼代理	件	26	568	1221	1790	1364	1090
非诉讼代理	件	129	1045	3016	3837	2537	1549
人民调解委员会	个	904	813	750	814	1586	1552
调解人员	人	3664	3466	3644	4556	16248	17438
调解民间纠纷	件	2005	2632	2642	15210	16042	15239
四、参加普法教育人数	**万人**	**80**	**170**	**79**	**571**	**154.3**	**288**

12-33 历年计划生育情况

Basic Statistics on Family Planning over Years

年　份	已婚育龄妇女人数(人)	女性初婚人数(人)			落实各种节育措施	
			23周岁及以上	不　足20周岁	育龄夫妇(对)	节育率(%)
1978	130438	10974			103414	79.3
1979	134483	11914			104612	77.8
1980	136742	9270	8920		101190	74.0
1981	141079	13714			112956	80.1
1982	142324	8729			115302	81.0
1983	149928	12664			129035	86.1
1984	156444	9579			138785	88.7
1985	159985	11208			142974	89.4
1986	168611	13983	11899		150545	89.3
1987	176868	13492	11252		158857	89.8
1988	183022	12419	10072		164889	90.1
1989	196042	13691	10228	15	172799	88.2
1990	202505	13264	9670	29	177425	87.6
1991	211544	13790	10834	12	184254	87.1
1992	224624	15295	10375	13	190151	84.7
1993	235150	13932	9793	6	200673	85.3
1994	243456	13213	9833	9	208234	85.5
1995	252627	13921	10430	26	215339	85.2
1996	258873	13556	10114	20	221805	85.7
1997	263646	12968	9623	9	226674	85.98
1998	267982	12366	9260	7	233007	86.95
1999	280455	12114	8999	4	249368	88.92
2000	285244	11122	7050	14	249741	87.55
2001	295395	10903	6755	14	260077	88.04
2002	303134	11635	7082	8	268243	88.49
2003	306157	12441	7767	5	266832	87.16
2004	312941	13957	9318	2	273387	87.36
2005	317062	13251	9057	5	275685	86.95
2006	323479	12460	9117	3	279246	86.33
2007	331556	13621	10333	1	293733	85.29
2008	343051	14485	11053	1	291049	84.84
2009	352115	14450	11157	5	297559	84.51
2010	367607	14265	11019	4	309054	84.07

12-33 续表

年　份	领取独生子女证		人口出生率（‰）		计　划 生育率 (%)	多孩率（%）
	累　计 (人)	领证率 (%)	省计划 指　标	实　际 完　成		
1978			13.0	18.73		
1979			12.0	24.13		
1980	423	1.84	13.0	24.41	69.72	23.38
1981			11.9	21.86		
1982			18.1	19.07		
1983			17.0	16.74		
1984			15.5	15.54		
1985	1954	1.22	15.3	15.37	88.94	4.27
1986	2029	1.20	16.5	16.44	92.45	2.93
1987	2257	1.28	16.0	16.11	93.16	1.97
1988	2408	1.32	17.0	16.75	93.58	2.14
1989	2116	1.10	17.0	17.06	92.35	2.54
1990	2288	1.13	17.5	17.07	89.08	3.71
1991	2514	1.19	20.0	17.91	89.55	3.65
1992	2335	1.04	19.8	19.31	86.08	4.44
1993	2905	1.24	20.0	18.38	87.29	4.50
1994	3245	1.33	19.2	17.88	86.50	4.71
1995	3389	1.34	19.3	17.76	85.09	4.33
1996	4028	1.63	18.3	17.05	83.83	4.87
1997	4514	1.71	18.0	16.50	83.98	4.68
1998	4971	1.85	16.6	15.31	90.01	2.92
1999	21228	7.57	15.8	14.55	89.31	2.92
2000	30921	10.84	15.3	12.11	90.17	1.77
2001	41636	14.10	14.9	11.16	91.75	1.57
2002	49188	16.23	14.3	10.35	91.80	1.31
2003	51814	16.92	12.5	10.34	92.45	1.24
2004	55425	17.71	12.5	10.86	93.48	1.14
2005	60426	19.06	11.5	10.62	94.32	0.80
2006	69507	21.49	11.6	10.14	94.69	0.71
2007	73766	22.25	11.0	10.39	95.48	0.63
2008	77919	22.71	11.0	10.77	96.28	0.54
2009	80738	22.93	11.0	10.67	96.75	0.75
2010	81736	22.23	11.5	10.90	96.97	0.99

注：领证率是期末已领取独生子女证人数除以全市已婚育龄妇女人数。

12-34 主要年份优抚和社会救济、福利事业

Basic Statistics on Special Care, Social Relief and Welfare in Main Years

项　　目	单位	1990年	1995年	2000年	2005年	2009年	2010年
一、优抚事业							
优抚收养性事业单位数	个	1	1	1	1	1	1
#民政部门办	个	1	1	1	1	1	1
优抚收养性单位收养人数	人次	19	11	7	8	7	8
优抚事业费用	万元	340	213	412	2400	4258	4555
二、社会救济							
社会救济人数	人次	4433	7273	19914	23886	40438	36516
年末社会散居孤老残幼人数	人	2026	2444	1596	875	379	11
#定期救济对象	人	142	569	29	18	379	11
社会救济福利事业费	万元		190	993	6955	23729	21199
自然灾害生活救济费	万元	4.6	70	50	744	235	139
三、社会福利							
社会福利事业单位数	个	1	1	3	36	36	38
#民政部门办	个	1	1	3	4	3	3
社会福利事业单位收养人数	人	363	351	406	2240	2570	2609
#民政部门办	人	363	351	406	893	1106	1715
社会福利企业单位	个	9	15	20	20	10	10
安排“四残”人员就业数	人	199	239	393	351	247	321
社会福利事业单位费用支出	万元					9129	9770
四、敬老院情况							
全市敬老院个数	个			32	31	33	35
年末敬老院供养人数	人			833	1347	1464	894
五、“五保户”情况							
年末列入“五保户”户数	户			1545	1575	1364	1254
年末列入“五保户”人数	人			1587	1575	1364	1263
全年“五保户”费用支出	万元			2198	1594	999	1536
六、城乡基层社会保障							
建立社会保障网络镇街数	个	33	24	32	32	32	32
城镇社会服务设施数	个	215	225	342	48	398	405

注：“五保户”人数及费用支出含敬老院供养人数及费用支出。

12-35 主要年份婚姻登记情况

Basic Statistics on Marriage Registration in Main Years

项　　目	单位	1985年	1990年	1995年	2000年	2005年	2009年	2010年
准予登记结婚	对	11870	13668	14170	10535	14293	18604	11415
#涉外、华侨、港澳台同胞	对	638	709	510	213	113	116	79
准予登记离婚	对				448	1319	2277	1856
#涉外、华侨、港澳台同胞	对						19	9
计划生育率	%						96.8	97.0

12-36 主要年份环境保护基本情况

Basic Statistics on Environmental Protection in Main Years

项　　目	单 位	1985年	1990年	1995年	2000年	2005年	2009年	2010年
一、废水								
废水排放总量	万吨	3100	5259	9681	40703	69049	74612	87953
#工业废水	万吨	2686	4124	5511	11753	21355	29960	29742
工业废水排放达标率排放量	%	55.0	46.1	85.4	72.0	92.1	97.8	96.3
城镇生活污水处理率	%						67	71.5
二、废气								
工业废气排放量	亿标立方	34	307	556	1318	1695	2135	2340
三、工业固体废物								
固体废物产生量	万吨	16	112	108	149	284	318	313
固体废物处置量	万吨	8	2	1	5	12	15	15
固体废物处理率	%	48.2	1.8	0.9	66.9	99.8	4.8	4.8
固体废物利用率	%	37.5	17.9	18.2	63.8	86.5	95.0	95.0
四、城市环境质量及污染控制								
空气污染指数	范围值				21-87	24-123	14-104	14-108
交通干线噪声平均值	db(A)				68.4	67.9	63.8	67.7
汽车尾气达标率	%				81.2	88.1	83.5	81.0
市区城市生活垃圾无害化处理率	%						100.0	100.0

12-37 主要年份社会保险事业情况

Basic Statistics on Social Insurance in Main Years

项　　目	单 位	1995年	2000年	2005年	2009年	2010年
一、社会保险						
参加各种社会保险人数	万人次	149.33	338.33	804.71	2397.83	2726.37
#失业保险人数	万人	6.49	17.84	177.78	259.15	279.90
养老保险人数	万人	8.46	82.95	182.49	315.81	421.84
地方养老保险人数	万人				310.87	371.01
医疗保险人数	万人	7.60	88.21	189.40	536.57	592.27
工伤保险人数	万人	126.78	136.53	235.10	438.87	469.08
社会保险基金总收入	万元	18155	127964	491540	1201283	1544112
#失业保险基金收入	万元	60	2732	28954	25488	27008
养老保险基金收入	万元	7697	85245	343429	714507	976257
地方养老保险基金收入	万元				122869	144699
医疗保险基金收入	万元	2057	23488	82138	281366	333342
工伤保险基金收入	万元	8341	15891	35073	57053	62806
社会保险待遇总支出	万元	10520	40454	217413	604796	547470
#失业保险待遇支出	万元	16	440	6676	17388	9681
养老保险待遇支出	万元	7450	24130	135958	241649	194055
地方养老保险待遇支出	万元				43190	1849
医疗保险待遇支出	万元	1436	3694	51021	267092	299975
工伤保险待遇支出	万元	1618	11703	22220	35477	41910
二、农民基本养老保险						
实际参保人数	万人		58.51	51.55	45.83	
实际申领人数	万人		16.45	18.63	24.48	
保费征缴金额	万元			33845	175470	
养老支付金额	万元		2467	33411	74542	

注：1. 1997年起养老保险因口径调整，与以前年份不可比。
2. 参加各种社会保险总人数包含生育保险人数。
3. 2010年起，农（居）民基本养老保险并入职工养老保险。

12-38 主要年份最低生活保障情况

Basic Statistics on Minimum Income Relief in Main Years

项　　目	单 位	2005年	2006年	2007年	2008年	2009年	2010年
居民最低生活保障线	元/人月	320	320	320	400	400	440
村民最低生活保障线	元/人月	300	300	300	400	400	440
居民最低生活保障户数	户	1911	2433	3079	1531	1606	1599
居民最低生活保障人数	人	4885	6091	7574	3653	3770	3643
居民最低生活保障金支出	万元	789.5			1052.0	726.7	673.4
村民最低生活保障户数	户	6705	7133	6844	12125	13106	12214
村民最低生活保障人数	人	17426	19050	18534	33384	33549	30785
村民最低生活保障金支出	万元	2318			9747	6295.3	5922.3

12-39 主要年份市政建设情况

Basic Statistics on Municipal Construction in Main Years

项　　目	单 位	1995年	1999年	2000年	2005年	2009年	2010年
水厂日供水能力	万吨	66	182	187	480	700	700
年末供水管道总长度	公里	1580	2011	2106	3680	12668	16268
全年供水量	万吨	18802	66268	70046	155100	160782	165607
#生活用水量	万吨	7361	29530	21433	51100	46099	28560
园林绿地面积	公顷	800	1229	1396	10298	29497	33092
#公园绿地面积	公顷					10266	9075
建成区绿化覆盖面积	公顷	1885	1556	1364	9436	31865	35571
建成区土地面积	平方公里	82.00	126.14	147.68	657.17	780.15	798.48
公园数	个		249	273	931	777	1004
公园面积	公顷		827	1423	2887	5919	11130

12-40 主要年份液化石油气及天然气供应情况

Basic Statistics on Supply of Liquefied Petroleum Gas and Natural Gas in Main Years

项　　目	单 位	1995年	2000年	2005年	2008年	2009年	2010年
年末液化石油气用户数	户	63419	110172	144797	912026	892874	956018
#家庭用气户数	户	62246	106910	144035	876622	873246	870921
全年液化石油气供应量	吨	25935	58287	161930	394510	351893	344762
#家庭用量	吨	18948	22104	24354	233183	215357	188108
年末天然气用户数	户			5027	82916	112230	147047
#家庭用气户数	户			5000	82303	111501	116239
全年天然气供应量	万立方米			350	18808	29255	23414
#家庭用量	万立方米			45	924	1078	1600
年末汽车天然气加气站	个					8	10
年末汽车天然气加气站全年供气量	万立方米					1955	5324

注：本表2000-2006年为市喜威液化石油气有限公司与市中液石油气有限公司的业务量,2007年起调整为市城市管理局统计口径。

12-41 历年环境保护基本情况

Basic Statistics on Environmental Protection over Years

年 份	全市降水PH均值(范围值)	全市酸雨PH均值(范围值)	全市酸雨频率(%)	全市酸雨占总降水量(%)	交通十线噪声平均值(db)	工业废水排放量(万吨)	工业废水排放达标量(万吨)	工业废水排放达标率(%)
1982						1842	1381	74.97
1983						2068	1564	75.63
1984	6.53					2127	1203	56.56
1985						2686	1483	55.21
1986					76.8	2416	596	24.67
1987	6.64	5.38		38.4	78.9	3501	1843	52.64
1988	4.85	4.72	63.6	75.1	77.6	3029	2349	77.55
1989	5.44	5.21	31.0	31.8	74.1	3976	2473	62.21
1990	6.15	5.30	29.5	43.3	75.9	4124	1900	46.07
1991	5.24	4.78	35.4	30.4	72.2	5506	3560	64.70
1992	5.10	4.71	36.8	35.9	76.0	5849	3501	59.90
1993	4.93	4.41	22.5	29.1	75.8	6500	4175	64.23
1994	5.33	4.81	23.2	25.5	72.6	7057	5361	75.97
1995	5.89	5.49	9.2	13.7	70.3	5511	4706	85.40
1996	5.83	5.40	14.7	10.9	70.4	6033	4790	79.40
1997	4.94	4.84	56.6	76.4	70.6	8930	5697	63.80
1998	4.79	4.70	60.3	80.4	70.3	7989	3683	46.10
1999	4.97	4.68	40.0	50.5	69.1	11719	6258	53.40
2000	4.90	4.67	50.7	56.6	68.7	11753	8468	72.00
2001	5.06	4.74	31.6	43.9	68.2	11694	8168	69.90
2002	5.47	5.09	29.3	28.8	68.0	25587	23179	90.60
2003	4.55	4.44	60.5	77.2	67.9	23389	19761	84.49
2004	4.47	4.41	69.6	85.7	68.0	22501	20274	90.10
2005	4.07	4.00	65.7	86.2	67.9	21355	19667	92.10
2006	3.57-6.57	4.70	50.0	42.4	68.0	24134	22344	92.58
2007	5.21	4.36-7.59	54.2	59.2	67.9	91260	88072	96.51
2008	4.83	4.65	60.1	63.6	63.6	33359	31560	94.61
2009	5.03	4.88	51.8	67.3	63.8	29960	29309	97.82
2010	5.11	4.97	52.2	65.3	67.7	29742	28639	96.29

注：2007年工业废水排放量和工业废水排放达标量两个指标统计口径变更，与往年不可比。

主要统计指标解释

Explanatory Notes on Main Statistical Indicators

工程技术人员 指在国民经济各行业从事工程技术工作的自然科学技术专业人员，包括：高级工程师、工程师、助理工程师、技术员和未评定职称的技术人员。

农业技术人员 指在国民经济各行业从事农业技术工作的自然科学技术专业人员，包括：高级农艺师、农艺师、助理农艺师、技术员和未评定职称的技术人员。

科学研究人员 指在国民经济各行业从事科学技术活动的科学技术专业人员，包括：正副研究员、助理研究员、研究实习员、技术员和未评定职称的技术人员。

专利申请量 指企业当年向国家知识产权局提出专利申请并被受理项数。

专利授权量 指企业当年获国家知识产权局授予专利权的项数。

发明 专利法及其实施细则所称的发明是指对有关产品、方法或其改进所提出的新的技术方案。

实用新型 专利法及其实施细则所称的实用新型是指对产品的形状、构造或者其结合所提出的适于实用的新的技术方案。

外观设计 专利法及其实施细则所称的外观设计是指对产品的形状、图案、色彩或者其结合所作出的富有美感并适于工业上应用的新设计。

毕业生数 毕业生数是指上学年内，具有学籍的学生学完教学计划规定的全部课程，考试及格，实际毕业的学生数。不包括结业生和肄业生。

招生数 招生数是指新学年开始时，按规定实际招收入学的新生数，不包括重读生和复学生（高等教育包括春秋两季招收的学生）。

在校学生数 是指具有学籍的注册学生总数。

学龄儿童入学率 指调查范围内已入小学学习的学龄儿童占校内外学龄儿童总数（包括弱智儿童在内，但不包括盲聋哑儿童）的比重。

电影放映单位 指具有放映机器设备、固定或不固定的放映场所与专职或兼职的放映技术人员，经有关部门登记批准，经常为一定的观众对象放映电影的机构。包括经批准对外开放进行营业，并与电影发行放映管理机构分帐的专用放映单位和军委系统租片单位。

公共图书馆藏书量 是指本馆已编目的古籍、图书、期刊和报纸的合订本、小册子、手稿，以及缩徽制品、录像带、录音带、光盘等视听文献资料数量之和。

医疗机构 是指根据《医疗机构管理条例》的规定，经登记取得《医疗机构执业许可证》的机构。包括医院、社区卫生服务中心（站）、卫生院、门诊所、诊疗所、医务室、村卫生室、妇幼保健院（所、站）、专科疾病防治院（所、站）、急救中心、临床检验中心。

医院 指设有固定床位能收容病人住院并能为病人提供医疗、护理服务的医疗机构。包括县及县以上医院、农村乡卫生院、其他医院三部分。按所属性质分为卫生部门、工业及其他部门、集体经济单位三类。其中县及县以上医院按业务性质分为综合医院和专科医院。

实有床位 是指报告期末固定实有床位数，包括正规床、简易床、监护床、正在消毒和修理床位、因扩建或修理而停用的床位，不包括产科新生儿床、待产室待产床、库存床、观察床、临时加床和病人家属陪伴床。

诊疗人数 是指所有诊疗工作的总人数。包括病人来院就诊的门诊、急诊人次和出诊、下地段、赴家庭病床、到工厂、农村、工地、会议、集体活动等外出诊疗的人次数，以及外出进行的单项健康检查及健康咨询指导人次数。并包括本院职工的诊疗的人次数及局部的单项健康检查人数。

卫生技术人员 指卫生事业机构支付工资的全部固定职工和合同制职工中现任职务为卫生技术工作的专业人员。包括中医师、西医师、中西医结合高级医师、护师、中药师、西药师、检验师、其他技师、中医士、西医士、护士、助产士、中药剂士、西药剂士、检验士、其他技士、其他中医、护理员、中药剂员、西药剂员、检验员，其他初级卫生技术人员。

治愈率 是指年内治愈（并经治疗后，疾病症状消失，功能完全恢复。）出院病人数占年内出院人数的比例。

病死率 是指年内住院病人中死亡人数占出院人数的比例。

刑事案件立案 是指实施违反我国刑事法律的行为，构成犯罪的案件。根据《关于公安机关办理刑事案件程序规定》第一百六十二条，公安机关受理案件后，经过审查，认为有犯罪事实需要追究刑事责任，且属于自己管辖的，由接受单位制作《刑事案件立案报告书》，经县级以上公安机关负责人批准，予以立案。

刑事案件破案 根据《关于公安机关办理刑事案件程序规定》第一百六十六条的规定，刑事案件破案应当具备下列条件：（一）犯罪事实已有证据证明；（二）有证据证明犯罪事实是犯罪嫌疑人实施的；（三）犯罪嫌疑人或者主要犯罪嫌疑人已经归案。

治安案件查处 是指触犯了《中华人民共和国治安管理处罚条例》规定，给社会或个人造成一定危害，公安机关依照相关法律、法规和规定，应当给予处罚的行为事件。

律师 指受聘参加法律顾问处工作，担任法律顾问、刑（民）事代理人、刑事辩护人，办理非诉讼事件、解答法律询问，代写法律事务文书等主要从事律师业务的专职法律工作者和兼职律师。

公证人员 指在国家公证机关依法办理公证事务的司法人员。包括公证员、助理公证员和在公证处工作的其他人员。

调解人员 在人民调解委员会担负调解民间一般民事纠纷和轻微违法行为所引起的纠纷的工作人员。包括调解委员会的委员和调解小组的调解员。

社会保险基金收入 是指根据国家规定，由纳入基本社会保险范围的单位，按照国家规定的缴费基数和缴费比例缴纳的社会统筹基金，以及通过其他方式取得的形成基金来源的收入，包括：单位缴纳的社会统筹基金收入、财政补贴收入、利息收入、其他收入。

社会保险基金支出 是指按照国家政策规定的开支范围和开支标准从社会统筹基金中支付给参加基本社会保险人员个人的费用，以及由于保险关系转移、上下级之间调剂资金等原因而发生的支出。

社会福利事业单位 指集中收养社会孤老、残、幼的机构。包括由民政部门管理的社会福利院、儿童福利院、精神病人福利院和城镇集体办的福利院，以及农村集体举办的敬老院。

社会福利事业单位收养人数包括民政部门管理的和城镇及农村集体举办的社会福利事业单位中收养的老人、少年儿童、缺乏生活自理能力的残疾人员和精神病人。

废水排放总量 包括工业废水和生活污水。工业废水指工业企业在生产、科研过程中向企业外部排放的所有排放口的废水量总和。生活污水指居民或职工在饮用、洗涤、烹饪、清洁卫生等过程中排放的污水量。

十三、能　源

Energy

13-1 能源主要指标(2005-2010年)

Main Indicators of Energy (2005-2010)

项　　目	单　位	2005年	2006年	2007年	2008年	2009年	2010年
地区能源消费总量(等价值)	万吨标准煤	1885.78	2138.97	2393.92	2589.66	2603.52	2812.65
地区能源消费总量(当量值)	万吨标准煤	1800.14	2010.20	2154.52	2280.31	2311.86	2438.84
电力消耗	亿千瓦时	419.83	472.01	515.40	514.16	495.58	562.00
单位GDP能耗(等价值，2005年可比价)	吨标准煤/万元	0.864	0.822	0.778	0.738	0.705	0.691
单位GDP能耗(当量值，2005年可比价)	吨标准煤/万元	0.825	0.772	0.700	0.650	0.626	0.599
单位GDP电耗(2005可比价)	千瓦小时/万元	1923.00	1813.46	1674.45	1465.25	1341.26	1380.10
规模以上工业综合能源消费量(当量值)	万吨标准煤	1203.77	1329.05	1437.94	1452.85	1367.94	1496.06
规模以上工业增加值能耗(当量值,2005年可比价)	吨标准煤/万元	1.14	1.02	0.92	0.82	0.82	0.73
规模以上工业发电量	亿千瓦时	378.81	410.54	402.54	362.53	342.29	368.26
全社会用电量	亿千瓦时	419.83	472.01	515.40	514.16	495.58	562.00
火力发电转换效率	%	37.05	36.97	36.68	37.59	39.24	38.91
供热转换效率	%				87.75	89.74	91.18
能源消费比上年增长	%		13.43	11.92	8.18	0.54	8.03
电力消费比上年增长	%		12.43	9.19	-0.24	-3.61	13.40
生产总值比上年增长	%		19.22	18.26	14.00	5.25	10.27
能源消费弹性系数			0.70	0.65	0.58	0.10	0.78
电力消费弹性系数			0.65	0.50			1.30

13-2 综合能源平衡表(2005-2010年)

Overall Energy Balance Sheet (2005-2010)

单位：万吨标准煤

项　　目	2005年	2006年	2007年	2008年	2009年	2010年
可供本地区消费的能源量	**1885.78**	**2138.97**	**2393.92**	**2589.66**	**2603.52**	**2812.65**
年初库存量	77.54	67.21	77.91	87.19	158.56	133.72
一次能源生产量						31.61
回收能	1.31	5.51	13.81	13.67	13.31	
外省调入量	1866.72	2139.88	2328.67	2537.65	2493.23	2564.50
进口量	9.31	1.71	60.72	100.59	83.79	205.75
境内轮船和飞机在境外加油量						
本省调出量(-)						-7.31
出口量(-)						
境外轮船和飞机在境内加油量(-)						
年末库存量(-)	-69.11	-75.35	-87.19	-149.43	-145.37	-115.62
加工转换投入(-)产出(+)量	**-0.08**					**-15.28**
火力发电						
供热						-13.93
洗选煤						
炼焦						
炼油						
制气						
损失量	**63.74**	**63.40**	**84.93**	**65.64**	**34.59**	**42.12**
运输和输配损失	63.74	63.40	84.93	65.64	33.77	42.12
终端消费量	**1821.96**	**2075.57**	**2308.98**	**2524.02**	**2568.93**	**2755.25**
第一产业	5.04	6.61	6.46	4.74	6.17	6.86
农、林、牧、渔业	5.04	6.61	6.46	4.74	6.17	6.86
第二产业	1334.30	1491.65	1654.16	1782.54	1790.15	1952.34
工业	1305.42	1459.54	1617.24	1742.08	1749.90	1913.74
#用作原材料、燃料						
建筑业	28.88	32.11	36.92	40.46	40.25	38.59
第三产业	304.16	366.00	409.89	459.67	475.19	483.54
交通运输、仓储及邮政业	84.47	97.27	114.30	129.63	134.83	139.41
批发、零售业和住宿、餐饮业	137.35	172.82	178.02	193.99	200.60	198.74
其他	82.34	95.91	117.57	136.05	139.76	145.39
生活消费	178.45	211.31	238.48	277.07	297.42	312.51
城镇	178.45	211.31	238.48	277.07	297.42	312.51
乡村						
平衡差额						
消费量合计	**1885.78**	**2138.97**	**2393.92**	**2589.66**	**2603.52**	**2812.65**

13-3 石油平衡表(2005-2010年)

Petroleum Balance Sheet (2005-2010)

单位：万吨

项　　目	2005年	2006年	2007年	2008年	2009年	2010年
一、可供量	**413.06**	**461.36**	**444.13**	**460.89**	**445.10**	**401.11**
生产量						
外省(区、市)调入量	408.02	462.31	448.20	472.40	442.12	394.75
进口量	1.82	1.20				0.03
境内轮船和飞机在境外加油量						
本省(区、市)调出量(−)						2.09
出口量(−)						
境外轮船和飞机在境内加油量(−)						
年初年末库存差额	3.22	-2.15	-4.07	-11.51	2.98	8.42
年初库存量	18.64	15.42	17.57	21.64	33.15	28.29
年末库存量(−)	15.42	17.57	21.64	33.15	30.17	19.87
二、消费量	**413.06**	**461.36**	**444.13**	**460.89**	**445.10**	**401.11**
消费量分组一						
农林牧渔业	1.23	2.36	2.22	1.10	2.21	2.47
工业	249.88	269.49	227.73	196.77	172.29	135.08
建筑业	14.49	16.17	16.18	14.89	16.69	14.55
交通运输、仓储和邮政业	54.93	63.34	73.81	83.33	85.93	85.15
批发、零售业和住宿、餐饮业	28.76	33.17	37.70	55.53	52.47	48.56
其他	21.91	25.00	27.44	34.45	33.86	33.18
生活消费	41.86	51.83	59.05	74.82	81.65	82.11
消费量分组二						
终端消费	266.62	286.63	320.59	381.24	414.02	389.49
#工业	103.76	95.08	104.24	117.23	141.34	123.56
加工转换损失	146.12	174.41	123.49	79.54	30.93	11.53
火力发电	146.12	174.41	123.49	79.54	30.85	11.53
供热					0.08	
炼油损耗						
制气						
损失量	0.32	0.32	0.05	0.11	0.15	0.09
三、平衡差额						

13-4 煤炭平衡表(2005-2010年)

Coal Balance Sheet (2005-2010)

单位：万吨

项　　目	2005年	2006年	2007年	2008年	2009年	2010年
一、可供量	**1596.99**	**1738.97**	**1849.66**	**1924.57**	**1916.83**	**2039.07**
生产量						
外省(区、市)调入量	1582.15	1746.25	1769.23	1847.82	1906.10	1750.92
进口量	9.40		85.00	140.82		287.97
本省(区、市)调出量(-)						8.02
出口量(-)						
年初年末库存差额	5.44	-7.28	-4.57	-64.07	10.73	8.20
年初库存量	70.80	65.36	72.64	77.21	141.28	129.63
年末库存量(-)	65.36	72.64	77.21	141.28	130.55	121.43
二、消费量	**1596.99**	**1738.97**	**1849.66**	**1924.57**	**1916.83**	**2039.07**
消费量分组一						
农林牧渔业						
工业	1596.99	1738.97	1849.66	1924.57	1914.73	2037.77
建筑业						
交通运输、仓储和邮政业						
批发、零售业和住宿、餐饮业					2.10	1.20
其他						
生活消费						
消费量分组二						
终端消费	132.22	184.22	233.99	441.92	481.42	374.94
#工业	132.22	184.22	233.99	441.92	479.32	373.74
用于加工转换	1464.76	1554.75	1615.67	1482.65	1434.21	1664.03
火力发电	1464.76	1554.75	1615.67	1459.21	1335.14	1448.61
供热				23.44	101.71	217.88
洗煤损耗						
炼焦						
制气						
型煤加工损耗					-2.64	-2.46
损失量	0.01				1.20	0.10
三、平衡差额						

13-5 全社会用电量（2005-2010年）

Total Consumption of Electricity (2005-2010)

单位：万千瓦时

项　　目	2005年	2006年	2007年	2008年	2009年	2010年
全社会用电量总计	**4198289**	**4720112**	**5154025**	**5141578**	**4955750**	**5619996**
#各行业用电量合计	3855742	4329080	4718336	4651348	4409908	5036303
#第一产业	9761	9514	9643	9584	9354	10279
第二产业	3397588	3761186	4101528	4019849	3724455	4317267
第三产业	448393	558380	607165	621915	676099	708757
城乡居民生活用电量合计	342547	391032	435689	490230	545842	583693
各行业用电分类						
农、林、牧、渔业	9761	9514	9643	9584	9354	10279
工业	3374306	3735651	4061784	3962669	3673716	4262339
#轻工业	1357858	1502077	1656565	1675707	1590781	1821542
重工业	2016448	2233574	2405219	2286962	2082935	2440797
#采矿业	8112	6024	8796	8607	6865	8044
制造业	3044575	3381692	3625554	3567232	3382129	3953169
#电力、燃气及水的生产和供应业	321619	347935	427434	386830	284722	301126
#电力、热力的生产和供应业	240737	272067	328413	268378	173866	183361
#电厂生产全部耗用电量	41656	75606	75090	68094	67286	51096
线路损失电量	190736	189347	253318	200284	106573	132265
燃气生产和供应业	654	845	895	917	1433	1778
水的生产和供应业	80228	75023	98126	117535	109423	115987
建筑业	23282	25535	39744	57180	50739	54928
交通运输、仓储和邮政业	14425	15508	19789	22453	23358	26524
#交通运输业	8614	9387	12512	13868	13997	16173
仓储业	2084	2300	3122	3890	4459	5774
邮政业	3727	3821	4155	4695	4902	4577
信息传输、计算机服务和软件业	15277	17376	22259	26429	31172	35085
批发、零售业和住宿、餐饮业	282238	364478	356196	337296	364374	376037
#批发和零售业	148555	193891	177435	162736	177608	194549
住宿和餐饮业	130153	170587	178761	174560	186766	181488
金融、房地产、商务及居民服务业	65223	79917	101327	110630	114305	117690
#金融业	16158	16225	16870	16178	15073	14156
房地产业	21976	25083	25846	23986	23111	23489
租赁和商务服务、居民服务和其他服务	27089	38609	58611	70466	76121	80045
公共事业及管理组织	71230	81101	107594	125107	142890	153421
#科学研究、技术服务和地质勘查业	4550	3206	3012	2691	2675	2950
#地质勘查业	248	23	17	15	30	45
水利、环境和公共设施管理业	26633	30069	33736	38338	49440	56514
#水利管理业	12157	11650	6618	2443	4127	5208
教育、文化、体育和娱乐业	13596	15417	21112	24582	27728	29655
#教育	4793	4871	5988	6295	7208	8615
卫生、社会保障和社会福利业	12151	15088	7522	4012	5889	8964
公共管理和社会组织、国际组织	14300	17321	42212	55484	57158	55338

13-6 规模以上工业综合能源消费量（2005-2010年）

Overall Energy Consumpiton of Industrial Enterprises above Designated Size (2005-2010)

单位：吨标准煤

指　　标	2005年	2006年	2007年	2008年	2009年	2010年
合　计	**12037714**	**13290543**	**14379411**	**14528511**	**13679420**	**14960593**
(一)采矿业	769	675	706	361	160	193
煤炭开采和洗选业						
石油和天然气开采业						
黑色金属矿采选业						
有色金属矿采选业						
非金属矿采选业	769	675	706	114	160	193
其他采矿业				247		
(二)制造业	5273612	6365772	7492792	8140697	7848902	8743936
农副食品加工业	59666	94383	139017	146621	169496	190698
食品制造业	51949	75174	84197	85670	89657	100257
饮料制造业	34764	48904	60046	59173	54740	62258
烟草制品业						
纺织业	876658	842201	932175	856952	758755	809179
纺织服装、鞋、帽制造业	165413	144783	138591	99994	83779	58020
皮革、毛皮、羽毛(绒)及其制品业	92086	183236	203600	160892	142298	188284
木材加工及木、竹、藤、棕、草制品业	8684	11324	12470	17024	17524	31901
家具制造业	106972	105694	100380	99529	75372	96883
造纸及纸制品业	1452027	2246173	2889078	3477439	3708558	4155618
印刷业和记录媒介的复制	38855	41457	49755	63425	58184	49990
文教体育用品制造业	150581	138360	136963	143387	108321	116821
石油加工、炼焦及核燃料加工业	67	29939	92308	56016	696	2306
化学原料及化学制品制造业	149516	156848	162108	174693	165849	215692
医药制造业	4950	6075	6443	7111	6932	6972
化学纤维制造业	17288	25988	22388	4378	4179	8430
橡胶制品业	42554	41997	41964	61100	51890	41861
塑料制品业	326872	320924	342762	424140	383414	418696
非金属矿物制品业	333262	409912	539683	612137	657556	716487
黑色金属冶炼及压延加工业	22399	27459	28448	20815	10287	17037
有色金属冶炼及压延加工业	26412	34052	41856	55869	33015	41801
金属制品业	180098	171235	180663	138760	115815	133152
通用设备制造业	45760	48845	57133	81424	57777	69724
专用设备制造业	104801	80444	89690	112887	103566	74432
交通运输设备制造业	14488	13571	16419	51812	38347	45462
电气机械及器材制造业	283994	305746	318329	301393	252323	270507
通信设备、计算机及其他电子设备制造业	578746	659829	702659	697227	585042	710090
仪器仪表及文化、办公用机械制造业	78158	69880	72045	65574	62713	68411
工艺品及其他制造业	26474	31338	31624	65255	52816	42966
废弃资源和废旧材料回收加工业	117					
(三)电力、燃气及水的生产和供应业	6763334	6924096	6885913	6387453	5830358	6216464
电力、热力的生产和供应业	6728304	6859857	6817766	6323666	5775585	6162853
燃气生产和供应业				21	184	231
水的生产和供应业	35030	64238	68147	63766	54589	53380

主要统计指标解释

Explanatory Notes on Main Statistical Indicators

能源生产总量 指一定时期内全国（地区）一次能源生产量的总和，是观察全国（地区）能源生产水平、规模、构成和发展速度的总量指标。一次能源生产量包括原煤、原油、天然气、水电、核能及其他动力能（如风能、地热能等）发电量。不包括低热值燃料生产量、生物质能、太阳能等的利用和由一次能源加工转换而成的二次能源产量。

能源消费总量 指一定时期内全国（地区）生产和生活消费的各种能源的总和，是观察能源消费水平、构成和增长速度的总量指标，能源消费总量包括原煤和原油及其制品、天然气、电力等。能源消费总量分为三部分，即终端能源消费量、能源加工转换损失量和损失量。

(1)终端能源消费量 指一定时期内全国（地区）生产和生活消费的各种能源在扣除了用于加工转换二次能源消费量和损失量以后的数量。

(2)能源加工转换损失量 指一定时期内全国（地区）投入加工转换的各种能源数量之和与产出各种能源产品之和的差额。它是观察能源在加工转换过程中损失量变化的指标。

(3)能源损失量 指一定时期内能源在输送、分配、储存过程中发生的损失和由客观原因造成的各种损失量。不包括各种气体能源放空、放散量。

能源生产弹性系数 是研究能源生产增长速度与国民经济增长速度之间关系的指标。计算公式：

$$\text{能源生产弹性系数}=\frac{\text{能源生产总量增长速度}}{\text{国民经济增长速度}}$$

国民经济增长速度，可根据不同的目的或需要，用国民生产总值，国内生产总值等指标来计算，本资料是采用国内生产总值指标计算的。

电力生产弹性系数 是研究电力生产增长速度与国民经济增长速度之间关系的指标。计算公式：

$$\text{电力生产弹性系数}=\frac{\text{电力生产量增长速度}}{\text{国民经济增长速度}}$$

能源消费弹性系数 是反映能源消费增长速度与国民经济增长速度之间比例关系的指标。计算公式：

$$\text{能源消费弹性系数}=\frac{\text{能源消费量增长速度}}{\text{国民经济增长速度}}$$

电力消费弹性系数 是反映电力消费增长速度与国民经济增长速度之间比例关系的指标。计算公式：

$$\text{电力消费弹性系数}=\frac{\text{电力消费量增长速度}}{\text{国民经济增长速度}}$$

能源加工转换效率 指一定时期内能源经过加工、转换后，产出的各种能源产品的数量与同期内投入加工转换的各种能源数量的比率。它是观察能源加工转换装置和生产工艺先进与落后、管理水平高低等的重要指标。计算公式：

$$\text{能源加工转换效率}=\frac{\text{能源加工、转换产出量}}{\text{能源加工、转换投入量}}\times 100\%$$

十四、镇街主要指标

Main Indicators of Towns

14-1 镇街生产总值

Gross Domestic Product by Town

单位：万元

镇街	(1991年) 地区生产总值	第一产业	第二产业	第三产业	(1992年) 地区生产总值	第一产业	第二产业	第三产业
全市	**959073**	**134523**	**503220**	**321330**	**1108922**	**144115**	**592701**	**372106**
莞城	22046	174	16612	5260	28881	108	22263	6510
石龙	25154	907	17669	6578	29467	1026	21163	7278
虎门	44900	10059	16412	18429	56539	10336	24781	21422
东城	23500	7179	13793	2528	32770	7362	21392	4016
万江	18518	3874	11653	2991	27997	3968	18928	5102
南城	13339	2219	8181	2939	18147	1973	12681	3493
中堂	14889	3300	9065	2524	19902	4360	10669	4873
望牛墩	11950	2794	7394	1762	13789	2854	8683	2252
麻涌	24449	10489	11478	2482	26907	9797	14294	2816
石碣	12556	2686	7660	2210	16967	2888	11140	2939
高埗	11546	3352	5163	3031	14295	4017	6503	3775
道滘	15659	4540	9542	1577	19009	4805	12003	2201
洪梅	6492	3879	1872	741	6906	2441	3435	1030
沙田	12616	6467	4552	1597	16779	6511	7850	2417
厚街	31303	5679	22403	3221	38272	6064	28528	3680
长安	24850	7961	13185	3704	36298	8980	21883	5435
寮步	23700	9030	8979	5691	30083	9256	12627	8200
大岭山	10557	5918	3123	1516	16175	6342	4928	4905
大朗	19481	11277	4870	3334	24694	10104	9836	4754
黄江	20403	2765	15888	1750	28355	3244	22864	2247
樟木头	10515	10515	2107	6426	13972	2212	8536	3224
清溪	8673	2076	4428	2169	12742	2405	6936	3401
塘厦	17826	6128	9049	2649	30454	6300	19988	4166
凤岗	8676	2698	5550	428	12119	3257	8146	716
谢岗	9472	2019	5197	2256	7178	2339	4236	603
常平	38008	13134	14511	10363	45046	11625	20103	13317
桥头	14030	4083	8114	1833	22099	5429	10336	6334
横沥	11125	2499	6349	2277	15673	2710	9342	3621
东坑	16245	3544	11393	1308	22332	3368	17294	1670
企石	16155	3731	9575	2849	21159	4699	13097	3363
石排	16123	2350	10727	3046	18091	2704	11839	3548
茶山	13328	3385	7146	2797	16377	4160	8782	3435

注：各镇街合计不等于全市数，下同。

14-1 续表 1

单位：万元

镇街	(1993年) 地区生产总值	第一产业	第二产业	第三产业	(1994年) 地区生产总值	第一产业	第二产业	第三产业
全市	**1570491**	**143953**	**873114**	**553424**	**2170340**	**174796**	**1194928**	**800616**
莞城	41307		32838	8469	55021		43120	11901
石龙	34182	582	21188	12412	48891	216	32738	15937
虎门	74808	11281	37710	25816	103070	14350	51597	37123
东城	37567	4379	25901	7287	44963	5223	30065	9675
万江	39317	4818	26939	7561	45953	5499	31186	9268
南城	23341	2767	16312	4262	46416	2811	38511	5094
中堂	31352	7282	16982	7089	34819	6271	19472	9076
望牛墩	15717	2642	10196	2879	18449	2796	11974	3679
麻涌	34553	9305	22223	3025	42676	9160	27917	5599
石碣	23877	2542	16311	5024	34401	2816	24582	7003
高埗	17843	4751	8347	4745	22368	5495	10877	5996
道滘	24306	5086	15471	3749	37062	5698	27835	14072
洪梅	8069	2265	4292	1512	9020	2406	4756	1858
沙田	24446	6574	14434	3438	31950	6196	20646	5107
厚街	57912	6707	44408	6796	101289	7615	77637	16037
长安	49862	9995	31962	7905	68914	11024	46939	10951
寮步	46311	9423	21926	14962	63089	12428	30205	20456
大岭山	22611	6717	7660	8234	27722	6725	11258	9739
大朗	32720	10237	15152	7331	46550	13958	21052	11540
黄江	37008	3021	30171	3816	47096	3254	39031	4811
樟木头	18265	1361	13994	2910	23438	1680	18008	3750
清溪	19533	3299	12076	4158	30510	4230	20391	5889
塘厦	41635	4353	31001	6281	80870	6396	65620	8854
凤岗	16961	3282	12778	901	24520	4166	19054	1300
谢岗	12063	2367	8997	699	16093	3365	11143	1585
常平	67921	12564	34518	20839	100294	13561	62109	24624
桥头	27654	5023	15085	7546	40632	6225	22445	11962
横沥	23825	23825	2604	13815	33565	3922	17444	12198
东坑	33565	4073	25007	4485	36161	4245	26665	5251
企石	28573	5167	17684	5722	34915	6545	21854	6516
石排	25462	2992	17949	4521	31920	3699	21172	7049
茶山	21196	4908	12096	4192	30233	6017	18221	5995

14-1 续表 2

单位：万元

镇街	(1995年) 地区生产总值	第一产业	第二产业	第三产业	(1996年) 地区生产总值	第一产业	第二产业	第三产业
全市	**2962892**	**214306**	**1669723**	**1078863**	**3617502**	**248645**	**1994826**	**1374031**
莞城	69318		52710	16608	72335		50523	21812
石龙	70501	318	46550	23633	72190	303	36303	35584
虎门	130282	18388	68784	43110	158257	25193	85444	47620
东城	85114	6208	57257	21649	100581	6744	66136	27701
万江	55648	6705	37884	11059	63649	8488	40934	14227
南城	83707	2938	63407	17362	103785	3667	79347	20771
中堂	41537	6593	23358	11585	50533	7418	28908	14206
望牛墩	21961	3197	14061	4703	25963	3440	16512	6011
麻涌	47340	11783	28584	6973	49764	15494	26884	7386
石碣	46831	3332	33206	10293	66081	3495	45532	17054
高埗	28324	6213	14403	7708	36274	6945	19348	9981
道滘	47605	5698	27835	14072	55596	6031	35931	13634
洪梅	15209	2667	6923	5619	16733	2908	7657	6168
沙田	42922	7741	29376	5806	49023	10655	32354	6015
厚街	118353	9670	90642	18041	140036	10906	83151	45979
长安	93323	12505	65233	15585	131672	12882	97066	21724
寮步	75398	14727	32311	28360	85876	15651	37022	33203
大岭山	39228	8485	17265	13478	49383	9773	21083	18527
大朗	66807	17319	25844	23644	78506	16982	29641	31883
黄江	61098	3708	46392	10998	63391	3929	46558	12904
樟木头	31914	2662	24710	4543	41323	3443	32232	5647
清溪	52550	5721	35627	11202	82953	6083	55419	21451
塘厦	112158	6909	90588	14661	139903	9900	112916	17087
凤岗	37051	4767	30135	2149	48015	5521	39670	2824
谢岗	18872	4356	12655	1861	25536	5213	18242	2081
常平	135315	18444	87856	29015	146594	19303	86033	41258
桥头	54012	7206	30626	16180	64694	8418	38393	17883
横沥	44663	4484	23559	16620	54922	4717	29045	21161
东坑	34654	5179	19727	9748	50965	5274	32218	13473
企石	44588	7760	28861	7967	54066	8947	35535	9584
石排	34349	4898	20547	8904	37946	5718	21459	10769
茶山	41484	6017	18221	5995	51339	7159	24892	9433

14-1 续表 3

单位：万元

镇街	(1997年)				(1998年)			
	地区生产总值	第一产业	第二产业	第三产业	地区生产总值	第一产业	第二产业	第三产业
全市	**4485981**	**256388**	**2432816**	**1796777**	**5579965**	**259437**	**3056779**	**2263749**
莞城	80298		49962	30336	110076		49677	60399
石龙	95560	293	48361	46906	133953	116	77910	55927
虎门	246823	25799	130963	90061	362826	29535	176729	156562
东城	125730	5850	78959	40921	161819	5246	105142	51431
万江	69516	8749	42333	18434	82239	9424	50075	22922
南城	130392	3490	103126	23776	160524	3933	128850	27741
中堂	61741	7610	35991	18140	76980	7727	45359	23894
望牛墩	30854	3780	19390	7684	36531	3941	22769	9821
麻涌	52217	15965	29345	6907	62531	16443	35485	10603
石碣	85990	3782	54674	27534	109255	3852	70872	34531
高埗	46630	7586	26579	12465	60242	8235	36383	15624
道滘	69424	6383	47525	15516	80887	6756	54039	20092
洪梅	20052	4501	7602	7949	23134	4607	9569	8958
沙田	54881	11342	36602	6936	71203	16829	42167	12207
厚街	184205	11448	96880	75877	247177	12150	146229	88798
长安	180377	13111	134235	33031	245676	13562	183031	49083
寮步	103656	17341	45112	41203	129731	18768	60452	50511
大岭山	65246	10538	31884	22824	83268	9134	45040	29094
大朗	95301	19093	38996	37212	122409	15008	53085	54316
黄江	67618	4139	47073	16406	83585	4244	58492	20849
樟木头	55682	4725	43020	7936	71299	5333	51615	14351
清溪	120961	7519	84276	29166	160483	7802	115314	37367
塘厦	178757	11467	140870	26420	230580	12121	177569	40890
凤岗	63066	5925	51486	5655	79286	6187	65440	7659
谢岗	29488	6379	20521	2588	34881	6958	24888	3035
常平	185390	20195	98068	67127	231059	19811	131252	79995
桥头	79685	8523	51919	19243	96661	9712	61140	25809
横沥	67894	6411	34892	26591	81263	5364	45427	30472
东坑	63718	4810	44682	14226	78576	5726	54359	18491
企石	62625	9562	42240	10823	72065	9827	47551	14687
石排	43477	6463	23530	13484	53842	6606	28932	18304
茶山	63955	9321	39524	15110	77319	9878	47785	19656

14-1 续表 4

单位：万元

镇　街	(1999年)				(2000年)			
	地区生产总值	第一产业	第二产业	第三产业	地区生产总值	第一产业	第二产业	第三产业
全　市	**6672386**	**257863**	**3670519**	**2744004**	**8202531**	**259087**	**4507072**	**3436372**
莞　城	131005		58104	72901	184225		67030	117195
石　龙	157715	349	86171	71195	184256	189	98240	85827
虎　门	442633	31013	213607	198014	532946	30479	263928	238539
东　城	207432	4126	125159	78147	262854	4233	153667	104954
万　江	97379	9435	59636	28308	138724	11604	85526	41594
南　城	198820	2756	149678	46386	233013	3119	171413	58481
中　堂	94412	7001	57217	30194	123213	7032	76571	39610
望牛墩	43303	4012	26738	12553	51516	4072	31399	16045
麻　涌	75449	12466	44768	18215	90816	12213	45965	32638
石　碣	137148	3866	88152	45130	175180	4021	111038	60121
高　埗	78709	8792	50131	19786	102516	9155	67888	25473
道　滘	93751	7151	61687	24913	109999	7569	67841	34589
洪　梅	26118	4162	11872	10084	29921	4383	14095	11443
沙　田	86339	12167	53505	20667	109128	12714	71503	24911
厚　街	300721	12412	171495	116814	405317	12705	221947	170665
长　安	332335	13820	240690	77825	419347	14256	299650	105441
寮　步	161782	19944	82582	59256	202379	20732	110577	71070
大岭山	108469	9238	67662	31569	138789	9742	89991	39056
大　朗	156427	16699	69193	70535	201504	17826	94065	89613
黄　江	97621	4410	67206	26005	123331	5243	83748	34340
樟木头	94385	4225	64138	26021	147697	4639	71921	71138
清　溪	206524	8790	151219	46515	303131	9984	231303	61844
塘　厦	288110	12783	217897	57430	363971	13486	272234	78251
凤　岗	100753	6267	61392	33094	128298	6336	79138	42824
谢　岗	42142	3610	29017	9515	50174	3975	35779	10420
常　平	302805	15703	166347	120755	395318	16116	218229	160974
桥　头	111892	9062	69595	33235	130380	9093	82261	39026
横　沥	97209	6178	55276	35756	116749	8593	62314	45842
东　坑	101287	5363	65010	30913	118430	6241	76250	35940
企　石	85313	10000	51789	23524	99467	11339	58897	29231
石　排	69030	6772	37874	24384	87817	6913	48532	32372
茶　山	90250	9514	55468	25268	105432	10712	64726	29994

14-1 续表 5

单位：万元

镇街	(2001年)				(2002年)			
	地区生产总值	第一产业	第二产业	第三产业	地区生产总值	第一产业	第二产业	第三产业
全市	**9918905**	**260968**	**5405092**	**4252845**	**11869374**	**248791**	**6488109**	**5132474**
莞城	222233		80203	142030	312742		76890	235852
石龙	215738	150	115691	99897	248664	144	135163	113357
虎门	618557	30469	304781	283307	717425	26838	350636	339951
东城	342044	3785	188628	149631	466960	2110	232502	232348
万江	175693	13015	90857	71821	213919	11026	106945	95948
南城	286473	2929	211622	71922	350029	2711	262431	84887
中堂	153366	7155	95677	50533	194263	5908	122819	65536
望牛墩	60921	3540	36872	20509	73104	3591	43299	26214
麻涌	127061	12298	74806	39957	173557	1002	120426	43079
石碣	243163	4139	150613	88411	340162	4141	209830	126191
高埗	133362	9477	90730	33155	173004	9701	120415	42888
道滘	128327	8011	76692	43624	153201	8479	87039	57683
洪梅	34245	4587	16543	13115	41756	4793	21676	15287
沙田	142060	13641	92266	36153	182363	13912	119778	48673
厚街	483117	13088	253149	216880	583689	13976	297707	272006
长安	529219	14496	371263	143460	679022	14622	469032	195368
寮步	252526	21246	143824	87456	314871	20276	182688	111907
大岭山	194021	10089	133489	50443	251078	5741	178811	66526
大朗	264929	17764	128283	118882	341930	15525	181234	145171
黄江	154595	5176	98438	50981	199781	5288	122001	72492
樟木头	176062	4460	84195	87407	210845	5545	101237	104063
清溪	393471	10517	302613	80341	501941	11106	382584	108251
塘厦	457175	13796	335872	107507	573947	13603	425078	135266
凤岗	162854	6400	97540	58914	205006	2035	126903	76068
谢岗	58323	4115	41585	12623	71092	5665	40790	24637
常平	493419	16451	272983	203985	557039	16077	310537	230425
桥头	151979	8366	98054	45559	179442	7245	118564	53633
横沥	140251	9252	74148	56851	168932	9380	90576	68976
东坑	132805	6013	84256	42535	149147	5438	92587	51122
企石	115314	12403	63421	39490	127616	9088	68807	49721
石排	107585	6925	61859	38801	131394	6967	75798	48629
茶山	123931	9801	75341	38789	153215	9801	91916	51498

14-1 续表 6

单位：万元

镇　街	(2003年)				(2004年)			
	地区生产总值	第一产业	第二产业	第三产业	地区生产总值	第一产业	第二产业	第三产业
全　市	**14525187**	**228165**	**7981954**	**6315068**	**18060258**	**227087**	**10160382**	**7672789**
莞　城	415993		80802	335191	552370		94035	458335
石　龙	287713	116	167126	120471	317521	51	186652	130820
虎　门	905165	27106	462105	415954	1139827	27168	598000	514659
东　城	652408	1657	314094	336657	897727	900	411172	485655
万　江	269593	9622	129625	130346	329849	5617	156431	167801
南　城	452911	2743	314752	135416	741609	1869	349496	390244
中　堂	256251	7013	162945	86292	338808	5956	206693	126159
望牛墩	87872	3520	50846	33506	106086	3550	59709	42827
麻　涌	234612	8769	177540	48303	292911	8664	226131	58116
石　碣	463023	4253	290495	168275	590604	3649	381862	205093
高　埗	224078	9891	157949	56238	282716	9943	202317	70456
道　滘	178954	8975	100566	69413	217400	9499	119688	88213
洪　梅	53960	5113	29668	19179	76686	4770	41140	30776
沙　田	236769	13944	155438	67387	310921	13975	202383	94563
厚　街	721188	12275	374482	334431	878666	12341	454284	412041
长　安	887947	14863	603308	269776	1162826	15040	759582	388204
寮　步	394322	13167	234806	146349	498253	5327	303435	189491
大岭山	322872	4937	226565	91370	447412	4571	313857	128984
大　朗	443891	10640	240983	192268	574604	6986	325826	241792
黄　江	258682	4567	152903	101212	331432	3294	187369	140769
樟木头	250877	4863	119145	126869	291893	4350	139729	147814
清　溪	645553	11218	495035	139300	848426	9610	660589	178227
塘　厦	710030	13565	526730	169735	882099	13700	653816	214583
凤　岗	284608	2048	170574	111986	373309	2015	220434	150860
谢　岗	91482	4266	51312	35904	119007	4328	69024	45655
常　平	657385	12627	377679	267079	796109	10792	468642	316674
桥　头	213712	5419	134937	73356	264849	4495	144282	116072
横　沥	205872	9602	117554	78716	253887	9075	153884	90928
东　坑	181394	8423	113270	59701	230057	7943	145998	76116
企　石	142717	5216	72284	65217	167279	3848	80461	82970
石　排	157729	7144	92020	58565	190127	7259	109953	72915
茶　山	195098	8607	118895	67596	268473	7413	161070	99990

14-1 续表 7

单位：万元

镇街	(2005年) 地区生产总值	第一产业	第二产业	第三产业	(2006年) 地区生产总值	第一产业	第二产业	第三产业
全市	**21831961**	**205546**	**12278624**	**9347791**	**26279791**	**120089**	**15065985**	**11093717**
莞城	617849		153367	464482	712319		230144	482174
石龙	349301	141	194749	154411	384329	35	213392	170902
虎门	1283052	22937	668632	591483	1492628	11446	763086	718096
东城	1049758	480	473888	575389	1264850	427	571728	692694
万江	375471	4209	164099	207164	440346	4711	187932	247702
南城	1016644	1900	440431	574313	1229016	1995	508223	718798
中堂	424212	6122	276399	141691	507968	6428	332766	168774
望牛墩	126751	3511	73191	50049	156949	3480	87638	65831
麻涌	387211	8588	310275	68348	494018	7106	398466	88445
石碣	728816	3782	491498	233535	868731	3091	588622	277018
高埗	366593	10020	254017	102556	456695	6552	320225	129918
道滘	255589	8753	143285	103551	301036	9568	174820	116648
洪梅	102660	3939	61138	37583	123863	4082	77274	42507
沙田	364800	13695	240822	110283	442784	12585	293854	136345
厚街	1033929	11722	531019	491188	1199117	6929	609223	582965
长安	1339428	9492	917732	412204	1539236	7505	1042139	489592
寮步	598969	7765	364261	226943	739610	1136	451671	286803
大岭山	547734	4102	370108	173524	675091	2329	431260	241502
大朗	707369	14112	411161	282096	850356	1491	499588	349277
黄江	364377	3065	220654	140658	441152	741	276062	164349
樟木头	330537	3463	157434	169640	393688	600	185556	207532
清溪	984943	9036	761281	214626	1097986	8012	828219	261755
塘厦	1057175	13661	771724	271790	1186644	12312	830537	343794
凤岗	517427	1762	320177	195488	623929	1750	373375	248804
谢岗	148917	4467	91026	53424	192841	4795	118714	69332
常平	951464	10062	556932	384470	1119659	6338	644544	468777
桥头	287240	4495	168473	114271	388604	1387	210763	176454
横沥	304870	8593	195659	100619	373304	7274	242406	123624
东坑	261238	11543	165441	84254	295233	5703	194653	94877
企石	200581	3129	102183	95269	244027	2266	129255	112506
石排	234709	7268	128132	99308	294009	7283	154259	132467
茶山	305183	6652	190620	107911	384988	3215	245078	136695

14-1 续表 8

单位：万元

镇 街	(2007年)				(2008年)			
	地区生产总值	第一产业	第二产业	第三产业	地区生产总值	第一产业	第二产业	第三产业
全 市	**31600489**	**118991**	**17546573**	**13934924**	**37036004**	**148251**	**19016068**	**17871685**
莞 城	897597		298250	599347	1015311		294311	721000
石 龙	427216	10	235821	191385	475742	7	239943	235792
虎 门	1846638	10373	936639	899626	2153489	11940	1093014	1048535
东 城	1559123	377	699730	859017	1816793	339	773623	1042831
万 江	520636	3405	221314	295917	604659	3702	262498	338459
南 城	1425257	2015	583496	839747	1632407	1285	618209	1012913
中 堂	588085	6553	379181	202351	659949	6760	419455	233734
望牛墩	193635	3462	105983	84190	236495	3359	127759	105377
麻 涌	651344	5985	537412	107947	834681	7564	693959	133158
石 碣	994532	3096	670790	320646	1082524	2795	694349	385380
高 埗	568276	6530	384637	177109	690604	6526	442377	241701
道 滘	362268	8202	211240	142826	439328	7218	240510	191600
洪 梅	163384	4281	110958	48145	206785	4381	147969	54435
沙 田	515106	12403	327706	174997	588063	12863	337140	238060
厚 街	1420026	7270	719643	693113	1616483	7971	797404	811108
长 安	1770272	7746	1152474	610052	2029075	4979	1158887	865209
寮 步	886584	1118	531815	353650	1038493	2141	584767	451585
大岭山	822554	2241	502679	317634	960138	2248	554712	403178
大 朗	1025864	2098	592111	431655	1100875	877	688340	411658
黄 江	556305	740	347972	207593	721414	724	438204	282486
樟木头	461719	505	228647	232567	507743	311	253050	254382
清 溪	1266762	6207	924401	336153	1417816	5170	966538	446108
塘 厦	1365736	11206	903107	451422	1602945	10447	980030	612468
凤 岗	747757	1752	409163	336843	901696	1725	472782	427189
谢 岗	239771	5178	143093	91500	273944	9273	160217	104454
常 平	1311744	6665	747353	557726	1495652	6058	796227	693366
桥 头	467790	1326	242928	223536	536868	2692	254438	279737
横 沥	443014	4350	275399	163265	522130	6972	300380	214778
东 坑	320991	4532	204804	111654	372361	4017	231268	137076
企 石	291765	2868	150052	138844	320630	2314	159252	159064
石 排	360806	7308	187787	165711	417073	7313	216033	193727
茶 山	476010	3131	293991	178888	593265	4327	353036	235902

14-1 续表 9

单位：万元

镇街	(2009年) 地区生产总值	第一产业	第二产业	第三产业	(2010年) 地区生产总值	第一产业	第二产业	第三产业
全市	**37639142**	**147877**	**18230836**	**19260428**	**42464527**	**165719**	**21608153**	**20690656**
莞城	1054949		318447	736502	1196478		386025	810453
石龙	502973	6	249848	253119	559487	14	301186	258287
虎门	2437582	13180	1213679	1210723	2840349	17635	1410761	1411953
东城	1989067	386	742171	1246510	2309506	391	952986	1356129
万江	611916	3578	241005	367333	688921	3590	271769	413562
南城	1841809	1235	706141	1134433	2135136	1173	654285	1479678
中堂	662727	6965	396592	259170	771405	7035	478834	285536
望牛墩	288697	3395	162960	122342	306900	3498	166207	137195
麻涌	932351	8332	788621	135398	1109110	9248	934928	164934
石碣	1094432	2667	641983	449782	1280125	2954	858482	418689
高埗	609392	6228	387053	216111	698532	7337	451425	239770
道滘	449115	8024	234381	206710	515731	8181	289160	218390
洪梅	253003	4612	186637	61754	341015	4626	263103	73286
沙田	614104	12894	360064	241146	726957	12903	470002	244052
厚街	1695963	8373	880274	807316	1981416	9108	1063475	908833
长安	2083662	4532	1196987	882143	2371479	4959	1450285	916235
寮步	1120641	1866	630705	488070	1335015	2395	774425	558195
大岭山	975717	2255	505238	468224	1107869	2407	613793	491669
大朗	1160519	1242	675946	483331	1352689	1352	807882	543455
黄江	768073	720	419897	347456	890211	745	493492	395974
樟木头	524759	378	251340	273041	550388	404	234874	315110
清溪	1363307	5410	873074	484823	1498135	5864	967020	525251
塘厦	1713803	11448	1059192	643163	1948397	11713	1278441	658243
凤岗	1013446	1220	513090	499136	1170248	1222	599388	569638
谢岗	294969	9452	166712	118805	358653	8230	216560	133863
常平	1516942	6725	799850	710367	1686376	7102	861382	817892
桥头	535223	3546	251952	279725	593138	5738	286829	300571
横沥	538610	6294	326010	206306	624788	3982	370547	250259
东坑	387579	2118	237522	147939	459962	1760	293723	164479
企石	318197	1974	172565	143658	373899	1976	224958	146965
石排	438939	7500	243190	188249	507685	7520	299884	200281
茶山	620174	4327	360862	254985	710237	2878	415234	292125

14-2 镇街第三产业增加值（2010年）

Value-added of the Tertiary Industry by Town (2010)

单位：万元

镇街	第三产业增加值	#交通运输及仓储业	批发和零售业	住宿和餐饮业	金融业	房地产业
全市	**20690656**	**810778**	**4058051**	**1476753**	**1752289**	**3164428**
莞城	810453	60651	209618	27780	149682	165643
石龙	258287	16138	56797	25009	33968	44977
虎门	1411953	56345	415049	114053	96503	132217
东城	1356129	66658	174536	104872	152356	357568
万江	413562	22329	66937	36205	32728	70014
南城	1479678	31168	180745	64600	247983	269539
中堂	285536	12522	70271	30717	24051	30542
望牛墩	137195	26135	20916	7495	12887	8826
麻涌	164934	25403	21621	9173	17562	16534
石碣	418689	17347	79801	30760	37432	54021
高埗	239770	27855	43243	25731	16176	38617
道滘	218390	11077	30824	17820	17146	62109
洪梅	73286	8861	11854	8331	5126	10053
沙田	244052	27368	42028	25182	16904	35045
厚街	908833	25808	123824	95679	67091	141126
长安	916235	16812	246691	97122	66120	87230
寮步	558195	41960	96126	52456	40655	98616
大岭山	491669	12715	196843	36379	32177	59341
大朗	543455	8167	96472	65666	44078	104571
黄江	395974	18217	76146	43681	28769	86081
樟木头	315110	8306	71375	29146	30353	64126
清溪	525251	13212	59478	48530	35508	117237
塘厦	658243	19321	92791	81387	49390	114895
凤岗	569638	10245	77589	63548	40290	142674
谢岗	133863	8987	24134	12921	12190	29822
常平	817892	28654	130215	116212	63125	169886
桥头	300571	8450	45788	32654	17208	39426
横沥	250259	3709	44025	30644	19745	51870
东坑	164479	1441	28798	17402	15272	36161
企石	146965	7900	17905	12679	9941	30700
石排	200281	6110	37362	25262	19339	39348
茶山	292125	25631	46525	29062	23068	63409

14-3 镇街户籍户数与人口数(2010年)

Population of Household Town (2010)

单位：人

镇街	户数(户)			人口数	按性别分		按农业、非农业分		总人口中未落户籍的人口数
		农业户	非农业户		男	女	农业人口	非农业人口	
全市总计	**530497**	**259691**	**270806**	**1817709**	**922666**	**895043**	**896789**	**920920**	**4360**
莞城	38361	1	38360	172290	88462	83828	1892	170398	113
石龙	21187	2385	18802	70770	35175	35595	8919	61851	791
虎门	35029		35029	127556	64344	63212		127556	2
东城	24446		24446	87657	44770	42887		87657	21
万江	23843		23843	77123	39196	37927		77123	297
南城	19714		19714	71991	37684	34307		71991	29
中堂	21731	15169	6562	74846	38082	36764	55532	19314	84
望牛墩	11774	10016	1758	45881	22860	23021	39669	6212	820
麻涌	21699	17513	4186	72332	36307	36025	62223	10109	708
石碣	14833	11133	3700	43887	22441	21446	37119	6768	68
高埗	11365	10642	723	37832	19103	18729	35087	2745	135
道滘	16907	12403	4504	55841	27966	27875	44176	11665	64
洪梅	6433	5908	525	21963	11125	10838	20719	1244	236
沙田	12654	11447	1207	40697	20496	20201	36415	4282	70
厚街	29142	23347	5795	96939	48644	48295	84206	12733	8
长安	13475		13475	43697	22547	21150		43697	1
寮步	20323	13023	7300	68524	34701	33823	42795	25729	1
大岭山	13210	11539	1671	44480	22361	22119	38956	5524	
大朗	18646	16281	2365	70192	36231	33961	62036	8156	14
黄江	7933	5835	2098	24735	12566	12169	18351	6384	2
樟木头	7912		7912	27434	13911	13523		27434	6
清溪	11426	9129	2297	35682	17821	17861	29517	6165	
塘厦	17381		17381	45569	23048	22521		45569	97
凤岗	6957	4955	2002	24245	11807	12438	17524	6721	8
谢岗	5322	4168	1154	20441	10182	10259	17140	3301	158
常平	24871	17997	6874	73738	37951	35787	57797	15941	3
桥头	11825	4966	6859	35887	17995	17892	16351	19536	186
横沥	11664	8861	2803	36760	18820	17940	30454	6306	12
东坑	10845	9071	1774	30102	15460	14642	27060	3042	170
企石	13011	10895	2116	41830	21386	20444	36586	5244	27
石排	12987	11420	1567	42811	21550	21261	39090	3721	197
茶山	13459	11587	1872	44639	22520	22119	37175	7464	32
松山湖	132		132	9338	5154	4184		9338	

14-4 镇街户籍人口自然变动情况（2010年）

Population Household by Town (2010)

镇　街	出　生		死　亡		自然增长	
	人　数（人）	出生率（‰）	人　数（人）	死亡率（‰）	人　数（人）	自然增长率（‰）
全市总计	**19509**	**10.90**	**8367**	**4.68**	**11142**	**6.23**
莞　城	1398	8.33	752	4.48	646	3.85
石　龙	541	7.73	350	5.00	191	2.73
虎　门	1296	10.24	782	6.18	514	4.06
东　城	840	11.43	366	4.98	474	6.45
万　江	468	10.32	187	4.12	281	6.20
南　城	713	9.48	334	4.44	379	5.04
中　堂	484	11.12	176	4.04	308	7.07
望牛墩	415	11.03	146	3.88	269	7.15
麻　涌	796	11.11	322	4.49	474	6.62
石　碣	502	11.75	246	5.76	256	5.99
高　埗	532	12.81	205	4.94	327	7.88
道　滘	500	8.99	298	5.36	202	3.63
洪　梅	238	10.99	124	5.73	114	5.27
沙　田	1167	12.13	356	3.70	811	8.43
厚　街	1115	16.16	185	2.68	930	13.48
长　安	838	9.91	301	3.56	537	6.35
寮　步	778	11.60	381	5.68	397	5.92
大岭山	538	12.54	164	3.82	374	8.72
大　朗	782	11.25	361	5.19	421	6.06
黄　江	314	13.00	98	4.06	216	8.94
樟木头	321	11.85	102	3.77	219	8.09
清　溪	405	11.43	217	6.13	188	5.31
塘　厦	493	11.18	188	4.26	305	6.92
凤　岗	286	11.91	87	3.62	199	8.29
谢　岗	298	14.84	99	4.93	199	9.91
常　平	735	10.10	387	5.32	348	4.78
桥　头	430	12.09	196	5.51	234	6.58
横　沥	468	12.85	192	5.27	276	7.58
东　坑	291	9.67	174	5.78	117	3.89
企　石	505	12.05	213	5.08	292	6.97
石　排	499	11.82	154	3.65	345	8.17
茶　山	493	11.07	224	5.03	269	6.04
松山湖	30	3.40			30	3.40

注：本表按户籍人口统计。

14-5 镇街人口迁移变动情况（2010年）

Population Migration by Town (2010)

单位：人

镇街	迁移总计	省内	省外	迁入总计	省内迁入	省外迁入	迁出总计	迁往省内	迁往省外
全市总计	**35185**	**13301**	**21884**	**28534**	**10602**	**17932**	**6651**	**2699**	**3952**
莞城	4865	1212	3653	2970	915	2055	1895	297	1598
石龙	833	440	393	674	353	321	159	87	72
虎门	1658	687	971	1440	594	846	218	93	125
东城	3588	1141	2447	3381	1069	2312	207	72	135
万江	1465	409	1056	1378	371	1007	87	38	49
南城	5084	1638	3446	4169	1214	2955	915	424	491
中堂	458	208	250	406	183	223	52	25	27
望牛墩	211	113	98	186	96	90	25	17	8
麻涌	487	175	312	376	136	240	111	39	72
石碣	760	310	450	588	243	345	172	67	105
高埗	116	53	63	100	44	56	16	9	7
道滘	168	67	101	144	59	85	24	8	16
洪梅	167	71	96	139	59	80	28	12	16
沙田	362	137	225	327	127	200	35	10	25
厚街	738	254	484	660	222	438	78	32	46
长安	1430	418	1012	1240	359	881	190	59	131
寮步	1086	347	739	1011	325	686	75	22	53
大岭山	623	217	406	551	193	358	72	24	48
大朗	845	355	490	762	335	427	83	20	63
黄江	601	254	347	567	241	326	34	13	21
樟木头	705	273	432	618	244	374	87	29	58
清溪	580	275	305	480	243	237	100	32	68
塘厦	1737	708	1029	1447	633	814	290	75	215
凤岗	912	423	489	850	405	445	62	18	44
谢岗	160	74	86	131	67	64	29	7	22
常平	1085	438	647	994	391	603	91	47	44
桥头	339	133	206	285	109	176	54	24	30
横沥	361	138	223	339	134	205	22	4	18
东坑	164	54	110	119	43	76	45	11	34
企石	242	123	119	202	111	91	40	12	28
石排	338	151	187	291	142	149	47	9	38
茶山	284	117	167	213	100	113	71	17	54

注：本表按户籍人口统计。

14-6 镇街土地面积和人口密度（2010年）

Land Area and Population Density by Town (2010)

镇街	土地面积（平方公里）	人口密度（人/平方公里）	
		户籍人口	常住人口
莞城	11.2	15383	14473
石龙	13.8	5128	10283
虎门	166.5	766	3836
东城	105.1	834	4690
万江	48.5	1590	5047
南城	56.6	1272	5111
中堂	59.9	1250	2331
望牛墩	31.6	1452	2684
麻涌	87.2	829	1354
石碣	36.2	1212	6823
高埗	34.6	1093	6283
道滘	54.3	1028	2635
洪梅	33.2	662	1750
沙田	78.8	516	2253
厚街	125.7	771	3487
长安	89.4	489	7430
寮步	72.5	945	5774
大岭山	95.5	466	2926
大朗	97.5	720	3189
黄江	92.9	266	2491
樟木头	118.8	231	1118
清溪	140.1	255	2231
塘厦	128.2	355	3761
凤岗	82.4	294	3871
谢岗	91.0	225	1092
常平	103.3	714	3741
桥头	56.0	641	2979
横沥	44.7	822	4582
东坑	23.7	1270	5857
企石	58.2	719	2091
石排	48.7	879	3290
茶山	45.4	983	3447
松山湖	58.1	161	648

14-7 镇街常住人口(2010年)

Permanent Population by Town(2010)

单位：万人

镇　街	2010年	镇　街	2010年
莞　城	16.21	寮　步	41.86
石　龙	14.19	大岭山	27.94
虎　门	63.87	大　朗	31.09
东　城	49.29	黄　江	23.14
万　江	24.48	樟木头	13.28
南　城	28.93	清　溪	31.26
中　堂	13.96	塘　厦	48.21
望牛墩	8.48	凤　岗	31.90
麻　涌	11.81	谢　岗	9.94
石　碣	24.70	常　平	38.64
高　埗	21.74	桥　头	16.68
道　滘	14.31	横　沥	20.48
洪　梅	5.81	东　坑	13.88
沙　田	17.75	企　石	12.17
厚　街	43.83	石　排	16.02
长　安	66.42	茶　山	15.65

注：2010年镇街常住人口数为东莞市第六次全国人口普查数据，以2010年11月1日零时为标准时点。

14-8 镇街新莞人人口数（2009-2010年）

Migrant Population by Town (2009-2010)

单位：人

镇街	2009年			2010年		
	新莞人	男	女	新莞人	男	女
全市总计	**4299615**	**2093055**	**2206560**	**4114745**	**2010869**	**2103876**
莞城	64884	32270	32614	54037	26954	27083
石龙	63193	29035	34158	56289	26242	30047
虎门	426320	212155	214165	418140	205782	212358
东城	229981	131924	98057	209982	114118	95864
万江	84867	43202	41665	61928	32077	29851
南城	141752	68240	73512	130877	71174	59703
中堂	53967	27489	26478	48260	24351	23909
望牛墩	37873	17901	19972	35173	15932	19241
麻涌	32805	19013	13792	34798	19145	15653
石碣	113228	47335	65893	100760	42537	58223
高埗	128976	78766	50210	129189	77513	51676
道滘	75937	33625	42312	65833	29151	36682
洪梅	27437	13687	13750	24050	12058	11992
沙田	68777	35191	33586	65890	34489	31401
厚街	297107	138679	158428	289037	135689	153348
长安	542680	250483	292197	401157	182837	218320
寮步	182566	94938	87628	181021	95214	85807
大岭山	109817	60343	49474	100485	55816	44669
大朗	175068	82722	92346	130003	61428	68575
黄江	168781	82890	85891	153006	72294	80712
樟木头	113253	56654	56599	100900	48987	51913
清溪	151264	54283	96981	133927	50250	83677
塘厦	199882	93729	106153	351027	164772	186255
凤岗	141798	73150	68648	132568	69732	62836
谢岗	56013	25685	30328	44025	20755	23270
常平	142572	67152	75420	201978	95393	106585
桥头	60891	26512	34379	61003	26591	34412
横沥	103502	53847	49655	94048	52017	42031
东坑	68027	29817	38210	72268	33556	38712
企石	42256	20856	21400	36727	18078	18649
石排	92178	43825	48353	94447	45281	49166
茶山	76048	33836	42212	77380	36336	41044
其他单位	25915	13821	12094	24532	14320	10212

14-9 镇街计划生育情况（2010年）

Basic Statistics on Family Planning by Town (2010)

镇街	已婚育龄妇女人数(人)	女性初婚人数(人)	#23周岁及以上	落实各种节育措施 育龄夫妇(对)	节育率(%)	领取独生子女证 累计(人)	领证率(%)	计划生育率(%)	多孩率(%)
全市总计	**367607**	**14265**	**11019**	**309054**	**84.07**	**81736**	**22.23**	**96.97**	**0.99**
莞城	36093	1080	943	30441	84.34	9810	27.18	96.78	0.86
石龙	14280	462	370	12178	85.28	4002	28.03	95.75	0.92
虎门	25210	998	781	20188	80.08	5363	21.27	96.99	1.93
东城	14032	624	501	11617	82.79	3046	21.71	97.02	0.48
万江	8189	361	278	6891	84.15	1595	19.48	97.44	0.43
南城	15124	598	498	13126	86.79	4423	29.24	97.05	0.84
中堂	8574	358	259	7075	82.52	2074	24.19	96.90	0.21
望牛墩	6724	244	182	5880	87.45	1229	18.28	97.83	1.20
麻涌	13068	633	501	10474	80.15	2903	22.21	97.61	0.38
石碣	9059	360	291	7587	83.75	1613	17.81	98.01	1.79
高埗	8763	412	310	7285	83.13	1891	21.58	97.93	2.07
道滘	10563	333	248	8974	84.96	2162	20.47	96.00	0.80
洪梅	4041	136	91	3453	85.45	915	22.64	96.64	
沙田	19313	798	649	16196	83.86	3652	18.91	96.40	1.29
厚街	17252	919	820	14127	81.89	3234	18.75	96.95	0.54
长安	18667	488	412	15804	84.66	3353	17.96	97.14	0.95
寮步	13913	486	340	11904	85.56	2960	21.28	96.02	1.29
大岭山	9511	492	354	8120	85.37	1765	18.56	97.58	1.67
大朗	14012	549	375	11572	82.59	3271	23.34	97.31	0.90
黄江	5632	226	163	4848	86.08	1379	24.49	97.13	0.96
樟木头	6405	240	183	5280	82.44	1080	16.86	96.88	0.93
清溪	8083	265	186	6926	85.69	1484	18.36	97.53	1.48
塘厦	8662	382	298	7134	82.36	2106	24.31	97.36	0.81
凤岗	5736	234	179	4825	84.12	888	15.48	97.20	0.35
谢岗	4396	181	137	3779	85.96	883	20.09	97.32	1.34
常平	15247	554	405	13157	86.29	3961	25.98	97.28	0.82
桥头	7447	261	181	6434	86.40	2112	28.36	96.51	0.70
横沥	7671	298	210	6444	84.00	1907	24.85	96.15	1.07
东坑	5718	216	156	4864	85.06	1351	23.63	96.56	1.37
企石	8566	368	229	7514	87.72	1695	19.79	97.23	0.59
石排	8378	374	252	7062	84.29	1668	19.91	96.99	0.60
茶山	8917	307	209	7847	88.00	1909	21.41	95.94	1.22
松山湖	361	28	28	48	13.30	52	14.40	100.00	

14-10 镇街农业总产值（2010年，按当年价格计算）

Gross Output Value of Agriculture by Town (2010, at Current Prices)

单位：万元

镇街	农业总产值	种植业产值	林业产值	牧业产值	渔业产值	服务业产值
石龙	33				33	
虎门	29891	6879	131	10420	12461	
东城	2327	1584	111		632	
万江	6093	5406	1		686	
南城	2437	2345		15	67	10
中堂	12504	9657	1	1273	1573	
望牛墩	5448	4480		572	396	
麻涌	14284	11235	43	200	2805	
石碣	4409	3525			454	430
高埗	10717	9543			1024	150
道滘	13948	5895	4	5146	2842	61
洪梅	8853	3055		3945	1853	
沙田	25323	7101		3330	14892	
厚街	15516	12450	25	198	2843	
长安	7594	798	13	190	6593	
寮步	4115	2176	16	51	1872	
大岭山	4639	2982	48	10	1599	
大朗	2333	1557	9	98	670	
黄江	945	558	74		314	
樟木头	793	467	37	217		72
清溪	9119	6287	111		264	2457
塘厦	22154	11066	43	7316	812	2916
凤岗	2222	2054	10		158	
谢岗	13950	2944	13	6381	4476	135
常平	18213	8616	2	7770	1824	
桥头	9810	3775	5	4325	1705	
横沥	6960	2323		3327	1310	
东坑	2870	2481			389	
企石	5378	3436	18	509	1415	
石排	10610	3912	1	3035	3462	199
茶山	4878	1853		270	2755	

14-11 镇街主要农产品生产及产品产量（2010年）

Production and Output of Main Agricultural Products by Town (2010)

镇街	粮食播种面积(亩)	粮食总产量(吨)	稻谷播种面积(亩)	稻谷产量(吨)	蔬菜播种面积(亩)	蔬菜产量(吨)	水果总面积(亩)	水果总产量(吨)
石龙								
虎门	1722	408	885	319	19030	19787	5247	2657
东城	1439	644	1439	644	3209	5330	255	151
万江	862	359	545	191	12204	19948	154	247
南城					62	27	790	425
中堂	2268	687	1617	576	18321	33510	6172	6493
望牛墩	439	143	408	137	2841	4178	7294	12360
麻涌	9698	2815	8231	2571	12547	12223	22174	26202
石碣	389	132	200	84	10800	13644	301	458
高埗	1593	486	1238	408	22683	33963	90	180
道滘	3200	1171	3200	1171	10992	21733	121	227
洪梅	4102	1302	4015	1244	510	659	6984	10258
沙田	3506	1122	3506	1122	14970	15972	5057	4464
厚街	1103	273			40694	44263	11642	2405
长安					1034	913	2000	584
寮步	88	16			3360	5695	2235	492
大岭山	453	157			6561	7231	6747	894
大朗	238	52			3877	4284	11580	691
黄江					685	744	4920	499
樟木头					985	1398	5174	116
清溪	798	198			12350	13215	11774	761
塘厦	911	129	40	20	28719	35683	14528	953
凤岗	548	63			5241	4461	13216	903
谢岗	881	196	103	40	5200	8196	9921	1781
常平	612	177			17300	28850	9507	200
桥头	1670	463			7041	10104	1974	431
横沥	856	210			7450	7520	3494	86
东坑	353	103			7190	8950	1310	88
企石	2559	751	677	233	5784	10122	2643	50
石排	858	241			12785	13488	215	192
茶山	776	184	20	8	6197	6813	3017	292

14-11 续表 1

(2010年)

镇街	香(大)蕉面积(亩)	香(大)蕉产量(吨)	荔枝面积(亩)	荔枝产量(吨)	林业用地面积(亩)	当年种植面积(亩)	生猪年末存栏量(头)	肉猪出栏量(头)
石龙					150			
虎门	315	189	3310	869	31524		27000	73000
东城			127	28	10914	450		
万江	118	219	9	3				
南城			370	130	15653	500		
中堂	6077	6469					3457	5850
望牛墩	7219	12272					3200	4160
麻涌	20889	24962					197	140
石碣	250	450	51	8				
高埗								
道滘	121	227					29117	40083
洪梅	6984	10258					12714	31328
沙田	3771	3903	50	8	500		3952	8122
厚街	252	116	9235	2051	55370	500		
长安			1802	514	19451	220	1641	1558
寮步	35	63	1489	235	14670	800		
大岭山			5830	606	54386	1600		
大朗			10730	549	34466	170		
黄江			4230	485	71448	1000		
樟木头			4470	62	54123	1250		1015
清溪	80	4	9140	350	71984	1850		
塘厦	10	1	13412	816	36426	1600	5000	27350
凤岗	30	7	9890	710	41550	4499		
谢岗	1050	860	8000	449	61799	971	39817	43816
常平	3	1	7712	87	30176		18408	35810
桥头	120	122	820	41	10446		13302	34763
横沥	15	6	3322	62	6150		15000	25000
东坑	9		1040	49	5222			
企石			2323	32	9293	610	2128	4428
石排	30	70	70	9	767			
茶山	42	37	2704	113	9980			

注：林业用地面积、当年种植面积指标采用林业局数据。

14-11 续表 2

(2010年)

镇街	三鸟年末存栏量(只)	三鸟出栏量(只)	畜牧总肉量(吨)	#猪肉	禽蛋产量(吨)	淡水养殖面积(亩)	水产品产量(吨)	#淡水产量
石龙						102	51	51
虎门	105576	452213	5663	5109	11	8812	12254	4459
东城						1761	851	851
万江						2125	976	976
南城	1395	5492	6		1	225	110	110
中堂	491	30410	612	400		3622	1934	1613
望牛墩	34000	18300	296	278	32	1302	458	458
麻涌	34921	72138	82	10	20	4131	2026	2026
石碣						900	563	563
高埗						3013	1356	1356
道滘	53749	93757	2813	2698	75	6772	3206	3206
洪梅	22344	33715	2185	2144		3755	1782	1782
沙田	278800	968148	1511	559	14	17146	14357	7071
厚街						6036	1850	1850
长安	8045	31397	93	62		2636	4340	442
寮步			2			2526	2003	2003
大岭山						2175	2013	2013
大朗	22058	34564	39			3435	789	789
黄江						4545	387	387
樟木头	8300	35542	108	71				
清溪						855	313	313
塘厦	434759	1507028	3426	1913	189	3889	1304	1304
凤岗						1574	225	225
谢岗	135000	871600	3588	2281		18690	7068	7068
常平	510297	1630695	3800	2434	35	4079	2407	2407
桥头	22610	36860	2396	2363	1	3976	2420	2420
横沥	21000	60000	1818	1750	8	2887	1732	1732
东坑						3120	736	736
企石			278	268		2925	1658	1658
石排						7494	4163	4163
茶山	7000	24000	115			4305	2936	2936

14-12 镇街农机总动力、机耕面积及农村用电量（2010年）

Basic Statistics on Total Power of Agricultural Machinery, Area of Tractor Ploughing and Electricity Consumption in Rural Areas by Town (2010)

镇　街	农机总动力（千瓦）	#耕作机械	排灌机械	农村用电量（万千瓦时）	化肥施用实物量（吨）	农药使用量（吨）
石　龙				1661		
虎　门	31250	144	946	390844	1902	92
东　城	9000	154		58913	213	2
万　江	566	26	140	108200	1092	8
南　城				8041	98	1
中　堂	9555	696	2830	131490	2747	26
望牛墩	2326	263	370	61681	1757	18
麻　涌	4514	1184	164	11092	6893	37
石　碣	2127	213	1393	155977	1112	31
高　埗	13059	4161	2004	136221	1325	38
道　滘	2294	549	310	115000	1913	9
洪　梅	588	129	90	891	1799	15
沙　田	48729	1787	1170	46795	5240	120
厚　街	2691	132	306	327126	2906	116
长　安				445426		
寮　步	143	7	136	21858	434	7
大岭山	8756	3650	466	25224	523	18
大　朗	788	512	64	205067	1237	36
黄　江	122	23	2	62588	243	30
樟木头				91847	81	9
清　溪	2371	1075	1107	232461	960	77
塘　厦	669	143	109	313133	2215	26
凤　岗	376	108	190	205623	229	10
谢　岗	2512	1098	1330	4571	803	16
常　平	150			176153	787	10
桥　头	2484	180	1882	129957	1394	15
横　沥	2133		2133	101000	350	8
东　坑	25		25	79599	639	3
企　石	435	360	75	66918	343	
石　排	2628	375	1146	106747	1273	34
茶　山	1137	25	974	128382	937	7

14-13 镇街农村集体(经联社、经济社两级合计)经济收益分配(2010年)

Income Distribution of Rural Economy by Town (2010)

单位：万元

镇　街	经营总收入	经营总费用	经营纯收入
全市总计	**1433841**	**664547**	**769294**
莞　城	14885	4220	10665
石　龙	16309	8141	8168
虎　门	137790	65042	72748
东　城	97549	47994	49555
万　江	52650	24360	28290
南　城	53627	25271	28357
中　堂	53166	15640	37526
望牛墩	8046	3799	4247
麻　涌	16801	7430	9371
石　碣	60792	28519	32274
高　埗	24260	9049	15211
道　滘	21707	9304	12403
洪　梅	5309	2978	2331
沙　田	21149	9698	11451
厚　街	108942	58616	50326
长　安	150589	65688	84901
寮　步	64766	33033	31732
大岭山	36345	15602	20743
大　朗	53604	25760	27844
黄　江	22076	8512	13564
樟木头	18932	16355	2577
清　溪	48183	20719	27465
塘　厦	57305	24818	32486
凤　岗	62051	19511	42541
谢　岗	8102	3166	4936
常　平	66482	30164	36318
桥　头	29305	15318	13987
横　沥	23364	14292	9072
东　坑	19890	10898	8992
企　石	13857	9158	4699
石　排	28973	12099	16874
茶　山	37039	19396	17643

14-14 镇街规模以上工业企业主要经济指标（2010年）

Main Indicators of Industrial Enterprises above Designated Size by Town (2010)

单位：万元

镇　　街	企业单位数（个）	亏损企业	工业销售产值	工业增加值
莞　　城	49	10	953789	224875
石　　龙	75	18	1706183	299200
虎　　门	432	68	5010191	1190171
东　　城	264	30	2934575	740250
万　　江	161	24	1011409	216549
南　　城	84	14	2305262	466780
中　　堂	115	9	1788020	386466
望 牛 墩	107	20	672124	137922
麻　　涌	85	13	4720454	930401
石　　碣	174	33	3529479	721918
高　　埗	134	23	1514605	516339
道　　滘	165	21	1045591	237050
洪　　梅	75	13	1545249	270400
沙　　田	141	19	1650964	371282
厚　　街	292	47	3841719	843814
长　　安	384	113	5612508	1275471
寮　　步	232	35	3911161	688076
大 岭 山	240	44	2167291	474245
大　　朗	338	42	2548752	635103
黄　　江	162	35	1783637	391645
樟 木 头	126	32	808435	152717
清　　溪	302	42	4262830	840851
塘　　厦	404	60	4370450	1016180
凤　　岗	210	54	1747770	398308
谢　　岗	122	24	575026	128889
常　　平	268	45	2961843	676805
桥　　头	145	33	966751	173966
横　　沥	112	25	957924	229588
东　　坑	74	19	1250229	226985
企　　石	100	14	704984	120305
石　　排	140	24	622758	172932
茶　　山	156	21	1304355	253300

14-14 续表 1

(2010年)

单位：万元

镇　街	资产总额	流动资产	固定资产净值	负债总额
莞　城	980140	402151	415977	564467
石　龙	996759	729371	209315	486644
虎　门	3701976	2527173	939244	2079013
东　城	2574453	1656120	789669	1444314
万　江	834538	566613	160852	555865
南　城	1788472	1280891	396326	1051406
中　堂	1581047	944829	531311	946515
望牛墩	495423	340266	128691	348331
麻　涌	4699865	2388875	1683733	2929170
石　碣	1781230	1312925	397822	988630
高　埗	1127156	764317	306954	724842
道　滘	882599	672833	181184	420114
洪　梅	1831189	1169269	523132	1070146
沙　田	1154762	794188	280417	717649
厚　街	2435422	1809316	525885	1545553
长　安	4341860	2838117	1300391	3048464
寮　步	2371529	1759754	492462	1492634
大岭山	1909130	1292736	477509	1210273
大　朗	1937681	1431665	417074	1292602
黄　江	1437329	992621	382203	909294
樟木头	762462	493334	236335	422677
清　溪	3063990	2038491	718476	1593827
塘　厦	2999365	2144452	679851	1787453
凤　岗	1537179	962085	498003	847995
谢　岗	534763	361923	153273	333489
常　平	2511688	1778339	585729	1470336
桥　头	840687	604772	195347	541026
横　沥	727854	514774	182893	485833
东　坑	791635	553500	212127	523272
企　石	622974	484703	98968	414182
石　排	477071	350052	104598	290490
茶　山	1118263	750651	312490	647136

14-14 续表 2

(2010年)

单位：万元

镇街	主营业务收入	#主营业务税金及附加	利润总额	利税总额	本年应交增值税	职工平均人数（人）
莞城	953664	2583	68322	90958	20053	23812
石龙	1703096	1998	90677	121101	28426	39511
虎门	5003883	5503	225780	349144	117861	206298
东城	2927583	7960	201173	265512	56380	117623
万江	1009802	1738	39992	61773	20043	38839
南城	2302234	782	154793	206692	51117	60031
中堂	1785696	3038	199854	229987	27095	39355
望牛墩	669477	1048	36320	55037	17669	22103
麻涌	4707297	1822	262449	335947	71676	37893
石碣	3521662	1776	124463	143085	16846	100336
高埗	1517446	1353	69583	84546	13610	132832
道滘	1041573	1375	37182	59858	21301	43031
洪梅	1538661	518	132503	154251	21231	21162
沙田	1644118	790	82242	100610	17578	46465
厚街	3828964	5561	142664	180554	32328	190840
长安	5590724	5186	162125	254788	87477	272748
寮步	3896403	1859	165998	193149	25291	125900
大岭山	2163490	1501	39501	71815	30813	103121
大朗	2542148	4099	79433	119329	35798	102190
黄江	1763873	915	44435	58754	13404	85372
樟木头	805006	514	19693	29396	9189	48212
清溪	4257610	7889	232771	263396	22736	152536
塘厦	4369786	3504	182740	225505	39261	191711
凤岗	1744604	994	27702	44842	16146	100649
谢岗	572928	409	22188	29178	6582	32027
常平	2954001	2886	222047	252751	27818	124805
桥头	964649	1204	16116	25012	7693	48272
横沥	947504	424	33985	41760	7351	59392
东坑	1241704	643	29400	34069	4027	42182
企石	703712	654	12638	22353	9062	27484
石排	623575	745	17858	31150	12546	45953
茶山	1303024	2081	43259	67152	21813	45377

14-15 镇街规模以上工业企业主要经济效益指标（2010年）

Main Indicators on Economic Benefit of Industrial Enterprises above Designated Size by Town (2010)

镇　街	工业增加值率 (%)	总资产贡献率 (%)	资产负债率 (%)	流动资产周转率 (次/年)	成本费用利润率 (%)	全员劳动生产率 (元/人)	产品销售率 (%)
莞　城	23.1	10.6	57.6	2.4	7.7	94437	98.1
石　龙	17.2	12.2	48.8	2.3	5.6	75726	98.2
虎　门	22.9	9.8	56.2	2.0	4.7	57692	96.5
东　城	24.4	10.7	56.1	1.8	7.4	62934	96.7
万　江	21.5	8.2	66.6	1.8	4.1	55756	100.5
南　城	19.6	12.1	58.8	1.8	7.1	77757	96.5
中　堂	22.4	15.7	59.9	1.9	12.6	98200	103.7
望牛墩	20.8	11.8	70.3	2.0	5.7	62400	101.6
麻　涌	19.5	7.7	62.3	2.0	5.9	245534	98.7
石　碣	20.5	8.1	55.5	2.7	3.7	71950	100.2
高　埗	33.9	8.2	64.3	2.0	4.8	38872	99.3
道　滘	22.7	7.2	47.6	1.6	3.7	55088	100.2
洪　梅	17.5	8.7	58.4	1.3	9.4	127776	99.9
沙　田	22.2	9.3	62.2	2.1	5.2	79906	98.8
厚　街	21.5	7.8	63.5	2.1	3.9	44216	97.8
长　安	22.2	6.1	70.2	2.0	3.0	46764	97.9
寮　步	17.2	8.6	62.9	2.2	4.4	54653	97.6
大岭山	21.9	4.2	63.4	1.7	1.9	45989	99.8
大　朗	24.5	6.6	66.7	1.8	3.2	62149	98.3
黄　江	22.1	4.3	63.3	1.8	2.6	45875	100.5
樟木头	18.2	4.7	55.4	1.6	2.4	31676	96.4
清　溪	19.5	8.6	52.0	2.1	5.8	55125	98.9
塘　厦	22.9	7.7	59.6	2.0	4.4	53006	98.4
凤　岗	22.7	3.1	55.2	1.8	1.6	39574	99.5
谢　岗	22.3	5.9	62.4	1.6	4.0	40244	99.4
常　平	22.8	10.3	58.5	1.7	8.1	54229	99.7
桥　头	17.9	3.4	64.4	1.6	1.7	36039	99.7
横　沥	24.1	6.1	66.8	1.8	3.8	38656	100.7
东　坑	18.1	4.5	66.1	2.2	2.4	53811	99.5
企　石	17.2	4.5	66.5	1.5	1.8	43773	100.8
石　排	27.9	7.0	60.9	1.8	2.9	37632	100.4
茶　山	19.1	6.5	57.9	1.7	3.4	55821	98.2

14-16 镇街规模以上工业企业R&D人员情况(2010年)

R&D Personnel of Industrial Enterprises above Designated Size by Town (2010)

镇 街	有R&D活动的工业企业数（个）	R&D人员合计（人）	#参加项目人员	#女性	#研究人员	#全时人员	非全时人员
全市总计	**436**	**36064**	**32438**	**6393**	**6095**	**27710**	**8354**
莞 城	5	300	222	35	161	164	136
石 龙	13	578	550	116	124	482	96
虎 门	39	2134	1809	322	425	1395	739
东 城	21	2713	2475	792	573	2634	79
万 江	13	889	795	151	191	757	132
南 城	13	841	764	186	275	688	153
中 堂	8	299	221	70	102	200	99
望 牛 墩	2	45	45	6	4	42	3
麻 涌	24	1597	1464	214	295	829	768
石 碣	19	7526	6908	345	748	6793	733
高 埗	4	53	49	7	13	39	14
道 滘	10	303	289	41	60	241	62
洪 梅	6	308	273	41	54	116	192
沙 田	12	310	297	38	59	208	102
厚 街	14	749	657	46	134	596	153
长 安	27	3191	2892	720	264	2375	816
寮 步	22	869	762	156	234	682	187
大 岭 山	11	375	326	35	40	226	149
大 朗	20	1621	1494	466	168	1496	125
黄 江	14	838	695	108	166	386	452
樟 木 头	11	478	446	43	78	210	268
清 溪	12	1375	1296	220	189	1208	167
塘 厦	33	3849	3469	1190	483	2451	1398
凤 岗	8	575	489	161	150	524	51
谢 岗	5	222	205	32	91	185	37
常 平	19	1355	1200	285	368	1119	236
桥 头	7	100	99	12	16	52	48
横 沥	7	216	186	43	50	168	48
东 坑	3	42	40	2	6	6	36
企 石	7	607	592	112	129	176	431
石 排	9	259	227	43	36	185	74
茶 山	10	245	226	58	52	149	96
松 山 湖	8	1202	976	297	357	928	274

14-17 镇街规模以上工业企业R&D人员全时当量情况(2010年)

R&D Personnel Full-time-equivalent of Industrial Enterprises above Designated Size by Town (2010)

镇　街	有R&D活动的工业企业数(个)	R&D人员全时当量(人年)	#研究人员	#应用研究人员	#试验发展人员
全市总计	**436**	**26634**	**4542**	**463**	**26171**
莞　城	5	300	161		300
石　龙	13	430	77		430
虎　门	39	1723	344	99	1624
东　城	21	804	331		804
万　江	13	668	127		668
南　城	13	525	99	29	495
中　堂	8	271	98		271
望牛墩	2	33	2		33
麻　涌	24	999	231	28	971
石　碣	19	6684	624	50	6634
高　埗	4	30	7		30
道　滘	10	239	52		239
洪　梅	6	296	41		296
沙　田	12	206	37	6	200
厚　街	14	599	109		599
长　安	27	2811	197	22	2789
寮　步	22	568	179	24	544
大岭山	11	308	27		308
大　朗	20	1504	149	68	1437
黄　江	14	634	107	34	601
樟木头	11	439	72		439
清　溪	12	1201	148	27	1174
塘　厦	33	1734	295	67	1667
凤　岗	8	557	144		557
谢　岗	5	164	69		164
常　平	19	901	306		901
桥　头	7	77	11		77
横　沥	7	188	38	2	186
东　坑	3	40	5		40
企　石	7	299	58		299
石　排	9	118	17		118
茶　山	10	192	38	7	184
松山湖	8	1089	343		1089

14-18 镇街规模以上工业企业R&D经费情况(2010年)

The R&D Funds of Industrial Enterprises above Designated Size by Town (2010)

镇街	R&D经费内部支出合计(万元)	按活动类型分组		按资金来源分组			R&D经费外部支出合计(万元)
		应用研究支出	试验发展支出	政府资金	企业资金	境外资金	
全市总计	**495099**	**9740**	**485360**	**20388**	**455496**	**10021**	**11050**
莞城	4431		4431	778	3566		50
石龙	8097		8097	1134	6963		121
虎门	27350	1687	25663	1688	23966	1696	772
东城	43831		43831	1846	41040	944	307
万江	19360		19360	1162	18105	43	473
南城	18494	313	18182	756	17668		2227
中堂	3832		3832	149	3683		16
望牛墩	672		672	20	652		
麻涌	39871	974	38898	837	38918		774
石碣	79100	330	78770	624	73980	3679	996
高埗	1669		1669	26	1491		54
道滘	2820		2820	238	2572		35
洪梅	8541		8541	73	8468		53
沙田	6958	858	6100	199	6600	160	20
厚街	7804		7804	468	7336		22
长安	31522	163	31359	1244	26293	459	1388
寮步	15829	1092	14737	730	14418	681	504
大岭山	4075		4075	284	3739	34	2
大朗	12975	1436	11539	894	12081		170
黄江	12807	249	12558	1162	10943		
樟木头	3191		3191	15	3142		
清溪	14043	1329	12714	950	13094		255
塘厦	42537	402	42136	975	38293	736	797
凤岗	5810		5810	68	5423		79
谢岗	2918		2918	159	1888	843	23
常平	14352	453	13899	571	12393	747	262
桥头	1143		1143		1053		29
横沥	2519	83	2436	333	2185		11
东坑	1604		1604		1604		10
企石	12069		12069	1647	10422		191
石排	3686		3686	92	3594		
茶山	5422	373	5049	159	5263		36
松山湖	35769		35769	1108	34661		1375

14-19 镇街规模以上工业企业全部R&D项目情况(2010年)

Basic Statistics on R&D Projects of Industrial Enterprises above Designated Size by Town (2010)

镇街	项目数(个)	参加项目人员(人)	项目人员折合全时当量(人年)	全部项目经费内部支出(万元)
全市总计	**1955**	**32438**	**24050**	**444812**
莞城	21	222	222	3181
石龙	44	550	411	7865
虎门	230	1809	1436	24636
东城	104	2475	680	42572
万江	54	795	591	11373
南城	76	764	492	16475
中堂	27	221	197	3748
望牛墩	5	45	33	672
麻涌	93	1464	926	36835
石碣	102	6908	6339	76581
高埗	5	49	28	1646
道滘	35	289	230	2455
洪梅	20	273	263	8151
沙田	34	297	198	6833
厚街	73	657	521	7157
长安	134	2892	2550	28747
寮步	80	762	519	13960
大岭山	44	326	270	3491
大朗	73	1494	1389	12419
黄江	55	695	520	7181
樟木头	25	446	410	2792
清溪	92	1296	1143	11758
塘厦	119	3469	1531	34177
凤岗	25	489	473	5711
谢岗	12	205	151	2886
常平	162	1200	797	13704
桥头	15	99	76	1131
横沥	22	186	162	2246
东坑	7	40	38	1604
企石	27	592	290	10799
石排	23	227	105	3113
茶山	18	226	177	4550
松山湖	99	976	884	34362

14-20 镇街规模以上工业企业办科技机构情况(2010年)

Basic Statistics on Scientific and Technological Institutions of Industrial Enterprises above Designated Size by Town (2010)

镇街	有科技机构的工业企业数（个）	机构数（个）	机构人员合计（人）	#博士毕业	#硕士毕业	#本科毕业	机构经费支出（万元）
全市总计	**314**	**376**	**26376**	**287**	**1071**	**10105**	**330015**
莞城	2	2	127	1	3	77	1473
石龙	10	11	536	7	18	163	7261
虎门	24	26	1517	24	86	554	15151
东城	17	22	2872	11	46	984	36961
万江	8	9	604	4	26	286	12551
南城	12	16	387	10	37	291	9462
中堂	5	5	260	1	16	119	3032
望牛墩	2	2	45	3	3	17	673
麻涌	20	24	2301	14	70	594	30629
石碣	13	13	3565	8	31	1107	43855
高埗	3	4	143		4	98	803
道滘	8	8	345	5	12	88	2434
洪梅	3	6	798		3	102	528
沙田	8	9	267	1	4	107	3065
厚街	14	19	928	10	18	303	8717
长安	11	13	870	6	36	540	14836
寮步	15	21	753	8	49	290	11293
大岭山	8	10	233	3	19	102	4744
大朗	15	16	1107	11	32	767	10984
黄江	13	14	887	10	39	466	8176
樟木头	8	8	262	2	13	115	1566
清溪	13	15	1435	17	21	336	11969
塘厦	18	23	1647	15	44	659	9064
凤岗	7	9	685	2	28	203	3384
谢岗	4	4	92	2	1	80	1413
常平	14	17	643	22	46	283	6062
桥头	3	3	29	2	1	21	272
横沥	7	9	265	4	8	88	2422
东坑	3	3	34		4	15	1796
企石	6	10	339	11	18	172	7601
石排	3	3	140	4	5	30	1630
茶山	9	10	247	4	5	144	1233
松山湖	8	12	2013	65	325	904	54976

14-21 镇街规模以上工业企业高新技术产品情况(2010年)

Basic Statistics on High-tech Products of Industrial Enterprises above Designated Size by Town (2010)

镇　街	高新产品个数(个)	高新产品产值(万元)	高新产品销售收入(万元)	#高新产品出口销售收入	高新产品实现利税(万元)
全市总计	**1430**	**23536957**	**23167434**	**15108731**	**1168241**
莞　城	34	371195	350288	127561	33651
石　龙	51	1290337	1245631	653839	76000
虎　门	117	967915	932021	480807	42946
东　城	66	1132680	1082247	698589	116890
万　江	54	372923	380910	78859	30943
南　城	37	755184	712712	320810	46294
中　堂	17	49387	48280	4847	3350
望牛墩	13	67360	67652	37095	3608
麻　涌	16	288642	289230	126426	25591
石　碣	110	2236262	2263787	1945164	100101
高　埗	18	518656	515526	332983	33109
道　滘	22	93402	94355	33057	3149
洪　梅	6	15707	14168		2010
沙　田	19	59527	58303	20026	2491
厚　街	39	885187	878748	778777	42922
长　安	169	2630442	2567120	1378265	89665
寮　步	58	1974363	1929588	1814774	60108
大岭山	67	728772	715035	353433	90555
大　朗	52	428299	407519	138036	34124
黄　江	26	805046	832071	712377	23082
樟木头	27	175541	157743	114696	4849
清　溪	54	1220752	1190184	1180813	33613
塘　厦	78	1382266	1380488	1129933	21589
凤　岗	30	418562	413413	258050	30004
谢　岗	17	146908	145343	111718	3083
常　平	86	1355223	1356373	1153031	61004
桥　头	28	110229	110471	74747	3378
横　沥	24	216774	217775	169444	13750
东　坑	15	376971	375598	306397	8303
企　石	10	22487	23574	10815	1456
石　排	22	103878	103581	51980	5489
茶　山	27	431703	419811	213441	14996
松山湖	21	1904377	1887893	297940	106138

14-22 镇街固定资产投资总额（2010年）

Total Investment in Fixed Assets by Town(2010)

单位：万元

镇　街	全社会固定资产投资	第二产业	#工　业	第三产业	民营
莞　城	165197	57172	57085	108025	84187
石　龙	194445	41691	41691	152754	77716
虎　门	722791	214939	214939	507852	459541
东　城	529521	119536	119536	409985	237035
万　江	228008	96425	95125	131583	163712
南　城	659114	134522	134522	524592	262993
中　堂	196167	76198	76198	119899	159922
望牛墩	119540	76584	76584	42661	64910
麻　涌	284849	171532	171532	113317	131838
石　碣	171208	72892	72892	98316	75189
高　埗	175654	71676	71676	103978	92423
道　滘	117897	43974	43874	73308	93275
洪　梅	298750	168283	168283	130467	192025
沙　田	203184	102083	101410	101101	91842
厚　街	378074	158773	158773	219301	193012
长　安	505163	132836	132836	372327	294187
寮　步	241274	88529	88529	152745	100844
大岭山	326038	91702	91702	234336	212063
大　朗	391952	139786	139786	252166	242599
黄　江	251363	111422	111422	139941	105994
樟木头	159721	33295	32874	126426	77194
清　溪	219724	136580	136580	82894	79248
塘　厦	271924	59887	59887	212037	69708
凤　岗	310244	109585	109585	200659	154227
谢　岗	85586	62515	62515	23071	25727
常　平	299915	47778	47778	252137	217550
桥　头	126566	91475	91475	35091	52399
横　沥	109725	55437	55437	54288	55352
东　坑	110282	61798	61798	48484	55939
企　石	56643	15864	15864	40779	43735
石　排	174179	86127	85712	87360	47294
茶　山	173325	105052	104722	68273	90493
松山湖	237169	81966	81966	155203	32542

14-23 镇街邮电局、所通信能力及服务网点(2009-2010年)

Communication Capacity and Service Establishments of Telecommunication Offices by Town (2009-2010)

镇　街	邮电局(所、综合营业厅)(处)		服务网点(含报刊亭)(处)		固定电话用户(含小灵通)(户)	
	2009年	2010年	2009年	2010年	2009年	2010年
全市总计	**546**	**555**	**2884**	**2916**	**3783993**	**3324166**
市　区	68	68	501	497	1068619	761545
石　龙	13	13	51	49	88613	84263
虎　门	35	36	234	232	234892	219265
中　堂	9	9	55	57	60311	51254
望牛墩	5	4	23	23	31460	27283
麻　涌	4	6	18	21	41759	36237
石　碣	26	26	91	87	88743	78810
高　埗	12	12	53	50	43436	39219
道　滘	7	7	38	40	49467	44691
洪　梅	4	4	14	16	22331	19523
沙　田	10	9	46	48	46892	40998
厚　街	30	30	164	164	184767	169658
长　安	41	42	254	257	234830	221734
寮　步	19	19	94	98	110901	104412
大岭山	19	19	91	95	74564	70008
大　朗	19	20	117	119	138082	134157
黄　江	14	15	80	82	91769	86574
樟木头	16	16	82	83	75931	64361
清　溪	20	21	114	116	106105	95309
塘　厦	33	34	146	150	150228	139256
凤　岗	26	23	88	83	95527	88055
谢　岗	7	7	42	45	34095	29659
常　平	34	37	169	176	172123	160024
桥　头	13	13	66	67	65064	56518
横　沥	16	17	55	56	66433	58087
东　坑	11	11	37	38	42630	36586
企　石	9	9	45	48	45987	40267
石　排	12	12	64	65	61139	53533
茶　山	14	14	52	52	76501	74941

注：市区指莞城、南城、东城、万江四个街道。

14-24 镇街社会消费品零售总额（2010年）

Total Retail Sales of Consumer Goods by Town (2010)

镇　街	社会消费品零售总额（万元）	限额以上批发零售和住宿餐饮业		
		企业数（个）	年末从业人员（人）	销售额/营业额（万元）
莞　城	899828	197	9348	1834109
石　龙	230009	66	2401	132630
虎　门	1009489	238	10800	533356
东　城	727171	199	9936	1566464
万　江	319865	105	4209	413743
南　城	1166657	209	16904	2770566
中　堂	157159	59	2618	363111
望牛墩	48853	25	530	181023
麻　涌	73891	28	896	128639
石　碣	177018	55	2487	599647
高　埗	137637	52	1858	185528
道　滘	91305	60	2526	159894
洪　梅	35895	17	780	26630
沙　田	112983	67	1837	679970
厚　街	678036	205	10677	459789
长　安	544764	201	7596	453554
寮　步	1020929	129	5976	1115053
大岭山	335201	51	2477	160913
大　朗	404381	133	4698	489397
黄　江	188626	52	3940	121750
樟木头	330520	97	4423	495208
清　溪	276625	85	2181	75532
塘　厦	480527	102	5039	587358
凤　岗	222052	93	3262	214831
谢　岗	68954	30	544	185798
常　平	583649	241	8418	405499
桥　头	146777	73	2406	75159
横　沥	152151	62	1154	48805
东　坑	85875	45	870	47021
企　石	83592	48	834	30663
石　排	162460	45	714	69096
茶　山	162570	62	1679	171878
松山湖	9726	13	1076	355143

注：限额以上批发零售和住宿餐饮业企业数为产业活动单位数，不是法人企业数。

14-25 镇街注册工商企业及个体户数（2010年）

Registered Industrial & Commercial Enterprises and Self-employed Individuals by Town (2010)

单位：户

镇　街	总户数	国有集体	三资企业	三来一补	私营企业	个体户
全市总计	**497260**	**12451**	**10490**	**4887**	**89037**	**380395**
莞　城	15684	714	223	18	3814	10915
石　龙	8904	248	110	29	832	7685
虎　门	51833	649	721	255	6051	44157
东　城	34773	1035	614	159	7898	25067
万　江	14592	330	207	41	3771	10243
南　城	21992	994	509	34	7764	12691
中　堂	8999	294	92	28	1259	7326
望牛墩	3157	144	105	20	555	2333
麻　涌	4195	207	76	20	607	3285
石　碣	13219	279	186	156	2013	10585
高　埗	7638	203	155	48	1007	6225
道　滘	5551	176	173	47	1220	3935
洪　梅	2228	83	77	11	292	1765
沙　田	7302	279	205	22	1198	5598
厚　街	30088	449	567	185	4335	24552
长　安	46152	735	944	665	10167	33641
寮　步	20113	542	409	149	4327	14686
大岭山	18857	343	326	89	3102	14997
大　朗	21451	487	379	209	3097	17279
黄　江	11129	295	324	171	2366	7973
樟木头	13292	317	214	114	2208	10439
清　溪	13842	238	531	283	1968	10822
塘　厦	23562	458	810	424	4813	17057
凤　岗	16711	367	404	480	2244	13216
谢　岗	5230	128	188	111	658	4145
常　平	22939	622	573	316	3637	17791
桥　头	8980	265	297	139	1345	6934
横　沥	10400	282	329	191	1604	7994
东　坑	5575	248	136	110	782	4299
企　石	6546	269	151	91	985	5050
石　排	10851	279	211	145	1374	8842
茶　山	10789	326	188	127	1423	8725
松山湖	686	166	56		321	143

注:本表数据来源于市工商局。

14-26 镇街集市贸易市场数及私营个体户注册资金额(2009-2010年)

Fair Trades and Registered Capital of Private Enterprises & Self-employed Individuals by Town (2009-2010)

镇 街	集市贸易市场数(个)		个体工商户注册资金额(万元)		私营企业注册资金额(万元)	
	2009年	2010年	2009年	2010年	2009年	2010年
全市总计	**923**	**792**	**884958**	**851416**	**10215756**	**12049270**
莞 城	41	28	23337	19560	833668	902764
石 龙	15	13	10834	11951	135396	168064
虎 门	95	77	86049	90668	678679	773379
东 城	72	57	47243	47339	1205057	1344802
万 江	41	33	24237	22389	406859	473474
南 城	31	31	20664	23369	1585654	1772515
中 堂	26	22	19037	18347	182020	215908
望牛墩	8	7	6349	6361	71589	84017
麻 涌	17	14	7133	7637	112191	147227
石 碣	28	21	21313	22517	130666	145934
高 埗	14	13	11877	13627	144425	161587
道 滘	12	10	12029	11559	130511	175758
洪 梅	3	4	3045	3015	60562	78000
沙 田	22	21	12098	13834	176957	209840
厚 街	53	50	50605	53051	510579	649934
长 安	51	46	79310	71128	628921	776228
寮 步	41	32	29157	30255	454272	532916
大岭山	22	17	43309	33361	197154	250459
大 朗	29	25	43093	44905	287323	342680
黄 江	29	26	19122	18806	170843	203708
樟木头	30	24	21570	21536	120164	161989
清 溪	22	20	19039	20086	131484	172901
塘 厦	32	27	37397	34851	417246	530896
凤 岗	21	22	25748	28448	161983	206664
谢 岗	8	8	10693	10870	51673	64422
常 平	42	40	85514	55223	321045	392536
桥 头	21	16	19220	18606	151088	173397
横 沥	20	17	19893	19766	115676	139932
东 坑	16	16	11014	12002	85573	117178
企 石	15	14	15142	15607	132718	153408
石 排	25	22	28640	27294	88434	111860
茶 山	21	19	21037	23000	127506	169827
松山湖			197	449	154576	245066

注:本表数据来源于市工商局。

14-27 镇街来料加工装配签约宗数、出口值及引进设备价值（2010年）

Contracts of Processing and Assembling of Import Materials, Export Value and Value of Equipments Imported by Town (2010)

镇　街	新签协议宗数（宗）	累计投产宗数（宗）	出口值（万美元）	引进设备价值（万美元）
莞　城		14	5334	33
石　龙		14	8534	144
虎　门		201	18231	176
东　城		93	15764	106
万　江		49	3615	29
南　城		31	115954	6721
中　堂		20	3452	1
望牛墩		11	2125	
麻　涌		17	1278	
石　碣		127	15792	282
高　埗		46	73521	1408
道　滘		34	6632	53
洪　梅		9	5640	19
沙　田		10	450	
厚　街		152	112858	977
长　安	2	670	250798	10555
寮　步		70	167642	448
大岭山		70	82665	2920
大　朗		184	26596	1726
黄　江		175	270825	8283
樟木头		98	43748	480
清　溪		238	186023	3079
塘　厦	1	348	60254	2081
凤　岗	1	413	66999	1436
谢　岗		105	8630	782
常　平		251	42639	1463
桥　头		109	88923	1940
横　沥	2	160	26945	2108
东　坑		91	27610	345
企　石		63	3006	9
石　排		121	9184	1304
茶　山		94	16469	203

注：本表为外经贸局口径。

14-28 镇街“三资”企业签约、实际利用外资及出口值(新口径)(2010年)

Contracts, Foreign Capital Actually Utilized and Export Value of Enterprises with Foreign Investment by Town (2010)

镇　街	签约宗数(宗)	投产企业宗数(宗)	协议(合同)规定外商投资总额(万美元)	外商实际投资总额(万美元)	出口值(万美元)
莞　城	9	58	3589	2415	27878
石　龙	5	54	1499	6866	169358
虎　门	75	498	9560	11390	205864
东　城	28	326	13046	10923	175136
万　江	10	147	1030	1537	18608
南　城	26	197	7859	6755	41150
中　堂	3	80	491	2087	18806
望牛墩	9	108	3236	2254	13865
麻　涌	2	46	10710	25469	162265
石　碣	10	134	2000	5135	316954
高　埗	9	140	2746	5608	49432
道　滘	17	135	3130	1242	29786
洪　梅	4	57	7637	10145	18238
沙　田	13	132	2100	3009	73482
厚　街	43	382	14313	12120	386920
长　安	76	550	21155	20509	388581
寮　步	27	287	11343	8563	308381
大岭山	13	259	3056	11274	127747
大　朗	54	324	11096	11442	79199
黄　江	35	262	7463	11123	148352
樟木头	20	182	4065	5564	47076
清　溪	42	477	12688	15467	381873
塘　厦	48	628	14979	16043	300171
凤　岗	41	343	24909	13367	106547
谢　岗	20	164	4907	5022	36853
常　平	55	280	10070	6365	304167
桥　头	33	269	5052	3018	61277
横　沥	46	262	12904	8795	97259
东　坑	19	120	13264	5198	110787
企　石	15	108	2357	2673	32983
石　排	24	184	4225	4207	36557
茶　山	22	163	5096	6801	33529

注：本表为外经贸局口径。

14-29 镇街进出口总额（2009-2010年，海关口径）

Total Value of Exports and Imports by Town (2009-2010, Custom Statistics)

单位：万美元

镇街	2009年			2010年		
	进出口总额	进口	出口	进出口总额	进口	出口
莞城	85582	40686	44896	112212	50754	61458
石龙	194629	63959	130670	272041	93465	178576
虎门	295900	102666	193234	369333	142234	227099
东城	241425	84012	157413	373441	154607	218834
万江	37851	11650	26201	44842	13774	31068
南城	396951	255365	141587	563209	350966	212243
中堂	64313	37801	26512	76507	47189	29318
望牛墩	23724	9494	14230	28343	9331	19012
麻涌	279163	160068	119095	363189	199176	164013
石碣	407283	150471	256812	550904	214570	336334
高埗	158594	54513	104081	198511	69848	128663
道滘	59679	24857	34822	72156	33568	38588
洪梅	106517	86428	20089	159488	135083	24405
沙田	133146	67872	65273	186453	106939	79514
厚街	632162	217617	414546	784427	277270	507157
长安	856901	357322	499579	1149654	499704	649950
寮步	654579	272451	382128	940627	403534	537093
大岭山	300518	117480	183038	353467	135691	217776
大朗	215453	89158	126296	273352	112295	161057
黄江	650028	250790	399238	704122	282814	421308
樟木头	122033	47877	74156	151400	58980	92420
清溪	842272	344308	497963	968780	393677	575103
塘厦	511018	194792	316226	591603	223821	367782
凤岗	264985	105032	159953	320932	137308	183624
谢岗	49514	17324	32191	72620	27053	45567
常平	516360	221717	294643	603192	249694	353498
桥头	293935	110268	183668	248480	95428	153052
横沥	149721	54713	95009	192652	64329	128323
东坑	161084	67420	93664	245115	103078	142037
企石	35088	10260	24827	53068	16299	36769
石排	58601	16515	42086	72626	19908	52718
茶山	70211	30612	39599	97605	43150	54455

14-30 镇街实际利用外资（2009-2010年）

Foreign Capital Actually Utilized by Town (2009-2010)

单位：万美元

镇　　街	2009年	2010年	镇　　街	2009年	2010年
莞　　城	1989	2415	寮　　步	6488	8563
石　　龙	4446	6866	大 岭 山	10636	11274
虎　　门	10595	11390	大　　朗	7709	11442
东　　城	10131	10923	黄　　江	10493	11123
万　　江	3618	1537	樟 木 头	4070	5564
南　　城	6117	6755	清　　溪	15594	15467
中　　堂	1668	2087	塘　　厦	14705	16043
望 牛 墩	1871	2254	凤　　岗	10369	13367
麻　　涌	24114	25469	谢　　岗	4062	5022
石　　碣	4688	5135	常　　平	13167	6365
高　　埗	5203	5608	桥　　头	5934	3018
道　　滘	1547	1242	横　　沥	8038	8795
洪　　梅	10825	10145	东　　坑	4796	5198
沙　　田	6769	3009	企　　石	2333	2673
厚　　街	9917	12120	石　　排	4101	4207
长　　安	16062	20509	茶　　山	6330	6801

14-31 镇街工商税收总额（2009-2010年）

Taxes by Town (2009-2010)

单位：万元

镇街	2009年			2010年		
	工商税收总额	国税	地税	工商税收总额	国税	地税
莞城	283194	117527	165668	332872	159046	173826
石龙	90648	47080	43568	107372	55570	51802
虎门	294875	167357	127518	375602	227265	148337
东城	409819	181570	228249	468433	217508	250926
万江	90481	46878	43603	98898	55338	43560
南城	403738	134057	269681	491596	139932	351664
中堂	80296	63220	17076	93651	72187	21464
望牛墩	33077	24505	8572	49557	37803	11753
麻涌	141902	91278	50624	165502	106116	59387
石碣	115017	77819	37198	142838	88837	54001
高埗	65630	45980	19650	83324	57706	25619
道滘	62168	42541	19627	78408	55847	22561
洪梅	37022	28760	8261	41802	30467	11335
沙田	70505	42406	28098	82215	47759	34457
厚街	196626	110592	86033	245523	151094	94429
长安	297627	185970	111657	388497	254602	133895
寮步	165236	98908	66328	207707	129670	78037
大岭山	116655	69358	47296	150110	89818	60293
大朗	108582	67943	40639	139088	87125	51963
黄江	89158	55717	33441	108441	66151	42290
樟木头	60170	35837	24333	72119	42832	29288
清溪	121867	79997	41870	155687	96966	58721
塘厦	231760	115971	115789	295451	148998	146453
凤岗	125419	61146	64273	156927	80508	76419
谢岗	26452	17624	8828	35506	23457	12048
常平	176827	92095	84732	188201	93186	95015
桥头	54685	33891	20794	64461	40409	24053
横沥	54509	34994	19514	78913	53714	25199
东坑	39418	24837	14581	49934	29701	20234
企石	34949	23628	11321	42649	28817	13832
石排	43170	29825	13345	48281	33054	15227
茶山	70053	47294	22759	79876	54322	25555

14-32 镇街本级可支配财政收入和财政支出（2009-2010年）

Disposable Government Revenue and Expenditure by Town (2009-2010)

单位：万元

镇　　街	可支配财政收入		财政支出	
	2009年	2010年	2009年	2010年
莞　　城	62678	56626	58854	56865
石　　龙	46016	52727	45683	52010
虎　　门	143368	169952	140236	143662
东　　城	120067	138353	115288	132646
万　　江	50204	54033	54592	55407
南　　城	129219	154062	115052	115563
中　　堂	50262	55757	50245	54023
望 牛 墩	30595	33845	30459	33823
麻　　涌	49852	55622	49843	55622
石　　碣	40184	47054	40589	47037
高　　埗	35842	39141	35596	38842
道　　滘	48323	50046	48102	49602
洪　　梅	21541	23020	21564	23039
沙　　田	41230	44093	41557	38545
厚　　街	79103	93565	79101	93660
长　　安	123864	131282	124335	125357
寮　　步	79610	87284	79235	86202
大 岭 山	70502	77270	70128	77056
大　　朗	59843	64159	60311	62693
黄　　江	48715	104843	48633	104466
樟 木 头	38265	43794	67533	71637
清　　溪	50467	60191	51415	60737
塘　　厦	97842	113876	97614	113770
凤　　岗	52001	60044	48012	59017
谢　　岗	27543	30808	26351	31068
常　　平	89126	94628	90722	93458
桥　　头	35626	40533	48521	38798
横　　沥	40429	42368	41604	42357
东　　坑	41362	48245	41099	48078
企　　石	23806	26006	23791	26000
石　　排	36078	36685	35603	36576
茶　　山	40174	44297	40001	44766

14-33 镇街资产负债总额（2009-2010年）

Total Assets and Liabilities by Town (2009-2010)

单位：万元

镇　街	资产总额		负债总额	
	2009年	2010年	2009年	2010年
莞　城	479675	471634	153561	134020
石　龙	301583	295689	153871	146703
虎　门	826800	907252	64956	129739
东　城	242500	247500		
万　江	261766	284496	99694	116344
南　城	498392	508712	135739	87251
中　堂	330849	336504	164836	171279
望牛墩	169113	190694	100863	119232
麻　涌	209375	252382	96992	105555
石　碣	353126	355313	182181	175398
高　埗	183016	222424	94860	112753
道　滘	197778	217726	64277	95009
洪　梅	156272	125257	92982	100053
沙　田	270128	278508	95044	94338
厚　街	377148	393263	118648	141027
长　安	546912	593557	53005	54376
寮　步	277494	378749	88847	118069
大岭山	281317	314502	94226	116678
大　朗	206610	236617	34826	34363
黄　江	253963	290636	79312	93003
樟木头	248885	243045	149188	152033
清　溪	290077	308305	122940	123553
塘　厦	606634	679358	182578	203905
凤　岗	354382	397103	158325	180386
谢　岗	136487	161391	71750	84253
常　平	535082	591685	163922	165689
桥　头	177880	219675	79300	90981
横　沥	206051	230625	104282	127694
东　坑	202954	237399	113876	122805
企　石	154620	157720	59848	55983
石　排	208932	238128	75590	120235
茶　山	140001	335948	53561	92061

14-34 镇街各项人民币存贷款余额与城乡居民储蓄存款余额（2009-2010年）

Balance of Deposits and Loans by Town and Savings Deposit of Urban and Rural Household (2009-2010)

单位：万元

镇街	年末各项存款余额		年末各项贷款余额		城乡居民储蓄存款余额	
	2009年	2010年	2009年	2010年	2009年	2010年
莞城	6413744	6836386	5314985	4975504	2087825	2266112
石龙	1190569	1390116	488305	594022	808199	905687
虎门	4084004	4695398	1690341	2082215	3213867	3590249
东城	3849488	4816053	2508767	2501542	2188415	2611030
万江	1020666	1250488	758795	786033	725482	833149
南城	7028632	9162540	5790360	7409222	1858000	2233097
中堂	714301	834866	436289	581732	494051	574883
望牛墩	349813	395863	126699	162056	245156	281740
麻涌	567709	728228	262127	343243	302623	355550
石碣	1293160	1360772	427950	471764	846502	937744
高埗	621829	695656	146334	159044	432531	502032
道滘	518720	640928	170566	214599	375379	436287
洪梅	182227	255573	98322	129454	111857	142493
沙田	727804	869695	265791	348131	383528	430431
厚街	2567309	2937956	1838245	2044178	1894020	2143817
长安	3285949	4195678	1463433	1767091	2253195	2746995
寮步	1150222	1395674	574138	693107	781796	969146
大岭山	880373	1022520	433206	589130	622434	743551
大朗	1492982	1810578	768526	936551	1105730	1317177
黄江	876372	1081735	360363	478777	619018	755117
樟木头	844491	979395	566392	635996	664447	767445
清溪	1049565	1241391	407992	488079	710980	846646
塘厦	1813651	2245018	976916	1187364	1180713	1433273
凤岗	1215656	1396353	557951	641814	786894	933126
谢岗	324139	388859	97656	143019	228236	276067
常平	2074004	2386186	994423	1092646	1478324	1734354
桥头	612109	721245	283866	339180	499079	578266
横沥	618282	724335	247083	291954	484785	569499
东坑	455310	518500	166085	179983	337088	384164
企石	398386	485141	243495	291320	309910	367920
石排	619247	698930	199583	241336	456423	522528
茶山	743269	870723	225654	267398	530999	625931

注：本表是按人民银行东莞支行口径。

14-35 镇街普通中学情况（2010年）

Basic Statistics on Regular Secondary Schools by Town (2010)

镇街	学校数（所）	毕业生数（人）	#普通高中	招生数（人）	#普通高中	在校学生数（人）	#普通高中	教职工数（人）	#专任教师
全市总计	**190**	**73810**	**20816**	**93196**	**24668**	**258276**	**70398**	**16946**	**14572**
莞城									
石龙	4	1413		1589		4662		307	271
虎门	7	3712	242	4353	329	12347	1026	901	822
东城	9	2625		3587		9521		535	491
万江	7	3291	651	3618	692	10841	2237	633	573
南城	7	2466	617	3328	720	8985	2082	634	513
中堂	7	2188	135	2563	182	6844	474	466	388
望牛墩	3	1436		1491		4443		224	208
麻涌	3	1530	294	1433	377	4577	1065	327	297
石碣	8	1518	218	2390	315	6254	840	385	337
高埗	5	1045		1281		3509		222	196
道滘	4	1665	477	2058	492	5966	1481	376	294
洪梅	1	390		231		858		82	61
沙田	3	1170	254	1538	552	4108	1191	310	282
厚街	8	2161		2744		7540		488	435
长安	5	1683		2773		7014		425	352
寮步	7	2642	406	3741	499	10277	1413	592	512
大岭山	6	1943	313	2256	329	6235	973	398	320
大朗	7	2281	417	3345	536	8981	1600	551	471
黄江	3	905		1072		2856		174	162
樟木头	3	1063	316	1452	315	3929	908	252	213
清溪	6	1252	190	1551		4062		307	264
塘厦	4	1600		2773	340	7099	511	400	328
凤岗	8	1777	492	2768	242	7060	797	501	397
谢岗	3	676		681		2241		148	126
常平	11	1976		3072		7864		510	416
桥头	5	1182	173	2166	490	5717	1342	506	378
横沥	4	743	90	1355		3345		260	199
东坑	4	957		1313		3351		227	175
企石	3	1292	344	1602	325	4265	986	288	262
石排	4	1082		1215		3378		247	215
茶山	7	1676	434	2802	731	7217	1919	438	381
松山湖	1			198		339		4806	4208

14-36 镇街小学情况（2010年）

Basic Statistics on Primary Schools by Town (2010)

镇 街	学校数 (所)	毕业生数 (人)	招生数 (人)	在校学生数 (人)	教职工数 (人)	
						#专任教师
全市总计	**330**	**77429**	**108900**	**552377**	**28298**	**23733**
莞 城	9	2429	2162	13126	790	756
石 龙	6	1666	1666	9796	488	448
虎 门	24	5634	6464	35944	2033	1670
东 城	14	4420	6416	31530	1446	1280
万 江	16	3720	4573	24237	1108	1026
南 城	10	2643	4136	20703	1093	935
中 堂	8	2285	2737	14396	808	692
望 牛 墩	4	1214	950	5907	392	363
麻 涌	8	1249	1154	6713	457	418
石 碣	8	2482	3637	18148	747	680
高 埗	6	1329	2042	10236	511	469
道 滘	6	1642	1769	10284	504	413
洪 梅	3	355	244	1944	136	119
沙 田	4	1084	1227	7120	375	325
厚 街	14	3377	4351	23159	1354	1133
长 安	22	3512	7911	34626	1708	1374
寮 步	17	3368	5372	25908	1249	1011
大 岭 山	9	2140	3229	15724	832	646
大 朗	18	3351	5699	27394	1174	990
黄 江	9	1469	2482	11586	538	483
樟 木 头	7	1768	2390	11971	546	444
清 溪	9	1909	3362	16223	767	699
塘 厦	13	3450	5041	26340	1348	1060
凤 岗	15	2808	5070	24303	1151	969
谢 岗	3	881	1196	6186	297	260
常 平	18	3972	5830	29363	1325	1160
桥 头	7	1707	2619	12808	706	556
横 沥	7	1701	2954	13481	713	573
东 坑	7	1533	2548	11914	565	447
企 石	8	1547	1917	9828	483	429
石 排	9	1797	2400	11916	664	567
茶 山	7	2311	3036	15288	738	666
松 山 湖	2	334	480	2472	168	150

14-37 镇街卫生事业机构、床位及人员数（2010年）

Number of Health care Institutions, Beds and Personnel by Town (2010)

镇街	机构数（个）	#医院	病床床位（张）	卫生工作人员（人）	#卫生技术人员	#执业(助理)医师	注册护士	药剂人员	检验人员
全市总计	**2229**	**71**	**19980**	**46102**	**37487**	**13214**	**14689**	**2284**	**1412**
莞城	59	7	2993	6008	5045	1661	2171	367	185
石龙	28	3	1478	2111	1636	546	647	104	44
虎门	187	7	1834	4172	3509	1185	1422	229	149
东城	159	5	1491	2879	2343	839	963	129	111
万江	64	3	320	991	744	265	283	50	29
南城	89	4	1088	3279	2357	945	906	92	130
中堂	52	1	271	639	574	185	220	20	16
望牛墩	33	1	120	347	284	78	76	21	7
麻涌	26	2	400	482	404	139	158	27	17
石碣	42	1	265	826	702	250	295	69	34
高埗	60	2	298	761	591	214	216	28	19
道滘	64	1	120	515	428	135	114	34	20
洪梅	12	1	50	259	210	57	73	18	12
沙田	48	2	165	541	431	154	137	31	15
厚街	133	2	1022	2289	1941	670	837	87	63
长安	112	5	989	2539	2065	742	826	132	73
寮步	116	2	784	1763	1384	495	541	85	38
大岭山	93	2	330	1023	865	300	328	65	30
大朗	111	3	732	1515	1235	463	458	74	38
黄江	51	2	458	1211	948	353	343	73	47
樟木头	35	2	470	1024	823	287	343	48	35
清溪	74	1	474	1194	961	362	349	45	44
塘厦	81	2	617	1742	1458	538	540	104	39
凤岗	57	2	952	1618	1295	454	496	69	54
谢岗	23	1	120	289	243	101	87	12	9
常平	133	1	356	1575	1299	506	480	66	42
桥头	52	1	350	752	649	221	234	32	18
横沥	64	1	305	844	667	235	229	33	20
东坑	47	1	130	558	469	161	166	23	18
企石	35	1	448	739	610	182	242	41	16
石排	43	1	250	867	683	241	284	39	17
茶山	44	1	300	661	564	223	203	29	18
松山湖	2			89	70	27	22	8	5

注：本表不含省、市属医疗机构。

14-38 镇街优抚和社会救济基本情况（2010年）

Basic Statistics on Special Care and Social Relief by Town(2010)

镇　街	敬老院个　数（个）	敬老院供养人数（人）	最低生活保障户数（户）	最低生活保障人数（人）	最低生活保障费支出（万元）
全市总计	**35**	**894**	**13813**	**34428**	**6595.71**
莞　城	1	32	456	1184	201.80
石　龙	1	33	342	885	202.31
虎　门	1	16	488	1289	321.08
东　城	1	22	52	148	22.01
万　江	1	52	1015	2131	411.98
南　城		6	76	180	37.63
中　堂	1	13	1216	2940	549.49
望牛墩	1	97	530	1460	361.13
麻　涌	1	12	1844	3805	700.90
石　碣	1	38	119	356	73.62
高　埗	1	23	362	1082	157.46
道　滘	1	43	651	1664	339.77
洪　梅	1	31	645	1320	288.48
沙　田	1	35	1020	1893	426.90
厚　街	2	36	631	1832	273.35
长　安	3	25	8	22	3.31
寮　步	1	28	430	1249	149.38
大岭山	1	29	241	709	119.43
大　朗	1	34	391	1155	244.95
黄　江	1	36	160	429	79.80
樟木头	1	60	129	354	76.61
清　溪	1	33	208	543	109.74
塘　厦	1	17	178	405	84.02
凤　岗	2	8	23	60	12.54
谢　岗	1	13	294	1050	137.97
常　平	1	16	260	620	127.20
桥　头	1	32	218	562	74.33
横　沥	1	9	307	827	182.63
东　坑	1	26	327	927	175.28
企　石	1	14	438	1267	241.28
石　排	1	8	529	1438	317.37
茶　山	1	17	225	642	91.95

14-39 镇街专利申请与授权数（2010年）

Basic Statistics on Patents Application Accepted and Granted by Town (2010)

单位：件

镇街	专利申请数	#发明	实用新型	外观设计	专利授权数	#发明	实用新型	外观设计
全市总计	**21654**	**3143**	**7677**	**10834**	**20397**	**442**	**7529**	**12426**
莞城	360	130	134	96	278	13	152	113
石龙	169	30	99	40	177	11	104	62
虎门	784	81	401	302	804	20	342	442
东城	5363	664	534	4165	3719	41	539	3139
万江	507	117	223	167	493	17	224	252
南城	1305	339	581	385	845	45	461	339
中堂	121	26	62	33	125	5	55	65
望牛墩	72	14	42	16	68	3	31	34
麻涌	140	34	71	35	170	15	116	39
石碣	344	44	189	111	332	6	218	108
高埗	199	44	76	79	211	21	87	103
道滘	474	46	145	283	476	6	118	352
洪梅	78	15	26	37	69	1	24	44
沙田	281	22	105	154	248	4	69	175
厚街	1393	76	374	943	2031	9	391	1631
长安	1586	190	769	627	2388	51	856	1481
寮步	740	123	441	176	843	13	434	396
大岭山	908	55	160	693	881	6	152	723
大朗	325	49	168	108	384	15	250	119
黄江	440	61	293	86	423	10	236	177
樟木头	274	27	89	158	365	6	121	238
清溪	567	70	353	144	675	8	318	349
塘厦	975	121	529	325	799	15	460	324
凤岗	285	19	123	143	275	8	137	130
谢岗	48	7	17	24	60	2	37	21
常平	664	117	323	224	641	22	311	308
桥头	271	34	118	119	243	2	112	129
横沥	626	27	204	395	366	1	180	185
东坑	560	69	293	198	650	8	407	235
企石	198	25	113	60	256	7	125	124
石排	359	25	136	198	452	5	110	337
茶山	313	40	167	106	281	2	148	131
松山湖	913	397	313	203	339	43	197	99
其他	12	5	6	1	30	1	7	22

14-40 镇街总用电量和总供水量（2009-2010年）

Gross Electicity Comsumption and Water Supply by Town(2009-2010)

镇　　街	总用电量（万千瓦时）		总供水量（万吨）	
	2009年	2010年	2009年	2010年
莞　　城	47942	53903	18154	17699
石　　龙	65765	70228	2464	2489
虎　　门	352310	390844	12023	11996
东　　城	166402	256029	7710	7015
万　　江	107257	119324	4746	4831
南　　城	88056	95732	1028	1139
中　　堂	232846	269112	2721	2937
望 牛 墩	58063	61681	1761	1765
麻　　涌	92288	116520	2278	2458
石　　碣	141371	155976	3795	3855
高　　埗	117113	133411	2961	3066
道　　滘	104837	125724	3096	3282
洪　　梅	46272	52489	1400	1528
沙　　田	92370	105815	3235	3738
厚　　街	282486	327126	11079	11069
长　　安	473889	540192	12631	13277
寮　　步	189748	219715	4410	4634
大 岭 山	145699	169086	3884	3967
大　　朗	175774	205043	7384	7584
黄　　江	140385	159909	5354	5124
樟 木 头	82898	91847	1772	1883
清　　溪	200401	232463	5966	6163
塘　　厦	270126	313145	9225	9869
凤　　岗	167916	205623	4734	4758
谢　　岗	55327	66888	1939	2039
常　　平	232874	264291	10732	10351
桥　　头	113423	127799	3336	3240
横　　沥	102224	119845	3435	3488
东　　坑	69358	79618	2222	2260
企　　石	62449	71391	1625	1636
石　　排	94567	109237	2985	3029
茶　　山	114743	128337	4202	4272

十五、村（居）委会主要指标

Main Indicatory of Villagers' (Neighborhood) Committees

15 村(居)委会主要指标（2010年）

Main Indicators of Villagers'(Neighborhood) Committees (2010)

村(居)委会	土地面积(平方公里)	户籍人口(人)	外来暂住人口(人)	户籍从业人数(人)	全部企业及个体户数(个)	#工业企业	当年可支配财政收入(万元)	资产总额(万元)	负债总额(万元)	资产负债率(%)
莞　城										
市　桥	0.9	31396	1620	10160	2714	1	525	592	67	11.3
东　正	1.7	21110	3956	12563	696	26	410	483	46	9.5
罗　沙	1.8	14630	3685	5780	1798	19	590	276	55	19.9
西　隅	0.6	11215	772	3438	208	3	279	944	235	24.9
北　隅	1.1	28856	10348	18146	1580	6	521	870	196	22.5
博　厦	1.0	8890	770	3510	250	32	390	324	49	15.1
兴　塘	2.6	12562	11046	7263	4026	15	382	351	124	35.3
创　业	1.5	18682	4250	9982	2423	20	461	262	55	21.0
罗沙联合社							1840	24157	1273	5.3
博厦联合社							471	6060	952	15.7
细村联合社							2123	15501	935	6.0
石　龙										
忠维村	0.8	992	3668	473	108	12	1471	10732	7351	68.5
林屋村	0.7	648	1485	295	105	29	1175	5557	1614	29.0
新维村	0.6	548	1208	316	482	40	2147	14724	3786	25.7
蒲溪村	0.7	617	369	174	10		797	3360	417	12.4
西湖村	3.5	2786	4560	1438	600	85	5860	78699	6288	8.0
王屋洲村	3.2	1566	3572	587	265	16	1500	14418	644	4.5
黄家山村	2.5	1924	2123	624	158	6	859	8788	4398	50.1
中山东	0.5	16951	18568	9657	305	25	204	1756	1143	65.1
中山西	0.5	20228	4545	9515	663	19	325	5711	3883	68.0
兴　龙		18237	7685	8560	1580	14	466	1783	1008	56.5
虎　门										
树　田	4.0	1468	10755	720	401	395	1732	11683	3714	31.8
怀　德	13.8	6202	27195	3703	896	176	5744	33314	3344	10.0
居　岐	1.8	1306	13500	709	672	76	3076	13408	1804	13.5
村　头	1.3	809	7158	417	194	52	2009	13607	5815	42.7
陈　村	1.3	787	4000	200	35	32	790	5738	1533	26.7
黄　村	0.9	563	4500	362	83	28	686	2809	1760	62.7
大　宁	5.4	2737	21000	1086	550	200	10907	61309	6593	10.8
北　栅	5.9	4557	24800	2967	2032	336	6177	34781	9571	27.5
龙　眼	3.0	2733	42500	1081	996	280	10687	94818	4350	4.6
赤　岗	7.5	4352	4600	2676	203	80	2751	24893	11020	44.3
博　涌	5.9	7005	27000	3580	3450	305	1399	9225	5393	58.5
新　联	0.6	1157	12000	565	425	65	1253	6098	705	11.6
白　沙	7.8	7033	17026	3610	1351	212	3579	30058	12867	42.8
镇　口	1.8	3132	12613	1392	425	125	3410	15369	713	4.6
金　洲	4.8	3779	23000	1041	1988	75	2981	31017	9910	32.0

15　续表 1

(2010年)

村(居)委会	土地面积(平方公里)	户籍人口(人)	外来暂住人口(人)	户籍从业人数(人)	全部企业及个体户数(个)	#工业企业	当年可支配财政收入(万元)	资产总额(万元)	负债总额(万元)	资产负债率(%)
小捷滘	2.0	892	9781	567	418	105	2034	15928	5888	37.0
南栅	8.2	5284	59000	4213	1564	305	9691	95339	29840	31.3
东风	2.8	1752	11000	1002	473	62	1527	12925	6327	49.0
宴岗	1.3	1109	6318	554	175	29	907	5533	1537	27.8
路东	5.6	3107	17500	1975	902	197	6922	44640	4145	9.3
沙角	11.5	5692	21600	2960	1335	340	4832	40397	18300	45.3
虎门寨	2.0	7555	10000	3960	6950	39	4021	22043	1903	8.6
九门寨	2.6	1432	4200	675	30	28	1033	8227	1783	21.7
南面	7.3	2773	3550	1510	120	18	2963	19781	2169	11.0
北面	5.5	2523	4825	1600	78	73	480	9126	3208	35.2
武山沙	2.9	2256	4332	822	185	60	774	7688	4312	56.1
东方	0.7	9334	3000	6067	736	9	273	482	84	17.4
则徐	1.2	15744	10510	8400	2044	61	674	1264	115	9.1
新湾	1.0	9788	3330	4200	202	46	818	2664	2283	85.7
东城										
温塘	11.6	9510	25100	5705	612	65	2411	24067	2187	9.1
桑园	4.0	3694	42000	2422	445	135	1604	11570	410	3.5
周屋	2.8	2317	10000	1391	364	60	1193	6586	404	6.1
余屋	2.0	1639	3800	1028	285	65	1118	5599	223	4.0
鳌峙塘	2.0	1033	4500	512	220	80	703	3352	353	10.5
峡口	1.6	1214	3650	655	373	85	2878	5879	222	3.8
柏洲边	1.0	1071	3850	649	217	58	1176	5977	124	2.1
上桥	1.0	1383	2600	810	188	40	3104	3593	462	12.9
下桥	2.0	2404	7100	1520	870	47	1018	6617	1061	16.0
樟村	3.0	3039	3000	1693	528	43	2287	17682	1624	9.2
梨川	1.0	1635	4030	1180	564	90	1548	6035	563	9.3
堑头	1.5	3078	430	1945	263	30	2018	9139	392	4.3
主山	6.6	5987	30060	3672	595		1820	14570	600	4.1
石井	6.7	2005	2980	1006	145	60	1168	13044	4955	38.0
同沙	4.6	2414	5000	1675	395	125	1996	11450	627	5.5
光明	1.9	1407	2461	954	132	28	1998	9287	86	0.9
牛山	11.0	4089	14666	3055	455	95	1688	14726	4604	31.3
立新	2.5	3002	5000	1550	580	47	1103	5912	3989	67.5
火炼树	1.2	1325	5780	792	485	403	1419	8326	4387	52.7
岗贝	1.7	12712	2850	4850	1350		1578	1253	260	20.8
花园新村	0.8	1255	1400	860	742		1046	2376	325	13.7
东泰	1.4	13377	5450	5500	620		810	4167	219	5.3
万江										
万江	2.6	4149	3528	2896	86	67	2519	13114	2217	16.9
石美	2.5	4018	3310	1690	220	69	2867	15033	2215	14.7
莫屋	1.0	1453	2315	870	155	84	806	5747	1682	29.3
拔蛟窝	1.3	2022	2275	878	240	66	4354	20779	3148	15.2

15　续表 2

(2010年)

村(居)委会	土地面积(平方公里)	户籍人口(人)	外来暂住人口(人)	户籍从业人数(人)	全部企业及个体户数(个)	#工业企业	当年可支配财政收入(万元)	资产总额(万元)	负债总额(万元)	资产负债率(%)
黄粘洲	0.3	788	1308	490	36	23	836	3662	858	23.4
蚬涌	2.0	1971	2316	1281	243	98	505	5748	1509	26.3
谷涌	2.0	2966	1133	2124	168	27	2491	21227	721	3.4
小享	3.8	4947	1946	3396	161	121	4688	16837	561	3.3
滘联	2.1	3393	1307	2036	75	36	812	6792	4317	63.6
金泰	1.0	2028	1500	1129	130	30	1537	5871	1898	32.3
曲海	1.2	1556	768	950	32	3	776	14301	153	1.1
牌楼基	1.6	1595	1067	1013	156	39	1148	18596	1669	9.0
大莲塘	0.8	1021	1196	663	75	37	1464	8794	307	3.5
水蛇涌	1.5	2040	1456	985	142	39	1808	15449	1421	9.2
共联	1.3	1926	5548	1042	174	51	820	6074	673	11.1
新谷涌	1.4	2140	1230	1265	86	40	1285	14356	1346	9.4
坝头	1.4	1538	1543	971	18	13	1296	14154	4173	29.5
胜利	0.9	929	6078	471	29	26	806	3164	284	9.0
官桥滘	1.9	1624	2170	715	54	52	1318	9776	801	8.2
简沙洲	1.6	1690	2207	900	127	116	490	5694	3561	62.5
新和	3.7	2628	3500	1891	157	115	1372	9262	995	10.7
上甲	1.4	2420	1430	1192	72	70	925	8036	2065	25.7
严屋	0.7	1069	706	671	41	31	741	4928	1293	26.2
大汾	2.6	3378	1321	2156	183	67	1825	13300	621	4.7
新村	5.9	7963	2310	5565	173	169	2430	15159	2210	14.6
流涌尾	2.5	2290	1504	1660	69	50	738	4811	1313	27.3
万江墟	1.0	5420	1126	2316	240	23	742	4425	2509	56.7
新城		4784	5830	3374	616		274	694	31	4.5
南城										
胜和	4.0	6552	29967	4085	2650	7	2303	43047	27799	64.6
亨美	0.5	1800	2200	1035	31	9	2303	30508	10375	34.0
三元里	0.4	1083	856	565	30	9	1893	25229	1412	5.6
篁村	1.0	3005	6500	2048	690	12	1309	28232	2410	8.5
新基	2.0	2711	6532	1702	1325	36	19610	108801	39875	36.7
周溪	5.0	3874	5125	2215	159	25	15316	51409	8761	17.0
袁屋边	2.0	1904	3500	1012	360	28	4936	36477	3353	9.2
白马	4.0	3317	6640	2155	847	42	9375	36131	3968	11.0
石鼓	2.0	1759	6831	913	253	24	4107	34111	7108	20.8
蛤地	8.0	2736	5530	1448	105	26	2191	30933	14056	45.4
西平	3.9	3502	5709	2281	567	12	29981	71899	47300	65.8
水濂	6.0	2012	1650	1023	76	17	1653	16947	10901	64.3
雅园	1.8	1207	2382	627	136	45	2241	21379	982	4.6
元美	0.4	2604	2130	1157	106	14	7180	17620	15856	90.0
鸿福		8211	3264							
宏远	1.0	7451	21000	4796	691	5				
新城	4.5	2180	1199	1100	4900		287	341	193	56.6

15 续表 3

(2010年)

村(居)委会	土地面积(平方公里)	户籍人口(人)	外来暂住人口(人)	户籍从业人数(人)	全部企业及个体户数(个)	#工业企业	当年可支配财政收入(万元)	资产总额(万元)	负债总额(万元)	资产负债率(%)
中　堂										
潢涌村	9.3	9192	5762	6283	943	95	30421	198110	8787	4.4
三涌村	4.0	3723	2310	2650	359	67	1240	8683	4805	55.3
湛翠村	1.8	2311	1005	1510	124	39	765	4344	1761	40.5
袁家涌村	4.0	5575	2320	3518	438	87	1253	7631	2496	32.7
吴家涌村	3.4	2696	1668	1515	397	71	1526	9726	3452	35.5
凤冲村	1.3	1624	628	1029	87	38	331	1711	899	52.5
鹤田村	2.2	2210	1709	1406	374	77	522	3503	1716	49.0
东　泊	2.9	3728	3875	1812	687	132	3565	20934	6871	32.8
中堂村	1.1	1924	935	1107	159	53	288	1330	472	35.5
一　村	0.7	1754	8166	998	280	30	1299	5678	121	2.1
东向村	2.4	3248	1620	2238	343	86	531	3074	577	18.8
斗　朗	2.5	2584	946	1687	191	40	1281	9192	3894	42.4
江　南	2.1	2412	3716	1795	704	120	2256	12578	228	1.8
蕉利村	4.6	4912	3311	3172	575	120	1013	6394	2598	40.6
槎滘村	9.4	9992	2346	6428	632	143	2788	27368	3037	11.1
下芦村	1.3	1186	336	681	65	24	1693	2773	1095	39.5
马沥村	1.9	1965	506	1358	60	10	3963	8592	1668	19.4
四乡村	4.2	3170	300	1916	46	14	410	2565	1343	52.4
红　锋	0.1	771	87	496	53	4	196	1226	822	67.1
居　民	0.7	8779	6599	4833	1516	24	178	1927	1636	84.9
望牛墩										
李屋村	0.6	631	1840	376	72	30	324	2159	1224	56.7
望东村	1.4	2044	2200	942	192	21	370	2756	1615	58.6
扶涌村	0.6	885	1300	498	76	11	422	2991	1185	39.6
赤滘村	1.9	2945	3050	1780	60	38	1317	9571	2802	29.3
五涌村	1.4	1527	2300	820	70	38	612	2496	1224	49.0
下漕村	3.5	4226	4240	2261	108	41	644	4537	3198	70.5
上合村	1.9	2928	1950	1250	46	34	452	6585	4230	64.2
聚龙江村	0.7	941	2290	468	220	18	951	7530	1401	18.6
望联村	2.8	5088	2633	3062	429	24	876	3926	1295	33.0
洲湾村	1.6	1903	1200	860	42	15	325	2678	1705	63.7
洲涡村	1.9	2538	532	965	32	22	301	3116	1824	58.5
寮厦村	1.4	1420	812	592	23	12	427	4291	2795	65.1
官桥涌村	0.7	946	900	563	22	14	501	3610	376	10.4
芙蓉沙村	0.8	1038	450	635	32	17	407	4582	2157	47.1
杜屋村	1.8	2340	1160	1505	92	32	516	5060	1835	36.3
横沥村	1.8	2232	400	1527	35	7	623	3419	1565	45.8
福安村	0.6	1059	312	613	18	5	489	5508	3507	63.7
官洲村	1.0	1056	470	639	41	13	336	2164	1459	67.4
石排村	0.4	619	400	330	16	7	230	1910	1031	54.0
朱平沙村	2.7	3310	2890	1936	50	14	886	4893	4131	84.4
锦涡村	2.2	1529	730	942	39	7	698	4573	2828	61.8
居　民		4676		2050						

15 续表 4

(2010年)

村(居)委会	土地面积(平方公里)	户籍人口(人)	外来暂住人口(人)	户籍从业人数(人)	全部企业及个体户数(个)	#工业企业	当年可支配财政收入(万元)	资产总额(万元)	负债总额(万元)	资产负债率(%)
麻　涌										
麻一村	4.0	4080	2500	2910	245	14	1105	3835	3076	80.2
麻　二	6.8	3587	786	2221	82	4	2624	15170	186	1.2
麻三村	3.7	3777	1092	2238	717	16	1024	9336	863	9.2
麻四村	4.5	4783	980	2820	188	17	1745	12131	1443	11.9
大步村	10.7	7173	4138	4094	392	66	7333	20433	981	4.8
东太村	4.8	4507	1376	2638	177	12	1519	6127	1223	20.0
新基村	4.4	5653	4526	3370	345	39	3572	8233	369	4.5
川槎村	3.0	3930	2026	2357	225	50	112	578	534	92.4
鸥涌村	2.8	3822	4300	2236	174	10	511	542	287	53.0
黎滘村	1.3	1317	412	693	32	9	351	1326	552	41.6
华阳村	5.5	5288	1336	3223	111	10	2281	8588	1123	13.1
南洲村	3.4	2764	1513	1649	181	20	2682	13144	723	5.5
大盛村	6.9	2803	8000	1790	410	21	1742	19302	2853	14.8
漳澎村	29.6	12292	1813	8296	202	9	3767	32324	2161	6.7
居　民		6513		4640						
石　碣										
唐洪村	1.0	1790	3395	879	394	37	2199	11041	2103	19.1
水南村	2.8	3517	6429	1554	1160	153	1900	20686	6472	31.3
石碣村	4.6	5216	11560	2975	1498	226	2779	19752	6949	35.2
刘屋村	4.9	4463	3920	2559	512	105	1939	9975	3389	34.0
横滘村	1.6	1931	4165	1085	576	97	2225	11112	5281	47.5
鹤田厦村	2.5	1887	6597	1148	238	25	2111	12320	4711	38.2
四甲村	4.0	4640	7175	2683	820	135	2921	15414	3855	25.0
沙腰村	4.0	3521	3215	2295	251	56	2950	14107	2439	17.3
梁家村	1.9	2437	1541	1315	153	69	1911	12063	5442	45.1
桔洲村	1.2	1442	9054	869	443	78	5775	34315	1687	4.9
单屋村	2.3	1310	2800	783	175	94	2634	13188	2830	21.5
涌口村	1.6	1733	4550	964	497	143	2744	20512	7053	34.4
西南村	2.6	2032	6500	1073	1042	83	7042	42670	4942	11.6
黄泗围村	1.2	705	2255	379	324	79	1903	11210	1298	11.6
居　民		7263	6136	4955	1225	35	836	7679	8875	115.6
高　埗										
冼沙村	7.5	7360	22305	4450	442	139	1652	13726	9639	70.2
卢溪村	2.3	1696	10500	802	51	35	927	4120	266	6.5
宝莲村	0.7	1046	1615	645	40	16	293	1397	299	21.4
塘厦村	2.7	1887	2530	1123	102	19	400	2147	419	19.5
草墩村	0.8	801	1275	453	25	22	678	3841	1645	42.8
护安围村	1.9	1112	483	667	90	41	686	4329	413	9.5
保安围村	2.3	2339	1560	1416	72	32	3119	24402	16228	66.5

15　续表 5

(2010年)

村(居)委会	土地面积(平方公里)	户籍人口(人)	外来暂住人口(人)	户籍从业人数(人)	全部企业及个体户数(个)	#工业企业	当年可支配财政收入(万元)	资产总额(万元)	负债总额(万元)	资产负债率(%)
三联村	2.1	1382	650	830	23	5	366	2912	1314	45.1
横滘头村	0.9	1083	831	725	16	8	1021	4850	1951	40.2
低涌村	2.2	2864	11501	1692	398	21	829	5515	2102	38.1
朱磡村	1.0	1468	1206	895	24	14	187	1211	639	52.8
欧邓村	0.7	948	780	553	25	9	521	2947	1686	57.2
芦村	1.3	1719	450	768	55	19	265	1563	640	41.0
高埗村	2.1	3254	12145	2008	281	53	1209	8068	4737	58.7
凌屋村	1.2	1256	1875	712	39	8	672	5103	1787	35.0
上江城村	1.9	2314	14950	1272	118	13	902	7737	2945	38.1
下江城村	1.5	1470	2015	990	132	27	1532	5521	2495	45.2
新联村	1.3	1634	900	983	150	9	217	2633	1239	47.1
居民		2199	2000	1100	350	1				
道滘										
南城村	7.1	4370	4256	2672	606	84	2462	17135	1117	6.5
闸口村	5.2	2805	8900	1713	444	42	2200	12506	994	8.0
北永村	6.3	3672	4860	2274	243	117	3113	21032	2817	13.4
永庆村	3.1	1673	3055	1166	153	99	1717	8409	493	5.9
厚德村	4.2	2468	5500	1695	180	38	1868	12289	1668	13.6
蔡白村	5.5	4713	5050	2879	290	62	1753	18552	7502	40.4
南丫村	6.8	4123	16500	2728	403	101	4375	27685	6203	22.4
九曲村	4.6	3073	3086	1985	165	48	990	5938	1326	22.3
大罗沙村	4.5	2848	4531	1730	55	20	1595	9549	3334	34.9
小河村	6.1	5716	5512	3560	212	68	741	5884	1462	24.9
昌平村	3.8	3376	3181	2360	166	34	807	2554	2687	105.2
大岭丫村	4.1	3539	5625	2157	289	76	3610	25233	6478	25.7
大鱼沙村	1.7	1725	2500	1072	213	33	746	4292	911	21.2
居民		11665		6027			97	236	187	79.2
洪梅										
洪屋涡村	14.1	6771	2906	4305	149	145	1673	15485	2862	18.5
新庄村	1.0	867	580	500	33	20	444	3193	1614	50.6
梅沙村	3.5	3965	2200	2468	68	25	559	6793	2572	37.9
金鳌沙村	2.3	1355	410	901	28	8	605	4532	2744	60.6
乌沙村	1.5	2152	2600	1322	34	5	692	8888	962	10.8
尧均村	0.8	606	1856	402	45	11	442	2277	1158	50.9
夏汇村	0.8	695	125	455	7		330	1992	1372	68.9
氹涌村	1.6	1894	3030	955	63	9	1163	4789	2578	53.8
黎洲角村	1.6	2631	2588	1798	349	10	2193	9138	2007	22.0
居民	1.0	958	2315	671			83	27		
沙田										
中围村	0.9	1725	32	985	23	1	3633	11950	3683	30.8
和安村	0.8	3169	227	1860	59	4	866	9495	2582	27.2
大流村	0.5	2020	119	1211	45	1	355	10323	7096	68.7

15 续表 6

（2010年）

村(居)委会	土地面积(平方公里)	户籍人口(人)	外来暂住人口(人)	户籍从业人数(人)	全部企业及个体户数(个)	#工业企业	当年可支配财政收入(万元)	资产总额(万元)	负债总额(万元)	资产负债率(%)
泥洲村	0.3	3777	191	2450	30	1	753	19308	13185	68.3
杨公洲村	3.9	1886	3026	1092	489	243	3964	9078	3376	37.2
阁西村	5.4	2200	7385	1133	447	54	2429	20620	9587	46.5
民田村	5.2	2537	7500	1520	694	115	1546	11381	3027	26.6
大泥村	4.4	1863	6848	725	832	217	1194	7087	703	9.9
福禄沙村	3.5	1940	2400	1079	167	50	1048	7880	3705	47.0
西大坦村	0.9	2080	132	1079	18	1	414	8259	2547	30.8
穗丰年村	5.9	2718	1800	1763	247	95	2997	19994	6253	31.3
齐沙村	3.8	2075	8485	1117	839	125	1885	15676	2730	17.4
稔洲村	4.7	2469	11066	1552	1281	203	1776	8647	3046	35.2
义沙村	5.1	1905	5840	1080	338	110	1708	11796	3349	28.4
西太隆村	4.5	1999	7429	1191	462	263	975	7264	2869	39.5
横流	1.0	4296	3200	2153	1249	41	612	6756	2086	30.9
先锋村	0.4	2038	210	957	35	8	440	4965	2294	46.2
厚街										
厚街村	8.0	9038	16197	5830	2192	69	2880	25513	12972	50.8
珊美村	2.1	2428	9204	1377	467	12	764	9348	2733	29.2
寮厦村	2.5	2360	6652	1460	745	26	2536	15686	2609	16.6
河田村	9.1	6160	14541	3354	752	51	2600	19334	8449	43.7
汀山村	4.3	1938	15822	1248	772	58	2153	16320	4904	30.1
环冈村	4.2	2063	7950	1435	215	39	4982	23120	7605	32.9
三屯村	4.5	2656	15673	1605	908	71	2769	24577	7675	31.2
宝屯村	3.0	2542	8199	1408	442	112	2920	21702	10394	47.9
陈屋村	2.0	1520	3592	1002	570	53	2945	18718	3364	18.0
赤岭村	5.3	3595	16504	2393	816	68	4052	40434	24347	60.2
桥头村	10.0	7842	10423	4521	889	56	3850	36056	5616	15.6
南五村	1.6	1469	4668	610	118	29	1433	7247	2631	36.3
溪头村	4.1	3726	13700	1221	945	105	5193	29975	4433	14.8
沙塘村	1.5	2057	3635	1339	165	29	2630	16754	5850	34.9
宝塘村	1.7	1541	5800	958	300	29	9604	25018	5324	21.3
下汴村	2.2	1746	6113	1135	407	60	2602	20203	3601	17.8
白濠村	5.3	5285	15988	2615	920	118	3459	20579	5422	26.4
新塘村	4.4	5675	12192	3388	782	55	3196	28364	4707	16.6
双岗村	4.2	6872	5079	4409	782	49	1503	14184	3318	23.4
涌口村	4.0	5531	1120	3318	837	88	4186	32135	7846	24.4
大迳村	11.8	3624	2316	2160	155	15	1129	5998	1982	33.0
新围村	15.1	4538	2397	2801	143	15	611	5071	2201	43.4
居民		12733	5080	5692	3421	115	368	5332	348	6.5
长安										
涌头	4.1	1731	17935	675	1269	120	5203	30566	14188	46.4
霄边	7.6	3456	36964	1961	2137	119	14612	126919	8167	6.4
咸西	4.0	1258	10188	587	1132	83	13479	78817	17065	21.7

15 续表 7

(2010年)

村(居)委会	土地面积(平方公里)	户籍人口(人)	外来暂住人口(人)	户籍从业人数(人)	全部企业及个体户数(个)	#工业企业	当年可支配财政收入(万元)	资产总额(万元)	负债总额(万元)	资产负债率(%)
锦厦	9.7	4245	49246	2212	1909	203	14923	124180	24769	20.0
新安	8.6	3405	45725	1750	1961	325	4429	91156	6799	7.5
乌沙	7.3	3843	65293	2091	3836	499	9394	61033	6701	11.0
新民	1.5	923	17350	242	966	156	3520	33398	15967	47.8
沙头	9.9	6188	41330	3380	4073	400	13691	127447	55861	43.8
上沙	5.2	2854	31991	1505	2675	365	6901	64756	13967	21.6
厦岗	5.3	3199	28312	1532	1938	425	9786	46847	1908	4.1
厦边	4.4	2480	15358	1302	2404	290	5708	25912	6088	23.5
上角	3.9	1303	19564	736	1126	199	8860	58774	25241	43.0
长盛	0.7	6291	21091	5321	1576	2	6258	13447	6882	51.2
寮步										
塘边	0.7	1638	3000	855	250	30	1342	8676	4702	54.2
西溪村	4.5	4594	8200	2166	338	163	1428	16781	2986	17.8
凫山村	4.0	5903	7025	3645	480	75	1581	12598	5538	44.0
石步村	4.7	4474	1970	1930	220	58	1925	24728	16177	65.4
良边村	2.7	3217	3500	2018	420	265	1286	6285	1128	18.0
富竹山村	3.5	1915	2600	1226	75	38	1896	12879	3364	26.1
塘唇村	3.4	2253	2700	1365	115	54	2276	27810	8279	29.8
向西村	2.9	2556	3800	1065	115	26	966	9909	4078	41.2
下岭贝村	1.8	1501	7682	911	221	13	2025	10815	501	4.6
岭厦	0.9	1020	4500	583	135	110	2678	20055	3081	15.4
新旧围	1.4	981	1850	620	215	210	1250	6898	686	9.9
霞边村	1.3	833	900	420	68	19	1672	6601	987	15.0
横坑	5.9	4787	17982	2785	478	466	9205	90790	22517	24.8
竹园村	1.5	883	1200	422	130	32	1591	7004	2286	32.6
上屯村	4.5	3301	3150	1867	188	42	1501	12382	562	4.5
石龙坑村	1.9	3677	5000	2324	215	206	2279	6806	416	6.1
牛杨	1.2	1499	5500	773	118	62	2828	9560	2762	28.9
泉塘	2.3	1538	5000	947	82	58	851	6548	2153	32.9
坑口	1.6	1175	2500	660	200	30	1311	14324	1887	13.2
浮竹山村	3.4	1496	2500	928	140	30	1938	16203	5322	32.9
上底村	2.0	1461	1250	740	86	11	282	3484	1666	47.8
刘屋巷村	1.6	569	1720	317	42	29	1569	5948	1252	21.1
药勒村	2.4	1122	3100	622	111	37	2724	10388	1534	14.8
陈家埔村	1.6	847	2500	359	63	18	673	6238	2718	43.6
缪边	1.6	1188	3000	742	168	36	1883	10937	2180	19.9
居民	1.7	9242	5000	6165	2611	18	994	2165	793	36.6
小坑村	1.5	817	1300	400	45	20	912	5662	280	5.0
长坑村	1.0	926	450	405	23	10	899	6025	505	8.4
井巷村	1.1	897	1201	514	32	23	1001	6033	926	15.4

15 续表 8

(2010年)

村(居)委会	土地面积(平方公里)	户籍人口(人)	外来暂住人口(人)	户籍从业人数(人)	全部企业及个体户数(个)	#工业企业	当年可支配财政收入(万元)	资产总额(万元)	负债总额(万元)	资产负债率(%)
大岭山										
马蹄岗村	0.8	2186	3968	1421	137	38	600	6485	2363	36.4
大塘朗村	3.0	1592	2140	1063	51	38	637	4038	858	21.3
新塘村	2.0	2172	6690	1401	269	93	1816	10173	2167	21.3
元岭村	0.3	974	605	462	54	3	1106	15405	405	2.6
金桔村	4.3	3621	6550	2390	540	62	2844	23615	6026	25.5
鸡翅岭村	4.5	1322	3200	701	177	16	1954	5455	1700	31.2
大沙村	3.0	1816	2000	1377	157	150	1986	8401	2697	32.1
旧飞鹅村	3.1	457	1000	290	37	32	712	3703	84	2.3
连平村	7.2	2887	16000	1084	275	72	1192	5166	1823	35.3
梅林村	1.5	535	7500	286	127	62	865	4420	1114	25.2
下高田村	0.5	475	1700	255	63	44	514	2143	469	21.9
大环村	2.0	588	841	398	25	15	594	3286	1137	34.6
太公岭村	2.2	1675	4198	1155	140	51	908	3746	1199	32.0
百花洞村	4.8	1299	6800	635	48	41	1577	12207	3143	25.8
大片美村	2.6	1010	6000	480	178	18	977	3611	154	4.3
矮岭冚村	5.5	3590	10987	2238	819	108	6500	16295	6032	37.0
大岭村	7.0	2363	850	1431	77	62	633	4125	1113	27.0
农场	1.0	734	3500	350	470	13	710	4165	795	19.1
水朗村	4.5	1359	2901	628	24	16	1629	6340	1091	17.2
大塘村	8.5	3236	20000	2150	190	180	2365	12051	3579	29.7
杨屋村	12.0	4844	15500	3178	630	135	1433	10779	1675	15.5
颜屋村	3.0	742	6600	308	150	70	848	5566	813	14.6
居民	10.0	3904	6214	1862	545	13	242	905	556	61.4
大朗										
竹山	1.3	1639	2818	790	396	140	1259	11627	811	7.0
高英村	1.7	1836	4178	1022	267	95	1507	16680	5319	31.9
巷头	3.5	4344	14463	2495	2308	478	4972	47096	11831	25.1
巷尾	1.6	1980	6356	1148	920	225	13876	36063	3349	9.3
求富路	1.4	1425	6283	836	490	121	3348	20026	2286	11.4
长塘	2.7	4687	10689	2795	1574	424	7096	59655	14850	24.9
大井头	4.1	5727	7655	2716	2310	319	20990	69102	10895	15.8
圣堂	0.9	1583	2537	954	1222	35	2407	22424	584	2.6
蔡边村	6.1	4182	5057	2252	1018	295	4180	31699	7360	23.2
水口村	3.3	2953	6735	1527	836	268	2649	27045	5153	19.1
洋乌村	2.1	1691	2875	1080	458	196	835	6548	4251	64.9
洋坑塘村	1.1	1075	5650	682	365	142	1298	11631	999	8.6
松柏朗村	2.5	4155	4499	2342	540	108	1387	15925	7853	49.3
黄草朗	1.5	2319	4712	1087	791	352	1566	16698	7470	44.7
黎贝岭村	1.9	2245	3502	1433	466	185	1736	14094	947	6.7
佛子凹村	1.1	2410	1045	1220	134	60	1471	7967	841	10.6
佛新	0.6	868	608	420	236	119	874	12130	5166	42.6
松木山村	2.7	2599	7360	1600	763	300	2305	20849	2313	11.1
犀牛陂村	8.0	3240	8314	1794	946	550	2014	15018	1150	7.7

15　续表 9

(2010年)

村(居)委会	土地面积(平方公里)	户籍人口(人)	外来暂住人口(人)	户籍从业人数(人)	全部企业及个体户数(个)	#工业企业	当年可支配财政收入(万元)	资产总额(万元)	负债总额(万元)	资产负债率(%)
水平村	7.9	1904	4634	1254	382	147	2301	16597	4564	27.5
屏山	2.3	506	400	282	32	12	373	2270	196	8.6
宝陂村	0.5	706	119	231	31	6	711	13114	5761	43.9
石厦村	8.0	2952	5128	1730	511	239	6342	17585	2127	12.1
杨涌村	1.5	1362	3798	777	368	114	754	4082	261	6.4
沙步村	3.1	2266	3427	1273	571	308	365	1505	1223	81.3
新马莲村	6.6	1597	3808	1162	285	136	626	2399	1380	57.5
大朗	0.3	6631	3053	3949	928	30	397	2098	473	22.6
长富	1.5	1310	300	931	10					
黄江										
社贝村	4.0	1100	14816	668	546	72	1267	8120	210	2.6
鸡啼岗村	3.0	1429	8352	859	87	52	1685	10190	952	9.3
合路村	1.4	898	7100	415	125	120	1631	10577	730	6.9
袁屋围村	0.6	363	1080	230	61	8	1573	8061	2545	31.6
北岸村	3.5	1570	8136	971	273	58	1673	8645	1175	13.6
田心村	4.0	1614	12000	968	639	67	2237	12472	1152	9.2
大冚村	6.4	799	2850	488	78	35	840	3492	319	9.1
龙见田村	3.0	883	4425	336	194	49	1091	7779	949	12.2
长龙村	18.0	2488	8000	1410	250	56	1630	8251	2328	28.2
星光村	3.3	1123	6000	1123	77	15	441	3860	1342	34.8
新市	1.6	6009	6800	4037	500		337	915	270	29.5
旧村	1.5	278	2430	148	42	35	663	4655	719	15.5
田美	7.4	3376	28294	1884	600	323	2728	24305	4040	16.6
三新	16.0	2805	13212	1520	684	132	2654	14466	1481	10.2
樟木头										
圩镇	4.3	9619	11748	6289	2924	161	1915	19469	12909	66.3
樟罗	6.8	3493	21360	1969	2799	70	4423	37872	13472	35.6
百果洞	2.4	889	5300	512	1562	26	2087	19061	7416	38.9
樟洋	13.5	2431	30352	1139	1623	32	2411	18896	5888	31.2
石新	7.3	2308	10807	1080	1698	135	4212	47478	30448	64.1
柏地	6.6	1385	7087	699	900	90	1509	22510	7178	31.9
官仓	3.0	1103	2936	575	323	36	1009	8158	3228	39.6
裕丰	10.0	1990	11000	895	523	57	2283	10617	5785	54.5
金河	14.0	1715	12270	950	822	127	1732	10141	3930	38.8
清溪										
罗马村	7.0	1850	7350	1160	339	50	630	3872	1654	42.7
长山头村	4.3	1133	6800	700	96	41	2799	13040	5540	42.5
荔横村	3.4	1515	11596	823	252	59	1388	11583	7344	63.4
浮岗村	3.0	1955	7500	890	710	60	1505	12879	5960	46.3
松岗村	3.9	1266	3758	510	76	43	903	2495	842	33.8
上元村	4.3	920	42	645	223	29	905	3787	1780	47.0
重河村	8.4	2661	8000	1320	360	30	910	7865	1011	12.9

15 续表 10

(2010年)

村(居)委会	土地面积(平方公里)	户籍人口(人)	外来暂住人口(人)	户籍从业人数(人)	全部企业及个体户数(个)	#工业企业	当年可支配财政收入(万元)	资产总额(万元)	负债总额(万元)	资产负债率(%)
清厦村	2.3	1544	4876	893	578	40	1483	8316	4323	52.0
铁松村	5.6	2537	10880	1168	168	85	1708	12411	5005	40.3
铁场村	7.4	783	182	443	13		653	5099	2537	49.8
九乡村	7.5	1707	3000	1053	200	62	594	6597	5489	83.2
大埔村	1.8	728	3000	360	99	30	647	3388	1044	30.8
大利村	9.6	2649	16572	1662	1002	68	2011	13835	4292	31.0
渔樑围村	2.5	1062	17000	553	285	63	1932	11727	3634	31.0
三星村	2.5	1086	3725	523	102	24	736	3948	3292	83.4
厦坭村	1.7	881	5986	476	340	28	863	8690	2538	29.2
土桥村	1.2	581	7030	310	328	51	1513	11048	6380	57.8
谢坑村	3.2	777	4000	483	84	59	1429	4569	2377	52.0
三中村	9.0	1770	58120	980	661	131	1389	10068	5356	53.2
青皇村	6.5	1124	3800	674	65	33	1111	2607	389	14.9
居民	7.0	7153	12813	3603	1912	18	1645	4375	2732	62.5
塘厦										
林村	21.0	5385	44000	3725	1821	243	8779	61168	5562	9.1
莲湖	9.0	2183	21000	542	452	206	2610	19175	6376	33.3
石潭埔	6.8	1611	9301	1569	140	65	2530	17025	3280	19.3
横塘	4.0	1099	70007	698	114	96	2092	8546	2258	26.4
莆心湖	6.1	2044	7500	1146	165	75	4540	29332	3636	12.4
诸佛岭	2.4	1114	12630	695	296	50	3020	29832	6175	20.7
振兴围	2.4	967	10000	652	164	54	6421	15872	699	4.4
四村	4.0	1066	10780	503	439	285	1904	15007	5451	36.3
蛟乙塘	4.9	1416	9980	710	325	93	2141	20933	6793	32.5
沙湖	4.0	595	5893	222	95	77	2050	13056	2504	19.2
大坪	13.0	1346	11367	750	65	58	7013	22789	6165	27.1
田心	4.5	849	7800	472	96	93	1412	16349	2112	12.9
龙背岭	8.2	957	8155	528	252	69	2283	12892	3393	26.3
石鼓	6.4	2510	15000	1270	302	96	5601	30136	6510	21.6
石马	2.7	489	5900	312	170	45	737	5578	1907	34.2
清湖头	4.1	1354	15200	835	194	148	3770	21992	4122	18.7
平山	4.8	765	8025	493	112	105	1737	14906	921	6.2
桥陇	2.8	1018	7250	668	143	62	2289	12572	6166	49.1
凤凰岗	3.5	1331	9569	708	314	80	2136	13640	5681	41.7
塘厦	0.9	14689	46300	6462	2200	355	376	2247	352	15.7
三局		2678								
凤岗										
雁田村	22.0	3646	27864	1675	3654	508	15797	260851	35420	13.6
官井头村	10.1	1875	9881	1123	600	175	7018	101207	10980	10.9
油甘埔村	7.4	2014	14938	955	761	493	4394	38634	10848	28.1
凤德岭村	3.3	1264	5542	582	362	84	1914	11546	2416	20.9

15 续表 11

(2010年)

村(居)委会	土地面积(平方公里)	户籍人口(人)	外来暂住人口(人)	户籍从业人数(人)	全部企业及个体户数(个)	#工业企业	当年可支配财政收入(万元)	资产总额(万元)	负债总额(万元)	资产负债率(%)
塘沥村	6.5	1913	12651	830	270	68	1163	6954	2099	30.2
黄洞村	11.9	2246	13259	1288	214	211	1140	11952	831	7.0
竹塘村	5.6	1292	14226	499	365	130	1332	7597	2463	32.4
竹尾田村	1.6	737	8900	275	155	15	1320	7984	366	4.6
三联村	3.3	1500	9788	797	826	40	682	3533	1946	55.1
五联村	5.6	1334	2767	596	251	151	1637	16127	8936	55.4
天堂围村	4.1	1104	9952	679	334	124	2329	20195	1557	7.7
居民	1.3	5320	2800	2983	438	23	79	554	55	9.9
谢岗										
黎村	11.0	3742	3173	2135	90	21	2143	8566	1323	15.4
南面村	39.6	1493	768	730	39	15	621	2709	471	17.4
窑山村	11.3	525	1607	364	27	22	261	2140	450	21.0
大龙村	5.6	1027	2500	636	54	23	373	2468	1234	50.0
大厚村	5.6	1018	5200	575	116	57	557	3683	226	6.1
谢山村	4.0	572	2600	330	135	50	2534	4995	478	9.6
谢岗村	14.0	2941	3260	1885	110	70	1011	8209	1021	12.4
赵林村	3.8	1695	5262	685	131	65	1325	5316	1372	25.8
曹乐村	6.6	2154	5863	1302	217	109	851	4993	955	19.1
五星村	1.6	1287	4175	1027	50	22	328	1739	1446	83.2
稔子园村	2.5	634	1763	375	56	32	441	2399	153	6.4
泰园		3353	7854	1842	640	4	176	598	751	125.6
常平										
居民	4.0	15940	25219	9077	798	29	889	1613	865	53.6
下墟村	0.4	826	2000	455	210	34	607	3713	2512	67.7
岗梓村	2.7	2545	8600	1570	125	68	1566	10005	5784	57.8
桥梓村	2.0	2484	5984	1519	208	85	2575	23473	6582	28.0
塘角村	1.1	957	8970	498	150	126	2136	9773	2191	22.4
苏坑村	4.0	3581	5282	1370	216	136	1266	8646	2397	27.7
袁山贝村	5.0	3553	8750	1244	631	303	4471	21457	5248	24.5
金美村	3.0	2416	8500	1137	312	145	4711	43431	15905	36.6
还珠沥村	5.5	2769	17025	1652	393	153	2928	14069	5175	36.8
朗贝村	4.0	1952	6000	705	293	85	978	6058	221	3.7
板石村	3.4	1928	11000	1134	660	45	928	5159	670	13.0
桥沥村	9.8	3474	33000	1512	743	210	1989	13001	2009	15.5
卢屋村	3.0	838	3700	490	180	160	538	2083	431	20.7
土塘村	8.7	2814	31306	1542	1080	144	4730	25504	1364	5.4
麦元村	2.4	1079	3308	386	150	20	1799	10051	921	9.2
九江水村	9.0	1413	7035	702	364	71	7877	21399	755	3.5
朗洲村	4.1	621	1243	398	110	29	1498	3923	1214	31.0
陈屋贝村	2.2	1111	5720	696	178	40	1395	10334	990	9.6
司马村	8.0	2790	15660	1449	527	84	3644	24191	3651	15.1

15 续表 12

(2010年)

村(居)委会	土地面积(平方公里)	户籍人口(人)	外来暂住人口(人)	户籍从业人数(人)	全部企业及个体户数(个)	#工业企业	当年可支配财政收入(万元)	资产总额(万元)	负债总额(万元)	资产负债率(%)
霞坑村	1.6	734	4337	387	235	30	730	4909	386	7.9
漱旧村	2.0	1129	4200	687	135	28	784	4418	295	6.7
漱新村	2.4	1258	5900	800	561	150	1044	6737	2020	30.0
黄泥塘村	1.0	896	2000	448	119	55	479	2637	1457	55.3
元江元村	1.9	1483	6000	905	145	49	1532	8903	1986	22.3
横江厦村	5.0	2785	4716	1685	232	90	1019	7960	3487	43.8
田尾村	2.1	1557	4350	827	56	36	707	4118	2007	48.7
白花沥村	1.0	695	212	159	10	10	420	1970	1314	66.7
沙湖口村	1.4	1022	3631	690	91	28	526	4528	2609	57.6
白石岗村	5.0	3773	6106	1231	110	101	1036	6722	4224	62.8
松柏塘村	3.8	2337	5731	1073	85	35	764	7243	3653	50.4
上坑村	1.3	922	1900	520	140	47	1523	11121	4128	37.1
木棆村	3.5	2066	6124	1047	521	60	4558	25722	2096	8.2
桥头										
东江村	4.8	2365	1927	1518	187	40	1272	7687	3652	47.5
山和村	2.5	966	2650	498	56	24	1066	6159	1572	25.5
屋厦村	2.0	693	1350	437	105	36	1118	5799	1949	33.6
岗头村	0.6	485	2791	306	50	30	710	3489	1155	33.1
李屋村	2.3	1608	2395	835	51	40	1444	17585	6327	36.0
邓屋村	2.7	1865	10200	1002	59	38	4020	25800	9478	36.7
朗厦村	4.1	1594	5500	831	108	78	3022	17682	4376	24.8
邵岗头村	1.3	859	1290	493	36	34	908	5333	2423	45.4
桥头	1.0	1320	2100	504	282	47	2695	20819	2401	11.5
迳联	1.5	1755	3350	808	108	46	3897	20171	2136	10.6
田新	2.2	2185	3750	1040	382	240	3862	22056	7166	32.5
岭头	1.3	1160	3530	691	260	68	2385	15185	2404	15.8
石水口村	7.0	4461	7300	2385	580	115	4357	30152	7200	23.9
大洲	4.6	3232	3505	1582	148	75	2626	20879	4551	21.8
禾坑村	1.5	990	1150	602	72	21	1005	5999	1628	27.1
田头角村	1.0	750	1816	430	68	43	1303	6618	2107	31.8
居民	15.6	9599	51245	4800			92			
横沥										
石涌村	3.9	1768	6083	1060	658	158	2241	15408	4262	27.7
隔坑村	1.8	2673	5620	1714	720	69	2305	14242	7190	50.5
半仙山村	1.5	1592	2863	930	1083	45	2180	19916	14358	72.1
横沥村	3.5	2901	3225	1856	578	53	1388	15452	6686	43.3
田头村	4.0	2504	6386	1483	757	53	2161	12922	4524	35.0
田坑村	5.0	2797	4882	1808	964	76	2001	7537	1956	26.0
村头村	4.0	2306	4150	685	509	87	1975	10291	3394	33.0
长巷村	2.4	1641	805	942	50	23	490	4793	2229	46.5
田饶步村	2.4	1820	1865	835	185	51	1025	14857	7465	50.3

15 续表 13

(2010年)

村(居)委会	土地面积(平方公里)	户籍人口(人)	外来暂住人口(人)	户籍从业人数(人)	全部企业及个体户数(个)	#工业企业	当年可支配财政收入(万元)	资产总额(万元)	负债总额(万元)	资产负债率(%)
六甲村	1.5	1087	3300	657	157	38	735	6921	3638	52.6
村尾村	2.3	1461	3560	980	454	45	1505	9480	3756	39.6
水边村	5.0	2727	4630	1946	271	37	720	6416	2894	45.1
新四村	3.8	2053	6449	1325	423	108	235	2315	1861	80.4
山厦村	2.7	1063	2324	533	236	42	1370	11966	781	6.5
月塘村	2.8	1101	953	535	107	24	1432	13110	1311	10.0
张坑村	1.0	615	1400	362	82	33	578	6816	1222	17.9
居民	3.0	6524	1584	3785	1783	26	177	1303	768	58.9
东坑										
东坑村	2.0	3028	13000	1823	233	68	1898	16344	8635	52.8
黄麻岭村	0.7	1074	3250	418	46	43	605	6308	3468	55.0
长安塘村	1.2	1853	900	1165	115	90	1362	7639	5519	72.3
寮边头村	0.8	1582	2146	737	240	25	1463	6864	3218	46.9
塔岗村	1.7	1755	5300	1097	74	60	1735	8698	2257	26.0
坑美村	2.0	1930	2580	945	125	66	669	5770	1408	24.4
新门楼村	1.4	1701	7256	841	142	11	939	9810	5880	59.9
井美村	1.9	2496	2896	1548	521	50	2342	9871	4545	46.0
初坑村	2.5	2462	8251	1397	428	55	560	2516	1473	58.6
凤大村	0.3	735	2760	480	321	14	272	2443	2084	85.3
丁屋村	1.1	1076	2500	521	12	8	763	3785	1751	46.3
彭屋村	2.3	1878	5300	1177	212	8	812	4236	1288	30.4
黄屋村	1.8	1948	4795	1039	519	28	1645	9832	2735	27.8
角社村	2.5	3384	4800	2221	175	68	1483	24968	766	3.1
居民	0.1	3030	330	1765	95	4				
企石										
铁岗村	5.7	2466	1872	1520	33	16	1323	10965	3440	31.4
深巷村	4.1	2222	2446	1230	130	52	750	5987	2599	43.4
湖美村	1.0	804	431	380	34	15	457	3910	2005	51.3
博夏村	6.7	3534	625	1668	49	15	745	6487	947	14.6
上洞村	5.3	2651	1803	1928	145	25	436	4695	936	19.9
清湖村	4.6	2011	1459	878	35	24	722	5826	2304	39.6
江边村	5.0	2958	1568	1500	65	23	634	4681	1009	21.6
旧围村	3.8	1898	1082	900	45	25	887	3772	936	24.8
东平村	1.5	723	3216	476	212	28	619	3625	2564	70.7
上截村	0.8	1141	1061	504	53	10	662	5518	4197	76.1
下截村	1.2	1439	829	786	45	18	1106	6359	2811	44.2
东山村	6.2	4296	5839	1455	403	89	3648	27373	10115	37.0
铁炉坑村	3.4	3037	2135	1598	130	88	1220	9722	3286	33.8
企石村	1.5	1362	612	761	39	18	705	6791	2314	34.1
杨屋村	0.8	643	396	320	45	10	344	3641	1983	54.5
莫屋村	1.0	1219	752	610	51	21	300	2177	1112	51.1
霞朗村	1.0	883	2586	175	253	32	1977	13032	5166	39.6
新南村	2.8	2092	1200	1378	303	41	1271	8437	2801	33.2
南坑村	1.5	1207	1084	810	91	27	934	7114	415	5.8

15　续表 14

(2010年)

村(居)委会	土地面积(平方公里)	户籍人口(人)	外来暂住人口(人)	户籍从业人数(人)	全部企业及个体户数(个)	#工业企业	当年可支配财政收入(万元)	资产总额(万元)	负债总额(万元)	资产负债率(%)
居　　民	0.5	5244	5731	3610	435		129	105	57	54.3
石　　排										
石排村	2.4	3614	4705	1720	701	66	896	2341	931	39.8
下沙村	3.4	2608	3715	1170	501	80	618	3904	1307	33.5
庙边王村	3.7	2390	7834	1509	952	201	881	5005	1172	23.4
福隆村	5.6	5822	10665	3698	1035	306	1981	21077	9693	46.0
沙角村	3.4	2576	4496	1742	318	32	1047	3486	881	25.3
黄家壆村	2.4	1925	2800	1214	186	30	1578	11752	254	2.2
赤坎村	3.2	1401	2617	690	279	53	1576	8507	2349	27.6
向西村	2.0	1202	5323	561	492	58	1369	7263	1680	23.1
水贝村	3.5	3234	4102	1803	336	85	982	5985	727	12.1
田寮村	3.3	1955	1588	1150	219	45	6558	6142	658	10.7
横山村	3.8	2031	4336	1322	366	45	765	2885	889	30.8
谷吓村	3.1	1870	3851	985	315	62	460	4458	1814	40.7
埔心村	2.2	1581	10298	741	868	689	1769	9430	319	3.4
塘尾村	1.6	1090	4563	650	228	76	843	8027	566	7.1
李家坊村	0.9	936	3338	538	196	60	571	4623	1377	29.8
田边村	4.2	2108	3169	1027	229	75	545	2498	1287	51.5
中坑村	3.2	2320	3480	1578	201	29	851	10799	587	5.4
燕窝村	4.3	1723	6227	1005	414	87	1289	6819	813	11.9
太　　和		2425		1549			335	1305	954	73.1
茶　　山										
上元村	4.5	3155	5000	1888	120	115	469	2607	970	37.2
茶山村	1.3	1724	4570	1093	71	43	1293	12609	5422	43.0
下朗村	1.0	1385	3000	942	68	29	1873	13203	2011	15.2
横江村	3.7	3052	4500	2128	131	66	2002	13778	3003	21.8
卢边村	3.3	2721	2210	1646	90	85	2227	10469	2010	19.2
寒溪水村	1.3	960	3126	539	59	42	759	3771	827	21.9
增埗村	6.0	7098	12310	4057	316	171	1077	11086	6711	60.5
南社村	6.9	3559	13510	2162	148	98	2302	32513	3848	11.8
塘角村	4.7	2923	9580	1558	155	135	1607	11684	1294	11.1
京山村	3.5	2444	4760	1389	328	41	1587	15821	5983	37.8
博头村	1.2	633	1736	355	38	15	923	4953	464	9.4
冲美村	0.8	752	1893	426	78	38	1051	7126	284	4.0
粟边村	3.2	1970	3600	1027	183	58	665	7302	1186	16.2
刘黄村	0.8	998	5220	614	258	71	1239	7710	2990	38.8
孙屋村	0.6	715	1085	470	41	24	280	2474	943	38.1
超朗村	8.2	2939	2088	1735	89	81	1193	21246	715	3.4
茶山圩	1.0	7610	3200							

十六、历年国民经济和社会发展主要指标

Main Indicators of National Economy and Social Development over Years

16 历年国民经济和社会发展主要指标

Main Indicators of National Economy and Social Development over Years

年份	户籍人口(万人)	常住人口(万人)	新莞人人口(万人)	人口自然增长率(‰)	户籍从业人员(万人)	新莞人从业人员(万人)	城镇在岗职工人数(万人)	城镇在岗职工平均工资(元)
1949	68.24							
1952	71.68							
1957	77.48				37.57		3.90	400
1962	79.64				36.78		2.93	552
1965	86.46			29.60	40.56		3.17	524
1970	98.56			20.60	49.97		3.29	534
1975	107.94			14.51	51.44		3.80	577
1978	111.23			13.81	54.97		8.20	474
1979	112.04			19.00	56.51		9.68	650
1980	112.70			19.31	57.86		9.86	750
1981	114.46			16.57	59.42		10.66	887
1982	116.19			14.14	61.76		11.41	1095
1983	117.59			11.53	63.25		11.59	1197
1984	118.95			10.60	65.51		11.76	1383
1985	120.85			10.83	67.35		12.30	1456
1986	123.01		15.62	11.56	69.68	10.41	13.27	2616
1987	124.86		25.29	11.67	71.63	18.03	13.67	2067
1988	126.76		36.89	12.09	71.99	29.25	12.71	2757
1989	128.76		47.19	12.39	73.95	40.53	13.10	3320
1990	131.85	175.62	65.59	12.31	75.10	57.20	13.16	3552
1991	133.65	200.01	80.58	13.34	76.99	70.20	14.59	3777
1992	136.06	227.78	114.48	14.50	77.55	107.10	15.47	4531
1993	138.92	259.41	121.70	13.41	79.36	112.68	17.66	6228
1994	141.40	295.43	139.09	13.37	81.02	124.18	16.09	8360
1995	143.65	336.45	142.18	12.75	82.40	126.54	17.87	9682
1996	145.25	383.17	143.32	11.97	83.52	127.66	17.50	10382
1997	147.12	436.38	144.68	12.09	84.78	130.73	16.50	10691
1998	148.77	496.97	199.11	10.86	85.98	183.19	16.40	11422
1999	150.82	565.98	244.81	10.22	87.82	216.15	16.39	12557
2000	152.61	644.84	254.72	7.52	88.62	244.84	16.41	14051
2001	153.89	654.43	457.82	7.01	90.80	449.68	16.42	16183
2002	156.19	654.84	433.65	5.91	92.93	426.01	16.42	17804
2003	158.96	655.25	440.45	5.65	95.64	432.73	16.60	22598
2004	161.97	655.66	486.95	5.96	98.36	473.39	17.54	25326
2005	165.65	656.07	584.98	6.02	101.30	553.42	18.86	28253
2006	168.31	685.66	586.76	5.86	103.76	566.98	19.99	31135
2007	171.26	717.02	557.80	5.98	106.65	538.95	20.56	35284
2008	174.87	750.60	552.50	6.23	109.67	530.30	20.72	39516
2009	178.73	786.08	429.96	6.31	112.18	413.46	22.60	42585
2010	181.77	822.48	411.47	6.23	114.44	391.23	22.63	46576

注：城镇在岗职工人数与平均工资1952－1975年是全所有制单位资料，1978－1999年为城镇职工资料，2000年起为城镇在岗职工资料。

16 续表 1

年 份	地区生产总值(万元)	第一产业	第二产业	工 业	建筑业	第三产业	人均地区生产总值(元)
1949							
1952							
1957							
1962							
1965							
1970							
1975							
1978	6.11	2.72	2.68			0.71	553
1979	6.62	2.65	2.92			1.05	593
1980	7.22	2.63	3.33			1.26	643
1981	9.11	3.28	4.30			1.54	802
1982	11.43	3.73	5.81			1.89	991
1983	13.03	3.98	6.90			2.15	1115
1984	15.96	4.57	7.81			3.59	1350
1985	22.60	6.15	11.66			4.80	1885
1986	30.02	8.14	13.57	10.54	3.03	8.30	2462
1987	39.29	9.82	17.72	14.24	3.49	11.74	3170
1988	55.46	11.89	28.28	25.05	3.23	15.29	4408
1989	60.92	12.66	27.97	27.22	0.75	20.29	4768
1990	80.44	13.28	40.53	39.18	1.34	26.63	6173
1991	95.91	13.45	50.32	48.34	1.98	32.13	5095
1992	110.89	14.41	59.27	56.63	2.64	37.21	5038
1993	157.05	14.40	87.31	82.89	4.42	55.34	5850
1994	217.03	17.48	119.49	110.77	8.72	80.06	6357
1995	296.29	21.43	166.97	154.19	12.78	107.89	7421
1996	361.75	24.86	199.48	187.85	11.63	137.40	8444
1997	448.60	25.64	243.28	230.79	12.50	179.68	9747
1998	558.00	25.94	305.68	290.69	14.99	226.37	11265
1999	667.24	25.79	367.05	349.53	17.52	274.40	12494
2000	820.25	25.91	450.71	430.45	20.25	343.64	13679
2001	991.89	26.10	540.51	517.03	23.48	425.28	15268
2002	1186.94	24.88	648.81	621.86	26.96	513.25	18131
2003	1452.52	22.82	798.20	757.18	41.01	631.51	22174
2004	1806.03	22.71	1016.04	968.01	48.03	767.28	27554
2005	2183.20	20.55	1227.86	1173.23	54.63	934.78	33287
2006	2627.98	12.01	1506.60	1441.69	64.91	1109.37	39173
2007	3160.05	11.90	1754.66	1681.83	72.83	1393.49	45057
2008	3703.60	14.83	1901.61	1819.22	82.38	1787.17	50471
2009	3763.91	14.79	1823.08	1741.53	81.55	1926.04	48988
2010	4246.45	16.57	2160.82	2078.45	82.37	2069.07	52798

注：1. 本表按当年价格计算。
2. 人均生产总值1990年及以前年份按年平均户籍人口计算，1991年起按年平均常住人口计算。

16　续表 2

上年＝100

年　份	地区生产总值指　数	第一产业	第二产业			第三产业	人均地区生产总值指　数
				工　业	建筑业		
1949							
1952							
1957							
1962							
1965							
1970							
1975							
1978							
1979	99.5	86.5	107.0			146.4	98.6
1980	102.7	90.3	117.3			113.9	102.0
1981	116.6	115.0	122.1			110.8	115.4
1982	116.9	105.3	131.0			117.6	115.1
1983	110.4	104.8	115.7			111.3	108.9
1984	114.2	109.0	107.0			140.9	112.9
1985	132.3	118.9	144.5			132.7	130.5
1986	126.1	111.9	110.3			174.7	124.0
1987	122.5	111.6	127.7	125.8	147.0	126.0	120.5
1988	115.7	90.6	143.7	151.4	77.9	103.0	114.0
1989	107.1	99.8	106.2	106.4	103.7	113.7	105.5
1990	123.2	104.4	127.6	130.6	76.4	128.0	120.8
1991	117.5	103.1	121.5	121.8	113.2	118.6	108.8
1992	108.3	100.0	112.6	113.7	78.0	105.1	92.6
1993	127.9	79.4	139.2	138.5	168.1	129.0	104.8
1994	122.5	107.2	124.7	124.3	138.5	122.3	96.3
1995	127.4	110.5	135.1	135.3	128.3	116.8	108.9
1996	117.5	109.4	115.5	116.2	91.2	123.5	109.5
1997	119.6	104.5	119.8	120.1	106.1	121.8	111.3
1998	121.8	100.9	122.1	122.2	115.1	124.5	113.1
1999	119.7	102.3	120.6	120.7	115.2	120.3	111.0
2000	119.7	99.8	120.7	120.9	110.5	120.0	106.6
2001	119.9	103.0	121.6	122.0	113.0	118.9	110.7
2002	120.5	97.6	122.6	123.0	114.1	119.1	119.6
2003	120.5	90.2	122.3	121.4	143.5	119.7	120.4
2004	121.0	90.0	125.6	126.5	106.8	115.8	120.9
2005	119.5	102.3	120.0	120.2	113.5	119.3	119.4
2006	119.2	58.9	121.9	122.0	118.7	117.1	116.6
2007	118.3	89.9	114.8	115.0	108.7	123.3	113.1
2008	114.0	110.6	106.1	106.4	100.9	124.0	109.0
2009	105.3	102.3	99.7	99.4	104.7	111.4	100.5
2010	110.3	101.6	116.7	117.5	97.1	104.1	105.3

注：本表按可比价格计算。

年　份	全社会固定资产投资(亿元)	地方财政一般预算收入(亿元)	地方财政一般预算支出(亿元)	居民消费价格指数(上年=100)	商品零售价格指数(上年=100)	农林牧渔业总　产　值(亿元)	农林牧渔业总产值指数(1978=100)
1949						0.54	
1952		0.28	0.02			0.66	
1957		0.32	0.04			0.78	
1962		0.31	0.07			0.76	
1965		0.47	0.07			1.28	
1970		0.48	0.08			1.47	
1975		0.65	0.11			2.53	
1978	0.23	0.66	0.18		100.4	4.24	100.0
1979	0.16	0.66	0.19		102.6	4.15	96.5
1980	0.24	0.67	0.20		110.9	4.19	98.0
1981	0.38	0.68	0.21		109.3	5.04	102.1
1982	1.81	0.81	0.26		101.2	5.59	117.6
1983	1.84	0.86	0.28		99.6	5.64	117.4
1984	3.01	0.85	0.30	99.3	98.6	7.02	126.7
1985	7.06	1.11	0.50	106.5	106.9	9.12	138.9
1986	11.52	1.61	0.99	104.2	104.4	12.30	174.6
1987	14.19	2.02	1.25	112.0	112.2	14.84	186.4
1988	16.55	2.71	1.75	136.0	132.8	20.37	182.1
1989	5.01	3.19	2.16	122.0	122.4	22.11	181.9
1990	7.51	3.57	2.28	96.6	94.9	23.64	195.3
1991	13.75	4.44	2.75	102.4	101.4	24.26	199.5
1992	18.88	5.62	3.82	109.2	107.7	27.13	211.3
1993	32.76	9.38	7.29	121.8	119.5	28.45	175.5
1994	140.76	7.69	8.90	123.5	118.4	34.75	188.4
1995	63.14	11.56	12.42	113.9	109.7	42.69	207.8
1996	67.62	9.65	12.41	106.8	104.7	49.72	216.3
1997	65.89	11.41	14.85	101.5	99.7	51.44	225.0
1998	77.00	15.10	17.91	99.9	98.7	53.60	227.3
1999	88.32	18.26	21.26	97.9	95.9	53.74	242.8
2000	102.89	30.47	33.61	101.5	100.1	54.64	243.3
2001	125.49	45.02	47.86	96.6	97.8	55.93	246.3
2002	191.57	55.29	64.96	98.1	99.1	53.67	263.2
2003	319.39	67.45	76.52	100.7	101.7	49.02	209.7
2004	454.87	82.64	94.16	103.0	103.2	44.19	213.5
2005	597.24	103.97	117.04	102.4	103.0	42.05	222.2
2006	705.45	128.94	147.90	101.2	102.8	21.26	121.0
2007	841.21	186.45	193.10	103.1	104.2	19.98	105.6
2008	944.34	209.22	218.26	105.5	107.9	25.53	118.3
2009	1094.08	231.16	232.62	96.9	95.3	25.31	122.2
2010	1114.98	277.84	289.83	102.8	103.2	28.31	126.2

注：农林牧渔总产值1952—1970年按1957年不变价计算，1975年按1970年不变价计算，1978年起按当年价计算。

年 份	农作物总播种面积(千公顷)	#粮食	粮食产量(万吨)	油料产量(万吨)	水果产量(万吨)	肉类产量(万吨)	水产品产量(万吨)
1949	141.26	127.26	21.07	0.15			0.32
1952	167.61	149.68	26.95	0.35			0.34
1957	188.98	165.53	28.80	0.33			0.42
1962	155.97	138.18	33.12	0.38			0.63
1965	158.97	121.64	43.71	0.72	4.54		0.99
1970	174.60	127.25	45.08	0.96	6.95		1.62
1975	202.00	137.03	50.72	1.11	3.68		2.19
1978	190.63	138.15	53.23	1.42	2.65	2.69	3.09
1979	172.36	129.16	53.53	1.91	2.33	2.92	2.23
1980	162.41	117.12	52.94	2.90	2.37	2.77	2.55
1981	151.17	107.13	44.75	3.55	4.69	2.80	2.49
1982	146.96	106.68	54.33	2.99	5.82	3.30	2.77
1983	146.21	109.02	56.12	1.97	7.72	3.57	3.03
1984	144.35	105.12	55.82	2.31	10.59	3.33	3.25
1985	130.01	93.05	48.87	2.10	18.94	3.33	3.26
1986	119.41	83.81	45.52	2.01	30.77	4.33	4.65
1987	119.73	83.40	46.28	1.70	36.31	4.61	6.57
1988	119.53	82.42	46.09	1.51	26.37	5.61	6.81
1989	122.27	85.61	48.76	1.37	22.14	5.86	6.23
1990	123.25	85.74	49.43	1.34	28.24	6.22	6.85
1991	119.42	81.77	47.37	1.15	34.32	6.88	6.90
1992	104.10	64.26	36.81	0.93	34.48	6.80	7.32
1993	71.20	36.74	20.21	0.56	27.13	7.66	6.50
1994	67.30	35.75	20.24	0.37	26.49	8.54	6.74
1995	71.89	39.90	22.74	0.37	24.32	9.76	7.48
1996	72.23	41.89	24.32	0.31	20.63	11.61	8.11
1997	72.17	41.61	24.69	0.29	16.50	12.90	9.19
1998	73.46	41.63	24.72	0.26	11.41	15.35	9.69
1999	72.59	41.77	24.73	0.22	13.63	15.99	9.40
2000	65.73	35.18	20.41	0.20	12.94	17.90	9.51
2001	56.95	22.56	12.84	0.16	15.01	19.84	8.96
2002	42.28	9.88	5.37	0.09	18.93	18.88	8.24
2003	33.97	5.65	3.05	0.04	14.64	15.46	7.58
2004	30.82	5.41	3.04	0.02	17.54	14.62	7.15
2005	27.38	4.14	2.00	0.01	15.13	17.17	6.74
2006	22.26	2.29	1.00	0.01	13.96	3.49	4.71
2007	21.37	2.15	0.99	0.01	13.16	2.03	4.73
2008	23.48	2.72	1.20	0.01	10.15	2.41	7.23
2009	24.72	2.77	1.19	0.01	9.15	2.55	7.33
2010	24.62	2.79	1.25	0.01	7.55	2.88	7.63

年　份	工业企业单位数(个)	工　业增加值(亿元)	工业增加值指数(上年=100)	规模以上工业增加值(亿元)	总　供电　量(亿千瓦时)	总　售电　量(亿千瓦时)	建筑业总产值(亿元)	建筑业增加值(亿元)
1949	1							
1952	3522							
1957	262							
1962	280				0.08	0.07		
1965	260				0.36	0.32		
1970	220				0.71	0.60		
1975	324				1.24	1.11		
1978	1290				1.64	1.49		
1979	1250				1.93	1.73		
1980	1293				2.17	1.97		
1981	1479				2.22	1.99		
1982	1862				2.69	2.35		
1983	1964				3.15	2.75		
1984	2329				3.26	2.84		
1985	4187				3.82	3.39		
1986	5949	10.54		6.96	3.93	3.51		3.03
1987	8106	14.24	125.8	8.68	6.43	5.71		3.49
1988	8408	25.05	151.4	15.03	9.48	8.47		3.23
1989	8757	27.22	106.4	15.54	12.09	10.84	1.03	0.75
1990	9892	39.18	130.6	23.76	18.01	16.15	1.27	1.34
1991	10094	48.34	121.8	31.54	24.05	21.67	2.19	1.98
1992	11639	56.63	113.7	38.21	32.00	28.87	3.19	2.64
1993	12449	82.89	138.5	59.08	43.62	39.40	5.39	4.42
1994	14086	110.77	124.3	78.43	58.58	53.02	7.99	8.72
1995	15215	154.19	135.3	111.02	68.00	61.68	9.49	12.78
1996	15326	187.85	116.2	140.89	80.03	72.71	9.66	11.63
1997	16857	230.79	120.1	177.71	94.93	86.65	28.73	12.50
1998	16406	290.69	122.2	240.22	109.48	100.91	35.92	14.99
1999	16877	349.53	120.7	292.58	132.78	123.42	40.73	17.52
2000	16975	430.45	120.9	360.11	178.03	169.06	40.45	20.25
2001	18094	517.03	122.0	410.67	207.72	196.59	50.13	23.48
2002	21313	621.86	123.0	542.03	258.55	246.97	65.84	26.96
2003	21935	757.18	121.4	673.59	321.65	283.54	76.48	41.01
2004	22156	968.01	126.5	826.58	372.84	350.28	77.01	48.03
2005	21868	1173.23	120.2	979.34	415.66	396.59	84.35	58.61
2006	22447	1441.69	122.0	1186.20	464.45	445.52	94.58	64.91
2007	22587	1681.83	115.0	1388.34	507.89	482.56	112.87	72.83
2008	25656	1819.22	106.4	1602.98	507.35	487.32	108.81	82.38
2009	31160	1741.53	99.4	1453.37	488.85	478.19	99.40	81.55
2010	38273	2078.45	117.5	1708.31	556.89	543.66	122.06	82.37

16 续表 6

年　份	公路通车里程(公里)	民用汽车拥有量(万辆)	旅客周转量(万人公里)	货物周转量(万吨公里)	邮电业务收入(万元)	本地电话用户(万户)	移动电话用户(万户)
1949	204	0.002					
1952	219	0.002	1350	139			
1957	373	0.005	2100	195			
1962	598	0.007	4120	293			
1965	882	0.010	4725	457			
1970	1134	0.012	2800	900			
1975	1173	0.025	3890	694			
1978	1259	0.06	9425	15148	686	0.20	
1979	1225	0.11	11162	15290	790	0.21	
1980	1225	0.20	13584	16353	927	0.31	
1981	1225	0.30	13845	15606	962	0.34	
1982	1225	0.34	16026	17185	940	0.35	
1983	1225	0.45	54075	108634	1018	0.39	
1984	1240	0.61	62107	140113	1263	0.48	
1985	1240	0.79	95237	171591	1560	0.77	
1986	1248	0.86	127458	126898	2015	0.88	
1987	1261	1.00	159117	174942	3410	1.63	
1988	1302	1.36	173335	169112	5728	2.52	
1989	1325	1.63	240999	186626	9620	4.30	0.02
1990	1325	1.94	322236	184700	17555	4.90	0.05
1991	1759	2.07	373284	194101	27733	7.50	0.11
1992	2055	3.26	503973	232752	42155	9.70	0.30
1993	2260	4.81	577800	248230	65699	14.98	0.72
1994	2292	6.16	595134	273053	102238	23.19	2.41
1995	2327	8.83	446230	264605	152761	31.57	4.77
1996	2330	9.08	477466	267193	207573	36.91	8.24
1997	2330	10.34	511592	278649	284278	42.65	15.29
1998	2377	11.34	577452	285889	376708	50.13	26.17
1999	2467	12.70	804278	300410	515916	60.87	51.01
2000	2518	15.37	1001906	404678	724593	78.12	123.68
2001	2570	18.36	1031579	406247	1225474	98.96	295.76
2002	2641	22.01	1091821	420684	1816802	127.93	412.39
2003	2688	25.56	1126964	422822	1051220	206.11	660.86
2004	2759	31.97	1166262	423669	1207778	281.35	856.09
2005	2871	40.66	1185290	424829	1328172	384.52	1016.41
2006	3891	48.93	1213809	336783	1466871	461.31	1216.34
2007	3924	60.89	1264982	356677	1619048	469.17	1408.23
2008	4001	70.16	2248521	1747489	1723829	439.41	1454.29
2009	4713	79.56	1053469	1016490	1563077	378.40	1409.29
2010	4751	92.08	1290692	1090340	1553352	332.42	1607.60

注：1. 公路通车里程2006年起含专用公路和村道。
　　2. 邮电业务收入2003年以前为邮电业务总量，按1990年不变价计算，2003年起为邮电业务收入。

16　续表 7

年　份	社会消费品零售总额(亿元)	进出口总额(亿美元)	出口额	进口额	协议(合同)规定外商投资额(亿美元)	实际利用外资(亿美元)	#外商直接投资
1949							
1952							
1957			0.02				
1962			0.04				
1965			0.08				
1970			0.10				
1975			0.25				
1978	2.13		0.39				
1979	2.50		0.54		0.05	0.02	
1980	3.16		0.77		0.11	0.09	
1981	4.02		0.92		0.08	0.05	0.001
1982	4.81		1.09		0.08	0.07	0.005
1983	5.23		1.19		0.16	0.09	0.003
1984	7.39		1.30		0.32	0.19	0.07
1985	9.36		1.75		0.68	0.35	0.14
1986	12.24		2.33		0.34	0.45	0.15
1987	15.05		2.68		1.85	1.32	0.21
1988	24.65		3.18		6.22	2.99	0.64
1989	27.04		3.49		2.34	2.73	0.84
1990	31.97	10.82	5.68	5.14	3.02	2.56	1.00
1991	36.50	31.75	16.52	15.23	6.45	2.83	1.47
1992	44.35	50.90	26.03	24.87	20.88	4.81	3.29
1993	63.69	67.56	32.11	35.45	35.55	10.49	7.92
1994	85.16	88.30	42.94	45.36	34.97	11.95	7.79
1995	113.01	153.91	77.99	75.92	33.09	11.58	6.72
1996	125.53	178.42	91.87	86.55	20.89	13.10	6.95
1997	146.04	212.99	113.68	99.31	12.14	15.16	8.80
1998	175.16	232.73	130.61	102.13	16.37	15.48	9.30
1999	202.30	284.63	151.54	133.09	14.72	17.89	9.71
2000	235.16	320.45	171.59	148.86	18.36	19.54	10.87
2001	275.71	344.55	189.89	154.65	20.98	20.29	11.47
2002	321.24	442.47	237.36	205.11	24.89	23.48	14.59
2003	369.78	521.06	280.02	241.04	32.56	27.72	17.54
2004	426.47	645.18	351.92	293.25	41.32	33.47	21.39
2005	506.29	743.72	409.29	334.42	47.52	42.48	14.68
2006	599.32	842.21	473.76	368.45	55.28	50.04	18.08
2007	722.45	1068.73	602.32	466.41	62.51	60.07	21.18
2008	881.15	1132.99	655.37	477.62	39.37	47.09	24.47
2009	959.07	941.55	551.69	389.86	20.30	42.12	25.94
2010	1108.06	1213.38	695.98	517.40	30.73	31.63	27.32

注：1. 出口总额1990年起为海关口径，1990年以前为外经贸口径。
2. 实际外商直接投资2004年起为新口径，是以验资作为统计标准，与往年数不可比。

16 续表 8

年 份	入境旅游人数(万人次)	国际旅游外汇收入(万美元)	接待国内游客人次(万人次)	旅 游总收入(亿元)	各项人民币存款余额(亿元)	城乡居民储蓄存款余额	各项人民币贷款余额(亿元)
1949							
1952						0.003	0.004
1957						0.02	0.26
1962					0.08	0.04	0.75
1965					0.16	0.09	0.81
1970					0.39	0.16	0.87
1975					0.96	0.41	1.39
1978					1.05	0.54	1.96
1979					1.49	0.72	2.13
1980					2.61	1.17	3.08
1981					3.80	2.03	4.02
1982					4.51	2.77	4.55
1983					6.05	3.86	5.76
1984					11.03	6.18	12.19
1985					13.49	9.19	14.24
1986	80	554	69		19.59	13.14	20.68
1987	107	453	87		28.48	18.97	31.24
1988	125	710	105		38.05	24.91	41.58
1989	115	504	97		46.82	32.57	49.37
1990	125	1025	98		68.07	45.51	63.04
1991	155	2443	118		94.97	61.47	78.40
1992	172	2473	125		147.34	81.54	105.98
1993	169	2888	117		179.83	107.17	134.31
1994	119	3464	75		249.78	151.54	173.44
1995	89	5679	62		383.68	232.97	254.85
1996	175	6464	139		489.65	318.02	312.81
1997	171	6778	112		671.17	425.82	382.66
1998	216	6601	141		864.01	533.75	442.74
1999	253	7055	156		1040.84	616.34	524.37
2000	291	7617	185		1228.67	672.07	630.84
2001	327	8200	217	39.80	1458.65	799.18	750.18
2002	930	11847	822	72.51	1790.18	1001.69	933.41
2003	1086	13825	1006	79.92	2126.78	1231.06	1206.72
2004	1131	23437	982	85.70	2462.87	1431.68	1405.25
2005	1156	28189	987	90.72	2933.40	1728.28	1500.52
2006	1363	33180	1170	96.01	3365.65	2013.40	1730.56
2007	1725	42702	1477	118.88	3751.83	2120.74	2154.77
2008	1872	45614	1604	128.69	4354.53	2638.04	2380.36
2009	2037	51756	1751	151.49	4986.61	2904.57	2903.80
2010	2251	67592	1924	191.32	5943.39	3386.85	3329.82

16 续表 9

年份	在校学生数（万人）				学龄儿童入学率(%)	高考入围人数(人)		病床床位数(张)
	普通高等学校	普通中等学校	#普通中学	小学			#省线入围人数	
1949		0.21	0.20	5.28				219
1952		0.39	0.34	7.04				179
1957		0.72	0.67	8.80				403
1962		1.01	0.97	12.00				1376
1965		1.08	1.05	16.09				1308
1970		6.02	6.02	11.81				1476
1975		5.03	4.96	16.82				1970
1978		7.66	7.60	16.11	98.36	846	250	2257
1979		6.27	6.23	15.80	98.70	566	166	2271
1980		5.52	5.48	15.49	98.85	222	140	2207
1981		4.40	4.35	15.09	98.72	239	154	2210
1982		4.23	4.17	14.48	99.06	252	115	2292
1983		4.37	4.28	13.54	99.75	245	150	2098
1984		4.76	4.65	13.46	99.65	619	220	2231
1985		5.00	4.66	13.44	99.83	534	285	2323
1986		5.33	4.94	14.07	99.90	595	228	3054
1987		6.03	5.44	14.43	99.94	644	297	3393
1988		6.64	5.93	15.01	99.93	925	315	3640
1989		6.98	6.20	15.59	99.92	977	284	3677
1990		7.01	6.12	16.27	99.94	759	224	3866
1991		7.11	6.01	17.01	99.92	861	268	4085
1992		7.83	6.52	17.52	99.94	994	312	4517
1993	0.11	8.95	7.53	18.01	99.95	1102	423	4940
1994	0.15	10.19	8.58	18.62	99.96	1823	586	5365
1995	0.16	11.12	9.25	19.51	99.99	2095	809	5798
1996	0.18	11.78	9.52	20.60	99.98	2160	1093	5288
1997	0.20	12.28	9.80	22.18	99.99	2212	1215	5505
1998	0.22	12.68	10.12	23.58	99.99	2348	1315	5892
1999	0.22	13.06	10.55	24.88	99.99	3501	1790	6241
2000	0.32	13.56	11.24	27.28	99.99	5017	2646	7081
2001	0.38	14.58	12.21	29.54	100.00	5651	3225	7474
2002	0.51	16.06	13.53	34.28	100.00	6873	3759	8641
2003	0.69	17.73	14.97	38.69	100.00	9167	4509	9820
2004	0.91	19.98	17.13	44.83	100.00	10756	5452	10797
2005	1.66	22.05	19.10	48.09	100.00	11196	6455	11972
2006	2.20	25.00	21.46	49.68	100.00	11359	7652	13293
2007	2.52	27.50	23.46	52.07	100.00	13275	9185	15227
2008	2.87	29.39	24.84	52.86	100.00	15047	9987	16778
2009	3.40	29.60	24.95	51.12	100.00	17487	12569	18080
2010	3.83	30.58	25.83	55.24	100.00	18845	13761	19980

年 份	卫生机构技术人员数(万人)	#执业(助理)医师	每万人口拥有 床位数(张)	每万人口拥有 执业(助理)医师(人)	年末参加基本养老保险人数(万人)	年末参加基本医疗保险人数(万人)	城镇居民最低生活保障人数(人)
1949	0.02		3.21				
1952	0.01		2.50				
1957	0.03		5.20				
1962	0.13		17.28				
1965	0.16		15.13				
1970	0.17		14.98				
1975	0.23		18.25				
1978	0.26	0.08	20.29	6.90			
1979	0.29	0.10	20.27	8.67			
1980	0.30	0.12	19.58	10.35			
1981	0.31	0.11	19.31	9.63			
1982	0.33	0.11	19.73	9.44			
1983	0.33	0.11	17.84	9.25			
1984	0.34	0.11	18.76	9.52			
1985	0.33	0.12	19.22	9.94			
1986	0.35	0.12	24.83	9.58			
1987	0.35	0.13	27.17	10.44			
1988	0.38	0.15	28.72	12.13			
1989	0.39	0.16	28.56	12.58			
1990	0.39	0.17	22.01	9.80			
1991	0.39	0.18	20.42	8.77			
1992	0.41	0.18	19.83	8.04			
1993	0.45	0.20	19.04	7.80			
1994	0.49	0.22	18.16	7.52	7.55	7.77	
1995	0.53	0.23	17.23	6.83	8.46	7.60	
1996	0.58	0.24	13.80	6.39	9.16	7.65	
1997	0.63	0.26	12.62	5.97	7.53	8.29	
1998	0.71	0.30	11.86	5.95	7.84	9.05	
1999	0.76	0.31	11.03	5.44	8.35	9.95	
2000	0.81	0.33	10.98	5.13	82.95	88.21	1825
2001	0.81	0.34	11.42	5.24	83.01	84.99	2003
2002	0.90	0.35	13.20	5.38	103.19	105.19	2711
2003	0.98	0.38	14.99	5.74	104.13	105.90	2876
2004	1.31	0.49	16.47	7.43	104.44	105.95	4968
2005	1.88	0.69	18.25	10.52	182.49	189.40	4885
2006	2.29	0.86	22.21	12.58	204.08	212.16	6091
2007	2.88	1.04	21.24	14.57	227.98	236.32	3129
2008	3.31	1.19	22.35	15.81	262.63	513.25	3653
2009	3.58	1.29	23.00	16.39	315.81	536.57	3770
2010	3.75	1.32	24.29	16.07	421.84	592.27	3643

注：每万人口拥有床位数、执业(助理)医师数按常住人口计算。

16 续表 11

年 份	专 利 申请量 (件)	专 利 授权量 (件)	城市居民 人均可支 配收入 (元)	农 民 人 均 纯收入 (元)	城镇人均 住房使用 面 积 (平方米)	农村人均 生活用房 使用面积 (平方米)
1949						
1952						
1957						
1962						
1965						
1970						
1975						
1978				149		
1979				188		
1980				272		
1981				463		
1982				567		
1983				618		
1984				691		
1985			791	803	11	
1986			1033	951	12	
1987			1247	1142	13	
1988			1778	1325	15	
1989			2282	1424	17	
1990	34	30	2508	1542	16	
1991	70	50	3068	1673	16	
1992	102	78	4026	2290	17	
1993	100	90	5970	2903	20	
1994	104	100	8270	3769	23	
1995	325	262	9588	4769	20	
1996	333	312	10824	5554	21	20
1997	725	321	11032	6132	21	41
1998	890	709	11506	6830	26	43
1999	1221	819	12954	7704	29.7	46
2000	1653	1399	14142	8484	31.1	47
2001	2914	1753	16938	9383	39.9	48
2002	3100	2680	16949	10178	41.8	55
2003	3865	2858	18471	11033	41.4	58
2004	4325	3167	20526	11941	41.6	65
2005	6694	3114	22882	13076	42.7	65
2006	9879	4872	25320	14313	45.2	60
2007	13842	6752	27025	15747	43.1	59
2008	14406	8093	30275	16904	40.3	55
2009	19106	12918	33045	18098	40.4	56
2010	21654	20397	35690	20486	44.1	52

十七、东莞与全国、全省及三角洲城市主要指标比较

Comparison of Main Indicators between Dongguan and China, Guangdong Province, the Cities of the Pearl River Delta

17-1 主要年份全国国民经济与社会发展指标

Main Indicators on National Economy and Social Development of China

指　　标	单 位	1980年	1985年	1990年	1995年	2000年	2005年	2009年	2010年
一、人口与劳动力									
年末总人口	万人	98705	105851	114333	121121	126743	130756	133474	133972
年末从业人员人数	万人	42361	49873	64749	68065	72085	75825	77995	
#城镇从业人员	万人	10525	12808	17041	19040	23151	27331	31120	
二、经济总量									
国内生产总值	亿元	4518	8964	18548	60794	99215	182321	340507	397983
第一产业增加值	亿元	1359	2541	5017	12020	14716	22718	35226	40497
第二产业增加值	亿元	2192	3867	7717	28679	45556	86208	157639	186481
第三产业增加值	亿元	967	2556	5814	20094	38942	73395	147642	171005
人均国内生产总值	元	460	853	1634	5046	7858	13985	25575	29762
三、农业									
主要农产品产量									
粮食	万吨	32056	37911	44624	46662	46218	48402	53082	54641
水果	万吨	679	1164	1874	4215	6225	16120	20396	21401
肉类	万吨		1927	2857	5260	6125	7743	7650	7925
水产品	万吨	450	705	1237	2517	4278	5106	5116	5366
四、工业									
工业增加值	亿元	1997	3449	6858	24951	40034	77231	135240	160030
主要工业产品产量									
机制纸及纸板	万吨	535	911	1372	2812	2487	5404	9389	10036
彩电	万台	3	435	1033	2058	3936	8283	9899	11830
发电量	亿千瓦时	3006	4107	6212	10070	13556	24747	37147	42065
成品钢材	万吨	2716	3693	5153	8980	13146	39692	69626	79776
水泥	亿吨	0.80	1.46	2.10	4.76	5.97	10.64	16.50	18.80
五、运输邮电									
货运量	亿吨	54.65	74.58	97.06	123.49	135.87	186.21	282.52	320.30
货物周转量	亿吨公里	12026	18365	26208	35909	44321	80258	122133	137329
客运量	亿人	34.18	62.02	77.27	117.26	147.86	184.70	297.69	328.00
旅客周转量	亿人公里	2281	4437	5628	9002	12261	17467	24835	27779
邮电业务总量	亿元	13	30	82	989	4793	12029	27193	32940
年末固定电话用户	万户		312	685	4071	14483	35043	31373	29438
年末移动电话用户	万户			1.8	363	8453	39343	74721	85900

注：1. 2010年年末人口数为第六次全国人口普查数据。
2. 城镇从业人员1998年起为城镇在岗职工人数。
3. 邮电业务总量1999年及以前年份按1990不变价计算，2000年起按2000年不变价计算。

17-1 续表

指　　标	单　位	1980年	1985年	1990年	1995年	2000年	2005年	2009年	2010年
六、固定资产投资									
全社会固定资产投资总额	亿元	911	2543	4517	20019	32918	88604	224846	278140
#房地产开发	亿元			253	3149	4984	15759	36232	48267
七、商业									
社会消费品零售总额	亿元	2140	4305	8300	20620	34153	67177	132678	156998
八、物价总指数									
商品零售价格指数	上年=100	106.0	108.8	102.1	114.8	98.5	100.8	98.8	103.1
居民消费价格指数	上年=100		109.3	103.1	117.1	100.4	101.8	99.3	103.3
九、外贸外经									
海关进出口总额	亿美元	381	696	1154	2809	4743	14221	22075	29728
进口额	亿美元	200	423	533	1321	2251	6601	10059	13948
出口额	亿美元	181	273	621	1488	2492	7620	12016	15779
实际利用外资	亿美元		20	38	378	494	603	918	1057
十、财政、金融									
财政收入	亿元	1160	2005	2937	6242	13395	31649	68518	83080
财政支出	亿元	1229	2004	3084	6824	15887	33930	76300	89575
各项人民币存款余额	亿元				53882	123804	287163	597741	71.8万
各项人民币贷款余额	亿元				50544	99371	194690	399685	47.9万
十一、人民生活									
在岗职工人均工资	元	762	1148	2140	5500	9371	18405	32736	
城市居民人均可支配收入	元	478	739	1510	4283	6280	10493	17175	19109
农民人均纯收入	元	191	398	686	1578	2253	3255	5153	5919
城乡居民人民币储蓄存款余额	亿元	400	1623	7120	29662	64332	141051	260772	303302
十二、教育									
在校学生数									
普通高等学校	万人	114	170	206	291	556	1562	2145	2232
普通中学	万人	5508	4706	4586	5371	7369	8624	7875	
小学	万人	14627	13370	12241	13195	13013	10864	10072	9941
十三、卫生									
医院床位数	万张	198	223	262	284	295	307	396	437
卫生技术人员	万人	280	341	390	426	449	446	522	584
#执业（助理）医师	万人	115	141	176	192	208	194	216	237

注：实际利用外资不含对外借款，2005年起为实际使用外商直接投资口径。

17-2　主要年份广东省国民经济与社会发展指标

Main Indicators on National Economy and Social Development of Guangdong Province

指　　标	单　位	1980年	1985年	1990年	1995年	2000年	2005年	2009年	2010年
一、人口与劳动力									
年末常住人口	万人			6347	7387	8650	9194	10130	10441
年末从业人员人数	万人	2368	2731	3118	3551	3989	5023	5652	5723
#城镇从业人员	万人	564	661	785	912	759	904	1055	1105
二、经济总量									
地区生产总值	亿元	250	577	1559	5933	10741	22367	39483	46013
第一产业增加值	亿元	83	172	385	864	986	1428	2010	2287
第二产业增加值	亿元	103	230	616	2900	5000	11440	19420	23015
第三产业增加值	亿元	64	176	559	2168	4755	9598	18053	20712
人均地区生产总值	元	481	1026	2484	8129	12736	24647	39436	44736
三、农业									
主要农产品产量									
粮食	万吨	1682	1604	1896	1803	1822	1395	1315	1317
水果	万吨	29	116	329	415	644	832	1062	1129
肉类	万吨	63	128	202	305	324	384	427	441
水产品	万吨	63	109	208	354	593	695	703	731
四、工业									
工业增加值	亿元	90	186	523	2449	4463	10490	18092	21463
主要工业产品产量									
机制纸及纸板	万吨	31	53	104	288	260	691	1316	1435
彩电	万台	1	79	262	764	1532	4090	4093	4495
发电量	亿千瓦时	109	167	344	821	1293	2163	2666	3101
成品钢材	万吨	45	79	134	247	406	1366	2286	2919
水泥	万吨	387	1120	2071	5318	5872	8032	10029	11537
五、运输邮电									
货运量	万吨	14201	58726	85809	111063	119216	134101	179722	203089
货物周转量	亿吨公里	1413	1608	2214	4643	3065	3919	4943	5915
客运量	万人	21444	49848	78046	130998	164791	161357	428705	491548
旅客周转量	亿人公里	114	270	453	936	1219	2043	2853	3331
邮电业务总量	亿元	2	4	26	205	602	2177	3938	5084
年末程控电话用户	万户		24	113	591	1415	3443	3367	3169
年末移动电话用户	万户			1	99	1357	6407	8939	9708

注：1. 2010年年末人口数为第六次全国人口普查数据。
　　2. 邮电业务总量1999年及以前年份按1990不变价计算，2000年起按2000年不变价计算。

17-2 续表

指标	单位	1980年	1985年	1990年	1995年	2000年	2005年	2009年	2010年
六、固定资产投资									
全社会固定资产投资总额	亿元	38	185	381	2327	3234	7164	13353	16113
#房地产开发	亿元			33	564	859	1592	2961	3660
七、商业									
社会消费品零售总额	亿元	118	289	667	2478	4380	7883	14892	17415
八、物价总指数									
商品零售价格指数	上年=100	108.5	113.6	95.6	111.6	99.9	101.8	96.8	103.3
居民消费价格指数	上年=100		114.8	97.5	114.0	101.4	102.3	97.7	103.1
九、外贸外经									
海关进出口总额	亿美元	26	54	419	1040	1701	4280	6111	7849
进口额	亿美元	4	24	197	474	782	1898	2522	3317
出口额	亿美元	22	30	222	566	919	2382	3590	4532
实际利用外资	亿美元	2	9	20	121	146	152	203	210
十、财政、金融									
地方财政一般预算收入	亿元	38	69	131	382	911	1807	3650	4516
地方财政一般预算支出	亿元	27	67	151	526	1070	2289	4334	5415
各项人民币存款余额	亿元				7090	16908	35784	66766	78286
各项人民币贷款余额	亿元				5496	11717	20745	38893	46099
十一、人民生活									
在岗职工人均工资	元	789	1393	2929	8250	13823	23959	35965	40253
城市居民人均可支配收入	元	473	954	2303	7439	9762	14770	21575	23898
农民人均纯收入	元	274	495	1043	2699	3654	4690	6907	7890
城乡居民人民币储蓄存款余额	亿元	30	155	752	3885	8667	19051	31346	36219
十二、教育									
在校学生数									
#普通高等学校	万人	4	7	10	15	30	87	133	143
中等职业教育学校	万人	6	18	45	67	66	71	120	155
普通中学	万人	252	236	234	339	461	612	696	709
小学	万人	749	671	747	883	930	1067	888	849
十三、卫生									
医院及卫生院床位数	万张	8	10	11	14	16	19	25	28
卫生技术人员	万人	14	18	19	23	27	30	41	45
#执业（助理）医师	万人	6	7	8	10	11	12	16	17

注：海关进出口总额1985年及以前年份为外贸部门统计数字。

17-3 主要经济指标东莞占全国、全省的比重（2010年）

Proportion of Main Indicators of Dongguan to China and Guangdong Province (2010)

指　标	单 位	绝对值			东莞占全国的比重(%)	东莞占全省的比重(%)
		全 国	全 省	东 莞		
一、人口						
年末常住人口	万 人	133972	10441	822.48	0.61	7.88
二、经济总量						
生产总值	亿 元	397983	46013	4246.45	1.07	9.23
第一产业增加值	亿 元	40497	2287	16.57	0.04	0.72
第二产业增加值	亿 元	186481	23015	2160.82	1.16	9.39
第三产业增加值	亿 元	171005	20712	2069.07	1.21	9.99
三、工业						
工业增加值	亿 元	160030	21463	2078.45	1.30	9.68
主要工业产品产量						
发电量	亿千瓦时	42065	3101	356.00	0.85	11.48
机制纸及纸板	万 吨	10036	1435	933.18	9.30	65.04
彩　电	万 台	11830	4495	535.90	4.53	11.92
四、农业						
主要农产品产量						
粮　食	万 吨	54641	1317	1.25	0.002	0.09
水　果	万 吨	21401	1129	7.55	0.04	0.67
肉　类	万 吨	7925	441	2.88	0.04	0.65
水产品	万 吨	5366	731	7.63	0.14	1.04
五、固定资产投资额						
全社会固定资产投资额	亿 元	278140	16113	1114.98	0.40	6.92
六、运输邮电						
货物周转量	亿吨公里	137329	5915	109.03	0.08	1.84
旅客周转量	亿人公里	27779	3331	129.07	0.46	3.88
年末固定电话用户	万 户	29438	3169	298.04	1.01	9.40
年末移动电话用户	万 户	85900	9708	1607.60	1.87	16.56
七、财政、金融						
地方财政收入	亿 元	83080	4516	277.84	0.33	6.15
财政支出	亿 元	89575	5415	289.83	0.32	5.35
各项人民币存款余额	亿 元	71.8万	78286	5943.39	0.83	7.59
各项人民币贷款余额	亿 元	47.9万	46099	3329.82	0.70	7.22
八、外经外贸						
进出口总额	亿美元	29728	7849	1213.38	4.08	15.46
进口总额	亿美元	13948	3317	517.40	3.71	15.60
出口总额	亿美元	15779	4532	695.98	4.41	15.36
实际利用外资	亿美元	1057	210	27.32	2.58	12.99
九、商业、物价						
社会消费品零售总额	亿 元	156998	17415	1108.06	0.71	6.36
商品零售价格指数	上年=100	103.1	103.3	103.2		
居民消费价格指数	上年=100	103.3	103.1	102.8		
十、人民生活						
在岗职工人均工资	元		40253	46576		
城市居民人均可支配收入	元	19109	23898	35690		
农民人均纯收入	元	5919	7890	25733		
城乡居民人民币储蓄存款余额	亿 元	303302	36219	3386.85	1.12	9.35

17-4 主要经济指标东莞占全国、全省的比重（2009年）

Proportion of Main Indicators of Dongguan to China and Guangdong Province (2009)

指标	单位	绝对值			东莞占全国的比重(%)	东莞占全省的比重(%)
		全国	全省	东莞		
一、人口						
年末常住人口	万人	133474	10130	786.08	0.59	7.76
二、经济总量						
地区生产总值	亿元	340507	39483	3763.91	1.11	9.53
第一产业增加值	亿元	35226	2010	14.79	0.04	0.74
第二产业增加值	亿元	157639	19420	1823.08	1.16	9.39
第三产业增加值	亿元	147642	18053	1926.04	1.30	10.67
三、工业						
工业增加值	亿元	135240	18092	1741.53	1.29	9.63
主要工业产品产量						
发电量	亿千瓦时	37147	2666	337.00	0.91	12.64
机制纸及纸板	万吨	9389	1316	866.67	9.23	65.88
彩电	万台	9899	4093	514.00	5.19	12.56
四、农业						
主要农产品产量						
粮食	万吨	53082	1315	1.19		0.09
水果	万吨	20396	1062	9.15	0.04	0.86
肉类	万吨	7650	427	2.55	0.03	0.60
水产品	万吨	5116	703	7.33	0.14	1.04
五、固定资产投资额						
全社会固定资产投资额	亿元	224846	13353	1094.08	0.49	8.19
六、运输邮电						
货物周转量	亿吨公里	122133	4943	101.65	0.08	2.06
旅客周转量	亿人公里	24835	2853	105.35	0.42	3.69
年末固定电话用户	万户	31373	3367	272.03	0.87	8.08
年末移动电话用户	万户	74721	8939	1409.29	1.89	15.77
七、财政、金融						
地方财政收入	亿元	68518	3650	231.16	0.34	6.33
财政支出	亿元	76300	4334	232.62	0.30	5.37
各项人民币存款余额	亿元	597741	66766	4986.61	0.83	7.47
各项人民币贷款余额	亿元	399685	38893	2903.80	0.73	7.47
八、外经外贸						
进出口总额	亿美元	22075	6111	941.55	4.27	15.41
进口总额	亿美元	10059	2522	389.86	3.88	15.46
出口总额	亿美元	12016	3590	551.68	4.59	15.37
实际利用外资	亿美元	918	203	25.94	2.83	12.78
九、商业、物价						
社会消费品零售总额	亿元	132678	14892	959.07	0.72	6.44
商品零售价格指数	上年=100	98.8	96.8	95.3		
居民消费价格指数	上年=100	99.3	97.7	96.9		
十、人民生活						
在岗职工人均工资	元	32736	35965	42585		
城市居民人均可支配收入	元	17175	21575	33045		
农民人均纯收入	元	5153	6907	13064		
城乡居民人民币储蓄存款余额	亿元	260772	31346	2904.57	1.11	9.27

17-5 主要经济指标人均水平东莞与全国、全省的比较(2010年)

Comparison of Per Capita Level of Main Economic Indicators between Dongguan and China, Guangdong Province (2010)

指　　标	单 位	人 均 水 平			东莞相当于全国(%)	东莞相当于全省(%)
		全 国	全 省	东 莞		
生产总值	元	29762	44736	52798	177.4	118.0
财政收入	元	6213	4390	3455	55.6	78.7
出口总额	美元	1180	4406	8653	733.4	196.4
各项人民币存款余额	元	53593	74979	72262	134.8	96.4
居民储蓄存款余额	元	22639	34689	41179	181.9	118.7
固定资产投资额	元	20800	15666	13863	66.7	88.5
社会消费品零售总额	元	11741	16931	13777	117.3	81.4
实际利用外资	美元	79	204	340	429.7	166.2
在岗职工人均工资	元		40253	46576		115.7
城市居民可支配收入	元	19109	23898	35690	186.8	149.3
农民人均纯收入	元	5919	7890	25733	434.8	326.1
粮食产量	公斤	409	128	2	0.4	1.2
水产品产量	公斤	40	71	9	23.6	13.4
水果产量	公斤	160	110	9	5.9	8.6
工业发电量	千瓦时	3146	3015	4426	140.7	146.8
医院卫生院床位数	张/千人	3.26	2.65	2.38	72.9	89.7
卫生技术人员数	人/千人	4.36	4.28	4.56	104.6	106.6

注：本表人均指标时点数按常住人口计算，时期数按年平均常住人口计算。

17-6 主要经济指标人均水平东莞与全国、全省的比较(2009年)

Comparison of Per Capita Level of Main Economic Indicators between Dongguan and China, Guangdong Province (2009)

指　　标	单 位	人 均 水 平			东莞相当于全国(%)	东莞相当于全省(%)
		全 国	全 省	东 莞		
生产总值	元	25575	39436	48988	229.4	137.5
财政收入	元	5146	3646	3009	67.6	91.4
出口总额	美元	903	3586	7180	919.1	221.6
各项人民币存款余额	元	44783	65909	63436	174.9	112.8
居民储蓄存款余额	元	19537	30944	36950	230.0	137.2
固定资产投资额	元	16888	13338	14240	97.4	118.2
社会消费品零售总额	元	9965	14875	12482	153.2	92.9
实际利用外资	美元	69	203	338	577.1	184.0
在岗职工人均工资	元	32736	35965	42585	130.1	118.4
城市居民可支配收入	元	17175	21575	33045	192.4	153.2
农民人均纯收入	元	5153	6907	13064	253.5	189.1
粮食产量	公斤	399	131	2	0.4	1.3
水产品产量	公斤	38	70	10	28.7	15.0
水果产量	公斤	153	106	12	7.8	12.6
工业发电量	千瓦时	2790	2663	4386	181.6	182.3
医院卫生院床位数	张/千人	2.97	2.47	2.30	91.4	104.2
卫生技术人员数	人/千人	3.91	4.05	4.66	137.2	124.8

注：本表人均指标时点数按常住人口计算，时期数按年平均常住人口计算。

17-7 珠江三角洲国民经济和社会发展主要指标（2010年）

指　　标	单 位	广州市	深圳市	珠海市
一、综合				
行政区域土地面积	平方公里	7287	1953	1654
年末常住人口	万人	1270.96	1037.20	156.16
年末户籍人口	万人	806.14	259.87	104.74
地区生产总值	亿元	10748.28	9581.51	1208.60
第一产业增加值	亿元	188.56	6.47	32.36
第二产业增加值	亿元	4002.27	4523.37	662.01
#工业增加值	亿元	3644.96	4233.23	619.39
第三产业增加值	亿元	6557.45	5051.67	514.23
人均生产总值(按常住人口计算)	元	87458	94296	77888
二、农村经济				
农业产值	亿元	322.13	15.05	57.62
粮食产量	万吨	43.04		4.18
水果产量	万吨	39.92	0.32	12.11
水产品产量	万吨	44.14	3.09	19.72
三、工业				
规模以上工业企业数	个	6969	8249	1347
规模以上工业增加值	亿元	4073.35	5015.33	683.98
规模以上工业企业主营业务收入	亿元	13624.65	18813.72	3058.87
规模以上工业企业利润总额	亿元	1031.27	1599.02	191.24
规模以上工业产品销售率	%	98.0	99.0	92.1
四、固定资产投资				
全社会固定资产投资总额	亿元	3263.57	1944.70	501.55
#房地产开发投资额	亿元	983.66	458.47	179.51
商品房屋销售面积	万平方米	1405.13	465.59	282.78
商品房屋销售额	亿元	1674.99	892.55	293.01
五、交通、邮电				
民用汽车拥有量	万辆	159.89	166.97	20.97
年末固定电话用户数	万户	601.81	508.93	80.20
年末移动电话用户数	万户	2329.19	2008.60	241.31
全年总用电量	亿千瓦时	625.90	655.46	102.26
#工业用电量	亿千瓦时	349.72	395.42	65.08

Main Indicators of National Economy and Social Development of the Pearl River Delta Economic Zone (2010)

佛山市	惠州市	肇庆市	江门市	东莞市	中山市
3848	11356	14822	9541	2460	1800
719.91	460.11	392.22	445.08	822.48	312.27
370.89	337.28	422.41	392.28	181.77	149.18
5651.52	1729.95	1085.87	1570.42	4246.45	1850.65
105.40	102.38	190.26	117.03	16.57	50.74
3542.49	1019.57	456.67	872.21	2160.82	1074.10
3419.18	960.82	411.87	833.28	2078.45	1022.01
2003.63	608.00	438.94	581.18	2069.07	725.81
80313	38650	27987	35622	52798	60797
211.17	166.30	291.96	214.73	28.31	86.82
9.70	58.68	110.51	87.20	1.25	7.31
5.35	54.92	103.87	22.01	7.55	17.69
56.47	14.33	32.90	67.30	7.63	33.90
7684	1853	1131	3246	5899	5063
3915.12	881.16	434.51	1053.39	1708.31	1263.08
13733.60	3892.63	1689.05	3639.89	7708.17	4710.39
1073.34	196.32	98.18	251.08	352.36	273.96
95.7	97.6	98.3	94.5	97.8	95.8
1719.63	894.02	625.21	631.77	1114.98	660.37
485.52	267.90	91.14	111.72	298.99	241.79
885.47	627.30	342.24	382.52	511.25	670.55
668.13	311.17	140.31	179.17	373.77	350.38
91.24	25.64	14.74	27.88	92.08	37.13
266.03	139.80	79.65	110.00	298.04	96.20
1076.00	562.10	206.86	390.66	1607.60	454.64
463.08	192.46	105.08	165.21	543.66	187.05
351.59	132.03	78.33	115.63	435.57	128.94

17-7 续表

(2010年)

指　　标	单 位	广州市	深圳市	珠海市
六、金融、贸易、财政				
年末金融机构人民币存款余额	亿元	23384.50	20210.75	2542.56
#城乡居民储蓄存款余额	亿元	9069.26	6717.05	957.58
年末金融机构人民币贷款余额	亿元	14987.73	13708.16	1203.85
全社会消费品零售总额	亿元	4500.28	3000.76	486.03
预算内地方财政收入	亿元	872.65	1106.82	124.53
预算内地方财政支出	亿元	977.32	1266.07	166.41
七、对外经济				
海关进口总额	亿美元	553.96	1425.66	226.18
海关出口总额	亿美元	483.80	2041.84	208.62
外商直接投资项目	个	978	1929	213
合同利用外资金额	亿美元	49.68	56.52	12.58
实际利用外商直接投资	亿美元	39.79	42.97	12.24
八、人民生活、物价				
在岗职工年平均工资	元	54807	50456	34405
城市居民年人均可支配收入	元	30658	32381	25382
城市居民年人均消费支出	元	25012	22807	20370
农民人均纯收入	元	12676		10187
居民消费价格总指数(以上年为100)	%	103.2	103.5	103.0
九、教育、卫生				
学校数				
高等学校	所	77	8	
中等职业技术学校	所	94	13	10
普通中学	所	476	295	60
小学	所	1004	340	124
在校学生数				
高等学校	万人	84.39	6.73	11.50
中等职业技术学校	万人	24.81	2.97	1.99
普通中学	万人	57.23	33.48	9.53
小学	万人	82.48	61.85	12.63
医院医疗机构数	个	2387	2456	510
#医院	个	216	114	31
医院床位数	张	53227	21196	5075
执业(助理)医师	人	33575	21295	4615

佛山市	惠州市	肇庆市	江门市	东莞市	中山市
8335.04	2038.58	1057.38	2214.97	5943.39	2603.02
4407.92	1031.64	650.26	1461.98	3386.85	1443.74
4749.09	1096.21	642.04	973.75	3329.82	1329.89
1687.13	582.53	332.89	655.86	1108.06	648.11
306.05	131.23	76.80	104.29	277.84	139.38
363.35	185.44	127.66	132.98	289.83	145.85
186.16	140.00	17.94	39.28	517.40	86.14
330.39	202.33	25.96	104.10	695.98	225.05
238	362	113	194	869	147
21.90	14.80	16.29	8.20	25.97	7.55
19.68	14.38	9.34	11.08	27.32	6.68
37079	29599	30114	27497	46576	40578
27245	23565	16832	21153	35690	25357
21995	19741	12164	15561	25733	18833
12202	9077	7524	8589	20486	14928
103.1	103.2	102.8	103.2	102.8	103.0
3	1	4		5	
38	30	30	31	25	13
180	209	174	195	190	99
424	689	753	340	330	211
3.97	1.43	4.22	2.33	3.83	3.53
7.84	6.99	7.73	5.33	4.46	2.54
32.34	30.87	32.84	26.39	25.83	15.29
43.82	39.80	36.82	30.24	55.24	23.78
1071	719	678	750	985	470
59	46	42	31	91	45
13894	7523	6808	8355	19571	10009
11646	6223	4762	6472	11769	5383

17-8 长江三角洲国民经济和社会发展主要指标（2010年）

指 标	单 位	上海市	南京市	苏州市	无锡市	常州市	镇江市
一、综合							
行政区域土地面积	平方公里	6341	6582	8488	4788	4375	3847
年末常住人口	万人	2301.91	800.47	1046.60	637.26	459.20	311.34
年末户籍人口	万人	1412.32		637.66	466.56	360.80	270.75
地区生产总值	亿元	16872.42	5010.36	9168.90	5758.00	2976.70	1956.64
第一产业增加值	亿元	114.15	142.02	155.53	104.94	99.80	81.58
第二产业增加值	亿元	7139.96	2327.76	5294.07	3208.79	1667.20	1124.52
第三产业增加值	亿元	9618.31	2540.57	3719.31	2444.27	1209.70	750.54
二、农村经济							
农业总产值	亿元	287.03	244.75	269.73		174.50	122.72
三、工业							
工业增加值	亿元	6456.78	2005.26	4956.75	2986.52	1514.34	1043.67
规模以上工业企业主营业务收入	亿元		8536.80	24300.00	12783.13		
规模以上工业企业利润总额	亿元	2216.55	467.97	1400.00	891.63	405.80	
四、固定资产投资							
全社会固定资产投资总额	亿元	5317.67	3306.05	3617.82	2985.65	2103.55	1327.08
#房地产开发投资额	亿元	2119.46	754.76	935.80	612.67	446.96	114.88
五、交通、邮电							
民用汽车拥有量	万辆	169.56	83.05	124.96	73.48	45.40	
年末固定电话用户数	万户	935.90	290.14		215.76	159.60	113.74
年末移动电话用户数	万户	2361.60	931.34	1309.40	790.41	501.40	273.88
六、金融、贸易、财政							
年末金融机构本外币存款余额	亿元	52190.04	12887.43	14225.49	8827.20	4672.02	2242.89
#城乡居民储蓄存款余额	亿元	16249.29	3572.07	4701.31	3109.44	2024.15	1002.51
年末金融机构本外币贷款余额	亿元	34154.17	10915.34	10831.62	6487.13	3098.24	1617.07
全社会消费品零售总额	亿元	6036.86	2267.77	2380.06	1809.08	1044.73	559.52
预算内地方财政收入	亿元	2873.58	518.80	900.55	511.89	286.18	138.10
预算内地方财政支出	亿元	3302.89	542.73	820.75	468.47	273.44	154.86
七、对外经济							
海关进口总额	亿美元	1880.85	456.01	1209.70	249.51		34.03
海关出口总额	亿美元	1807.84	248.85	1531.18	362.72	155.58	47.51
实际利用外商直接投资	亿美元	111.21	26.76	85.35	33.00	24.43	16.15
八、人民生活、物价							
城市居民年人均可支配收入	元	31838	28312	29219	27750	26269	23075
城市居民年人均消费支出	元	23200	18156	17879	15867	17124	14080
农民人均纯收入	元	13746	11128	14460	14002	12637	10874
居民消费价格总指数(以上年为100)	%	103.1	104.2	103.4	103.4	103.4	103.7

注：1. 2010年年末人口数为第六次全国人口普查数据。
2. 杭州民用汽车拥有量为机动车拥有量。

Main Indicators on National Economy and Social Development of the Yangtze River Delta Economic Zone(2010)

南通市	扬州市	泰州市	杭州市	宁波市	嘉兴市	湖州市	绍兴市	舟山市	台州市
8001	6634	5793	16596	9817	3915	5818	8256	1440	9411
728.28	445.98	461.86	870.04	760.57	450.17	289.35	491.22	112.13	596.88
762.92	459.12	504.65	689.12	574.10	341.60	259.98	438.91	96.77	583.14
3417.88	2207.99	2002.58	5945.82	5125.82	2296.00	1301.56	2782.74	633.45	2415.12
262.43	159.25	148.45	207.96	218.43	126.30	104.61	149.28	62.44	159.99
1908.56	1229.34	1125.85	2844.47	2848.23	1342.12	714.61	1582.87	288.55	1262.66
1246.89	819.40	728.28	2893.39	2059.16	827.58	482.34	1050.59	282.46	992.47
463.31	284.30		316.34	339.00	213.88	176.90	225.80	121.27	276.02
1568.49	1074.61	981.02	2500.29	2569.60	1191.02	637.18	1414.33	213.78	1144.08
7306.19			11002.30		4899.30	2611.83			
536.80	369.50	342.35	753.48	654.20	311.10	132.96	398.43	45.87	169.08
2168.38	1331.85	1538.03	2753.13	2206.48	1518.56	764.95	1253.6	413.84	950.24
272.78	165.16	153.76	956.20	557.27	270.75	142.79	297.80	58.98	196.08
35.53	23.84	22.17	183.25			21.80			56.59
240.75		143.03	365.74		163.09	107.83	201.80	54.94	178.72
552.03	393.44	339.32	1236.38		468.22	286.93	436.45	128.94	719.60
4957.83	2430.55	2359.79	16957.94	9723.11	3590.82	1805.61	4948.32	1143.25	3588.48
2693.99	1252.40	1164.18	4990.97	3312.17	1629.71	821.68	1945.72	410.80	1730.67
2964.58	1486.06	1531.07	14936.65	9392.28	2753.64	1461.32	3934.27	1017.72	3055.82
1265.36	719.48	550.29	2146.08	1704.51	799.36	516.09	852.89	212.54	960.45
290.81	167.78	165.54	671.34	530.93	176.83	97.27	193.23	61.04	164.88
327.94	193.94	207.35	616.58	600.74	199.06	127.12	222.03	105.03	222.76
69.89	21.83	27.08	170.18	309.30	67.80	10.67	59.27	37.95	30.47
140.85	60.55	58.77	353.37	519.67	160.41	58.61	210.89	69.37	139.63
20.61	20.56	13.63	43.56	23.13	16.10	9.19	9.53	0.98	1.32
23541	21766	21359	30035	30166	24815	25572	30164	26848	28583
14492	13679	13445	20219	19420	15979	16207	17399	16375	19626
9914	9462	9324	13186	14261	14365	13288	13651	14265	11307
103.7	103.4	103.8	103.9	103.7	104.0	104.0	104.0	104.1	104.6

第三部分　基本单位情况

Part Three　Basic Units

1-1 按行业分的法人单位、产业活动单位数（2010年）

Number of Corporate Units and Industrial Establishments by Sector (2010)

项目	法人单位数（个）	单产业法人单位	多产业法人单位	产业活动单位数（个）	多产业法人单位的产业活动单位数
合计	**77059**	**75375**	**1684**	**88479**	**11420**
采矿业	**12**	**12**		**12**	
煤炭开采和洗选业					
石油和天然气开采业	2	2		2	
黑色金属矿采选业					
有色金属矿采选业	3	3		3	
非金属矿采选业	6	6		6	
其他采矿业	1	1		1	
制造业	**36133**	**35939**	**194**	**36432**	**299**
农副食品加工业	183	177	6	197	14
食品制造业	268	262	6	277	9
饮料制造业	63	58	5	70	7
烟草制品业					
纺织业	1737	1728	9	1756	19
纺织服装、鞋、帽制造业	2052	2032	20	2076	24
皮革、毛皮、羽毛(绒)及其制品业	1439	1434	5	1448	9
木材加工及木、竹、藤、棕、草制品业	338	335	3	343	5
家具制造业	1087	1080	7	1098	11
造纸及纸制品业	1831	1828	3	1837	6
印刷业和记录媒介的复制	1282	1280	2	1284	2
文教体育用品制造业	1112	1108	4	1120	8
石油加工、炼焦及核燃料加工业	36	34	2	39	3
化学原料及化学制品制造业	874	865	9	886	12
医药制造业	41	38	3	42	1
化学纤维制造业	69	69		69	
橡胶制品业	754	753	1	757	3
塑料制品业	4208	4195	13	4223	15
非金属矿物制品业	590	587	3	596	6
黑色金属冶炼及压延加工业	127	127		127	
有色金属冶炼及压延加工业	253	250	3	255	2
金属制品业	4256	4245	11	4274	18
通用设备制造业	1747	1729	18	1765	18
专用设备制造业	2376	2367	9	2391	15

1-1 续表 1

(2010年)

项目	法人单位数(个)	单产业法人单位	多产业法人单位	产业活动单位数(个)	多产业法人单位的产业活动单位数
交通运输设备制造业	294	291	3	302	8
电气机械及器材制造业	2574	2558	16	2606	32
通信设备、计算机及其他电子设备制造业	4393	4369	24	4436	43
仪器仪表及文化、办公用机械制造业	517	514	3	523	6
工艺品及其他制造业	1603	1598	5	1605	2
废弃资源和废旧材料回收加工业	29	28	1	30	1
电力、燃气及水的生产和供应业	**147**	**145**	**2**	**178**	**31**
电力、热力的生产和供应业	30	30		32	2
燃气生产和供应业	28	27	1	33	5
水的生产和供应业	89	88	1	113	24
建筑业	**2528**	**2500**	**28**	**2812**	**284**
房屋和土木工程建筑业	414	411	3	560	146
建筑安装业	709	699	10	776	67
建筑装饰业	1062	1052	10	1105	43
其他建筑业	343	338	5	371	28
交通运输、仓储和邮政业	**1297**	**1257**	**40**	**1913**	**616**
铁路运输业	6	6		6	
道路运输业	424	405	19	575	151
城市公共交通业	69	68	1	72	3
水上运输业	50	49	1	53	3
航空运输业	9	9		12	3
管道运输业	1	1		2	1
装卸搬运及其他运输服务业	542	529	13	663	121
仓储业	101	100	1	104	3
邮政业	95	90	5	426	331
信息传输、计算机服务和软件业	**1389**	**1367**	**22**	**1677**	**288**
电信和其他信息传输服务业	305	296	9	527	222
计算机服务业	822	814	8	867	45
软件业	262	257	5	283	21
批发和零售业	**16215**	**15948**	**267**	**19564**	**3349**
批发业	7759	7660	99	8707	948
零售业	8456	8288	168	10857	2401
住宿和餐饮业	**1116**	**1006**	**110**	**1795**	**679**
住宿业	563	480	83	683	120
餐饮业	553	526	27	1112	559
金融业	**231**	**184**	**47**	**1788**	**1557**
银行业	34	22	12	1156	1122
证券业	11	9	2	46	35
保险业	78	48	30	400	322

1-1 续表 2

(2010年)

项目	法人单位数(个)	单产业法人单位	多产业法人单位	产业活动单位数(个)	多产业法人单位的产业活动单位数
其他金融活动	108	105	3	186	78
房地产业	**2567**	**2489**	**78**	**2926**	**359**
房地产业	2567	2489	78	2926	359
租赁和商务服务业	**8215**	**8085**	**130**	**9433**	**1218**
租赁业	95	95		98	3
商务服务业	8120	7990	130	9335	1215
科学研究、技术服务和地质勘查业	**831**	**822**	**9**	**904**	**73**
研究与试验发展	171	168	3	176	5
专业技术服务业	514	508	6	576	62
科技交流和推广服务业	139	139		143	4
地质勘查业	7	7		9	2
水利、环境和公共设施管理业	**329**	**322**	**7**	**371**	**42**
水利管理业	59	59		62	3
环境管理业	82	79	3	106	24
公共设施管理业	188	184	4	203	15
居民服务和其他服务业	**1940**	**1919**	**21**	**2181**	**241**
居民服务业	627	619	8	766	139
其他服务业	1313	1300	13	1415	102
教　育	**1556**	**1519**	**37**	**1931**	**375**
教育	1556	1519	37	1931	375
卫生、社会保障和社会福利业	**526**	**471**	**55**	**940**	**414**
卫生	478	424	54	888	410
社会保障业	5	5		5	
社会福利业	43	42	1	47	4
文化、体育和娱乐业	**390**	**385**	**5**	**463**	**73**
新闻出版业	13	13		14	1
广播、电视、电影和音像业	58	58		63	5
文化艺术业	107	106	1	110	3
体育	35	35		36	1
娱乐业	177	173	4	240	63
公共管理与社会组织	**1635**	**1003**	**632**	**3157**	**1522**
中国共产党机关	54	54		56	2
国家机构	579	528	51	1353	774
人民政协和民主党派	11	11		11	
群众团体、社会团体和宗教组织	357	349	8	475	118
基层群众自治组织	634	61	573	1262	628
国际组织	**2**	**2**		**2**	
国际组织	2	2		2	

1-2 按注册类型分的法人单位、产业活动单位数（2010年）

Number of Corporate Units and Industrial Establishments by Registration Status(2010)

项　　目	法　人 单位数 （个）	单 产 业 法人单位	多 产 业 法人单位	产业活动 单 位 数 （个）	多产业法 人单位的 产业活动 单 位 数
合　　计	**77059**	**75375**	**1684**	**88479**	**11420**
内资企业	**65523**	**63961**	**1562**	**76126**	**10603**
国有	1451	1340	111	3193	1742
集体	2259	2165	94	3074	815
股份合作	239	233	6	780	541
国有联营	9	9		10	1
集体联营	63	62	1	72	9
国有与集体联营	19	18	1	55	36
其他联营	45	43	2	57	12
国有独资公司	37	37		44	7
其他有限责任公司	17101	16838	263	19433	2332
股份有限公司	857	812	45	1944	1087
私营独资	9423	9374	49	9669	246
私营合伙	2523	2512	11	2574	51
私营有限责任公司	23697	23353	344	25313	1616
私营股份有限公司	977	964	13	1035	58
其他内资	6823	6201	622	8873	2050
港澳台投资企业	**8268**	**8204**	**64**	**8702**	**434**
与港澳台商合资经营	423	415	8	512	89
与港澳台商合作经营	399	399		424	25
港澳台商独资	7206	7151	55	7517	311
港澳台商投资股份有限公司	240	239	1	249	9
外商投资企业	**3268**	**3210**	**58**	**3651**	**383**
中外合资经营	264	247	17	368	104
中外合作经营	130	127	3	156	26
外资企业	2740	2703	37	2981	241
外商投资股份有限公司	134	133	1	146	12

1-3 按地域分的法人单位、产业活动单位数（2010年）

Number of Corporate Units and Industrial Establishments by District (2010)

项目	法人单位数（个）	单产业法人单位	多产业法人单位	产业活动单位数（个）	多产业法人单位的产业活动单位数
全市	**77059**	**75375**	**1684**	**88479**	**11420**
东城街道	4980	4853	127	5792	812
南城街道	4056	3917	139	4701	645
万江街道	2577	2516	61	2909	332
莞城街道	3572	3414	158	4308	736
石碣镇	2217	2165	52	2552	335
石龙镇	945	897	48	1292	347
茶山镇	1869	1833	36	2102	233
石排镇	1635	1600	35	1868	233
企石镇	1109	1077	32	1291	182
横沥镇	1738	1705	33	1982	244
桥头镇	1772	1744	28	2066	294
谢岗镇	1034	1016	18	1169	135
东坑镇	828	795	33	1044	216
常平镇	3551	3482	69	4169	618
寮步镇	3661	3600	61	4046	385
樟木头镇	1991	1954	37	2359	368
大朗镇	3786	3726	60	4280	494
黄江镇	1728	1696	32	1952	224
清溪镇	2354	2307	47	2635	281
塘厦镇	4149	4092	57	4521	372
凤岗镇	2263	2228	35	2506	243
大岭山镇	2641	2603	38	2916	275
长安镇	6058	5990	68	6838	780
虎门镇	5505	5421	84	6244	739
厚街镇	3006	2943	63	3547	541
沙田镇	1718	1685	33	1938	220
道滘镇	1256	1223	33	1450	194
洪梅镇	471	454	17	581	110
麻涌镇	957	926	31	1144	187
望牛墩镇	680	655	25	808	128
中堂镇	1422	1387	35	1689	267
高埗镇	1176	1138	38	1370	194
松山湖	316	296	20	367	51
虎门港	38	37	1	41	3
东莞生态园				2	2

1-4　营业收入超5000万元的内资企业（2010年）

Domestic-funded Enterprises with Business Revenue over RMB 50 Million (2010)

单位名称	所属镇街	联系电话	主要产品(或服务)
农副食品加工业			
东莞市东糖中轻糖业有限公司	中堂镇	88118099	单晶冰糖
东莞市太粮米业有限公司	樟木头镇	87703313	大米
东莞市富之源饲料蛋白开发有限公司	洪梅镇	88436030	豆粕
东莞市双胞胎饲料有限公司	大岭山镇	82760188	饲料
东莞市永益食品有限公司	厚街镇	85811111	食用油
东莞市樟木头食品有限公司	樟木头镇	87718596	牲猪
东莞市穗丰食品有限公司	麻涌镇	88224098	小麦粉
东莞市制糖厂有限公司	中堂镇		制糖
东莞市银华生物科技有限公司	万江街道	22188099	饲料
东莞市湘大骆驼饲料有限公司	万江街道	23175022	饲料
中纺粮油(东莞)有限公司	麻涌镇	88235183	豆油
东莞市海大饲料有限公司	麻涌镇	88237100	畜禽饲料
东莞市东美食品有限公司	高埗镇	88872108	淀粉
东莞市虎门日隆食品厂	虎门镇	85564450	豆制品糕点
东莞市康达尔饲料有限公司	莞城街道	22236928	饲料
东莞市金良稻丰米业有限公司	樟木头镇	87709579	谷物磨制
东莞市煌上煌食品有限公司	洪梅镇	88430678	肉制品
东莞市沙田顺发畜禽实业有限公司	沙田镇	88686610	饲料
中储粮油脂工业东莞有限公司	麻涌镇	88236688	豆油
东莞市华南油脂工业有限公司	麻涌镇	88235666	棕榈油
东莞市新泰粮食有限公司	樟木头镇	87123620	粮食
食品制造业			
广东丹宝利酵母有限公司	中堂镇	88812123	高活性干酵母
东莞市来一口食品有限公司	谢岗镇	87637375	果冻
内蒙古伊利实业集团股份有限公司东莞分公司	道滘镇	88835173	冰淇淋
东莞市华美食品有限公司	茶山镇	86643036	饼干
东莞市广利饲料有限公司	大岭山镇	83352060	混合饲料
广东一品鲜生物科技有限公司	中堂镇	22613911	酵母抽提物
东莞市百味佳食品有限公司	寮步镇	83285888	鸡精
东莞市金富士食品有限公司	东城街道	22621998	饼干
东莞市今麦郎食品有限公司	中堂镇	88118372	方便面
东莞市金娃食品工业有限公司	谢岗镇	87636739	果冻
饮料制造业			
东莞市福地纯水有限公司	南城街道	22404191	饮用水
东莞爱维蒸馏水有限公司	虎门镇	85519666	蒸馏水
东莞日之泉蒸馏水有限公司	中堂镇	88815015	蒸馏水
东莞市珠江啤酒有限公司	常平镇	83553033	啤酒
纺织业			
东莞市盛泰针织制衣有限公司	大朗镇	83206828	针织服装
东莞市辉骏针织时装有限公司	大朗镇	83183029	针织时装
东莞市长源毛织制衣有限公司	大朗镇	83200838	针织服装
东莞市盈邦针织有限公司	大朗镇	83482998	针织服装
东莞市凯纳德针织服饰有限公司	大朗镇	83110775	毛衣

1-4 续表 1

(2010年)

单位名称	所属镇街	联系电话	主要产品(或服务)
东莞市广昌隆毛织时装有限公司	大朗镇	83197153	毛织服装
东莞市雅路家用纺织品有限公司	凤岗镇	87509191	床褥(单)类
东莞市宝丰服装实业有限公司	寮步镇	83216003	毛织品
东莞市环宇织造有限公司	大朗镇	83112688	毛织服装
东莞市晶晖针织有限公司	大朗镇	83116573	针织服装
东莞市英伟实业有限公司	大朗镇	83102266	针织服装
东莞市琪然电脑刺绣有限公司	虎门镇	85726660	刺绣、服装辅料
东莞市大朗伟航针织制衣厂	大朗镇	83128091	针织品
东莞市精英针织有限公司	大朗镇	86262888	毛针织品
东莞市翔兴针织有限公司	大朗镇	83186788	毛衣
东莞市力豪针织服饰有限公司	大朗镇	83017168	毛织品
东莞市金泽服装有限公司	大朗镇	83181322	针织服装
东莞市施丹娜服饰有限公司	大朗镇	83315639	毛织品
东莞市颖祺实业有限公司	大朗镇	83180838	针织服装
东莞长联新材料科技有限公司	寮步镇	81259388	印花染色粘合剂
东莞市金凌印刷有限公司	塘厦镇	87881585	丝印染精
东莞市安盛针织制衣有限公司	大朗镇	83137868	毛织品
东莞市寮步镇上屯嘉顺针织厂	寮步镇	81112666	羊毛针织毛衫
东莞市正卉毛织有限公司	大朗镇	83137868	针织毛衫
东莞市超翔服饰有限公司	大朗镇	38879801	针织服装
东莞市悠派户外用品制造有限公司	茶山镇	84596111	帐篷
东莞市瑞麟毛织有限公司	寮步镇	83280312	毛织品
东莞市明威包装材料有限公司	高埗镇	84996493	绳、索、缆
东莞市新阳织造有限公司常平分公司	常平镇	38838288	毛织品
东莞市和辉针织有限公司	大朗镇	83133988	针织品
东莞市大朗民源生毛织制衣有限公司	大朗镇	83186260	针织服装
东莞市拓展实业有限公司	茶山镇	86485888	化学纤维
东莞市大朗骏松服饰厂	大朗镇	81119288	针织品
东莞市兴业针织有限公司	大朗镇	83311479	针织服装
东莞市胜兴针织有限公司	大朗镇	83189100	针织女毛衫
东莞市富士达针织有限公司	大朗镇	83319826	毛衫
东莞市科纺纺织有限公司	中堂镇	88115588	牛仔布
东莞市瑞锋服饰有限公司	大朗镇	86260003	针织毛衣
东莞市华轩针织制衣有限公司	大朗镇	83181838	针织服装
东莞市众圣针织有限公司	大朗镇	83111739	毛衫
东莞市稳丰纺织有限公司	中堂镇		纺织品
东莞市常平满利针织有限公司	常平镇	83977300	毛衣
东莞市东林制衣有限公司	寮步镇	83238080	毛织品
东莞市圣旗路时装有限公司	常平镇	89851115	针织品
东莞市民生纺织有限公司	中堂镇	88188870	气流纺纱
东莞市建盛针织有限公司	大朗镇	83110188	针织服装
东莞市颖和祺服饰有限公司	大朗镇	81125303	毛衣
东莞市众达针织制衣有限公司	大朗镇	83109181	毛衫
东莞市入世丰针织有限公司	东坑镇	88905668	针织衫
东莞市欧佳特服饰有限公司	大朗镇	86262988	毛衣

1-4 续表 2

(2010年)

单位名称	所属镇街	联系电话	主要产品(或服务)
东莞市大朗和利达针织制衣厂	大朗镇	83133988	针织毛衫
纺织服装、鞋、帽制造业			
东莞市百思特服饰有限公司	虎门镇	85709002	服装
东莞市永豪制衣实业有限公司	寮步镇	83327589	针织服装
东莞市茶山伟博纺织服装厂	茶山镇	86648311	服装
东莞市添翔制衣厂	万江街道	22277218	服装
东莞市业联制衣有限公司	大朗镇	81069908	牛仔服装
东莞市源源制衣有限公司	中堂镇	88126801	裤子
东莞市以纯集团有限公司	虎门镇	85520146	纺织服装
东莞市经纬制衣实业有限公司	中堂镇	88411698	牛仔裤
东莞市时艺时装制衣有限公司	虎门镇	85260068	针梳织服装
东莞市中堂稳发制衣厂	中堂镇	88881891	棉制梳织服装
东莞中玉服装有限公司	常平镇	86997999	纺织
东莞市原野服装有限公司	虎门镇	85226693	纺织服装
东莞市鸿锦服饰有限公司	虎门镇	86091828	制衣
东莞市雅酷服装有限公司	中堂镇	88111626	牛仔裤
东莞市星达实业有限公司	虎门镇	88620008	服装
东莞市搜于特服装股份有限公司	道滘镇	88320269	设计服装
东莞市斌斌时装有限公司	虎门镇	88923858	服装
东莞市稳发制衣有限公司	中堂镇	88881891	棉梳织服装
东莞市寮步登辉鞋厂	寮步镇	81199856	鞋材
东莞市都市丽人实业有限公司	凤岗镇	82691609	内衣
广东金盾服装公司	南城街道	22404168	警察服装
东莞市极奇制衣有限公司	企石镇	86664648	衣服
东莞市卓越实业有限公司	石排镇	86550111	针织服装
东莞市松鹰实业有限公司	虎门镇	85561999	棉织服装
东莞市惠琪针织有限公司	寮步镇	88909698	毛衣制品
东莞市成功针织制衣厂	东城街道	22265157	纺织服装
东莞市尚景服装有限公司	石排镇		纺织服装
东莞市中玲实业有限公司	万江街道	22175828	纺织品服装
东莞市由美制衣有限公司	望牛墩镇	88562339	服装
东莞市凫山新兴发针织有限公司	寮步镇	83321465	毛衫
东莞市东城嘉文制衣厂	东城街道	22267333	梳织服装
皮革、毛皮、羽毛(绒)及其制品业			
东莞黄江成元鞋材制品厂	黄江镇	83363017	鞋材(皮)
东莞市新虎威鞋厂	虎门镇	85198313	皮鞋
东莞市琪胜鞋业有限公司	厚街镇	88632999	皮鞋
东莞厚街鹏利鞋厂	厚街镇	85906088	皮鞋
东莞市优秀鞋业有限公司	厚街镇	83088530	鞋类、女鞋
东莞市跨日鞋业集团有限公司	厚街镇	85584408	皮鞋
东莞市江顺箱包袋配件有限公司	塘厦镇	87912965	箱包袋配件
东莞市龙运鞋业有限公司	厚街镇	85933911	鞋类制品
东莞黄江裕成制鞋厂	黄江镇	83363017	运动鞋
东莞长安霄边兴鹏鞋厂	长安镇	85531541	男女装皮鞋

1-4　续表 3

(2010年)

单位名称	所属镇街	联系电话	主要产品(或服务)
东莞市莎米特箱包有限公司	樟木头镇	87712545	旅行袋
东莞市中盛针织实业有限公司	横沥镇	83716818	毛衫
木材加工及木、竹、藤、棕、草制品业			
东莞市凯旋木器制品有限公司	高埗镇	81300168	胶合卡板
东莞市德曼木业有限公司	桥头镇	81037666	木门
东莞市南兴木工机械有限公司	厚街镇	89982033	木工机械、木工刀具
东莞市易辉纤维板有限公司	桥头镇	81039118	纤维板
东莞市冠宇木业有限公司	中堂镇	81163188	木制品
东莞市东上板业有限公司	中堂镇	88128816	硅酸钙板
家具制造业			
东莞市光润家具制造有限公司	东城街道	86216333	办公家具
东莞市桥新家私有限公司	桥头镇		木制家具
东莞市富宝沙发制造有限公司	大岭山镇	85611985	家具
东莞市慕思寝室用品有限公司	厚街镇	85058288	沙发
东莞市嘉梦家具有限公司	常平镇	83826528	床垫、床上用品
东莞市森盛家具有限公司	厚街镇	85593555	套房家具
东莞市远大家具有限公司	大岭山镇	85617870	木制家具
东莞市美迪家具有限公司	洪梅镇	88843128	木质家具
东莞市星港家具有限公司	南城街道	22901327	家具
东莞市广纳家具制造有限公司	大朗镇	83136198	家具
东莞市好好家具有限公司	寮步镇	81120825	木器家具
东莞市利普家具有限公司	厚街镇	83082222	家具居配套用品
东莞市盛世家具有限公司	东城街道	23161906	木床
东莞市荣圣家具有限公司	凤岗镇	87842272	办公椅
东莞市协力钢构工程有限公司	厚街镇	85919838	钢构件
东莞市时兴家具制造有限公司	高埗镇	88872168	家具
东莞市德美家具有限公司	大岭山镇	85606228	玻璃酒柜、茶几、餐台
东莞市大宇家具有限公司	中堂镇	88180888	办公椅、办公桌
东莞市卓之神家具厂	高埗镇	88704226	木家具
东莞市鸿福家具有限公司	沙田镇	88663836	木质家具
东莞市华辉家具实业有限公司	厚街镇	85592833	家具
东莞市东品家具有限公司	凤岗镇	87842343	软体家具
东莞市千顺五金有限公司	清溪镇	87313028	铁制家具
东莞市明晟家具有限公司	东城街道	22653163	实木家具
东莞市银通家具有限公司	沙田镇	88686466	玻璃家具
东莞市广丰家具有限公司	厚街镇	85595163	家具
东莞市元宗家具有限公司	大岭山镇	85610588	家具
东莞市华晟家具制造有限公司	东城街道	22653163	家具
造纸及纸制品业			
东莞市华通包装有限公司	道滘镇	81332988	纸制品
东莞市中联纸业有限公司	中堂镇	88811357	包装用纸
东莞市旭丰纸业有限公司	中堂镇	88121293	瓦楞原纸
东莞东兴纸品厂	南城街道	86228785	瓦楞纸板、瓦楞纸箱
东莞市裕元纸品包装有限公司	沙田镇	82270888	纸箱

1-4 续表 4

(2010年)

单位名称	所属镇街	联系电话	主要产品(或服务)
东莞市银桦纸品有限公司	中堂镇	81163388	包装材料、纸箱
东莞市雄东纸业有限公司	洪梅镇	88844928	造纸
东莞市永安造纸有限公司	望牛墩镇	88818068	瓦楞纸
东莞市天赐纸品有限公司	高埗镇	88734233	纸板
东莞市顺丰纸品制造有限公司	茶山镇	86176968	纸板
东莞市建桦造纸有限公司	中堂镇		箱板纸
东莞市常联造纸厂有限公司	常平镇	83337837	机制瓦楞纸
东莞市胜源纸品厂	高埗镇	89910165	纸制品
东莞市易创实业有限公司	寮步镇	81118021	纸制品
东莞市振兴造纸有限公司	高埗镇	88949288	高强芯纸
东莞市晋邦纸业有限公司	大朗镇	81123388	纸板
东莞市全方圆纸制品有限公司	万江街道	87076226	纸制品
东莞市天盛特种纸品有限公司	虎门镇	85169458	无碳复写纸
东莞市顺通纸品有限公司	道滘镇	88328608	纸板
东莞市智达纸业制品有限公司	沙田镇	88862222	纸类制品
东莞市骏业纸业有限公司	道滘镇	88830822	中卡纸
东莞市大田包装有限公司	虎门镇	85269998	纸板
东莞市上隆纸业有限公司	中堂镇	88187688	高强瓦楞纸
东莞市顺兴造纸有限公司	道滘镇	88328608	瓦楞芯纸
东莞市潢涌银洲纸业有限公司	中堂镇	88899113	挂面箱板纸
东莞市天全纸品有限公司	高埗镇	81338828	纸板
东莞市盈泰纸品厂	望牛墩镇	88552289	生活用纸
东莞市道滘东发纸品有限公司	道滘镇	88839018	灰板纸
东莞市华深包装材料有限公司	寮步镇	81197702	木质包装箱
东莞市贝辉装饰材料有限公司	大朗镇	83199339	装饰材料(浸渍纸)
东莞市双洲纸业有限公司	中堂镇	88182618	瓦楞纸
东莞市恒伟纸业有限公司	道滘镇	88323168	纸板
东莞市白天鹅纸业有限公司	万江街道	22172128	纸制品
东莞市同力纸业有限公司	中堂镇		瓦楞芯纸
东莞市东保纸业有限公司	高埗镇	88786298	瓦楞纸挂面纸
东莞市华柏纸品有限公司	中堂镇	88112269	彩纸
东莞市祥兴纸业有限公司	中堂镇	88815238	瓦楞纸
东莞市高埗东保纸品厂	高埗镇	88734233	纸板
东莞市新富发纸业有限公司	万江街道	22711928	灰纸板
东莞市大步纸业有限公司	麻涌镇	88286883	机制纸及纸制品
东莞市裕杨纸品实业有限公司	茶山镇	86411555	纸箱
东莞市龙腾纸业有限公司	麻涌镇	88826898	纸制品
东莞市同兴纸品有限公司	高埗镇	81303788	瓦楞纸板
东莞市鸿业造纸有限公司	中堂镇	88814848	机制纸
东莞清溪现代纸品厂	清溪镇	87295802	纸箱
东莞市厚威包装有限公司	大朗镇	82228320	纸箱
东莞市伟虹纸业有限公司	望牛墩镇	88558198	造纸
东莞市达成纸品有限公司	麻涌镇	88289898	纸制品
东莞市深联造纸有限公司	中堂镇	88818778	瓦楞芯纸
广东玉兰装饰材料有限公司	东城街道	22652789	墙纸
东莞市旗峰纸业有限公司	道滘镇	88328212	纸

1-4　续表 5

(2010年)

单位名称	所属镇街	联系电话	主要产品(或服务)
东莞市鸿晖实业有限公司	石碣镇	86382008	纸制品
东莞市中堂镇吴家涌有利造纸厂	中堂镇	88412438	瓦楞纸
东莞荣辉纸类制品厂	清溪镇	87321128	咭套装
东莞市金田纸业有限公司	万江街道	22280688	灰板纸
东莞市华利纸品有限公司	高埗镇	88703832	纸板
东莞市凤岗新达纸品有限公司	凤岗镇	87750288	机制纸及纸板
东莞市建航纸业有限公司	中堂镇	88129488	包装纸
东莞市泰昌纸业有限公司	望牛墩镇	88852607	仿牛卡纸
印刷业和记录媒介的复制			
东莞市天华创展印刷有限公司	凤岗镇	87862122	出版物印刷
东莞长安锦厦怡兴柯式印刷厂	长安镇	85094628	彩合印刷
东莞市新广联数码科技有限公司	麻涌镇	88289688	只读类光盘复制
东莞市二轻包装彩印厂有限公司	东城街道	22699213	包装彩盒
东莞市东彩印刷包装有限公司	厚街镇	85820822	包装、装潢印刷品印刷
东莞市金剑模具制造有限公司	虎门镇	86093538	五金模具
文教体育用品制造业			
东莞市石碣易辉玩具厂	石碣镇		填充玩具
东莞市智高文具有限公司	石碣镇	86634176	彩泥
东莞市蓝宇玩具有限公司	厚街镇	88919828	玩具
东莞长安美泰玩具二厂	长安镇	85312683	塑胶玩具
东莞市丰泽文具有限公司	虎门镇	85506636	文件夹
东莞市天宇玩具制品有限公司	桥头镇	83429729	塑胶玩具
东莞清溪华创玩具电子厂	清溪镇	87314418	玩具线路板
东莞市智乐堡儿童玩具有限公司	石排镇	86550188	玩具
东莞伟易达电子厂	厚街镇	85581806	电子玩具
石油加工、炼焦及核燃料加工业			
东莞市安美化学有限公司	松山湖管委会	83210707	润滑油
东莞市安美润滑科技有限公司	松山湖管委会	83213232	环保清洗溶剂、润滑材料
东莞市晔联道路改性沥青有限公司	洪梅镇	88439822	改性石油沥青
东莞市荣高废油处理有限公司	麻涌镇	88221178	润滑油
化学原料及化学制品制造业			
东莞市罗孚化工有限公司	洪梅镇		万能胶
东莞市威亮实业有限公司	中堂镇	88886988	合成洗衣服
东莞市立顿洗涤用品实业有限公司	望牛墩镇	88999999	肥皂、合成洗涤剂制品
东莞市贝特利新材料有限公司	麻涌镇	88283198	油墨
东莞市保得生物工程有限公司	南城街道	22886693	生物有机肥
东莞市三联科技实业有限公司	寮步镇	83215622	颜料
广东省福利龙复合肥有限公司	高埗镇	88739816	复合肥料
东莞市金成化工有限公司	茶山镇	86486982	聚丙烯树脂
东莞市盛和化工有限公司	黄江镇	87132012	苯酐
东莞市汇美淀粉科技有限公司	麻涌镇	88287968	纺织HM391、HM328变性淀粉
东莞市瑞德丰生物科技有限公司	大岭山镇	83359225	农药复配
东莞市英科水墨有限公司	茶山镇	86481155	水性墨
东莞市芙蓉化工有限公司	望牛墩镇	88857923	分散松香胶
东莞市竣成化工有限公司	厚街镇	85595702	胶水
化学纤维制造业			

1-4 续表 6

(2010年)

单位名称	所属镇街	联系电话	主要产品(或服务)
东莞市源丰纤维制品有限公司	茶山镇	86645703	条纶短纤
医药制造业			
广东华南药业集团有限公司	石龙镇	86100111	银翘解毒口服液
广东众生药业股份有限公司	石龙镇	86100111	众生丸
橡胶制品业			
东莞市日源盛橡胶绝缘制品有限公司	石碣镇		绝缘材料
东莞市石碣东英塑胶制品厂	石碣镇	86631490	塑胶鞋底
塑料制品业			
东莞市百分百科技有限公司	东城街道	88754800	塑胶开关
东莞长安上角广迎五金塑胶制品有限公司	长安镇	85413055	塑胶机壳
东莞市富利时塑胶制品有限公司	东城街道	22653193	塑胶
东莞市朝阳实业有限公司	企石镇	86722142	塑料制品
东莞市晟美包装制品有限公司	南城街道	86228778	塑料制品
东莞市冠宏包装实业有限公司	望牛墩镇	88518756	BOPP封箱皮
东莞凤岗五联威达利塑胶制品厂	凤岗镇	87753728	吸塑罩
东莞市华瀚儿童用品有限公司	清溪镇	87867129	婴儿车
东莞冠诚塑胶模具有限公司	清溪镇	87739270	遥控器
东莞市泰和塑胶制品有限公司	桥头镇	83450238	塑料制品
东莞市汇美实业有限公司	长安镇	85412223	DVD、VCD塑胶面壳
东莞市华源包装有限公司	茶山镇	86646996	塑料包装袋
东莞市巨祺包装有限公司	常平镇	81093697	塑料瓶盖
东莞市荣辉塑料粒有限公司	虎门镇	85154933	塑料粒
东莞市华立实业股份有限公司	常平镇	83333239	塑料板
东莞新航包装材料有限公司	清溪镇		发泡胶(泡沫)包装材料
东莞市沃捷塑胶原料有限公司	常平镇	83504992	塑胶
东莞市泰至塑料五金有限公司	茶山镇	81821668	PVC管材
东莞市港源胶粘带制品有限公司	寮步镇	81111360	胶粘带
东莞市博美包装制品有限公司	塘厦镇	86255725	小型包装制品
东莞市惠德丽实业有限公司	企石镇	86728338	塑料杂品
东莞市兄奕塑胶制品有限公司	樟木头镇	87792188	塑胶制品
东莞清溪三钢电器制造厂	清溪镇	87732437	五金塑胶制品
东莞市丸万塑料包装有限公司	东城街道	22024286	塑料制品
东莞市铭丰包装品制造有限公司	万江街道	22171188	首饰盒
东莞清溪旺普登电子厂	清溪镇	87291877	液晶用背光板
东莞市正新包装制品有限公司	东城街道	22650889	塑料制品
东莞市瑞丰实业有限公司	寮步镇	81192789	聚乙烯环保薄膜
深圳市航天远东实业有限公司东莞分公司	凤岗镇	82100375	塑胶制品
东莞市合鑫电子厂	石排镇	86537079	塑胶
东莞市日泰鞋材有限公司	万江街道	23036108	鞋材
东莞长安乌沙新永塑胶零件模具厂	长安镇	85548081	塑胶制品
东莞市天宝五金塑胶制品有限公司	塘厦镇	87914500	五金

1-4 续表 7

(2010年)

单位名称	所属镇街	联系电话	主要产品(或服务)
非金属矿物制品业			
东莞市华佳能电器玻璃有限公司	桥头镇	81029258	钢化玻璃
东莞市茶山和兴粉磨站	茶山镇	86404633	粉磨水泥
东莞市增联有机玻璃制品有限公司	常平镇	81081968	有机玻璃制品
东莞市唯美陶瓷工业园有限公司	高埗镇	81133333	马可波罗瓷砖
东莞市东成石材有限公司	厚街镇	85596328	大理石花岗的切割
东莞市唯美装饰材料有限公司	东城街道	22650006	陶瓷制品
东莞市银泰玻璃有限公司	虎门镇	85708866	钢化玻璃
东莞市银通玻璃有限公司	沙田镇	88868988	玻璃制品
黑色金属冶炼及压延加工业			
东莞市东上钢材有限公司	中堂镇	88815968	钢材
东莞市丰源钢铁制品有限公司	大朗镇	83130830	钢铁制品
东莞市锦上钢材有限公司	中堂镇	88186778	PC钢棒
广东万濠精密仪器股份有限公司	长安镇	85316127	投影仪
有色金属冶炼及压延加工业			
东莞市华雨金属材料有限公司	大朗镇	83131757	铝棒延压
东莞市华昌铝合金制品厂	东城街道	22265108	铝材
东莞市金龙珠宝首饰有限公司	厚街镇	85832107	黄金饰品
东莞市亿鑫钢业有限公司	企石镇	86768769	钢结构材料
东莞市宏顺金属材料有限公司	企石镇	86764001	电镀锌钢板
东莞市永铖铝业有限公司	万江街道	22175338	铝挤型材
东莞市宏发钢铁结构材料有限公司	企石镇	86737153	钢结构材料
东莞市东城东联金属制品厂	东城街道	22291760	铝制品
金属制品业			
东莞市博丰塑胶五金制品有限公司	企石镇	86739662	吸塑
东莞市汇雅实业有限公司	厚街镇	85830032	五金制品
东莞市通旺达五金制品有限公司	凤岗镇	87561911	金属制品
东莞市硕泰实业有限公司	大岭山镇	81516875	金属压力容器
东莞市人本五金有限公司	塘厦镇	86856789	金属制品
东莞市坚朗五金制品有限公司	塘厦镇	87943311	点支撑幕墙配件
东莞市精丽制罐有限公司	石排镇	81702261	日用不锈钢制品
东莞市锐嘉精密机械制造有限公司	寮步镇	88908188	机箱
东莞市千岛金属锡品有限公司	塘厦镇	87880129	锡线
东莞市奥达铝业有限公司	大岭山镇	81621188	铝材制品
东莞市广成五金塑胶实业有限公司	桥头镇	81023992	五金塑胶制品
东莞市扬明精密塑胶五金电子有限公司	长安镇	85338940	塑胶五金电子制品
广东华宇钢结构工程有限公司	寮步镇	83218928	金属结构工程、网架工程
东莞市汇昌金属制品厂	寮步镇	83307988	铝制品
东莞市东兴铝材制造有限公司	中堂镇	88813671	铝合金型材
东莞科力钢铁线材有限公司	望牛墩镇	88557276	金属丝绳及其制品
东莞市冠辉五金有限公司	长安镇	85413848	五金配件
东莞市金翔电器设备有限公司	万江街道	22704478	电脑机箱
东莞市宏力实业有限公司金属结构加工厂	沙田镇	88861110	空心导轨
通用设备制造业			

1-4 续表 8

(2010年)

单位名称	所属镇街	联系电话	主要产品(或服务)
东莞厚街科技电业厂	厚街镇		电钻、电锯、工具
东莞市TR轴承有限公司	莞城街道	22461784	滚动轴承
东莞市铁志电子有限公司	寮步镇	82311308	碎纸机
东莞市三和兴模具钢材有限公司	塘厦镇	82016100	模具钢材
东莞市优富利电子有限公司	大岭山镇	85784995	风扇
东莞市快意施耐德电梯有限公司	清溪镇	87736443	电梯
东莞市宝特模具钢加工有限公司	望牛墩镇	88516020	金属制品
东莞市大岭山长虹弹簧厂	大岭山镇	85612812	弹簧
东莞市勤上金属制品有限公司	常平镇	83395678	铁线
东莞市鸿金顺机械制造有限公司	虎门镇	85558848	机械数控设备
东莞市台冠起重机械设备有限公司	大朗镇	83019666	桥式起重机
东莞市力宇燃气动力有限公司	虎门镇	85015288	发电机
东莞市快意电梯有限公司	清溪镇	87731075	电梯
东莞市寮步兆峰轴承有限公司	寮步镇	83328819	轴承
东莞市科达机电设备有限公司	万江街道	22188788	蒸发式降温换气机组
东莞市三友联众电器有限公司	厚街镇	85914551	继电器
东莞市东城永强弹簧厂	东城街道	22261357	弹簧
东莞市石排同利五金厂	石排镇	86659735	锌合金
东莞市富士电梯有限公司	东城街道	23062593	电梯
东莞市莱钢钢结构有限公司	黄江镇	83666666	钢结构件
东莞市三联机械有限公司	寮步镇	83321381	铸铁件
东莞市有同电器有限公司	南城街道	22401688	电子变压器用铁心电
东莞市得鑫五金有限公司	大朗镇	81124006	螺丝
东莞市庆新安制冷设备配件有限公司	桥头镇	83341457	制冷空调器
专用设备制造业			
东莞市虎门铭锋五金塑胶制品厂	虎门镇	38835099	模具、五金塑胶、运动器材
东莞市大族粤铭激光科技有限公司	万江街道	22771433	激光雕刻机
东莞晓达模具科技有限公司	大岭山镇	81881522	模具
东莞市金祥源环境治理工程技术有限公司	东城街道	88057088	
东莞市隆泰实业有限公司	石碣镇		煤矿机械
东莞科威医疗器械有限公司	东城街道	21985698	膜式氧合器
东莞市康达机电工程有限公司	寮步镇	88996233	机电工程
东莞市泰康电子科技有限公司	长安镇	85322066	电子连接器
东莞立诚电子有限公司	石排镇	86532010	电线
东莞市三洋电梯有限公司	厚街镇	85884455	电梯
东莞市方达实业有限公司	长安镇	85338842	PVC排水器材
东莞市虎门机械厂	虎门镇	85711932	B24小型拉伸机
东莞市雄丰配电设备有限公司	茶山镇	86647816	高压配电柜
东莞市道滘兴隆造纸厂	道滘镇	88381933	制浆
交通运输设备制造业			
广东永强奥林宝国际消防汽车有限公司	寮步镇	83269740	消防汽车
东莞市大裕摩托车有限公司	中堂镇	88883627	摩托车
东莞市永强汽车制造有限公司	寮步镇	83307688	罐式车
东莞市旗丰消声器有限公司	东城街道	22658795	汽车及摩托车消声器

1-4 续表 9

(2010年)

单位名称	所属镇街	联系电话	主要产品(或服务)
电气机械及器材制造业			
东莞市凯晟灯头实业有限公司	企石镇	86787878	铜灯头
东莞市大忠电子有限公司	东城街道	22630563	电子产品
东莞樟木头津地本电子厂	樟木头镇	87707507	电线连接头
东莞市昊恩装饰品有限公司	道滘镇	88328732	台灯
东莞塘厦新联电器厂	塘厦镇	87910170	电器、风筒
东莞市北航电机有限公司	虎门镇	85157468	电机
东莞市雷洋电子科技有限公司	长安镇	85391369	电子设备
东莞安尚光源有限公司	道滘镇	88311915	节能灯
东莞市日新传导科技股份有限公司	桥头镇	85425888	电子电器配件
东莞市锐升电线电缆有限公司	虎门镇	86092388	电线
东莞市特宝电子五金有限公司	清溪镇	87322805	电源
东莞市科菱电线有限公司	虎门镇		电线
东莞市瑞桥电器有限公司	企石镇	81358668	电器产品及连接线
高达粤电安信电力检修安装有限公司	虎门镇	85561893	机电设备安装
东莞市乐科电子有限公司	塘厦镇	87289666	电子产品
广东美林电线电缆有限公司	虎门镇	88920098	电线、电缆
东莞清溪荔横峻凌电子厂	清溪镇	87734725	电子产品
东莞市凌力电池有限公司麻涌电池厂	麻涌镇	88822642	干电池
东莞市奥源电子科技有限公司	长安镇	81589595	电子产品及零配件
广东康菱动力科技有限公司	松山湖管委会	22895555	发电机及发电机组
广东省东莞电机有限公司	南城街道	22810778	交流电动机
东莞长安迅诚电业制品厂	长安镇	85413308	漏电保护器插座
广东五星太阳能有限公司	万江街道	22176388	太阳能热水器
东莞市梅兰电器有限公司	寮步镇	83300022	电器器材
东莞市石龙富华电子有限公司	石龙镇	86022222	电源适配器
东莞清溪光荣电业制品厂	清溪镇	87300000	吸尘器
东莞勤上光电股份有限公司	常平镇	83395678	LED路灯
东莞市益达实业有限公司	茶山镇	86412628	漆包绕组线
东莞市理士奥电源核技术有限公司	塘厦镇	87925180	阀控式蓄电池
广东领亚电子科技有限公司	虎门镇	85510688	电线
东莞市迈科新能源有限公司	大朗镇	83197555	锂离子电池
东莞市中亚电缆有限公司	中堂镇	88111000	电线、电缆
东莞市通宝电线电缆有限公司	大朗镇	83315034	电线
东莞市绿雅家用电器有限公司	万江街道	88991088	电扇
东莞市亿丰电池有限公司	万江街道	22179288	干电池
东莞市金达照明有限公司	万江街道	22284761	水晶灯
广东中德电缆有限公司	东坑镇	81181482	电缆
东莞市开关厂有限公司	寮步镇	83300801	高低压开关屏
东莞市朗迪格林特电器有限公司	长安镇	85538815	空调风扇叶
东莞市高能电气股份有限公司	东城街道	22291876	绝缘体制品
东莞市宾士机电设备有限公司	寮步镇	89161688	发电机组
东莞市奥维漆包线有限公司	茶山镇	81810183	漆包绕线组
东莞市民兴电缆有限公司	凤岗镇	87510316	电线、电缆

1-4 续表 10

(2010年)

单位名称	所属镇街	联系电话	主要产品(或服务)
广东明家科技股份有限公司	横沥镇	87061828	插座
广东钜龙电力设备有限公司	石龙镇		油浸式电力变压器
东莞市杉杉电池材料有限公司	南城街道	22035233	锂离子电池材料
东莞市科慧电子有限公司	清溪镇	87326186	高频变压器
东莞华旭电线电缆有限公司	虎门镇	85526356	电线电缆、插头
东莞市凌力电池有限公司	万江街道	22271791	干电池
东莞市联升电线电缆有限公司	虎门镇	85253317	电线、铜线、插头电源线
东莞市欧雷玛电源有限公司	塘厦镇	87865169	铅酸蓄电池
东莞市迈科科技有限公司	大朗镇	83015380	镍氢电池
东莞市石碣志业电子有限公司	石碣镇	86318226	电线制品
东莞市奇声电子实业有限公司	麻涌镇	88231648	音响
东莞市华达电缆厂	大岭山镇	85617836	电缆
通信设备、计算机及其他电子设备制造业			
东莞市金正数码科技有限公司	寮步镇	81111299	DVD
东莞市光普实业发展有限公司	清溪镇	87339849	电脑机箱
东莞清溪欣冠电子厂	清溪镇	87311298	调制解调器
东莞市奥莱克电子有限公司	麻涌镇	88226006	组合音响
东莞市佳禾电子有限公司	石排镇	86596918	耳机
东莞市顺茂塑胶电子制品有限公司	虎门镇	85232518	塑胶电子制品
东莞市德生通用电器制造有限公司	东城街道	23167118	收音机
东莞市时唛特电器有限公司	塘厦镇	87987070	电子设备
东莞市茵莉电子有限公司	石碣镇	86314889	变压器
东莞市凯运电子有限公司	虎门镇	86232178	电子工线材
东莞市飞尔液晶显示器有限公司	大朗镇	83106619	电子元器件
东莞清溪显讯电子制品厂	清溪镇	87893556	电子
东莞市金锐显数码科技有限公司	塘厦镇	86858666	液晶电视主板
东莞市方达电子工业有限公司	长安镇	85410922	电子产品
东莞市耐福电子有限公司	清溪镇	87739261	散热风扇
东莞市楚东电子科技有限公司	塘厦镇	82133122	电子元件
东莞市亚力通电子科技有限公司	塘厦镇	82080288	电子元件
广东易事特电源股份有限公司	松山湖管委会	22897777	不间断电源
东莞厚街下汴电子厂	厚街镇	85591388	CD唱盘及收音机
东莞厚街新塘早川电子厂	厚街镇	85901115	电子配件
东莞海益机械配件有限公司	寮步镇	83220188	传感器零件
东莞市石碣东诚电子有限公司	石碣镇	86319827	电子材料
东莞市奕联实业有限公司	长安镇	86064988	连接线、连接器
东莞市亿达音响制造有限公司	东城街道	22665300	组合音箱
东莞黄江达裕科技电子厂	黄江镇	83531877	液晶显示器
东莞市森特电子有限公司	石碣镇	86329018	电脑机箱
东莞市粤林电脑科技有限公司	清溪镇	87890888	电脑机箱
东莞石龙华南电子五金制品厂	石龙镇	86624941	电子元件
聚信科技有限公司	松山湖管委会	22898612	通信产品
东莞市佰利电子有限公司	高埗镇	88708002	发光二极管
东莞市数字印数码科技有限公司	凤岗镇	87510868	数码音乐播放器

1-4 续表 11

(2010年)

单位名称	所属镇街	联系电话	主要产品(或服务)
东莞市腾易电子科技有限公司	常平镇	83509289	电话线
东莞市嘉田五金塑胶制品有限公司	凤岗镇	87774386	电脑机箱
东莞大岭山光顺电子厂	大岭山镇	83352904	电子产品
东莞市步步高通信设备有限公司	长安镇	85540688	有绳电话机
东莞市旭田电子有限公司	石碣镇	86300036	键盘
东莞市龙光电业有限公司	长安镇	85338787	机箱
东莞科德电子有限公司	常平镇	83391340	铭板
东莞市晖速天线技术有限公司	长安镇	85388505	天线配件
东莞市煜弘电子制造有限公司	虎门镇	85014888	音箱电脑
东莞伟易达电子元器件制造厂	寮步镇	85581806	电子元件
东莞伟易达电子通讯设备厂	寮步镇	85581806	室内无线电话
郡懋电子(东莞)有限公司	塘厦镇	87282000	微晶合金
东莞嘉财电业制造厂	大岭山镇	83359040	电业制造
东莞市塘厦克琛达塑胶电子厂	塘厦镇	86851777	电子元件
东莞市欧珀电子工业有限公司	长安镇	85545555	影碟机
东莞市盈聚电子有限公司	石碣镇	86327382	电子配件
东莞市奕东电子有限公司	东城街道	22200329	电子连接器
东莞市东方科技有限公司	厚街镇	85586389	电脑周边设备
东莞南城添迪制品厂	南城街道	22417969	电脑磁头臂
东莞市石碣德昌电子制品厂	石碣镇	88488080	电源线插头
东莞市金铭电子有限公司	大岭山镇	85656666	手机
广东步步高电子工业有限公司	长安镇	85545555	手机
东莞市步步高视听电子有限公司	长安镇	85545555	影碟机
东莞市步步高教育电子产品有限公司	长安镇	85540888	语言复读机
东莞市大朗迅田视讯设备厂	大朗镇	83482898	锌合金分路线
东莞道滘镇协益电子厂	道滘镇	88831848	电气机械
东莞市前锋电子有限公司	石碣镇	86633990	电磁炉
东莞市金业电子科技有限公司	寮步镇	83261111	VCD机
东莞厚街普光液晶显示厂	厚街镇	81520001	手机用液晶显示模组
东莞市福地电子材料有限公司	南城街道	22406025	LED芯片
东莞市芊和电子有限公司	石碣镇	81803262	耳机
东莞市铭基电子有限公司	厚街镇	83096688	电脑连接线
东莞市众誉电子有限公司	虎门镇	85554168	鼠标键盘
东莞市金河田实业有限公司	厚街镇	85585691	电脑外部设备
东莞市美声电器有限公司	茶山镇	83369888	液晶电视
东莞佳汇电子厂	大岭山镇	85602828	电脑显示器
东莞市华康电脑科技有限公司	横沥镇	83723860	电脑机箱
东莞市铭普实业有限公司	石排镇	81701560	网络变压器
广东志成冠军集团有限公司	塘厦镇	87722374	不间断电源
东莞清溪富崴电子厂	清溪镇	87313668	电脑扫描器
东莞市亚通光电有限公司	塘厦镇	82006088	光电子器件
仪器仪表及文化、办公用机械制造业			
东莞市邦泽电子有限公司	沙田镇	89191288	碎纸机

1-4 续表 12

(2010年)

单位名称	所属镇街	联系电话	主要产品(或服务)
东莞市华兰海电子有限公司	麻涌镇	88823105	便携式轴重台
广东正业科技有限公司	高埗镇	86279158	电子材料耗材
东莞寮步铨讯电子厂	寮步镇	83527668	数码相机
工艺品及其他制造业			
东莞市腾浦隆电子有限公司	常平镇	83903917	电位器
东莞三思化妆品有限公司	常平镇	83758028	化妆品
东莞市昌晖印染器材有限公司	虎门镇	85555020	印刷、印染机械
东莞太平电镀元件厂	虎门镇	85511047	拉链
东莞市钮成服装辅料有限公司	东城街道	22625327	钮扣
东莞市冠炜塑胶五金制品有限公司	常平镇	83981763	塑胶制品
东莞市阳光树脂制品有限公司	石碣镇	86633666	胶粘剂
东莞市华辉玻璃制品有限公司	石排镇	86656791	玻璃镀银、镀铝
东莞市雅居乐日用制品有限公司	石排镇	86598000	PVC台布
东莞市金叶珠宝有限公司	厚街镇	85822216	珠宝首饰
电力、热力的生产和供应业			
东莞市常平供电公司	常平镇	83399778	电力供应管理
东莞市城郊供电所	莞城街道	22336600	电力供应管理
广深沙角B电力有限公司沙角B火力发电厂	虎门镇		火力发电
东莞市基宁发电有限公司	虎门镇	85136442	火力发电
广东省粤电集团有限公司沙角C电厂	虎门镇	85165698	发电
东莞市石碣供电公司	石碣镇	86317627	电力供应管理
广东电力发展股份有限公司沙角A电厂	虎门镇	85136679	火力发电
东莞市三联热电有限公司	中堂镇	88812123	火力发电
燃气生产和供应业			
东莞市寮步新奥燃气有限公司	寮步镇		天然气、管道燃气
东莞市九丰能源有限公司	虎门港管委会	88866301	液化石油汽
水的生产和供应业			
东莞市东江自来水有限公司	莞城街道	22214443	自来水供应
东莞市寮步自来水公司	寮步镇	83328899	自来水供应
东莞市大朗镇自来水公司	大朗镇	83318306	自来水供应
东莞市横沥镇自来水公司	横沥镇	83375146	自来水供应
东莞市清溪自来水有限公司	清溪镇	87733362	自来水供应
东莞市常平镇自来水公司	常平镇	83335588	自来水供应
东莞市东江水务有限公司	东城街道	22609238	自来水供应
东莞市沙田自来水厂	沙田镇	88862620	自来水供应
东莞市长安镇自来水公司	长安镇	85535689	自来水供应
东莞市虎门自来水有限公司	虎门镇	85525510	自来水供应
东莞市塘厦自来水公司	塘厦镇	87724614	自来水供应
东莞市东城自来水公司	东城街道	22612699	自来水供应
房屋和土木工程建筑业			
东莞市正大建筑工程有限公司	万江街道	22278818	建筑工程
东莞市宏达建设工程有限公司	东城街道	22380008	房屋建筑工程

1-4　续表 13

(2010年)

单位名称	所属镇街	联系电话	主要产品(或服务)
东莞市瑞安建筑工程有限公司	万江街道	22386908	建筑工程
东莞市华源建筑工程有限公司	厚街镇	85596888	建筑工程
东莞市南粤建筑工程有限公司	万江街道	22020079	房屋建筑施工
东莞市中厚建筑工程公司	厚街镇	85582766	房屋工程建筑
东莞市石龙建筑工程公司	石龙镇	86116908	房屋建筑(二级)
东莞市凤岗建筑工程公司	凤岗镇	87860335	房屋工程建筑
东莞市健升建筑工程有限公司	南城街道	22302222	房屋建筑工程
东莞市建工集团有限公司	南城街道	22427888	房屋建筑工程
东莞市莞城建筑工程公司	莞城街道	22229020	工业和民用建筑工程
东莞市东城建筑公司	东城街道	22319001	房屋建筑
东莞市高业建设工程有限公司	高埗镇	88788633	水利工程建筑
东莞市经纬公路工程有限公司	东城街道	22083210	公路工程施工
东莞市鸿高建设工程有限公司	企石镇	86664882	房屋工程建筑
东莞市恒泰建筑工程有限公司	横沥镇	83378981	房屋建筑工程
东莞市方中建筑工程有限公司	莞城街道	86222001	建筑工程施工
东莞市南城区建筑工程有限公司	南城街道	22413912	房屋建筑
广东省水利水电第三工程局	塘厦镇	87721441	水利水电工程施工
东莞市裕欣国建筑工程有限公司	高埗镇	88781698	房屋工程建筑
东莞市百分百建设工程有限公司	东城街道	88754008	房屋建筑工程施工
东莞市茗鑫路桥建设养护有限公司	莞城街道	81115196	公路、路桥建设、养护
东莞市城区市政工程公司	莞城街道	22225634	建筑房屋
东莞市金斗建造工程有限公司	寮步镇	83300000	工业与民用建筑施工
建筑安装业			
东莞市广安电器安装工程有限公司	东城街道	82266666	电器工程安装
东莞市顺源机电安装工程有限公司	莞城街道	22490699	机电、电表、冷暖通风
广东集明电力工程有限公司	莞城街道	22492728	建筑装饰
湖南望新建设集团股份有限公司东莞分公司	南城街道	22999910	建筑
东莞市虎门煤气有限公司	虎门镇	85111140	燃气
东莞市粤发电气安装有限公司	石龙镇	86118998	承修电力设施
东莞市石龙第二建筑工程有限公司	石龙镇	86600222	房屋工程建筑
东莞市高宝电气安装工程有限公司	高埗镇	88786869	安装电力设备
东莞市输变电工程公司	寮步镇	83237889	电力安装
东莞市建安集团有限公司	东城街道	22986086	房屋建筑
东莞市虎门建设发展有限公司	虎门镇	85188631	建筑
东莞市景安电器安装工程有限公司	长安镇	81762299	电器安装
东莞市顺安电力消防工程有限公司	莞城街道	22481077	消防设施工程
东莞市安利来电气安装有限公司	大朗镇	83010013	电力设施承装
东莞市塘厦水电空调设备安装工程有限公司	塘厦镇	87913322	机电设备工程安装
东莞市名雕装饰有限公司	莞城街道	22029268	室内装饰
东莞市誉荣建材有限公司	东城街道	23321108	室内精装
东莞市小杨装饰工程有限公司	清溪镇		建筑装饰
其他建筑业			
东莞市凤安电力工程有限公司	凤岗镇	82082968	电力设施工程
东莞市福华建筑工程有限公司	沙田镇	88866688	房屋建筑
东莞市东塘电气安装有限公司	塘厦镇	87905273	承装电力设施
东莞市东方动力拆迁有限公司	南城街道	22991778	建筑拆迁

1-4　续表 14

(2010年)

单位名称	所属镇街	联系电话	主要产品(或服务)
东莞市广强建筑基础工程有限公司	东城街道	22464088	建筑基础工程
东莞市力丰钢结构有限公司	厚街镇	85916822	钢结构安装
东莞市岭南园林建设有限公司	莞城街道	22450507	园林绿化工程
东莞市国贸水电安装工程有限公司	东城街道	22760555	水电安装
道路运输业			
东莞市旺盆运输有限公司	厚街镇	81694271	运输
东莞市三和物流有限公司	寮步镇	83214617	货运
东莞市高埗客运站有限公司	高埗镇		客运
东莞市汽车运输有限公司	莞城街道	22463079	道路旅客运输
东莞市长城客运有限公司	莞城街道	22461975	公路客运
顺丰速运(东莞)有限公司	寮步镇	88981336	普通货物道路运输
东莞市飞马物流有限公司	黄江镇	86916838	普通货运
东莞市嘉达快运服务有限公司	东城街道	22981833	货物快递
东莞市交通集团有限公司	万江街道	22701663	交通运输服务
东莞市万隆华禹运输有限公司	厚街镇	85967555	货运
东莞市正泰运输服务有限公司	麻涌镇	88222278	货物中转
东莞市玖龙运输有限公司	麻涌镇	88234888	公路货运
城市公共交通业			
东莞市城巴运输有限公司	莞城街道	22492259	交通运输
东莞市华悦客运集团有限公司	莞城街道	27231596	小汽车
东莞市公共汽车有限公司	莞城街道	22211806	交通运输
水上运输业			
东莞市丰海海运有限公司	塘厦镇	87926329	港澳航线运输
广州港集团新沙港务有限公司	麻涌镇	82159033	货物装卸堆存
东莞市海昌船务有限公司	石碣镇	86018810	货物运输
装卸搬运及其他运输服务业			
东莞市德邦货运有限公司	南城街道	22907828	货运代理
东莞市南城南方物流有限公司	南城街道	22986935	运输
仓储业			
东莞市百安石化仓储有限公司	虎门港管委会	88666030	化工品仓储
中央储备粮广东新沙港直属库	麻涌镇	88231111	粮食储备
东莞市业荣威通贸易有限公司	洪梅镇	88431919	石化产品仓储
邮政业			
东莞市邮政局	莞城街道	22330782	函件
电信和其他信息传输服务业			
中国铁通集团有限公司东莞分公司长安营业厅	长安镇	86249800	电信业务
广东省电信实业集团东莞市有限公司	莞城街道	22482870	电信业务
中国网络通信集团公司东莞市分公司	南城街道	89826085	通讯服务
中国电信股份有限公司东莞分公司	南城街道	22808888	固定电话服务
广东省广播电视网络股份有限公司东莞洪梅分公司	洪梅镇	88430100	有线广播电视传输服务
中国铁通集团有限公司东莞分公司	莞城街道	86272388	电信固定电话
软件业			
东莞市智宇计算机科技有限公司	东城街道	23609655	系统集成
广东力优环境系统股份有限公司	松山湖管委会	23076888	冷冻空调
东莞市泰阳实业有限公司	虎门镇	85136389	计算机网络工程

1-4 续表 15

(2010年)

单位名称	所属镇街	联系电话	主要产品(或服务)
批发业			
东莞市建晖燃料有限公司	莞城街道	22348877	煤炭
广东省东莞五金矿产进出口有限公司	莞城街道	22227420	进出口代理
广东省东莞国药集团有限公司	莞城街道	22337200	药品
东莞市大通电脑有限公司	东城街道	23071386	计算机软、硬件
东莞市金杯供销有限公司	南城街道	22409128	汽车
东莞市建森废纸回收有限公司	中堂镇	88121098	废纸回收
东莞市萃华商贸有限公司	桥头镇	83342322	贸易管理
东莞市加利石油产品有限公司	沙田镇	88689922	润滑油
东莞主致医药有限公司	南城街道	22036911	医药
东莞市拓顺贸易有限公司	莞城街道	23032773	五金配件
东莞市银河废纸回收有限公司	中堂镇	88188108	废纸回收
东莞市恒镒钢铁有限公司	中堂镇	88189477	钢材
东莞市金汇废纸回收有限公司	中堂镇		废纸回收
东莞市兴盛废纸回收有限公司	中堂镇	88881402	废纸回收
东莞市源来废纸回收有限公司	中堂镇	88117972	废纸
东莞市双丰废纸回收有限公司	中堂镇	88182628	废纸回收
东莞市明泰贸易有限公司	南城街道	22824398	国际商业贸易
广东省东莞丝绸进出口有限公司	南城街道	22482892	服装
东莞市中堂废旧物资回收有限公司中联分公司	中堂镇	88120732	废纸收购
广东省东莞化工进出口有限公司	莞城街道	22231118	进出口代理
广东洛贝电子科技有限公司	松山湖管委会	22895186	电磁炉
东莞市伟明贸易有限公司	南城街道	23033918	泡棉、全棉涂色布
东莞市溢源对外贸易有限公司	东城街道	22201203	代理进出口
东莞市宇阳科技发展有限公司	凤岗镇	87506458	电容
广东鸿程油库有限公司	万江街道	88016809	石油及制品
东莞市东普贸易有限公司	石碣镇	86604338	钢材
东莞市永信药业有限公司	南城街道		中成药
东莞市东达汽车有限公司	厚街镇	85935999	汽车
东莞市中堂废旧物资回收有限公司银洲分公司	中堂镇	88120732	废纸收购
东莞市天牛塑胶原料有限公司	常平镇	86998877	塑胶原料
东莞市银洲燃料有限公司	中堂镇	88181366	煤炭
广东省东莞纺织品进出口有限公司	莞城街道		服装进出口
东莞市乾洋机电设备有限公司	中堂镇	81139232	五金机电
东莞市华银贸易有限公司	道滘镇	88311866	煤炭
东莞市仲源化工有限公司	谢岗镇		甲醇
东莞市永祥贸易有限公司	大岭山镇		燃料油
东莞市科裕钢铁贸易有限公司	沙田镇	88867777	钢材
东莞市津盈实业有限公司	虎门镇	85121693	钢材
东莞市文成酒业有限公司	东城街道	22111386	酒类
东莞市东悦机电设备有限公司	中堂镇	88188200	钢材
东莞市天昌塑胶原料有限公司	常平镇	86992933	塑胶原料
东莞市智丰贸易有限公司	大朗镇	83015809	服装
东莞市大洲进出口有限公司	大朗镇	83032998	服装

1-4 续表 16

(2010年)

单位名称	所属镇街	联系电话	主要产品(或服务)
东莞市东建浆纸有限公司	莞城街道	22623930	纸张
东莞市祥兴针车有限公司	石龙镇	86882006	缝纫设备
东莞市中堂废旧物资回收有限公司同力分公司	中堂镇	88120732	废纸收购
东莞东风南方东益汽车服务有限公司	虎门镇	85133806	汽车
东莞市汇鸿纸业有限公司	石碣镇	86010920	纸张
东莞市银图贸易有限公司	中堂镇	88412888	塑料
东莞市万通化工有限公司	万江街道	22187777	聚氯乙烯
东莞市德利石油化工有限公司	松山湖管委会	85516299	石油及制品
东莞市建筑材料进出口有限公司	莞城街道	22816022	鞋帽
深圳市庆鹏石油化工经销有限公司东莞分公司	沙田镇	88864889	成品油
东莞市鸿越实业有限公司	虎门镇	85261330	粉煤灰渣
东莞市中堂废旧物资回收有限公司东江分公司	中堂镇	88120732	废纸收购
东莞市合联进出口贸易有限公司	大朗镇	83125556	出口毛衣
东莞市泰昌石油化工贸易有限公司	樟木头镇	87710980	罐装润滑油
东莞市东伟石油化工有限公司	望牛墩镇	88855108	油
东莞市文一实业有限公司	道滘镇	88327025	文具
东莞市诚昌纸业有限公司	长安镇	85311598	文具
东莞市恒泰石油制品贸易有限公司	长安镇	85322068	重油
东莞市金马经贸有限公司	莞城街道	22307188	进出口代理
东莞市凯盈贸易有限公司	南城街道	23188808	机电产品
东莞市年丰饮料有限公司	东城街道	22256391	饮料
东莞市宝信实业有限公司	高埗镇	88731100	服装
东莞市正诚贸易有限公司	东城街道	22680808	进出口业务
东莞市糖酒集团东方配销有限公司	南城街道	22184011	小食
广东省东莞市厚街供销社	厚街镇	85581485	日用百货建材
东莞市君科进出口贸易有限公司	南城街道	22299128	货物及技术出口
东莞市中堂废旧物资回收有限公司珠江分公司	中堂镇	88120732	废纸收购
东莞市麒麟机械有限公司	莞城街道	22473938	轴承
东莞市惠顺贸易有限公司	东城街道		建材
广东省东莞国药集团药材有限公司	莞城街道	22239530	中药材
东莞市旗峰对外贸易有限公司	东城街道	22633592	进出口业务
东莞市中堂废旧物资回收有限公司建桦分公司	中堂镇	88120732	废纸收购
东莞市电力燃料有限公司	万江街道	22475222	石油及制品
东莞市溢安贸易有限公司	麻涌镇	88280993	重油
东莞市东辉贸易有限公司	黄江镇	83364788	化工原料
东莞市德凯经贸有限公司	南城街道	23027769	服装出口贸易
东莞市糖酒集团美宜佳便利店有限公司	南城街道	22465830	小食品
东莞市友华机电工程有限公司	莞城街道	23050801	中央空调
东莞市港源贸易有限公司	南城街道	22488703	工艺品进出口
东莞市中堂废旧物资回收有限公司建晖分公司	中堂镇	88120732	废纸收购
东莞市永椿净化设备工程有限公司	寮步镇	81107819	净化设备工程
东莞市新技术进出口有限公司	南城街道	22428678	各类商品和技术的进出口
东莞市科大贸易有限公司	沙田镇	88867777	钢材
东莞市长安利源石油有限公司	长安镇	85416068	石油

1-4 续表 17

(2010年)

单位名称	所属镇街	联系电话	主要产品(或服务)
东莞市明盛能源有限公司	石碣镇	86313666	煤炭
东莞市佳森能源有限公司	麻涌镇	88235233	煤炭
东莞市中堂废旧物资回收有限公司	中堂镇	88811203	收购废品
东莞市中凯进出口有限公司	大朗镇	83101855	毛衫
东莞中茂石油化工贸易有限公司	塘厦镇		甲醇
广东省东莞机械进出口有限公司	莞城街道	22222040	进出口机电产品
东莞市雄峰特殊钢有限公司	凤岗镇	87559810	模具钢材
东莞市宏川化工有限公司	松山湖管委会	22893998	化工产品
东莞市利士石油化工有限公司	高埗镇	88731368	石油
东莞市科虹金属有限公司	石碣镇	86309328	铜材
东莞市华树电脑有限公司	莞城街道	22313954	电子计算机及其配件
广东省东莞轻工业品进出口有限公司	莞城街道	22212413	各类电器
东莞市隆兴纸业有限公司	石龙镇	86088777	文化用纸
东莞市天锐贸易有限公司	长安镇	85545555	电子元件
东莞市美德石化产品有限公司	谢岗镇	87682025	溶剂油
东莞市一君医药有限公司	高埗镇	81306988	中成药
东莞市南洋计算机软件有限公司	东城街道	22505550	计算机应用软件
东莞市创丰科技发展有限公司	南城街道	22855300	自动化设备
东莞市泽通贸易有限公司	莞城街道	22224050	电器
东莞市汇众进出口有限公司	大朗镇	83209503	针织制品
东莞市昱方钢材有限公司	长安镇	85349788	模具钢材
东莞市伟业石油化工有限公司	望牛墩镇	88850666	柴油
东莞市恒生进出口有限公司	南城街道	23181991	泡棉机进出口
东莞市振东医药有限公司	东城街道	22323888	药品
东莞市同汇贸易有限公司	东城街道	23360488	化工产品
东莞市永盛燃料有限公司	万江街道	22287225	石油及制品
东莞市百业兴经贸有限公司	南城街道	22421328	一般贸易
广东省东莞快宜外经发展有限公司	南城街道	22421003	商品进出口
东莞市寮步根记五金贸易部	寮步镇	83219698	铜制品
东莞市华麟贸易有限公司	莞城街道	22313101	食用香精料
东莞市莞晟贸易有限公司	中堂镇	88110155	煤炭
东莞市力宏贸易有限公司	中堂镇	88411005	化工产品
东莞市彩虹塑胶颜料有限公司	凤岗镇	87777113	塑胶颜料
东莞市瑞展皮革贸易有限公司	厚街镇	85825996	皮革
东莞市柏百顺石油化工有限公司	樟木头镇	87781216	化工燃料及产品
东莞市海川进出口有限公司	大朗镇	83113663	服装
东莞市益发贸易有限公司	东城街道	22508736	服务
东莞市锦茂进出口有限公司	东城街道	22339829	国内商业服务
东莞市顺盈钢材贸易有限公司	中堂镇	88188790	钢材、五金
广东省东莞市新华书店有限公司	莞城街道	22115138	教材图书
东莞市同舟化工有限公司	沙田镇	22365733	甲苯
东莞市万红贸易有限公司	东城街道	22316751	进出口贸易
东莞市对外贸易发展有限公司	东城街道		代理进出口
东莞市荣兴纸业有限公司	石碣镇	86013903	纸

1-4 续表 18

(2010年)

单位名称	所属镇街	联系电话	主要产品(或服务)
东莞市先锋特殊钢有限公司	凤岗镇	87777097	钢材
东莞市糖酒集团丰裕贸易有限公司	南城街道	22481231	食品
东莞市广弘医药有限公司	万江街道	88899033	中药材及中成药
东莞市巨树食品有限公司	万江街道	22422166	副食
东莞市长成纸张有限公司	虎门镇		纸张
东莞市中泰纸业有限公司	长安镇	85415136	纸张
东莞市信佳贸易有限公司	南城街道	23186737	热轧卷板
东莞市中堂废旧物资回收有限公司深联分公司	中堂镇	88120732	废纸收购
东莞市中堂废旧物资回收有限公司汇达分公司	中堂镇	88120732	废纸收购
东莞市东孚商贸有限公司	万江街道	22772277	化妆品及卫生用品
广东省东莞盐业总公司	莞城街道	22380236	盐产品
广东省东莞市谢岗食品公司	谢岗镇	87687328	生猪
东莞市达明发展有限公司	东城街道	22363006	出口家具
东莞市嘉宝石油化工有限公司	樟木头镇	87711087	甲基苯
广东省东莞医药保健品进出口有限公司	南城街道	22802920	出口服装
东莞市天泰控股集团有限公司	东城街道	23138888	成品油
东莞市中堂废旧物资回收有限公司振桦分公司	中堂镇	88120732	废纸收购
东莞市翔顺妇幼用品有限公司	麻涌镇	88281327	奶粉
东莞市世发贸易有限公司	南城街道	22800368	化工原料
东莞市东源投资实业有限公司	南城街道	22855416	煤炭
中国石油天然气股份有限公司东莞销售分公司	南城街道	22022155	成品油
东莞市宇兴贸易有限公司	大朗镇	83109968	毛衣
东莞市允新贸易有限公司	寮步镇	83039670	模具钢
东莞市中堂废旧物资回收有限公司金洲分公司	中堂镇	88120732	废纸收购
东莞市健宇塑胶原料有限公司	常平镇	86991001	塑胶原料
广东烟草东莞市有限公司	东城街道	22210936	烟草
东莞市厚龙燃气有限公司	厚街镇	85817336	液化石油气
东莞市澳洁贸易有限公司	常平镇	83750888	日用百货
东莞国药集团仁济堂药业有限公司	莞城街道	22484521	中药材
东莞市广通贸易有限公司	南城街道	22407968	汽车轮胎
东莞市中堂废旧物资回收有限公司双洲分公司	中堂镇	88120732	废纸收购
东莞市鼎鑫贸易有限公司	东城街道	22314016	贸易
东莞市源源钢铁贸易有限公司	大朗镇	83130830	钢材材料
东莞市永联化工贸易有限公司	大朗镇	83112349	过氧化氢
东莞市常平好必来塑胶贸易有限公司	常平镇	86992038	塑胶原料
东莞市东物剧毒化学物品有限公司	莞城街道	22383672	物流流通
东莞市中彦进出口有限公司	大朗镇	83315888	服装
广东省东莞市海东石油有限公司	麻涌镇	88232325	油品
东莞市华江石油化工有限公司	樟木头镇	82119266	石油化工
东莞市东塑进出口有限公司	东坑镇	83862338	货物进出口贸易
东莞市洋通饮料贸易有限公司	茶山镇	86110722	啤酒
广东省东莞包装进出口有限公司	南城街道	22802861	纺织品进出口
东莞市建安贸易有限公司	莞城街道	22321232	轻纺产品服装
东莞市富励贸易有限公司	凤岗镇		化工产品

1-4 续表 19

(2010年)

单位名称	所属镇街	联系电话	主要产品(或服务)
东莞市彬源塑胶贸易有限公司	厚街镇	85904198	塑胶
东莞市瑞腾贸易有限公司	莞城街道	22223639	农副产品
东莞市成泰化工有限公司	南城街道	22884548	EVA
东莞市润泰纸业有限公司	长安镇	85499268	纸张
东莞市朝阳药业有限公司	道滘镇	88327952	中成药、中药材
东莞市金仙峰实业有限公司	南城街道	22416577	白砂糖
东莞市广济医药器械有限公司	南城街道	22906161	药品
东莞市创兴糖业贸易有限公司	万江街道	22784583	糕点、糖果及糖
东莞市东江石油化工有限公司	万江街道	87076081	石油及制品
东莞市中堂废旧物资回收有限公司有利分公司	中堂镇	88120732	废纸收购
东莞市道滘珠洲石油气有限公司	道滘镇	88389233	液化石油气
东莞市中堂废旧物资回收有限公司鸿业分公司	中堂镇	88120732	废纸收购
东莞市三方贸易有限公司	东城街道	23051611	食品
广东省东莞市虎门供销社	虎门镇	85513008	家用电子类
东莞市华穗石化有限公司	麻涌镇	88283682	重油
东莞市康盈贸易有限公司	东城街道	22784583	食糖
东莞市虎门粮食有限公司	虎门镇	85511250	粮油
东莞市环球工艺进出口贸易有限公司	南城街道	22802312	出口家具
东莞市东安石油化工有限公司	沙田镇	88865128	汽油
东莞市豪景商贸有限公司	石龙镇	86118181	机电产品
东莞市利兴糖业贸易有限公司	万江街道	22784583	糕点、糖果及糖
东莞市百业进出口有限公司	南城街道	22421328	一般贸易
东莞市金鹏塑料原料有限公司	樟木头镇	87126666	化学产品
东莞市海华五金矿产进出口有限公司	莞城街道	22243170	进出口代理
东莞市日之泉物流有限公司	中堂镇	88815015	钢材
东莞市汇富进出口贸易有限公司	南城街道	22389322	家具
东莞市南腾贸易有限公司	中堂镇	88122189	有机溶剂
东莞市信立实业有限公司	大岭山镇	85633333	农产品贸易
东莞市东糖集团有限公司	东城街道	22613931	成品糖
东莞市中信化工有限公司	黄江镇	86918388	塑胶粒
东莞市乘风实业有限公司	石排镇	86615001	购销包
上海凯群贸易有限公司东莞分公司	厚街镇	85750312	塑胶、塑样及制品
东莞市卓远发展经贸有限公司	黄江镇	87132056	苯酐
东莞市百维食品化工原料实业有限公司	寮步镇	83263989	食品添加剂
东莞市鑫泉石油化工有限公司	樟木头镇		化工产品
东莞市日之泉贸易有限公司	中堂镇	88815015	钢材
东莞市超捷实业有限公司	麻涌镇	88228979	重油
东莞市华润涂料有限公司	东城街道	22363331	油漆
东莞市瑞峰纸业有限公司	东城街道	22623952	纸张
东莞市华辉金属材料有限公司	莞城街道	22468979	金属材料
广东大地通讯连锁服务有限公司	莞城街道	23066666	通讯设备
东莞市亿丰行洗涤产品有限公司	茶山镇	86311487	洗涤用品
东莞市星辰塑胶有限公司	常平镇	86991286	塑胶原料
东莞市顺安废纸回收有限公司	望牛墩镇	88851243	废纸回收

1-4 续表 20

(2010年)

单位名称	所属镇街	联系电话	主要产品(或服务)
东莞市广联通信器材有限公司	石排镇		手机
东莞市泓海贸易有限公司	莞城街道	22340699	纺织品染料
中铝洛阳铜业有限公司东莞分公司	虎门镇	85562885	有色金属
广东省东莞畜产进出口有限公司	东城街道	22206023	五金
东莞市华闽金属材料有限公司	横沥镇	83792951	金属贸易
东莞市辉明石化产品有限公司	谢岗镇	23183527	石油
东莞市欢盈投资有限公司	东城街道		空调
东莞市广利食品进出口有限公司	莞城街道	22223344	食品
东莞市华发纸张有限公司	石碣镇	86313868	白纸板
东莞市华丰盛塑料有限公司	中堂镇	88411688	PC塑料
东莞市美星塑胶材料有限公司	南城街道	23120868	塑胶原料
东莞市伟力地坪材料有限公司	企石镇		地称材料
东莞市创辉进出口贸易有限公司	寮步镇	81106328	毛织品
东莞市广招贸易有限公司	中堂镇	88893567	锌锭、铝锭
东莞市港汇钢业有限公司	厚街镇	85883322	钢材
东莞市美的日用家电有限公司	莞城街道	22666432	美的电饭煲
东莞市恒旭达塑胶贸易有限公司	樟木头镇		塑胶
东莞市创维电器发展有限公司	东城街道	22292742	家用电器
东莞市岭南进出口有限公司	寮步镇	81197620	电脑配件
东莞市东长石油化工有限公司	望牛墩镇		重油
鞋柜商贸有限公司东莞经销部	厚街镇		鞋帽
永恩投资(集团)有限公司广东经销部	厚街镇	83085323	服装
东莞市盈邦贸易有限公司	沙田镇	81631398	重油
东莞市麻涌利南废纸回收有限公司	麻涌镇	88234888	废纸收购
东莞市合泊进出口贸易有限公司	东城街道	23609238	代理进出口
零售业			
东莞市粤美特加油站有限公司	大岭山镇	83351331	汽油、柴油
东莞市东宝能源有限公司	塘厦镇	87905808	重油
东莞市嘉誉电子有限公司	清溪镇	82692990	电子产品
东莞市寮步新城国际汽车城	寮步镇	88126605	食品
东莞市顺电商贸有限公司莞城威尼斯分店	莞城街道		食品
东莞市志诚汽车服务有限公司	寮步镇	83228331	汽车
东莞市兴华燃料贸易有限公司大朗高英供应站	大朗镇	83187988	液化石油气
广东钻石世家国际珠宝有限公司	南城街道	22028888	钻石
东莞市大参林连锁药店有限公司	南城街道	22884901	药品
广州市好又多(天利)百货商业有限公司世博分公司	东城街道	22763201	百货超市
东莞东风南方汽车服务有限公司樟木头分公司	樟木头镇	83841307	品牌汽车
东莞市国贸超级市场有限公司	莞城街道	22117591	副食品
东莞市君通汽车贸易有限公司	寮步镇	83226599	汽车
东莞市励骏实业有限公司	厚街镇	21123920	皮鞋
东莞市广物正通达汽车贸易有限公司	寮步镇	83269019	长安品牌汽车
东莞市塘厦林村加油站	塘厦镇	87902608	成品油
东莞市广物君豪实业投资有限公司	万江街道	22703999	汽车
东莞市东奥汽车服务有限公司	寮步镇		汽车

1-4 续表 21

(2010年)

单位名称	所属镇街	联系电话	主要产品(或服务)
东莞市中科能源有限公司	黄江镇	83600900	润滑油
东莞市骐骏汽车销售服务有限公司	樟木头镇	87798302	汽车
东莞东美丰田汽车销售服务有限公司	塘厦镇	82087662	汽车
东莞市森和纸业有限公司	厚街镇	85588818	纸制品
上海嘉定乐购生活购物有限公司东莞市厚街分公司	厚街镇	88913888	百货
东莞市周通泰汽车贸易有限公司	常平镇	83333390	汽车
东莞市中昌贸易有限公司	大朗镇	81123383	汽车
东莞市骏宇汽车贸易有限公司	南城街道	22851778	汽车及配件
东莞市东悦汽车销售服务有限公司	大朗镇	81069990	整车
东莞市万江国威加油站	万江街道	22275846	机动车燃料
东莞市新天地汽车销售服务有限公司	寮步镇	83523008	汽车
东莞市新日水果食品有限公司	莞城街道	22489993	水果、食品
东莞市龙成汽车销售服务有限公司	万江街道	22779999	汽车
东莞市东部丰田汽车销售服务有限公司	寮步镇	83285989	丰田品牌汽车
东莞市海雅百货有限公司	东城街道	22031333	百货
东莞市桥头加桥加油站有限公司	桥头镇	22367236	机动车燃料
东莞市志达汽车销售服务有限公司	虎门镇	85226333	汽车
东莞市世纪骏丰频谱科技有限公司	莞城街道		频谱仪
东莞市立诚立信贸易有限公司	黄江镇	86919417	塑胶
东莞市恒波商业有限公司	大朗镇	83018679	通讯产品
东莞凯润丰田汽车销售服务有限公司	虎门镇	85133988	汽车
东莞市悦海实业投资有限公司	寮步镇	81254225	服装
上海大众汽车东莞销售服务有限公司	莞城街道	22337006	汽车
东莞市南城丰田汽车销售服务有限公司	南城街道	22987090	汽车
东莞市新大地汽车贸易有限公司	莞城街道		汽车
东莞市同庆汽车贸易有限公司	寮步镇	83300188	汽车
广东省东莞国药集团长安医药有限公司	长安镇	85308840	药品
东莞市苏宁电器有限公司	莞城街道	22320266	家用电器
东莞市时尚电器有限公司	莞城街道	22342220	家用电器
东莞市华美汽车销售服务有限公司	虎门镇	85017927	汽车
东莞市安信丰田汽车销售服务有限公司	大岭山镇	81870333	汽车
东莞市合信汽车销售服务有限公司	南城街道	23188228	汔车
东莞市恒信汽车销售服务有限公司	东城街道	22767228	汽车
东莞市永佳丰田汽车销售服务有限公司	厚街镇	81691107	汽车维修
东莞东风南方汽车销售有限公司	南城街道	22985916	东风日产品牌汽车
东莞市博雅贸易有限公司	常平镇	81090360	长安福特品牌汽车
东莞市华升汽车有限公司	虎门镇	85246601	汽车
东莞东风南方东升汽车销售服务有限公司	厚街镇	85089656	汽车
深圳市华德石油化工有限公司东莞分公司	沙田镇	88866342	石油化工产品
东莞市中油迅兴实业有限公司	中堂镇	88412338	柴油
东莞市志和汽车销售服务有限公司	寮步镇	81103821	汽车
东莞市骏标汽车销售有限公司	南城街道	22850962	小轿车
东莞市天虹商场有限公司	莞城街道	23164880	百货
东莞市合禾汽车销售服务有限公司	常平镇	82201168	丰田汽车

1-4 续表 22

(2010年)

单位名称	所属镇街	联系电话	主要产品(或服务)
东莞市常平供销社	常平镇	83331117	超级市场
东莞市大兴汽车贸易有限公司	东城街道	22662646	汽车
东莞市黄江镇江南加油站有限公司	黄江镇	83629433	汽油
东莞市东城中油柏洲边加油站	东城街道	22263969	汽油
东莞市中油国威油品有限公司	虎门镇	85503019	汽油
东莞市金美汽车服务有限公司	常平镇	83553927	汽车
东莞市鸿鹰汽车服务有限公司	南城街道	22981108	汽车
东莞市银星实业发展有限公司	清溪镇	87737539	柴油
东莞市志祥汽车服务有限公司	寮步镇	83226599	汽车
东莞市天下行丰田汽车服务有限公司	常平镇	83558216	汽车
东莞市遂通汽车服务有限公司	南城街道	22850555	汽车
东莞市冠丰汽车有限公司	寮步镇	83525630	汽车
东莞市虎门石油公司虎威加油站	虎门镇	85109138	柴油
东莞市锦多宝能源有限公司	樟木头镇	87780788	汽油、重油、润滑油
东莞龙华丰田汽车服务有限公司	万江街道	22773388	汽车
东莞市鸿业石化有限公司	企石镇	86663789	液化石油气
东莞市南城区农机服务站宏伟加油站	南城街道	22404202	汽油
东莞市昌发汽车贸易有限公司虎门分公司	虎门镇	85131831	汽车
东莞市人人乐商业有限公司	厚街镇	81633337	食品
东莞市南城海雅百货有限公司	南城街道	23027222	服装
东莞市三益汽车有限公司	寮步镇	83526653	汽车
东莞市丰华汽车服务有限公司	樟木头镇	87193088	汽车
东莞市大朗镇松木山加油站	大朗镇	83128021	汽油
深圳市海王星辰健康药房连锁有限公司东莞分公司	莞城街道	22366079	药品
东莞市捷达通贸易有限公司	南城街道	22971218	汽车
东莞市锦华汽车贸易有限公司	厚街镇	85990730	小汽车
东莞市东富实业有限公司	寮步镇	83220559	汽车
东莞东风南方汽车服务有限公司寮步分公司	寮步镇	83523042	汽车
东莞市骏捷汽车贸易有限公司	厚街镇	83080019	东风本田汽车
东莞市长久汽车贸易有限公司	东城街道	22663933	汽车
东莞市星高达汽车服务有限公司	寮步镇	81105588	斯柯达品牌汽车
东莞市南菱汽车服务有限公司	南城街道	22909591	汽车
东莞市江铃汽车有限公司	寮步镇	83220527	汽车
东莞市合宝汽车服务有限公司	南城街道	22851228	宝马轿车
东莞市汇天源汽车服务有限公司	寮步镇	83528753	汽车
东莞市永成加油站有限公司	厚街镇	85588949	汽油
东莞市中油西溪加油站有限公司	寮步镇	83328508	汽油
东莞市东众汽车服务有限公司	寮步镇	83230999	汽车
东莞市顺昌贸易有限公司	凤岗镇		机动车燃料
东莞市常平液化石油气供应有限公司	常平镇	83337820	液化石油气
东莞市兴隆汽车贸易有限公司	寮步镇	82315618	汽车
东莞市和盈商贸有限公司	万江街道	22422218	日用品
东莞市东盛超市有限公司	东城街道	23139067	日用百货
东莞中汽南方汽车服务有限公司	南城街道	86225930	汽车
东莞市天和商贸有限公司	樟木头镇	22508941	百货
东莞市大朗世达汽车有限公司	大朗镇	81116716	汽车

1-4 续表 23

(2010年)

单位名称	所属镇街	联系电话	主要产品(或服务)
东莞华多利汽车有限公司	寮步镇	83523000	汽车
东莞市厚街涌口加油站有限公司	厚街镇	85050598	柴油
东莞市万华皮革有限公司	厚街镇	85876266	皮革
东莞市骏丰汽车有限公司	寮步镇	83229371	汽车
东莞市大新汽车贸易有限公司	东城街道	22672268	汽车
东莞市羚丰汽车贸易有限公司	东城街道	22981618	汽车
东莞市华力冷气工程有限公司	莞城街道	23067567	制冷电器
东莞市金逸贸易有限公司	东城街道	22367303	电脑音相
东莞市常平镇朗贝加油站	常平镇	83330019	汽油
东莞市奇旺商贸有限公司	东坑镇	83887138	服装
东莞市常平石油供应有限公司	常平镇	83022221	汽油、煤油
东莞市百力恒丰田汽车销售服务有限公司	长安镇	81603800	汽车
中域电讯连锁集团股份有限公司	南城街道	22888888	手机通讯产品
东莞市东城加成加油站有限公司	东城街道	22489229	汽油、柴油、润滑油
东莞市虎门煤气有限公司	虎门镇	85111140	燃气
东莞市鸿燕贸易有限公司	南城街道	23303318	汽车
东莞市桥南加油站有限公司	厚街镇	85882970	汽油
东莞市虎门镇嘉燃加油站	虎门镇	85110933	汽油
东莞市聚成汽车技术服务有限公司	南城街道	22406200	汽车
东莞市天泰石油化工有限公司	南城街道	22028726	润滑油
东莞市同兴涂料有限公司	高埗镇	88739118	二甲苯
东莞市永奥汽车贸易有限公司	寮步镇	83261895	汽车
东莞市渝庆汽车销售服务有限公司	寮步镇	83300138	汽车
东莞市万威水上加油站有限公司	中堂镇	88823882	柴油
东莞市骏鸣汽车销售服务有限公司	寮步镇	81112813	汽车
广东省东莞市医药有限公司	莞城街道	22507881	西药
东莞市正欣科技有限公司	南城街道	22023588	软件设计
上海嘉定乐购生活购物有限公司东莞市常平分公司	常平镇	81896969	百货
东莞市南方汽车博览有限公司	樟木头镇	87707666	汽车
东莞市永怡汽车贸易有限公司	南城街道	22904057	汽车
东莞市华美乐建材超市有限公司	南城街道	22901188	瓷砖
东莞市凯润东成汽车销售服务有限公司	寮步镇	82223988	广州本田品牌汽车
上海嘉定乐购生活购物有限公司东莞市虎门分公司	虎门镇	81613268	百货
东莞市彩怡百货有限公司	莞城街道	22497688	百货
东莞市永升汽车贸易有限公司	寮步镇	81128180	汽车
东莞市加南石油供应有限公司	中堂镇		柴油、汽油
东莞市汇福轮胎有限公司	石龙镇	86180598	汽车轮胎
东莞市福丰汽车有限公司	南城街道	22850001	长安福特品牌汽车
东莞市宏宝汽车销售服务有限公司	寮步镇	81106028	汽车
东莞市金实力油料有限公司	清溪镇		重油
东莞市永濠汽车销售服务有限公司	南城街道	22904888	汽车
东莞市昊安汽车有限公司	长安镇	85223818	汽车

1-4 续表 24

(2010年)

单位名称	所属镇街	联系电话	主要产品(或服务)
东莞市嘉荣超市有限公司	南城街道	22808810	家用百货
东莞市中堂镇东泊加油站	中堂镇	88885838	柴油
东莞市华隆加油站有限公司	寮步镇	22367236	汽油、柴油
中国石油化工股份有限公司广东东莞石油分公司	莞城街道	22506200	汽油
东莞市寮步横坑加油站有限公司	寮步镇	83301011	汽油
东莞市常平木抡加油站	常平镇	83988331	机动车燃料
东莞市东仁汽车销售服务有限公司	南城街道	86228588	汽车
东莞市中维商贸有限公司	东坑镇	83887138	西装
东莞市新东联汽车贸易有限公司	寮步镇	83527292	汽车
深圳市国美电器有限公司 东莞市分公司	莞城街道	22807391	家用电器
东莞市冠骏汽车销售服务有限公司	寮步镇	83230777	汽车
东莞市东鑫汽车销售服务有限公司	塘厦镇	82089077	汽车
东莞市愉康超市有限公司	长安镇	85536488	百货
广东省东莞国药集团虎门医药有限公司	虎门镇	85511364	药品
东莞市万昌燃气有限公司	凤岗镇		生活用燃料
住宿业			
东莞市蒂豪花园酒店有限公司	大朗镇	83122222	住宿服务
东莞市昌明实业有限公司喜来登酒店	厚街镇	85988888	饮食服务
东莞市东城国际酒店有限公司	东城街道		星级酒店
东莞市凯景酒店有限公司	中堂镇	88883333	酒店管理服务
东莞市塘厦三正半山酒店有限公司	塘厦镇	87299333	旅游饭店
东莞市嘉华酒店有限公司	厚街镇	85928888	餐饮
东莞市会展国际大酒店	南城街道	22889999	旅游饭店
东莞市龙泉国际大酒店	虎门镇	85188688	餐饮
东莞市太子酒店有限公司	黄江镇	83363333	住宿
东莞市宏远酒店有限公司	南城街道	22418888	餐饮
东莞市松山湖酒店有限公司凯悦酒店分公司	松山湖管委会	22891234	住宿
东莞市长安国际酒店有限公司	长安镇	85333333	餐饮服务
东莞市悦莱花园酒店有限公司	寮步镇	81118888	餐饮
东莞市富盈酒店有限公司	厚街镇	85888888	餐饮
东莞市丰泰花园酒店有限公司	虎门镇	85708888	旅业
东莞宾馆有限公司	莞城街道	22222222	正餐服务
东莞市汇华饭店	常平镇	83938888	旅游饭店
东莞市汇景酒店有限公司	洪梅镇	88848888	餐饮
餐饮业			
真功夫餐饮管理有限公司	长安镇	38792952	快餐饮食服务
东莞市桥头新鸿酒店	桥头镇		西餐服务
福州德克士食品有限公司石龙餐厅	石龙镇	86185991	食品
东莞世博唐宫海鲜舫有限公司	东城街道	22762802	中西餐服务
东莞市花园粥城服务有限公司	东城街道	22612051	餐饮服务
银行业			
招商银行股份有限公司东莞分行	东城街道	22303888	金融业务
广东发展银行股份有限公司东莞分行	莞城街道	22477888	金融业务
兴业银行股份有限公司东莞分行	南城街道	22809988	金融业务

1-4 续表 25

(2010年)

单位名称	所属镇街	联系电话	主要产品(或服务)
交通银行股份有限公司东莞分行	莞城街道	22505643	金融业务
东莞市农村商业银行股份有限公司	莞城街道	22103131	金融业务
中国银行股份有限公司东莞分行	南城街道	22819888	金融业务
东莞银行股份有限公司	莞城街道	22118010	吸收公众存款
中国建设银行股份有限公司东莞市分行	南城街道	22816118	金融业务
中国农业银行股份有限公司东莞分行	南城街道	23305742	金融业务
中信银行股份有限公司东莞分行	东城街道	22667876	金融业务
中国工商银行股份有限公司东莞分行	南城街道	22481728	金融业务
东莞农村商业银行股份有限公司石碣西南分理处	石碣镇	86631724	金融业务
证券业			
东莞证券有限责任公司	莞城街道	22119350	证券经纪业务
广发证券股份有限公司东莞虎门证券营业部	虎门镇	85521178	证券经纪
保险业			
中国人寿保险股份有限公司东莞分公司	莞城街道	22488488	人寿保险业务
中国人民人寿保险股份有限公司东莞市中心支公司	东城街道	22306285	人寿保险
中国人民财产保险股份有限公司东莞市分公司	东城街道	22313601	财产保险业务
中国平安财产保险股份有限公司东莞分公司	南城街道		财产保险业务
中国太平洋财产保险股份有限公司东莞中心支公司	南城街道	22807699	金融保险
天平汽车保险股份有限公司东莞中心支公司	南城街道	22992063	车辆保险
中国太平洋人寿保险股份有限公司东莞中心支公司	莞城街道	22321518	承保各种人身保险业务
中华联合财产保险股份有限公司东莞中心支公司	莞城街道	22605888	财产保险经营业务
中国平安人寿保险股份有限公司东莞中心支公司	南城街道	21683205	人寿保险
永安财产保险股份有限公司东莞中心支公司	南城街道	22996100	企业财产损失保险
中国大地财产保险股份有限公司东莞中心支公司	东城街道	22361158	财产保险
泰康人寿保险股份有限公司东莞中心支公司	南城街道	22994019	人寿保险
中国人民健康保险股份有限公司东莞中心支公司	东城街道	22328887	健康保险业务
新华人寿保险股份有限公司东莞中心支公司	莞城街道	22498243	寿险营销
太平保险有限公司东莞中心支公司	莞城街道	22476688	财产保险业务
太平人寿保险有限公司东莞中心支公司	南城街道	23188161	经营人寿保险业务
阳光人寿保险股份有限公司东莞中心支公司	南城街道	88981959	人寿保险
其他金融活动			
东莞信托有限公司	莞城街道	22366101	信托业务
中国邮政储蓄银行有限责任公司东莞分行	莞城街道	22116366	金融业务
房地产业			
东莞市莞深长城地产有限公司	松山湖管委会	22891428	房地产开发
东莞市长银房地产开发有限公司	塘厦镇	87287398	房产开发经营
东莞市富鹏置业有限公司	凤岗镇	87862310	房地产开发经营
东莞市丰盛房地产开发有限公司	南城街道	23183800	房地产开发经营
东莞市万盛房地产开发有限公司	望牛墩镇	88561185	房地产开发
广东南峰房地产有限公司	莞城街道	22383796	房地产经营
东莞市龙城房地产开发有限公司	石龙镇	86111268	房地产开发
东莞市樟木头镇物业管理公司	樟木头镇	87713517	物业管理
东莞市信义房地产开发有限公司	长安镇	81888880	房地产开发经营
东莞市丰华房地产开发有限公司	莞城街道	22629333	房地产开发
东莞市新世纪房地产开发有限公司	大岭山镇	83053693	房地产

1-4 续表 26

(2010年)

单位名称	所属镇街	联系电话	主要产品(或服务)
东莞市桃源商住建造有限公司	松山湖管委会	22986086	房地产开发
东莞市新世纪丽江豪园商住开发有限公司	茶山镇	86409800	房地产开发经营
东莞市丰泰建设房地产有限公司	虎门镇	85221133	房地产开发
东莞市瀚森房地产开发有限公司	横沥镇	81010511	房地产开发
东莞市商业中心发展有限公司	南城街道	22422888	开发建造东莞商业中心
东莞市塘厦镇房地产开发公司	塘厦镇	87722361	房地产开发
东莞市粤海村(单项)房地产开发有限公司	东城街道	22611621	房地产开发
东莞市塘盛房地产开发有限公司	塘厦镇	87917238	房地产开发
东莞市濠兴逸苑商住开发有限公司	石龙镇		房地产开发
东莞市翠云轩房地产开发有限公司	寮步镇	22679733	其它房地产活动
东莞宏远工业区股份有限公司	南城街道	22414228	开发经营工业区
中惠熙元房地产集团有限公司	东城街道	22360398	房地产开发经营
东莞市金泓地产有限公司	大朗镇	83485807	房地产开发
东莞市捷利物业投资有限公司	虎门镇	85124488	房地产开发经营
东莞市三元盈晖投资发展有限公司	万江街道		房地产项目经营
东莞市东沙港建设发展有限公司	中堂镇	88661823	房地产开发
东莞市金众房地产有限公司	南城街道	22820205	房地产开发
东莞市中信康华房地产开发有限公司	南城街道	22482388	房地产
东莞市中惠香樟绿洲房地产开发有限公司	樟木头镇	22360398	房地产开发
东莞市鼎峰房地产开发有限公司	企石镇	86666016	房地产开发
东莞市广源房地产开发有限公司	寮步镇		房地产开发经营
广东宏远集团房地产开发有限公司	南城街道		城市综合开发
东莞市凯蓝房地产开发有限公司	虎门镇	85716483	房地产
东莞市东田丽园房地产开发有限公司	常平镇	83989677	开发经营
东莞市长佳长安花园开发有限公司	长安镇	85338777	房地产项目开发
东莞市鸿景房地产有限公司	南城街道	22821111	房地产开发
东莞市丰泰华园山庄建造有限公司	虎门镇	85188896	房地产开发
广东丰泰集团有限公司	虎门镇	85221133	房地产
东莞市碧水天源物业有限公司	大朗镇	83131976	房地产开发
东莞市新世纪科教拓展有限公司	凤岗镇	87555552	房地产活动
东莞市麻涌镇房地产开发公司	麻涌镇	88233288	房地产开发经营
东莞市致富物业管理有限公司	沙田镇	88868218	物业管理
东莞市星河传说商住区有限公司	东城街道	22031328	房地产开发
东莞市富麟实业有限公司	凤岗镇	87568889	房地产开发
东莞市汇景房地产开发有限公司	厚街镇	85923777	房地产开发
东莞市庆丰房地产咨询服务有限公司	东城街道	22619005	房地产开发
东莞市聚豪名轩商住开发有限公司	石龙镇	86088001	房地产投资
东莞市永江集团有限公司	凤岗镇	87840888	实业投资
东莞市宝田实业有限公司	沙田镇	88689966	厂房出租

1-4 续表 27

(2010年)

单位名称	所属镇街	联系电话	主要产品(或服务)
东莞市新世纪房地产有限公司	大朗镇	88237666	房地产开发
东莞市万科阳光房地产开发有限公司	常平镇	83916852	房地产经营
东莞市建工集团房地产开发有限公司	南城街道	22427888	房地产开发
东莞市玉泉投资开发有限公司	凤岗镇	87508188	土地开发
东莞市松山湖房地产有限公司	松山湖管委会	22892336	房地产开发
东莞市凤岗房地产开发公司	凤岗镇	87753308	房地产开发经营
东莞市美居广场建造有限公司	万江街道	22777795	房地产开发经营
东莞市凯沣房地产策划有限公司	东城街道	23110366	房地主市场调查
东莞市松湖居置业有限公司	松山湖管委会	23013547	房地产开发
东莞市中信广场建造有限公司	东城街道	23282506	商品房
东莞市阳龙房地产有限公司	长安镇		房地产开发
东莞市田禾房地产投资有限公司	莞城街道	23030787	房地产开发
东莞华美新村建造有限公司	万江街道		房地产开发经营
东莞市东城区房地产开发公司	东城街道	22483788	房地产开发
东莞市新世纪润城实业投资有限公司	塘厦镇	88991899	房地产开发
东莞市东城区房地产开发公司	东城街道	22470531	商品房
东莞市莞都可苑房地产开发有限公司	中堂镇	22211908	房地产开发
东莞市盈锋房地产开发有限公司	莞城街道	22495555	房地产开发
东莞市万科房地产有限公司	莞城街道	23013547	房地产开发经营
东莞市幸福花苑开发有限公司	南城街道	23129388	项目开发经营
东莞市深城投实业投资有限公司	万江街道	23185306	物业投资
东莞市华建物业投资有限公司	南城街道	22820769	房地产开发
东莞景天房地产开发有限公司	东城街道	22667836	开发建设
东莞市阳光海岸实业有限公司	虎门镇	81615333	房地产
东莞市汇盈豪苑房地产开发有限公司	厚街镇	22388601	房地产开发
东莞市铭可达商住中心开发有限公司	莞城街道	22309112	房地产开发
东莞市孚泰房地产开发有限公司	南城街道		房地产开发经营
东莞市大绿地房地产开发有限公司	清溪镇	87388810	房地产开发
中信华南(集团)东莞有限公司	东城街道	22482388	房地产开发
东莞市康联房地产开发有限公司	厚街镇	85753088	房地产开发
东莞市佳驹实业有限公司	南城街道	22679733	房地产开发
东莞市松山居置业有限公司	松山湖管委会	22303989	房地产开发
东莞市惠明盛香缤房地产开发有限公司	寮步镇		房地产开发经营
东莞市利丰房地产投资有限公司	石排镇	86555829	房地产开发
东莞市新世纪怡岛花园商住开发有限公司	道滘镇	88638888	房地业开发
东莞市山水雅居房地产开发有限公司	常平镇	82206266	房地产开发经营
东莞市丽水佳园开发有限公司	道滘镇	88318806	房地产开发
东莞市合盛房地产开发有限公司	虎门镇	85705222	房地产开发
广东三正集团有限公司	桥头镇	82470333	房地产开发
东莞市广盈服务有限公司企石分公司	企石镇		服务业
东莞市山语湖房地产投资有限公司	常平镇	22032016	房地产开发
东莞市鹏程物业投资有限公司	长安镇	81667958	房地产开发

1-4　续表 28

(2010年)

单位名称	所属镇街	联系电话	主要产品(或服务)
东莞市城市中心区开发建设总公司	南城街道	22414280	房地产开发
东莞市佳驹实业有限公司	南城街道	22360088	房地产开发
东莞市锋尚公寓房地产开发有限公司	南城街道	22820000	房地产开发
东莞市星城国际房地产开发有限公司	寮步镇	26276301	房地产开发
东莞市中润投资实业有限公司	万江街道		房地产开发
东莞市盈盛房地产开发有限公司	石龙镇	22801111	房地产开发
东莞市东逸物业管理有限公司	厚街镇	85883333	房地产开发
东莞市富怡房地产开发有限公司	厚街镇	85832206	房地产开发经营
中信华南东莞有限公司	东城街道	22482388	房地产
东莞市三盈房地产开发有限公司	寮步镇	83221883	房地产开发
东莞市中惠沁林山庄房地产开发有限公司	大岭山镇		实业项目开发投资
东莞市同方房地产开发有限公司	东城街道	22483998	房地产开发
东莞市光大房地产开发有限公司	东城街道	22986086	房地产开发
东莞市金贤房地产开发有限公司	厚街镇	85936698	房地产开发
东莞市中天广场建造有限公司	常平镇	82328296	房地产开发
东莞市新世纪长盛广场商住开发	大朗镇		房地产开发
东莞市丰泰建设房地产有限公司	寮步镇	85188701	房地产开发
东莞市神鹰塑料有限公司	常平镇	86991888	物业管理
东莞市深国投房地产开发有限公司	南城街道		房地产开发
东莞市三正房地产开发有限公司	塘厦镇	87299333	房地产开发
东莞市龙泉房地产开发有限公司	长安镇	85112323	房地产开发
东莞市金色家园开发建造有限公司	常平镇		金色家园项目开发经营
东莞市新世纪明上居商住开发有限公司	大朗镇	23013547	房地产开发
东莞市石龙镇房地产公司	石龙镇	86116822	镇域房地产监管
东莞市陶然居房地产开发有限公司	长安镇		房地产开发
东莞市瀚森投资集团有限公司	莞城街道	22333488	房地产投资
东莞市新世纪房地产开发有限公司	东城街道	22382251	房地产开发
东莞市富盈房地产开发有限公司	厚街镇	81226161	房地产开发
东莞市篁城开发有限公司	南城街道	22113388	房地产项目开发
商务服务业			
东莞市山淙劳务派遣有限公司	桥头镇		劳务派遣服务
广东华强三洋集团有限公司	塘厦镇		投资、管理属下企业
东莞市凯信知识产权代理有限公司	莞城街道		商标申请代理
东莞市丰华集团有限公司	莞城街道	22629333	酒店投资
东莞市宏图工业开发公司	南城街道	22415322	宏图工业区内土地开发
东莞市凤岗镇官井头股份经济联合社	凤岗镇	87771352	企业管理服务
东莞市合鑫膳食管理服务有限公司	东城街道	23111916	膳食管理
东莞市大朗供电公司	大朗镇	83316187	电力供应管理
东莞市石碣镇桔洲股份经济联合社	石碣镇	86332030	经联社经济管理
东莞市沙田经济发展总公司	沙田镇	88861003	机构商务代理服务
东莞市青年国际旅行社有限公司	莞城街道	22239388	旅游

1-4 续表 29

(2010年)

单位名称	所属镇街	联系电话	主要产品(或服务)
东莞市虎门城郊供电公司	虎门镇	85527786	电力供应管理
东莞市石龙镇西湖股份经济联合社	石龙镇	86113078	合作社经济管理
城区资产办	莞城街道	22102722	政府内资产物业管理
东莞市鸿信实业有限公司	东坑镇	83383786	投资实业
东莞市长安镇咸西经济联合社	长安镇	85533868	合作社经济管理
东莞市长安镇综合市场	长安镇	85535310	农贸市场管理
东莞市国际旅行社有限公司	莞城街道	22458168	旅行社
东莞市粤龙物业发展有限公司	石龙镇	86181222	企业管理咨询
东莞市桥头供电公司	桥头镇	83341212	电力供应
东莞市沙田对外经济开发总公司	沙田镇	88689966	对外资用地办理立项
东莞市盈丰报关服务有限公司	寮步镇	81100932	代理报关服务
东莞市家宝园林绿化有限公司	厚街镇	85088699	商务服务
东莞市瑞中会计税务服务有限公司石碣分公司	石碣镇	81812200	代理记帐
东莞市瑞翔旅行社有限公司	东城街道	88996666	旅游
东莞市桥头镇桥头股份经济联合社	桥头镇	83342308	合作经济管理
东莞市虎门镇北栅经济联合社	虎门镇	85551481	资产管理
富盈集团有限公司	厚街镇	81568888	综合
东莞市南城区资产经营管理有限公司	南城街道	22417250	管理区属资产
东莞市长安供电公司	长安镇	85313828	电力供应管理
东莞市虎门镇路东经济联合社	虎门镇	85567032	合作经济管理
东莞市虎门镇资产经营管理有限公司	虎门镇	85522409	镇属资产产权的管理
东莞市大朗镇长塘股份经济联合社	大朗镇	83318030	合作社经济管理
东莞市中堂供电公司	中堂镇	88893288	电力供应
东莞市常平镇资产经营管理有限公司	常平镇	83331431	企业资产管理
东莞市虎门镇虎门寨股份经济联合社	虎门镇	85509032	合作经济管理
东莞市企石振华开发总公司	企石镇	86765688	外引内联企业的咨询洽谈
上沙股份经济联合社	长安镇	85547208	合作社经济管理
东莞市长安镇沙头经济联合社	长安镇	85544888	经济管理工作
东莞市望牛墩资产经营管理有限公司	望牛墩镇	88853008	产权管理
东莞市清溪镇经济联合总社	清溪镇	87733292	咨询服务
东莞市南枫佳誉保险代理有限公司	南城街道	22995003	保险产品
东莞市桥头镇资产经营管理有限公司	桥头镇	83342135	企业管理服务
东莞市华源集团有限公司	厚街镇	85928888	酒店
东莞市智能市场管理服务有限公司	清溪镇	87738170	市场管理
东莞市中国旅行社有限公司	南城街道	22218288	旅游业
东莞市塘厦镇资产经营有限公司	塘厦镇	82087792	资产经营管理
东莞市松山湖工业发展有限公司	松山湖管委会	22891044	房产管理
东莞市寮步经济发展总公司	寮步镇	83328387	经济贸易咨询
东莞市建华贸易有限公司	清溪镇	87733209	日用品
东莞市虎门名铺城	虎门镇	85113665	商铺管理
东莞市凤岗镇资产经营有限公司	凤岗镇	87759398	资产管理

1-4 续表 30

(2010年)

单位名称	所属镇街	联系电话	主要产品(或服务)
东莞市清溪对外经济发展有限公司	清溪镇	87732058	外引内联企业咨询
东莞市清溪供电公司	清溪镇	87314148	电力供应
东莞市天纬企业管理咨询服务有限公司	莞城街道	22482678	劳务派遣
东莞市黄江供电公司	黄江镇	83361290	电力供应管理
东莞市电化实业集团公司	莞城街道	22461466	实业投资
东莞市中堂镇潢涌股份经济联合社	中堂镇	88881002	合作社经济管理
广东宏远集团有限公司	南城街道	22414228	各类商品的进出口业务
东莞市横沥镇经济联合总社	横沥镇	83717663	企业管理咨询
东莞市方达集团有限公司	长安镇	85330098	兴办实业
东莞市长安镇霄边经济联合社	长安镇	81882222	合作社经济管理
东莞市常平镇土塘股份经济联合社	常平镇	83553233	合作社经济管理
东莞市中之进出口有限公司	南城街道	23182111	各类商品和技术的进出口
东莞市东城供电公司	东城街道	22669826	电力供应管理
东莞市樟木头资产经营管理有限公司	樟木头镇	87188978	镇属资产产权管理
东莞市桥头镇田新股份经济联合社	桥头镇	83341032	合作社经济管理
东莞市大莹物业管理有限公司	虎门镇	85151566	市场管理
东莞市石碣镇经济发展总公司	石碣镇	86631048	进出口服务
东莞市寮步镇横坑股份经济联合社	寮步镇	83301024	企业管理服务
东莞市东坑镇经济联合总社	东坑镇	83889698	企业管理机构
东莞市长安镇锦厦经济联合社	长安镇	85301960	企业管理
东莞市谢岗供电公司	谢岗镇	87761224	电力供应管理
东莞市桥头镇邓屋股份经济联合社	桥头镇	83341073	合作社经济管理
东莞市塘厦镇林村股份经济联合社	塘厦镇	87721501	企业管理咨询
东莞市厚街经济发展总公司	厚街镇	85990333	物业租赁
东莞市大岭山供电公司	大岭山镇	83350287	电力供应管理
东莞市南城区工业发展公司	南城街道	22415322	办理开办厂场业务
东莞市万江区资产经营管理有限公司	万江街道	22273273	投资与资产管理
东莞市集源资产经营管理有限公司	黄江镇	83633322	出租房屋服务
东莞康辉国际旅行社有限公司	莞城街道	22001168	国内旅游服务
东莞市东城实业发展总公司	东城街道	22331385	实业投资
东莞市桥光实业集团公司	桥头镇	83341012	外引内联企业的咨询
东莞市景鸿物业管理有限公司	莞城街道	22381011	劳务派遣
东莞市聚龙物业投资发展有限公司	石龙镇	86116908	物业投资
东莞市鸿弋进出口有限公司	厚街镇	85037999	货物进出口
东莞市黄河集团房地产开发有限公司	虎门镇	85222222	实业投资
东莞市新远高速公路发展有限公司	东城街道	22083200	投资开发东莞高速公路网
东莞市明煜管理咨询有限公司	南城街道	22408845	企业管理服务
东莞市福临门企业咨询服务有限公司	石碣镇	86330555	代办企业登记
东莞市群策外商投资服务有限公司	南城街道	22813652	企业登记代理咨询服务
东莞市大岭山镇资产经营管理有限公司	大岭山镇	85788362	经济管理

1-4 续表 31

(2010年)

单位名称	所属镇街	联系电话	主要产品(或服务)
东莞市凤岗供电公司	凤岗镇	87756877	电力供应
东莞市塘厦供电公司	塘厦镇	87727425	电力供应管理
东莞市虎门镇南栅股份经济联合社	虎门镇	85561938	合作社经济管理
东莞市高埗供电公司	高埗镇	88781518	电力供应管理
东莞市昌明实业有限公司	厚街镇	85598888	实业投资
东莞市清溪经济发展公司	清溪镇	87366293	企业管理服务
东莞市石排供电公司	石排镇	86550387	电力供应
东莞市石龙粤龙实业公司	石龙镇	86181222	电机、金属机械
东莞市厚街供电公司	厚街镇	85585368	电力供应管理
东莞市南城供电公司	南城街道	22414348	电力供应管理
东莞市江南市场经营管理有限公司	中堂镇		市场管理服务
东莞市麻涌镇经济发展总公司	麻涌镇	88239336	企业管理服务
东莞市石碣镇发展实业公司	石碣镇	86631030	企业咨询
东莞市东城资产经营管理有限公司	东城街道	22331385	资产管理
东莞市松山湖控股有限公司	松山湖管委会	22898178	第一产业投资
东莞市寮步供电公司	寮步镇	81113608	电力供应
东莞市中堂资产经营管理有限公司	中堂镇	88811116	资产经营管理
东莞市凤岗镇雁田经济联合社	凤岗镇	87774631	合作社经济管理
东莞市长安镇长实发展总公司	长安镇	85310368	企业管理
东莞市光华医院有限公司	寮步镇	22668152	医疗卫生
广东智通人才连锁股份有限公司	莞城街道	87078157	人才信息咨询服务
东莞市桥头镇石水口股份经济联合社	桥头镇	83428823	企业管理咨询
东莞市虎门镇龙眼股份经济联合社	虎门镇	85553988	投资和资产投资
东莞市万江供电公司	万江街道	22788971	企业管理机构
研究与试验发展			
东莞市万科建筑技术研究有限公司	松山湖管委会	22890188	建筑技术开发
专业技术服务业			
东莞市公路桥梁开发建设总公司	东城街道	22083269	规划建设公路桥梁
东莞市清溪工业开发有限公司	清溪镇	87732058	工业开发
科技交流和推广服务业			
东莞市方达环宇环保科技有限公司	长安镇	89998656	环保技术的开发转让服务培训
水利管理业			
东莞市万江区水利管理所	万江街道	22275920	水利工程管理
公共设施管理业			
东莞市松山湖公用事业有限公司	松山湖管委会	23306078	园林绿化维护
居民服务业			
东莞市大华沐足保健中心	莞城街道		足浴保健
东莞市东保押运有限公司	寮步镇	83528016	贵重物品押运
其他服务业			
东莞市虎门大宁企业发展公司	虎门镇	85553188	办理、开办厂场业务

1-4　续表 32

(2010年)

单位名称	所属镇街	联系电话	主要产品(或服务)
广州志诚科技工程服务有限公司东莞凤岗分公司	凤岗镇		服务
东莞市塘厦林村工业发展公司	塘厦镇	87722262	外引内联企业的咨询及洽谈
东莞市桥供废品回收有限公司	桥头镇	83341037	废旧物资回收
东莞市酷极动漫设计有限公司	东城街道		动漫设计
教育			
东莞市黄江镇中心小学	黄江镇	83601630	初等教育
东莞市东华小学	东城街道	22659823	初等教育
东莞市先进电脑横机技术推广中心	常平镇	89851116	咨询与指导
东莞市东华初级中学	东城街道	22659333	初中教育
东莞市东华高级中学	东城街道	22637808	普通高中教育
东莞市北师大翰林实验学校	万江街道	22702988	高中教育
东莞市第一中学	东城街道	22666280	高中教育
东莞市新民实业投资有限公司	石碣镇		教育投资
东莞市通圣机动车驾驶员培训有限公司	高埗镇		职业技能培训
卫生			
东莞市黄江医院	黄江镇	83636323	综合医院
东莞市长安医院	长安镇	85531104	医疗
东莞市南城医院	南城街道	22415129	非盈利性医疗服务
东莞康华医院有限公司	南城街道	22823018	医疗事业服务
东莞广济医院	凤岗镇	87866333	医疗服务
东莞市茶山医院	茶山镇	86642066	基本医疗
东莞市樟木头镇石新医院	樟木头镇	87710449	医疗服务
东莞东华医院有限公司	东城街道	22333333	医疗服务
东莞市东坑医院	东坑镇	83381754	医院服务
东莞市寮步医院	寮步镇	83321545	医疗卫生
东莞市桥头医院	桥头镇	81037663	医疗护理保健服务
东莞市厚街医院	厚街镇	81529815	综合医疗
东莞市东城医院	东城街道	22213790	综合医院
东莞市太平人民医院	虎门镇	85111525	医疗服务
东莞市石龙博爱医院	石龙镇	86118320	综合医院
东莞市石排医院	石排镇	86556333	诊疗
东莞市企石医院	企石镇	86661371	医疗保健
东莞市石龙人民医院	石龙镇	81368808	医疗保健
东莞市凤岗医院	凤岗镇	87510815	综合医院
新闻出版业			
东莞日报社	南城街道	23126688	报纸采写编
广播、电视、电影和音像业			
广东省广播电视网络股份有限公司东莞大朗分公司	大朗镇	83019778	广播电视网络规划建设
东莞市桥头镇文化广播电视服务中心	桥头镇		文化
娱乐业			
东莞市滨河游乐有限公司	樟木头镇		

1-5 营业收入超5000万元的外资企业（2010年）

Foreign-funded Enterprises with Business Revenue over RMB 50 Million (2010)

单位名称	所属镇街	联系电话	主要产品(或服务)
农副食品加工业			
东莞市飞亚达益富可华南油脂有限公司	麻涌镇	88230055	棕榈油精炼
东莞卡尔吉蛋白饲料有限公司	麻涌镇	88236732	豆油
东莞兴业生物科技有限公司	东城街道	22652130	饲料
东莞益海嘉里粮油食品工业有限公司	麻涌镇	88238760	饲料蛋白
东莞欧陆食品有限公司	长安镇	86246898	西式肉类食品
统一嘉吉(东莞)饲料蛋白科技有限公司	麻涌镇	88225888	豆油
中粮新沙粮油工业(东莞)有限公司	麻涌镇	88825601	豆油
东莞光华饲料有限公司	中堂镇	88817756	猪饲料
东莞顶志食品有限公司	麻涌镇	88238262	芝麻油
食品制造业			
东莞福满多食品有限公司	麻涌镇	88230290	粮食制品
东莞徐记食品有限公司	东城街道	22259888	糖果
东莞荣华饼家有限公司	石碣镇	86633692	月饼
华嘉食品有限公司	南城街道	22464101	饼干
广东太阳神集团有限公司	黄江镇	83621288	猴头菇胃肠口服液
爱兰特糖果(东莞)有限公司	常平镇	83552285	糖果
东莞万好食品有限公司	横沥镇	81016222	点心食品
东莞锦泰食品有限公司	南城街道	22400818	饼干
饮料制造业			
可口可乐装瓶商生产(东莞)有限公司	南城街道	22401678	茶饮料及果汁饮料
东莞雀巢有限公司	南城街道	22404088	速溶咖啡
东莞石龙津威饮料食品有限公司	石龙镇	86625388	葡锌乳酸菌饮料
金威啤酒(东莞)有限公司	松山湖管委会	22898999	啤酒
华润雪花啤酒广东有限公司	东城街道	88772999	啤酒
广东加多宝饮料食品有限公司	长安镇	85331688	王老吉
纺织业			
东莞合迅服装设计有限公司	长安镇	86244388	针织化纤胸围
东莞福安纺织印染有限公司	长安镇		棉针织折用纱线
沛恒制衣(东莞)有限公司	石龙镇	86617980	胸围
东莞明辉商标织造有限公司	樟木头镇	87797688	布商标
东莞福珍针织制衣有限公司	道滘镇	88321475	针织服装
东莞东兴商标织绣有限公司	长安镇	85545888	商标
东莞达利盛时装有限公司	凤岗镇	87756188	服装
东莞励发制衣厂	厚街镇	85822228	全棉男装针织长袖T恤
东莞超盈纺织有限公司	麻涌镇	88231808	双拉布
东莞弘裕纺织科技有限公司	望牛墩镇	88563858	特多龙塑胶布
宏达纺织(东莞)有限公司	塘厦镇	87982238	灯芯绒坯布、全棉坯布
东莞忆凯制衣有限公司	大朗镇	83185898	全绵婴儿毛衫
东莞东美线业有限公司	道滘镇	88339333	缝纫线、涤纶短纤维线
东莞贰发毛绒有限公司	樟木头镇	87718080	静电毛绒
东莞通盈纺织制衣有限公司	中堂镇	88188015	梳织布
东莞富达染厂有限公司	洪梅镇	88844490	棉针织色布
东莞百宏实业有限公司	沙田镇	88869615	鞋材、特殊粘扣带、织带等

1-5 续表 1

(2010年)

单位名称	所属镇街	联系电话	主要产品(或服务)
东莞永联弹力织物有限公司	望牛墩镇	88852801	橡筋
东莞麻涌联德毛纺织厂	麻涌镇	88287782	毛织纱线
东莞明海整染厂有限公司	道滘镇	38831553	染色布
广东联发毛纺织有限公司	东城街道	22262232	纺织
东莞宝达日用品制造有限公司	大朗镇	83311690	布手套
东莞同广纺织品有限公司	厚街镇	85933301	各类针织胚布
东莞晶苑毛织制衣有限公司	常平镇	83982212	纺织品
东莞市远梦家用纺织品有限公司	厚街镇	85991010	床上用品
东莞市小猪班纳服饰有限公司	樟木头镇	87125086	针织服装
东莞胜丰针织有限公司	高埗镇	88879742	纺织服装
东莞富山纺织漂染有限公司	洪梅镇	88841755	漂染针织布、梳织布
东莞康俊胶布有限公司	常平镇	83913222	胶尼龙布
东莞联丰巨川纤维腈棉有限公司	黄江镇	86914666	人造纤维制品
东莞世丽纺织有限公司	洪梅镇	88843806	全棉针织色布
东莞富阳针织有限公司	大朗镇	88603688	毛衣
东莞广成线业有限公司	长安镇	85428511	织线
东莞德福制衣有限公司	常平镇	83335273	毛衣针织
东莞如成服装有限公司	虎门镇	88709991	针织服装
东莞德永佳纺织制衣有限公司	麻涌镇	88821738	棉针织染整布
东莞联庆纺织有限公司	企石镇	86784606	棉、化纤纺织
联亚制衣(东莞)有限公司	凤岗镇	82081818	梭织服装
东莞百和织造有限公司	沙田镇	88862371	粘扣带
东莞虎门科艺纺织印花有限公司	虎门镇	85561798	丝绸印花
东莞嘉鹏纺织有限公司	麻涌镇	88826666	毛
东莞沙田丽海纺织印染有限公司	沙田镇	88866583	印染布
东莞厚宏制衣有限公司	桥头镇	83341382	针织服装
东莞乐升植绒有限公司	企石镇	86668899	棉、化纤印染精
东莞裕发纺织漂染有限公司	望牛墩镇	88850188	纺织漂染
多宝针织服装(东莞)有限公司	常平镇	83820563	针织毛衣
东莞奥康德思宏针织品有限公司	常平镇	83828858	毛衣(针织)
东莞润达弹性织造有限公司	厚街镇	85593366	织带
东莞业基工业有限公司	常平镇	83915577	服装
东莞茂志针织有限公司	大朗镇	83209838	针织服装
东莞念辉家饰用品有限公司	常平镇	83392366	桌巾
纺织服装、鞋、帽制造业			
得福(东莞)制衣有限公司	中堂镇		服装
东莞通威服装有限公司	凤岗镇	86808613	成衣
东莞菲力制衣有限公司	高埗镇	88786698	服装
东莞怡力制衣有限公司	横沥镇	81011666	服装
东莞精致针织有限公司	常平镇	86836260	各类服装
联业制衣(东莞)有限公司	清溪镇	87738280	衬衫
东莞迅捷环球制衣有限公司	长安镇	85441918	服装
东莞雄业制衣有限公司	茶山镇	86178938	婴儿全棉针织哈衣
东莞众信制衣有限公司	道滘镇	88318125	服装

1-5 续表 2

(2010年)

单位名称	所属镇街	联系电话	主要产品(或服务)
东莞启松服装有限公司	塘厦镇	87722174	服装
东莞联泰制衣有限公司	凤岗镇	86808117	衣服
东莞澳思制衣有限公司	常平镇	83332225	毛衣及针梭织服装
东莞福泉制衣有限公司	沙田镇	88666698	棉针织服装
东莞时利制衣有限公司	虎门镇	85709662	服装
东莞洋得服饰有限公司	寮步镇	83288888	手套
东莞聚龙制衣有限公司	长安镇	85538846	各类服装
东莞益豪时装有限公司	石龙镇	86618323	服装
东莞成笑服装有限公司	高埗镇	88709991	服装
东莞永信鞋业有限公司	厚街镇	85918310	运动鞋
东莞宝升制衣有限公司	长安镇	85549971	衣服
东莞利来远东针织有限公司	南城街道	22851333	服装
东莞高品服装有限公司	常平镇	83501111	服装
东莞海琪运动服装有限公司	虎门镇	85701202	化纤成人运动装
东莞丰泰制衣有限公司	茶山镇	86179848	纺织服装
东莞朗福皮鞋有限公司	谢岗镇	87761380	皮鞋
东莞凯威针织制衣有限公司	常平镇	86830510	布料服装
东莞奇兴服装有限公司	东坑镇	83382968	西装衫
东莞宏大制衣有限公司	高埗镇	88468668	各类针织衣服
东莞冠丽时装有限公司	石碣镇	86016001	服装
东莞三骏时装有限公司	长安镇	85326098	针梳织服装
东莞大明制衣有限公司	虎门镇	85192121	服装
东莞亿城服装有限公司	长安镇	85311107	各类纺织品、服装
东莞永嘉盛针织有限公司	南城街道	22407788	纺织毛衫
东莞昱胜鞋业有限公司	沙田镇	88808168	皮鞋
东莞励进制衣有限公司	厚街镇	85822228	全棉男装针织长袖T恤
东莞富坊制衣有限公司	虎门镇	85159988	服装
东莞宝基鞋业制造有限公司	厚街镇	85582985	鞋
东莞泰富服装有限公司	道滘镇	88830780	服装
东莞东浩制衣有限公司	东城街道	22265009	服装
东莞邦胜鞋业有限公司	厚街镇	85835990	各类鞋及鞋面
东莞茶山永联织造厂	茶山镇	88655088	婴儿服装
东莞励新制衣有限公司	道滘镇	88318081	棉针织衫
智诚国际东莞实业有限公司	万江街道	23175238	服装
东莞种子制衣厂	高埗镇	88876660	内衣裤
东莞美商制衣有限公司	南城街道	22902688	服装
东莞怡信针织有限公司	常平镇	86836268	服装
东莞市东方叶杨实业有限公司	东城街道	22634282	羊绒衣服
东莞大森鞋材有限公司	厚街镇	85901546	鞋材
东莞高业制衣有限公司	万江街道	22784602	服装
东莞胜德织造有限公司	高埗镇	88738293	毛织品
东莞邦西纺织制衣有限公司	茶山镇	88655083	针织服装
东莞绰荣制衣有限公司	常平镇	83936788	针梳织服装

1-5 续表 3

(2010年)

单位名称	所属镇街	联系电话	主要产品(或服务)
长江西服东莞有限公司	东坑镇	83384250	西服及西服套装
东莞盈升制衣有限公司	石排镇	86655401	服装
东莞上杰鞋业有限公司	长安镇	81663185	鞋
东莞四海时装有限公司	虎门镇	85113514	服装
东莞富程鞋业有限公司	东城街道	22265418	休闲鞋
乐活制衣(东莞)有限公司	横沥镇	83729200	成衣
东莞诠立鞋业有限公司	厚街镇	85992586	女装便鞋
皮革、毛皮、羽毛(绒)及其制品业			
东莞亮智服装有限公司	寮步镇	83305288	皮革服装
金进鞋业(东莞)有限公司	厚街镇	83085185	皮鞋
东莞威霖鞋业有限公司	厚街镇	83093999	运动鞋
东莞华宝鞋业有限公司	南城街道	22908300	鞋
东莞兆鑫鞋业有限公司	南城街道	88998989	PU童鞋
东莞绿扬鞋业有限公司	厚街镇	85876969	鞋以及鞋材
东莞宏国制鞋有限公司	虎门镇	85559400	皮鞋
东莞旭冠皮具有限公司	东城街道	22251741	手袋
东莞汇博鞋业有限公司	厚街镇	85826256	成品鞋
东莞超丰手袋有限公司	东城街道	22627688	手袋
东莞博励图鞋业有限公司	寮步镇	83266168	女鞋
东莞朝冠鞋业有限公司	厚街镇	85588915	皮鞋
东莞麦斯鞋业有限公司	横沥镇	83375950	皮鞋
东莞诚达鞋业有限公司	沙田镇	88806888	休闲鞋
东莞澳利高太平洋手袋有限公司	常平镇	83824000	手袋
东莞黄江宝亮鞋材厂	黄江镇	83367386	PU人造皮
东莞钜盛鞋业有限公司	寮步镇	83214345	皮鞋
东莞绿洲鞋业有限公司	厚街镇	85880975	皮鞋女鞋以及运动鞋
东莞高埗裕元制造厂第一分厂	高埗镇	88874202	鞋
雄进塑料制品(东莞)有限公司	寮步镇	83320081	PVC造革
东莞华南皮革有限公司	茶山镇	86642187	轻革
东莞聚保手袋有限公司	东城街道	22252261	旅行袋
东莞万鑫鞋业有限公司	南城街道	86226699	皮鞋
东莞福聚皮革有限公司	道滘镇	88326331	皮革鞣制
东莞市汉皇鞋业有限公司	横沥镇	83790019	鞋类
东莞奥天奴皮草服装有限公司	企石镇	86786993	皮草服装
东莞昌健鞋业有限公司	厚街镇	85581860	鞋类
东莞韦旭鞋业有限公司	长安镇	85321666	皮鞋
东莞卫仕皮具有限公司	道滘镇	88386228	皮具制品
东莞安阳鞋业有限公司	大朗镇	83318919	牛皮鞋
东莞力凯鞋业制造有限公司	厚街镇	85583101	运动鞋
东莞环艺实业有限公司	东城街道	88755578	手袋
东莞协和鞋业有限公司	厚街镇	85595058	人造革童鞋
东莞好利包袋制品有限公司	塘厦镇	87906032	钱包、手袋
东莞东禾鞋业有限公司	东城街道	22662588	鞋类
新百丽鞋业(深圳)有限公司东莞分公司	虎门镇	85261438	皮鞋

1-5 续表 4

(2010年)

单位名称	所属镇街	联系电话	主要产品(或服务)
东莞金莹鞋业有限公司	厚街镇	85900471	皮鞋
东莞源亨皮具制品有限公司	大朗镇	83312003	手袋
东莞永盛鞋业有限公司	厚街镇	85918310	运动鞋
东莞雄师皮具有限公司	长安镇	81663838	皮带
宏盛皮具(东莞)有限公司	东城街道	22665668	皮箱
东莞爱莉莎皮具有限公司	沙田镇	88868969	皮箱、包袋
东莞台育鞋业有限公司	石碣镇	86323168	皮鞋
东莞伯产合成皮革有限公司	麻涌镇	88820807	PU合成皮革
东莞邦荣鞋业有限公司	厚街镇	85835990	各类鞋
东莞祥昱鞋业有限公司	寮步镇	88906888	鞋类
东莞台威运动用品有限公司	长安镇	85534587	运动鞋、滑板
安迈特提箱(东莞)有限公司	大岭山镇	83356051	旅行箱包
东莞大邦鞋业有限公司	东城街道	23066010	成品鞋
东莞泰亿袋业有限公司	凤岗镇	87862228	皮箱
东莞建成鞋业有限公司	清溪镇	87734968	运动鞋
东莞时代皮具制品厂有限公司	厚街镇	85911900	手袋
东莞联增鞋业有限公司	厚街镇	85824668	人造革鞋
东莞市怡捷手袋有限公司	望牛墩镇	88569888	手袋
东莞瑞辉鞋业有限公司	东城街道	22656056	女装牛皮鞋
东莞朝代鞋业有限公司	厚街镇	85588915	皮鞋
东莞聚美手袋有限公司	长安镇	85374168	手袋
东莞昕晋手袋制造有限公司	长安镇	85379861	手袋旅行袋
东莞尚野皮具制品有限公司	长安镇	85382481	各类皮具
东莞宏业制鞋有限公司	塘厦镇	86859812	运动鞋、皮鞋
东莞飞力达鞋业有限公司	寮步镇		女式皮鞋
东莞星浩手袋有限公司	塘厦镇	87939288	各类手袋
东莞大田鞋业有限公司	清溪镇	87732488	皮鞋
东莞利威鞋业有限公司	南城街道	22009999	成品鞋
东莞捷希皮革制品有限公司	横沥镇	83731678	手袋鞋
东莞联运鞋业有限公司	寮步镇	83303350	鞋类
东莞泽荣箱包有限公司	寮步镇	83228386	旅行袋
东莞嘉应制鞋有限公司	石碣镇	86631175	皮鞋
东莞鼎力鞋业有限公司	厚街镇	85586102	运动鞋
东莞兆成鞋业有限公司	厚街镇	81693311	皮鞋
东莞威腾皮革有限公司	厚街镇	85080096	皮革
东莞钜旺鞋业有限公司	东城街道	22251840	皮鞋
圣马可(东莞)制革皮草有限公司	中堂镇	88124610	皮革
木材加工及木、竹、藤、棕、草制品业			
东莞承达木材制品有限公司	樟木头镇	87712640	木门
东莞市嘉声音响器材制造有限公司	中堂镇		木制音箱
东莞中城木业有限公司	道滘镇	88331338	装饰板
京木木制品(东莞)有限公司	石排镇	86516096	木制家具
亿丰(东莞)制帘有限公司	常平镇	83988300	木制百叶窗
广东富林木业科技有限公司	常平镇		造板

1-5 续表 5

(2010年)

单位名称	所属镇街	联系电话	主要产品(或服务)
家具制造业			
东莞上丰家具有限公司	寮步镇	83221455	电视架
东莞康桥家具有限公司	大岭山镇	83054021	木制家具
东莞柚隆木业有限公司	大岭山镇	83358666	木制品家具
东莞天山金属家具有限公司	寮步镇	83305743	金属家具
东莞宜庆家具有限公司	东城街道	22632705	家具
东莞宏展家具有限公司	桥头镇	83433133	家具
东莞朝阳家俱有限公司	黄江镇	83621515	家具
瑞丰木业(东莞)有限公司	清溪镇	86810555	家具
东莞中铤家具厂有限公司	塘厦镇	87727725	钢木家具
东莞威捷家具制品有限公司	塘厦镇	87943088	家具配件
东莞莱富家具有限公司	桥头镇	83432299	咖啡茶几桌
东莞新雅美家具有限公司	常平镇	83021686	家具
东莞台升家具有限公司	大岭山镇	83352715	木制家具
东莞稳耐五金塑胶制品有限公司	凤岗镇	87778036	电脑桌
东莞超信金属有限公司	寮步镇	83320898	铁制家具
东莞永鹏家具有限公司	大岭山镇	85617546	家具
东莞诺华家具有限公司	道滘镇	88313444	木质家具
东莞英记夹万家私厂有限公司	寮步镇	88908999	沙发
东莞米德兰五金塑胶制品有限公司	清溪镇	87312071	金属椅子
东莞明昌家俱有限公司	沙田镇	88687918	金属家具
富鼎木业(东莞)有限公司	大岭山镇	83357899	家具
东莞铭晋家具有限公司	东城街道	22653362	木质家具
优先家具(东莞)有限公司	东城街道	22691495	家具
东莞泰冠时钟有限公司	清溪镇	87730352	婴儿床
东莞益新家俬装饰有限公司	大岭山镇	83351335	家具
东莞长欣电子科技有限公司	沙田镇	88687888	金属家具配件
东莞大欣家具有限公司	东城街道	23160288	沙发
东莞巨千家具有限公司	石碣镇	86306168	铁制家具
东莞辰森木制品有限公司	黄江镇	83627078	木制家具
东莞雅克沙发有限公司	厚街镇	85087789	沙发
东莞超艺家具有限公司	凤岗镇	87555491	家具
东莞富运家私有限公司	大岭山镇	83055888	客厅家具
瑞丰木业(东莞)有限公司三中分公司	清溪镇	87310180	家具
东莞爱迪家私有限公司	大岭山镇	83051999	书架
东莞震兴家私有限公司	虎门镇	85551784	家具
东莞润丰金属塑胶有限公司	寮步镇	83320898	五金家具
东莞志佳木业有限公司	黄江镇	83623301	家具
东莞马山五金塑胶制品有限公司	清溪镇	87312780	五金塑胶家具
东莞美时家具有限公司	塘厦镇	82031091	办公家具
东莞明辉家私有限公司	大岭山镇	83351928	木制家具
东莞新兴钢具厂有限公司	高埗镇	88872618	办公家具
造纸及纸制品业			
泓达纸业(东莞)有限公司	黄江镇	83633276	纸板

1-5 续表 6

(2010年)

单位名称	所属镇街	联系电话	主要产品(或服务)
东莞市振兴纸品有限公司	高埗镇	88871188	纸板
东莞骏佳纸业有限公司	樟木头镇	87712467	纸类制品
安姆科国际容器(广东)有限公司	寮步镇	83303343	纸制品
东莞新森奇纸品有限公司	常平镇	83391366	纸箱
东莞利通包装有限公司	南城街道	22408186	纸箱纸板
广东理文造纸有限公司	洪梅镇	88432168	造纸
东莞中兴造纸厂有限公司	道滘镇	88323518	原色瓦楞芯纸
东莞地龙纸业有限公司	麻涌镇	88234888	牛卡纸
正隆(广东)纸业有限公司	厚街镇	82273288	纸板
怡高纸品印刷(东莞)有限公司	大朗镇	83122188	纸箱
东莞金洲纸业有限公司	中堂镇		瓦楞纸
东莞扬铭纸品有限公司	万江街道	22773061	纸张裁切
东莞顺诚纸品有限公司	中堂镇		纸板
东莞龙成纸业有限公司	大朗镇	81125111	瓦楞纸板
东莞大华纸品有限公司	塘厦镇	87885611	瓦楞制品
东莞恒基纸品有限公司	常平镇	83391999	纸板
东莞建晖纸业有限公司	中堂镇	88888363	涂布白板纸
东莞瑞麒婴儿用品有限公司	石龙镇	88492212	成人尿裤
东莞佳木纸品有限公司	横沥镇	83375868	纸板
东莞大新彩印纸品有限公司	清溪镇	87736060	纸制品
东莞华南印刷有限公司	清溪镇	82098700	纸盒
永丰余纸业(东莞)有限公司	凤岗镇	87566668	高档纸
东莞浩文纸品有限公司	樟木头镇	87198718	坑纸
永固(东莞)纸业有限公司	塘厦镇	87932383	纸箱
东莞力捷纸品有限公司	清溪镇	87313089	纸类印刷品
东莞玖龙纸业有限公司	麻涌镇	88234888	牛卡纸
东莞中世拓纸业有限公司	厚街镇	85033228	数码打印纸
东莞顺裕纸业有限公司	望牛墩镇	88560003	瓦楞纸
东莞正隆纸制品有限公司	黄江镇	83630032	纸箱
东莞市中堂江南造纸厂	中堂镇	88184305	包装用纸
东莞顺盈纸业有限公司	中堂镇	88112123	瓦楞原纸
东莞长安昌众造纸有限公司	长安镇	85534024	铜板纸
东莞海龙纸业有限公司	麻涌镇	88234888	灰底白板纸
有余纸品(东莞)有限公司	大岭山镇	85630000	纸箱
东莞理文造纸厂有限公司	中堂镇	88888168	纸及纸制品
东莞骏成纸业有限公司	凤岗镇	87505300	纸制品
东莞永联工艺包装有限公司	长安镇	86064889	纸制品
东莞映佳纸业有限公司	万江街道	22277747	纸品
东莞进益纸品有限公司	凤岗镇	87758302	纸箱
东莞合意印刷有限公司	樟木头镇	87138221	纸制品
斯默菲石东包装(东莞)有限公司	道滘镇	81331300	瓦楞芯纸
东莞寮步中大纸品有限公司	寮步镇	83211760	纸箱
东莞理文纸品有限公司	中堂镇	88888168	纸板
东莞明彩纸品有限公司	樟木头镇	87713003	纸制品

1-5 续表 7

(2010年)

单位名称	所属镇街	联系电话	主要产品(或服务)
印刷业和记录媒介的复制			
贝迪科技(东莞)有限公司	莞城街道	23169500	标签印刷
东莞金华印刷有限公司	常平镇	83398868	包装装潢
东莞勤和纸品有限公司	长安镇	85544224	纸制品
东莞大朗中编印刷厂	大朗镇	83314723	书籍印刷
东莞市智源彩印有限公司	望牛墩镇	88556888	包装装潢印刷
永发印务(东莞)有限公司	大岭山镇	85650898	包装装潢印刷品
东莞派克奇包装有限公司	茶山镇	85585950	纸制品
东莞佳艺包装制品有限公司	万江街道	22285667	彩色包装印刷品
东莞新扬印刷有限公司	东城街道	22259209	印刷成品书
东莞冠文彩印有限公司	万江街道	22278166	纸板印刷
敬业(东莞)印刷包装厂有限公司	虎门镇	85551734	纸盒
东莞忠柏彩印工艺制品有限公司	东城街道	22024071	纸浆
东莞新丰印刷有限公司	凤岗镇	87142581	书、报、刊印刷
东莞恒业印刷制品有限公司	长安镇	85099366	包装装潢印刷品
东莞永洪印刷有限公司	樟木头镇	87711961	彩色纸盒
东莞石华堂纸品印刷有限公司	寮步镇	88951100	印刷书本
东莞当纳利印刷有限公司	寮步镇	81126499	印刷服务
东莞新洲印刷有限公司	大岭山镇	85625222	包装印刷
美锐电路(东莞)有限公司	塘厦镇	87724932	印刷电路板
东莞兴年彩印有限公司	长安镇	85543667	纸品印刷
利丰雅高包装印刷东莞有限公司	大岭山镇	85630000	包装印刷
东莞晨光印刷有限公司	石排镇	86551928	纸张塑料工艺商标印刷品
东莞运城制版有限公司	常平镇	83395297	凹印版辊
东莞广发印刷钉装有限公司	道滘镇	88339316	书籍
东莞澳科实业有限公司	厚街镇	88566222	印刷
东莞虎彩印刷有限公司	虎门镇	85252189	包装印刷品
东莞昌明印刷有限公司	大岭山镇	83356851	包装物
建泰印刷(东莞)有限公司	长安镇	85375818	彩盒说明书
东莞金杯印刷有限公司	常平镇	83394888	印刷书刊
东莞明泰彩色包装印刷有限公司	长安镇	85316011	说明书印刷
东莞隽思印刷有限公司	樟木头镇	87712112	彩色纸箱
文教体育用品制造业			
东莞大德电子有限公司	长安镇	85544242	各类玩具
东莞威保运动器材有限公司	寮步镇	88953278	运动手套、护具
东莞盈利幼童用品有限公司	清溪镇	87736157	儿童三轮车
东莞中岳旅行用品有限公司	塘厦镇	87925791	文具饰品
东莞龙昌玩具有限公司	东城街道	86836266	玩具
东莞虎门南栅国际文具制造有限公司	虎门镇	85561686	文具夹
东莞怡迪电子塑胶制品有限公司	凤岗镇	87777708	塑胶玩具产品
明珠高尔夫制品(东莞)有限公司	清溪镇	86812699	高尔夫球
东莞百进五金塑料有限公司	石碣镇	81382666	模具
富国运动器材(东莞)有限公司	虎门镇	85252033	运动器材
宝钜(中国)儿童用品有限公司	清溪镇	87893231	婴儿手推车

1-5 续表 8

(2010年)

单位名称	所属镇街	联系电话	主要产品(或服务)
东莞南辉塑胶电子有限公司	沙田镇	88861619	塑胶玩具
东莞广声五金塑胶制品有限公司	长安镇	86061888	木制玩具
高仕文具(东莞)有限公司	厚街镇	85585588	文具
东莞大发玩具厂有限公司	长安镇	85315256	玩具
东莞虎门南栅国际文具制造厂	虎门镇	85561686	文具夹
东莞巨佑体育用品有限公司	沙田镇	85582170	运动鞋
东莞峰达电子有限公司	中堂镇	88811559	玩具
东莞冠越玩具有限公司	虎门镇	89968888	塑胶玩具
东莞易达文具有限公司	常平镇	81032000	文件夹类文具
东莞联欣运动器材有限公司	虎门镇	85259998	溜冰鞋
东莞利达运动用品有限公司	沙田镇	88806900	运动用品
东莞广德运动用品有限公司	寮步镇	83236641	背包
东莞宝熊渔具有限公司	塘厦镇	87722967	渔具
东莞镇扬玩具有限公司	清溪镇	87736471	玩具(电子塑胶)
盛昌布艺品(东莞)有限公司	望牛墩镇	88516028	塑胶电子玩具
东莞佳畅玩具有限公司	塘厦镇	86856166	塑胶玩具
东莞大迪音响器材有限公司	寮步镇	83326201	音箱
东莞胜辉健身器材有限公司	清溪镇	82098838	训练健身器材
锦美运动用品(东莞)有限公司	清溪镇	87333971	高尔夫球具
东莞稳健高尔夫球用品有限公司	清溪镇	87739826	高尔夫球用品
东莞美联玩具有限公司	茶山镇	86648128	填充玩具
东莞东耀玩具有限公司	虎门镇	81619866	塑胶及毛绒玩具
东莞祥兴玩具有限公司	长安镇	85541020	塑胶玩具
山打根实业(东莞)有限公司	万江街道	22272416	塑胶电子玩具
长荣玩具(东莞)有限公司	清溪镇	87314418	玩具
东莞力克玩具有限公司	大朗镇	83111005	锌合金塑料玩具车
东莞意志高纸品有限公司	东城街道	22259730	笔记本
东莞建力体育器材有限公司	清溪镇	87739848	高尔夫球具
明安运动器材(东莞)有限公司	虎门镇	85555321	高尔夫球类用品
东莞康博复材科技有限公司	常平镇	83028181	体育器材及配件
东莞御丰文具有限公司	虎门镇	85154611	文具
东莞东发玩具厂有限公司	长安镇	85315256	玩具
联志玩具礼品(东莞)有限公司	横沥镇	83737875	塑胶玩具
东莞兴发玩具厂有限公司	东城街道	22201697	塑胶玩具
东莞鑫达玩具礼品有限公司	横沥镇	83375750	合金塑胶玩具
东莞凤岗竹尾田玩具厂	凤岗镇	87753128	玩具
东莞富美高文具制品有限公司	清溪镇	87898682	文具
东莞华杰工业制品有限公司	东城街道	22265020	玩具
东莞乐迪卡游戏机制造厂有限公司	虎门镇	85159455	游戏机、电子液晶体显示器
东莞康贝童车玩具有限公司	塘厦镇	87720591	童车
东莞兴利五金塑胶有限公司	石排镇	86551728	玩具
东莞登富鞋业有限公司	清溪镇	87736010	运动鞋
东莞润田服装工艺制品有限公司	石碣镇	86633899	儿童玩具
东莞惠丰鞋业有限公司	厚街镇	85589441	运动鞋

1-5 续表 9

(2010年)

单位名称	所属镇街	联系电话	主要产品(或服务)
东莞永湖复合材料有限公司	塘厦镇		棒球棒
东莞龙昌数码科技有限公司	常平镇	86836266	玩具
东莞长安港芝电子塑胶制造厂有限公司	长安镇	85543500	健身器材
东莞华兴塑胶制品有限公司	清溪镇	87369935	塑胶玩具
明门(中国)幼童用品有限公司	清溪镇	87733251	婴儿手推车
东莞柏辉玩具有限公司	沙田镇	88861619	玩具
东莞太联运动器材有限公司	长安镇	85535757	曲根球中管、曲根球球杆
东莞金冠运动器材有限公司	寮步镇	83526163	体育器材及配件
东莞联弘玩具有限公司	横沥镇	83376123	玩具
东莞宝柏新威玩具有限公司	东坑镇	83384113	玩具
展恒玩具电子(东莞)有限公司	石排镇	86655372	塑胶玩具
东莞冠贺运动器材有限公司	虎门镇	85551210	球类产品及用具
东莞南栅利高文具制品厂有限公司	虎门镇	85561878	五金文件夹
东莞源泰运动器材有限公司	塘厦镇	87722669	网球拍、高尔夫球杆
东莞凯元高尔夫用品有限公司	东城街道	22699619	高尔夫球袋
东莞大扬运动器材有限公司	厚街镇	85594466	棒球
东莞飞达鞋业有限公司	桥头镇	83344547	运动鞋皮鞋
东莞长安锦厦邦劲电子厂	长安镇	85535441	塑胶发声玩具
东莞广达塑胶制品有限公司	大朗镇	83318515	塑胶玩具
东莞银辉玩具有限公司	虎门镇	85551910	玩具
东莞桥头中星电器厂	桥头镇	83344504	电器配件
东莞达宇运动器材有限公司	东坑镇	83882808	运动器材
东莞龙鑫运动用品有限公司	塘厦镇	86851318	运动器材
东莞飞达玩具制造有限公司	桥头镇		塑胶玩具
东莞开达电子有限公司	中堂镇	88811559	玩具
东莞兴华玩具有限公司	石排镇	81818839	玩具
石油加工、炼焦及核燃料加工业			
东莞太平洋博高润滑油有限公司	南城街道	88823886	发动机油
东莞泰和沥青产品有限公司	沙田镇	88803013	普通沥青
化学原料及化学制品制造业			
东莞大宝化工制品有限公司	大岭山镇	83352051	涂料
高宝化妆品(中国)有限公司	常平镇	83392980	护肤品
广东中成化工股份有限公司	麻涌镇	88822402	保险粉
东莞秉顺制漆有限公司	凤岗镇	86801888	油漆
东莞丽利涂料有限公司	大岭山镇	83353187	钢木家具涂料
东莞永达彩印有限公司	道滘镇	88830968	印刷彩盒
汉高胶粘剂技术(广东)有限公司	虎门镇	85563700	粘合剂
益海(东莞)油化工业有限公司	麻涌镇	88238729	皂粒
东莞三星道达尔工程塑料有限公司	大岭山镇	82781999	尼龙塑胶
东莞宏石功能材料科技有限公司	沙田镇	88808241	树脂
日立化成工业(东莞)有限公司	茶山镇	86413898	线路板专用光致抗蚀工膜
维布络安舍(广东)日用品有限公司	东城街道	22253908	合成洗涤刘
欧利生东邦涂料(东莞)有限公司	茶山镇	81866000	化工涂料
东莞威威日用品有限公司	石碣镇	86632080	合成洗涤剂

1-5 续表 10

(2010年)

单位名称	所属镇街	联系电话	主要产品(或服务)
大丰电研科技(东莞)有限公司	石碣镇	88487888	油墨
宣伟涂料(东莞)有限公司	寮步镇	83220251	油漆
东莞新长桥塑料有限公司	沙田镇	88663077	工程塑料
东莞毅兴塑胶原料有限公司	厚街镇	85588755	精色粉
东莞立茂化工有限公司	道滘镇	88330956	化学用品
东莞东交沥青有限公司	沙田镇	88807929	改进沥青
阿克苏诺贝尔涂料(东莞)有限公司	大岭山镇	86520333	工业涂料
罗门哈斯电子材料(东莞)有限公司	东城街道	86225511	铜添加剂
东莞宏德化学工业有限公司	长安镇	85533620	胶桨树脂化工类
鲁道夫化工(东莞)有限公司	高埗镇	88466888	纺织品助剂
东莞普立万氯乙烯聚合体有限公司	厚街镇	85878800	化合物
东莞誉展化工有限公司	凤岗镇	87509919	涂料油漆
东莞荣和化工有限公司	道滘镇	88337898	橡胶助剂
东莞杜邦华佳高性能涂料有限公司	万江街道	22288858	涂料
东莞鸥哈希化学涂料有限公司	大朗镇	83317997	塑胶涂料
东莞华宝树脂有限公司	厚街镇	85587517	胶水
东莞新东方化工有限公司	黄江镇	83639068	硅橡胶
东莞高宝化工有限公司	常平镇	83392980	印染助剂
东莞宝丽美化工有限公司	常平镇	83392980	印染助剂
集美化妆品(东莞)有限公司	塘厦镇		化妆品
东莞瑞安高分子树脂有限公司	长安镇	85533620	聚丙烯树脂
医药制造业			
东莞奥美医疗用品有限公司	黄江镇	83630000	医用敷料
化学纤维制造业			
东莞东港化纤有限公司	东城街道	89505888	丙纶制品
橡胶制品业			
东莞市圣皇鞋材有限公司	厚街镇	81691206	鞋材
东莞宝建鞋材有限公司	黄江镇	83631221	PU树脂
中星婴儿用品(东莞)有限公司	石排镇	86652872	婴儿用品
东莞富华鞋业有限公司	高埗镇	88788166	鞋类制品
东莞国信鞋业有限公司	塘厦镇	87721640	EVA拖(凉)鞋
东莞胜百吉鞋业有限公司	长安镇	81608888	成品鞋
东莞英树电子科技有限公司	中堂镇	88642999	塑胶制品
东莞市安德固塑料包装物有限公司	东城街道	22259888	塑胶制品
东莞新桥鞋业有限公司	万江街道	22184688	橡胶鞋底
东莞太洋橡塑制品有限公司	樟木头镇	87197979	硅胶制品
东莞铧冠橡塑制品有限公司	厚街镇	85876868	复合橡胶
东莞德州鞋业有限公司	长安镇	85531584	鞋
东莞万泰橡胶有限公司	道滘镇	88833021	橡胶靴、鞋
东莞南阳橡胶制品有限公司	寮步镇	83236641	加硫鞋
星海丰电子有限公司	虎门镇	85196313	橡胶制品
东莞亚华胶粘带有限公司	石碣镇	86316960	橡胶带
诠立电子科技(东莞)有限公司	清溪镇	87294721	橡胶制品

1-5 续表 11

(2010年)

单位名称	所属镇街	联系电话	主要产品(或服务)
东莞彰昱实业有限公司	东城街道	22260168	各类鞋材
东莞冠昱实业有限公司	东城街道		橡胶粒
东莞捷讯橡胶有限公司	企石镇	86724551	硅橡胶制品
广东银禧科技股份有限公司	虎门镇		改性塑料
塑料制品业			
东莞维鸿化工有限公司	桥头镇	83342979	聚素胶树脂成型粉
东莞井上高分子材料有限公司	茶山镇	86176861	聚氨酯橡胶
信国五金电子(东莞)有限公司	石碣镇	86316760	电脑零配件
东莞高成精密注塑科技有限公司	黄江镇	83632679	工程塑料及塑料合金
东莞塘厦三局建钛塑胶制品厂	塘厦镇	87911516	文件夹
东莞兴昂鞋业有限公司	大岭山镇	85631888	鞋材和鞋
东莞荣泰塑化材料有限公司	茶山镇	86869211	PVC塑胶粒
东莞威塑可塑胶原料有限公司	樟木头镇	87719561	塑胶原料
泽冠塑胶电子(东莞)有限公司	厚街镇	83086666	塑胶配件
东莞光群雷射科技有限公司	大岭山镇	85601301	塑料软包装
东莞裕元制造厂	高埗镇	88874202	运动鞋
光明(东莞)柯式印务纸品厂有限公司	虎门镇	85553368	彩盒
东莞百代塑胶制品有限公司	企石镇	86767688	塑胶玩具
东莞茂德塑胶制品有限公司	虎门镇	85015628	塑胶制品
东莞协宇塑胶制品有限公司	长安镇	85495868	塑胶制品
东莞尚科思工艺制品有限公司	寮步镇	81192118	手机套
东莞中央化学有限公司	企石镇	86788666	塑料包装容器
舒尔曼塑料(东莞)有限公司	桥头镇	83422777	工程塑料
东莞虎邦五金塑胶制品有限公司	长安镇	85544660	运动器材塑胚配件
东莞利富高塑料制品有限公司	石龙镇	86106920	汽车零部件
东莞华通发泡塑料制品有限公司	企石镇	86789888	泡沫包装和薄膜
永塑(东莞)塑料有限公司	清溪镇	87331245	塑胶粒
鸿特利塑胶制品(东莞)有限公司	清溪镇	87738200	塑胶制品
东莞泛昌窗帘制品有限公司	常平镇		塑胶百叶窗帘
东莞华心塑胶制品厂	凤岗镇	87775513	PVC袋
品翔电子塑胶制品(东莞)有限公司	石碣镇	86636668	电子塑胶制品
东莞大银塑胶制品有限公司	长安镇	85412001	塑料制品
银禧工程塑料(东莞)有限公司	道滘镇	38855188	工程塑料
东莞劲胜精密组件股份有限公司	长安镇	82288188	塑胶制品
赫比(东莞)电子科技有限公司	长安镇	81886111	模具塑胶制品
东莞康佳包装材料有限公司	凤岗镇	86202288	泡沫胶袋产品
海格五金(东莞)有限公司	石排镇		五金制品
东莞衍青塑胶五金制品有限公司	清溪镇	87733701	水杯
东莞洲进电子塑胶五金有限公司	虎门镇	85724011	塑胶配件
东莞东锋达电脑零配件有限公司	塘厦镇	87987390	塑料制品
东莞兴腾鞋材有限公司	大岭山镇	83058898	鞋材鞋底
东莞市佑忠电子有限公司	塘厦镇		发泡胶
康扬塑胶(东莞)有限公司	长安镇	85305187	塑胶配件类
东莞保利文塑胶制品有限公司	常平镇	83989198	胶花

1-5 续表 12

(2010年)

单位名称	所属镇街	联系电话	主要产品(或服务)
昌煜塑胶(东莞)有限公司	凤岗镇	87750453	塑胶产品
东莞信柏塑胶有限公司	塘厦镇	82016888	塑料原料
东莞利士包装有限公司	常平镇	83910878	塑料罐
东莞华源玩具有限公司	东坑镇	88455176	塑胶五金玩具
杰斯比塑料(东莞)有限公司	松山湖管委会	88011818	发泡聚丙烯粒子EPP
东莞厚街创机塑胶制品厂	厚街镇	82728888	塑料制品
东莞合旺塑胶颜料有限公司	凤岗镇	87758710	颜料塑胶鞋
东莞伟嘉塑胶电子制品有限公司	麻涌镇	88232838	塑胶制品
东莞荒井橡胶制品有限公司	塘厦镇	87925725	传真机、复印机、打印机等
东莞家宝生活用品有限公司	企石镇	86666668	塑料披覆
东莞高文内衣制品有限公司	横沥镇	83792939	海棉、脯棉
东莞桥历电子有限公司	桥头镇	86937682	塑胶五金
亚化科技(东莞)胶粘制品有限公司	长安镇	85312270	胶粘带
东莞冠晖塑胶制品有限公司	南城街道	22404249	塑胶充气制品
东莞黄江福泰塑料厂	黄江镇	83363017	塑料
东莞进升塑料制品有限公司	长安镇	85357081	CD袋
东莞金金碧电子有限公司	横沥镇	87574026	塑胶制品
东莞华庆塑料有限公司	东城街道	22295808	泡沫塑料
东莞凡进工业模具有限公司	常平镇	81895181	塑胶模具
兆丰(东莞)制帘有限公司	企石镇	86716666	门框形百叶窗
东莞同成塑胶五金制品有限公司	茶山镇	86640256	塑胶五金配件
东莞增立塑料制品有限公司	沙田镇	88680500	PVC人造革
东莞市立新塑胶有限公司	石排镇	86658588	塑胶制品、五金制品
东莞三和塑胶制品有限公司	常平镇	83392589	手握箱
东莞三阳塑胶有限公司	凤岗镇	87515998	塑胶浴帘
东莞百信塑胶制品有限公司	桥头镇	83456081	塑胶制品
东莞南星塑胶有限公司	樟木头镇	87713408	聚乙烯胶袋(筒)
东莞伸丰人造革有限公司	道滘镇	88315005	人造革
东莞富增泡棉塑胶有限公司	高埗镇	88462258	塑胶泡棉
东莞竞业塑胶五金制品厂有限公司	中堂镇	88812843	塑料餐具及厨具
富裕注塑制模(东莞)有限公司	横沥镇	83378570	塑胶模具
东莞欣仪五金塑胶制品有限公司	桥头镇	83439116	五金塑胶制品
东莞万善美耐皿制品有限公司	桥头镇		美耐皿制品
东莞欣意医疗保健制品厂	黄江镇	83361381	医疗用品
东莞稻畑工程塑料有限公司	石龙镇	86188280	工程塑料
东莞胜乔鞋业有限公司	塘厦镇	87887018	各类鞋
东莞恒骏吸塑制品有限公司	长安镇	85350072	塑胶盖
东莞普能塑料科技实业有限公司	高埗镇	88735183	塑料再生胶粒
东莞誉铭电业科技有限公司	长安镇	85373322	塑胶制品
东莞金富包装材料有限公司	虎门镇	85182565	塑料制品
东莞盛泓五金塑胶制品有限公司	凤岗镇	87772450	复印机等塑胶五金配件
东莞万豪五金电子有限公司	横沥镇	83379213	数码相机上盖
东莞群福塑胶制品有限公司	厚街镇	85827756	塑胶制品
东莞斯曼塑胶制品有限公司	石排镇	86551920	纤维胶粒

1-5 续表 13

(2010年)

单位名称	所属镇街	联系电话	主要产品(或服务)
东莞益卓电子科技有限公司	大朗镇	86263266	塑胶外壳
晋德塑料科技(东莞)有限公司	塘厦镇	87929956	工程塑料
千代达电子制造(东莞)有限公司	大岭山镇	88961122	海棉
乔福塑胶(东莞)有限公司	樟木头镇	87787166	塑胶塑料
东莞骏威电子制品有限公司	大朗镇	81119390	塑胶门钟
日本电产日新(东莞)工机有限公司	长安镇	87085211	数码相机镜片
东莞富采包装制品有限公司	虎门镇	85551972	吸塑
伟易达(东莞)塑胶制品有限公司	厚街镇	85581806	塑胶制品
东莞汇景塑胶制品有限公司	长安镇	85546080	塑胶制品
台翰模具制品(东莞)有限公司	长安镇	87087888	精冲模模具
东莞三联热缩材料有限公司	寮步镇	81120158	热缩套管
东莞卓越光像薄膜有限公司	常平镇	83395440	光像薄膜
东莞市翔和塑胶电子有限公司	黄江镇	83056968	塑胶制品
健富塑胶五金制品(东莞)有限公司	清溪镇	87338807	电脑机箱
关西毡子电子(东莞)有限公司	石龙镇	86117447	塑胶制品
东莞辰泰实业有限公司	清溪镇	87737400	塑胶产品
东莞绿树塑胶制品有限公司	东城街道	22765001	塑胶配件
加福塑胶制品(东莞)有限公司	长安镇	85310681	塑胶原料
东莞厚街溪头塑料厂	厚街镇	85599076	新塑胶粒
东莞丽骏塑胶制品有限公司	塘厦镇	87811708	衣架
东莞长安乌沙日新钜升塑胶电子厂	长安镇	85547460	精密塑胶模具
东莞富利达塑胶制品有限公司	凤岗镇	87750770	PVC薄膜
东莞加能鞋材有限公司	南城街道	22400092	鞋材
东莞三荣日化容器有限公司	茶山镇	86415046	塑料容器瓶
金旺塑胶制品(东莞)有限公司	凤岗镇	87515170	窗帘配件
东莞卓荣实业有限公司	东坑镇	83698138	塑胶衣架
中侨路易塑胶制品(东莞)有限公司	东城街道	22655287	塑胶袋
广东紫泉包装有限公司	东城街道	22679188	瓶盖
东莞永捷塑胶制品有限公司	石排镇	86920526	塑胶玩具
东莞嘉多利塑胶制品有限公司	凤岗镇	87504968	PVC薄膜
东莞穗联包装制品有限公司	凤岗镇	87559119	塑胶瓶
圣诺盟聚氨酯(东莞)有限公司	塘厦镇	87881068	海棉制品
东莞南新塑胶制品有限公司	常平镇	83996222	塑胶玩具制品
东莞美哲塑胶制品有限公司	中堂镇	88181588	塑胶地砖
东莞祥曜塑胶制品有限公司	凤岗镇	87758622	塑胶制品
东莞德源塑胶制品有限公司	虎门镇	85566181	塑胶制品
东莞顶钧塑胶模具有限公司	清溪镇	86815666	塑胶零配件
东莞奇妙包装有限公司	大朗镇	83034888	塑料软包装
东莞恒发五金塑胶制品有限公司	桥头镇	83345000	五金塑胶制品
东莞敬记容器有限公司	虎门镇	85151012	塑料制品
东莞贯新幼童用品有限公司	清溪镇		婴幼儿车及制品
东莞高富达塑料制品有限公司	东城街道	22636148	塑胶材料
东莞珂维斯日用品有限公司	东城街道	22089885	化妆品
东莞木村塑胶制品有限公司	沙田镇	88865581	打印机塑胶配件

1-5 续表 14

(2010年)

单位名称	所属镇街	联系电话	主要产品(或服务)
港龙包装制品(东莞)有限公司	塘厦镇	87903336	塑料薄膜
东莞贺捷塑胶有限公司	常平镇	83392512	旅行箱塑胶配件
东莞高登鞋材有限公司	道滘镇	88830578	塑料鞋
东莞丰佳塑胶有限公司	厚街镇	85999799	PCC胶粒
东莞普隆塑胶制品有限公司	石碣镇	88181588	塑胶地砖(软体)
东莞建航精密模具塑胶五金有限公司	寮步镇	88934111	塑料零件
非金属矿物制品业			
台玻华南玻璃有限公司	洪梅镇	88841000	浮法玻璃
益龙建材东莞有限公司	东坑镇	83885678	轻型建材及配套产品
东莞南玻工程玻璃有限公司	麻涌镇	88288656	中空玻璃
东莞万德镜片科技有限公司	东城街道	22676816	镜片
东莞中威预制混凝土产品有限公司	沙田镇	88682290	预制件产品
环球石材(东莞)有限公司	长安镇	85544338	石材
东莞金鲤水泥有限公司	麻涌镇	81206633	水泥
信义汽车玻璃(东莞)有限公司	虎门镇	85266666	汽车玻璃
东莞华润混凝土有限公司	道滘镇	88326100	水泥
西斯尔(广东)岩棉制品有限公司	石龙镇	86111401	岩棉制品
信义超白光伏玻璃(东莞)有限公司	虎门镇	85266666	超白光伏玻璃
东莞华润丰诚混凝土有限公司	茶山镇	88326100	预拌商品混凝土
东莞住秀电子有限公司	凤岗镇	87552682	钕铁硼磁铁
信义汽车部件(东莞)有限公司	虎门镇	85266666	汽车玻璃
东莞泰升玻璃有限公司	沙田镇	85557608	玻璃
东莞艺华弧形钢化玻璃有限公司	桥头镇	83346884	玻璃
信义超薄玻璃(东莞)有限公司	虎门镇	85266666	玻璃
东莞华润水泥厂有限公司	沙田镇	88867510	水泥
广东可耐福新型建筑材料有限公司	麻涌镇	88222708	环保石膏板
东莞可见优玻璃制品有限公司	清溪镇	87315335	玻璃转盘
信义玻璃工程(东莞)有限公司	虎门镇	85266666	建筑玻璃
东莞南玻太阳能玻璃有限公司	麻涌镇	88281785	光伏发电盖板玻璃
黑色金属冶炼及压延加工业			
东莞富威钢铁分条有限公司	凤岗镇	87512068	钢铁分条
滨川金属(东莞)有限公司	长安镇	85322971	电脑零配件
爱思开钢铁(东莞)有限公司	寮步镇	81112111	金属材料剪切
东莞宇新钢材制品有限公司	清溪镇	87313331	电镀锌铁(钢)板
东莞谦华五金厂有限公司	长安镇	85537869	焊接钢管
东莞川电钢板制品有限公司	长安镇	85543073	矽钢片
朋胜五金制品(东莞)有限公司	清溪镇	87995999	冷轧铁板
东莞大洲钢铁有限公司	虎门镇	85557451	五金铁片
东莞住商益安金属制品有限公司	沙田镇	88863093	剪切钢卷
东莞住金物产金属制品有限公司	洪梅镇	88439668	铝材
东莞伟腾五金塑胶有限公司	厚街镇	85599181	不锈钢餐具、厨具
东莞华联五金厂有限公司	凤岗镇	87777777	钢材分条
有色金属冶炼及压延加工业			
东莞升洋焊锡材料有限公司	谢岗镇	82126112	锡线、助焊剂

1-5 续表 15

(2010年)

单位名称	所属镇街	联系电话	主要产品(或服务)
东莞鼎翰铝制品有限公司	谢岗镇	87769786	铝制品
东莞中鸿钢铁制品有限公司	清溪镇	82068001	钢铁制品
东莞联茂电子科技有限公司	虎门镇	88623268	覆铜板
来利眼镜制品(东莞)有限公司	樟木头镇	82339955	眼镜配件
东莞合立五金制品有限公司	虎门镇	85520161	五金制品
阪和钢板加工(东莞)有限公司	茶山镇	81821038	电镀锌钢板
东莞铁和金属制品有限公司	南城街道	22903361	镀钢板
元生有色金属(东莞)有限公司	寮步镇	83281886	铝合金管材
东莞瑞城压铸制品有限公司	凤岗镇	87511225	铝合金制品
东莞翔腾金属制品有限公司	寮步镇	83036688	金属制品
日立金属(东莞)特殊钢有限公司	茶山镇	81869783	模具钢材
东莞日鑫铜材有限公司	中堂镇		裸铜杆
东莞兆隆五金有限公司	凤岗镇	87751742	铜线和铝线
东莞金昌金属加工有限公司	虎门镇		有色金属
东莞珂霓钢制品有限公司	长安镇	85417742	不锈钢棒
东莞升贸锡制品有限公司	虎门镇	85508193	锡制品
东莞三星钢材加工有限公司	大朗镇	81129215	电镀锌板深产品
东莞新文钦金属有限公司	中堂镇	88810666	铝合金条
东莞市石碣华丰五金厂	石碣镇	86313720	铝合金
东莞裕升薄板有限公司	沙田镇	88807688	镀锌薄板
东莞宜安电器制品有限公司	清溪镇	87737777	镁铝合金精密铸件
金属制品业			
东莞洲亮通讯科技有限公司	道滘镇	88326318	金属餐具
东莞颖新五金制品有限公司	长安镇	85533709	金属钮扣
东莞承光五金制品有限公司	厚街镇	85926110	塑胶制品
东莞顺牛金属制品有限公司	厚街镇	85931595	金属制品
东莞精锐电器五金有限公司	高埗镇	88941998	金属制品
东莞圣雅洁具有限公司	沙田镇	88863568	有机玻璃按摩池
东莞以利沙五金塑胶制品有限公司	塘厦镇	87811756	五金塑胶制品
东莞才誉五金有限公司	长安镇	81558628	五金配件
东莞马士基集装箱工业有限公司	麻涌镇	88826668	集装箱
东莞番尔康金属制品有限公司	凤岗镇	86803388	铁五金制品
东莞永冠铸造厂有限公司	清溪镇	87739480	五金铸件
东莞井上橡塑加工有限公司	茶山镇		五金
锌辉扬热浸锌(东莞)有限公司	沙田镇	88661928	热浸锌钢铁件
东莞雅康皮塑五金有限公司	塘厦镇	86957222	金属制品
东莞华震电器有限公司	寮步镇	83218666	喇叭金属零件
东莞欣鼎五金塑胶制品有限公司	清溪镇	87338888	沙滩桌椅
东莞兴铜五金有限公司	清溪镇	87091803	铜卷片
东莞四方技研五金制品有限公司	塘厦镇	87811636	精密冲模
东莞翡致伟五金制品有限公司	道滘镇	88837504	金属工具
东莞荣成塑胶五金制品有限公司	茶山镇	81811503	塑胶五金配件
东莞璋泰五金制品有限公司	清溪镇		铁制品
东莞韦腾五金塑胶制品有限公司	大岭山镇	85785101	烤肉炉

1-5 续表 16

(2010年)

单位名称	所属镇街	联系电话	主要产品(或服务)
东莞维信五金塑胶制品有限公司	长安镇	85411861	金属家具
东莞华尔泰装饰材料有限公司	万江街道	22716312	铝塑复合板
永金金属材料(东莞)有限公司	长安镇	85330095	锡条
东莞雄罐印铁制罐有限公司	寮步镇	83226869	马口铁制品、铁罐
东莞嘉丰机电设备有限公司	寮步镇	83226777	五金机箱机动性柜
东莞尚馥散热系统有限公司	虎门镇	88623999	铝散热片
东莞万成模具五金制品有限公司	高埗镇	88731998	电脑配件
东莞清溪鸿益五金厂	清溪镇	87732903	五金半成品
美达王板和精密金属(东莞)有限公司	松山湖管委会	22893015	电子、电器零件金属材料
东莞圆晟塑胶五金制品有限公司	清溪镇	87316948	五金杂物架
东莞虎门路东昌华五金制造厂	虎门镇	85561811	电镀五金文具夹
毅昌金型(东莞)五金制品有限公司	谢岗镇	87761209	塑胶模具
自力钢构(东莞)有限公司	石碣镇	86310711	钢构房屋承建
东莞欣晟五金制品有限公司	清溪镇	87890000	烤炉
东莞长谷川金属制品有限公司	横沥镇	83721269	铝梯
东莞智信五金制品有限公司	塘厦镇	87925656	五金制品
东莞茂盈五金科技有限公司	清溪镇	82038300	五金制品及配件
志联钢线钢缆(东莞)有限公司	长安镇	85312723	钢材
合胜五金制品(东莞)有限公司	清溪镇	87383625	五金制品
东莞亿量五金制品有限公司	大朗镇	81160085	线材
东莞塘厦保发珠宝首饰厂	塘厦镇	82621838	18K镶钻石首饰
东莞世泉家电五金制品有限公司	东坑镇	83885906	五金制品
日立粉末冶金(东莞)有限公司	茶山镇	86170115	气门导管
东莞精明五金科技有限公司	凤岗镇	87862898	五金配件
东莞蕾洛五金制品有限公司	凤岗镇	87750224	商用厨具
东莞惠昌电子有限公司	长安镇	85542566	电子
东莞陇亿自行车配件有限公司	塘厦镇	87723781	铁车架
东莞建兴塑胶五金制品有限公司	凤岗镇	87753012	五金日用品
东莞凤岗雁田财迎五金电子厂	凤岗镇	87770958	摄录机机芯
英联卫浴器材(东莞)有限公司	东坑镇	83387970	水槽
东莞台端电子有限公司	长安镇	85419090	各种端子
东莞恒旺五金有限公司	横沥镇	83737616	冷板
东莞佳男五金电镀有限公司	虎门镇	85713636	连续端子、电镀五金制品
大量(东莞)五金制品有限公司	大朗镇	83110970	金属丝
东莞东记金属制品有限公司	塘厦镇	87725811	高档建筑五金件
东莞正升五金制品有限公司	塘厦镇		折合桌椅
东莞鸿辉五金有限公司	塘厦镇	87933801	铁线
东莞清溪光华制锁厂有限公司	清溪镇	87731333	锁具产品
东莞泛亚金属制造有限公司	虎门镇	82888138	铝合金接头
同明金属制品(东莞)有限公司	塘厦镇	87903150	铜带片
东莞泉睿精密五金有限公司	麻涌镇	85315643	五金轨制设备
东莞肯上精密五金有限公司	长安镇	85335705	五金塑胶件
东莞特迪五金科技有限公司	清溪镇	86814789	五金配件、散热片
东莞智得电子制品有限公司	塘厦镇	87883069	五金配件

1-5 续表 17

(2010年)

单位名称	所属镇街	联系电话	主要产品(或服务)
东莞铿利五金制品有限公司	樟木头镇	87790560	五金配件
东莞众富五金制品有限公司	塘厦镇	87945998	电脑电器散热片
东莞良佳五金塑胶制品有限公司	塘厦镇	87725096	五金塑胶制品
东莞振华特种包装有限公司	麻涌镇	88828115	特种包装铁桶
东莞力群金属厂有限公司	麻涌镇	88826058	铁管
东莞顺传五金制品有限公司	清溪镇	87732273	自行车五金零件
灿荣五金(东莞)有限公司	石碣镇	88488118	电视架
东莞益鑫电子科技有限公司	大朗镇	86263266	手提打钉机
东莞冠德五金制品有限公司	横沥镇	83723626	冷扎铁马口铁
东莞华新五金家具有限公司	东坑镇	83385013	五金制品
东莞东旭金属表面处理有限公司	虎门镇	85565111	电镀
东莞济安塑胶五金制品有限公司	高埗镇	88870555	五金饰品
东莞茂森金属冲压有限公司	塘厦镇		金属冲压件及组件
米亚精密金属科技(东莞)有限公司	凤岗镇	86802888	高档五金件
通用设备制造业			
东莞钜升塑胶电子制品有限公司	长安镇	88611111	手机模型
成行精密部件(东莞)有限公司	塘厦镇	87282609	精密部件
东莞鸿达机械工业有限公司	道滘镇	88313008	机床
东莞厚街鸿亮机电设备有限公司	厚街镇	83099888	剪草机
东莞鹏驰五金制品有限公司	黄江镇	83668128	螺丝
东莞龙佑五金机械制造有限公司	虎门镇	85518848	精密精铣机床
东莞市高亿电子五金配件有限公司	塘厦镇	87923840	螺丝
东莞浦和冶金有限公司	虎门镇	85150321	轴承
广东欧科空调制冷有限公司	黄江镇	83660888	制冷设备
东莞宏彰机械有限公司	东坑镇	81170866	数控车床
东莞今富五金机械有限公司	谢岗镇	87632358	针织机
东莞塘厦林村太阳茂森金属制造厂	塘厦镇	87929299	金属冲压
东莞冠翔电机有限公司	常平镇		汽车空压机
东莞玖骏五金有限公司	虎门镇	88622999	轴心
东莞长益五金制品有限公司	横沥镇	83723671	铁管
东莞三美空调配件有限公司	东坑镇	83862444	空调配件接管
东莞万顺昌钢铁制品有限公司	虎门镇	85520198	不锈钢片
东莞家利来电器有限公司	常平镇	83390188	风筒
东莞益新五金有限公司	常平镇	83393762	五金制品
东莞珉强五金塑胶制品有限公司	清溪镇	89137168	铁管
协隆(东莞)塑胶电子有限公司	塘厦镇	87916200	金属机械
东莞邦达五金有限公司	常平镇	83818660	光控开关
东莞千石家电有限公司	横沥镇	83732881	冷气机
东莞吉田塑料制品有限公司	常平镇	83395533	机芯塑料件
大船科技(东莞)有限公司	松山湖管委会	22899666	精密轴承
东莞君雄精密五金制造有限公司	企石镇	86710181	钢铁铸件
东莞广泽汽车饰件有限公司	厚街镇	85903898	汽车饰件
东莞泰德电机有限公司	东坑镇	83020111	吊扇
东莞双叶金属制品有限公司	大岭山镇	85658197	汽车部件

1-5 续表 18

(2010年)

单位名称	所属镇街	联系电话	主要产品(或服务)
东莞日技金属加工有限公司	常平镇	83394631	钢材
东莞艾尔发自动化机械有限公司	大朗镇	83180326	机械手(注塑机)
春雨(东莞)五金制品有限公司	大朗镇	83310921	钢材
东莞瑞电电器有限公司	高埗镇	88703880	工业用空调
东莞耐力五金配件有限公司	长安镇	85338531	铁螺丝
东莞星志厨具厂有限公司	石碣镇	86634017	厨具
东莞富鸿齐电子有限公司	樟木头镇	87187028	各类主机轴承
东莞百利达健康器材有限公司	南城街道		电子机械衡具
东莞建越精密轴承有限公司	洪梅镇	88431300	轴承
希克斯电子(东莞)有限公司	大岭山镇	85601508	充电器
瑞智制冷机器(东莞)有限公司	虎门镇	85528857	制冷空调设备
东莞瑞智压缩机有限公司	虎门镇	85528857	气体压缩机
东莞保来得粉末冶金有限公司	大朗镇	83133077	轴承零配件
东莞东成空调设备有限公司	黄江镇	83632222	中央冷水机
东莞群马电子有限公司	东坑镇	83860001	电子零配件
东莞信易电热机械有限公司	大朗镇	83313588	干燥机
东莞庆安制冷设备配件有限公司	桥头镇	83341457	分离皿
东莞邑鸿金属有限公司	寮步镇	88959666	铁金属复合材料的分条裁切
东莞百乐仕汽车精密配件有限公司	塘厦镇	87987779	汽车配件
专用设备制造业			
东莞柏兆电子有限公司	长安镇	85540381	电脑主板机
东莞宏威数码机械有限公司	南城街道	22901516	旋涂机
东莞大泉传感器有限公司	寮步镇	88953366	传感器
忠信制模(东莞)有限公司	横沥镇	83732298	非金属制品模具
大宇(东莞)电器有限公司	东坑镇	83020257	榨汁机
东莞丰裕电机有限公司	塘厦镇	87902888	喷涂环保工业自化设备
先锐模具配件(东莞)有限公司	长安镇	85376810	热流管
永大精密模具(东莞)有限公司	长安镇	85312541	精密模具
东莞佑能工具有限公司	洪梅镇	88848901	钻头
东华机械有限公司	南城街道	22806233	注塑机
东莞伊斯丹电子有限公司	清溪镇	87338301	变压器
东莞胜美达(太平)电机有限公司	虎门镇	85111118	电子原件
东莞塘厦光裕灯泡厂	塘厦镇	87727255	灯泡
东莞安联电器元件有限公司	虎门镇	85500410	电器开关
东莞井上五金橡塑有限公司	沙田镇	88863344	印刷机部件
一胜百模具(东莞)有限公司	松山湖管委会	22897888	精密型模具
东莞添威电子制品有限公司	凤岗镇	87779805	电源供应器
东莞明利钢材模具制品有限公司	大朗镇	83316878	精密型腔模
东莞富强鑫塑胶机械制造有限公司	大朗镇	83313753	机械
东莞康佳模具塑胶有限公司	凤岗镇	82071360	模具
东莞东坑富港电子制品厂	东坑镇	83882225	电子制品
台光五金制品(东莞)有限公司	谢岗镇	87685123	精密五金模具
东莞东洋塑胶制品有限公司	塘厦镇	87880688	精密塑胶模具
东莞泛邦电子有限公司	长安镇	85310926	各类电子产品

1-5　续表 19

(2010年)

单位名称	所属镇街	联系电话	主要产品(或服务)
长成电子(东莞)有限公司	东城街道	22035023	非金属制品模具
东莞万德电子制品有限公司	东城街道	88775555	硅胶按键
东莞顺兴电子有限公司	寮步镇	83039160	电子塑胶零配件
东莞骆恒塑胶制品有限公司	清溪镇	87312310	精密成型钢模
东莞保康电子科技有限公司	樟木头镇	87780831	血糖检测器
比美高精密模具(东莞)有限公司	凤岗镇	87753128	橡胶模具
捷荣模具工业(东莞)有限公司	长安镇	82387988	模具
东莞鑫佑光电科技有限公司	石排镇	86534198	背光板
东莞毅昌模具制造注塑有限公司	谢岗镇	87761209	五金模具
东莞富强电子有限公司	东坑镇	83882225	耳机
东莞佳鸿机械制造有限公司	望牛墩镇	88859861	吹瓶机
东莞胜方电子有限公司	东城街道	86216886	导电薄膜
东莞极盛电子有限公司	寮步镇	88953118	激光头塑料配件
东莞塘厦顺扬精密五金厂	塘厦镇	87989888	五金模具
东莞天祥塑胶有限公司	东城街道	88990909	电视机外壳
东莞鸿图金属压铸电器制造有限公司	长安镇	86062888	汽车零部件
科广电子(东莞)有限公司	寮步镇	83302929	微型二极管
东莞乙宏精密模具有限公司	塘厦镇	87919391	精密模具
伟易达(东莞)电子产品有限公司	厚街镇	85581806	电子玩具
交通运输设备制造业			
东莞龙达科技有限公司	塘厦镇		自行车配件
东莞杰腾造船有限公司	厚街镇	85921699	FRP游艇
东莞果升电子有限公司	常平镇	82207988	汽车影音设备
东莞恩斯克转向器有限公司	东城街道	22620960	汽车零部件及配件
小仓离合机(东莞)有限公司	石碣镇	86361603	离合器
格尔翰汽车配件(东莞)有限公司	石排镇	81828988	汽车配件
东莞井上建上汽车部件有限公司	沙田镇	88682171	汽车零部件
东莞泰合复合材料有限公司	黄江镇	86913288	自行车零配件
东莞方皓汽车配件有限公司	塘厦镇	87725576	捆绑器
东莞联志五金制品有限公司	大朗镇	83195767	汽车刹车盘零件
东莞鸿益雨刷有限公司	茶山镇	86646707	汽车雨刷
东莞京滨汽车电喷装置有限公司	东城街道	22658290	汽车零部件及配件
东莞大和化成汽车零配件有限公司	桥头镇		汽车固件
美尔顿车业(东莞)有限公司	寮步镇	81118000	电动助力车
爱地雅(东莞)自行车有限公司	寮步镇	88951888	自行车
东莞山口实业有限公司	樟木头镇	87128480	汽车塑胶制品
东莞山多力汽车配件有限公司	企石镇	86722101	汽车雨刷
广东中远船务工程有限公司	麻涌镇	88286988	金属船
东莞鸿图精密压铸有限公司	长安镇	86062888	铝合金压铸件
电气机械及器材制造业			
东莞钜鸿林实业有限公司	谢岗镇	82126070	电子玩具及其配件
东莞优电电线电缆有限公司	石碣镇	86632563	电线电缆
东莞裕新灯饰有限公司	虎门镇	82887578	灯饰产品
万宝至精工(东莞)有限公司	虎门镇	85564792	电镀轴芯

1-5 续表 20

(2010年)

单位名称	所属镇街	联系电话	主要产品(或服务)
京瓷爱克(东莞)电子有限公司	石龙镇	88495099	新型机电元件
东莞清溪合力电器制造厂	清溪镇	87731111	搅拌机
东莞福登机电有限公司	东坑镇	81035111	电机和小型电器
东莞创机电业制品有限公司	厚街镇	82728888	电动工具
世雅电子科技(东莞)有限公司	长安镇	85414388	高效率变频器
东莞万迪电子有限公司	常平镇	82988519	输配电及控制设备
东莞金山电池有限公司	塘厦镇	87723007	锂离子电子
京都电工(东莞)有限公司	长安镇	85428288	电子元器
东莞小泉照明有限公司	石龙镇	86189569	灯饰制品
桑野电子(东莞)有限公司	横沥镇	82329818	连接天线
东莞爱思丽灯饰有限公司	横沥镇	81012302	灯饰
东莞景盛电线材料有限公司	虎门镇	85157538	PVC胶粒
东莞合力电器制品有限公司	清溪镇	87731111	搅拌器
东莞杰光灯饰有限公司	东城街道	22674459	台灯落地灯
东莞鹰江电子有限公司	黄江镇	83635662	稳压电源
东莞市雅科精密线材有限公司	东坑镇	83888869	电线、电缆
东莞迅德电器有限公司	清溪镇	87739411	小型变压器
东莞德宏电线电子有限公司	塘厦镇	87724535	电线
东莞广宇精密电子有限公司	虎门镇	85509706	电线
东莞荣星电线有限公司	塘厦镇	87913003	漆包线
东莞维盟电子绝缘材料有限公司	清溪镇	87315040	耐高温电容器
东莞海韵电子有限公司	东城街道	22610501	电子设备
光宝电子(东莞)有限公司	长安镇	86070888	电源供应器
东莞华兴电器有限公司	清溪镇	82995698	小型变压器
东莞泽龙线缆有限公司	石龙镇	81388600	特种漆包线
东莞澳利电器制品有限公司	常平镇	83330419	变压器
益伸电子(东莞)有限公司	横沥镇	83796198	五金电子
东莞毓华电子科技有限公司	企石镇	86668107	开关电源
东莞库柏电子有限公司	长安镇	81605288	变压器
东莞庆泰电线电缆有限公司	常平镇	83330265	电线、电源
东莞威煌电器制品有限公司	塘厦镇	87727984	电动剪发器
东莞华新电线电缆有限公司	大朗镇	83195252	8.0铜杆
东莞林发电子有限公司	厚街镇	83085888	音响插头线
东莞新光电线有限公司	道滘镇	88316705	电线、电缆
东莞泰德灯饰有限公司	黄江镇	83620988	灯饰
智宝电子(东莞)有限公司	塘厦镇	87914676	电解电容器
东莞长联电线电缆有限公司	虎门镇	85703585	电线电缆
春迅电子(东莞)有限公司	寮步镇	88955688	感应灯
东莞宏大电器制品有限公司	东城街道	22269073	家用电器
正规电线电缆(东莞)有限公司	黄江镇	83624357	电源线连插头
东莞松藤电子有限公司	桥头镇	83457291	电吹风
东莞永力电业有限公司	常平镇	83335989	电源线插头
东莞宇隆电工材料有限公司	茶山镇	86642861	漆包线
金霸王(中国)有限公司	南城街道	22403615	电池AA、AAA

1-5 续表 21

(2010年)

单位名称	所属镇街	联系电话	主要产品(或服务)
易达威锐电源设备科技(东莞)有限公司	东城街道	22651108	智能化电源设备系统
东莞宏桦电器有限公司	塘厦镇	87935001	电风扇
东莞大通电线有限公司	大朗镇	83132896	PVC塑料粒(电线接口用)
东莞美群电器制品有限公司	塘厦镇	87981800	家用电力器具
东莞永大电子有限公司	常平镇	83339366	插头连接线
东莞光距电子有限公司	塘厦镇	87288988	网络产品(网络线)
东莞维升电子制品有限公司	黄江镇	83622694	电源线连插头
东莞金星电线有限公司	大朗镇	83195297	电线电缆
东莞苏泊尔电器有限公司	石碣镇	86365011	电磁炉
丽宾电子通讯(东莞)有限公司	寮步镇	81112051	耳机线材
港芝(东莞)电子制造厂有限公司	塘厦镇	87720639	健身器材
东莞巨汉灯饰有限公司	莞城街道	22096948	灯饰
东莞万利信新材料元件有限公司	长安镇	81882000	铝电解电容器
东莞宏翔电器有限公司	凤岗镇	87772581	电风扇
东莞华明灯具有限公司	清溪镇	87311200	灯具
东莞晋原电子有限公司	大岭山镇	85601899	塑胶制品
东莞川电电机有限公司	东坑镇	83020001	定子
东莞杰扬五金电器有限公司	东坑镇	83020011	吊灯
东莞可比世电子有限公司	黄江镇	83623093	变压器
东莞日线线缆有限公司	桥头镇	83344845	铜材
东莞信浓马达有限公司	凤岗镇	87772818	微电机
东莞塘厦伊南电器制品厂	塘厦镇	87880237	连接线
东莞大东电业有限公司	桥头镇	83340838	电线电缆
东莞宏智电器配件有限公司	谢岗镇	87136136	家用电器配件
东莞京洲灯饰有限公司	寮步镇		嵌灯
东莞南玻光伏科技有限公司	麻涌镇	88288808	晶体硅太阳能电池
东莞行特电子有限公司	清溪镇	87388642	连接器
东莞钜权电器有限公司	万江街道	22183056	厨房电器及其它零配件
东莞安硕电子有限公司	塘厦镇	87882595	电子式镇流器、微型变压器
东莞新南利电业有限公司	长安镇	85318758	电源线
东莞世福电器有限公司	塘厦镇	87923483	电源控制盒
东莞莞城协益电子厂	莞城街道	22264550	微型电机及零部件
万泰光电(东莞)有限公司	虎门镇	88620666	单模光纤
东莞东进照明有限公司	东城街道	22024968	灯饰
东莞贵名精密电子有限公司	虎门镇	85152555	电子绝缘配件
东莞金波罗电业科技有限公司	中堂镇	88886808	电线电缆
福华电子设备(东莞)有限公司	大朗镇	83193767	开关
东莞启益电器机械有限公司	塘厦镇	87989065	变压器
东莞进泰电子有限公司	塘厦镇	87725650	音响
东莞恒忻电子有限公司	塘厦镇	87915567	电感线圈
东莞蒂雅克电子有限公司	长安镇	85548848	音响视听设备
实盈电子(东莞)有限公司	清溪镇	87318688	连接器
富士林电子(东莞)有限公司	东坑镇	83882225	连接线
东莞文邦电线有限公司	清溪镇	87731000	电线电缆

1-5 续表 22

(2010年)

单位名称	所属镇街	联系电话	主要产品(或服务)
东莞怡盛电业有限公司	大朗镇	83016688	电线电缆
东莞大得电线电缆有限公司	企石镇	86787888	电线电缆
东莞桥梓周氏电业有限公司	常平镇	83332731	电线电缆PVC胶粒
东莞富美康电器科技有限公司	谢岗镇	87631613	直发器
东莞九州电器有限公司	大朗镇	83188854	筒灯
东莞实英电子有限公司	厚街镇	88630999	电脑接插件
东莞创宝达电器制品有限公司	常平镇	83335747	漏电保护器
东莞明电电气工程有限公司	万江街道	88750012	高压配电柜
杰群电子科技(东莞)有限公司	黄江镇	83635267	新型电子元器件
东莞艾天电池科技有限公司	横沥镇	88973706	锂离子电池
东莞高力电池有限公司	清溪镇	87739390	干电池
东莞联立电器实业有限公司	塘厦镇	87721921	小家电
奇烨电子(东莞)有限公司	石排镇	86925028	变压器
东莞统元电源连接有限公司	大朗镇	83101598	电源线连插头
东莞柏杰灯饰有限公司	虎门镇	85551219	塑料五金灯饰
东莞汉华金属制品有限公司	大朗镇	83188845	铜线
东莞华巨特殊线材有限公司	道滘镇	88389008	镀锡线
太阳电线东莞有限公司	南城街道	22401739	电线、电缆
东莞汇勋电器制品有限公司	塘厦镇		电风扇、暖风机、增湿机
东莞永德电业制品有限公司	塘厦镇		电线
荣文灯饰(东莞)有限公司	长安镇	81667888	灯饰及配件
长青林电子(东莞)有限公司	桥头镇	83340851	电线
东莞达晨电业制品有限公司	石碣镇	86631818	电线
东莞积信电器有限公司	樟木头镇	87799639	电烤炉
东莞嘉盛照明科技有限公司	虎门镇	85700057	灯具
易事特电力系统技术有限公司	松山湖管委会		不间断电源
东莞大新科技有限公司	沙田镇	88865753	气量测试器
东莞昭和机电有限公司	东城街道	23068915	电子连接线
亚士吉灯饰(东莞)有限公司	石龙镇	88492087	灯具、照明装置
东莞东峰铝型材制品有限公司	塘厦镇	87913344	铝型材
三诚东莞电子有限公司	东坑镇	83690222	液晶显示屏背光源组件
东莞佑茂五金塑胶有限公司	谢岗镇	87686300	电脑五金塑胶配件
日立蓄电池(东莞)有限公司	茶山镇	86400790	汽车铅酸蓄电池
东莞莹辉灯饰有限公司	虎门镇	85551445	灯饰
四国电线(东莞)有限公司	清溪镇	87735432	同轴电线
东莞港电电器制品有限公司	石排镇	86518228	直发器
飞宏(东莞)电子有限公司	清溪镇	87319026	电源供应器及半成品
东莞瀚宇电子有限公司	大朗镇	83193666	KF线
古河汽车配件(东莞)有限公司	清溪镇	87295600	汽车用电线
东莞三雄电业制造有限公司	桥头镇	83436611	电源线
日本电产三协电子(东莞)有限公司	石龙镇	86114520	微电机
东莞市井南电子有限公司	中堂镇	88410266	新型电子材料
东莞道滘建和五金制品厂	道滘镇	88836680	开关电线接插件
东莞新能源电子科技有限公司	南城街道	88989052	电池

1-5 续表 23

(2010年)

单位名称	所属镇街	联系电话	主要产品(或服务)
东莞光旭太阳能灯饰有限公司	大朗镇	86261866	太阳能电池板
东莞怡高塑胶五金电子制品有限公司	常平镇	83394988	汽车CD收放机
东莞亿得电器制品有限公司	虎门镇	85554635	电热炉
东莞吉联电线电缆有限公司	虎门镇	85551155	PVC电线
东莞市东阳光电容器有限公司	长安镇	85315188	电容器
东莞首资宝电器制造有限公司	谢岗镇	87130808	电暖器
东莞常禾电子有限公司	虎门镇	85551202	音箱、喇叭、扬声器
东莞志丰电子有限公司	大朗镇	83183457	蜂鸣器
东莞理士电源制品有限公司	塘厦镇	87325187	高能阀控密封蓄电池
东莞岳丰电子科技有限公司	石碣镇	86634236	电话线连插头
东莞永成电器制品厂有限公司	清溪镇	87738870	吸尘器
东莞固邦灯饰电线有限公司	虎门镇	85553167	节日灯饰、红铜线
东莞光晋灯饰有限公司	厚街镇	85586035	灯饰及灯饰配件
东莞清溪华晖五金电器厂	清溪镇	86817099	油炸锅
东莞三星电机有限公司	寮步镇	83305000	电源
东莞基立线缆有限公司	塘厦镇	82061078	电脑连接线
东莞力达电机有限公司	塘厦镇		微电机及其它电机
东莞市银晖电制品有限公司	塘厦镇	87723007	开发锂离子电池
东莞新隆漆包线有限公司	茶山镇	86415025	漆包线
东莞超霸电池有限公司	塘厦镇	87910215	电池
东莞威霸清洁器材有限公司	寮步镇	83283988	清地机
东莞冠宏电子有限公司	长安镇	88619858	放大器、音响、电子钢琴
东莞劲捷电子有限公司	厚街镇	85895863	电池充电器
东莞航升实业有限公司	黄江镇	83668283	家用电器用品
东莞卡妮尔灯饰有限公司	塘厦镇	87723088	台灯
东莞丰盛电线电缆有限公司	桥头镇	83343591	漆包线
东莞赫升机电有限公司	塘厦镇	82095588	各类机电设备
谊邦电工材料(东莞)有限公司	东城街道	22654837	漆包线
东莞升隆电线塑胶有限公司	黄江镇	83608118	电线
东莞卡斯特照明有限公司	茶山镇	88655066	照明灯具及其配件
东莞珀韵电子有限公司	横沥镇	83720950	音圈
东莞润泰电线电缆有限公司	虎门镇	88620999	电线
呈威电子(东莞)有限公司	横沥镇	83377756	微型变压器
东莞新元电子有限公司	塘厦镇	87815229	锂离子电池
东莞万宝至电机设备制造有限公司	东城街道	22267409	微电机其他电机
东莞苏扬电器有限公司	常平镇	83391502	圣诞灯串
东莞启东电线电缆有限公司	沙田镇	88867234	电线、电缆
台达电子电源(东莞)有限公司	石碣镇	86639008	电源供应器
东莞利通电器二厂	长安镇	86070888	电源供应器
东莞强盛电线电缆有限公司	石碣镇	86633470	电线电缆
东莞苏扬灯饰有限公司	桥头镇	83342116	圣诞饰品
东莞宏致电子有限公司	长安镇	85393066	电子零配件
万裕三信电子(东莞)有限公司	长安镇	86069888	电子电容器
立信杰(东莞)精密模具制造有限公司	凤岗镇	86800088	汽车线材

1-5 续表 24

(2010年)

单位名称	所属镇街	联系电话	主要产品(或服务)
东莞亿泰电线电缆有限公司	虎门镇	85500951	电线
东莞安达电器制品有限公司	凤岗镇	87771128	不锈钢咖啡壶
亚弘(东莞)电器有限公司	塘厦镇	86851766	家用电器
东莞鸿呈电子有限公司	厚街镇	88636000	电脑连接插头
海蓝星光学科技(东莞)有限公司	樟木头镇	87184998	镇流器
东莞威德电子科技有限公司	东城街道	23061648	背部按摩椅座垫
东莞新能源科技有限公司	松山湖管委会	88989162	高技术绿色电池
东莞乐域塑胶电子制品有限公司	石排镇	86550011	光管手提灯
大盛照明(东莞)有限公司	凤岗镇	87503918	各种灯具及配件
东莞泰欣照明有限公司	黄江镇	87135999	灯饰
东莞明晖不锈钢厨具有限公司	清溪镇	87313210	高身雪柜
金淞制冷设备(东莞)有限公司	常平镇	83394468	移动式冷气机
东莞元太电业有限公司	塘厦镇	87881778	电线
通信设备、计算机及其他电子设备制造业			
康展电子(东莞)有限公司	塘厦镇	87915950	电子原件
东莞首利科技五金有限公司	清溪镇	86812888	线路板组件
东莞普光液晶显示有限公司	厚街镇	81520001	手机液晶显示屏
凌进电子(东莞)有限公司	黄江镇	89769000	手机
东莞艾埤特电子有限公司	寮步镇	82815981	电子元器件
东莞捷盛电子有限公司	东城街道		零件印制电路板
东莞国瑞电子有限公司	塘厦镇	82063511	电感器
东莞立德电子有限公司	塘厦镇		变压器
泰科电子(东莞)有限公司	厚街镇	85817613	通讯终端设备
宝罗电子科技(东莞)有限公司	横沥镇	83712772	新型电子元件
东莞技嘉电子有限公司	黄江镇	83367140	电脑主板
东莞通华液晶有限公司	东城街道	88774388	液晶显示板
东莞歌乐东方电子有限公司	东坑镇	83387001	汽车音响
东莞微迅电子科技有限公司	清溪镇	87735130	数字音、视频编解码设备
东莞迈虹电子有限公司	长安镇	85378311	印刷线路板
东莞船井电机厂	黄江镇	83665999	液晶电视机
东莞三协精工科技有限公司	高埗镇	88787202	电子产品
东莞长安上角福摩斯托电子厂	长安镇	85541200	组合音响
东莞时力科技电子厂	长安镇	85415668	电子元件
东莞鹏龙光电有限公司	石碣镇	88787202	平板显示器件
东莞怡辉五金有限公司	清溪镇	87386488	五金制品、钢材
东莞康特尔电子有限公司	高埗镇	88462888	数字电视机
东莞柏能电子厂	厚街镇	85822002	计算机主板和显卡
东莞柏狮赛格精密电子有限公司	麻涌镇	88233068	半导体
东莞长安厦岗成铭电子制品厂	长安镇	85419999	电脑机箱
东莞长安日发电子厂	长安镇	85348787	磁头弹性臂
东莞爱铭数码电子有限公司	寮步镇	83038000	DVD激光头
东莞彩显有机发光科技有限公司	清溪镇	87738875	新型平放显示器
诺基亚通信有限公司东莞分公司	南城街道	22402844	移动电话
东莞奕华电子有限公司	东城街道	88759333	电子产品

1-5 续表 25

(2010年)

单位名称	所属镇街	联系电话	主要产品(或服务)
东莞顺晟电脑实业有限公司	凤岗镇	86801188	电脑机箱
东莞钨珍电子科技有限公司	谢岗镇	82126950	手机配件
东莞荃宝电子制品有限公司	清溪镇	87383811	电脑机箱
东莞常平土塘大根电子光学制品厂	常平镇	83395446	扫描器镜头
东莞栢能电子科技有限公司	厚街镇	85822002	电脑主机
东莞市王氏港建电子有限公司	常平镇	83903333	电子产品
东莞尔来德通讯有限公司	黄江镇	87097800	手机按键
大东俊通(东莞)电子有限公司	常平镇	83394379	组合音响
东莞大雅电子科技有限公司	长安镇	85448999	光磁盘驱动器
东莞冠坤电子有限公司	清溪镇	87318000	片式电容
伟易达(东莞)电讯有限公司	寮步镇	83231806	电源控制口
东莞伟易达卫星设备有限公司	寮步镇	83231806	室内无线电话
东莞微端电子科技有限公司	常平镇	83975888	新型平板显示器
东莞中探探针有限公司	虎门镇	85151668	电子测试探针
东莞航大电子有限公司	常平镇	83392291	电话单机
东莞明瑞电子有限公司	长安镇	86072000	调解器
东莞东远机械制造有限公司	常平镇	83501527	制版设备
东莞安美时电子有限公司	常平镇	83394581	网络控制设备
亚电电子(东莞)有限公司	塘厦镇	87982616	黑胶唱机
东莞庆帮电子有限公司	大朗镇	83319425	喇叭
东莞巨群光学镜片有限公司	寮步镇	82233688	光电子器件
东莞卓翰光电科技有限公司	横沥镇	81180610	模具光磁盘驱动器及其部件
东莞天钺科技有限公司	厚街镇	85889488	3C产业产品
东莞成铭电子有限公司	长安镇	85419999	电子零配件
东莞令特电子有限公司	虎门镇	81518186	压敏电阻、敏感元器件
东莞阳天电子科技有限公司	塘厦镇	82062778	电子元件
东莞锦富迪奇电子有限公司	东城街道	23116179	背光模组的增光片
广东生益科技股份有限公司	松山湖管委会	22271828	覆铜板
东莞南阳电子有限公司	寮步镇	83222875	电子元器件
东莞德利信电子有限公司	常平镇	83395111	各种机芯产品
东莞广通事务机有限公司	长安镇	85312190	电子元件及组件
平易电子(东莞)有限公司	常平镇	83820333	印刷电路板
东莞新洋电子有限公司	茶山镇	86171021	手机外壳
东莞辉城电子有限公司	望牛墩镇	88520218	电子组件
东莞建永数码科技有限公司	塘厦镇	87880818	CD镭射机
东莞黄江瑞升科技电子厂	黄江镇	83633303	电脑及周边产品
东莞石排联鑫电子厂	石排镇	86591818	彩色电视机
永胜电脑五金(东莞)有限公司	东坑镇	83387140	电脑机箱
美信音响器材(东莞)有限公司	塘厦镇	86856188	音箱(含喇叭)
东莞东骏电器有限公司	南城街道	22401688	电子变压器用铁心片
东莞加玮华电子有限公司	东城街道	22257469	耳机
升荣电子(东莞)有限公司	清溪镇	87311036	电脑周边产品
东莞谢岗钨珍电子厂	谢岗镇	82126950	手机外壳
东莞嘉茂电子科技有限公司	大朗镇	88606888	喇叭

1-5 续表 26

(2010年)

单位名称	所属镇街	联系电话	主要产品(或服务)
东莞全策电器有限公司	凤岗镇	82069922	收音机
飞比达电子元器件(东莞)有限公司	横沥镇	83725088	新型电子元器件
东莞建冠塑胶电子有限公司	虎门镇	85162899	连接器
泓凯电子科技(东莞)有限公司	黄江镇	83365942	电脑机箱
东莞石龙粤龙光学制品厂	石龙镇		收、放音机
东莞泰山电子有限公司	虎门镇	85564813	印刷线路版
东莞石碣源利电子厂	石碣镇	86638923	液晶显示器
棠裕电子(东莞)有限公司	清溪镇	87332588	液晶显示器
东莞创盟电子有限公司	虎门镇	85505799	电脑连接线
东莞建通电子五金有限公司	虎门镇	85565684	端子
东莞凡振工业电子有限公司	谢岗镇	87635181	电子音响
东莞信丰五金机械塑胶工业有限公司	长安镇	85411186	相机镜头连接垫
达创科技(东莞)有限公司	石碣镇	86637008	集线器
业强科技(东莞)有限公司	长安镇	85421928	新型电子元器件
东莞三星视界有限公司	厚街镇	85582000	液晶显示片
东莞泰富电子有限公司	高埗镇	88730138	电话
东莞利保迅电子有限公司	茶山镇	86408844	变压器
奥托仑光电子(东莞)有限公司	茶山镇	86401060	玻璃光学镜片
东莞加炜电子有限公司	石碣镇	86310071	电子连接器
东莞洲磊电子有限公司	谢岗镇	87631888	电子产品
富相电子科技(东莞)有限公司	高埗镇	88737888	液晶显示器件
东莞超悦电子有限公司	寮步镇	83305007	电脑键盘
东莞全特电子科技有限公司	虎门镇	85555526	塑胶电子制品
东莞爱美达电子有限公司	横沥镇	83377651	电脑散热器
东莞首富电子有限公司	樟木头镇	87710688	电子产品
东莞永保电子有限公司	桥头镇	81176991	锂离子电子
东莞黄江精成科技电子一厂	黄江镇	83632679	电脑主板
东莞凤岗三和盛科技电子厂	凤岗镇	87862222	计算机及周边设备
东莞领航电子有限公司	塘厦镇		变压器、整流器
东莞华盛音响制品有限公司	石排镇	86528327	汽车收放音机
东莞高盛电子有限公司	常平镇	83813136	电话机
东莞宏邦光电有限公司	清溪镇	87322250	扩散片
东莞铭异精密电子有限公司	石碣镇	86387383	电脑支架
东莞南城新科磁电制品厂	南城街道	22810033	电脑磁头
东莞呈越电脑配件有限公司	大朗镇	86913168	液晶显示器支架
东莞长安镇时力电子厂	长安镇	85533151	磁臂组合半成品
兴科电子(东莞)有限公司	虎门镇	85106058	手机按键
思林菲加热器材(东莞)有限公司	虎门镇	88629188	电子元器件
东莞高信电子有限公司	寮步镇	83283743	印刷电路板
东莞相川铁龙电子有限公司	常平镇	83395551	电子元件
世擎光电(东莞)有限公司	茶山镇	81821666	手机摄像模组
东莞山技光电科技有限公司	清溪镇	87388658	扩散膜
东莞沛波电子有限公司	石碣镇	86310316	小型变压器
奥泰斯电子(东莞)有限公司	黄江镇	83365026	防盗热感应器

1-5 续表 27

(2010年)

单位名称	所属镇街	联系电话	主要产品(或服务)
东莞长安涌头富贵电子厂	长安镇	85328418	电位器
雅新电子线路板(东莞)有限公司	石碣镇	86331999	印刷线路板
东莞宣得电子有限公司	长安镇	85546400	电子元器件
东莞市捷伟讯电子有限公司	厚街镇	85993708	手机
品基电子(东莞)有限公司	塘厦镇	87910231	电子元件
恩智浦半导体广东有限公司	黄江镇	83668268	半导体
台达电子(东莞)有限公司	石碣镇	86639008	线圈
东莞达宏电子有限公司	清溪镇	87736405	电源供应器
东莞红板多层线路板有限公司	长安镇	86060111	电子元器件
东莞天意电子有限公司	石龙镇	86080328	彩票终端机
东莞矽德半导体有限公司	清溪镇	87313240	集成电路
天弘(东莞)科技有限公司	松山湖管委会	22899333	网络游戏机
东莞万年富电子有限公司	塘厦镇	87724667	线路板
东莞华强三洋电子有限公司	塘厦镇	87910998	彩电
东莞利源电子有限公司	横沥镇	83723988	灯光控制器
东莞狮龙电子有限公司	寮步镇	83283391	DVD
广东南方宏明电子科技股份有限公司	南城街道	22407479	电容器
东莞电创电子有限公司	道滘镇	88834807	电子接插件
东莞首邦电子有限公司	石碣镇	86632772	变压器
智嘉通讯科技(东莞)有限公司	常平镇	83335430	通讯配件
东莞泰峰电子有限公司	桥头镇	83437030	汽车音响高频头
东莞华龙电子有限公司	横沥镇	83376575	变压器
东莞优威王电子塑胶五金有限公司	虎门镇	85701800	计算机用PC塑胶配件
东莞太华半导体有限公司	寮步镇	83263688	手机用液晶显示器部件
康舒电子(东莞)有限公司	塘厦镇	87915950	电源供应器
良特电子科技(东莞)有限公司	常平镇	83914041	通讯器材配件
中名(东莞)电子有限公司	虎门镇	85559636	耳机
唯耀电子(东莞)有限公司	石龙镇		电源板
品佳电子(东莞)有限公司	沙田镇	88800318	液晶显示器
东莞华春电子有限公司	中堂镇	88888850	电脑显示卡
东莞华科电子有限公司	大朗镇	83115168	片式电容
茂瑞电子(东莞)有限公司	东城街道	87077888	键盘
东莞东英电子工业有限公司	清溪镇	87328201	DVD机蕊
东莞欧珀移动通信有限公司	长安镇	85545555	手机
三井高科技(广东)有限公司	长安镇	86070008	新型电子元器件
东莞同昌电子有限公司	大朗镇	83318960	PCB
东莞能率科技有限公司	寮步镇	83527668	手机摄像头
东莞高埗昭和电子厂	高埗镇	88873451	遥控器
东莞德竹电子科技有限公司	虎门镇	85258301	电子零配件
东莞清溪三清半导体厂	清溪镇	87734139	半导体晶体管
东莞为勤电子有限公司	长安镇	85542016	电子元器件
矽谷电子科技(东莞)有限公司	黄江镇	83366696	液晶显示器
东莞裕佳电子有限公司	清溪镇	87739418	光盘驱动器
东莞友华电子有限公司	寮步镇	83326171	端子连接器

1-5 续表 28

(2010年)

单位名称	所属镇街	联系电话	主要产品(或服务)
东莞泉声电子有限公司	石碣镇	86325251	新型电子元器件
乐依文半导体(东莞)有限公司	长安镇	85647662	集成电路
东莞新动电子有限公司	大岭山镇	88962920	汽车组合仪表
旭丽电子(东莞)有限公司	石碣镇	86638923	键盘
东莞骅国电子有限公司	厚街镇	85597201	连接器
东莞辉煌电子有限公司	塘厦镇	87727680	电脑连线
松普科技(东莞)有限公司	塘厦镇	87937608	宽带接入网通信系统设备
东莞华强三洋马达有限公司	塘厦镇	87720523	微型马达
东莞市旭进光电有限公司	长安镇	85413789	光学镜头
东莞康创电子科技有限公司	厚街镇	85889989	收音机
东莞万士达液晶显示器有限公司	东城街道	22668178	光电子器件及其他电子器件
东莞高美电子有限公司	寮步镇	83300880	电子配件
东莞裕光数码电子有限公司	道滘镇	88382101	手机LCD电路板
太阳诱电(广东)有限公司	石碣镇	86636888	电容器
东莞亚锋电脑零配件有限公司	塘厦镇	87727888	橡胶电脑零配件
东莞伍联电子科技有限公司	凤岗镇	82097852	电子计算机外部设备
东莞东原电子有限公司	寮步镇	83228000	手机充电器
东莞全台电子有限公司	东坑镇	83697606	平板显示器
东莞康佳电子有限公司	凤岗镇	87758888	彩色电视
东莞音音电子绘本有限公司	黄江镇	83668068	电子式音乐卡
联一小原光学(东莞)有限公司	长安镇	86240666	光学玻璃毛胚
东莞芝浦电子有限公司	长安镇	85412371	热敏电阻
东莞厚街溪头资科电脑线材厂	厚街镇	85599076	电线
东莞光阵显示器制品有限公司	清溪镇	87738870	摄像头
东莞动利电子有限公司	常平镇		电脑散热风扇
东莞樟木头十和田电子厂	樟木头镇	87713119	收音机
东莞普思电子有限公司	长安镇	85538871	高频滤波器
高效电子(东莞)有限公司	寮步镇	88901888	电脑零配件
东莞昆盈电脑制品有限公司	厚街镇	85825810	鼠标器
东莞协盈电脑有限公司	厚街镇	85880090	鼠标器
东莞生益电子有限公司	万江街道	22272074	多层印刷电路板
东莞盛和电子有限公司	长安镇	86076988	电子
东莞雅图士电子科技有限公司	塘厦镇	82001800	电子器件
国巨电子(东莞)有限公司	塘厦镇	87720275	电阻器
东莞福摩斯托电子有限公司	长安镇	85541200	家用电子元件
东莞奇力新电子有限公司	清溪镇	87730251	线圈
东莞创慈磁性元件有限公司	石碣镇	86327771	变压器
东莞新进电子有限公司	大岭山镇	85613846	电子计算机外部设备
东莞旺宏科技有限公司	长安镇		鼠标
东莞黄江威成科技电子厂	黄江镇	83632679	液晶显示屏
永捷电路版(东莞)有限公司	厚街镇	85812542	印制电路板
特新微电子(东莞)有限公司	茶山镇	86403328	电路板钻孔
富加宜连接器(东莞)有限公司	沙田镇	88682108	电子连接器
东莞益衡电子有限公司	凤岗镇	87755689	电源供应器

1-5 续表 29

(2010年)

单位名称	所属镇街	联系电话	主要产品(或服务)
立维腾电子(东莞)有限公司	桥头镇	81038888	电子元件及组件
东莞弘电电子有限公司	虎门镇	85550979	新型电子元器件
东莞嘉耀电子有限公司	厚街镇	85930034	电脑功能卡
东莞中钜资讯光电有限公司	厚街镇	85994660	电子原配件
东莞陆和电子有限公司	中堂镇	88885117	键盘
台达电子零组件(东莞)有限公司	石碣镇	86639008	散热风扇(电脑)
东莞宝桥电子科技有限公司	黄江镇	83632679	新型平板显示器件
东莞市宝盛五金制品有限公司	清溪镇	87315888	电脑外壳
富港电子(东莞)有限公司	东坑镇	83882225	变压器
东莞美隆电声器材有限公司	塘厦镇	86856288	各类型喇叭
东莞展翊五金电器有限公司	清溪镇	87735052	电脑机箱
振曜电子(东莞)有限公司	大朗镇	83188470	网络交换机
东莞艾利博电子有限公司	松山湖管委会	22899100	电子词典和显示器
东莞黄江中盈科技电子厂	黄江镇	83663518	电脑主板
东莞近江电子有限公司	桥头镇	81036276	线路主板
东莞健益五金制品有限公司	茶山镇	86487999	DVD机芯五金件
快捷达通信设备(东莞)有限公司	常平镇	83936688	数据通信设备
东莞贯达电子有限公司	高埗镇	88786000	电感
东莞友华汽车配件有限公司	寮步镇	83326172	各种开线塑胶配件
东莞成乐电子有限公司	横沥镇	83713213	电子产品
东莞长安发利达电子厂	长安镇	85531414	电子元件
新豪(东莞)电子有限公司	寮步镇	83216200	电脑键盘
嘉益电子(东莞)有限公司	东城街道	22207821	印制电路板
乔日电业制品(东莞)有限公司	虎门镇	85562003	开关断路器
东莞诚信电子塑胶有限公司	虎门镇	85507263	变压器胶架
东莞美捷电业有限公司	常平镇	83903378	镭射收录机
东莞台霖电子通讯有限公司	大岭山镇	85655858	电脑线连插头
东莞宝山电子有限公司	樟木头镇	87712264	电子产品
东莞友华通信配件有限公司	南城街道	22982285	天线
东莞高埗微太电子科技有限公司	高埗镇		数码产品
东莞前盛电子有限公司	塘厦镇	87910575	电源供应器
东莞翊凯电器制品有限公司	清溪镇	86812999	电脑机箱外壳
成翔电子(东莞)有限公司	清溪镇	87733511	电源供应器
东莞广濑拓展电子有限公司	石龙镇		复印线路办
东莞联桥电子有限公司	茶山镇	86485066	印刷电路板
极讯电子(东莞)有限公司	寮步镇	88953310	电子元件
东莞市科隆威自动化设备有限公司	寮步镇	83228201	无铅流焊
联德电子(东莞)有限公司	石碣镇	83072288	电子电源供应器
东莞创群石英晶体有限公司	大朗镇	83119395	石英晶体谐振器
东莞东力电子有限公司	塘厦镇	87723276	DVD机
东莞清溪晶达电子制品厂	清溪镇	87320077	液晶器件
广东升威电子制品有限公司	塘厦镇	87287777	电位器编码器

1-5 续表 30

(2010年)

单位名称	所属镇街	联系电话	主要产品(或服务)
东莞福哥电子有限公司	茶山镇	86649438	电子产品电位器
东莞联宝光电科技有限公司	企石镇	86786368	电子产品
东莞怡科电子有限公司	长安镇	87086668	汽车移动电话充电器
东莞大朗辉鸿电子厂	大朗镇	83018938	喇叭半成品
东莞爱电电子有限公司	桥头镇	83434525	线路板
旗利得电子(东莞)有限公司	谢岗镇	87766645	印刷线路板
东莞七盟电子有限公司	黄江镇	83621007	电子专用设备
群光电子(东莞)有限公司	清溪镇	87311688	电脑键盘
东莞森泰电子有限公司	凤岗镇	87751663	手机
东莞长江电脑制品有限公司	清溪镇	87736209	电脑机箱
东莞塘厦建永塑胶电子厂	塘厦镇	87880818	CD镭射机
东莞东聚电子电讯制品有限公司	石碣镇	86631652	鼠标
东莞汇和电子有限公司	谢岗镇	87768410	印刷线路板
东莞亨域电子有限公司	望牛墩镇	88859838	恒温器
东莞山本电子科技有限公司	麻涌镇	88227094	印刷线路板
东莞致力电脑有限公司	清溪镇	87312821	电脑配件
盛恒达电子(东莞)有限公司	石碣镇	86633718	ADLS路由器
东莞友池精密机械有限公司	清溪镇	87369900	背光涯
东莞鸿万电子有限公司	企石镇	86785330	游戏机配件
东莞泰硕电子有限公司	大岭山镇	85321851	连接器
东莞稀世电子有限公司	道滘镇	88383096	空气净化器
东莞东骅电子科技有限公司	清溪镇	33336888	电脑机箱
圣华电子(东莞)有限公司	塘厦镇	87882707	电脑连接线
东莞益新实业有限公司	塘厦镇	87811000	电子零配件
东莞保力电子有限公司	石排镇	86511770	充电器
东莞怡发塑胶制品有限公司	常平镇	83392238	电话充电器胶件
东莞雅士电子有限公司	长安镇	85545115	收放组合机
东莞东煦五金电镀厂有限公司	虎门镇	85564222	LED引线架
雅邦电子(东莞)有限公司	石碣镇	86331999	电子成品组装
东莞力音电子有限公司	石碣镇	86637826	电子线圈
东莞智富五金制品有限公司	塘厦镇	86853888	电器外壳、散热片等
东莞明鑫电子有限公司	企石镇	86731868	电子元件及组件
东莞塘厦裕华电路板厂	塘厦镇		空白线路板
东莞德英电子通讯设备有限公司	莞城街道	22024422	婴儿监督器
东莞世技电子有限公司	寮步镇	83224133	防盗器
东莞旭福电脑有限公司	清溪镇	87318190	电脑主机板
东莞盛世科技电子实业有限公司	黄江镇	86914800	电子元器件
东莞嘉德电子科技有限公司	桥头镇	83025777	塑胶配件
东莞长安科得电子有限公司	长安镇	85546130	主板机
先锋信泰(东莞)光学有限公司	长安镇	85535435	精密光电电器件
东莞得泰电子有限公司	石碣镇	86316090	耳机
锦旭电子(东莞)有限公司	清溪镇	87737118	电脑周边产品

1-5　续表 31

(2010年)

单位名称	所属镇街	联系电话	主要产品(或服务)
飞磁电子材料(东莞)有限公司	清溪镇	87382420	磁芯、磁环
东莞仲屏电子有限公司	石排镇	81868166	扬声器
东莞富鼎塑胶五金有限公司	高埗镇	86279588	电脑托架
东莞诠盛电器有限公司	厚街镇	85825373	电源插座
东莞石龙京瓷光学有限公司	石龙镇	86119611	液晶部品
东莞巨丰铜线有限公司	东城街道	22266314	漆包线
东莞艾斯光电科技有限公司	东城街道	22667703	新型电子元器件
东莞常平桥沥大东大明电子厂	常平镇	83914086	塑胶制品
东莞美城电子电器有限公司	莞城街道	22250946	收、录音机
东莞建玮电子制品有限公司	清溪镇	87734800	电脑连接线
东莞宏松精密组件有限公司	清溪镇	28129588	键盘
东莞日矿富士电子有限公司	洪梅镇	88431720	液晶背光源用电极
东莞翔国光电科技有限公司	茶山镇	81833588	印刷电路板
东莞森玛仕格里菲电路有限公司	茶山镇	81822047	多层线路板
东莞企达电器制品有限公司	横沥镇	83715169	电子元件
东莞宏笙电子有限公司	塘厦镇	87919270	鼠标器
东莞高伟光学电子有限公司	寮步镇	83307113	手机摄像头
东莞太阳诱电有限公司	石碣镇	86636888	电容器
东莞广原电子有限公司	石碣镇	86366010	扬声器
东莞福满生电子有限公司	常平镇	82207777	电脑显示器托架
东莞成谦音响科技有限公司	长安镇	85380808	喇叭
华容电子(广东)有限公司	石碣镇	83075098	电容器
艾利和电子科技(中国)有限公司	松山湖管委会	22899100	MP3和MP4
东莞宇球电子有限公司	寮步镇	83529888	电子插接件
东莞英格尔电子有限公司	塘厦镇	87934928	电子元件
华磁电子(东莞)有限公司	石碣镇		电感器
东莞凯升电子有限公司	塘厦镇	87883521	电脑机箱
吉嘉电子东莞有限公司	樟木头镇	87790197	多媒体音箱
东莞耀升机电有限公司	清溪镇	87338900	电子零件、压铸产品
东莞耀胜电子有限公司	横沥镇	83737691	电脑周边产品
东莞欧陸电子有限公司	长安镇	87088788	电子元件
东莞市兴奇宏电子有限公司	企石镇	86731868	电脑主机
东莞精恒电子有限公司	横沥镇	88977068	公共广播器材
东莞樟洋电子有限公司	樟木头镇	87197011	数字摄录机
东莞惠伦顿堡电子有限公司	黄江镇	83362809	电子元器材
东莞亿润电子制品有限公司	高埗镇	88730855	光电子元器件
东莞鸿达电子有限公司	塘厦镇	87727438	电话机
广东佳彩数码科技有限公司	企石镇	86727181	机顶盒
东莞清溪德丽电子厂	清溪镇	87311036	电脑键盘
东莞勤德五金制品有限公司	塘厦镇		计算机五金制品
东莞易迅电子制品有限公司	高埗镇	88788261	开关电源器CAC、DC换能器
雅新电子(东莞)有限公司	石碣镇	86331999	空白印刷电器板

1-5 续表 32

(2010年)

单位名称	所属镇街	联系电话	主要产品(或服务)
东莞李洲电子科技有限公司	谢岗镇	87762548	数码管
东莞新劲电子有限公司	塘厦镇	87810780	电脑周边产品
东莞上端电子有限公司	长安镇	85099191	电脑配件
东莞科达五金制品有限公司	石碣镇	86313419	精密驱动器部件
东莞捷仕美电子有限公司	大朗镇	83125678	电子连接器
协发(东莞)电子有限公司	塘厦镇	87720745	电源供应器
先锋高科技(东莞)有限公司	寮步镇	83287704	磁盘驱动器
东莞康源电子有限公司	虎门镇	85562002	线路板
东莞环亚高科电子有限公司	长安镇	85316946	个人数码助理
东莞致通电脑有限公司	清溪镇	87312821	数据机网络卡
东莞基杰五金制品有限公司	清溪镇	87735140	电脑机箱
东莞捷讯电子有限公司	樟木头镇	87712009	手提标签机
东莞亚联科技电子有限公司	塘厦镇	87727680	电脑及其周边配件充电器
东莞艾笛森光电有限公司	横沥镇		电子产品
东莞明泰电讯设备有限公司	大岭山镇	83356898	各类电话机
瑞讯电子(东莞)有限公司	东城街道	88753288	网络卡路由器
东莞宇宙电路板设备有限公司	凤岗镇	87569928	电路板水平机组
东莞宝星电子有限公司	寮步镇	83288770	微型麦克风
东莞莫仕连接器有限公司	石碣镇	86310328	电脑连接线
最上(东莞)电子有限公司	塘厦镇	87883718	喇叭鼓纸
东莞科泰电子有限公司	南城街道		合路器
祥发电子(东莞)有限公司	石碣镇	86331999	电源供应器
东莞友讯电子有限公司	长安镇	85318000	网络卡
东莞隆盛达电子有限公司	万江街道	22706295	影碟机
东莞彩嘉电子有限公司	谢岗镇	87762803	录放机
品嘉电子(东莞)有限公司	厚街镇	85903505	电脑显示卡
东莞磁威电子科技有限公司	企石镇	86787388	宽带网络活音分歧器
日本电产(东莞)有限公司	高埗镇	88873011	大容量光磁盘驱动器
东莞联聿电子有限公司	长安镇	85322996	电脑机箱
东莞百音电子有限公司	南城街道	22984320	扬声器
东莞正阳电子有限公司	塘厦镇	87916258	音箱
东莞长安华南电子厂	长安镇	85307366	磁性产品
东莞冠诚塑胶模具有限公司清溪分厂	清溪镇	87315088	遥控器
东莞东源光电有限公司	东城街道	22633913	光纤跳接线
东莞美维电路有限公司	东城街道	86228000	印制线路板
东莞鸿爱斯通信科技有限公司	高埗镇	88783009	电子元件
东莞美京电子有限公司	寮步镇	83222370	散热片
东莞科乐波电子有限公司	寮步镇	83281822	变压器
东莞合宝电器制品有限公司	横沥镇	83715169	电器开关
东莞三诺科技有限公司	清溪镇	86816099	电脑机箱
仪器仪表及文化、办公用机械制造业			
东莞虎门泰达电子有限公司	虎门镇	85558622	电子计算器

1-5 续表 33

(2010年)

单位名称	所属镇街	联系电话	主要产品(或服务)
东莞信泰光学有限公司	长安镇	85535435	数码相机
京瓷美达办公设备(东莞)有限公司	石龙镇	86112525	打印机
东莞贝盈激光仪器有限公司	樟木头镇	86907088	激光仪器
东英精密轴承(东莞)有限公司	沙田镇	88666101	打印机配件
优利德科技(东莞)有限公司	虎门镇	85729892	电器仪表
东莞清溪优品电子厂	清溪镇	87311417	计数机
东京光学(东莞)科技有限公司	石龙镇	86185458	镜头组件
东莞富鼎兴精密电子科技有限公司	谢岗镇	87686518	电脑周边配件
东莞新溢眼镜制造有限公司	长安镇	85540945	眼镜
东莞精熙光机有限公司	长安镇	85312190	照相机、复印机主要零部件
东莞均益精密五金制品有限公司	石排镇	88937100	表带表壳
东莞富国橡塑工业有限公司	大岭山镇	85656968	防振垫
东莞长安新民冠利精密钟表厂	长安镇	85387288	钟表
陆逊梯卡华宏(东莞)眼镜有限公司	高埗镇	88870241	金属塑胶眼镜
东莞宝元数控科技有限公司	高埗镇	88874202	控制器
东莞雄福五金有限公司	横沥镇	83723390	数码相机零配件
盈利时表业(东莞)有限公司	大朗镇	83103333	表带
宏达光电玻璃东莞有限公司	大岭山镇	81625988	TFT-LCD显示屏材料
东莞侨运表业有限公司	厚街镇	83086066	手表
希比希真空电子(东莞)有限公司	长安镇	82389200	数码相机零配件
广东尼康照相机有限公司	长安镇	85535435	相机
金宝电子(中国)有限公司	长安镇	85321555	电子计算机
东莞泰联光学有限公司	长安镇	85535435	照相
东莞力维时钟有限公司	清溪镇	87732284	时钟
东莞日精电子有限公司	塘厦镇	86857999	遥控器、打印机等控制面板
万金机械配件东莞有限公司	凤岗镇	82039188	复印机零配件
东莞快灵通卡西尼电子科技有限公司	寮步镇	83039222	计算器
东莞华仪仪表科技有限公司	清溪镇	87309005	仪器仪表
东莞新旭光学有限公司	长安镇	86240898	光学镜片组
东莞晓视眼镜制造厂有限公司	凤岗镇	87754133	眼镜
高铁检测仪器(东莞)有限公司	南城街道	22400899	试验机
三和盛电子科技(东莞)有限公司	凤岗镇	87862222	数码相机关键件
东莞石龙粤龙办公设备制造厂	石龙镇	86181222	影印机
东莞应华精密金属有限公司	寮步镇	82316661	数码相机外壳
镰仓光学(东莞)有限公司	虎门镇	85562870	望远镜及其配件
东莞大泰光电科技有限公司	虎门镇	85503858	照相机配件
柯尼卡美能达商用科技(东莞)有限公司	石龙镇		复印机
工艺品及其他制造业			
东莞大信装饰礼品有限公司	常平镇	86293999	蜡烛灯
东莞赛诺家居用品有限公司	塘厦镇	87881068	软件家具用品
三铃制线(东莞)有限公司	常平镇	83395435	铜线
东莞台新纤维制品有限公司	清溪镇	87311541	汽车地毯

1-5 续表 34

(2010年)

单位名称	所属镇街	联系电话	主要产品(或服务)
东莞隆富精密模具有限公司	长安镇	85311526	手机按键
东泰机械工具(东莞)有限公司	常平镇	83939183	冲床
东莞三大电子科技有限公司	常平镇	83997278	电脑零件
东莞大洋硅胶制品有限公司	樟木头镇	87712088	硅胶制品
东莞优立化工有限公司	塘厦镇	87727642	电泳涂料
东莞西文商标织绣有限公司	长安镇	81767999	商标织绣
永泰电子(东莞)有限公司	常平镇	83918040	电脑连接线
东莞华昌导体有限公司	虎门镇	85507296	红铜线
阿基里斯电子材料(东莞)有限公司	长安镇	85308801	防静电处理
东莞安泰玩具有限公司	樟木头镇	87790368	塑胶玩具
东莞安居家饰有限公司	清溪镇	87306597	窗帘
东莞永腾电子制品有限公司	凤岗镇	87755269	铝制散热片及散热器
欣泰家具(东莞)有限公司	清溪镇	87313008	太阳伞、户外伞
东莞海金杜门五金制品有限公司	南城街道	22401768	特殊五金冲压件
东莞星系手袋厂有限公司	塘厦镇	87939288	日用杂品
东莞华艺铜业有限公司	常平镇	83918628	铜杆
东莞大日化工厂有限公司	虎门镇	85556675	ABS粒
广濑电机(东莞)有限公司	常平镇	83817840	连接器
东莞婴宝幼童用品有限公司	清溪镇	87738800	童车
东莞宝峰金属制品有限公司	谢岗镇	87136078	铁制品
东莞素艺儿童用品有限公司	道滘镇	88382301	婴儿手推车
东莞富钢电子有限公司	常平镇	83399000	电路板组件
东莞晟富电子科技有限公司	寮步镇	81100168	降频器
东莞华生精密制品有限公司	樟木头镇	87187900	组装音响
东莞杜邦电子材料有限公司	南城街道	22852951	电子材料
大毅科技电子(东莞)有限公司	常平镇	83394790	新型电子元器件
东莞庆章光机有限公司	清溪镇	87381610	分光镜
东莞宇源精密金属实业有限公司	黄江镇	86968798	金属工艺品
东莞利冠光学电子有限公司	石碣镇	86387600	镜片
电力、热力的生产和供应业			
广东广合电力有限公司沙角发电厂C厂	虎门镇	85135124	火力发电
东莞天明电力有限公司	道滘镇	22788336	火力发电
深南电(东莞)唯美电力有限公司	高埗镇	88463006	天然气发电
东莞通明电力有限公司	寮步镇	83525188	天然气发电站的建设经营
东莞深能源樟洋电力有限公司	樟木头镇	87198888	发电
东莞市科伟环保电力有限公司	横沥镇	83715838	垃圾焚烧发电
东莞虎门电厂	虎门镇	85042288	火力发电
东莞中科环保电力有限公司	南城街道	22667772	垃圾余热发电
燃气生产和供应业			
东莞新奥燃气有限公司	莞城街道	88992299	管道燃气输配
建筑安装业			
东莞安泰电业工程有限公司	莞城街道	22465497	高低压输变电等设备安装

1-5 续表 35

(2010年)

单位名称	所属镇街	联系电话	主要产品(或服务)
道路运输业			
广东省虎门大桥有限公司	虎门镇	85509333	高速公路管理养护
东莞发展控股股份有限公司	东城街道	22083225	高速收费
水上运输业			
东莞虎门龙威客运有限公司	虎门镇	85511759	沿海旅客运输
仓储业			
东莞三江港口储罐有限公司	虎门港管委会	88862888	液体化工仓储服务
东莞永得利仓储有限公司	麻涌镇	88236909	物流服务
电信和其他信息传输服务业			
中国联通有限公司东莞分公司	南城街道	89826239	通信服务
中国移动通信集团广东有限公司东莞分公司	东城街道	13926888888	移动通信业务
批发业			
东莞金丰物流设备有限公司	道滘镇	88333981	叉车
东莞喜威液化石油气有限公司	东城街道	22497388	液化气
东莞柳道贸易有限公司	长安镇	85394466	热流道条流及配件
金光纸业(广州)有限公司东莞分公司	南城街道	22992511	纸品
莎罗雅(东莞)清洁用品有限公司	长安镇	85358605	清洁用品
隆原(东莞)机电贸易有限公司	长安镇	81607192	柴油发电机
锦江麦德龙现购自运有限公司东莞万江商场	万江街道	22178888	商品
嘉顿食品贸易(中国)有限公司	南城街道	23024830	蛋糕
东莞加德士石油产品有限公司	东城街道	22367236	石油产品
大同机械(东莞)销售有限公司	东城街道	22806163	机械设备
东莞华港国际贸易有限公司	长安镇	85416451	塑胶原料
东莞润德商业有限公司	厚街镇	89788109	百货
东莞市创盛贸易有限公司	长安镇	82289868	钢材制品
零售业			
东莞德现汽车销售服务有限公司	寮步镇	81117637	现代品牌轿车
东莞永佳中通汽车服务有限公司	厚街镇	81633000	汽车零配件
东莞中升雷克萨斯汽车销售服务有限公司	南城街道	23190999	雷克萨斯汽车
青岛润泰事业有限公司东莞大朗分公司	大朗镇	83034798	百货
东莞仁孚溢华汽车服务有限公司	南城街道	22902080	汽车
东莞百安居装饰建材有限公司	万江街道	22719121	室内装修材料
东莞沃尔玛百货有限公司	莞城街道	22323055	超级市场
广东吉之岛天贸百货有限公司东莞花园广场分公司	东城街道		百货
安利(中国)日用品有限公司东莞分公司	莞城街道	22556455	日用品
东莞仁孚华星汽车服务有限公司	寮步镇	82222080	奔驰轿车
东莞意美汽车服务有限公司	厚街镇	85050911	汽车
东莞美东汽车服务有限公司	寮步镇	82319819	汽车
东莞擎达汽车销售服务有限公司	厚街镇	85580180	汽车
东莞市洛加斯润滑油有限公司	大岭山镇	85617000	润滑油
中油碧辟石油有限公司东莞分公司	万江街道	88338556	机动车燃料
东莞家乐福商业有限公司	东城街道	22201897	百货

1-5 续表 36

(2010年)

单位名称	所属镇街	联系电话	主要产品(或服务)
住宿业			
东莞御景湾酒店	东城街道	22625029	旅业
东莞丽池海悦酒店有限公司	厚街镇	85885888	服务行业
东莞长安酒店	长安镇	85532388	餐饮服务
东莞新都会酒店有限公司	樟木头镇	87713333	餐饮
餐饮业			
东莞海悦花园大酒店有限公司	长安镇	85318888	餐饮服务
东莞豪门大饭店	虎门镇	85117888	餐饮
东莞麦华食品有限公司	莞城街道	22115051	西式快餐
东莞肯德基有限公司	莞城街道	83588288	快餐
东莞泛亚饮食有限公司	樟木头镇	87708232	餐饮
银行业			
恒生银行(中国)有限公司东莞分行	东城街道	23138838	金融企业
汇丰银行(中国)有限公司东莞分行	南城街道	23093088	吸收公众存款
保险业			
信诚人寿保险有限公司东莞营销服务部	东城街道	22763188	人寿保险
美国友邦保险有限公司东莞支公司	南城街道	22418628	人寿保险
中德安联人寿保险有限公司广东分公司东莞营销服务部	南城街道	22827268	人寿保险
房地产业			
东莞骏豪房地产开发有限公司	塘厦镇	28022593	房地产开发经营
东莞时富花园开发有限公司	寮步镇	83232328	商品住宅
东莞御花苑商品住宅建造有限公司	南城街道	22402268	房地产开发经营
东莞庄士房地产开发有限公司	沙田镇	88660958	房地产开发经营
东莞市金地房地产投资有限公司	南城街道		开发、建设、经营普通住宅
东莞万科置业有限公司	莞城街道	23013547	房地产开发及建设
东莞雁田工业区发展有限公司	凤岗镇	87771905	房地产开发经营
东莞市庆丰房地产有限公司	东城街道	22619005	房地产中介
东莞水濂山水库商品住宅建造有限公司	南城街道		房地产开发经营
东莞东泰花园建造有限公司	东城街道	22482388	房地产
东莞市阳明渡假山庄开发有限公司	塘厦镇	82275828	房地产开发
东莞市乐富房地产开发有限公司	樟木头镇	87187088	房地产开发
商务服务业			
东莞康美雅咨询有限公司	凤岗镇	87513260	家庭电器用品的咨询
(丹麦)森海塞尔通信有限公司东莞代表处	东城街道	22360850	业务联络
东莞派诺蒙鞋业服务有限公司	东城街道	22491889	鞋类产品设计
研究与试验发展			
东莞新科技术研究开发有限公司	南城街道	22810033	研究开发磁电制品
娱乐业			
东莞峰景高尔夫有限公司	东城街道	22253459	高尔夫球
东莞长安今宇高尔夫球场俱乐部有限公司	长安镇	85539288	高尔夫球娱乐活动
东莞观澜湖高尔夫球会有限公司	塘厦镇	28020888	高尔夫球场及配套设施

1-6 星级酒店名单(2010年)

List of Star-ranking Hotels (2010)

酒店名称	星级	电话	地址
银城酒店	五星	22828888	南城区莞太大道48号
樟木头三正半山酒店	五星	87799333	樟木头镇石新大道
凤岗金凯悦大酒店	五星	87759888	凤岗镇凤深大道158号
龙泉国际大酒店	五星	85188688	虎门镇连升路金洲段
豪门大饭店	五星	85117888	虎门镇虎门大道
嘉华大酒店	五星	85928888	厚街镇家具大道1号
富盈酒店	五星	85888888	厚街镇赤岭路段
索菲特御景湾酒店	五星	22698888	东城区迎宾路8号
莲花山庄	五星	85538388	长安镇莲花山
长安海悦花园大酒店	五星	85318888	长安镇霄边管理区二环路
长安国际酒店	五星	85333333	长安镇锦绣路1号
石龙金凯悦大酒店	五星	86188888	石龙镇莞龙路西湖路段
喜来登大酒店	五星	85988888	厚街镇S256省道莞太路段
新都会怡景酒店	五星	87883888	塘厦镇环市东路6号
太子酒店	五星	83363333	黄江镇江北路32号
塘厦三正半山酒店	五星	87299333	塘厦镇迎宾大道
汇华国际饭店	五星	83938888	常平镇常平大道2号
帝豪花园酒店	五星	83122222	大朗镇美景中路769号
丰泰花园酒店	五星	85708888	虎门镇S358省道大板地路段
华尔登国际酒店	五星	81028888	桥头镇广场路3号
桥头三正半山酒店	五星	83341868	桥头镇碧莲路
悦莱花园酒店	五星	81118888	寮步镇香市路8号
寮步金凯悦大酒店	四星	83326328	寮步镇教育路1号
文华大酒店	四星	85911111	厚街镇莞太路新塘路段
珊瑚大酒店	四星	85826888	厚街镇S256省道莞太路段
东莞宾馆	四星	22222222	莞城区东正路11号
江龙大酒店	四星	85838888	厚街镇S256省道莞太路段
新都会酒店	四星	87713333	樟木头镇维多利商业大道38号
君爵酒店	四星	22288888	万江区石美广深路段
宏远酒店	四星	22418888	南城区宏远路1号
汇美酒店	四星	83918888	常平镇中元路9号
花园酒店	四星	87799888	樟木头镇南城广场

1-6　续表 1

（2010年）

酒店名称	星级	电话	地址
长安酒店	四星	85532388	长安镇中心S358省道旁
司马假日酒店	四星	83391888	常平镇司马管理区
新世纪酒店	四星	83338888	常平镇常平大道8号
梵尔赛酒店	四星	83816888	常平镇下墟工业区
厚街海悦花园大酒店	四星	85885888	厚街镇厚街大道东
华翔国际酒店	四星	83728888	横沥镇瑞康路
汇源华美达酒店	四星	85244888	虎门镇虎门大道
业丰大酒店	四星	83113888	大朗镇莞樟路金朗大道23号
万盈酒店	四星	88828888	麻涌镇麻涌大道
中汇文华酒店	四星	88788888	高埗镇振兴路
方中假日酒店	四星	86866666	茶山镇茶山大道西28号
半岛酒店	四星	83988888	常平镇北环路
华禧酒店	四星	85383888	长安镇S358省道上沙路段
嘉辉会酒店	四星	87563388	凤岗镇官井头嘉辉路
美怡登酒店	四星	83028888	常平镇中元路
石龙宾馆	三星	86613333	石龙镇绿化中路2号
广彩城酒店	三星	22402088	南城区莞太路
石碣豪华大酒店	三星	86633333	石碣镇新城区
金湖粤海酒店	三星	87869888	塘厦镇塘厦大道南99号
莲城酒店	三星	85536888	长安镇莲峰路接一环路口
乌沙大酒店	三星	85548888	长安镇乌沙环东路228号
黄江假日酒店	三星	83362888	黄江镇黄江大道3号
西湖大酒店	三星	22822888	南城区西平板岭
明苑大酒店	三星	85122918	虎门镇金龙大道南
盛御酒店	三星	86111888	石龙镇西湖大道1号
篁胜酒店	三星	22463888	南城区体育路11号
宝石大酒店	三星	86662188	企石镇振华路1号
恒丰酒店	三星	83343333	桥头镇恒丰新村2号
西湖酒店	三星	86112288	石龙镇西湖区
金岛山庄	三星	87729018	塘厦镇128工业区
绿洲酒店	三星	88832788	道滘镇振兴路156号
沙头酒店	三星	85418888	长安镇沙头管理区

1-6 续表 2

(2010年)

酒店名称	星级	电话	地址
华通城大酒店	三星	86732288	企石镇湖滨南路
丰田酒店	三星	87771199	凤岗镇雁田管理区怡安路
丽江酒店	三星	88872888	高埗镇捷达工业村13座
嘉福海港酒店	三星	88682888	沙田镇中心区港口大道17号
中明酒店	三星	88883368	中堂镇新兴路1号
乐怡酒店	三星	85823888	厚街镇康乐北路
御烽酒店	三星	22186888	万江区107国道拔蛟窝路段
莱莉雅酒店	三星	87507888	凤岗镇永盛商业大街中银大厦
东逸酒店	三星	85396388	长安镇莲峰路103号
鸿茂酒店	三星	83508888	常平镇常黄路
四季酒店	三星	88566666	望牛墩镇新电城A8座
宏信假日酒店	三星	87363888	清溪镇香芒西路
美景湾酒店	三星	83739888	横沥镇沿江路1号
天鹅湖酒店	三星	83338388	常平镇天鹅湖路8号
富豪酒店	三星	83998888	常平镇金美路256号
中青旅山水设计师酒店	三星	21988888	东城区东纵大道189号
亚都酒店	三星	85343888	长安镇长中路
金沙亚都酒店	三星	85413888	长安镇靖海中路36号
金澳花园酒店	二星	22496966	东城大道金澳花园A座
耀豪酒店	二星	88865333	沙田镇中心区
东海酒店	二星	83335484	常平镇东元路1号
银星酒店	二星	83987333	常平镇木棆大道9号
雄狮大酒店	二星	83911540	常平镇振兴路1号
盈丰酒店	二星	83333333	常平镇振兴路中段
新港大酒店	二星	83331000	常平镇新市一街6号
悦华大酒店	二星	83336888	常平镇东兴路275号
海霞酒店	二星	83815222	常平镇板石霞村路段
昇平酒店	二星	83812888	常平镇中元街
冠城酒店	二星	83337788	常平镇中元街常平广场
龙源大酒店	二星	85551028	虎门镇S358省道北栅路段
恒安酒店	二星	88682066	沙田镇横流中心区
海月酒店	二星	85926888	厚街镇涌口海月公园侧
悦凯酒店	一星	83398808	常平镇东元东路28号

1-7　高新技术企业名录（2010年）

List of High-tech Enterprises (2010)

企业名称	所在镇街	联系电话	行业类别
东华机械有限公司	东城街道	22806004	塑料加工专用设备制造
东莞宝丽美化工有限公司	常平镇	86290888	化学试剂和助剂制造
东莞创慈磁性元件有限公司	石碣镇	86327771	电子元件及组件制造
东莞贰发毛绒有限公司	樟木头镇	87718080	其他纺织制成品制造
东莞富强鑫塑胶机械制造有限公司	大朗镇	83313753	塑料加工专用设备制造
东莞光群雷射科技有限公司	大岭山镇	85601301	塑料薄膜制造
东莞宏威数码机械有限公司	南城街道	22909612	电工机械专用设备制造
东莞华科电子有限公司	大朗镇	83115168	电子元件及组件制造
东莞华仪仪表科技有限公司	清溪镇	81901668	电工仪器仪表制造
东莞科威医疗器械有限公司	东城街道	21985698	医疗诊断、监护及治疗设备
东莞昆盈电脑制品有限公司	厚街镇	85825810	电子计算机外部设备制造
东莞莫仕连接器有限公司	石碣镇	86310328	电子元件及组件制造
东莞勤上光电股份有限公司	常平镇	83395678	照明灯具制造
东莞泉声电子有限公司	石碣镇	86325251	电子元件及组件制造
东莞市瑞柯电机有限公司	清溪镇	87899858	汽车零部件及配件制造
东莞生益电子有限公司	东城街道	22272074	印制电路板制造
东莞市TR轴承有限公司	莞城街道	22469450	轴承制造
东莞市奥莱克电子有限公司	麻涌镇	88229781	家用音响设备制造
东莞市百分百科技有限公司	东城街道	88754582	照明灯具制造
东莞市柏百顺石油化工有限公司	樟木头镇	87787788	其他合成材料制造
东莞市邦泽电子有限公司	沙田镇	89191288	其他文化、办公用机械制造
东莞市大兴化工有限公司	谢岗镇		涂料制造
东莞市德生通用电器制造有限公司	东城街道	23167118	家用音响设备制造
东莞市东阳光电容器有限公司	长安镇	85315288	电子元件及组件制造
东莞市福地电子材料有限公司	南城街道	22406001	光电子器件及其他电子器件制造
东莞市高能电气股份有限公司	东城街道	22291876	绝缘制品制造
东莞市光华实业有限公司	石龙镇	81862888	变压器、整流器和电感器制造
东莞市广大制冷有限公司	虎门镇	81688909	制冷、空调设备制造
东莞市广益食品添加剂实业有限公司	中堂镇	88886882	食品及饲料添加剂制造
东莞市国菱机械有限公司	长安镇	85544423	金属成形机床制造
东莞市宏磊达电子塑胶有限公司	寮步镇	87070008	灯用电器附件及其他照明器具制造
东莞市华兰海电子有限公司	麻涌镇	88823550	电子元件及组件制造
东莞市环宇激光工程有限公司	常平镇	83364999	电子工业专用设备制造
东莞市晖速天线技术有限公司	东城街道	85388505	通信传输设备制造
东莞市金河田实业有限公司	厚街镇	85585691	电子计算机外部设备制造
东莞市金翔电器设备有限公司	万江街道	22704478	电子计算机外部设备制造
东莞市凯晟灯头实业有限公司	企石镇	86787878	电光源制造
东莞市蓝冠环保节能科技有限公司	寮步镇	83309068	燃气、太阳能及类似能源的器具制造
东莞市理士奥电源技术有限公司	塘厦镇	87925180	电池制造
东莞市迈科科技有限公司	大朗镇	83197555	电池制造
东莞市南兴木工机械有限公司	厚街镇	89982033	木材加工机械制造
东莞普思电子有限公司	长安镇		电子元件及组件制造

1-7 续表 1

(2010年)

企业名称	所在镇街	联系电话	行业类别
东莞市日新传导科技股份有限公司	桥头镇		电线电缆制造
东莞市盛和化工有限公司	黄江镇	87132000	有机化学原料制造
东莞市特尔佳电子有限公司	常平镇	89962233	电子元件及组件制造
东莞万成制药有限公司	万江街道	22282309	化学药品制剂制造
东莞市英科水墨有限公司	茶山镇	86179128	油墨及类似产品制造
东莞市永强汽车制造有限公司	寮步镇	83307688	汽车整车制造
东莞市友美电源设备有限公司	寮步镇	88953166	照明灯具制造
东莞市源殿电子科技有限公司	茶山镇	85317295	变压器、整流器和电感器制造
东莞市粤铭激光技术有限公司	万江街道	89838888	金属切割及焊接设备制造
东莞市众誉电子有限公司	虎门镇		电子计算机外部设备制造
东莞维升电子制品有限公司	黄江镇	83622694	电线电缆制造
东莞新能源电子科技有限公司	南城街道	88989114	电池制造
东莞信易电热机械有限公司	大朗镇	83313588	塑料加工专用设备制造
东莞星火机电设备工程有限公司	黄江镇	83666848	发电机及发电机组制造
东莞徐记食品有限公司	东城街道	22268955	糖果、巧克力制造
东莞宜安电器制品有限公司	清溪镇	87327777	常用有色金属压延加工
东莞益新五金有限公司	常平镇	87811000	移动通信及终端设备制造
东莞永洪印刷有限公司	樟木头镇	87711991	包装装潢及其他印刷
东莞友讯电子有限公司	长安镇	85318000	通信传输设备制造
东莞泽龙线缆有限公司	石龙镇	81388616	电线电缆制造
高铁检测仪器(东莞)有限公司	南城街道	22400899	实验分析仪器制造
广东丹宝利酵母有限公司	中堂镇	88896528	其他调味品、发酵制品制造
广东福利龙复合肥有限公司	高埗镇	88735305	复混肥料制造
广东宏达工贸集团有限公司	莞城街道	26888888	建筑安装业
广东科旺电源设备有限公司	南城街道	22900009	其他未列明的电气机械制造
广东升威电子制品有限公司	塘厦镇	87287777	电子元件及组件制造
广东万濠精密仪器股份有限公司	长安镇	85316127	电工仪器仪表制造
广东一品鲜生物科技有限公司	中堂镇		其他未列明的食品制造
广东智通人才连锁股份有限公司	莞城街道	87078398	职业中介服务
环球工业机械(东莞)有限公司	大朗镇	83118946	金属切削机床制造
金宝电子(中国)有限公司	长安镇	85321555	其他电子设备制造
品翔电子塑胶制品(东莞)有限公司	石碣镇	86636668	电子元件及组件制造
实盈电子(东莞)有限公司	清溪镇	87318688	电子元件及组件制造
泰阳电子(东莞)有限公司	石龙镇	81867666	电子元件及组件制造
万裕三信电子(东莞)有限公司	长安镇	85323339	电子元件及组件制造
信义汽车玻璃(东莞)有限公司	虎门镇	85266666	平板玻璃制造
智嘉通讯科技(东莞)有限公司	常平镇	83335430	通信交换设备制造
中名(东莞)电子有限公司	虎门镇	85709915	家用音响设备制造
达创科技(东莞)有限公司	石碣镇	86637008	计算机网络设备制造
东莞奥美佳电子有限公司	凤岗镇	87503835	其他电子设备制造
东莞德永佳纺织制衣有限公司	麻涌镇	88821738	棉、化纤印染精加工
东莞丰裕电机有限公司	塘厦镇	87902888	喷枪及类似器具制造

1-7 续表 2

(2010年)

企业名称	所在镇街	联系电话	行业类别
东莞光阵显示器制品有限公司	清溪镇	87738870	光电子器件及其他电子器件制造
东莞广泽汽车饰件有限公司	厚街镇	85903898	汽车零部件及配件制造
东莞海龙纸业有限公司	麻涌镇	88234888	机制纸及纸板制造
东莞虎彩印刷有限公司	虎门镇	85252189	包装装潢及其他印刷
东莞佳鸿机械制造有限公司	望牛墩镇	88850268	其他医疗设备及器械制造
东莞金波罗电业科技有限公司	中堂镇	88886808	电线电缆制造
东莞玖龙纸业有限公司	麻涌镇	88234888	机制纸及纸板制造
东莞市百思维软件有限公司	南城街道	22384201	应用软件服务
东莞市保得生物工程有限公司	南城街道	22814098	其他作物的种植
东莞市贝特利新材料有限公司	麻涌镇		油墨及类似产品制造
东莞市创普光电技术有限公司	企石镇	86730808	航空、航天及其他专用设备制造
东莞市大众农业科技有限公司	洪梅镇	88438227	农业科学研究与试验发展
东莞市东方科技有限公司	厚街镇	85583500	电子计算机外部设备制造
东莞市东兴铝材制造有限公司	中堂镇	88813671	其他未列明的金属制品制造
东莞市广安电气检测中心有限公司	石龙镇	86106683	技术检测
东莞市弘明空调服有限公司	莞城街道	22766088	纺织服装制造
东莞市华立实业股份有限公司	常平镇	83333239	其他家具制造
东莞骅国电子有限公司	厚街镇	85597201	电子元件及组件制造
东莞市开关厂有限公司	寮步镇	83233911	配电开关控制设备制造
东莞市开普互联信息有限公司	石龙镇	86117069	基础软件服务
东莞市康达机电工程有限公司	寮步镇	88996333	发电机及发电机组制造
东莞市科达机电设备有限公司	万江街道	22188788	制冷、空调设备制造
东莞市科隆威自动化设备有限公司	寮步镇	83228201	电子工业专用设备制造
东莞市龙记环保科技有限公司	厚街镇	85588479	其他环境治理
东莞市迈科新能源有限公司	大朗镇	83197555	电池制造
广东明家科技股份有限公司	横沥镇	88973888	社会公共安全设备及器材制造
东莞市前锋电子有限公司	石碣镇	88480108	家用厨房电器具制造
东莞市三联科技实业有限公司	寮步镇		其他专用化学产品制造
东莞市沙田顺发畜禽实业有限公司	沙田镇	88686605	农产品初加工服务
东莞市杉杉电池材料有限公司	南城街道	22035233	电池制造
东莞市神州视觉科技有限公司	东城街道	22629057	电工机械专用设备制造
东莞市石龙富华电子有限公司	石龙镇	86022222	其他电子设备制造
东莞市石龙联兴实业有限公司	石龙镇	88496069	纸和纸板容器的制造
东莞市太平洋计算机科技有限公司	莞城街道	22320368	其他计算机服务
东莞市万维网络科技信息有限公司	南城街道		应用软件服务
东莞市新雷神仿真控制有限公司	南城街道	22386051	计算机、软件及辅助设备零售
东莞市英芝堂生物工程有限公司	麻涌镇	88826118	生物、生化制品的制造
东莞市宇洁新材料有限公司	常平镇	83998003	其他未列明的制造业
东莞市至诚涂料有限公司	万江街道	22182252	涂料制造
东莞市中大科教网络科技有限公司	南城街道		应用软件服务
东莞宇宙电路板设备有限公司	凤岗镇	87569928	电子工业专用设备制造
东莞运城制版有限公司	常平镇	83501075	包装装潢及其他印刷

1-7 续表 3

(2010年)

企业名称	所在镇街	联系电话	行业类别
东莞正阳电子有限公司	塘厦镇	87916258	电子元件及组件制造
广东宏远集团药业有限公司	东城街道	22264813	化学药品制剂制造
广东华南药业集团有限公司	石龙镇	86100111	化学药品制剂制造
广东加多宝饮料食品有限公司	长安镇	85331688	茶饮料及其他软饮料制造
广东龙马化学有限公司	麻涌镇	88232288	涂料制造
广东五星太阳能有限公司	万江街道	22176388	燃气、太阳能及类似能源的器具制造
广东信力特种橡胶制品有限公司	麻涌镇	88220801	合成橡胶制造
广东银禧科技股份有限公司	虎门镇	88922988	初级形态的塑料及合成树脂制造
广东志成冠军集团有限公司	塘厦镇	87725486	电子工业专用设备制造
广东中成化工股份有限公司	麻涌镇	88229852	无机盐制造
广东众生药业股份有限公司	石龙镇	86100111	中成药制造
康舒电子(东莞)有限公司	塘厦镇	87915950	电子元件及组件制造
台达电子电源(东莞)有限公司	石碣镇	86639008	电子元件及组件制造
先锐模具配件(东莞)有限公司	长安镇	85376810	其他未列明的金属制品制造
东莞市银华生物科技有限公司	万江街道	22188099	水产饲料制造
广东星河生物科技股份有限公司	塘厦镇	82012345	蔬菜的种植
台达电子(东莞)有限公司	石碣镇	86631008	电子元件及组件制造
台达电子零组件(东莞)有限公司	石碣镇	86321008	电子元件及组件制造
东莞东运机械制造有限公司	常平镇	83500018	印刷专用设备制造
东莞广发制药有限公司	石碣镇	86385109	中成药制造
东莞华明灯具有限公司	清溪镇	87311200	照明灯具制造
东莞惠伦顿堡电子有限公司	黄江镇		电子元件及组件制造
东莞劲胜精密组件股份有限公司	长安镇	82288188	电子元件及组件制造
东莞康佳模具塑胶有限公司	凤岗镇	82071360	模具制造
东莞明鑫电子有限公司	企石镇	86944888	电子计算机外部设备制造
东莞三泰电器有限公司	常平镇	86836688	广播电视接收设备及器材制造
东莞市奥普特自动化科技有限公司	长安镇	86068128	工业自动控制系统装置制造
东莞市霸菱实业有限公司	虎门镇	85553636	金属结构制造
东莞市邦臣光电有限公司	东城街道	22086466	照明灯具制造
东莞市飞尔液晶显示器有限公司	大朗镇	38811180	电子元件及组件制造
东莞市佳景印刷材料有限公司	寮步镇	82318231	油墨及类似产品制造
东莞市坚朗五金制品有限公司	塘厦镇	87943311	其他未列明的金属制品制造
东莞市金银丰机械实业有限公司	厚街镇		皮革、毛皮及其制品加工专用设备制造
东莞市凯迪克高分子材料有限公司	中堂镇	81335656	涂料制造
东莞市凯格精密机械有限公司	东城街道	22767281	电子工业专用设备制造
东莞市凯诺德软件科技有限公司	南城街道	22024818	应用软件服务
东莞市康源节能科技有限公司	万江街道		制冷、空调设备制造
东莞市科达计算机系统工程有限公司	虎门镇	85109166	计算机系统服务
东莞市力凯科技发展有限公司	厚街镇	88910888	应用软件服务
东莞市领航通通信科技有限公司	南城街道	38959333	应用软件服务
东莞市龙基电子有限公司	石龙镇	81862666	电子元件及组件制造
东莞市瑞德丰生物科技有限公司	大岭山镇	85601568	化学农药制造

1-7 续表 4

(2010年)

企业名称	所在镇街	联系电话	行业类别
东莞市世通国际快件监管中心有限公司	常平镇	81088018	装卸搬运
东莞市兄奕塑胶制品有限公司	樟木头镇	87792188	塑料板、管、型材的制造
东莞市依时利科技有限公司	莞城街道	22333699	其他计算机服务
东莞市粤林电脑科技股份有限公司	清溪镇	87890888	电子计算机外部设备制造
东莞市智高文具有限公司	石碣镇	86316738	文具制造
东莞市智乐堡儿童玩具有限公司	石排镇	86550188	玩具制造
东莞市中一合金科技有限公司	大朗镇	88605666	贵金属压延加工
东莞市桦业土木基础工程有限公司	东城街道	22308398	其他土木工程建筑
东莞顺传五金制品有限公司	清溪镇	87732273	脚踏自行车及残疾人座车制造
东莞太平洋博高润滑油有限公司	麻涌镇	88823886	原油加工及石油制品制造
东莞盈拓科技实业有限公司	横沥镇	83796609	金属切削机床制造
东莞岳丰电子科技有限公司	石碣镇	81837666	电子工业专用设备制造
东莞致通电脑有限公司	清溪镇	87312821	计算机网络设备制造
东莞中探探针有限公司	虎门镇	85151668	电子元件及组件制造
东莞洲亮通讯科技有限公司	道滘镇	88326318	通信终端设备制造
广东楚天龙智能卡有限公司	凤岗镇	87509999	光电子器件及其他电子器件制造
广东迪奥技术工程有限公司	南城街道	22771688	建筑安装业
广东佳彩数码科技有限公司	企石镇		广播电视接收设备及器材制造
广东南方宏明电子科技股份有限公司	南城街道	22407479	电子元件及组件制造
广东省东莞电机有限公司	南城街道	22412480	电动机制造
环球石材(东莞)有限公司	长安镇	85544338	建筑用石加工
旭丽电子(东莞)有限公司	石碣镇	86638923	电子计算机外部设备制造
忠信制模(东莞)有限公司	横沥镇	83732298	模具制造
东莞东海龙环保科技有限公司	常平镇	83506181	照明灯具制造
东莞基业电气设备有限公司	万江街道		其他输配电及控制设备制造
东莞锦泰食品有限公司	南城街道	22400818	饼干及其他焙烤食品制造
东莞康视达自动化科技有限公司	东城街道	23395666	光电子器件及其他电子器件制造
东莞理文造纸厂有限公司	中堂镇	88888168	机制纸及纸板制造
东莞李洲电子科技有限公司	谢岗镇	89766888	光电子器件及其他电子器件制造
东莞龙昌数码科技有限公司	常平镇	86836266	游艺用品及室内游艺器材制造
东莞欧达电子有限公司	常平镇	83977722	光学仪器制造
东莞市达成机械设备制造有限公司	寮步镇	83217777	其他专用设备制造
东莞市大忠电子有限公司	东城街道	22630563	计算机网络设备制造
东莞市鼎聚光电有限公司	常平镇	86769535	电光源制造
东莞市虎门金山电线电缆有限公司	虎门镇		电线电缆制造
东莞市建邦计算机软件有限公司	东城街道	22499660	公证服务
东莞市快意电梯有限公司	清溪镇	82078888	起重运输设备制造
东莞市莱钢钢结构有限公司	黄江镇	83666666	钢铁铸件制造
东莞市力王电池有限公司	塘厦镇	86201111	电池制造
东莞市联升电线电缆有限公司	虎门镇	85554248	电线电缆制造
东莞市麦蒂科技有限公司	常平镇	81096262	应用软件服务
东莞市石龙万通实业有限公司	石龙镇	86117333	金属家具制造

1-7 续表 5

(2010年)

企业名称	所在镇街	联系电话	行业类别
东莞市台冠起重机械设备有限公司	大朗镇		起重运输设备制造
东莞市天盛特种纸制品有限公司	虎门镇	85169458	机制纸及纸板制造
东莞市铁志电子有限公司	寮步镇	82311301	其他文化用品制造
东莞市维信电脑科技有限公司	常平镇	22300106	应用软件服务
东莞市新时代新能源科技有限公司	大岭山镇	85653393	其他家用电力器具制造
东莞市旭田电子有限公司	石碣镇	86338696	电子计算机外部设备制造
东莞市亚洲制药有限公司	洪梅镇	23364693	中成药制造
东莞市一信通信科技有限公司	桥头镇	23171138	移动通信及终端设备制造
东莞市益达实业有限公司	茶山镇	86640198	电线电缆制造
东莞市盈聚电子有限公司	石碣镇	81837999	其他通信设备制造
东莞市远梦家用纺织品有限公司	厚街镇	83085188	其他针织品及编织品制造
东莞市兆明光电科技有限公司	企石镇	86720016	照明灯具制造
东莞市中实焊锡有限公司	虎门镇	85231818	其他未列明的金属制品制造
东莞市贻嘉光电科技有限公司	茶山镇		光电子器件及其他电子器件制造
东莞新东方化工有限公司	黄江镇	83639068	合成橡胶制造
东莞宇球电子有限公司	寮步镇	83529888	电子元件及组件制造
广东巨龙信息科技有限公司	石龙镇	86189876	应用软件服务
广东开心信息技术有限公司	南城街道	22023575	计算机系统服务
广东中远船务工程有限公司	麻涌镇		金属船舶制造
意拉德电子(东莞)有限公司	横沥镇	82208900	电子元件及组件制造
优利德科技(东莞)有限公司	虎门镇	85723888	电工仪器仪表制造
泓凯电子科技(东莞)有限公司	黄江镇	83365942	电子计算机外部设备制造
东莞康佳电子有限公司	凤岗镇	87758888	家用影视设备制造
东莞康源电子有限公司	虎门镇	88628888	印制电路板制造
东莞市奥其斯电器科技有限公司	虎门镇	38852099	变压器、整流器和电感器制造
东莞市广视通科教设备有限公司	万江街道	22710130	初中教育
东莞市宏德电子设备有限公司	黄江镇	83603488	其他专用设备制造
东莞市金隽机械有限公司	常平镇	83939588	塑料加工专用设备制造
东莞市康达尔饲料有限公司	麻涌镇		饲料加工
东莞市乐科电子有限公司	塘厦镇		集成电路制造
东莞市利安达环境科技有限公司	万江街道	22708610	环境污染防治专用设备制造
东莞市铭丰包装品制造有限公司	万江街道	22171188	其他未列明的制造业
东莞市千岛金属锡品有限公司	塘厦镇	87880129	锡冶炼
东莞市泰斗微电子科技有限公司	南城街道	21686601	应用软件服务
东莞市新泽谷机械有限公司	寮步镇	83286900	电子工业专用设备制造
东莞市雄丰配电设备有限公司	茶山镇	86402683	配电开关控制设备制造
东莞市亚力通电子科技有限公司	塘厦镇	82080288	移动通信及终端设备制造
东莞市政创软件科技有限公司	莞城街道		应用软件服务
东莞思威特电子有限公司	东城街道	22620160	电子元件及组件制造
东莞新科技术研究开发有限公司	南城街道	22810033	电子元件及组件制造
广东太阳神集团有限公司	黄江镇		营养、保健食品制造
信义玻璃工程(东莞)有限公司	虎门镇	85266666	其他玻璃制品制造

1-7 续表 6

(2010年)

企业名称	所在镇街	联系电话	行业类别
钰翔精密模具(东莞)有限公司	黄江镇	83360906	模具制造
大宝(东莞)模具切削工具有限公司	大朗镇	83182598	切削工具制造
东莞艾尔发自动化机械有限公司	大朗镇	83180326	其他未列明的电气机械制造
东莞常禾电子有限公司	虎门镇		其他电子设备制造
东莞超盈纺织有限公司	麻涌镇	88231808	棉、化纤印染精加工
东莞呈越电脑配件有限公司	大朗镇		电子计算机外部设备制造
东莞达电电子有限公司	石碣镇	86323500	电子元件及组件制造
东莞东聚电子电讯制品有限公司	石碣镇	86631652	电子计算机外部设备制造
东莞耳神电声科技有限公司	万江街道	89027886	电子计算机外部设备制造
东莞福泰电子有限公司	长安镇	85318100	其他电子设备制造
东莞广宏电子有限公司	长安镇	85317001	电子元件及组件制造
东莞鸿图精密压铸有限公司	长安镇	86066888	其他未列明的金属制品制造
东莞建玮电子制品有限公司	清溪镇	87734800	电子元件及组件制造
东莞利富高塑料制品有限公司	石龙镇	86105767	其他塑料制品制造
东莞龙杰电子有限公司	清溪镇	87734425	其他输配电及控制设备制造
东莞南玻工程玻璃有限公司	麻涌镇	88287668	平板玻璃制造
东莞市安默琳节能环保技术有限公司	万江街道		机床附件制造
东莞市奥达铝业有限公司	大岭山镇		金属结构制造
东莞市飞新达精密机械科技有限公司	寮步镇		其他非金属加工专用设备制造
东莞市丰远电器有限公司	南城街道	22414746	其他专用设备制造
东莞市富士达电子科技有限公司	石排镇	81828788	灯用电器附件及其他照明器具制造
东莞市冠辉五金有限公司	长安镇	85413848	建筑、家具用金属配件制造
东莞市宏达聚氨酯有限公司	高埗镇		初级形态的塑料及合成树脂制造
东莞市华南信息科技有限公司	莞城街道	22322788	应用软件服务
东莞市华鹰电子有限公司	长安镇	85540908	电子元件及组件制造
东莞市汇成真空科技有限公司	大岭山镇	85611172	泵及真空设备制造
东莞市慧达环保有限公司	东城街道	22691303	环境污染防治专用设备制造
东莞市慧通信息技术有限公司	南城街道	22026888	应用软件服务
东莞市嘉腾仪器仪表有限公司	东城街道	22677412	电子工业专用设备制造
东莞市捷联科技有限公司	莞城街道	22027000	应用软件服务
东莞市金培电子有限公司	桥头镇	81026999	电子计算机外部设备制造
东莞市骏朗自动化科技有限公司	洪梅镇	81336777	汽车及其他用计数仪表制造
东莞市骏泰精密机械有限公司	寮步镇	82317226	电池制造
东莞市力宇燃气动力有限公司	虎门镇		内燃机及配件制造
东莞市凌信电子科技有限公司	南城街道		电子工业专用设备制造
东莞市三友联众电器有限公司	厚街镇	85917501	电子元件及组件制造
东莞市胜蓝电子有限公司	长安镇	87094988	光电子器件及其他电子器件制造
东莞市事通达机电科技有限公司	东城街道	22627577	其他金属加工机械制造
东莞市适意机械有限公司	虎门镇	85705316	模具制造
东莞市硕源电子材料有限公司	万江街道	22780301	锦纶纤维制造
东莞市泰康电子科技有限公司	长安镇	85322066	电子计算机外部设备制造
东莞市腾宇龙机械科技有限公司	南城街道		皮革、毛皮及其制品加工专用设备制造

1-7　续表 7

(2010年)

企业名称	所在镇街	联系电话	行业类别
东莞市新铂铼电子有限公司	东城街道	38895239	电子真空器件制造
东莞市亚通光电有限公司	塘厦镇	82006088	电子元件及组件制造
东莞市亚勖电子科技有限公司	黄江镇	82020499	工程和技术研究与试验发展
东莞市扬明精密塑胶五金电子有限公司	长安镇	85338940	电子元件及组件制造
东莞市意利自动化科技有限公司	厚街镇	83083988	皮革、毛皮及其制品加工专用设备制造
东莞市永兴电子科技有限公司	大朗镇	82220180	光电子器件及其他电子器件制造
东莞市源兴光学仪器有限公司	东城街道	22084011	光学仪器制造
东莞市中村绝缘材料科技有限公司	道滘镇		其他通信设备制造
东莞通华液晶有限公司	东城街道	88774388	电子元件及组件制造
东莞拓扑实业有限公司	东城街道	22767756	涂料制造
东莞万德电子制品有限公司	东城街道	88775555	电子元件及组件制造
东莞信泰光学有限公司	长安镇	85535435	光学玻璃制造
东莞亿东机器有限公司	大岭山镇	85785000	铸造机械制造
广东华盈光达科技有限公司	莞城街道	22316555	应用软件服务
广东理文造纸有限公司	洪梅镇		机制纸及纸板制造
广东荣文照明集团有限公司	长安镇	82288988	灯用电器附件及其他照明器具制造
广东省东莞市亿达音响制造有限公司	大朗镇	89061666	其他电子设备制造
广东天新软件科技有限公司	南城街道	22851788	应用软件服务
佳辉设备(东莞)有限公司	塘厦镇		电子工业专用设备制造
金元宝弹簧设备(东莞)有限公司	中堂镇	88121891	紧固件、弹簧制造
模德模具(东莞)有限公司	清溪镇		其他金属加工机械制造
永泰电子(东莞)有限公司	常平镇	83918040	电力电子元器件制造
东莞市星火太阳能科技有限公司	松山湖	22891508	热力生产和供应
东莞市中之光电科技有限公司	松山湖	23183088	照明灯具制造
广东大普通信技术有限公司	松山湖	88010888	电子元件及组件制造
东莞市万科建筑技术研究有限公司	松山湖	22890188	其他专业技术服务
广东力优环境系统股份有限公司	松山湖	23076888	应用软件服务
广东领亚电子科技有限公司	松山湖	85550688	电子计算机外部设备制造
广东洛贝电子科技有限公司	松山湖	22895188	家用厨房电器具制造
广东正业科技有限公司	松山湖	88985555	光学仪器制造
东莞泛亚太生物科技有限公司	松山湖	22892600	食品及饲料添加剂制造
广东东阳光药业有限公司	松山湖		化学药品制剂制造
广东康菱动力科技有限公司	松山湖	22895555	发电机及发电机组制造
广东生益科技股份有限公司	松山湖	22271828	电子元件及组件制造
广东易事特电源股份有限公司	松山湖	22897777	电力电子元器件制造
东莞市科磊得数码光电科技有限公司	松山湖	23076156	光电子器件及其他电子器件制造
东莞新能源科技有限公司	松山湖	88989001	其他通信设备制造
广东雨林木风计算机科技有限公司	松山湖	23075555	计算机系统服务
广东电子工业研究院有限公司	松山湖	22891168	其他科技服务
广东华南工业设计院	松山湖	22890228	其他专业技术服务